Reshaping Criminology with AI

Fernando Ortiz-Rodriguez
Tamaulipas Autonomous University, Mexico

Shishir Kumar Shandilya
Devi Ahilya Vishwavidyalaya, India

Cynthia Marisol Vargas Orozco
Tamaulipas Autonomous University, Mexico

Juana Iris Ibarra Costilla
Tamaulipas Autonomous University, Mexico

Jersain Llamas Covarrubias
Guadalajara University, Mexico

IGI Global
Scientific Publishing
Publishing Tomorrow's Research Today

Vice President of Editorial	Melissa Wagner
Director of Acquisitions	Mikaela Felty
Director of Book Development	Jocelynn Hessler
Production Manager	Mike Brehm
Cover Design	Jose Rosado

Published in the United States of America by
IGI Global Scientific Publishing
701 East Chocolate Avenue
Hershey, PA, 17033, USA
Tel: 717-533-8845
Fax: 717-533-7115
Website: https://www.igi-global.com E-mail: cust@igi-global.com

Library of Congress Cataloging-in-Publication Data

Names: Ortiz-Rodriguez, Fernando, 1974- editor. | Shandilya, Shishir K., 1981- editor. | Vargas Orozco, Cynthia, 1982- editor. | Ibarra Costilla, Juana, 1982- editor. | Llamas Covarrubias, Jersain Zadamig, editor.
Title: Reshaping criminology with AI / edited by: Fernando Ortiz-Rodriguez, Shishir Kumar Shandilya, Cynthia Vargas Orozco, Juana Ibarra Costilla, Jersain Llamas Covarrubias.
Other titles: Reshaping criminology with artificial intelligence
Description: Hershey, PA : IGI Global Scientific Publishing, [2026] | Includes bibliographical references and index. | Summary: "This book aims to collect new insights and research on digital criminology and their use of technology aid. The new paradigm of crime is digital. The future of cybersecurity rests on a synergistic partnership between AI and human expertise, combining their strengths for more effective defense against evolving cyber threats"-- Provided by publisher.
Identifiers: LCCN 2024060502 (print) | LCCN 2024060503 (ebook) | ISBN 9798369388716 (hardcover) | ISBN 9798369388723 (paperback) | ISBN 9798369388730 (ebook)
Subjects: LCSH: Criminology--Technological innovations.
Classification: LCC HV6030 .R46 2025 (print) | LCC HV6030 (ebook) | DDC 364--dc23/eng/20250328
LC record available at https://lccn.loc.gov/2024060502
LC ebook record available at https://lccn.loc.gov/2024060503

British Cataloguing in Publication Data
A Cataloguing in Publication record for this book is available from the British Library.

Table of Contents

Detailed Table of Contents

consciously and responsibly, ensuring the protection of individual rights, protecting human rights, and preserving the confidentiality of the public in the judicial system.

This article examines the European Union's Artificial Intelligence (AI) Act, specifically its cybersecurity requirements for high-risk AI systems. The Act adopts a risk-based framework that classifies AI systems by societal impact, emphasizing cybersecurity for high-risk applications in fields like biometric recognition and critical infrastructure. Key principles, including transparency, resilience, and risk management, aim to protect AI from unique vulnerabilities such as adversarial manipulation and data poisoning. Findings highlight the Act's lifecycle-based approach, the importance of stakeholder engagement, and the need for adaptive standards to address evolving threats. The study underscores international collaboration and calls for continuous advancements in interpretability and privacy-preserving techniques, positioning the EU as a global leader in responsible AI regulation.

Crime and delinquency evolve, adapt, and transform alongside new "forms of social interaction." As society has significantly shifted from traditional ways of doing things to digitally integrated activities—storing our personal information in the cloud—individuals who engage in antisocial, criminal, or unlawful behavior have also evolved. As criminologists, we must become involved in understanding these "new forms" of antisocial conduct to ensure effective prevention.

From a broad perspective, it is important to highlight the influence of artificial intelligence on human daily life. As is well known, it has influenced and brought about major changes, which have contributed to the development of humanity, seen from the perspective of its positive contributions or aspects. On the other hand, society itself has become dependent on technology, and its usefulness has also led to negative consequences, as artificial intelligence has been used on several occasions to cause harm, even with catastrophic consequences.

Mental health in migrants is often influenced by challenges related to healthcare access, including difficulties in understanding medical information and uncertainty in seeking appropriate assistance. This study analyzes survey responses from 82 adults (50 women and 32 men) to examine healthcare access barriers and their impact on mental health, vaccination status, and dental hygiene. Principal Component Analysis (PCA) was employed to extract significant features from the dataset, highlighting patterns such as healthcare literacy gaps and demographic influences. These features were used to train an Artificial Neural Network (ANN) for predictive modeling. The ANN demonstrated high accuracy, with F1 scores exceeding 85%, effectively predicting mental health conditions, vaccination rates, and dental hygiene practices. The results underscore the importance of addressing healthcare access barriers to improve overall well-being among migrants

This chapter delves into the evolving role of international law in reshaping cyber criminology, explicitly focusing on the "Draft United Nations Convention Against Cybercrime 2024." The study analyzes the key provisions and objectives of the draft UN Convention, particularly its approach to combating cybercrime, strengthening international cooperation, and addressing human rights concerns. It discusses how the treaty aims to regulate cybercrime through standardized legal frameworks while considering the balance between national sovereignty and international collaboration. Additionally, the paper addresses the challenges of protecting fundamental freedoms, ensuring transparency in law enforcement practices, and safeguarding the rights of vulnerable populations. The research ultimately calls for a broader, human rights-focused approach to cybercrime legislation to ensure fair and equitable global legal standards in the digital era.

Cybersecurity is a significant concern in the present digital world. The increase in cybercrimes attracts attention of the whole globe. India is one of the top countries on the list of cybercrimes and cyberattacks. More than 1 billion people use smartphones in India and the focus on digital economy has also attracted many cyberattacks. This necessitates the need for a specific legal framework. India's Penal Code was almost 160 years old, and its provisions were not adequate to address the growing nature of cybercrime. Though the provisions of Information Technology Act, 2000 can be applied, India needed a criminal code addressing the latest trends of crimes. Many considered that the enactment of Bharatiya Nyaya Sanhita (BNS) will provide this required framework. In making a critical analysis the chapter tries to evaluate the provisions of BNS to examine whether it provided due protection to India's cyberspace.

In today's digital era, the rise in privacy infringement cases highlights the urgent need for robust legal frameworks and causations. This study focuses on predicting court verdicts in online privacy cases under the Digital Personal Data Protection Act (DPDPA) by combining advanced text processing and machine learning techniques. The textual data from court case judgments is transformed into numerical features using TF-IDF, followed by feature selection through Recursive Feature Elimination (RFE) to prioritize the most relevant information. A hybrid GRU+ANN model is proposed, leveraging the sequential processing capabilities of GRU and the deep learning strength of ANN to predict court outcomes effectively. The methodology enhances model accuracy, reduces feature redundancy, and provides insights into factors influencing judicial decisions. This approach demonstrates the potential of AI-driven models in legal analytics and decision prediction.

This chapter focuses on the relationship between green criminology, environmental cybercrime, and artificial intelligence (AI); it systematically examines how AI technologies repay environmental cyber threats. Environmental cybercrime is introduced as a subfield of green criminology before dedicating some time to explaining how it is one of the pressing issues of the modern world. The chapter discusses AI in fighting these crimes through the development of anomaly detection, predictive analytics, and auto-incident reaction applications. Specific solutions can be derived from modern companies' success in implementing AI in the real world and examples like the SolarWinds cyberattack and foiled attempts at eco-terrorism. The ethical, legal, policy, and other issues are discussed, emphasizing privacy, fairness, and regulation. The last chapter provides a technological and regulatory agenda and ultimately calls for an integrated approach to interaction between criminologists, technologists, and policymakers to build and regulate a stronger and more progressive tomorrow.

This chapter explores the impact of AI-powered solutions on cybersecurity within the context of cryptocurrency transactions in e-commerce. The primary objective is to investigate how AI can mitigate the growing cybersecurity risks associated with cryptocurrency fraud, enhancing the safety of e-commerce platforms. Targeting researchers, AI engineers, and e-commerce professionals, this study employs a mixed-method approach, combining case studies, expert interviews, and comparative analysis of AI-based tools and traditional security systems. The findings highlight the significant potential of AI, particularly in predictive analytics and real-time fraud detection, to combat cryptocurrency-related cybercrimes. The chapter also addresses

Preface

In the annals of intellectual inquiry, few disciplines have grappled with the complexities of human behavior as profoundly as criminology. For centuries, scholars, practitioners, and policymakers have striven to understand the origins of crime, its multifaceted manifestations, and the most effective means of prevention and intervention. From classical theories rooted in free will and deterrence to sociological perspectives emphasizing societal structures and inequalities, and psychological insights delving into individual pathology, criminology has evolved through a rich tapestry of theoretical frameworks and empirical investigations. Yet, despite these advancements, the persistent challenges of crime, its adaptability, and its profound societal impact continue to underscore the need for innovative approaches. We stand at the precipice of a new era, one defined by the transformative power of artificial intelligence (AI), and it is within this context that we must consider how AI is not merely augmenting but fundamentally *reshaping* criminology.

The journey of criminology, much like any scientific endeavor, has been characterized by both incremental progress and paradigm shifts. Early criminological thought, often intertwined with philosophy and moral reasoning, sought to define deviance and establish frameworks for justice. The Enlightenment brought forth concepts of rational choice and utilitarianism, laying the groundwork for classical criminology's emphasis on deterrence and punishment. The late 19th and early 20th centuries witnessed the rise of positivism, with its focus on empirical observation and the identification of biological, psychological, and social factors contributing to criminal behavior. This era introduced the notion of the “criminal man” and spurred the development of statistical methods for analyzing crime patterns. Subsequently, sociological perspectives gained prominence, highlighting the influence of social disorganization, strain, cultural deviance, and conflict on crime rates. Each of these theoretical waves, while offering valuable insights, also presented limitations, often struggling to provide comprehensive explanations for the heterogeneous nature of criminal activity and the dynamic interplay of individual and societal forces. The evolution continued with the emergence of developmental criminology, life-course theories, and environmental criminology, each adding further layers of complexity and nuance to our understanding.

However, the 21st century has introduced a new variable into this intricate equation: data. The digital age has unleashed an unprecedented deluge of information, from real-time crime data and social media interactions to demographic shifts and economic indicators. Traditional methods of data collection and analysis, while still valuable, are increasingly overwhelmed by the sheer volume, velocity, and variety of this data. This is where AI steps in as a powerful ally, offering computational capabilities far exceeding human capacity. AI, in its various forms – machine learning, deep learning, natural language processing, and predictive analytics – provides tools to sift through massive datasets, identify hidden patterns, uncover subtle correlations, and make predictions with a degree of precision previously unimaginable. The implications for criminology are profound, extending beyond mere efficiency gains to fundamentally altering how we conceptualize, investigate, and respond to crime.

The initial forays of AI into criminology have largely focused on practical applications, particularly in law enforcement. Predictive policing algorithms, for instance, aim to forecast crime hotspots, optimize resource allocation, and enhance patrol effectiveness. Facial recognition technology assists in identifying suspects and missing persons. Natural language processing aids in analyzing vast amounts of textual data from police reports, witness statements, and intelligence briefings. These applications, while demonstrating the immediate utility of AI, have also sparked critical debates concerning privacy, algorithmic bias, and the potential for reinforcing existing social inequalities. These concerns are not to be dismissed; indeed, they are central to the ethical and responsible integration of AI into any societal domain, especially one as sensitive as criminal justice. Yet, the current discourse often overlooks the deeper, more transformative potential of AI to reshape the *academic and theoretical foundations* of criminology itself.

This preface argues that AI is not merely a set of tools to be applied to existing criminological problems; rather, it is a catalyst for a paradigm shift, prompting us to rethink fundamental questions and pursue novel avenues of inquiry. Imagine a criminology that leverages AI to build more sophisticated causal models of crime, disentangling complex feedback loops between individual predispositions, social environments, and situational factors. Consider the possibility of AI identifying previously unrecognized risk factors or protective mechanisms, leading to more targeted and effective crime prevention programs. Envision a criminology that utilizes AI to analyze the narrative structures of criminal careers, revealing hidden pathways of desistance and recidivism with unprecedented detail. The sheer analytical power of AI allows us to move beyond broad correlations to uncover intricate causal mechanisms, offering a more nuanced and dynamic understanding of criminal behavior.

Furthermore, AI compels us to engage with data in new ways. It necessitates interdisciplinary collaboration between criminologists, computer scientists, statisticians, and ethicists. It demands a critical examination of the data we collect, how it is collected, and what inherent biases it may contain. The insights generated by AI are only as robust as the data they are trained on, underscoring the imperative for data quality, representativeness, and ethical sourcing. This is not a passive acceptance of AI; rather, it is an active engagement with its capabilities and limitations, a recognition that human expertise and critical judgment remain indispensable.

This book aims to explore the multifaceted ways in which AI is reshaping criminology, moving beyond superficial applications to delve into its profound theoretical and methodological implications. We will examine how AI can enhance our understanding of crime causation, improve crime prediction and prevention strategies, and inform evidence-based policy decisions. We will also critically address the ethical dilemmas and societal challenges posed by the integration of AI into the criminal justice system, emphasizing the importance of transparency, accountability, and fairness. The journey ahead is complex, filled with both immense promise and significant challenges. However, by embracing the transformative potential of AI with a critical and discerning eye, we can pave the way for a more insightful, effective, and ultimately, more just approach to understanding and addressing the enduring problem of crime in the 21st century. The reshaping of criminology with AI is not a distant possibility; it is a present reality, and this volume seeks to illuminate its contours and guide its responsible evolution

Chapter 1
Convergence Between Criminology and Artificial Intelligence

Enrique Ismael Meléndez Ruíz
https://orcid.org/0000-0002-9624-6675
Independent Researcher, Mexico

Mayra Elizabeth Brosig Rodríguez
Universidad Autónoma de Nuevo León, Mexico

Fernando Ortiz-Rodriguez
https://orcid.org/0000-0003-2084-3462
Tamaulipas Autonomous University, Mexico

ABSTRACT

This bibliometric study analyzes the convergence between artificial intelligence and criminology through the analysis of 955 documents indexed in Web of Science (2001- 2024). The results reveal exponential growth in scientific production, especially since 2018, coinciding with significant technological advances and their implementation in criminal justice systems. The analysis identifies the United States as a leader both in scientific production and in the impact of citations. The most influential documents reflect fundamental concerns about algorithmic interpretability, fairness in risk assessments, and institutional transformations derived from these technologies. This analysis provides a comprehensive view of the current state of research in this emerging interdisciplinary field.

DOI: 10.4018/979-8-3693-8871-6.ch001

INTRODUCTION

The intersection between artificial intelligence (AI) and criminology represents one of the most promising research fields within the current academic landscape (Dakalbab et al., 2022). This disciplinary crossover emerges in a context where technologies based on machine learning algorithms and neural networks are reconfiguring numerous aspects of social life, including those related to the prevention, detection, and investigation of criminal behaviors (Babuta & Oswald, 2021). The expansion of these technologies has generated a growing development of scientific research that deserves to be systematically analyzed to understand the trends, gaps, and possibilities within this emerging field (Chan & Bennet, 2017).

This growing academic interest is reflected in the historical evolution of the application of computational tools to the study of criminal phenomena. The trajectory of this disciplinary intersection reveals a progressive sophistication that has fundamentally transformed both the methods and objectives of contemporary criminological research. What began as a tentative approach between technology and criminality has matured into a field with its own identity, whose evolution deserves to be analyzed from a historical perspective to understand its current and future implications.

Early applications focused on statistical modeling for the analysis of criminal patterns (Cohen & Felson, 1978). However, what began as isolated applications has transformed into a comprehensive framework that challenges traditional criminological paradigms while offering opportunities for evidence-based interventions. As technological capabilities have expanded exponentially, criminal justice systems worldwide are increasingly integrating AI-driven tools into their operational frameworks, raising important questions about effectiveness, ethics, and governance (Miranda, 2022; Llinares, 2018).

The development of AI systems applied to criminology has experienced significant evolution in the last decade, transitioning from experimental tools to becoming instruments of daily use in various institutions of the criminal justice system (Ferguson, 2016). The range of contemporary applications is remarkably diverse; for example, predictive surveillance systems attempt to forecast critical points of crime and optimize resource allocation (Perry, 2013), while risk assessment algorithms inform judicial decision-making in areas ranging from bail determinations to sentencing (Berk et al., 2021). Computer vision technologies have revolutionized surveillance (Wang & Liu, 2022), while natural language processing facilitates the analysis of case documents, police reports, and online content related to criminal activities. Each of these applications represents a fundamental reconceptualization of criminological practice.

In this sense, scientific production in this field has experienced exponential growth, diversifying both in theoretical approaches and practical applications (Završnik, 2020). However, to date, few studies have systematically examined the characteristics, evolution, and intellectual structure of this literature (Meijer & Wessels, 2019). The absence of knowledge mapping in this area makes it difficult to identify the main research currents and leading institutions, as well as to detect knowledge gaps that require greater academic attention (Van Eck & Waltman, 2017).

Therefore, this study aims to analyze the scientific production at the convergence between AI and criminology. Using bibliometric analysis techniques (Aria & Cuccurullo, 2017), the temporal evolution of publications, the main thematic areas, and emerging trends are examined. This analysis will allow not only to establish an updated state of the art on the field but also identifying directions for future research (Donthu et al., 2021).

The relevance of this study transcends the academic sphere, as its results can guide political decisions and professional practices in an area where technological implementation often advances faster than reflection on its social implications (Mittelstadt et al., 2019). In a context where AI is profoundly modifying traditional criminological paradigms, it is essential to understand the dynamics of scientific production that underlie these transformations, as well as the epistemological, ethical, and methodological challenges they pose (Richardson et al., 2019).

METHODOLOGY

Regarding the methodological approach, it has been structured in various phases to ensure a comprehensive analysis of the existing literature, relying on specialized tools for the processing and analysis of bibliometric data (Aria & Cuccurullo, 2017) (Van Eck & Waltman, 2017).

Data collection was conducted through the Web of Science (WoS) platform, recognized for its comprehensive coverage and rigor in the indexing of scientific publications (Mongeon & Paul-Hus, 2016). To preserve the integrity of bibliometric information, data was extracted in .bib format directly from the WoS platform. For data processing and statistical analysis, R software was used, leveraging its advanced capabilities for scientific data analysis and visualization, following the methodological recommendations of Donthu et al. (2021).

The search was structured considering the following terms within the platform: (“criminology” OR “criminal justice” OR “crime”) AND (“artificial intelligence” OR “machine learning”). This search strategy was applied to the period 2001-2024 to capture the most recent trends in the field, resulting in the initial identification of 955 documents.

The analysis of the sample allowed for the classification of documents according to their typology, identifying 851 research articles, 58 review articles, 43 early access articles, and 3 book chapters. The processing of this data using R statistical software facilitated the generation of robust statistical analyses and comprehensive visualizations of trends and patterns in the literature (Cobo et al., 2011). The use of this statistical software, in conjunction with data extracted in .bib format from WoS, allowed for detailed analyses of co-citation, mapping of collaboration networks, and analysis of thematic trends (Zupic & Čater, 2015).

RESULTS

The analysis of scientific production reveals an upward trend during the 2001-2024 period (Figure 1). During the first two decades of the 21st century, production remained modest, with only one to four publications annually, reflecting the emerging stage of this interdisciplinary field. However, 2018 represents a clear turning point with 26 publications, marking the beginning of a phase of exponential growth.

Starting in 2019, with 38 articles, there is evidence of significant acceleration that reaches 96 publications in 2020 and consistently exceeds 150 annual publications since 2021. This development culminates in 2024 with a historic maximum of 216 articles, representing a 72% increase compared to the previous year. This notable growth temporally coincides with substantial advances in AI technologies and their progressive implementation in criminal justice environments.

The observed upward trajectory reflects not only the growing academic interest in this field but also its consolidation as a dynamic research area. The accelerated pace of publications in the last five years suggests the formation of an increasingly robust scientific community committed to analyzing the applications, implications, and ethical challenges derived from the convergence between artificial intelligence and criminology. This trend indicates that the field has surpassed its initial exploration phase to enter a stage of maturity characterized by deeper and more specialized research.

Figure 1. Annual scientific production

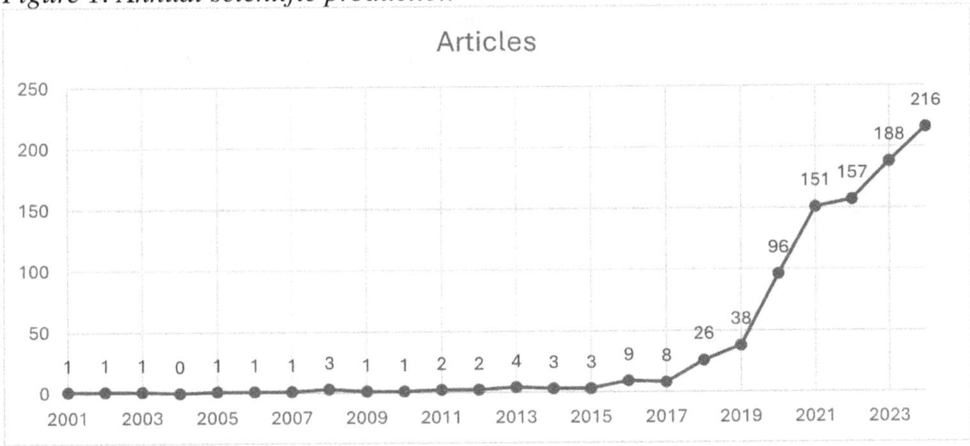

Source: Elaboration from integrated database of Web of Science platform

Most relevant journals in the study of the topic

The analysis of the main journals publishing on the topic in question reveals a distribution that reflects both the interdisciplinary nature of the area and certain patterns of academic specialization. The journal *IEEE ACCESS* emerges as the dominant publication with 91 documents, establishing a substantial difference compared to other journals in the field. This preeminence is significant given that *IEEE ACCESS* is an open access journal oriented toward multidisciplinary technological applications, suggesting that research at this intersection finds greater space in platforms focused on technological innovation than in traditional criminological publications.

At a second level of relevance, a group of specialized journals with moderate contributions is identified. *The International Journal of Advanced Computer Science* (15 documents), *Forensic Science International* (13 documents), *Multimedia Tools and Applications* (11 documents), *Electronics* (10 documents), and *ISPRS International Journal of Geo-Information* (10 documents) make up this intermediate group. This distribution demonstrates the convergence of multiple disciplines, integrating publications from the forensic field with others specialized in advanced computing, multimedia technologies, and geospatial information systems. A third group consists of journals that, although with fewer publications (9 documents each), represent a diversity of approaches: *AI & Society, Applied Sciences-Basel, Russian Journal of Criminology*, and *Scientific Reports*.

This distribution of publications (Figure 2) clearly illustrates the interdisciplinary character of research in AI and criminology. The notorious predominance of technological journals over specifically criminological ones suggests that the field is currently being driven mainly from the technological perspective, developing applications toward criminology, rather than from the traditional criminological discipline adopting and integrating AI tools. This imbalance represents a potential opportunity to strengthen the participation of criminological publications in this emerging field, promoting a more balanced dialogue between both disciplines.

Figure 2. Most Relevant Journals

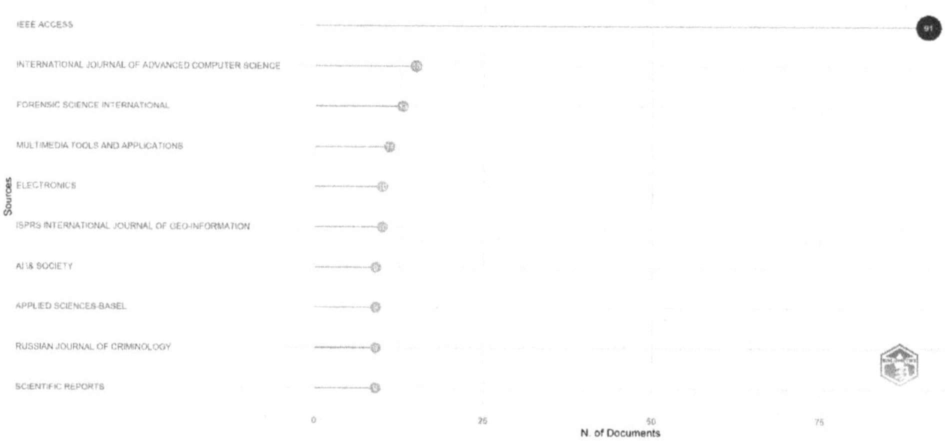

Source: Web of Science Platform

Corresponding author country

The analysis of the geographical distribution of corresponding authors in the field of artificial intelligence applied to criminology reveals significant patterns that reflect both dynamics of scientific leadership and trends of international collaboration in this emerging area (Figure 3).

The United States positions itself as the leader with approximately 200 documents, establishing a considerable advantage over other countries. This American preeminence can be attributed to several complementary factors: its historical leadership in the development of AI technologies, its robust tradition in criminological research, and the solid funding and research infrastructure available in its academic institutions and technological centers.

At a second level of scientific production are China and India, with approximately 100 and 80 documents respectively. China's prominent positioning reflects its strategic investment in AI technologies over the last decade and its particular interest in surveillance and public security applications. Meanwhile, India's presence likely responds to the convergence between its growing technological ecosystem and the specific challenges of citizen security in high population density contexts.

The United Kingdom occupies the fourth place with approximately 70 documents, followed by a group of countries with moderate contributions in the range of 30 to 50 documents, such as Korea, Italy, Spain, Russia, and Australia. This diversified geographical distribution evidences the global interest in this disciplinary intersection, integrating both consolidated technological powers and countries with advanced criminal justice systems.

Figure 3. Corresponding author country

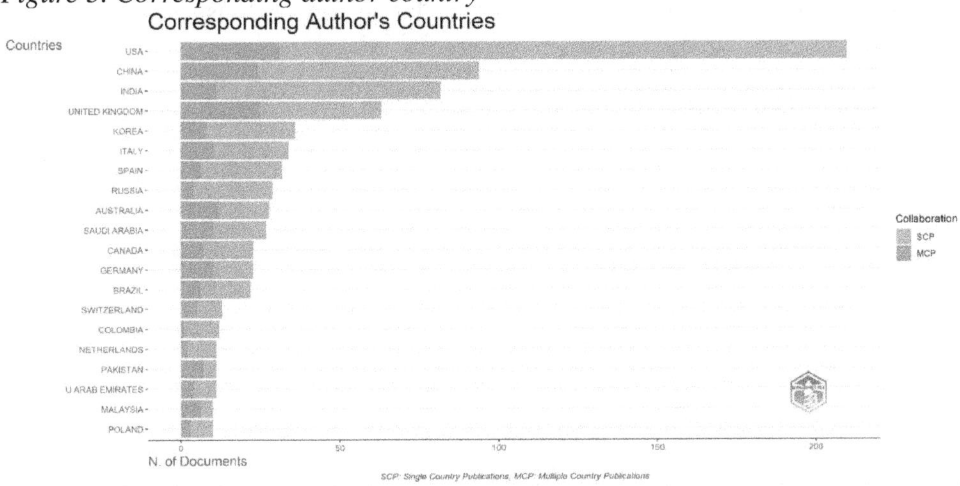

Source: Web of Science Platform

A particularly relevant aspect is the distinction between Single Country Publications (SCP) and Multiple Country Publications (MCP). The United States not only leads in terms of total volume but also maintains the highest proportion of international collaborations, suggesting its function as a central node in global research networks. This pattern of international collaboration is also significant in countries such as the United Kingdom, India, and China, although with different proportions between national and collaborative research.

This geographical configuration reflects both the current distribution of specialized knowledge and national priorities in research on security, justice, and technology. The predominance of countries with advanced economies and significant investment in technological R&D suggests that the development of this field is strongly conditioned by the availability of resources and specialized infrastructure, which could pose challenges of access and applicability for regions with less representation in scientific production.

Countries with the highest number of citations

Regarding the analysis of the most cited countries, Figure 4 reveals a distribution of academic influence that shows some similarities, but also notable differences compared to scientific production by country. The United States stands out as the most cited country, with approximately 9,655 citations, establishing a difference with the second country, China, which records approximately 1,500 citations. This disproportion is significantly greater than that observed in the number of publications, suggesting that American research is not only more numerous but also exerts a considerably greater influence in terms of academic impact measured by citations.

Figure 4. Most cited countries

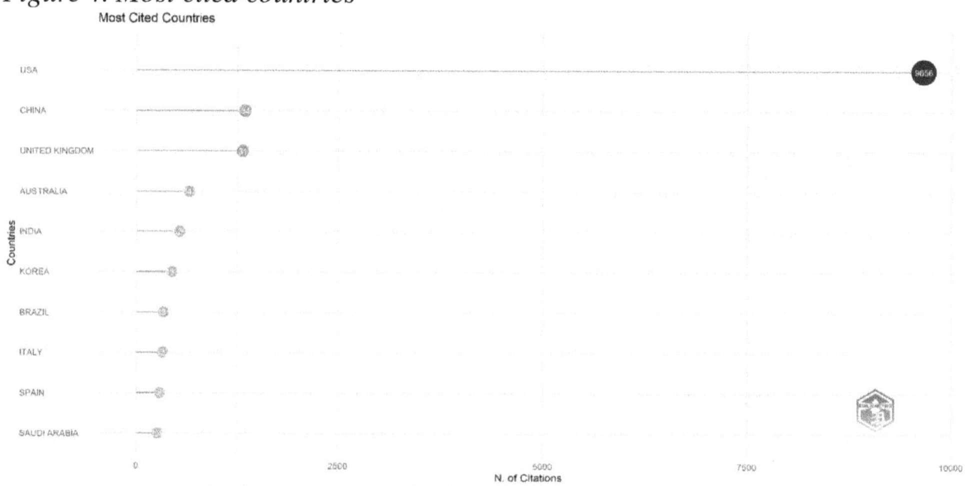

Source: Web of Science Platform

This distribution of citations suggests that, although research in AI applied to criminology is becoming geographically diversified in terms of production, academic recognition and influence remains primarily concentrated in the United States, with a substantial gap compared to the rest of the world. This poses significant challenges for the global scientific community in terms of visibility and impact of research developed outside the American sphere.

Most cited documents

The analysis of the most cited documents provides insight into the publications that have exerted the greatest intellectual influence on the subject of study (Table 1). This metric reveals those works that have established fundamental conceptual frameworks or generated significant debates within the scientific community. The following table presents the ten documents with the highest number of citations in this interdisciplinary field, highlighting both the most influential contributions and the thematic areas that have captured the greatest academic attention at the intersection between artificial intelligence and criminology.

Table 1. Most cited documents

Author	Article	Number of citations
Rudín, (2019)	*Stop explaining black box machine learning models for high stakes decisions and use interpretable models instead*	3860
Dressel & Farid, (2018)	*The accuracy, fairness, and limits of predicting recidivism*	525
Berk et al., (2018) (2021)	*Fairness in Criminal Justice Risk Assessments: The State of the Art*	427
Kleinber et al., (2018)	*Human Decisions and Machine Predictions*	347
Ferrag et al., (2022)	*Edge-IIoTset: A New Comprehensive Realistic Cyber Security Dataset of IoT and IIoT Applications for Centralized and Federated Learning*	303
Shaukat et al., (2020)	*A Survey on Machine Learning Techniques for Cyber Security in the Last Decade*	205
Burrel & Fourcader (2021)	*The Society of Algorithms*	202
Mohler et al., (2015)	*Randomized Controlled Field Trials of Predictive Policing*	201
Berk y Bleich (2013)	*Statistical Procedures for Forecasting Criminal Behavior. A Comparative Assessment*	119
Završnik (2019)	*Algorithmic justice: Algorithms and big data in criminal justice settings*	95

Source: Elaboration from the database of the Web of Science platform

The analysis of the ten most cited articles reveals the main trends. For example, Rudin's work (2019), with 3,860 citations, represents the epicenter of this debate by fundamentally questioning the use of "black box" models in high-impact decisions, advocating for inherently interpretable models that avoid perpetuating discriminatory practices in the justice system. This concern for accuracy and fairness is also reflected in Dressel and Farid (2018), who demonstrated that commercial software for recidivism risk assessment did not surpass predictions made by people without experience in criminal justice, thus questioning the need for complex systems when simpler solutions prove equally effective.

Berk et al. (2018) delve into the question of fairness by establishing a conceptual framework that demonstrates the impossibility of simultaneously maximizing accuracy and fairness in risk assessments, posing necessary trade-offs in the design of these systems. This tension between efficiency and fairness manifests in practical applications such as that investigated by Kleinberg et al. (2018), who demonstrated that machine learning can significantly improve bail decisions, with simulations indicating crime reductions of up to 24.7% without increasing incarceration rates.

The empirical effectiveness of these systems is evidenced in the work of Mohler et al. (2016) on predictive policing, where computational models outperformed human analysts in predicting crimes, achieving reductions of 7.4% in criminal volume through dynamic patrolling. However, these applications generate concerns about institutional transformation, as noted by Završnik (2019), who analyzes how "algorithmic justice" modifies the production of knowledge about crime and undermines traditional procedural safeguards.

Burrel and Fourcader (2021) examine these transformations from a sociological perspective. Meanwhile, works such as those by Ferrag et al. (2022) and Shaukat et al. (2020) represent emerging trends related to cybersecurity, developing datasets and techniques to combat the growing threat of cybercrime.

This research landscape reveals a dynamic interdisciplinary field focused on balancing the potential of AI to improve efficiency in the criminal justice system with fundamental concerns about fairness, transparency, and accountability. As these technologies continue to evolve, the integration of technical, ethical, and criminological perspectives is emerging as increasingly crucial for the responsible development of the subject.

Most frequent words

The analysis of the most frequent words in literature reveals the conceptual structure and dominant methodological priorities in this interdisciplinary field (Figure 5). "Crime" tops the list with 102 occurrences, almost doubling the frequency of the second most common word, which confirms the central focus on criminal phenomena as the primary object of study.

The term "model" appears as the second most frequent word with 52 occurrences, followed by "classification" with 48 occurrences, demonstrating the prominence of methodological approaches based on modeling and categorization of criminological data. This concentration reflects the emphasis on technical and operational aspects of applying AI to criminological problems, where the construction of predictive models constitutes a fundamental practice.

A second thematic group consists of the words “prediction” (39 occurrences), “impact” (34 occurrences), and “evidence” (33 occurrences), suggesting a substantial interest in the predictive capabilities of AI in criminological contexts, as well as in the evaluation of its effects and empirical foundations.

The term “artificial intelligence” explicitly appears as the seventh most frequent word (32 occurrences), followed by “models” (31 occurrences), “patterns” (31 occurrences), and “big data” (30 occurrences), completing the essential technological concepts that define the field. The prominence of “patterns” underscores the focus on detecting regularities in criminological data, while the inclusion of “big data” reflects the centrality of massive volumes of information as a fundamental resource for these applications.

This terminological distribution reveals a field strongly oriented toward practical and methodological applications, with emphasis on predictive modeling and classification of criminal phenomena.

Figure 5. Most frequent keywords

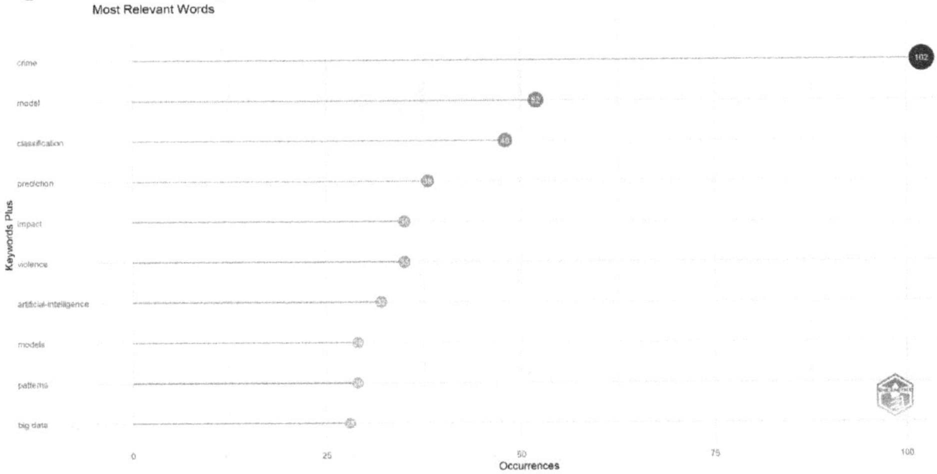

Source: Web of Science Platform

Keywords Cloud

The keyword cloud provides a visual representation of thematic priorities in the research (Figure 6). The term "crime" clearly dominates the center of the visualization with the largest size, confirming its function as the conceptual core of the field and the focal point around which this disciplinary intersection is articulated.

The distribution of terms reveals a conceptual structure in which technological and methodological aspects ("artificial intelligence", "model", "classification", "prediction", "patterns") are closely interrelated with the central object of study ("crime"). This visual pattern reinforces the interpretation that, in this emerging field, artificial intelligence technology is primarily conceived as an instrumental tool for modeling and predicting criminal phenomena.

Figure 6. Keyword cloud

Source: Web of Science Platform

The prominent but secondary presence of terms such as "impact" and "evidence" suggests a growing attention to the evaluation of results and empirical foundations of these applications. Simultaneously, the visualization allows us to appreciate how considerations about the social and ethical implications of these technologies are beginning to emerge, although with less prominence than technical and applied aspects.

This graphical representation complements the quantitative analysis of frequencies, offering a perspective on the conceptual structure of the field and confirming its practical and methodological orientation, where technology serves to address traditional criminological problems through new data-based approaches.

Keyword network

The analysis of the keyword network generated with *VOSviewer* software (Figure 7) reveals the conceptual structure of the field of artificial intelligence applied to criminology.

Figure 7. Red de términos clave

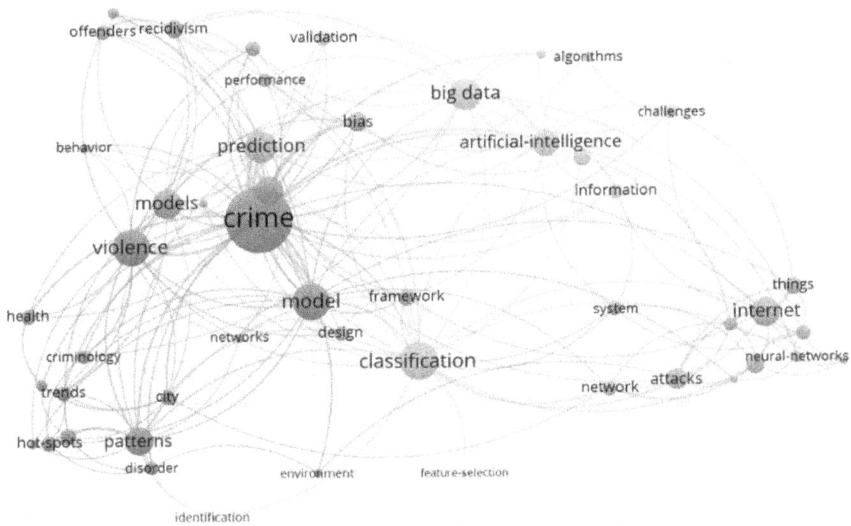

Source: Elaboración propia con Web of Science.

The visualization shows five interconnected thematic clusters that reflect the main lines of research. The first cluster, dominated by the central term "crime," focuses on urban and spatial criminology, including concepts such as "violence," "city," "hot-spots," and "patterns," evidencing AI applications oriented toward the analysis of spatial crime patterns and prevention strategies based on urban environments. The second cluster represents the field of cybersecurity, grouping terms such as "Internet," "attacks," and "neural-networks," showing the growing importance of cybercrime and AI applications for its detection and prevention. The third cluster centers on risk and recidivism assessment, with terms such as "offenders," "recidivism," and "risk-assessment," reflecting the use of predictive algorithms in judicial systems. The fourth cluster encompasses technological foundations and legal challenges, including "artificial intelligence," "big data," and "law," serving as the conceptual infrastructure that underpins specific applications. Finally, the fifth cluster represents methodology and system design, with "model" as a prominent element, connecting with "classification," "prediction," and "framework."

This thematic network reflects a developing interdisciplinary field, where traditional criminology, computer science, and data analysis converge, with lines of research ranging from very specific applications (such as intrusion detection) to broader methodological considerations. The structure of the network suggests that, although there are differentiated subfields, there is significant interconnection between them, indicating an integrated research area with multiple points of contact between disciplines.

CONCLUSION

This study reveals a rapidly growing interdisciplinary field that has experienced a notable expansion, particularly since 2018. This systematic analysis of scientific production allows for the identification of significant patterns that characterize the intellectual structure, geographic distribution, and thematic evolution of this disciplinary intersection.

The results demonstrate a marked acceleration in scientific production during the 2018-2024 period, coinciding with significant advances in AI technologies and their progressive implementation in criminal justice contexts. This exponential growth reflects not only increasing academic interest but also the consolidation of a scientific community dedicated to exploring the applications, implications, and challenges derived from this technological convergence.

The distribution of publications by sources reveals a predominance of technological journals over traditional criminological publications, with IEEE ACCESS as the dominant channel. This imbalance suggests that the field is being driven primarily from the technological perspective toward criminological applications, rather than from the criminological discipline adopting AI tools. This asymmetry represents an opportunity to strengthen the participation of specifically criminological publications, promoting a more balanced dialogue between both disciplines.

The geographic analysis shows an indisputable leadership of the United States, both in scientific production and, especially, in citation impact. The disproportion between the volume of citations received by American publications compared to those from other countries suggests the existence of a center-periphery structure in knowledge generation, where certain institutions exert a disproportionate influence on the conceptual configuration of the field.

The examination of the most cited documents reveals fundamental concerns that structure the academic debate: the interpretability of "black box" models in high-impact decisions (Rudin, 2019); accuracy and fairness in algorithmic risk assessments (Dressel & Farid, 2018; Berk et al., 2018); and the institutional transformations derived from the implementation of these technologies (Završnik, 2019; Burrel

& Fourcader, 2021). These seminal works articulate essential tensions between technological efficiency and ethical considerations that will characterize the future development of the field.

The analysis of key terms identifies five main thematic clusters: urban and spatial criminology, cybersecurity, risk and recidivism assessment, technological foundations and legal challenges, and methodology and system design. This conceptual structure reflects a multifaceted field with differentiated but interconnected subfields, where traditional criminological perspectives converge with advances in computational sciences and data analysis.

The relative absence, among the most frequent terms, of concepts related to ethical concerns or civil rights ("privacy," "bias," "fairness") is significant, suggesting that, although these considerations are present in influential works, they do not yet constitute the dominant conceptual core of the field. This finding raises questions about the balance between technological innovation and ethical reflection in the development of this disciplinary intersection.

The limitations of this study include the exclusive dependence on Web of Science as a data source, which could underestimate contributions in publications not indexed on this platform. Future research could incorporate complementary sources such as Scopus or qualitative content analysis, and exploration of co-authorship networks to better understand the social structure of the scientific community.

In synthesis, this study identifies an emerging field characterized by rapid growth, American leadership, technocentric orientation, and fundamental concerns about interpretability, fairness, and institutional transformation. The findings suggest the need to strengthen critical criminological perspectives, broaden the participation of researchers from less represented regions, and deepen the integration of ethical considerations in the design and implementation of AI technologies in criminal justice contexts. As these technologies continue to transform institutional practices, an interdisciplinary approach that balances technological innovation with ethical reflection and criminological contextualization is essential.

REFERENCES

Aria, M., & Cuccurullo, C. (2017). bibliometrix: An R-tool for comprehensive science mapping analysis. *Journal of Informetrics, 11*(4), 959–975. https://doi.org/https://doi.org/10.1016/j.joi.2017.08.007. DOI: 10.1016/j.joi.2017.08.007

Babuta, A., & Oswald, M. (2021). Machine learning predictive algorithms and the policing of future crimes: governance and oversight. In J. L. McDaniel, & K. Pease, *Predictive policing and artificial intelligence.* Routledge, Taylor & Francis Group.

Berk, R., Heidari, H., Jabbari, S., Kearns, M., & Roth, A. (2021). Fairness in criminal justice risk assessments: The state of the art. *Sociological Methods & Research, 50*(1), 3–44. https://doi.org/https://doi.org/10.1177/0049124118782533. DOI: 10.1177/0049124118782533

Berk, R., Heidari, H., Jabbari, S., Kearns, M., & Roth, A. (2021). Fairness in criminal justice risk assessments: The state of the art. *Sociological Methods & Research, 50*(1), 3–44. https://doi.org/https://doi.org/10.1177/0049124118782533. DOI: 10.1177/0049124118782533

Berk, R. A., & Bleich, J. (2013). Statistical procedures for forecasting criminal behavior: A comparative assessment. *Criminology & Pub. Pol'y, 12.*

Burrel, J., & Fourcader, M. (2021). The Society of Algorithms. *Annual Review of Sociology, 47*(1). https://doi.org/https://doi.org/10.1146/annurev-soc-090820-020800

Chan, J., & Bennet, M. L. (2017). Making sense of big data for security. *British Journal of Criminology, 57*(2), 299–319. https://doi.org/https://doi.org/10.1093/bjc/azw059

Cobo, M. J., López-Herrera, A. G., Herrera-Viedma, E., & Herrera, F. (2011). Science mapping software tools: Review, analysis, and cooperative study among tools. *Journal of the American Society for Information Science and Technology, 62*(7), 1382–1402. https://doi.org/https://doi.org/10.1002/asi.21525. DOI: 10.1002/asi.21525

Cohen, L. E., & Felson, M. (2010). Social Change and Crime Rate Trends: A Routine Activity Approach. *American Sociological Review, 44*(4), 588-608. https://doi.org/https://doi.org/10.2307/2094589

Dakalbab, F., Talib, M. A., Waraga, O. A., Nassif, A. B., Abbas, S., & Nasir, Q. (2022). Artificial intelligence & crime prediction: A systematic literature review. *Social Sciences & Humanities Open, 6*(1), 100342. https://doi.org/https://doi.org/10.1016/j.ssaho.2022.100342. DOI: 10.1016/j.ssaho.2022.100342

Donthu, N., Kumar, S., Mukherjee, D., Pandey, N., & Marc, W. (2021). How to conduct a bibliometric analysis: An overview and guidelines. *Journal of Business Research, 133*, 285–296. https://doi.org/https://doi.org/10.1016/j.jbusres.2021.04.070. DOI: 10.1016/j.jbusres.2021.04.070

Dressel, J., & Farid, H. (2018). The accuracy, fairness, and limits of predicting recidivism. *Science Advances, 1*(1), 4. https://doi.org/https://doi.org/10.1126/sciadv.aao5580. DOI: 10.1126/sciadv.aao5580 PMID: 29376122

Ferguson, A. G. (2016). Policing Predictive Policing. https://doi.org/Available at *SSRN*: https://ssrn.com/abstract=2765525

Ferrag, M. A., Friha, O., Hamouda, D., Maglaras, L., & Janicke, H. (2022). Edge-IIoTset: A New Comprehensive Realistic Cyber Security Dataset of IoT and IIoT Applications for Centralized and Federated Learning. *IEEE Access : Practical Innovations, Open Solutions, 10*, 40281–40306. https://doi.org/https://doi.org/10.1109/ACCESS.2022.3165809. DOI: 10.1109/ACCESS.2022.3165809

Garvie, C., Bedoya, A., & Franke, J. (2019). *The perpetual line-up: Unregulated police face recognition in America*. Georgetown Law Center on Privacy & Technology.

Kleinberg, J., Lakkaraju, H., Leskovec, J., Ludwig, J., & Mullainathan, S. (2018). Human decisions and machine predictions. *The Quarterly Journal of Economics, 133*(1), 237–293. https://doi.org/https://doi.org/10.1093/qje/qjx032 PMID: 29755141

Llinares, F. M. (2018). Inteligencia artificial y justicia penal: más allá de los resultados lesivos causados por robots. *Revista de Derecho Penal y Criminologia, 20*, 87-130. https://doi.org/https://doi.org/10.5944/rdpc.20.2018.26446

Meijer, A., & Wessels, M. (2019). Predictive Policing: Review of Benefits and Drawbacks. *International Journal of Public Administration, 42*(12), 1031–1039. https://doi.org/https://doi.org/10.1080/01900692.2019.1575664. DOI: 10.1080/01900692.2019.1575664

Miranda, H. (2022). Inteligencia artificial y justicia. *Revista de la Facultad de Derecho de México, 72*(284), 373-402. https://doi.org/http://10.22201/fder.24488933e.2022.284.83394

Mittelstadt, B., Russel, C., & Wachter, S. (2019). Explaining Explanations in AI. *Proceedings of the conference on fairness, accountability, and transparency*, (pp. 279-288). https://doi.org/https://doi.org/10.1145/3287560.3287574

Mohler, G. O., Short, M. B., Malinoswki, S., Johnson, M., Tita, G. E., Bertozzi, A. L., & Brantingham, P. J. (2015). Randomized Controlled Field Trials of Predictive Policing. *Journa of the American Statistical Association, 110*(512), 1399-1411. https://doi.org/https://doi.org/10.1080/01621459.2015.1077710

Mongeon, P., & Paul-Hus, A. (2016). The journal coverage of Web of Science and Scopus: A comparative analysis. *Scientometrics, 106*(1), 2013–2228. https://doi.org/https://doi.org/10.1007/s11192-015-1765-5. DOI: 10.1007/s11192-015-1765-5

Perry, W. L. (2013). *Predictive policing: The role of crime forecasting in law enforcement operations*. Rand Corporation. DOI: 10.7249/RR233

Richardson, R., Schultz, J. M., & Crawford, K. (2019). Dirty data, bad predictions: How civil rights violations impact police data, predictive policing systems, and justice. *NYUL Law Review Online, 91*.

Rudin, C. (2019). Stop explaining black box machine learning models for high stakes decisions and use interpretable models instead. *Nature Machine Intelligence, 1*(5), 206–215. https://doi.org/https://doi.org/10.1038/s42256-019-0048-x. DOI: 10.1038/s42256-019-0048-x PMID: 35603010

Shaukat, K., Luo, S., Varadjarajan, I., Hamed, A., & Xu, M. (2020). A Survey on Machine Learning Techniques for Cyber Security in the Last Decade. *IEEE Access : Practical Innovations, Open Solutions, 8*, 222310–222354. https://doi.org/https://doi.org/10.1109/ACCESS.2020.3041951. DOI: 10.1109/ACCESS.2020.3041951

Van Eck, N. J., & Waltman, L. (2017). Citation-based clustering of publications using CitNetExplorer and VOSviewer. *Scientometrics, 111*(2), 1053–1070. https://doi.org/https://doi.org/10.1007/s11192-017-2300-7. DOI: 10.1007/s11192-017-2300-7 PMID: 28490825

Završnik, A. (2019). Algorithmic justice: Algorithms and big data in criminal justice settings. *European Journal of Criminology, 18*(5), 623–642. https://doi.org/https://doi.org/10.1177/1477370819876762. DOI: 10.1177/1477370819876762

Završnik, A. (2020). Criminal justice, artificial intelligence systems, and human rights. *ERA Forum, 20*, 567-583. https://doi.org/https://doi.org/10.1007/s12027-020-00602-0

Zupic, I., & Čater, T. (2015). Bibliometric methods in management and organization. *Organizational Research Methods, 18*(3), 429–472. https://doi.org/https://doi.org/10.1177/10944281145626. DOI: 10.1177/1094428114562629

Chapter 2
Looking at the Influence of AI on Criminal Ethics

Ignacio Hernández Rodríguez
Autonomous University of Tamaulipas, Mexico

Gabriela Cervantes
Autonomous University of Tamaulipas, Mexico

Mario Alberto Morales
Autonomous University of Tamaulipas, Mexico

ABSTRACT

The impact of artificial intelligence (AI) on criminal ethics, examining both its advantages and the ethical challenges it poses. AI has transformed the way information is processed. Criminal investigations are carried out, optimizing the efficiency of data collection and analysis. However, its implementation has also had consequences, raising concerns about algorithmic bias, discrimination, and a lack of clarity in decision-making procedures. A critical analysis of the literature and case studies was conducted, highlighting the importance of a solid ethical framework to guide the application of criminology. The importance of implementing policies that promote equity and accountability, as well as appropriate training for experts in the sector, is emphasized. Consequently, it can be established that although AI offers essential possibilities for improving criminal practice, its incorporation must be done consciously and responsibly, ensuring the protection of individual rights, protecting human rights, and preserving the confidentiality of the public in the judicial system.

DOI: 10.4018/979-8-3693-8871-6.ch002

INTRODUCTION

Nowadays, it is important to use a wide range of techniques to identify irregularities and trends to make projections and enhance crime prevention, to guide solutions with new possibilities, which increases the use of computer tools that carry out complex operations and a large number of operations, which a human being could not or would carry out very slowly, taking weeks, months, years, decades or centuries, so the incorporation of artificial intelligence (AI) is an increasingly relevant issue as the use of cutting-edge technologies increases, for example in criminal investigations and in the judicial system (Golding & Nicola, 2019).

Before entering context, we must remember the four postulates that govern ethics: Non-maleficence, Beneficence, Justice, and Autonomy (López-Calva, 2024). Therefore, before using AI in different fields of hard, social, or human sciences, we should know if it is possible to apply these postulates in favor of using AI in a way that does not harm others with its use, that we benefit, that the application is valued equally in any case and that equal cases are treated equally, and finally, that we do not lose sight of the fact that the autonomy of the creation, development, instrumentation, use, and sale of AI (Gervais, 2023) will maintain the sensitivity of each individual without that use causing the loss of the free decision-making of each individual and that those who feel violated can stop using it at any time, without that affecting them, denigrating them, or degrading them in front of others. The above considering that these principles originated from the culture of medical health (Cottey, 2016).

Thus, AI, particularly machine learning -oriented algorithms, are present in several areas of knowledge. These algorithms examine large volumes of data and make predictions when necessary. Applied in the financial, health (Weidener, 2016), industry, economics, nutrition, criminal, and many other sectors (Schuklenk, 2020). Considering that prediction is also applied in the field of administration of justice, for example in important matters such as crime, through what are known as predictors, such as algorithms to foresee risks. Additionally, in recent decades, considerable progress in the legal research and AI community has developed from computer models. (Avella et al., 2022)

Specifically, AI is seen as a language of tools, like an Atlas for applying qualitative analysis to interview procedures, and in studies for automatically coding them, which saves time and reduces risks. (Lopezosa et al., 2023)

Currently, recent advances in AI have the capacity to analyze a broad spectrum of industrial sectors, including the military, national security, and intelligence. However, government use of this technology could entail dangers, ranging from large-scale surveillance, cyberattacks, and even the possibility of using it in deadly autonomous devices, such as programs or computers that control weapons of mass destruction, for which humans safeguard the code to activate them. Therefore, AI research can be generated and encouraged; for example, increasing security in the communication card supply chain in the United States of America. That government generates protocols so that intelligence agencies can prioritize the task of protecting American industry from those countries that intend to conduct international espionage or cause damage to key industries in that country. On the other hand, there are various types of AI-focused tools implemented primarily in police administration, which include surveillance systems with biometric signature recognition, license plate recognition, or text or natural language processing to search for specific patterns in social media messages, faces, and behavioral patterns that pose a threat to society and even the rest of the world. The introduction of AI services in this area allows for the detection, collection, and processing of data. Thus, some of the best-known systems include facial recognition systems, license plate systems, and tracking systems that are very popular in Europe (Riba, 2024) .

This chapter seeks to understand how AI relates to criminal ethics. This will be relevant by focusing on examining both the benefits and challenges. It will address the ethical trade-offs that arise in 1) the use of technologies, from algorithmic bias to the management of sensitive data; 2) as well as the regulations and best practices that can guide the responsible use of AI.

In studying this topic, it is considered essential to understand how to maintain the balance between technological innovation and the essential ethical principles governing justice. Critical reflection and a focus on ethical professionalism protect human rights and promote equitable justice that does not harm and that benefits its use.

BACKGROUND

In November 2021, UNESCO issued a recommendation aimed at providing nations with guidelines for addressing the impact of AI, a trend in human endeavor across all fields. AI is a dynamic, evolving, and comprehensive foundation. However, the establishment of current and future ethical and legal standards, along with government and global policies for these uses, is crucial. It is well known that the implementation of laws and government regulations does not apply to all countries, as each is considered autonomous. Therefore, consensus must be reached to ensure that agreements are applied to the largest possible number of countries and, in this sense, safeguard global protocols. Otherwise, a lack of understanding between countries, and even between states within the same country, can lead to tensions in the process of scientific and technological innovation, for example in the area of technology and communications. Therefore, discovering appropriate solutions will be a constant challenge for societies (Vásquez, 2023) .

AI implies greater efficiency and more efficient government. Something that must be constantly considered are the developers, the so-called specialists, who range from areas such as public health, security, human resources, customer service, border security, immigration, and certain features that reproduce the attributes of human intelligence, from decision-making to management, including the processing of those attributes. Issues of equity, ethics, justice, and fairness generate concern and are viewed as possible within democratic principles. As countries move forward, researchers question whether these preparations will include accountability tests (Nzobonimpa & Savard, 2023) .

Ethics in data protection in digital settings and criminal intelligence

It is crucial to emphasize that no system can supplant judgment. The position of the analyst element is examined below. It is essential to train analog individuals to navigate digital contexts and enhance their intelligence product skills. Digital tools in the context of " big data" (a massive and complex collection of data that is difficult to store, process, and analyze with traditional systems) and AI must be incorporated in accordance with the current legal framework of the country in question, which will safeguard personal information and restrict intelligence actions, with the challenge of managing more information in a short period of time, but with the uncertainty of whether the level of quality will be reduced. (De Paula, 2023) .

A study conducted in 2024 analyzed how AI can bring benefits in terms of accuracy, efficiency, access to advanced tools, and personalization of care, in addition to addressing important ethical considerations such as: Protection of patient data, transparency in decision-making, and adequate supervision and regulation of artificial intelligence systems (Zúñiga & Zúñiga, 2024) .

Likewise, the research entitled "Ethics in Artificial Intelligence from a Legal Perspective" showed that specialists and various international organizations, including the European Union, agreed to safeguard a prototype with autonomous AI features, which are perceived as cognitive or intelligent beings. (Zabala Leal, 2021) .

Another study aimed to evaluate the benefits of using AI in the public policy cycle and help fill this gap. To do so, a comparative study of eight global cases was conducted. According to the study, the greatest benefit of using AI was its ability to instantly handle and analyze large volumes of varied data, thus automating various processes within the public policy cycle. However, there are also drawbacks such as marginalization, biased calculations, lack of privacy, and limited transparency (Toache, 2023) .

The term criminology refers to the comprehensive study of crime and criminal behavior, as well as the criminal justice system and the processes that shape it, through the combination of several sciences or disciplines (Reyes *et al*., 2023). Each discipline provides unique resources and knowledge to criminology. For example, biology provides this area with tools to examine biological evidence such as DNA, fingerprints, and blood samples. Chemistry or biochemistry provides investigators with tools to examine chemical evidence such as substances, explosives, and chemicals. Physics provides the tools to examine evidence such as weapons, shoe prints, and vehicle wreckage, and other authors refer to AI as a scientific advance of great relevance, crucial to progress in some of the most significant discoveries of recent years in human history. (Parga, 2023) Under this approach, we understand that AI should not replace human beings. Furthermore, for the same reason, it must be used under appropriate parameters to prevent the danger of misuse.

A relevant and sensitive issue for every government is homicide. Homicide is a crime that is causing disorder in society, and there is a growing need to ensure that this type of conduct does not go unpunished. Therefore, criminology is an essential tool in the field of criminal law. By using scientific techniques, investigators can accurately determine whether a crime has occurred and who is allegedly responsible. Considering an example of the aforementioned, Ecuador's criminal investigation department has all the necessary equipment and personnel to assist in criminal investigations through the use of AI (Andrade Molina, 2009a).

In the legal field, the fusion of AI and forensics is generating various discussions in Latin America about how to attribute civil liability when these technologies cause prejudice. It is crucial to determine who should bear responsibility: the programmer, provider, or the user entity. The question also arises as to how these systems can be subject to strict oversight to ensure fair and impartial use. Although there are some attempts to incorporate artificial intelligence into criminal justice, for example throughout the Americas, it is understood that each country is sovereign and applies its laws according to its judicial system. However, civil liability regulations are still in their initial stages (Barrios, 2024).

METHODOLOGY

Various databases were consulted in documentary research such as Willey, Francis & Taylor, Google Scholar, Research rabbit, ebsco, science direct, PubMed. Considering terms such as artificial intelligence, ethics, applied methodologies, intelligence for decision-making, and data analysis in the field of forensics, a matrix was then created with information from various studies compiled in the research queries, such as author information, research objective, year of publication, location of the research, and the results that impacted the research. Considering that the search for information was limited to a 5-year period, from 2019 to 2024, a matrix of the literature consulted was created. Although the database consulted yields countless references, only a fraction of them were considered, which serve as support for this chapter of the book. See Table 1.

Table 1. Literature Matrix

Year and Author	Title of the research	Keywords	Objective	Impact of the results
Avella, M. del P. R., Sanabria-Moyano, J. E., & Dinas-Hurtado, K. (2022).	Use of the COMPAS algorithm in criminal proceedings and the risks to human rights.	Artificial intelligence; criminal justice; algorithms; human rights.	Identify the fundamental risk predictive algorithms. Main ones and the impact on human rights.	The results indicate that there are indeed risks when implementing intelligent predictive systems, focused on the lack of transparency.
(Lopezosa et al., 2024)	The use of artificial intelligence in editorial proposals and limitations.	Artificial intelligence; media; AI; journalism; scoping review; digital media.	Identifying the use of artificial intelligence.	The conclusion was evidence-based contributions to the debate on current and future effects.
(Riba, 2024)	Artificial Intelligence and Police Control Police	Control Police, technology, artificial intelligence, social sciences	It is essential to understand the basis of these expectations and their origin, as they are often rooted in economic interests and the promise of an objective and neutral application of technology in policing.	These expectations, promoted by economic interests, have emerged as a source of hope for the applications of artificial intelligence in policing.
(Vásquez, 2023)	Ethics of Artificial Intelligence. UNESCO Recommendation, November 2021	Inevitable tensions, human dignity, human rights, and fundamental freedoms.	Values, principles, and actions that seek to guide the development of AI in a direction focused on human dignity and human rights.	Investments were made in research that considers the ethics of using artificial intelligence for various sectors and develops incentives.
(Nzobonimpa & Savard, 2023)	Ready but irresponsible? Analysis of the Government Artificial Intelligence Readiness Index	Accountability, algorithms, artificial intelligence, government, irresponsible	Ethics, equity, disparate impact, opacity, privacy, and inconsistency in service delivery processes and the proliferation of algorithmic systems.	Two limitations of our study should be noted. The first is that the data were collected in 2020. Some countries may have improved or corrected some of the conditions highlighted in this research by the time of publication, given that the strategic adoption of AI by governments has followed rapid technological innovation.
(De Paula, G. 2023)	Decision-making, criminal intelligence, and new analysis tools: the use of artificial intelligence.	Criminal intelligence, decision-making, artificial intelligence.	AI interpretation of reality, and in the area of decision-making, a fundamental tool for strategic calculations.	AI for global public security can become part of the criminal intelligence cycle and enhance capabilities

continued on following page

Table 1. Continued

				including strategic decision-making, operational planning, and tactical support.
(Zabala Leal, 2021)	Ethics in Artificial Intelligence	Artificial intelligence, digitalization of law, ethics, smart contracts, blockchain, tokens, botsourcing, heuristics, algorithms, self-determination, biohacking, transhumanism.	Show the importance of working with ethics as a key factor in the implementation of AI.	Optimizing the quality of life of human beings, within the framework of human rights and laws, through the tools that AI provides.
(Toache, 2023)	Advantages and disadvantages of using Artificial Intelligence in the public policy cycle: analysis of international cases.	Artificial Intelligence; public policy cycle; e-government; smart public administration; open government.	Analyze the advantages and disadvantages of using AI in the public policy cycle to help fill this gap.	The advantages and benefits obtained from the application of AI were noted, such as the rapid processing and analysis of large amounts of data. However, areas for improvement were also identified, which are related to ethical principles, such as the lack of privacy and transparency.
(Parga, 2023)	Can artificial intelligence replace the human mind? Implications of AI for fundamental rights and ethics?	Artificial Intelligence, Humanism, Ethics, Human Rights, Social Responsibility	Analyze the problems generated and verify how AI is used and applied as an instrument at the service of human beings.	AI and its benefits must continue to be analyzed from a scientific perspective, as an aid to human endeavor, in order to avoid harming the natural order, while maximizing the benefits that can be obtained through its application.
(Andrade Molina, 2009b)	Application of forensic science methods to identify those responsible for homicide.	Criminal law; homicide. Criminalistics; procedural validity; forensic acoustics.	The key roles, procedures, and functions performed in these types of crimes will be analyzed and evaluated to verify the effectiveness of these established procedures, seeking a fair administration of justice.	It is established that with the proper implementation of models, procedures, the use of technologies and tools, and with the awareness of the relevant authorities, unpunished cases of this crime would decrease and would be handled with greater transparency.

continued on following page

Table 1. Continued

(Barrios, 2024)	Civil Liability of Artificial Intelligence. Its Transdisciplinary Application in Forensic Sciences.	Responsibility, ethics, judicial criminology.	Establish comprehensive standards of civil liability for potential failures or biases in judicial Artificial Intelligence.	The popularization of AI in forensics raises legal challenges that must be effectively addressed. The importance of AI for forensic analysis processes, suspect identification, and the prediction of criminal behavior was established. However, it was also concluded that it requires clear and comprehensive regulation for its successful implementation.
Mercan, G., & Varol Selçuk, Z. (2024).	Artificial intelligence (AI) activities in legal practices.	Artificial intelligence and the judiciary, decision-making algorithms, AI applications in law, AI in judicial processes.	Guide the responsible and ethical integration of AI technologies in the legal field, ensuring that technological advancement does not come at the expense of the fundamental principles of law and justice.	Seeks to inform policy decisions and the future development of AI technologies in the legal field.
P. Renukadevi, S. John and N. Shivani. (2024)	Forensic Science: AI-Powered Image and Audio Analysis	Ethics, Efficiency, Forensics, Instruments, Data Integrity, Data Model, Approach, Artificial Intelligence, Ethical AI.	Ethics, Efficiency, Forensics, Instruments, Data Integrity, Data Model, Approach, Artificial Intelligence, Ethical AI.	Demonstrate the possibility of integrating image and audio analysis to conclude forensic science cases such as murders.
Gangi, M. (2024).	The Impact of Artificial Intelligence Systems in Criminal Law: An Integral and Integrated Development Perspective	Criminal law, IA, Predictive Policing, Predictive Justice, Integral Development	Provide a proposal for developing AI systems in the field of criminal law.	It addresses the new challenges of using AI in political science, considering ethics in biotechnology.
Alijonov Mukhammadyusuf Jurabek Ugli. (2024)	The role of artificial intelligence as legal personality and some issues on this field: on the example of criminalistics, investigation and forensic examination	Information (digital) technologies; information and telecommunication system; war crimes investigation; forensic examination; forensic sciences.	Thoroughly research and analyze the potential for integrating AI into Ukraine's legal system to increase the efficiency of law enforcement agencies, reduce crime, and explore potential applications of AI in judicial proceedings.	Considers that the use of developing technologies in forensic science should be analyzed and supervised by experts in these fields, and their roles should be regulated.

RESULTS

Various facets were identified, considering responsibility and forensic ethics, which include important challenges from the area of criminal justice, as well as efficiency and improvement in data analysis. AI-related tools allow for the processing of patterns and connections between crimes, but it must be taken into account that their use does not accelerate investigations, because it must be considered to increase the precision in identifying the details of each case study. On the other hand, in recent years, artificial intelligence has been incorporated into the areas of forensics, leaving important advances, which are, from the way crimes are committed, how they are investigated and also in their prevention . On the other hand, it offers professionals opportunities to increase efficiency, improve the focus of legal processes and access to them. Different technologies are based on AI, among which is machine learning, which are revolutionizing traditional legal deceptions by automating the scrutiny of documents, functioning as a support for taking deceptions until being able to create hypotheses for the resolution of cases (Gangi, 2024; Mercan and Varol, 2024). An example of the applications would be the power to assist in the extraction of relevant information to identify fingerprints or deception patterns in order to take well-founded deceptions, obtain greater insight during the exercise of justice and quickly conclude the case without having to carry it out for months or years.

Similarly, it has been shown that through the use of AI it is deception to analyze information stored for years and of large size; to the aforementioned, we can add the development or improvement of AI models, through algorithms and thus be able to identify similar aspects or patterns, to make correlations in various crimes, which might not be identified with the naked eye by humans (Urvanová et al., 2021). Currently, developed and developing countries seek to implement these techniques in the exercise of judicial power, mainly to obtain fair results or to encourage their justice systems to be equitable and for people to have greater access to legal advice, for people in vulnerable situations (Shepitko et al., 2023).

However, the research identified that the use of AI algorithms can perpetuate and amplify existing biases. Models trained on historical data containing racial or socioeconomic biases can result in discriminatory decisions in law enforcement. This finding highlights the need for ongoing critical review of algorithms used in forensic science. Algorithmic algorithms are identified as a fundamental ethical challenge. The results suggest that without a clear understanding of how these systems operate, it is difficult to ensure accountability. The opacity of automated decisions and the findings indicate the imperative to develop a robust ethical framework to guide and include the creation of policies that explicitly address ethical dilemmas and promote equitable practices. Collaboration between technology, ethics, and criminal justice experts is essential to establish standards for protection, but fundamentally, to protect the sensitive data of every entity, person, or government that deposits their data in such systems. Finally, it is observed that the integration of AI into forensics is transforming the skills required by professionals in this field. Training in the ethical use of these technologies becomes essential, ensuring that researchers understand both the capabilities and limitations of AI (Howard, 2019).

DISCUSSION AND CONCLUSION

In conclusion, this chapter showed that the use of AI in forensics also raises important ethical questions that must be addressed proactively and with clearer laws for users, as well as for the companies or individuals who generate them.

The importance of human judgment in the administration of justice is also raised. Although AI can facilitate analytical tasks, the deep understanding of law and ethics that humans possess cannot be fully replicated by algorithms. Therefore, it is essential to balance the efficiency of AI with empathy and moral reasoning in legal decisions. To address these challenges, collaboration between legal professionals, technologists, ethicists, and legislators is necessary to establish ethical guidelines and regulatory frameworks that ensure the responsible use of AI in the legal field, recognizing its limitations and impacts on the principles of justice and equity (Danshin & Kostenko, 2020).

The findings highlight the urgent need to address inherent bias in algorithms and the lack of transparency in their processes, which can affect and make it imperative that the institutions involved develop robust ethical frameworks and clear policies to guide the use of AI, ensuring that human rights and social justice are prioritized, but at the same time, allowing such systems to be created, without impeding rules that limit them to the point where they cannot be used.

Throughout this article, we explored how AI tools have improved efficiency and the identification of criminal patterns, but we also highlighted the serious ethical challenges that arise from their use. We described examples where we saw the need to establish national and, of course, global agreements that allow every criminal activity to be judged equally and under ethical principles. Employers and governments should train their workers and raise awareness about these critical issues due to their application in decision-making, which, given the facts, could lead to irreversible damage to humanity if done incorrectly. These harms could be prevented if the laws, rules, and procedures governing AI are considered from the outset.

Furthermore, it is crucial that forensics professionals receive training in the ethical use of these technologies, integrating principles of justice and human rights, ethics, and morality into their daily practice. This will adequately address the dilemmas posed by AI in this field. The era of artificial intelligence in forensics presents both opportunities and challenges, as well as the effectiveness, integrity, and legitimacy of investigations. The future of forensics in an increasingly digitalized world will depend on our ability to balance innovation with ethical responsibility, ensuring that technology is used as a tool for the common good, rather than a means that perpetuates inequalities—that is, using ethical principles so that it does no harm, benefits all, is done fairly, and is done autonomously.

REFERENCES

Andrade Molina, D. E. (2009a). Application of methods from the science of forensics to identify those responsible for homicide [bachelor thesis, Universidad del Azuay]. https://dspace.uazuay.edu.ec/handle/datos/877

Andrade Molina, D. E. (2009b). Application of forensic science methods to identify perpetrators of homicide [bachelor thesis, Universidad del Azuay]. https://dspace.uazuay.edu.ec/handle/datos/877

Avella, M. del PR, Sanabria-Moyano, J.E., & Dinas-Hurtado, K. (2022). Use of the COMPAS algorithm in criminal proceedings and the risks to human rights. *Brazilian Journal of Criminal Procedural Law*, *8*(1), 275–310.

Cottey, A. (2016, April). Reducing Ethical Hazards in Knowledge Production. *Science and Engineering Ethics*, *22*(2), 367–389. DOI: 10.1007/s11948-015-9651-3 PMID: 25991087

Danshin, M. V., & Kostenko, M. V. (2020). Moral foundations of counteraction of criminality: ethical questions of criminalistics. *Publishing House "Baltija Publishing"*.

De Paula, G. (2023). Decision-making, criminal intelligence and new analysis tools: The use of artificial intelligence. *Journal of the National Intelligence School*, *1*(2), 133–149. DOI: 10.58752/AZFVQ42S

Gangi, M. (2024). The Impact of Artificial Intelligence Systems in Criminal Law: An Integral and Integrated Development Perspective. In *Intersections Between Rights and Technology* (pp. 61–83). IGI Global. DOI: 10.4018/979-8-3693-1127-1.ch005

Gervais, D. J. (2023). Towards an effective transnational regulation of AI. *AI & Society*, *38*(1), 391–410.

Golding, L. P., & Nicola, G. N. (2019, September). A Business Case for Artificial Intelligence Tools: The Currency of Improved Quality and Reduced Cost. *Journal of the American College of Radiology*, *16*(9, 9 Pt B), 1357–1361. DOI: 10.1016/j.jacr.2019.05.004 PMID: 31492415

Howard, J. (2019). Artificial intelligence: Implications for the future of work. *American Journal of Industrial Medicine*, *62*(11), 917–926. DOI: 10.1002/ajim.23037 PMID: 31436850

Lopezosa, C., Codina, L., & Boté-Vericad, J. J. (2023). *Testing ATLAS.ti with OpenAI: Towards a new paradigm for qualitative interview analysis with artificial intelligence*. http://repositori.upf.edu/handle/10230/56449

Lopezosa, C., Pérez-Montoro, M., Rey Martín, K., Lopezosa, C., Pérez-Montoro, M., & Rey Martín, K. (2024). The use of artificial intelligence in newsrooms: Proposals and limitations. *Journal of Communication*, *23*(1), 279–294. DOI: 10.26441/RC23.1-2024-3309

Mercan, G., & Varol Selçuk, Z. (2024). Artificial intelligence (AI) activities in legal practices. [PDF] [Artificial intelligence] [AI]. *International Journal of Eurasian Education and Culture*, *9*(25), 131–144. DOI: 10.35826/ijoecc.1824

Nzobonimpa, S., & Savard, J.-F. (2023). Ready but irresponsible? Analysis of the Government Artificial Intelligence Readiness Index. *Policy and Internet*, *15*(3), 397–414. DOI: 10.1002/poi3.351

Parga, M. O. (2023). CAN ARTIFICIAL INTELLIGENCE REPLACE THE HUMAN MIND? IMPLICATIONS OF AI FOR FUNDAMENTAL RIGHTS AND ETHICS. *Annals of the Francisco Suárez Chair*, *57*, 39–61. DOI: 10.30827/acfs.v57i.24710

Reyes, R. J. A., Poveda, M. Y. B., & Calderón, G. X. C. (2023). Criminalistics as a science and its importance in Ecuadorian criminal legislation. *LATAM Latin American Journal of Social Sciences and Humanities*, *4*(6), 6. Advance online publication. DOI: 10.56712/latam.v4i6.1531

Riba, J. M. L. (2024). Artificial intelligence and police control. *InDret*, *2*, 407–436. DOI: 10.31009/InDret.2024.i2.10

Schuklenk, U. (2020, February). On the ethics of AI ethics. *Bioethics*, *34*(2), 146–147. DOI: 10.1111/bioe.12716 PMID: 31943279

Shepitko, V., Shepitko, M., Latysh, K., Kapustina, M., & Demidova, E. (2023). Artificial intelligence in crime counteraction: From legal regulation to implementation. *Social & Legal Studies*, *7*(1), 135–144. DOI: 10.32518/sals1.2024.135

Toache, E. A. (2023). Advantages and disadvantages of using artificial intelligence in the public policy cycle: An analysis of international cases. *Acta Universitaria*, *33*, 1–26. DOI: 10.15174/au.2023.3891

Urbanová, P., Eliášová, H., & Dostálová, T. (2022). How accurate is forensic facial identification of surgically altered faces? *The Australian Journal of Forensic Sciences*, *55*(3), 406–425. DOI: 10.1080/00450618.2022.2032341

Vásquez, P. A. R. (2023). Ethics of Artificial Intelligence. UNESCO Recommendation, November 2021. *Compendium (Newtown, Pa.)*, *26*(50), 1–6.

Weitener, L., Fischer, M., & Teaching, A. I. (2023, October 16). Ethics in Medical Education: A Scoping Review of Current Literature and Practices. *Perspectives on Medical Education*, *12*(1), 399–410. DOI: 10.5334/pme.954 PMID: 37868075

Zabala Leal, T. D. (2021). Ethics in artificial intelligence from a legal perspective. *Via Inveniendi Et Iudicandi*, *16*(2). Advance online publication. DOI: 10.15332/19090528.6785

Zúñiga, L. A. L., & Zúñiga, M. A. R. (2024). The Ethics of Using Artificial Intelligence in the Psychological Assessment and Diagnosis of Patients in Durango, Mexico. *Ciencia Latina Multidisciplinary Scientific Journal*, *8*(4), 4. Advance online publication. DOI: 10.37811/cl_rcm.v8i4.12278

Chapter 3

Guiding Principles to Address Cybersecurity Requirements for High-Risk AI Systems Under the AI Act

Jersain Llamas Covarrubias
https://orcid.org/0000-0003-1965-2415
Universidad de Guadalajara, Mexico

Celina Díaz Michel
Universidad de Guadalajara, Mexico

ABSTRACT

This article examines the European Union's Artificial Intelligence (AI) Act, specifically its cybersecurity requirements for high-risk AI systems. The Act adopts a risk-based framework that classifies AI systems by societal impact, emphasizing cybersecurity for high-risk applications in fields like biometric recognition and critical infrastructure. Key principles, including transparency, resilience, and risk management, aim to protect AI from unique vulnerabilities such as adversarial manipulation and data poisoning. Findings highlight the Act's lifecycle-based approach, the importance of stakeholder engagement, and the need for adaptive standards to address evolving threats. The study underscores international collaboration and calls for continuous advancements in interpretability and privacy-preserving techniques, positioning the EU as a global leader in responsible AI regulation.

DOI: 10.4018/979-8-3693-8871-6.ch003

INTRODUCTION

Artificial Intelligence (AI) is reshaping technological, economic, and social landscapes worldwide, yet defining AI remains a complex task due to its inherent diversity and multidimensionality. Each field that employs AI tends to emphasize unique functionalities, ethical considerations, and potential societal impacts, creating challenges in establishing a unified regulatory approach. However, precision in defining AI is indispensable, as effective regulation relies on clear, measurable boundaries. Without such clarity, safeguarding AI applications becomes inherently difficult. As an initial step, international bodies have proposed frameworks that outline the AI lifecycle, emphasizing its iterative nature and the need for adaptive governance. For instance, the OECD conceptualizes AI development as a cyclical process, from initial design and data processing to deployment and ongoing monitoring that underscores AI's evolving nature and the necessity of continuous oversight (OECD, 2024). Similarly, the European Union's Artificial Intelligence Act (AI Act) provides a functional definition of AI as an autonomous, adaptable system capable of generating predictions, recommendations, or decisions that shape both digital and physical realms. Together, these frameworks provide foundational structure for regulatory efforts, marking an essential step toward safeguarding AI-driven innovations in critical fields.

As the first comprehensive and binding regulatory framework for AI, the AI Act introduces a risk-based approach that classifies AI systems according to their societal impact, ensuring oversight is proportionate to potential risks. Specifically, the Act prohibits applications deemed "unacceptable," while high-risk AI systems, those potentially impacting public safety, health, or fundamental rights, must comply with rigorous regulatory standards before entering the EU market. These requirements include robust transparency, cybersecurity, and risk management protocols to protect public welfare. Conversely, AI applications classified as limited or minimal risk, face only baseline requirements, such as voluntary codes of conduct. This calibrated approach balances innovation with necessary safeguards, establishing an intervention level aligned with the unique risks each AI system presents.

Cybersecurity is a cornerstone of the AI Act, reflecting the necessity of managing AI-specific vulnerabilities that diverge significantly from those found in traditional digital systems. AI systems are uniquely susceptible to novel attack vectors, such as adversarial manipulation, data poisoning, and model evasion, which can compromise the accuracy, integrity, and reliability of AI outputs. Addressing these vulnerabilities requires an innovative approach to cybersecurity that includes adversarial testing, continual model validation, and adaptive risk management strategies. Given AI's potential to transform high-stakes domains like healthcare, finance, and critical infrastructure, there is an urgent need to develop dedicated, AI-focused cybersecurity standards that can address these evolving threats effectively and comprehensively.

Despite advances in traditional cybersecurity frameworks, these measures often fall short of adequately protecting AI systems due to the specific, adaptive nature of AI vulnerabilities. Standardized cybersecurity protocols for AI applications are still in development, highlighting a pressing need for AI-specific security measures that go beyond foundational controls. This gap underscores the urgency of establishing mature cybersecurity practices tailored to AI, ensuring that AI systems across sectors remain secure and resilient while meeting regulatory demands.

In this context, this article explores the evolving regulatory landscape of AI, with a focus on the European AI Act and its implications for cybersecurity compliance. It begins by discussing the Scope and Significance of Cybersecurity and AI Systems, emphasizing the critical role of cybersecurity in managing AI-related risks. The section on Key Guiding Principles for Cybersecurity Compliance in AI Systems introduces foundational standards essential for practitioners to ensure secure AI deployment. Implementing Cybersecurity Practices on AI Systems provides actionable guidance aligned with regulatory requirements, while Data Governance and Stakeholder Assessment in Cybersecurity-Focused AI Systems highlights the importance of structured data management and ethical considerations. Following these sections, the article presents Materials and Methods, outlining the research approach and methodologies used to assess the AI Act's cybersecurity provisions. The Results section details key findings on regulatory impacts, protocol effectiveness, and real-world applications of cybersecurity standards in AI. In the Discussion, these findings are analyzed to highlight areas of regulatory strength, identify limitations, and suggest avenues for future research and adaptive security protocols. The article then addresses Challenges and Future Directions in AI Cybersecurity, examining unresolved issues and emerging trends. Finally, the Conclusion synthesizes these discussions, providing policymakers, industry leaders, and researchers with a nuanced perspective on AI cybersecurity, fostering the secure and responsible deployment of AI technologies across critical sectors.

SCOPE AND SIGNIFICANCE OF CYBERSECURITY AND AI SYSTEMS

The integration of AI into cybersecurity has catalyzed the development of a robust, interdisciplinary field that merges insights from AI research, adversarial machine learning, and traditional cybersecurity practices. This intersection spans three primary domains: (1) utilizing AI to strengthen cybersecurity defenses; (2)

addressing the potential misuse of AI for malicious purposes; and (3) securing AI systems themselves against cyber threats (Junklewitz et al., 2023).

The application of AI in cybersecurity operations has yielded substantial advancements across various domains. Within cybersecurity, AI enhances defense and response strategies, enabling proactive and precise threat mitigation. For instance, AI-powered malware detection leverages machine learning algorithms to recognize malicious software through behavioral analysis, offering an adaptive layer of defense (Munjal & Puri, 2024). AI also strengthens intrusion detection systems (IDS) by analyzing network traffic patterns, allowing for real-time anomaly detection and swift responses to potential threats (Raheja, 2024). In phishing detection, AI analyzes extensive datasets of email content, identifying suspicious patterns to intercept threats before reaching users (Jahnavi & Urvashi, 2024). Furthermore, in digital forensics, AI-driven solutions automate the collection and analysis of digital evidence, ensuring data integrity and expediting the processing of large datasets (Bhawna & Mahajan, 2024).

Beyond traditional cybersecurity applications, AI has extended its impact to traffic monitoring systems. Through computer vision and the integration of IoT sensors, AI enables real-time detection of traffic violations, analyzing video frames and sensor data to support enforcement efforts and enhance road safety (Jahnavi & Urvashi, 2024). In cybersecurity rating platforms, AI is increasingly incorporated within DevOps frameworks to automate vulnerability management. This integration facilitates continuous monitoring and remediation of security weaknesses across multiple vectors, including application, network, and endpoint security, thereby reinforcing an organization's overall cybersecurity posture (Pitre et al., 2024).

In the realm of Cyber-Physical Systems (CPS), AI has transformed interactions between physical and cyber domains, enabling the development of intelligent entities such as autonomous vehicles, robotics, and smart grids. These systems dynamically adapt to real-time data inputs, supporting predictive maintenance and early detection of cyber threats, which enhances resilience and operational sustainability (Stutz et al., 2024). Collectively, these applications underscore AI's critical role in automating complex processes, accelerating response times, and facilitating timely, accurate threat detection, thereby contributing to a resilient digital infrastructure.

Quantitatively, AI's role in security operations has demonstrated a significant impact: 28% of enterprises employ AI to automate threat detection and response processes, while 27% leverage it for endpoint security to identify and neutralize device-level threats effectively (ISACA, 2024). Additionally, 24% of enterprises use AI to automate routine security tasks, alleviating the workload on security personnel and enabling teams to prioritize complex threats. Despite these advancements, a persistent cybersecurity skills gap remains, with organizations increasingly relying on AI to offset workforce shortages. According to ISACA (2024), only 35% of security teams are involved in developing AI-related policies, indicating a gap in the integration of AI strategies within organizational governance. Thus, while AI is a pivotal asset in modern cybersecurity frameworks, its effective implementation and governance necessitate improved collaboration and policy alignment across cybersecurity teams and organizational structures.

Conversely, the misuse of AI by organized crime introduces new complexities, heightening the effectiveness of traditional criminal tactics and presenting unprecedented challenges for law enforcement. Criminal organizations in the region are increasingly employing AI-powered tools such as large language models (LLMs) and deep learning technologies to automate and enhance their operations. The widespread availability of generative AI has empowered these groups to scale fraudulent schemes and deceive victims with increased precision. As AI evolves, its misuse by organized crime demands renewed efforts from local and international law enforcement to adapt their strategies accordingly (Newton, 2024).

One significant concern is the use of AI to create deepfake audio and visual content for deception and extortion. Criminal groups in countries such as Peru have exploited AI's ability to imitate voices, using samples from social media to simulate a relative's voice in ransom calls. Similarly, at the US-Mexico border, criminal organizations have fabricated realistic images and videos of missing migrants, deceiving families into paying ransoms for their alleged safe return. These applications of deepfake technology amplify the psychological impact of scams, reducing the likelihood that victims will question the authenticity of the communication (Newton, 2024; Dawes Centre, 2020).

AI also enables organized crime to refine traditional phishing techniques, increasing both the sophistication and reach of these attacks. Using LLMs, cybercriminals can craft highly personalized and convincing emails that mimic the language and style of familiar contacts, making it difficult for recipients to detect fraudulent messages. This approach is particularly effective in social engineering attacks that aim to obtain sensitive information or credentials by imitating authoritative figures, such as employers or government officials. In Brazil, for instance, cybercriminal groups have used AI-generated emails to impersonate federal tax services, leading victims to download malware from what appears to be a legitimate government website (FBI, 2024; Newton, 2024).

AI-driven automation has also transformed financial fraud schemes, allowing organized crime to reach more victims with fewer resources. For example, AI-powered chatbots, like "LoveGPT," are used in dating scams, engaging victims in emotional manipulation before requesting financial assistance. This type of scam, known as "pig butchering" has gained traction among major criminal organizations, including Mexico's Jalisco New Generation Cartel (CJNG) and Brazil's First Capital Command (PCC). These groups exploit AI-driven tools to conduct large-scale fraud, amplifying both the reach and impact of their scams by generating highly convincing narratives (Newton, 2024; Dawes Centre, 2020).

The role of AI in organized crime extends to malware development, where it assists in creating and debugging malicious code. Criminal actors, sometimes bypassing safeguards in mainstream LLMs, develop custom AI models specifically for illegal purposes. These models are tailored to evade law enforcement detection, lowering barriers for novice actors to produce sophisticated malware efficiently. AI-fueled advancements in malware also include tools such as DeepExploit and AVPASS, which use reinforcement learning to adapt malicious code and evade detection, complicating efforts to combat cybercrime (Europol & UNICRI, 2023; Newton, 2024).

Moreover, organized crime has adopted a Crime as a Service (CaaS) model, where AI-driven criminal services are offered for rent or sale. This business model, initially seen in Denial of Service (DoS) attacks, now includes AI-enhanced phishing, deepfake impersonation, and automated financial fraud schemes. The scalability of these AI-enabled crimes enhances profitability for organized crime while posing significant challenges to regulatory frameworks and traditional law enforcement methods (Dawes Centre, 2020; Europol & UNICRI, 2023).

As AI becomes increasingly integral to public security, criminals are also targeting AI-based security systems directly. Criminals employ techniques to bypass or manipulate AI-driven surveillance systems, such as facial recognition, allowing them to evade detection. Additionally, the manipulation of autonomous systems, including drones and self-driving vehicles, enables remote criminal activities, such as smuggling contraband or gathering intelligence, without direct human intervention. These advancements underscore the need for robust regulatory measures to monitor and counter the criminal use of AI in autonomous systems (Europol & UNICRI, 2023).

Finally, securing AI systems themselves against cyber threats is crucial. AI systems inherit traditional cybersecurity risks common to digital systems but face unique vulnerabilities specific to their design and function. The emerging field of AI cybersecurity is actively addressing these risks, with global efforts aimed at adapting established cybersecurity practices and developing new tools tailored to AI's distinct landscape (Federal Office for Information Security, 2023). This approach includes the creation of risk management tools, specialized metrics, and tailored mitigation strategies to enhance the resilience of AI systems against complex threats.

AI systems are increasingly vulnerable to sophisticated attacks, each targeting different facets of their operation and decision-making processes. Evasion attacks, for example, involve manipulating inputs to deceive the AI model during inference, leading to incorrect classifications that are undetectable to human observers. These attacks can be targeted, forcing a specific incorrect output or untargeted, causing general inaccuracies (Federal Office for Information Security, 2023). Information extraction attacks, on the other hand, expose sensitive or proprietary data from the AI model. Techniques such as model stealing replicate a model's structure, while membership and attribute inference attacks seek to identify specific data points within training sets, potentially compromising sensitive information (Jarmul, 2023). Additionally, poisoning and backdoor attacks compromise the integrity of an AI system by embedding malicious data or triggers within the model, which can degrade performance or cause targeted misclassifications when specific conditions are met (MITRE, 2023).

Emerging threats like linkage and membership inference attacks present unique challenges. These attacks exploit auxiliary datasets to re-identify individuals or confirm their inclusion in training datasets, compromising both individual privacy and model integrity. Furthermore, model-stealing attacks pose serious risks to proprietary AI technologies, as attackers replicate or approximate models through extensive API queries, effectively acquiring valuable intellectual property (Jarmul, 2023). These sophisticated attack vectors highlight the need for implementing advanced protections, such as privacy-preserving techniques and differential privacy, to prevent data leakage and bolster defenses against evolving AI-specific vulnerabilities.

Incorporating AI into cybersecurity frameworks requires attention to these emerging, AI-specific threats. According to MITRE's ATLAS™ framework, AI security spans a range of protective measures aimed at safeguarding AI throughout its lifecycle, including defenses against data poisoning and evasion attacks that compromise AI model integrity (MITRE, 2023). Integrating secure practices into each phase of the AI development cycle, using frameworks such as MLOps and CRISP-ML(Q), is essential to ensure the confidentiality, integrity, and availability of AI systems.

Key Guiding Principles for Cybersecurity Compliance on AI systems

The European Union's AI Act (European Parliament and Council of the European Union, 2024a) sets forth a robust framework for the development and deployment of AI systems, focusing on transparency, accountability, and risk mitigation. One of the most critical aspects of the Act is its emphasis on cybersecurity, particularly for high-risk AI systems, which carry unique threats to public welfare, individual privacy, and the stability of essential infrastructure. This section provides an in-depth analysis of the cybersecurity requirements for high-risk AI systems under the AI Act, covering essential principles to ensure these systems operate securely, transparently, and responsibly.

The AI Act classifies high-risk AI systems based on their potential to affect public safety, health, and fundamental rights. High-risk AI applications include biometric recognition systems, AI in critical infrastructure management, and general-purpose AI models that present systemic risks (Recital 54, Article 6). Each category demands rigorous cybersecurity measures due to the potential for adverse societal impact should these systems be compromised, misused, or fail. For instance, biometric systems used in public spaces for remote identification are considered high-risk due to their sensitivity and potential for misuse, where even minor technical inaccuracies can lead to bias, discrimination, or privacy violations (Recital 54). Meanwhile, AI systems deployed in critical infrastructure, such as energy, water supply, or digital communication, carry significant cybersecurity risks because any failure could endanger public health and disrupt social stability (Recital 55). Consequently, these systems are subject to comprehensive regulatory oversight under the Act.

Central to the AI Act's cybersecurity framework are stringent requirements for risk management, accuracy, resilience, and transparency in system operation. High-risk AI systems must be developed with robust cybersecurity protocols that account for potential disruptions, whether they arise from technical limitations, environmental factors, or malicious intent. Providers are mandated to conduct systematic risk assessments to identify and manage risks throughout the AI system lifecycle (Article 15). The Act requires that all AI systems implement quality and relevance controls for datasets used in model training, testing, and validation, reducing the likelihood of biased or incorrect outputs (Article 10). For example, to avoid systemic errors and bias, biometric systems must be trained on data reflective of diverse populations. Additionally, AI providers must develop detailed technical documentation, ensuring that external auditors and regulators can evaluate the AI system's reliability and intended purpose effectively (Article 13).

Transparency plays a crucial role in cybersecurity compliance, as it enables deployers and users to interpret system outputs accurately and understand potential risks. The Act requires that all high-risk AI systems be accompanied by clear and accessible instructions, detailing system capabilities, limitations, accuracy, and security controls (Article 13). Providers are obliged to disclose any factors that may influence accuracy or reliability, including potential vulnerabilities. This level of transparency empowers deployers to make informed decisions, use AI systems responsibly, and recognize situations where human oversight may be necessary to mitigate risks (Article 14).

The AI Act also enforces a high standard of resilience in high-risk AI systems, mandating technical and organizational measures to prevent and address disruptions, such as errors, inconsistencies, or security breaches (Recital 75, Article 15).

Providers are required to integrate fail-safe mechanisms and redundancy solutions, particularly for AI applications that may interact with people or other systems in unpredictable environments. These resilience measures are especially crucial for AI systems that continue to learn after deployment, as there is a heightened risk of "feedback loops" wherein potentially biased outputs influence future system inputs. To prevent such issues, high-risk AI systems must be designed to identify and minimize these biases, ensuring that feedback loops do not adversely impact system performance or user trust (Recital 74).

A key element of the AI Act's cybersecurity requirements is the defense against adversarial attacks, which target vulnerabilities in AI models and training datasets. The Act outlines protocols for handling specific threats such as data poisoning, where malicious actors compromise training data to skew AI outputs; model poisoning, which involves tampering with pre-trained components; and adversarial examples, where inputs are designed to trick AI systems into making incorrect decisions (Recital 76, Article 15). To mitigate these risks, high-risk AI systems must incorporate detection and response mechanisms, preventing unauthorized third parties from altering their use, behavior, or performance. Furthermore, the Act underscores the importance of protecting the confidentiality of sensitive data and preventing model leakage, particularly in biometric and critical infrastructure systems.

The principle of mutual recognition within the AI Act introduces a streamlined approach to cybersecurity compliance, allowing high-risk AI systems that adhere to recognized EU cybersecurity standards, such as Regulation (EU) 2019/881, to automatically meet the AI Act's cybersecurity requirements (Recital 77, Article 42). This approach simplifies the compliance process for AI providers who already follow established cybersecurity protocols, thereby reducing redundant cybersecurity assessments across EU member states. In addition, the Act specifies that any significant modifications to an AI system must be documented and registered with the European Commission, ensuring that compliance is maintained as systems evolve.

To support continuous cybersecurity improvement, the AI Act introduces the concept of AI regulatory sandboxes; controlled environments where AI providers can test their systems under close regulatory supervision. These sandboxes offer an invaluable platform for AI developers to experiment, gather insights, and refine security controls before full-scale deployment (Recital 131, Article 58). Within these sandboxes, providers can collaborate with regulatory bodies, conduct real-world trials, and receive guidance on meeting compliance requirements. This proactive framework encourages innovation while ensuring that AI systems meet strict cybersecurity standards before they are used in public or commercial settings.

In the event of a cybersecurity incident involving a high-risk AI system, the AI Act mandates prompt reporting to relevant national authorities and the European Commission, detailing incident causes and corrective measures taken (Recital 115,

Article 55). This requirement allows regulators to address emerging security threats, collect data on common vulnerabilities, and enhance the regulatory framework accordingly. Such transparency is essential for maintaining public trust and ensuring that AI systems remain resilient against evolving cybersecurity risks.

The AI Act also requires ongoing monitoring and assessment of cybersecurity risks throughout the lifecycle of high-risk AI systems, underscoring the need for an adaptable security approach that evolves with the AI technology itself (Recital 114, Article 15). Cybersecurity provisions must address both the digital and physical aspects of AI deployment, ensuring that safeguards are in place to protect AI models, data, and infrastructure from unauthorized access and cyber threats. This includes measures to prevent unauthorized third-party access, data tampering, and attacks that could alter AI system performance, protecting both the integrity of the system and the safety of end-users.

Under the AI Act, cybersecurity requirements for AI systems reflect a broader ethical commitment to protecting individual rights and societal interests. By mandating transparent, resilient, and secure AI development practices, the Act seeks to balance innovation with accountability. Providers of high-risk AI systems are expected to adhere to principles of fairness, ensure that their systems respect privacy, and prevent discrimination (Recital 66, Article 9). These ethical considerations are integral to the EU's regulatory approach, emphasizing that AI technology must be safe, reliable, and aligned with public values.

In conclusion, the cybersecurity requirements established by the AI Act represent a significant advancement in AI regulation, particularly for high-risk applications. By enforcing strict security standards and lifecycle risk management, the Act provides a framework that aims to prevent misuse, enhance system integrity, and protect fundamental rights. The introduction of AI regulatory sandboxes, presumption of conformity, and requirements for incident reporting and real-time monitoring illustrate a comprehensive approach to AI cybersecurity that balances security with innovation. These provisions position the EU as a global leader in responsible AI regulation and provide a blueprint for other jurisdictions seeking to implement similar standards.

To build upon these regulatory advancements, Junklewitz et al. (2023) provide guiding principles that further clarify the implementation of the cybersecurity requirements outlined in the AI Act. These principles advocate for a comprehensive view of AI systems, emphasizing that the cybersecurity requirements apply to the system as a whole rather than individual components, such as AI models alone. This approach necessitates a security risk assessment within the broader Risk Management System, tailored to each system's unique design and intended application, facilitating compliance while recognizing the inherent complexities of AI-driven applications. Junklewitz et al. (2023) also emphasize an integrated, continuous security approach that combines proven cybersecurity practices with AI-specific controls, acknowledging that the current state of the art imposes certain limits on securing AI models, particularly with emerging AI technologies.

Together, the AI Act and these guiding principles represent a nuanced regulatory framework that not only addresses the immediate risks posed by AI systems but also encourages ongoing innovation in cybersecurity to accommodate AI's rapid technological progress. By synthesizing strict security requirements with adaptable principles, this framework underscores the EU's commitment to fostering responsible and resilient AI systems while setting a high standard for international AI governance.

Implementing Cybersecurity Practices on AI Systems

The AI Act underscores the essential role of European standards in strengthening the security and compliance of AI systems, particularly in the context of cybersecurity. Supporting this goal, the European Commission's 2023 standardization request drives the development of AI-specific standards that incorporate the latest technological and regulatory advancements. This initiative, led by key European standardization bodies like CEN-CENELEC and ETSI, aims to create comprehensive and widely recognized security measures tailored to AI's unique requirements. While existing standards, such as ISO 27000, provide a foundational framework, specific adaptations are necessary to address the complexities of AI applications, enhancing both resilience and public trust in these technologies (Junklewitz et al., 2023). Currently, the European Union is in the early phases of creating these specialized standards, intended to meet cybersecurity demands and reinforce the credibility of AI systems on a global scale.

In addition, harmonized standards play an indispensable role in translating the objectives of the AI Act into tangible compliance measures. Soler Garrido et al. (2024) argue that these standards should support the AI Act's goals by shifting the focus from organization-centered risk management to a more product-centric approach that prioritizes individual safety and fundamental rights. This shift ensures that standards for high-risk AI systems address societal risks and encompass AI-specific vulnerabilities, such as model manipulation and data poisoning. These standards are crafted with precision and clarity to facilitate compliance, allowing AI providers to navigate the complex AI risk landscape effectively and implement robust security measures across various applications.

By harmonizing cybersecurity requirements across sectors, these standards encourage a consistent approach to safeguarding AI systems while fostering innovation. As highlighted by Junklewitz et al. (2023) and Soler Garrido et al. (2024), this balanced emphasis on compliance and innovation positions the EU as a global leader in responsible AI governance, offering a model for other regions as they aim to integrate AI safety with technological advancement.

Alongside European efforts, the NIST AI Risk Management Framework (AI RMF 1.0), developed outside the EU, provides valuable guidance for organizations aiming to implement robust AI practices. This framework offers a comprehensive approach to managing AI-related risks by emphasizing transparency, accountability, and secure design. Structured around four core functions; govern, map, measure, and manage risks, the NIST AI RMF presents actionable guidelines to enhance the security, transparency, and accountability of AI deployments (National Institute of Standards and Technology, 2023a). While not a regulatory requirement within the EU, the NIST framework complements European standards by offering practical insights that mitigate risks, promote ethical AI use, and establish trust in AI systems.

Building upon this foundation, the NIST AI Risk Management Framework for Generative AI (NIST AI 600-1) provides additional guidance specifically tailored to generative AI systems. This framework addresses unique AI-specific risks, such as confabulation, biases, information integrity, and privacy concerns, and outlines strategies to manage these challenges. It also identifies the origins of these risks, including model design, training data, and human interaction, and suggests proactive steps that organizations can take to maintain governance, transparency, and accountability throughout the AI lifecycle. By promoting an adaptable risk management strategy based on risk tolerance and societal impact, this framework supports the development of AI systems that prioritize trustworthiness, reliability, and ethical considerations aligned with public expectations (National Institute of Standards and Technology, 2024).

To facilitate the practical application of the AI RMF principles, the NIST AI RMF Playbook operationalizes the framework's core functions, outlining specific actions organizations can adopt to implement effective AI governance. This playbook serves as a flexible, context-based guide that encourages voluntary adoption according to industry needs. By providing actionable steps within the "Govern, Map, Measure, and Manage" framework, the Playbook enhances legal compliance, transparency, and accountability in AI deployment. Additionally, it addresses critical challenges such as bias, system transparency, and incident management, underscoring the importance of structured policies to manage AI risks effectively across diverse operational contexts (National Institute of Standards and Technology, 2023b).

On the European side, the recently established ISO/IEC 42001:2023 standard provides a comprehensive framework for managing AI systems within organizations, emphasizing responsible use and alignment with core organizational objectives (ISO, 2023). This standard guides organizations in creating, implementing, and continuously improving an AI management system, detailing specific processes for risk management, governance structures, and ethical considerations. A key aspect of ISO/

IEC 42001:2023 is its integration of AI management with existing organizational processes, ensuring that AI applications not only meet regulatory requirements but also align with broader strategic goals and stakeholder expectations.

The ISO/IEC 42001:2023 standard also introduces a comprehensive risk management approach tailored for AI systems. Unlike traditional IT risk frameworks, this standard addresses technical risks alongside broader societal impacts, advocating for a risk assessment and mitigation process that considers the well-being of individuals and communities affected by AI deployments. By encouraging organizations to proactively manage both technical and societal risks, this standard enhances public trust in AI technologies and strengthens accountability through structured risk treatment plans and impact assessments, underscoring the need for ethical AI governance (ISO, 2023).

Another foundational element of ISO/IEC 42001:2023 is its lifecycle perspective on AI systems, which mandates that organizations manage AI assets across development, deployment, and decommissioning stages. This lifecycle-based approach includes comprehensive documentation requirements for AI-related resources such as data, computational tools, and human involvement, ensuring transparency and traceability at each phase. Additionally, the standard emphasizes clear role definitions and responsibilities within the AI management framework, ensuring that stakeholders are equipped to support the secure and ethical functioning of AI systems (ISO, 2023).

Finally, ISO/IEC 42001:2023 incorporates a continuous improvement model within the AI management system, setting specific objectives for enhancing organizational performance. This includes establishing measurable AI-specific goals, monitoring progress, and adjusting the management system based on observed outcomes. By aligning with ISO's overarching management principles, ISO/IEC 42001:2023 facilitates integration with other standards, such as ISO 9001 (Quality Management) and ISO 27001 (Information Security), enabling organizations to maintain secure, reliable, and ethically responsible AI systems through a cohesive and adaptable framework.

Data Governance and Stakeholder Assessment in Cybersecurity-Focused AI Systems

The integration of AI into cybersecurity has propelled significant advancements in threat detection and response mechanisms, providing organizations with enhanced capabilities to anticipate and mitigate complex cyber threats. However, the convergence of AI and cybersecurity also brings forth governance challenges that demand rigorous regulatory, ethical, and technical frameworks. Effective governance in AI-driven cybersecurity systems extends beyond technical optimization and requires a collaborative, multi-stakeholder approach that integrates ethical principles, regulatory standards, and continuous stakeholder engagement to address the social, legal, and organizational implications of these technologies.

As outlined in Microsoft's Responsible AI Standard, structured data governance is foundational to the responsible deployment of AI in cybersecurity, as it minimizes bias, safeguards sensitive data, and ensures transparency in data handling processes (Microsoft, 2022a). Microsoft's framework emphasizes the importance of continuously updating data and adapting models to respond to emerging cyber threats, fostering resilience in systems operating within rapidly evolving digital landscapes. This approach is particularly critical given that cyber threats continually diversify and grow in sophistication, requiring cybersecurity frameworks that are not only technically robust but also ethically responsible and adaptable to changing social contexts (Microsoft, 2022b).

This governance approach is closely aligned with the collaborative model proposed by Bowen, Sothinathan, and Bowen (2024), who argue that the integration of AI and cybersecurity necessitates a governance structure where state regulators, industry experts, non-profit organizations, and affected user communities all contribute to the development and oversight of these technologies. Such a framework, by ensuring that AI systems are continuously monitored and assessed from multiple perspectives, enhances both the technical and ethical soundness of cybersecurity systems. Bowen et al. (2024) emphasize the role of governments not just as regulatory authorities but as facilitators that collaborate with various sectors, including private organizations and civil society, to address the complex regulatory challenges posed by AI in cybersecurity. This partnership-based model encourages shared responsibility, where ethical and operational risks can be identified and addressed more comprehensively than by regulatory oversight alone.

Microsoft's Responsible AI Standard further supports this collaborative model by incorporating regular stakeholder assessments and structured impact evaluations through tools such as the Responsible AI Impact Assessment Template. This template provides a systematic process to document, evaluate, and proactively address potential risks, emphasizing ethical considerations such as fairness, inclusivity, and accountability (Microsoft, 2022c). By establishing clear documentation and proactive risk management procedures, organizations are better equipped to handle ethical and operational risks, particularly in high-stakes environments like cybersecurity, where errors can lead to severe societal and economic consequences. Bowen et al. (2024) similarly advocate for proactive stakeholder engagement and ethical oversight, stressing the importance of identifying potential biases and operational risks in AI systems, especially those impacting sensitive demographic groups. This approach helps prevent scenarios where AI-driven cybersecurity measures might disproportionately affect certain populations, thus fostering trust and compliance with legal standards.

Additionally, Microsoft's Responsible AI framework underscores the necessity for adaptable data governance practices to keep cybersecurity AI models aligned with real-time threat landscapes. This adaptive approach involves periodic reviews and updates of datasets, which are essential for AI models tasked with recognizing and responding to new threat vectors in a dynamic cybersecurity environment (Microsoft, 2022b). Bowen et al. (2024) further reinforce this adaptive requirement, noting that cybersecurity AI systems are subject to rapid technological advances and evolving regulatory landscapes. By aligning technical resilience with ethical integrity, both Microsoft's standards and the collaborative governance framework advocated by Bowen et al. (2024) demonstrate a comprehensive and resilient approach to the ethical deployment of AI in cybersecurity.

This integration of Microsoft's Responsible AI guidelines and the multi-stakeholder model proposed by Bowen et al. (2024) embodies a robust, adaptive, and ethically grounded governance framework. Through this balanced approach, AI systems in cybersecurity are not only designed to meet high technical standards but are also structured to uphold social responsibility, inclusivity, and ethical accountability. The convergence of these models reinforces the need for AI governance in cybersecurity that is proactive, adaptable, and inclusive, capable of safeguarding both digital infrastructures and public trust. Such an approach supports the development of AI in cybersecurity as a tool that serves society equitably, thereby fostering the resilience and credibility of digital security measures across a broad spectrum of sectors and communities.

CHALLENGES AND FUTURE DIRECTIONS IN AI CYBERSECURITY

The European Union's Cyber Resilience Act represents a progressive step toward enhancing cybersecurity standards for digital products, aligning closely with the objectives of the AI Act to secure AI systems and manage associated risks. This legislation mandates both organizational and technical measures for high-risk AI applications, requiring providers to implement proactive risk management strategies and adhere to harmonized cybersecurity standards before entering the EU market. By establishing these rigorous security measures, the EU aims to create a foundation for resilient AI systems capable of withstanding evolving threats. Acknowledging technological limitations, the Act also emphasizes that standards should reflect the current maturity of AI technology, recognizing that the fast pace of AI advancements requires adaptable cybersecurity practices. This approach foresees the continuous development of resilience-focused standards, preparing the EU for an adaptable and resilient cybersecurity landscape in AI (European Parliament and Council of the European Union, 2024b).

A key challenge in AI cybersecurity is implementing lifecycle security practices that accommodate the evolving nature of AI systems. Unlike traditional digital products, AI systems undergo continuous learning and adaptation, which presents unique risks across each lifecycle phase from development and deployment to real-time operation and eventual decommissioning. The Cyber Resilience Act establishes foundational requirements to ensure security throughout a product's lifecycle. This approach mandates that manufacturers conduct comprehensive cybersecurity risk assessments and integrate security measures into each stage of AI product development. This proactive strategy emphasizes addressing not only immediate risks but also potential misuse scenarios, requiring systems to have secure configuration options that prevent unauthorized access, along with mechanisms for real-time monitoring. As AI systems are increasingly integrated into critical infrastructures, such as healthcare, transportation, and finance, the need for a lifecycle-based approach to security becomes even more crucial. Addressing these lifecycle-specific needs involves regular updates to threat models, dynamic risk assessments, and continuous monitoring to detect emerging vulnerabilities, ensuring AI products remain resilient as they adapt to diverse operational contexts.

Vulnerability management is another core element under the Cyber Resilience Act, requiring manufacturers to implement continuous oversight and swift response to emerging security issues throughout a product's lifecycle. Given AI systems' unique vulnerabilities, such as adversarial attacks, model extraction, and evasion tactics, ongoing monitoring and vulnerability management are essential. The Act stipulates that products be free of known exploitable vulnerabilities at launch, with a systematic approach to identifying, disclosing, and mitigating newly discovered risks over time. By issuing timely security updates and sharing essential cybersecurity information with users, manufacturers encourage a collaborative approach to cybersecurity, empowering users to make informed security decisions. AI-specific vulnerabilities often target model weaknesses by exploiting data reliance or manipulating inputs, prompting an adaptive approach to vulnerability management. Adversarial testing, model auditing, and anomaly detection systems that can detect and mitigate these threats in real-time become essential components in securing AI systems.

A further significant challenge in AI cybersecurity is the complex supply chain that underpins many AI products. The Cyber Resilience Act mandates that manufacturers ensure third-party components meet established security standards, thereby preventing vulnerabilities from compromising the overall safety of the product. Given that AI systems often depend on a blend of proprietary and third-party data, algorithms, and hardware, this requirement is essential to maintaining a consistent security baseline across the entire supply chain. Practical measures for supply chain security may include conducting regular assessments and validations, performing supply chain audits, securing certifications for vendors, and vulnerability testing of third-party components before integration. These practices foster accountability across all entities involved in producing and deploying AI systems. The Act's emphasis on supply chain security mitigates risks linked to dependencies on third-party components, reducing the likelihood of security breaches originating from external sources.

Transparency is another cornerstone of the Cyber Resilience Act, which requires manufacturers to provide essential cybersecurity information to users, empowering them to address potential risks and limitations associated with AI products. By promoting transparency, the Act encourages users to take proactive security measures, thereby enhancing trust in AI system operations. For high-risk AI systems, transparency mandates include accessible documentation outlining the system's security measures, limitations, and any potential risks. This transparency mandate aligns with the AI Act's requirement for high-risk systems to maintain interpretability and auditability, allowing developers and users to track how AI systems generate outputs. As AI systems increase in complexity, especially those using deep learning and neural networks, enhanced interpretability becomes vital for transparency and user empowerment. Clear communication about system limitations and potential vulnerabilities equips users to use AI responsibly and recognize situations where human oversight may be necessary.

To further safeguard critical AI products, the Cyber Resilience Act introduces conformity assessments, classifying products as either Class I or Class II based on their cybersecurity implications. This classification system allows regulatory authorities to prioritize oversight based on the potential impact of each AI application, directing resources toward securing the most critical systems. High-risk AI products face stricter conformity requirements, involving thorough testing and certification to ensure compliance with cybersecurity protocols. Conformity assessments provide a structured pathway for developers to align their products with EU security regulations, establishing clear benchmarks for acceptable cybersecurity practices in high-stakes AI applications. Beyond certification, these assessments include reviewing security practices, risk management, and adherence to standards, creating a multifaceted approach that enhances security for high-risk AI applications.

Looking ahead, the landscape of AI cybersecurity will continue evolving, influenced by technological advancements and new regulatory frameworks. The Cyber Resilience Act recognizes that AI's technological maturity will vary over time, suggesting that adaptable standards and continuous research are necessary to keep pace with emerging threats. Establishing flexible regulatory standards that evolve as AI technology advances will be crucial to addressing future cybersecurity challenges.

One promising approach is integrating machine learning operations (MLOps) with cybersecurity frameworks. MLOps, which automates and standardizes the deployment of machine learning models, can streamline AI lifecycle management and strengthen security by embedding monitoring, auditing, and risk management directly into the development pipeline. This proactive strategy facilitates rapid responses to new vulnerabilities, minimizing risks associated with the dynamic nature of AI models.

Advancements in privacy-preserving techniques, adversarial resilience testing, and differential privacy will be critical in protecting sensitive data within AI systems. As threats like model inversion, which allows attackers to reconstruct training data from model outputs, become more prevalent, these privacy-preserving methods help organizations protect user data while meeting security and ethical standards. International collaboration in AI cybersecurity research will play a crucial role in setting global standards, as the cross-border nature of digital threats requires a cohesive response. Aligning on best practices and sharing threat intelligence across jurisdictions can enhance cybersecurity consistency, offering a clear framework for organizations operating globally and fostering greater compliance.

The Cyber Resilience Act and the AI Act represent significant advances toward a robust regulatory framework for AI cybersecurity. By enforcing rigorous security measures, fostering transparency, and ensuring accountability throughout the supply chain, these regulations provide a strong foundation for managing AI-specific risks. However, the future of AI cybersecurity will depend on adaptive standards, innovative security practices, and sustained collaboration across sectors and borders. Embracing these challenges will enable policymakers, developers, and industry leaders to create a resilient, secure digital ecosystem that can keep pace with the rapid evolution of AI technologies.

MATERIALS AND METHODS

This study explores the cybersecurity requirements for high-risk AI systems under the EU's AI Act, focusing on secure, transparent, and resilient AI deployment. It employs a multi-step methodology, integrating regulatory analysis, technical assessments, and stakeholder input to evaluate how standards address AI-specific vulnerabilities.

The first phase reviews the AI Act, emphasizing cybersecurity-related provisions like risk management, transparency, and resilience. This analysis is enriched by European Commission documents and expert commentary, situating the Act within the broader cybersecurity standards landscape.

A comparative analysis follows, examining frameworks like ISO/IEC 42001:2023, ISO 27001, and NIST AI RMF for applicability to high-risk AI systems, focusing on data integrity, model robustness, and privacy. Industry case studies, including AI-based traffic monitoring and biometric systems, contextualize regulatory requirements.

A key aspect is the development of a threat model identifying AI-specific vulnerabilities such as data poisoning and adversarial evasion. This informs the evaluation of risk management protocols mandated by the AI Act, complemented by assessments of technical measures like adversarial testing and model auditing.

A lifecycle-based approach examines security from development to decommissioning, leveraging MLOps frameworks for continuous monitoring, dynamic risk assessment, and model validation. MLOps ensures structured management of AI lifecycle risks in high-risk environments.

Data governance and stakeholder engagement are pivotal. Practices addressing data quality, bias mitigation, and privacy ensure alignment with transparency and accountability standards. Multi-stakeholder inputs capture ethical and operational challenges in managing AI cybersecurity risks.

Both quantitative and qualitative analyses support findings. Quantitative data highlights AI's role in threat detection and automation, while qualitative insights from stakeholder interviews and policy documents address ethical and technical challenges.

Finally, the study acknowledges limitations, including the rapid evolution of AI and regulatory landscapes, necessitating adaptable approaches. The structured framework presented offers practical insights for ensuring cybersecurity compliance under the AI Act.

RESULTS

The results of this study reveal the complexities and essential requirements in implementing cybersecurity for high-risk AI systems under the European Union's AI Act. Through a structured analysis of regulatory frameworks, threat modeling, and industry case studies, several key insights emerge on the application of effective cybersecurity measures in AI systems and the practical challenges they face in real-world contexts.

The AI Act's risk-based approach, particularly for high-risk AI systems, provides a comprehensive framework for ensuring security, resilience, and transparency. Findings indicate that the classification of high-risk systems, those with potential impacts on public safety, health, or fundamental rights, effectively identifies sectors with heightened cybersecurity needs. For example, AI-based biometric recognition systems, critical infrastructure AI, and general-purpose AI models with systemic risks require stringent cybersecurity protocols due to the significant societal consequences of misuse or failure. Case studies, such as those involving AI-driven biometric systems, underscore the necessity of security measures tailored to these applications, where even minor technical inaccuracies could lead to severe outcomes, such as discrimination or privacy violations.

The AI Act mandates several technical and organizational measures to manage the unique vulnerabilities of AI systems. The threat model developed in this study reveals that AI systems are particularly susceptible to adversarial manipulation, data poisoning, and model evasion. Examining the effectiveness of the Act's protocols, including adversarial testing, systematic risk assessments, and data quality controls, findings show that these measures, when effectively implemented, can significantly enhance the security and reliability of AI systems. Protocols for transparency, such as the requirement for detailed documentation and operational disclosures, also strengthen the deployers' and users' ability to understand system capabilities and limitations, reducing risks associated with incorrect usage or unintended outcomes.

The lifecycle-based approach mandated by the AI Act, which emphasizes security from initial development through deployment and eventual decommissioning, is shown to be crucial for maintaining cybersecurity in AI systems. The integration of MLOps frameworks into this lifecycle substantially improves security and monitoring capabilities. Findings demonstrate that MLOps frameworks allow for continuous assessment of AI models, effectively addressing dynamic threats and preserving system integrity over time. However, results also highlight certain limitations: while MLOps provide a structured approach to security, some emerging AI-specific vulnerabilities, such as adaptive adversarial attacks, require further refinement in security measures to maintain resilience as AI technologies evolve.

Data governance emerges as a foundational element for cybersecurity in AI systems, particularly in ensuring data quality and privacy compliance. Findings show that the AI Act's requirements for data governance align well with principles of transparency, accountability, and fairness, essential for mitigating biases and protecting user privacy. This study also reveals that stakeholder engagement, particularly involving regulators, industry experts, and civil society organizations, enhances the ethical and operational robustness of cybersecurity practices. Collaborative governance frameworks foster a proactive approach to cybersecurity, addressing potential biases and security risks in a more comprehensive manner than single-entity oversight could achieve.

Quantitative data highlights the growing reliance on AI within cybersecurity operations, with 28% of organizations using AI to automate threat detection and response, 27% employing it in endpoint security, and 24% leveraging it for routine security tasks. Despite these advancements, qualitative analysis indicates a persistent skills gap within cybersecurity teams, with only 35% actively involved in AI policy development. This gap suggests that while AI technologies are increasingly critical in cybersecurity operations, greater alignment is needed between cybersecurity governance and AI integration to fully realize AI's potential in enhancing security.

The study finds that AI misuse by criminal organizations, poses significant challenges for cybersecurity. Criminal groups are exploiting advanced AI tools, such as large language models and deepfakes, to enhance traditional criminal tactics. Case studies show how generative AI is used for voice manipulation in ransom schemes, personalized phishing attacks, and even large-scale financial fraud. These findings highlight the urgent need for law enforcement and cybersecurity policies to address criminal AI applications proactively. Results suggest that frameworks like the AI Act could benefit from additional provisions to counteract AI-enabled criminal activities and to support law enforcement adaptation to these advanced threats.

Several challenges in implementing cybersecurity for high-risk AI systems are underscored in the results. One major hurdle identified is the need for adaptive standards that evolve in response to rapidly advancing AI threats. For instance, adversarial attacks are becoming increasingly sophisticated, outpacing some existing defensive measures. While the lifecycle security requirements under the AI Act are essential, they are constrained by current technological limitations in adversarial resilience and privacy-preserving techniques. Findings suggest that future advancements in AI cybersecurity will likely necessitate continuous updates to threat models, regulatory standards, and real-time monitoring capabilities to effectively address these emerging vulnerabilities.

The AI Act's transparency and conformity assessment requirements are found to be pivotal in ensuring accountability and user trust. The transparency mandate requires deployers and users of high-risk AI systems to understand system limitations, security controls, and potential risks, thereby fostering a responsible deployment environment. Conformity assessments provide structured benchmarks for compliance, enhancing security and reducing risk in high-stakes applications. Findings indicate that these assessments, especially for AI products categorized as Class I or II, help prioritize security resources according to the potential impact of each system, achieving an effective balance between regulatory oversight and innovation.

Finally, the results underscore the importance of international collaboration in AI cybersecurity, given the global nature of AI threats that require cohesive responses. The study highlights the AI Act's potential to serve as a model for other jurisdictions but also suggests that collaborative standards and shared threat intelligence will be essential for consistent global cybersecurity practices. Future research should focus on refining AI-specific defenses, advancing adversarial resilience, and developing privacy-preserving techniques to address the unique risks of AI while supporting ethical, secure, and responsible AI deployment worldwide.

In conclusion, this study's findings affirm the AI Act's significant contributions to AI cybersecurity, particularly for high-risk applications, by establishing a comprehensive regulatory framework that balances innovation with accountability. However, the evolving nature of AI technologies demands that cybersecurity standards remain adaptive, encouraging continuous innovation in both technical measures and regulatory practices to safeguard public welfare and critical infrastructure against increasingly sophisticated AI-driven threats.

DISCUSSION

This study emphasizes the importance of comprehensive cybersecurity frameworks, such as the EU's AI Act, in protecting high-risk AI systems. The AI Act addresses vulnerabilities like adversarial manipulation, data poisoning, and model evasion, while underscoring the need for adaptable measures to counter evolving threats.

A key contribution of the AI Act is its lifecycle, risk-based approach, focusing on high-risk applications with societal implications. However, findings highlight the need for adaptive safeguards to address unforeseen threats, particularly in systems with continuous learning models prone to feedback loops. Integrating dynamic security protocols would enhance resilience.

Transparency is central to the Act, promoting informed decision-making and accountability. Yet, current standards may need refinement for complex models like deep learning. Requiring model interpretability tailored to high-dimensional systems would ensure transparency as AI grows more sophisticated.

Data governance and stakeholder engagement are critical for ethical AI practices. Adaptive data governance models responsive to evolving inputs align better with the Act's goals, ensuring robust standards for data quality and privacy. A broad stakeholder approach further reinforces operational and ethical standards.

Criminal misuse of AI, particularly by organized crime, presents an emerging challenge. Advanced AI tools, such as deepfakes and large language models, are increasingly used for social engineering and fraud. The study identifies a regulatory gap in addressing third-party criminal misuse, recommending expanded provisions and stronger cooperation with law enforcement.

While the Act's conformity assessments and security requirements are foundational, the rapid evolution of AI demands flexible, real-time security measures. Continuous threat modeling and adaptive resilience strategies would address limitations in current adversarial defenses and privacy-preserving techniques.

International collaboration is vital given AI's global nature. The AI Act sets a strong precedent, but cohesive international standards and shared threat intelligence are necessary. Formal agreements and cross-border protocols for AI-related threats could foster a unified global response.

Priority areas for future focus include developing interpretability standards for complex AI, refining adversarial defenses, and implementing privacy-preserving techniques like differential privacy. Flexible governance models and evolving security protocols are crucial for maintaining relevance as AI advances.

In conclusion, the AI Act provides a robust foundation for AI cybersecurity, prioritizing transparency, adaptive risk management, and data governance. To keep pace with technological progress, regulatory frameworks must evolve through advancements in interpretability, adaptive security, and international cooperation, ensuring secure and ethical AI deployment.

CONCLUSION

The integration of AI in cybersecurity has significantly advanced proactive threat detection and response by optimizing defense mechanisms through real-time analysis and predictive capabilities. However, this integration also introduces unique security challenges, as AI systems are susceptible to sophisticated attacks that demand tailored protections and continuous monitoring across their lifecycle. Addressing these vulnerabilities requires both organizational and technical solutions. Organizationally, efforts must focus on standardizing processes and adapting existing security frameworks to meet the specific needs of AI-driven systems.

A key challenge in AI cybersecurity lies in the adaptive nature of AI, which, while powerful, can introduce unpredictability. An AI system deemed secure in a controlled environment may evolve quickly post-deployment, potentially undermining prior validation efforts. Designing robust test environments that mirror real-world complexities presents a critical hurdle. To mitigate this, implementing iterative re-verification protocols in sandbox environments is essential, allowing for continuous assessment and adjustment to maintain reliability and security as algorithms adapt to new data inputs.

The misuse of AI by criminal organizations also intensifies cybersecurity challenges. These groups increasingly exploit advanced tools, such as deepfakes and personalized phishing, to amplify the reach and effectiveness of traditional criminal tactics. This presents new complexities for law enforcement, which must adopt innovative strategies to address these evolving threats effectively and ensure user protection.

Standardizing cybersecurity measures for AI systems will evolve alongside AI technology itself. Initial standards should concentrate on universally accepted technical controls, especially for high-risk applications, establishing a foundational framework for more sophisticated, outcome-based requirements. These standards are essential first steps in a continuous journey toward developing robust technical measures that can ensure long-term security for AI systems.

For high-risk AI systems that employ emerging technologies, current methods may not fully meet the cybersecurity requirements outlined in the AI Act. This underscores the need for parallel advancements in technological innovation and regulatory standards. The future of AI cybersecurity depends on fostering a regulatory environment that evolves in tandem with cutting-edge technology, allowing for a sustainable, adaptive response to the rapidly shifting landscape of AI-driven threats.

To further enhance the resilience and accountability of AI systems, future research should explore methods for measuring AI robustness, developing privacy-preserving techniques, and optimizing defenses against emerging vulnerabilities. By advancing research in these areas, the field of AI cybersecurity can better address the evolving complexities of AI applications, supporting a more secure and responsible deployment of AI technologies.

REFERENCES

Bhawna, & Mahajan, S. (2024). Artificial intelligence perspective on digital forensics. In S. Mahajan, M. Khurana, & V. V. Estrela (Eds.), *Applying artificial intelligence in cybersecurity analytics and cyber threat detection* (pp. 34-42). John Wiley & Sons.

Bowen, G., Sothinathan, J., & Bowen, R. (2024). Technological Governance (Cybersecurity and AI): Role of Digital Governance. In Jahankhani, H., Bowen, G., Sharif, M. S., & Hussien, O. (Eds.), *Cybersecurity and Artificial Intelligence: Transformational Strategies and Disruptive Innovation* (pp. 143–168). Springer. DOI: 10.1007/978-3-031-52272-7_6

Dawes Centre for Future Crime at UCL. (2020). *AI-enabled future crime*. UCL. Retrieved from https://www.ucl.ac.uk/jill-dando-institute/sites/jill-dando-institute/files/ai_crime_policy_0.pdf

European Parliament and Council of the European Union. (2024a). Regulation (EU) 2024/1689 of the European Parliament and of the Council of 13 June 2024 laying down harmonised rules on artificial intelligence and amending Regulations (EC) No 300/2008, (EU) No 167/2013, (EU) No 168/2013, (EU) 2018/858, (EU) 2018/1139, and (EU) 2019/2144 and Directives 2014/90/EU, (EU) 2016/797, and (EU) 2020/1828 (Artificial Intelligence Act). Official Journal of the European Union, L 1689, 12.7.2024. https://data.europa.eu/eli/reg/2024/1689/oj

European Parliament and Council of the European Union. (2024b). Regulation (EU) 2024/2847 of the European Parliament and of the Council of 23 October 2024 on horizontal cybersecurity requirements for products with digital elements and amending Regulations (EU) No 168/2013 and (EU) No 2019/1020 and Directive (EU) 2020/1828 (Cyber Resilience Act). Official Journal of the European Union, L 20/11/2024. https://data.europa.eu/eli/reg/2024/2847/oj

Europol & UNICRI. (2023). Malicious Uses and Abuses of Artificial Intelligence. Retrieved from https://www.ucl.ac.uk/jill-dando-institute/sites/jill-dando-institute/files/ai_crime_policy_0.pdf

Federal Office for Information Security. (2023). AI security concerns in a nutshell. Federal Office for Information Security. https://www.bsi.bund.de/SharedDocs/Downloads/EN/BSI/KI/Practical_Al-Security_Guide_2023.pdf

ISACA. (2024). *State of Cybersecurity 2024: Global update on workforce efforts, resources, and cyberoperations*. https://www.isaca.org/resources/reports/state-of-cybersecurity-2024

ISO. (2023). *ISO/IEC 42001:2023 Information technology—Artificial intelligence—Management system requirements*. International Organization for Standardization.

Jahnavi, & Urvashi. (2024). Review on machine learning-based traffic rules contravention detection system. In S. Mahajan, M. Khurana, & V. V. Estrela (Eds.), *Applying artificial intelligence in cybersecurity analytics and cyber threat detection* (pp. 45-57). John Wiley & Sons.

Jarmul, K. (2023). *Practical data privacy: Enhancing privacy and security in data. Sebastopol*. O'Reilly Media.

Junklewitz, H., Hamon, R., André, A., Evas, T., Soler Garrido, J., & Sanchez Martin, J. I. (2023). *Cybersecurity of Artificial Intelligence in the AI Act*. Publications Office of the European Union., DOI: 10.2760/271009

Microsoft. (2022a). Microsoft Responsible AI Standard v2. Microsoft Corporation. https://blogs.microsoft.com/wp-content/uploads/prod/sites/5/2022/06/Microsoft-Responsible-AI-Standard-v2-General-Requirements-3.pdf

Microsoft. (2022b). Microsoft Responsible AI Impact Assessment Guide. Microsoft Corporation. https://blogs.microsoft.com/wp-content/uploads/prod/sites/5/2022/06/Microsoft-RAI-Impact-Assessment-Guide.pdf

Microsoft. (2022c). Responsible AI Impact Assessment Template. Retrieved from Microsoft Responsible AI documentation. https://blogs.microsoft.com/wp-content/uploads/prod/sites/5/2022/06/Microsoft-RAI-Impact-Assessment-Template.pdf

MITRE. (2023). MITRE ATLAS™: AI security 101 and adversarial tactics for AI systems. MITRE. https://atlas.mitre.org

Munjal, G., & Puri, T. (2024). Analysis of malicious executables and detection techniques. In Mahajan, S., Khurana, M., & Estrela, V. V. (Eds.), *Applying artificial intelligence in cybersecurity analytics and cyber threat detection* (pp. 3–20). John Wiley & Sons. DOI: 10.1002/9781394196470.ch1

National Institute of Standards and Technology. (2023b). AI RMF Playbook. National Institute of Standards and Technology. https://airc.nist.gov/docs/AI_RMF_Playbook.pdf

National Institute of Standards and Technology (NIST). (2023a). Artificial Intelligence Risk Management Framework (AI RMF 1.0). https://doi.org/DOI: 10.6028/NIST.AI.100-1

National Institute of Standards and Technology (NIST). (2024). *NIST AI 600-1: AI Risk Management Framework for Generative AI*. U.S. Department of Commerce., DOI: 10.6028/NIST.AI.600-1

Newton, C. (2024). 4 Ways AI Is Shaping Organized Crime in Latin America. InSight Crime. Retrieved from https://insightcrime.org

OECD. (2024). OECD AI Principles overview. https://oecd.ai/en/ai-principles

Pitre, V., Joshi, A., Saladi, S., & Das, S. (2024). Enhancing cybersecurity ratings using artificial intelligence and DevOps technologies. In Mahajan, S., Khurana, M., & Estrela, V. V. (Eds.), *Applying artificial intelligence in cybersecurity analytics and cyber threat detection* (pp. 63–86). John Wiley & Sons. DOI: 10.1002/9781394196470.ch5

Raheja, S. (2024). Detection and analysis of botnet attacks using machine learning techniques. In Mahajan, S., Khurana, M., & Estrela, V. V. (Eds.), *Applying artificial intelligence in cybersecurity analytics and cyber threat detection* (pp. 20–30). John Wiley & Sons. DOI: 10.1002/9781394196470.ch2

San Francisco, F. B. I. (2024, May 8). FBI Warns of Increasing Threat of Cyber Criminals Utilizing Artificial Intelligence. FBI. Retrieved from https://www.fbi.gov/contact-us/field-offices/sanfrancisco/news

Soler Garrido, J., De Nigris, S., Bassani, E., Sanchez, I., Evas, T., André, A., & Boulangé, T. (2024). Harmonised standards for the European AI Act (JRC139430). European Commission. https://publications.jrc.ec.europa.eu/repository/handle/JRC139430

Stutz, D., de Assis, J. T., Laghari, A. A., Khan, A. A., Deshpande, A., Kulkarni, D., Terziev, A., & Grata, E. G. H. (2024). Cyber threat detection and mitigation using artificial intelligence – A cyber-physical perspective. In Mahajan, S., Khurana, M., & Estrela, V. V. (Eds.), *Applying artificial intelligence in cybersecurity analytics and cyber threat detection* (pp. 108–126). John Wiley & Sons. DOI: 10.1002/9781394196470.ch7

KEY TERMS AND DEFINITIONS

Adversarial Attacks: Tactics employed to manipulate AI models by altering inputs to produce incorrect outputs. These include evasion attacks, poisoning, and model inversion, which exploit AI-specific vulnerabilities.

AI Regulatory Sandbox: Controlled environments provided by regulators where AI systems can be tested under close supervision before public deployment, allowing developers to refine security and compliance measures.

Artificial Intelligence (AI): Machine-based systems that can autonomously interpret inputs and produce outputs, including predictions, recommendations, or decisions that affect physical or digital environments. Under the AI Act, AI systems are classified by risk, with high-risk systems subject to strict oversight.

Conformity Assessment: A process under the AI Act for verifying that high-risk AI systems meet regulatory requirements, involving testing, documentation, and certification to ensure cybersecurity compliance.

Cyber Resilience: The ability of an AI system to maintain operational integrity in the face of cybersecurity threats, including attacks that attempt to compromise system functionality or data security.

Cybersecurity: The practice of protecting systems, networks, and programs from digital attacks. In the context of AI, cybersecurity aims to safeguard AI systems against adversarial manipulation, data breaches, and unauthorized access.

Data Poisoning: A type of adversarial attack where malicious data is introduced during an AI system's training phase, compromising the integrity of the model and skewing its outputs.

Differential Privacy: A privacy-preserving technique in AI that ensures data confidentiality by adding noise to datasets, minimizing the risk of identifying individual data points in model outputs.

Incident Reporting: A regulatory requirement under the AI Act where providers of high-risk AI systems must promptly report cybersecurity incidents to authorities, detailing the causes and corrective actions taken. This ensures transparency and fosters rapid response to emerging threats.

Model Evasion: A form of adversarial attack where inputs are carefully crafted to evade detection by an AI model, commonly targeting security systems to bypass protections.

Model Stealing: An attack where an adversary replicates or approximates an AI model by making extensive API queries, threatening intellectual property and exposing potential vulnerabilities.

Risk Management: The process of identifying, assessing, and controlling threats to an organization's digital assets, including those presented by AI systems. It involves continuous assessment throughout the AI lifecycle to mitigate vulnerabilities and ensure compliance with regulations.

Transparency: In the AI Act, transparency refers to the clear and accessible disclosure of AI system functionalities, limitations, and security controls, enabling users to understand risks and make informed decisions.

Chapter 4
General Overview Cybersecurity and Artificial Intelligence

Carolina Landero Perez
https://orcid.org/0000-0001-7621-0053
Autonomous University of Tamaulipas, Mexico

Cynthia Marisol Vargas Orozco
https://orcid.org/0000-0002-7329-9475
Autonomous University of Tamaulipas, Mexico

Ignacio Hernández Rodríguez
Autonomous University of Tamaulipas, Mexico

ABSTRACT

Crime and delinquency evolve, adapt, and transform alongside new "forms of social interaction." As society has significantly shifted from traditional ways of doing things to digitally integrated activities—storing our personal information in the cloud—individuals who engage in antisocial, criminal, or unlawful behavior have also evolved. As criminologists, we must become involved in understanding these "new forms" of antisocial conduct to ensure effective prevention.

DOI: 10.4018/979-8-3693-8871-6.ch004

INTRODUCTION

Major advancements in technology often bring about implications beyond their original purpose. While many envision technological innovation as a means to achieve social well-being, there are always those who seek personal gain at the expense of others.

Human evolution manifests in every sphere of knowledge—technological evolution began with the Industrial Revolution in the 18th century, progressed through the 20th century with the advent of computers and information technology, and now propels us into the realms of quantum computing and artificial intelligence (Allende López, 2019).

Artificial Intelligence (AI) "can be a valuable tool in cybersecurity, but it can also be leveraged by cybercriminals to enhance their attacks" (BBVA, 2024). AI can play a noble role across various fields, particularly by assisting security teams in improving threat detection, reducing response time to attacks, minimizing damage caused by cyberattacks, automating repetitive tasks, and resolving vulnerabilities (Microsoft, n.d.).

Acknowledging both the benefits and the potential misuse of technology in cyberspace, this chapter applies a qualitative, exploratory, descriptive, and documentary methodology to explore the relationship between cybersecurity and artificial intelligence.

The scope of this phenomenon is vast, considering the wide variety of digital criminal activity that often goes unnoticed due to general unawareness. Every age group is now vulnerable, especially since 2020, when COVID-19—one of the deadliest pandemics in history—forced global lockdowns (WHO, 2023), and "the reliance on digital tools surged dramatically, not only for accessing public services but also for remote work" (Roseth, Reyes, & Yee Amézaga, 2021). As Rodríguez Abitia (2021) stated, "the health emergency pushed us ten years ahead in terms of adapting to technology—there was no choice."

To better understand the context, this chapter presents a description of key concepts including: Criminology vs. Criminalistics, antisocial behavior (crime and offense), cybercrime and cyberoffense, cybersecurity, artificial intelligence, computer forensics, and information and communication technologies (ICTs). These will be further analyzed in the following sections.

Criminology vs. Criminalistics

It is essential to distinguish Criminology from Criminalistics, as the terms are often mistakenly used interchangeably. The foundational definition in Mexico, coined by Ruiz Funes (1952) and later expanded by Quiroz Cuarón (1965), defines

Criminology as a synthetic, causal, explanatory, natural, and cultural science focused on antisocial behavior (Quiroz Cuarón, 1965, as cited in Rodríguez Manzanera, 2024). Its primary subject of study is antisocial behavior and those who commit it (Rodríguez Manzanera, 2024).

Rodríguez Manzanera (2024) classifies Criminology as a factual, material, or empirical science. According to Bunge (2013), factual sciences deal with "events and processes" and allow hypotheses to be confirmed through "observation and/or experimentation." In other words, factual sciences must observe their surroundings, deliberately alter or examine variables to determine "how well their hypotheses match reality" (Bunge, 2013), relying on rational and objective knowledge to "identify the causes and contributing factors behind a phenomenon, and therefore, how to prevent it" (Rodríguez Manzanera, 2024).

Criminology goes beyond analyzing operational concepts like cause, motive, and causal factors; it seeks to understand "causal chains." It doesn't just aim to identify the immediate cause but the deeper, underlying causes. By understanding antisocial behavior and its causal factors, it becomes possible to prevent or counteract it. Criminology is not merely about comprehending antisocial behavior—it seeks to prevent it. Its focus is on prevention, not repression (Rodríguez Manzanera, 2024).

There's a methodological need within Criminology to analyze different levels of interpretation of phenomena, which eventually converge into a single synthesis. These levels coexist and depend on each other: "there can be no crime without a criminal, nor a criminal without a crime. Criminality is the totality of crimes, obviously committed by criminals" (Rodríguez Manzanera, 2024).

Rodríguez Manzanera (2024) explains that:

"Criminological interpretations are especially valuable for jurists:

A. The behavioral level of interpretation (crime) is relevant in legal proceedings.

B. The personal level of interpretation (criminal) is essential for sentencing.

C. The general level of interpretation (criminality) is especially useful for legislation.

This does not mean that each level is irrelevant at other times—only that each has its moment of greatest importance."

In essence, Criminology is a social science that studies crime, the criminal, the victim, and the societal response to criminal behavior. Its goal is to understand the causes of a crime and how they manifest, considering factors such as criminal psychology.

On the other hand, Criminalistics focuses on the study of physical evidence—the material traces of a crime—to identify and uncover the presumed perpetrator and reconstruct the crime scene. Criminalistics answers six of the classic seven investigative questions: What? Who? Where? When? How? With what? The final question, Why?, is addressed by Criminology.

According to Rafael Moreno (2016), Criminalistics is the discipline that primarily applies knowledge, methods, and research techniques from the natural sciences to examine material evidence related to a suspected crime—its formal subject of study. Edmond Locard, a renowned French forensic scientist, referred to this evidence as "silent witnesses that do not lie," because they help reconstruct criminal events and identify those responsible (Moreno González, 2016).

Aguilar Ruiz (2016) states that the criminalistics method allows for the protection and preservation—through the chain of custody—of elements considered as evidence, which were previously located at the scene of the incident, documented, collected, and packaged for proper transportation to the corresponding laboratories for analysis:

In criminalistics, the chain of custody is fundamental. It must be applied to all physical elements that constitute evidence in order to guarantee their authenticity, ensuring their identity and original condition. The conditions under which these elements are collected, transported, handled, analyzed, and preserved, as well as the individuals involved in these processes, are of utmost importance. The chain of custody begins at the site where evidence is first obtained and concludes when the judicial authority determines that there is no longer a need for experts to analyze the elements related to the incident. Undoubtedly, the investigator must possess both intellectual and moral integrity (Aguilar Ruiz, 2016).

Among the most important topics in criminalistics are those related to technological advancements, which have become a key strategy in investigations to meet the challenges of ever-evolving criminal behavior. This is achieved through techniques and instruments that "surpass traditional chemical methods in speed, efficiency, and precision for analyzing physical evidence" (Moreno González, 2016).

Moreno González (2016) notes that:

The modern stage of criminalistics investigation begins with the instrumental analysis of physical evidence (chromatographic and spectroscopic techniques, mass spectrometry, X-ray diffraction, scanning electron microscopy); the integration of instruments to achieve greater analytical precision (e.g., gas chromatograph with mass spectrometer); the use of various types of computerized systems (software); and the establishment of quality control laboratories that define globally accepted standards.

These technologies enable the permanent preservation of recorded data for future analysis and allow for the measurement of phenomena that cannot be directly observed with the senses (Moreno González, 2016).

Two key breakthroughs have revolutionized scientific criminal investigation: DNA analysis and the application of computer science to forensic disciplines. These allow experts to "acquire, preserve, extract, and present data that has been electronically processed and stored on digital media" (Moreno González, 2016), interconnected via the internet, which in recent years has experienced rapid growth.

An example of the importance of computer science and digital media in the forensic field, as explained by Moreno González (2016), is the shift from "manual searches for records in fingerprint and name databases" to "computerized systems that significantly reduce the time required for such tasks: the Automated Fingerprint Identification System (AFIS)."

> *AFIS can digitize fingerprints without the use of ink. Latent fingerprints are scanned and converted into electronic images, which are then stored in a database for rapid retrieval. According to Eillen Albrech, a program analyst at the FBI, this system reduces the risk of blurred, smudged, or incomplete prints, which were common in the traditional ink-based method. The use of this digital system improves the quality of fingerprint records and facilitates their subsequent identification.*
>
> *However, despite the widespread recognition of the benefits of analytical instruments, it is wise to remember Lord Lister's important warning: "Always be sure that your instruments are not deceiving you." In other words: "Always work with controls to avoid errors" (Moreno González, 2016).*

Antisocial Behavior

When referring to behavior that is socially unacceptable because it violates either a social norm or a law, one may be referring to the terms *crime* or *offense*—both of which represent antisocial behavior.

Crime and offense are often considered synonymous by many, but their distinction lies in whether the infraction is codified in law. Dr. Rodríguez Manzanera (2024) explains:

> *"An offense is an act or omission punishable by criminal law; it is a conduct defined by law—it is the legal offense" (Rodríguez Manzanera, 2024, p. 22).*
>
> *"A crime, on the other hand, refers to conduct that may or may not be defined in criminal codes—it is any action that harms the common good, threatens the basic structure of society, destroys fundamental values, and violates elementary rules of coexistence. It is an event with a beginning, a development, and an end. This level of analysis involves examining all factors and causes that contributed to the incident, including biological, psychological, and anthropological aspects that led to the 'acting out.' It is also important to note that many antisocial behaviors are not codified, and that does not mean criminologists should ignore them" (Rodríguez Manzanera, 2024, p. 27).*

In short, antisocial behavior can be criminal—such as assault or theft—or non-criminal, like lying or disrespecting a superior or authority figure (García Álvarez, 2014). These antisocial behaviors are studied by what is known as *dynamic criminology*, because it "tends to evolve rapidly, as the reality it studies and the sciences that compose it evolve as well" (Rodríguez Manzanera, 2024). Therefore, it is essential to also focus on how antisocial behaviors are evolving into cyberspace.

Cyberspace and Cybercrime

According to the Royal Spanish Academy (RAE), *"cyberspace is a virtual realm created by computer means, especially the Internet. It is an imaginary space where communications within a computer network take place"* (RAE, 2014). It is an artificial environment developed through computer tools, meaning it cannot be physically touched—rather, it is a digital construct created via computers (Pérez Porto & Gardey, 2022).

Cyberspace is where users can share information, exchange ideas, interact, play, participate in various social forums, use social networks, send and receive emails, and browse websites. They can do business here and engage in different activities such as banking, completing procedures, shopping, or booking appointments. Essentially, any digital feature connected to the internet forms part of cyberspace. Any virtual interface that creates a form of digital reality is considered cyberspace (Cybersecurity, 2024).

Cyberspace is a global and dynamic domain that includes Information Technology (IT) infrastructures, computers, hardware, software, computing systems, networks, programs, data and data traffic, users, the Internet, information services, and telecommunications (Guerra García, 2014; Quintana, 2016).

Guerra García (2014) and Bacigalupo (2018) outline that cyberspace is composed of multiple layers. The main ones are:

1. The Physical Layer includes geographic components and physical network infrastructures, such as computers, servers, cables, fiber optics, and radio transmissions.

Figure 1. First layer of cyberspace

Note: The image represents the physical network and geographic environment. Adapted from "Nature of Cyberspace" (Bacigalupo, 2018).

2. The Logical Layer consists of logical network components—the connections between network nodes, where a "node" is any device connected to communication networks and information systems (see Figure 2). Cyberspace is built from components that provide services, and these services are designed to be combined into more complex services.

For example, by combining applications like word processors, databases, or the Web, we can create more complex services like Facebook. Facebook itself is a platform where additional applications are developed. The evolution of cyberspace will depend on the continuous and rapid development of new capabilities and services built upon logical structures supported by physical infrastructure.

Figure 2. Network nodes

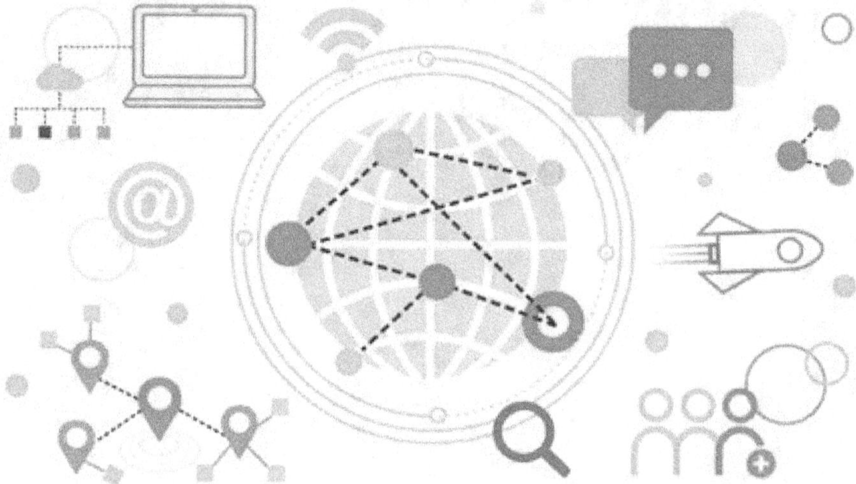

Note: The image represents the logical layer of cyberspace and the connections between various devices linked to communication networks and information systems. Adapted from "Illustration of the Concept of Social Networks" (www.freepik.com, 2024).

3) Third layer is the Social Layer, which includes the human component and cyber-identities. The human component consists of individuals who interact within cyberspace. People are no longer passive users—they contribute to Wikipedia, tweet, post on Facebook, and form professional networks on LinkedIn.

Participants in multiplayer games immerse themselves in virtual worlds, assume roles (avatars), earn money, make friends, debate governance, and often experience a sense of "reality" in these virtual environments.

Figure 3. Social Interaction layer in cyberspace

Note: The image illustrates the relationship between individuals and their cyber-identities. Adapted from "Cyberspace as a Social Environment" (NETiquette, 2024).

4) The Information Layer is the last one. This layer encompasses the creation, capture, storage, and processing of information in many forms: music, videos, business records, web pages, online books, photographs, metadata, and data created or collected during information searches (e.g., via Google). Information is no longer stored statically—it is dynamically generated. Websites are created on demand and personalized for each user based on information components stored in databases.

An important concept not to be overlooked is cyber-identity, which refers to "the identity created in cyberspace through social media and the internet. The construction of one or more cyber-identities may be influenced by the digital environment and the desire for approval from other users" (Mendoza Márquez & Fernández T., 2017). However, cyber-identities may also be false—created solely to attract attention or generate online impact.

Understanding how criminal behavior manifests in cyberspace means grasping the evolution of crime within "the other space" (www.ambitojuridico.com, 2012).

Miró Linares (2012), director of the Crimina Center at Miguel Hernández University of Elche, Spain—a research center focused on scientific analysis, prevention, and treatment of crime—explains: "Tell me what you do online, and I'll tell you what could happen to you in cyberspace. The more interaction and digital goals you have in cyberspace, the higher the chance of 'cyber-victimization.' The more self-protection, the lower the likelihood of victimization."

In other words, as technology advances and enables greater digital interaction—such as using email, online shopping, participating in forums or blogs, or conducting banking transactions—the risk of becoming a victim of antisocial behavior in cyberspace increases. Therefore, "those who lack antivirus software, don't update or change their passwords, are more likely to be victimized" (Miró Linares, 2012).

Among criminological theories, we find relevant application to our context in the *Routine Activity Theory* by Cohen and Felson (1979) (Redondo & Garrido Genovés, 2013), which states that *"a crime occurs when three elements coincide: the offender has the motivation to commit the act, the victim or target is accessible, and there is a failure in social control or protective mechanisms that would otherwise safeguard the victim or target"* (UNIR, 2022).

The first element—criminal behavior—applies in the virtual context. According to Miró Linares (2012), antisocial behavior in cyberspace can be categorized into three types:

- **Economic "cybercrime"**, which includes fraud and phishing, meaning the fraudulent acquisition of confidential information such as passwords or detailed information about credit cards or other banking data.
- **"Hacktivism"**, encompassing political and ideological crimes. This is understood as the non-violent use of illegal or legally ambiguous digital tools in pursuit of political goals, such as cyberterrorism or racially motivated attacks, among others.
- **Social "cybercrime"**, which is increasingly concerning. This includes cyberbullying, online harassment, and internet-based stalking as some of the most common manifestations (Miró Linares, 2012).

Cybercrime vs. Cyber Offenses

The terms *cybercrime* and *cyber offense* are often used interchangeably, much like *crime* and *offense* in general legal terminology. However, cyber offenses are grounded in established legal norms, which provide a basis for identifying them by considering the essential elements necessary for the application of jurisprudence (Díaz Aranda, 2016; UAS, 2023):

1. **Acts affecting protected legal interests** – without an action, there is no offense.

2. **Typification** – the conduct must match a legal description. In this regard, cybercrime has a particular advantage, since many cyber offenses do not "precisely align with the abstract definition laid out in the law."
3. **Unlawfulness** – the act violates legal norms, either endangering or destroying a legally protected interest.
4. **Culpability** – the direct relationship between the intent and awareness of the act and the actual conduct (UAS, 2023).

Cyber offenses or *computer crimes* refer to criminal acts carried out through digital means. These may include fraud, theft, virus creation, or distributed denial-of-service (DDoS) attacks, which do have corresponding legal classifications (Sanchis, 2018).

In **Mexico**, the main legal instruments regulating cyber offenses include:

- The Political Constitution of the United Mexican States (La Constitución Política de los Estados Unidos Mexicanos)
- The Federal Telecommunications and Broadcasting Law (La Ley Federal de Telecomunicaciones y Radiodifusión)
- The Federal Transparency and Access to Public Information Act (La Norma Federal de Transparencia y Acceso a la Información Pública)
- The Federal Copyright Law (La Ley Federal del Derecho de Autor)
- The Federal Law on Protection of Personal Data Held by Private Parties (La Ley Federal de Protección de Datos Personales en Posesión de Particulares)
- The Federal Criminal Code (El Código Penal Federal)(Ochoa Serafín, 2024)

It is important to note that **not all antisocial behaviors in cyberspace are covered by current legal frameworks**—but that does not mean they do not exist. This is why it is crucial to examine the diverse manifestations of cybercriminal behavior closely.

Cybercriminality

Cybercriminality refers to the set of **illegal activities or actions that harm the "common good" via cyber means**, using electronic devices and computer networks to target other cyber-persons. These acts are typically aimed at acquiring systems, digital assets, or legally protected interests. Cybercriminals may range from advanced hackers or organized groups to amateurs with access to basic technology (Kaspersky, 2024).

Table 1. Antisocial behaviors in cyberspace

Cybercriminality	
Illegal gambling	Ransomware attacks (a type of cyber extortion)
Violation of data confidentiality	Botnets through DoS and DDoS attacks
Cyber espionage (where hackers access government or corporate data)	Cyber extortion (demanding money to avoid a cyberattack)
Cyberterrorism	Gender-based cyber violence
Violation of privacy (Olimpia Law)	Cryptojacking (where hackers mine cryptocurrency using resources they do not own)
Cyberbullying and Happy Slapping	Crackings
Harassment or provoking fights	Doxing
Scams	Identity theft (in cases of stolen and misused personal information)
Email and Internet fraud	Computer fraud
Gossip (rumors)	Griefing
Grooming	Hacking or software piracy
Blocking or disrupting IT systems	Copyright infringement
Network interference (compromising a system)	Oversharing
Malware	Phishing or identity spoofing
Ransomware	Revenge porn
Data theft	Theft and sale of corporate data
Skimming (theft of financial/payment card data)	Virtual kidnapping
Child pornography (production, possession, distribution)	Sex-casting, Sexting, and Sextortion

Note: List of antisocial behaviors present in cyberspace. (SeguridadInformáticaHoy, 2024; FGJTam, 2024; Riestra Gaytán; SSPC, 2021; FGJCDMX, 2024)

Cybercriminals typically carry out one or two attacks at a time, often first targeting computers with viruses and then using them to spread malware to other devices or through a network. Some jurisdictions recognize a third category of cybercrime, in which a computer is used as an accessory to commit a crime (Kaspersky, 2024). To prevent cybercrime and ensure behaviors are legally categorized as cyber offenses, it is important to stay vigilant, report incidents, and preserve evidence.

Cybersecurity

The security of ourselves and our environment is crucial, especially given how vulnerable we are to cybercriminals. It is necessary to consider cybersecurity whenever we "navigate" through cyberspace.

When using the internet for online banking, social networks, or other services, there is a risk of exposing personal data—such as your name, address, or credit card number. Individuals with malicious intent can gain access through unsecured connections and misuse this information for personal gain (Ciberseguridad, 2024).

But what exactly is security and cybersecurity?

Security is defined as the state of being secure—free from danger, harm, or risk—and is associated with peace of mind and a sense of well-being (RAE, 2023).

Cybersecurity initially focused on protecting information from unauthorized access, use, disclosure, interruption, modification, or destruction—mainly through reactive measures. Over time, it evolved into a proactive protection strategy, aiming to prevent antisocial behaviors by "identifying and managing the risks that threaten cyberspace", while "promoting integration among all stakeholders and tools—public, private, and society as a whole" (Guerra García, 2014).

Cybersecurity—as well as cybercrime and cyber offenses—must be clearly differentiated from Information Security, IT Security, and Cyber Intelligence, for which the following table is included:

Table 2. Conceptualization of information security, data security, cybersecurity, and cyber intelligence

Information Security	These are preventive and reactive measures that store and protect information, whether processed or transmitted in different ways: electronically, verbally, or through written or printed messages. It can range from protecting a cabinet of important documents to protecting the database of a company, institution, organization, or individual.	It has a broader scope than Cybersecurity and IT Security, since the goal is to protect information from risks that may affect it in its different forms and states. It includes defensive aspects to protect interconnected information systems. Areas of competence include people and everything related to compliance with information security standards.
IT Security	Discipline that manages risks to protect the integrity and privacy of information stored in the IT system, its use, processing, and transmission, as well as the systems and processes involved in these activities. IT security, shorthand for Information Technology Security, is the practice of protecting an organization's IT assets—computer systems, networks, digital devices, data.	It provides services to the entire technical infrastructure of an organization, including hardware systems, software applications, and endpoints like laptops and mobile devices. IT security also protects the company's network and its components, such as physical and cloud-based data centers. Common IT security examples include endpoint security, cloud security, network security, and application security. It also includes physical security measures (e.g., locks, ID cards, surveillance cameras) to protect buildings and devices housing data and IT assets.
Cybersecurity	A set of actions, technologies, practices, and policies aimed at protecting and ensuring the functionality and integrity of data, networks, and systems against digital attacks, to prevent or mitigate the impact of cyberattacks. Cybersecurity aims to protect IT systems, applications, devices, data,	Primarily focuses on digital information, computing equipment, and interconnected systems that process, store, or transmit it, and on managing controls and measures to prevent attacks, which gives it strong overlap with IT Security. It is responsible for initiating
	financial assets, and individuals against ransomware and other malicious programs, phishing scams, data theft, and other cyber threats.	processes to solve issues caused by an attack or intrusion and conducting offensive actions against adversaries of digital security. Areas of competence include networks, software, hardware, services, and critical infrastructures such as technology infrastructure.
Cyber Intelligence	A branch of cybersecurity. It is the intelligence focused on identifying and countering criminal activities in IT or cyberspace. It involves collecting, analyzing, and applying information about cyber threats and malicious activities. Its goal is to prevent or mitigate cyberattacks and protect critical online infrastructures.	Focuses on collecting, analyzing, and applying information about cyber threats and malicious activities. It is externally focused, where potential threats are found. The goal is to develop and implement effective strategies to counter cyberattacks.

Note: The following table helps identify the main differences between the three types of security related to technology and cyberspace, which are currently applicable (Cybersecurity, 2024) (Microsoft, n.d.) (Kaspersky, 2024) (LISA Institute, 2024) (Lindemulder & Kosinski, 2024) (Salvador, n.d.)

Other important aspects in the development of the topic include the conceptualization of Artificial Intelligence, ICTs, and Forensic Computing.

Artificial Intelligence (AI)

AI has developed significantly, and without realizing it, it now permeates many of our daily activities. "The term Artificial Intelligence (AI) was coined during a conference organized by Marvin Minsky, John McCarthy, and Claude Shanon in

1956 at Dartmouth. This event can be considered the starting point of AI as a new scientific field" (Marvin Minsky, John McCarthy, and Claude Shanon, 1956, as cited in García Fernández, 2019).

AI is defined as "the capability of a system to correctly interpret external data, learn from it, and use those learnings to achieve specific goals and tasks through flexible adaptation" (Kaplan &

Haenlein, 2019). In other words, machines imitate human intellectual functions and knowledge, enabling them to present capabilities like "reasoning, learning, creativity, and planning" and offer objective solutions to problems (Kaplan & Haenlein, 2019) (European Parliament, 2021).

Currently, the application of AI is categorized based on its area of operation:

- **Software:** virtual assistants, image analysis software, search engines, or voice and facial recognition systems (European Parliament, 2021)
- **Embedded AI:** robots, drones, autonomous vehicles, or the Internet of Things (European Parliament, 2021)

Some applications of AI (European Parliament, 2021) (INESDI, 2023) include:

- Virtual voice assistants and personal digital assistants
- Web search engines
- Optimization of e-commerce, online shopping, and advertising
- Language translation software
- Smart homes or infrastructure
- Smart cars with AI-powered road safety features
- GPS navigation systems
- Cybersecurity
- Medicine
- Manufacturing optimization
- Agriculture
- Forensic science
- Public security, administration, and services

AI is transforming all sectors of human activity, proving to be highly effective in automating tasks and having an impact across healthcare, manufacturing, logistics, and retail—it is becoming our new necessity (Jewell, 2019).

Various authors highlight the benefits of AI, while also warning that control and protection systems are necessary:

- "All this change leads to a future transformation of information and its use," creating "a new way of seeing, doing, and managing that could be defined as a new form of professional knowledge and practice" (García Fernández, 2019).
- "We must avoid becoming victims of our own negligence" (Lira Arteaga, 2014).
- "For AI to reach its full potential, governments must prioritize citizen protection, while also allowing space for the positive innovation AI can bring" (Andrew Ng, 2019, as cited in Jewell, 2019).

INFORMATION AND COMMUNICATION TECHNOLOGIES (ICTS)

ICTs are "a set of technologies that enable access to, production, processing, and communication of information presented in different formats (text, image, sound...)" (Belloch Ortí, n.d.).

They encompass various technological devices, media, tools, or resources in which data is stored, modified, and shared, such as "cell phones, computers, tablets, video game consoles, the internet, and other tools" (CNDH Mexico, 2018). "They also include television and radio services" (CNDH Mexico, 2018).

While ICTs have improved our well-being, they have also introduced negative aspects. Companies that fail to implement safeguards have been involved in "fraud, bribery, corruption, and cybercrimes" (Caamaño Fernández & Gil Herrera, 2020), where cyber attackers gain political and/or economic advantages.

Forensic Computing

Since the invention of the first computer, "designed by German engineer Konrad Zuse between 1935 and 1936 and completed in 1938" (Jaimovich, 2019), and as it became a staple in daily life, cybercriminals have found gaps for committing antisocial and criminal acts. With the expansion of the internet, it became necessary to address this "new frontier of cybercrime. Law enforcement needed a system to investigate and analyze electronic data, and thus forensic computing was born" (IBM, n.d.).

Just like a forensic expert visits a crime scene and collects evidence, digital forensics also involves evidence collection. Forensic computing, also known as digital forensics or cyber forensics, "combines computing and legal forensic science to collect digital evidence in a way that is admissible in court" (IBM, n.d.).

Forensic computing has three objectives for which it gathers evidence (INFOSEC, n.d.):

1. To compensate for damages caused by criminals or intruders
2. To prosecute and bring criminals to justice
3. To create and implement measures to prevent similar incidents

Initially, digital evidence was found in "IT systems and devices: personal computers, servers, mobile phones, tablets, and electronic storage devices" (IBM, n.d.). With technological evolution, there's now a broader range of devices generating and storing data—from home IoT and operational technology (OT), to cars, appliances, doorbells, and even dog collars (IBM, n.d.) (CEPAL, 2021).

Investigating antisocial behavior or criminal activity involving computing, electronic, and/or telecommunications devices requires an expert with technical skills to track attacker activity and identify traces and logs that connect actions to outcomes (Lira Arteaga, 2014).

Cybersecurity and Artificial Intelligence Landscape

Initially, cybersecurity received little attention, but gained prominence with the technological boom. The digital era saw a significant increase in relevance due to the Coronavirus pandemic, which began on November 25, 2019, with a global state of emergency declared from January 30, 2020, to May 5, 2023 (WHO, 2023) (Legal Counsel of the Federal Executive, 2020). In Mexico, health confinement began on March 23, 2020, lasting until April 2021, followed by a staggered return with hygiene measures and social distancing (Legal Counsel of the Federal Executive, 2020) (Public Education Secretariat, 2021) (Tamaulipas Education Secretariat, 2021) (Albarrán Martíneza, 2021).

During this pandemic, remote work was largely adopted through ICTs (66%), with 90% of users increasing electronic device usage, 86% downloading new virtual tools, and 66% continuing their duties remotely. However, more than half of remote workers received no cybersecurity training from employers, and 44% of them experienced phishing attacks (Harán, 2020) (Bartolomé & Monteiro Lima, 2021).

Confirming the lack of cybersecurity awareness, Miller (2020) noted that the FBI reported a 400% increase in cyberattack complaints between the pandemic's start and April 2020 (Miller, 2020) (Harán, 2020). Adding to this, "Mexico ranks as the tenth most cyberattacked country in the world" (Albarrán Martíneza, 2021), signaling the need to implement new awareness and cybercrime prevention policies.

Cybersecurity in Mexico originated in response to computer crimes (not yet cybercrimes). Its pioneer institution was the **Center for Research and National Security (CISEN)**, created on February 13, 1989 (López Macedonio, 2018), developing a civil intelligence system aimed at warning of risks and threats to national security, especially during the transition to a more plural political system and an IT revolution. On December 1, 2018, CISEN was replaced by the **National Intelligence Center (CNI)** (Fernandez Bermejo & Martínez Atienza, 2018) (CNI, 2024).

The **Mexican Cyber Police** began with the creation of the **Cyber Unit in Mexico City on April 3, 2013**, aiming "to provide the public with preventive security measures for responsible use of technological tools" (Citizen Security Secretariat, 2024).

INTERPOL (2020) reported that cyber police forces faced significant pressure worldwide due to the "sharp increase in criminal activity on the web." In the private sector alone, between January and April 24, 2020, 907,000 spam emails, 737 malware-related incidents, and 48,000 malicious URLs were detected (INTERPOL, 2020).

Bartolomé and Monteiro present a historical record of security incidents. Until November 2017, there were fewer than 1,000 incidents per month, with a peak in December of that year reaching over 4,000. In 2018, all months recorded fewer than 1,000 incidents, while in the last quarter of 2019, the number of monthly incidents rose to between 3,000 and 4,000. In the second half of 2020, incidents exceeded 7,000 in a single month (Bartolomé & Monteiro Lima, 2021).

In case a cyber incident is detected, individuals can report it or request assistance from their corresponding cyber police unit. In Mexico, Cyber Police Units are present in all states across the country (CONAVIM, 2024).

According to the Third Government Report from the Governor of the State of Tamaulipas, the Cyber Police was established in July 2017 with the goal of investigating and addressing cybercrimes, reducing harm against children and adolescents, promoting community engagement, encouraging citizens to report crimes through digital and communication media, and preventing crimes such as extortion, threats, online fraud, and identity theft (García Cabeza de Vaca, 2019). Between July 2017 and July 2019, a total of 684 reports were filed (García Cabeza de Vaca, 2019).

Digital Violence

According to reforms to the General Law on Women's Access to a Life Free of Violence, digital violence is defined as:

"The deliberate act carried out through the use of information and communication technologies that exposes, distributes, displays, transmits, markets, offers, exchanges, or shares real or simulated intimate sexual content—images, audio, or video—of a person without their consent, approval, or authorization, causing psychological or emotional harm in any area of their private life or personal image. It also includes deliberate acts that harm the privacy, dignity, and/or intimacy of women committed through the use of information and communication technologies" (SIC, n.d., as cited by SSC, 2024).

Among the victims of digital violence, 60% of the reports received by the Cyber Police Unit nationwide are filed by women. The most affected demographic is women between 25 and 40 years of age, followed by those aged 18 to 25. The three most commonly reported incidents by women include romance-related scams, sexual violence-related behaviors, and cyberstalking (SSC, 2024).

Artificial Intelligence (AI)

Artificial Intelligence is a field of computer science aimed at developing systems capable of performing tasks that typically require human intelligence. It encompasses a wide range of disciplines, including data analytics, hardware and software engineering, linguistics,

neuroscience, philosophy, and psychology. AI relies heavily on machine learning and deep learning and is used for data analysis, prediction generation, object categorization, natural language processing, intelligent data retrieval, and more (Google, 2024).

AI is revolutionizing numerous fields, including forensic science. It offers advanced tools for forensic data analysis, enabling the identification of patterns and connections that might be missed using traditional methods. These tools not only speed up the analytical process but also enhance the accuracy of results (Ruiz Díaz, 2024).

Forensic technologies have become increasingly sophisticated, aiding in criminal investigations in various ways. According to the U.S. Bureau of Labor Statistics, employment for forensic science technicians is projected to grow by 13% from 2022 to 2032 (Gustafson, 2024).

As of 2024, several advances in forensic science technology have been documented (Gustafson, 2024), including:

- **Automated Firearm Identification**: The Integrated Ballistics Identification System (IBIS) is a cutting-edge solution for the analysis and comparison of ballistic markings on firearms and ammunition. It facilitates large-scale image capture and comparison, generating actionable data for firearm identification.
- **Blood Pattern Analysis Software (BPA)**: Emerging software designed to reconstruct crime scenes by analyzing bloodstains.
- **Mass Spectrometry Techniques**: Advanced methods used for identifying and quantifying synthetic cannabinoids through liquid chromatography-tandem mass spectrometry (LC-MS/MS). These techniques are essential in forensic toxicology due to their selectivity and sensitivity, allowing for the analysis of complex biological samples and the detection of cannabis-related compounds in urine.

- **High-Sensitivity Detection Methods**: Techniques like mass spectrometry, fluorescence detection, and molecular imaging are employed to detect trace substances or biological
  changes.
- **Omics Techniques in Forensic Entomology**: These include genomics, transcriptomics, proteomics, metabolomics, and microbiome analysis, offering comprehensive biological sample studies. They aid in species identification, phylogenetics, gene screening, and the analysis of forensic insect behavior at the genetic level.
- **Carbon Dot Powders**: A fluorescent carbon powder used to enhance fingerprint visibility at crime scenes. Under UV light, fingerprints glow in red, yellow, or orange, making them easier to analyze.
- **Artificial Intelligence**: Recent advances enable the use of AI across all forensic components of a criminal case. Although most common in digital forensics, AI is increasingly applied to crime scene analysis, fingerprint data comparison, photo comparison, and more.
- **Nanotechnology**: Forensic materials analysis at the atomic and molecular level provides scientists with new insights. Nanosensors are used to detect illicit drugs, explosives, and biological agents at a molecular scale.
- **Proteomes**: Beyond DNA, advances in protein detection and identification have made proteomics a crucial tool in forensic science. Proteomes are the complete set of proteins produced by an organism and can be found in blood, bones, and other biological materials. They help determine if a victim was exposed to poisons or link degraded biological samples to a suspect. Unlike DNA, proteomes change over time, offering valuable information about the time of death or environmental factors.

CONCLUSION

The use of technology is deeply integrated into nearly every aspect of modern life, enhancing communication, social interaction, and connectivity across business, governance, and family spheres. However, our increasing dependence on digital environments also demands robust security measures, as our personal, professional, and corporate data is stored in these virtual spaces.

The COVID-19 pandemic forced society to dive headfirst into the digital realm, often unprepared. While we adapted to various forms of digital crime, the preservation of digital evidence led to legal reforms and the creation of specific laws, such as the "Ley Olimpia."

As resilient actors in this digital transition, we must explore the potential of AI and cybertechnology in knowledge applications. For example, virtual reality could be adapted to scan and recreate suspected crime scenes for educational purposes in universities and for case review in the criminal justice system. Drones equipped with scanning technologies could be deployed to detect mass graves or locate missing persons across vast areas.

Much remains to be done in terms of public policy to fully integrate digital technologies and cyberspace processes into broader governmental and institutional frameworks.

REFERENCES

www.ambitojuridico.com. (10 de Septiembre de 2012). Cibercriminalidad: la delincuencia en "el otro espacio". *Legis. Ámbito Jurídico*, págs. https://www.ambitojuridico.com/noticias/penal/penal/cibercriminalidad-la-delincuencia-e n-el-otro-espacio.

www.freepik.com. (2024). Ilustración del concepto de redes sociales. *Vector gratis*. Obtenido de https://www.freepik.es/vector-gratis/ilustracion-concepto-redes-sociales_2806746.htm#fr omView=keyword&page=1&position=4&uuid=8e22b50d-4c32-4b2c-a89a-3da1bf6fcc19

Aguilar Ruiz, M. Ó. (2016). El método de la Criminalística, estrategia de la investigación. En S. García Ramírez, & O. V. Islas, *Temas de derecho penal, seguridad pública y criminalística: cuartas jornadas sobre justicia penal* (págs. 181-182). México: UNAM, Instituto de Investigaciones Jurídicas. Obtenido de https://biblio.juridicas.unam.mx/bjv/detalle-libro/1724-temas-de-derecho-penal-seguridad-publica-y-criminalistica

Albarrán Martíneza, E. E. (2021). Delitos cibernéticos. *revistatransregiones.com*, 93-104. Obtenido de https://revistatransregiones.com/web/index.php/tr/article/download/18/15/31

Allende López, M. (15 de Agosto de 2019). *La promesa de una nueva era tecnológica: la era cuántica*. Obtenido de Banco Interamericano de Desarrollo (BID): https://blogs.iadb.org/innovacion/es/impacto-de-las-tecnologias-cuanticas/

American Psychological Association. (s.f.). *Style and Grammar Guidelines*. Recuperado el 17 de enero de 2020, de Apastyle: https://apastyle.apa.org/style-grammar-guidelines

Bacigalupo, C. A. (2018). *Naturaleza del Ciberespacio*. Obtenido de CAB Group SRL: https://www.cabgroupsrl.com.ar/news/naturaleza-del-ciberespacio/

Bartolomé, M., & Monteiro Lima, A. G. (2021). El ciberespacio, antes, durante y después del COvID 19. La pandemia como una amenaza a la vida y a la. *Revista Academia de Guerra del Ejército Ecuatoriano*, *14*(1), 67–76. DOI: 10.24133/age.n14.2021.06

BBVA. (25 de Octubre de 2024). *La IA, en los dos lados de la ciberseguridad: aliada y amenaza en el mundo digital*. Obtenido de BBVA Innovación: https://www.bbva.com/es/innovacion/la-ia-en-los-dos-lados-de-la-ciberseguridad-aliada-y-amenaza-en-el-mundo-digital/

Bunge, M. (2013). *La ciencia: su método y su filosofía.* Editorial Laetoli. Obtenido de https://posgrado.unam.mx/musica/lecturas/LecturaIntroduccionInvestigacionMusical/epis temologia/Mario-Bunge-la-Ciencia-su-Metodo-y-Filosofia.pdf https://books.google.com.mx/books?id=OgmMDwAAQBAJ&pg=PT127&hl=es&source=gbs_selected_pages&cad=1#v=onepage&q&f=

Caamaño Fernández, E. E., & Gil Herrera, R. d. (2020). Prevención de riesgos por ciberseguridad desde la auditoria forense: conjugando el talento humano organizacional. *NOVUM, revista de Ciencias Sociales Apliacadas, 1*(10), 61-80. Obtenido de https://www.redalyc.org/journal/5713/571361695004/html/

CEPAL. (2021). *Tecnologías digitales para un nuevo futuro*. Obtenido de Naciones Unidas. Comisión Económica para América Latina y el Caribe (CEPAL): https://repositorio.cepal.org/server/api/core/bitstreams/879779be-c0a0-4e11-8e08-cf80b41a4fd9/content

CNI. (Octubre de 2024). *Centro Nacional de Inteligencia.* Obtenido de Gobierno de México: http://www.cni.gob.mx/transparencia/Centro-Nacional-Inteligencia.htm

CONAVIM. (Noviembre de 2024). *¿Has sufrido acoso cibernético? ¡Identifica sus modalidades y protégete!* Obtenido de Comisión Nacional para Prevenir y Erradicar la Violencia Contra las Mujeres: https://www.gob.mx/conavim/articulos/has-sufrido-acoso-cibernetico-te-decimos-a-donde-acudir#:~:text=Si%20quieres%20denunciar%20violencia%20cibern%C3%A9tica,los%20365%20d%C3%ADas%20del%20a%C3%B1o.

Díaz Aranda, E. (2016). *Lecciones de derecho penal (para el nuevo sistema de justicia en México).* UNAM, Instituto de Investigaciones Jurídicas.

Fernandez Bermejo, D., & Martínez Atienza, G. (2018). *Ciberseguridad, Ciberespacio y Ciberdelincuencia.* España: https://sistemabibliotecario.scjn.gob.mx/sisbib/2018/000295777/000295777.pdf

FGJCDMX. (Octubre de 2024). *Glosario de Delitos Cibernéticos.* Obtenido de Unidad de Inteligencia Cibernética: https://www.fgjcdmx.gob.mx/storage/app/media/Unidad%20de%20Inteligencia%20Ciber netica/delitos-ciberneticos.pdf

FGJTam. (22 de Octubre de 2024). *Delitos Cibernéticos.* Obtenido de Fiscalía General de Justicia del Estado de Tamaulipas: https://www.fgjtam.gob.mx/delitos-ciberneticos/

García Álvarez, M. F. (2014). Constelación de los sistemas que se relacionan con la violencia y la criminalidad femenina. *Archivos de Criminología, Seguridad Privada y Criminalística. Año 2, vol. III agosto-diciembre*, 26-32.

García Cabeza de Vaca, F. J. (25 de Septiembre de 2019). *3 Informe de Gobierno.* Obtenido de Gobierno del Estado de Tamaulipas: https://www.tamaulipas.gob.mx/wp-content/uploads/2018/01/tercer-informe-de-gobierno. pdf

García Fernandez, M. Á. (2019). Inteligencia artificial en imagen cardíaca: El futuro ya está aquí. *Revista Argentina de Cardiología, 87*(6), 491–495. DOI: 10.7775/rac.v87.i6.16997

González Miró, N. (2024). CLOUDS: Las nubes que almacenan la información que tu quieras. *El blog de Nacho González Miró.* Obtenido de https://nachogonzalezmiro.wordpress.com/blog/tecnologia/apps/las-nubes-que-almacenan-la-informacion-que-tu-quieras/

Google. (2024). *¿Qué es la inteligencia artificial o IA?* Obtenido de Google Cloud: https://cloud.google.com/learn/what-is-artificial-intelligence?hl=es-419

Guerra García, A. (2014). Ciberseguridad. *Universo.* Obtenido de https://www.uv.mx/universo/general/ciberseguridad/

Gustafson, K. (9 de Febrero de 2024). *Tecnologías modernas de las Ciencias Forenses.* Obtenido de Forensics Colleges: https://www.forensicscolleges.com/blog/resources/10-modern-forensic-science-technolog ies

Harán, J. M. (22 de Diciembre de 2020). *29 datos que deja el 2020 que hablan del estado actual de la ciberseguridad.* Obtenido de Welivesegurity. Cibercrimen: https://www.welivesecurity.com/la-es/2020/12/22/datos-2020-sobre-estado-actual-ciberse guridad/

INESDI. (07 de Septiembre de 2023). 5 ejemplos cotidianos de Inteligencia Artificial. *Blog.* Instituto de Innovación Digital de las Profesiones. Obtenido de https://www.inesdi.com/blog/ejemplos-cotidianos-de-ia/

INTERPOL. (Agosto de 2020). *Ciberdelincuencia: efectos de la COVID-19.* Obtenido de Secretaría General de INTERPOL: https://www.interpol.int/es/Noticias-y-acontecimientos/Noticias/2020/Un-informe-de-IN TERPOL-muestra-un-aumento-alarmante-de-los-ciberataques-durante-la-epidemia-de-C OVID-19

Jaimovich, D. (14 de Octubre de 2019). Cuál fue la primera computadora de la historia. *Infobae.* Obtenido de https://www.infobae.com/america/tecno/2019/10/14/cual-fue-la-primera-computadora-de-la-historia/

Jewell, C. (2019). Inteligencia artificial: la nueva electricidad. *OMPI Revista.* Obtenido de https://www.wipo.int/wipo_magazine/es/2019/03/article_0001.html

Kaplan, A., & Haenlein, M. (2019). Siri, Siri, en mi mano: ¿Quién es la más bella del mundo? Sobre las interpretaciones, ilustraciones e implicaciones de la inteligencia artificial. *Horizontes de negocios, 62*(1), 15-25. DOI: 10.1016/j.bushor.2018.08.004

Lindemulder, G., & Kosinski, M. (12 de Agosto de 2024). *¿Que es la ciberseguridad?* Obtenido de IBM: https://www.ibm.com/mx-es/topics/cybersecurity

Lira Arteaga, O. M. (2014). *Cibercriminalidad. Fundamentos de la investigación en México.* INACIPE.

LISA Institute. (2024). *Diferencia entre Ciberseguridad, Seguridad Informática y Seguridad de la Información.* Obtenido de LISA Institute - Seguridad, Ciberseguridad, Inteligencia y Geopolítica: https://www.lisainstitute.com/blogs/blog/diferencia-ciberseguridad-seguridad-informatica-seguridad-informacion?srsltid=AfmBOooR3vhA85MhfWaUbrSi_Qov73rpoKjwD9YE- 7acnTerY0aRY-8P

López Macedonio, M. N. (2018). *El archivo de la Dirección Federal de Seguridad: una fuente para escribir la historia de la segunda mitad del siglo XX mexicano.* Obtenido de Legajos. Boletín del Archivo General de la Nación. Núm. 15, pp. 71-82: https://archivos.gob.mx/Legajos/pdf/Legajos15/06Elarchivo.pdf

Mendoza Marquez, J. L., & Fernández, T. C. R. (2017). Ciberidentidades y redes sociales. En W. Aranguren, Y. Delgado, & B. Hamidian, *Venezuela en la mira de las Ciencias Económicas y Sociales. Encuentro de saberes* (pág. 522). Venezuela: Universidad de Carabobo. Obtenido de https://www.researchgate.net/publication/315445868_CIBERIDENTIDAD_Y_REDES_ SOCIALES

México, C. N. D. H. (Julio de 2018). *Derecho de acceso a las tecnologías de la información y la comunicación.* Obtenido de Comisión Nacional de los Derechos Humanos: https://www.cndh.org.mx/sites/all/doc/programas/ninez_familia/material/trip-derecho-acc eso.pdf

Miller, M. (16 de Abril de 2020). El FBI detecta un aumento en los informes de delitos cibernéticos durante la pandemia de coronavirus. *The Hill. Policía. Ciberseguridad.* Obtenido de https://thehill.com/policy/cybersecurity/493198-fbi-sees-spike-in-cyber-crime-reports-dur ing-coronavirus-pandemic/

Miró Linares, F. (10 de Septiembre de 2012). Cibercriminalidad: la delincuencia en “el otro espacio”. *Legis. Ámbito Jurídico.* Obtenido de https://www.ambitojuridico.com/noticias/penal/penal/cibercriminalidad-la-delincuencia-e n-el-otro-espacio

Moreno González, R. (2016). Temas de Criminalística. En S. García Ramírez, O. Islas, & L. A. Vargas Casillas, *Temas de derecho penal, seguridad pública y criminalística: cuartas jornadas sobre justicia penal* (págs. 175-180). México: UNAM, Instituto de Investigaciones Jurídicas. Obtenido de https://biblio.juridicas.unam.mx/bjv/detalle-libro/1724-temas-de-derecho-penal-seguridad-publica-y-criminalistica

Ochoa Serafín, M. (27 de Junio de 2024). Delitos informáticos en México: las leyes y las multas. *Ciberseguridad.* Obtenido de https://www.itmastersmag.com/ciberseguridad/delitos-informaticos-en-mexico-que-dice-l a-ley/#:~:text=En%20el%20C%C3%B3digo%20Penal%20Federal%20mexicano%2C%2 0se%20encuentra%20una%20secci%C3%B3n,se%20detallan%20las%20conductas%20ti pificadas.

Pérez Porto, J., & Gardey, A. (01 de Abril de 2022). Ciberespacio - Qué es, definición y concepto. Obtenido de //definicion.de/ciberespacio/

Quintana, Y. (2016). *Ciberguerra.* Editorial Catarata.

Redondo, S., & Garrido Genovés, V. (2013). *Principios de criminología.* Tirant lo Blanch.

Rodríguez Abitia, G. (16 de Mayo de 2021). *Boletín UNAM-DGCS-419. Pandemia acelera 10 años el uso de tecnologías digitales.* Obtenido de Boletín UNAM-Dirección General de Comunicación Social: https://www.dgcs.unam.mx/boletin/bdboletin/2021_419.html

Rodríguez Manzanera, L. (2024). *Criminología.* Editorial Porrúa.

Roseth, B., Reyes, A., & Yee Amézaga, K. (2021). *Servicios públicos y gobierno digital durante la pandemia: perspectivas de los ciudadanos, los funcionarios y las instituciones públicas.* América Latina y el Caribe: Banco Interamericano de Desarrollo. DOI: 10.18235/0003122

Ruiz Díaz, J. (08 de Junio de 2024). *Descubre cómo la IA está potenciando el campo de Forense.* Obtenido de Colegio Profesional de Criminalística: https://criminalisticamisiones.org/index.php/2024/06/08/descubre-como-la-ia-esta-potenciando-el-campo-de-forense/#:~:text=La%20IA%20ofrece%20herramientas%20avanzadas,la%20precisi%C3%B3n%20de%20los%20resultados

Sanchis, E. (Octubre de 2018). Ciberdelincuencia y ciberterrorismo, ciberdelitos y cibercrimen. *Peritos informáticos.* Obtenido de https://peritos-informaticos.com/blog/ciberdelincuencia-ciberterrorismo-ciberdelito-cibercrimen/#:~:text=Otra%20diferencia%20entre%20el%20cibercrimen,delitos%20de%20un a%20forma%20individual.

SSC. (2024a). *Policía Cibernética.* Obtenido de Gobierno de la Ciudad de México: https://www.ssc.cdmx.gob.mx/organizacion-policial/subsecretaria-de-inteligencia-e-inves tigacion-policial/policia-cibernetica#:~:text=Realizamos%20funciones%20de%20monito reo%20y,incidentes%20que%20ocurren%20en%20internet.

SSC. (2024b). *Policía cibernética.* Obtenido de Secretaría de Seguridad Ciudadana. Gobierno de la Ciudad de México: https://www.ssc.cdmx.gob.mx/organizacion-policial/subsecretaria-de-inteligencia-e-inves tigacion-policial/policia-cibernetica

SeguridadInformáticaHoy. (2024). *Los 10 delitos cibernéticos más comunes.* Obtenido de Seguridad Informática Hoy: https://seguridadinformaticahoy.com/delitos-ciberneticos/

SSPC. (10 de Junio de 2021). *Delitos cibernéticos.* Obtenido de Gobierno de México. Secretaría de Seguridad y Protección Ciudadana. Blog: https://www.gob.mx/sspc/articulos/conoce-los-principales-delitos-ciberneticos-y-sigue-nu estras-recomendaciones-para-prevenir-que-tus-hijas-e-hijos-sean-posibles-victimas

UAS. (10 de Mayo de 2023). *Análisis Sistemático del Delito.* Obtenido de Facultad de Derecho de Culiacan: https://derecho.uas.edu.mx/documentos/AnalisisSistematicodeDelito.pdf https://www.coursehero.com/file/202650345/AnalisisSistematicodeDelitopdf/

UNIR. (20 de Abril de 2022). *Teorías criminológicas: cuáles son las principales y en qué consisten.* Obtenido de La Universidad en Internet: https://mexico.unir.net/noticias/derecho/teorias-criminologicas/#:~:text=Teor%C3%ADa%20de%20las%20actividades%20cotidianas,a%20la%20v%C3%ADctima%20u%20obje tivo.

Chapter 5
Artificial Intelligence and Crime in the Use of Narcoterrorism

Maria Guadalupe Montoya
Autonomous University of Tamaulipas, Mexico

Abad Garcia Santiago
Autonomous University of Tamaulipas, Mexico

ABSTRACT

From a broad perspective, it is important to highlight the influence of artificial intelligence on human daily life. As is well known, it has influenced and brought about major changes, which have contributed to the development of humanity, seen from the perspective of its positive contributions or aspects. On the other hand, society itself has become dependent on technology, and its usefulness has also led to negative consequences, as artificial intelligence has been used on several occasions to cause harm, even with catastrophic consequences.

INTRODUCTION

Recently, the rapid development of technology has transformed economic and social dynamics, as well as the ways in which crimes are committed. The combined use of Artificial Intelligence (AI) and unmanned aerial vehicles—commonly known as drones—by drug trafficking groups has created new mechanisms that threaten a country's public security. These actions have allowed them to increase their opera-

DOI: 10.4018/979-8-3693-8871-6.ch005

tional capabilities, allowing them to monitor their territories, transport drugs, and carry out remote attacks from a distance, minimizing their exposure to direct risk.

These new forms of attack represent significant legal challenges for institutions responsible for ensuring public safety. In the context of Mexico, there has been a growing tactical use of drones to carry out violent actions against authorities or other criminal groups, as well as actions aimed at affecting the civilian population with the goal of instilling fear. The usefulness of these technologies by criminal organizations demands reflection regarding the need to create coordinated responses based on crime prevention.

The issue of extreme violence in Mexico practically began in 2006 with the militarization of public security, through a direct frontal attack on organized crime with the strongest force of the state: the Mexican army. Since then, most research has emphasized the number of homicides; that is, they focus on a quantitative approach. However, examining these events from the perspective of terrorism and/or narcoterrorism allows for a qualitative analysis.

In this sense, the levels of violence in Mexico can be classified as terrorist behavior, as they share the elements that doctrine and legislation recognize as inherent to the phenomenon. The significance of this omission is similar to what happens when an act of torture is treated as bodily harm or genocide as homicide: it hides an underlying reality that national crimes fail to address. Therefore, the core objective of this text is to study the emerging phenomenon in the Mexican context of the use of AI and drones by narco-terrorist criminal organizations.

To achieve this objective, the work will begin with some terminological clarifications. We will seek to establish some definitions, history, and usefulness of AI. Next, we will address conceptualizations of crime to unravel the usefulness of AI in criminality, especially when referring to the term narcoterrorism, as well as briefly review cases of these atrocities presented in Mexico. Finally, we will review some proposed legal reforms to the Mexican legal system, seeking to contribute to the academic understanding of the problem.

Overview of Artificial Intelligence

From a broad perspective, it is important to highlight the influence of AI on the daily lives of human beings, as it has influenced and developed major changes, which have contributed to the progress of humanity, seen from the perspective of its contributions or positive aspects. On the other hand, society itself has become dependent on technology, and its usefulness has also led to negative consequences, as AI has been used on several occasions to cause harm, even with catastrophic consequences.

The emergence of technology and the advances it has developed over the years constitute an evolutionary aspect of society. Therefore, it is important to clarify that, within the scope of technology, it has emerged and/or been applied in various ways. Therefore, its use and exploitation have been in medical, industrial, computer, social media, and other fields.

The topic of AI applications is vast, but this text, as already stated, will address its usefulness in criminal networks, which have left a sense of collective insecurity, originating from the crime rate in Mexico, partly caused by the drug market dispute, as well as the security control that authorities seek to exert.

Before embarking on a specific analysis, it is of great interest to address the concepts considered basic to understanding the impact and scope of AI. There is no universal definition of AI, so much depends on the area where it is applied. However, we can point out, according to the European Commission (2018), that it is used for "systems that exhibit intelligent behavior, as they are capable of analyzing their environment and taking action—with a certain degree of autonomy—in order to achieve specific objectives." Or, as Morente (2019) points out, they are "emerging or converging technologies. A new technology for data processing and analysis, a new method of information processing."

According to Nilsson (1998), AI "is related to intelligent behaviors in artifacts, and when behaviors are related, we speak of a system that acts rationally." It is a technology that allows computers to represent human intelligence and conflict-resolution capabilities. On its own or combined with other methods (sensors, geolocation, cybernetics), AI can perform tasks that would otherwise require human intelligence or intervention. Examples of AI in our daily lives include GPS, digital assistants, self-driving cars, and generative artificial intelligence tools (such as Open AI's Chat GPT), among others.

It can also be defined as a "scientific and technological discipline that results in organizing the processes of the mind and its connection with the body through computational metaphor, that is, through computer programs" (Pineda, 2024). As we can see, AI undoubtedly includes both the scientific and technological aspects, which, linked to the technologies and intentions of society, lead to the creation of positive projects, as well as negative actions due to their misuse.

AI is a branch of computer science that is often closely linked to machine learning and deep learning. These disciplines are based on algorithms designed to mimic the way the human brain makes decisions. By analyzing large amounts of data, these algorithms are able to improve performance over time, achieving increasingly accurate classifications and predictions.

Although AI has experienced moments of enormous enthusiasm followed by cycles of distrust, the arrival of tools like ChatGPT has signaled a turning point. Previously, major advances focused on machines' ability to decipher images. Now, the spotlight is on natural language processing: the ability of machines to understand and generate human language. And recently, it can also work with videos, images, categorization codes, and even scientific data such as molecular structures.

In this way, we can see those new ways of applying AI in different contexts are emerging every day. However, the progressive frenzy has also raised important questions about its ethical and responsible utility. These arguments are essential in the current conversation about the future of this technology. Here we must recall McCarthy's (2004) words, which accurately summarize the purpose of AI. “It is the science and engineering of making intelligent machines, especially intelligent computer programs. It relates to the similar task of using computers to understand human intelligence, but AI does not have to conform to observable biological methods.”

As the definition indicated in the preceding paragraph, it involves the use of intelligent machines, where both human intelligence and the intention to cause damage are simulated, since currently there are devices that, motivated by the invention and use of technological mechanisms, have been used and continue to be used by criminal groups to carry out illegal acts, thus generating greater violence in our country and through the loss of human lives of members of the armed forces, police institutions and civilian population.

AI has its beginnings in the 1950s, with Alan Turing's text *Computing Machinery and Intelligence* . In his article, Turing asks, *“Can machines think?”* From there, he offers a test, now known as the " *Turing Test* " (Turing, 1950). In this experiment, a human interrogator would attempt to differentiate between a computer text response and a human one. While this test has been the subject of much observation since its publication, it remains a substantial part of the history of AI.

For their part, Russell and Norvig (2021) when they published their work entitled *Artificial Intelligence: A Modern Approach*, this became one of the main books in the study of AI. They delved into four possible objectives or definitions of AI, which differentiate computer systems based on rationality and thought versus action:

Human approach:

- Systems that think like humans,
- Systems that act like humans,

Ideal approach:

- Systems that think rationally,
- Systems that act rationally.

In its simplest form, AI is a field that combines large amounts of data with computer science to enable problem-solving. It also encompasses the subfields of machine learning and deep learning. These disciplines are comprised of AI algorithms that seek to create expert systems that make predictions or classifications based on input data. There are currently many real-world applications for AI systems.

Below are some of the most common use cases:

Voice Recognition

It may be known as automatic speech recognition, computer speech recognition, or speech-to-text. They use Natural Language Processing (NLP) to transform the human voice into written words. Thus, many mobile devices incorporate speech recognition into their systems to perform speech searches or provide greater accessibility for sending text messages in different languages.

Customer Service

Online virtual assistants and chatbots are replacing humans throughout the customer journey. They frequently answer questions on topics like shipping, or provide personalized advice and size suggestions, changing the way we think about customer engagement on websites and social media platforms. Examples include messenger bots on e-commerce sites with virtual agents and messaging apps like Facebook Messenger.

Computer Vision

This AI technology allows computers and systems to generate meaningful information from videos, digital images, and other visual input, and then take action based on those inputs. This ability to provide recommendations distinguishes it from image recognition tasks. Thanks to convolutional neural networks, computer vision has applications in radiological image production in medicine, in self-driving cars in the automotive industry, and in photo tagging on social media.

From the Supply Chain

Adaptive robotics acts on information from Internet of Things (IoT) devices and on structured and unstructured data to make autonomous decisions. NLP tools can understand human speech and react to what is said. Predictive analytics is applied to demand responsiveness, inventory and network optimization, preventative maintenance, and digital manufacturing. Search and pattern recognition algorithms, no longer just predictive but hierarchical, analyze data in real time, helping supply chains react to machine-generated augmented intelligence while providing instant visibility and transparency.

Weather Forecast

The weather models broadcasters rely on for accurate forecasts consist of complex algorithms running on supercomputers. Machine learning techniques enhance these models, making them more applicable and accurate.

Anomaly Detection

AI models can analyze *big data* and uncover atypical data points within a data set. These anomalies can provide insight into faulty equipment, human error, or security breaches.

As can be seen, in this path that has been established in a timely manner, we see the level of progressiveness that AI has made as a contribution to humanity, however, each technological aspect has brought with it repercussions, some somewhat positive and others not with that purpose, since the Mexican State has wanted to confront insecurity through technology and until today it has not succeeded and, on the contrary, criminal groups have surpassed the Government itself in addressing this highly problematic issue.

ARTIFICIAL INTELLIGENCE AND CRIME

Regarding the term criminality, Rodríguez (2024) defines it as "the set of antisocial behaviors that occur at a specific time and place." In this regard, Gómez (2006) points out that it refers to "the statistical index of behaviors classified as criminal or morally prohibited, considered a reflection of the existence of a subculture of violence." The Royal Spanish Academy of Language (RAE) defines it as the "proportional number of crimes in a specific time and place."

That is, criminality refers to the body of actions that violate the provisions of criminal law, committed either individually or collectively within a specific period of time and territory . The term is attributed to armed groups and criminal organizations that produce and distribute drugs and use violence against state institutions and the civilian population, either individually or in coalition with other groups.

While it is true that AI has brought important advances in the field of public security, through its implementation through intelligent video surveillance systems or in other applications using systems capable of predicting where the next crime may occur, quickly analyzing a large amount of data (Perry et al., 2013). This same action would take a lot of time for officials, which is why AI has been very useful in preventing crime by providing quick and effective responses. However, according to Moussa et al. (2021), these same AI tools have been used by criminal organizations to avoid state surveillance, optimize illegal trafficking routes, among other activities.

At this point, it is necessary to establish a conceptualization of what terrorism means and thus manage the concepts and broaden the scope of AI, its application, and its scope. It should be noted that there is no globally agreed-upon conceptualization of terrorism, but there are various actions that are universally understood as expressions of this phenomenon.

For example, the United Nations Office on Drugs and Crime describes that the use of "politically motivated violence, aircraft seizure, attacks on naval fleets, the use of chemical or nuclear weapons, kidnapping and other forms of attacks directed towards the civilian population" can be considered terrorist acts (UNODC, 2025). Although terrorism is not a recent phenomenon, the beginning of the 21st century is characterized by an increasing number of such events . These acts are the conclusion of processes that often begin with "radicalization, the formation of extremist opinions and the acceptance of violence as a means to achieve change." (UNODC, 2025). Thus, terrorism represents a significant threat to international peace and security.

Terrorism is a complex phenomenon characterized by the systematic use of violence for religious, ideological, or political purposes, with the primary objective of instilling fear and exerting pressure on governments or civilian populations. Hoffman (2006) defines it as "premeditated violence against non-combatant targets with the purpose of generating a psychological and political impact." This tactic has been used by non-state actors in contexts of conflict or resistance, but also by criminal organizations, such as those involved in drug trafficking.

From the foregoing conceptualization, it is highlighted that the main characteristics of terrorism are that it is a threat to protected legal rights, such as peace, as well as security, which, in truth, could be national or international in nature. Several characteristics that we can identify in the aforementioned concept include its acceptance of violence, since this characteristic can lead to the commission of various criminal acts that cause fear in society.

Once the concepts that will serve as the central axis for the development of this chapter have been addressed, we will point out the usefulness and scope attributed to AI, in addition to the issue of crime, which, as is known, through the use of technology, is not only conducive to addressing the issue of security, whether national or public security, this taking into account the powers and, in turn, obligations that the Mexican State has in relation to the safeguarding of the protected legal assets of society.

The Mexican State, by constitutional mandate, is obliged, on the one hand, to provide protection to every person who is in national territory. To this end, it has legal systems that must be effectively enforceable. It also has institutions, authorities, and regulations applicable to each subject matter. This is done so that they are applied without any doubt and thus avoid compliance with Article 17 of the Constitution, that is, that society, fed up with taking justice into its own hands and thus relapsing into the era of barbarism.

IMPACT OF ARTIFICIAL INTELLIGENCE ON NARCOTERRORISM

According to Bagley (2012), the term narcoterrorism has been used in the Latin American context mainly since the 1980s to refer to criminal organizations dedicated to activities related to drug trafficking, since they have resorted to terrorist strategies through the use of explosives to kill officials and attack state institutions. The aim is to cause terror to protect their criminal interests and influence state decisions, as has been the case in Mexico and Colombia.

The RAE defines narcoterrorism as "terrorism linked to drug trafficking, from which it obtains its financing." In this regard, as Pelcastre (2024) points out regarding the usefulness of AI in the commission of crimes:

In recent years, organized crime in Latin America has adopted the use of Unmanned Aerial Vehicles (UAVs) or drones. These commercial robots have been modified to be equipped with remote-controlled grenades and explosives. They are then used to carry out airstrikes against authorities, rival gangs, and citizens who fail to comply with their criminal demands. This also exerts a new level of power and control, actions that represent a major challenge for law enforcement.

Along these same lines, we can describe that, at present, drones have ceased to be used merely for recreational purposes, or that the usefulness of these instruments no longer falls exclusively on military use in security tasks, but have become tools available to criminal organizations. This position is reaffirmed by Chaparro (2022) when he points out that "drug cartels have resorted to drones as instruments for transporting drugs, carrying out surveillance or patrolling their territories and, in cases of greater violence, to drop explosives.

Criminal organizations have turned to these unmanned aerial vehicles in part because of their low market value and the lack of a registry that would allow them to identify the owner of the drone, unlike weapons used exclusively by the military. Added to this is the practicality of modifying them, but above all, their ability to maneuver without a human pilot, which reduces the direct exposure of members of criminal networks.

In this regard, Gálvez (2005) points out that it is horrifying to observe "how these new technologies are used by criminal organizations as weapons of considerable power." This represents a change in the way these organizations operate, allowing them to avoid direct confrontations with other criminal groups or authorities. In this way, according to the same author, "the risk for criminals is minimized, but the violence and harm for all parties involved, including the civilian population, are increased."

AI addresses the aspects of human thought and behavior, as well as the rational aspect, so the combination of these elements has led to its use in carrying out narcoterrorist actions, thus leading to a Mexican state with a high level of insecurity.

ORGANIZED CRIME AND THE USE OF DRONES

Now, once we've defined the concepts in the field of AI, as well as its scope, usefulness, and impact on society, it's important to address the issue of narcoterrorism. The term AI used to be associated with futuristic narratives in practically unreal contexts. However, the current state of affairs is very different. Thanks to technological inventions and advances, AI has taken on a new meaning, becoming part of the daily lives of a large part of the world's population.

While it's true that technology is linked to human intellect, and with it, human beings have evolved toward positive actions, we mustn't overlook the fact that devices have also been created to cause harm to members of society. Therefore, if we talk about narcoterrorism, we are considering the idea that it encompasses various criminal acts.

Mexican cartels have begun to mutate into national and transnational organized crime. They have ventured into various crimes, such as money laundering, extortion, hydrocarbon theft, human trafficking, kidnapping, homicides (torture, dismemberment, burning, or dissolving bodies), etc., thus expanding their tentacles and control, creating new cartel factions that seek to dominate different territories.

With the cartels' new divisions, betrayals and score-settling emerge, leading each cartel to create its own armed wings, which provide security for the bosses and bribe various police or judicial authorities in exchange for protection to avoid capture. Even if they have been brought before the courts, they are released due to due process violations or poor integration of the investigation file due to a failure to establish proper traceability of arrest records or inconsistencies in the data. If they fail to co-opt high-level officials, they become targets for elimination. Journalist Anabel Hernández has described in her book how the Sinaloa Cartel's business model was created in its national and international drug distribution and sales network (Hernández, 2024).

It is important to consider the factors driving the increase in both crime and extreme violence. Thus, paramilitary groups or rival armed groups have begun to employ guerrilla tactics and techniques, employing explosive devices, car bombs, and weapons exclusively used by the military, capable of delivering lethal firepower against armored vehicles. We have observed this in various states (Tamaulipas, Nuevo León, Guanajuato, Guerrero, Michoacán, Sinaloa, Sonora, Jalisco, and Mexico City) against rivals and public officials. This is why citizens who are defenseless against this wave of extreme violence, caught in the crossfire or victimized by crime, are demanding justice.

In the Mexican context, according to Bunker and Sullivan (2021), cartels have been increasingly using drones in their criminal activities. Tactics and techniques have evolved as follows: in 2010, they began to be used exclusively for the transport of narcotics. After an experimental period, they used them to monitor their routes or territories. A few years later, in 2017, they used them as weapons; in 2020, as part of their propaganda; and finally, in 2021, they used them for night vision combat.

A report from the Ministry of National Defense (SEDENA) indicates that there has been a significant increase in attacks using explosive-laden drones. In 2020 alone, only five cases were recorded, but by the first half of 2023, 260 had already been reported, representing a 5,100 percent increase (Forbes, 2023). The attack strategy known as "narcodrones" is used by various drug cartels, including the Jalisco Nueva Generación Cartel (CJNG), the Sinaloa Cartel, and La Familia Michoacana (Animal Político, 2024).

These organizations carry out activities involving the manipulation of unmanned aerial vehicles, which they adapt to transport explosives. These explosives are then dropped on people and used in confrontations and against authorities at different levels of government. They are also used to transport drugs and in espionage to obtain private information about individuals, primarily those related to public order (Dibany, 2023).

For example, the Jalisco New Generation Cartel created a specialized unit for explosive attacks, a criminal group called "Drone Operators," to attack rival groups. However, they are not the only criminals in Mexico using this strategy. The Sinaloa Cartel has also used drones since 2021 to carry out aerial attacks in the north of the country (Gálvez, 2025).

There is evidence of the usefulness of drones as attack devices in different regions of Mexico, but especially in the state of Michoacán, where security forces and the community have been attacked with these instruments. Similarly, drones have been found modified to be used to launch explosives, which are dropped from the air against authorities or rival groups, but which end up affecting the entire community (La Silla Rota, 2024; El Universal, 2024; Tabasco Hoy, 2024). While it is true that the main objective of these attacks is to damage law enforcement infrastructure, they have also ended up damaging other types of public and private infrastructure, such as plazas, schools, and homes. The result of these attacks is the forced displacement of people from their communities, but the fear these attacks generate in them.

In a more aggressive move, the CJNG attacked members of several communities in Michoacán using drones to launch chemical explosives, causing physical reactions such as "itching, burning in the respiratory tract, and in some cases, a feeling of suffocation," which represents an enormous risk to the health of the general population (Proceso, 2024). The usefulness of these engineering tools is an example of how criminal groups take advantage of technological developments "to increase their operations and capabilities. This exploitation occurs especially when they have financial resources and develop specific technical skills" (Gálvez, 2025).

Unfortunately, this particular pattern of drone violence by criminal groups has also been present in other states in Mexico. Attacks have been documented in these states, or drones intended for use in criminal activities have been seized. These include Michoacán, Guerrero, Tamaulipas, Chihuahua, Baja California, Guanajuato, Chiapas, and others, according to media reports (Milenio, 2023; Vanguardia, 2023; La Jornada, 2024; El País, 2025).

These acts of violence are undoubtedly a major challenge for security authorities, both for the protection of their personnel and the public. In this regard, in order to detect and neutralize these devices, SEDENA is seeking to purchase technology that will allow it to prevent these attacks. In other words, it is necessary to "acquire technology to counter the action of drones and the rapid location of explosive devices, since according to reports, authorities in the state of Michoacán dismantle up to eight drones laced with explosives every day" (Tabasco Hoy, 2024).

The ease with which these criminal groups acquire these instruments makes it more difficult to track the origin of this acquisition and how authorities can confront them. Therefore, in Mexico, the lack of airspace regulation for drones puts authorities at a disadvantage.

CONTEXT OF MEXICAN REGULATIONS

From a legal perspective, criminal law faces legal gaps in regulating criminal conduct involving the use of autonomous or semi-autonomous systems. As Brenner (2010) points out, "the challenge lies in attributing criminal liability when technological tools execute actions without direct human supervision, as might be the case with drones programmed to attack."

In response to the increasing use of drones by organized crime groups and to guarantee the peace and security of Mexicans, in 2023 the federal executive branch received from the Permanent Commission of the Congress of the Union an initiative with a draft decree to modify the Federal Penal Code (CPF) and the Federal Law on Firearms and Explosives. Although the latter law regulates the possession, manufacture, and sale of weapons and explosives in Mexico, it does not specifically address the use of drones so far . However, it is imperative to mention that the Mexican State does have legal instruments to proceed in cases like these.

In 2024, the Federal Penal Code established legal provisions with specific penalties for those who misuse remotely piloted aircraft (drones). This provides authorities with a legal basis to justify their actions in cases where conduct related to the launching, activation, and detonation of explosives by drones is investigated. The law penalizes with 10 to 20 years in prison anyone who, through the use of these aircraft, drops "any explosive object or device, improvised explosive devices, or weapons, as well as chemical substances that, alone or in combination, are capable of being used as explosives against other people or property" (CPF, 2025).

The length of the sentence depends on the severity of the crime and whether the attack "affects any person or property," and whether the victims are property or people belonging to the armed forces or those responsible for public security.

It also provides for penalties of 5 to 10 years in prison for those who "import, manufacture, assemble, acquire or adapt remotely piloted aircraft for the transportation of improvised explosive devices, weapons, narcotics, synthetic drugs or other materials regulated by the Federal Law on Firearms and Explosives" (CPF, 2025).

Or when they are used in surveillance by the authorities.

Anyone who uses remotely piloted aircraft equipped with devices that allow photographing or making audio or video recordings, either physically or electronically, to monitor the activities of public servants in order to know or report their location in order to evade their action or carry out attacks against them (CPF, 2025).

This regulation aims to combat impunity in the use of these aircraft, as well as guarantee the peace and security of Mexicans. In other words, it seeks to prevent and punish the use of this type of aircraft in acts against public or private property or services; against the physical, emotional, or life of individuals; or that cause alarm, fear, or terror in the population in an attempt to undermine national security, pressure, or force an authority or a private individual to take a decision.

CONCLUSION

The lines described in this text have made it clear that the development of technology, specifically that related to the field of AI, has positively impacted the economic growth and security of countries. That is, its rapid rise has created new opportunities globally: from facilitating health diagnoses to increasing work efficiency through the systematization of tasks, as well as facilitating human connections through social media. However, these rapid changes also pose profound ethical dilemmas that force us to reflect on the potential that AI-based systems have to threaten respect for the human rights of the population. These risks add to existing structural inequalities, further harming historically marginalized groups.

The current state of AI is characterized by the search for solutions that are increasingly closer to human intelligence. Today, AI is composed of a set of knowledge that, combined with prior training, allows it to produce a result. While this is a fairly impressive achievement, the current goal is much more ambitious. AI professionals are working on deep learning to create algorithms capable of recognizing data and learning through examples. This seeks to enable AI to integrate skills inherent to human behavior (such as empathy and personality) to generate more personalized responses.

However, the impact of this type of technology has not been limited to the professional sphere; it has also reached the personal lives of a large portion of the population. However, its inappropriate use by criminal organizations opens the possibility of causing extremely serious damage. From a negative perspective, the link between AI and remotely piloted aircraft has changed the *modus operandi* of tactics and strategies used by organized crime to exert territorial control. By resorting to these tools, they have significantly increased their attack capacity to harm their opponents, which can be considered a new phase in the evolution of narcoterrorism.

Furthermore, reflecting on how Mexican society perceives terrorism, we knew that to recognize it, it couldn't be an attack on a somewhat dubious public space, a building or property with a public image devoid of reputation, like bars or rehabilitation centers. Nor could it be the mutilation and display of civilians—beheaded, dismembered, taped, half-naked, or completely naked—with threatening calligraphy inscribed on their bodies and, in other cases, with signs or banners labeling them members of another criminal group. No, that wouldn't be enough to counter the violence we're capable of tolerating and even endorsing in some cases, where everything could be hypocritically considered a valid enforcement of certain codes of communication between criminal groups, because that's how they are, and to a certain extent, that's how we Mexicans are. Deep down, we knew that terrorist intent would have to be too obvious for us to end up accepting that it also exists in drug trafficking.

The usefulness of AI through early detection and crime pattern detection systems represents a great opportunity for the State to counter and prevent these threats and thereby strengthen public security. However, the existing inequality between law enforcement and criminal groups remains a critical challenge. Therefore, the study of this phenomenon cannot be addressed exclusively from the perspective of national or international security; its complexity demands a combination of legal, technological, and social approaches.

In this regard, the Mexican state's legal framework has begun to adapt to the new criminal landscape through reforms to its laws to prohibit the use of drones in activities related to organized crime. This demonstrates that the levels of violence in Mexico could be classified as terrorist acts, but that the state has ignored the possibility of investigating and prosecuting crimes through two avenues: on the one hand, the option to investigate and prosecute crimes through criminal offenses other than terrorism, and on the other, the frank impunity of these actions.

However, these legal actions must be accompanied by significant investments in technology to prevent the spread of these types of narcoterrorist threats and narrow the technological gap between criminal organizations and the state.

REFERENCES

Animal Político. (2024, 26 de mayo). *Drones, la nueva tendencia en el arsenal de las organizaciones criminales*. https://www.animalpolitico.com/analisis/invitades/drones-tendencia-arsenal-crimen-organizado

Bagley, B. M. (2012). *Drug trafficking and organized crime in the Americas: Major trends in the twenty-first century*. Woodrow Wilson International Center for Scholars.

Brenner, S. W. (2010). *Cybercrime: Criminal threats from cyberspace*. Greenwood Publishing Group. DOI: 10.5040/9798400636554

Bunker, R. J., & Sullivan, J. P. (2021). *Evolved capabilities in Mexican drug trafficking: A 21st century profile of transnational organized crime*. Small Wars Journal. https://archive.smallwarsjournal.com/jrnl/art/evolved-capabilities-mexican-drug-trafficking-21st-century-profile-transnational-organized

Chaparro, J. (2022). *Drones and Organized Crime: A New War Front in Mexico*. Center for National Security Studies.

Congress of the United Mexican States. (2024). *Federal Penal Code*. Official Gazette of the Federation. https://www.diputados.gob.mx/LeyesBiblio/pdf/9_180324.pdf

Dibany, J. (2023). Use of drones in criminal activities could carry a sentence of 53 years in prison. *El Sol de México*. https://oem.com.mx/elsoldemexico/mexico/uso-de-drones-en-actividades-delictivas-podria-alcanzar-una-pena-de-53-anos-de-prision-16951763#!

El País. (2025, January 28). *Mexico investigates alleged attack by criminals on a U.S. patrol boat on the banks of the Rio Grande*. https://elpais.com/mexico/2025-01-28/mexico-indaga-un-supuesto-ataque-de-criminales-a-una-patrulla-estadounidense-en-la-ribera-del-rio-bravo.html

El Universal. (March 8, 2024). *Michoacán records the highest number of drone attacks by organized crime: Sedena*. https://www.jornada.com.mx/noticia/2024/03/08/politica/michoacan-registra-el-mayor-numero-de-ataques-con-drones-del-crimen-organizado-sedena-809

European Commission. (2018). *Artificial Intelligence for Europe*. https://eur-lex.europa.eu/legal-content/ES/TXT/?uri=CELEX%3A52018DC0237

Forbes Mexico. (2023, September 5). *Attacks with explosive-equipped drones are on the rise in Mexico*. https://www.forbes.com.mx/aumentan-en-mexico-los-ataques-con-drones-equipados-con-explosivos/

Gálvez, Y. (2025). It is extremely frightening to observe how these new technologies can be used by criminal organizations as weapons. *Dialogue Americas.* https://dialogo-americas.com/articles/organized-crime-and-its-use-of-drones-to-sow-terror/

Gómez Tagle, E. (2006). *Law and Society. Glossary of Criminology and Social Sciences.* Pontifical University of Mexico.

Hernández, A. (2024). *The Secret History: AMLO and the Sinaloa Cartel.* Grijalbo.

Hoffman, B. (2006). *Inside terrorism.* Columbia University Press.

La Jornada. (2024, January 5). *Guerrero: Drone attack reported in Heliodoro Castillo.*https://www.jornada.com.mx/noticia/2024/01/05/estados/guerrero-denuncian-ataque-con-drones-en-heliodoro-castillo-7596

La Silla Rota. (January 3, 2024). *Drones of Crime: How Cartels Are Arming Commercial Aircraft to Attack.* https://lasillarota.com

McCarthy, J. (2004). *What is Artificial Intelligence?*http://jmc.stanford.edu/articles.html

Milenio. (2023, May 5). *Guerrero: Drone attack reported in the mountains.* https://www.milenio.com/estados/guerrero-reportan-ataque-con-drones-en-la-sierra

Morente Parra, V. (2019). Big Data or the art of analyzing massive data. A critical reflection from the perspective of fundamental rights. *Rights and Freedoms, 41*(II), 225–253.

Moussa, R., Hernández, L., & Jiménez, P. (2021). Artificial Intelligence and Crime: A Rising Threat in Cyberspace. *Journal of Digital Security, 8*(2), 45–60.

Nilsson, N. J. (1998). *Artificial intelligence: A new synthesis.* Morgan Kaufmann Publishers.

Pelcastre, J. 2024. Organized Crime and Its Use of Drones to Spread Terror. *Dialogo Americas.* https://dialogo-americas.com/articles/organized-crime-and-its-use-of-drones-to-spread-terror/

Perry, W. L., McInnis, B., Price, C. C., Smith, S. C., & Hollywood, J. S. (2013). *Predictive policing: The role of crime forecasting in law enforcement operations.* RAND Corporation. https://www.rand.org/pubs/research_reports/RR233.html

Pineda Cortés, L. A. (2024). *AI, a metaphor for this and other times.* UNAM Gazette. https://www.gaceta.unam.mx/ia-metafora-de-este-y-otros-tiempos/

Proceso. (2024, April 9). *The CJNG adopts chemical explosives to break through in Michoacán.*https://www.proceso.com.mx/nacional/2024/04/09/el-cjng-adopta-explosivos-quimicos-para-abrirse-paso-en-michoacan-278664.html

Rodríguez Manzanera, L. (2024). *Criminology*. Porrúa.

Royal Spanish Academy. *Concept of Criminality*. https://dle.rae.es/criminalidad

Royal Spanish Academy. *Concept of Narcoterrorism*. https://dle.rae.es/narcoterrorismo

Russell, S. J., & Norvig, P. (2021). *Artificial Intelligence: A Modern Approach*. Pearson.

Segovia Marín, S. (2024, April 26). Military forces seized 197 explosives that were to be launched by drones by dissidents in Cauca. *El Colombiano.*https://www.elcolombiano.com/colombia/hallaron-197-explosivos-disidencias-farc-que-lanzarian-con-drones-cauca-FC24374661

Tabasco today. (March 8, 2024). Sedena prepares to purchase technology to counter drones. https://elmomentotabasco.mx/nacional/2024/03/08/alista-la-sedena-compra-de-tecnologia-para-contrarrestar-drones/

Turing, A. M. (1950). Computing Machinery and Intelligence. *Mind*, *59*(236), 433–460. DOI: 10.1093/mind/LIX.236.433

United Nations Office on Drugs and Crime. (2025). *Concept of terrorism*. https://www.unodc.org/e4j/es/secondary/terrorism.html

Vanguardia. (2023, July 16). *Drones modified by criminal groups are a new security challenge. Vanguardia*. https://vanguardia.com.mx/noticias/drones-modificados-por-grupos-criminales-son-un-nuevo-reto-para-la-seguridad-CB8571062

Chapter 6
Mental Health in Migrants:
Analyzing Healthcare Access Barriers Using AI-Based Techniques

Usharani Bhimavarapu
https://orcid.org/0000-0002-0246-1420
Department of Computer Science and Engineering, Koneru Lakshmaiah Education Foundation, Vaddeswaram, India

ABSTRACT

Mental health in migrants is often influenced by challenges related to healthcare access, including difficulties in understanding medical information and uncertainty in seeking appropriate assistance. This study analyzes survey responses from 82 adults (50 women and 32 men) to examine healthcare access barriers and their impact on mental health, vaccination status, and dental hygiene. Principal Component Analysis (PCA) was employed to extract significant features from the dataset, highlighting patterns such as healthcare literacy gaps and demographic influences. These features were used to train an Artificial Neural Network (ANN) for predictive modeling. The ANN demonstrated high accuracy, with F1 scores exceeding 85%, effectively predicting mental health conditions, vaccination rates, and dental hygiene practices. The results underscore the importance of addressing healthcare access barriers to improve overall well-being among migrants

DOI: 10.4018/979-8-3693-8871-6.ch006

INTRODUCTION

Mental health in immigrants is a critical area of study due to the unique challenges that this population faces, which can significantly impact their psychological well-being. Immigrants often experience a range of stressors related to their migration experience, including cultural adjustment, language barriers, economic hardships, and discrimination. These stressors can lead to higher rates of mental health conditions such as anxiety, depression, and post-traumatic stress disorder (PTSD). Furthermore, immigrants may encounter difficulties in accessing mental health services due to systemic barriers like lack of insurance, unfamiliarity with healthcare systems, and cultural stigma surrounding mental health. The transition to a new environment can also lead to social isolation, as immigrants may struggle to form support networks in unfamiliar surroundings. Additionally, the trauma experienced during migration, such as fleeing conflict or persecution, can further exacerbate mental health issues. Understanding mental health in immigrants requires a comprehensive approach that considers not only the psychological effects of migration but also the broader social, cultural, and economic factors that influence their mental health outcomes. Addressing these challenges is essential to promoting the well-being of immigrant populations and ensuring they receive the support they need for optimal mental health.

Medical evaluation in mental health cases is a comprehensive process that aims to assess an individual's psychological, emotional, and behavioral health. It begins with a thorough clinical interview, where a healthcare provider gathers information about the patient's mental health history, current symptoms, and any relevant life events, including stressors, trauma, or significant changes in behavior. This interview is crucial for establishing the context of the patient’s condition and understanding how their symptoms have evolved over time. The evaluation also includes a review of the patient's medical history, including any past mental health diagnoses, medications, or treatments, to identify any underlying physical health conditions or co-occurring disorders that could contribute to the mental health issue.

A physical examination may also be conducted to rule out any medical conditions that could present with psychological symptoms, such as thyroid disorders, neurological issues, or substance abuse. Lab tests, imaging studies, or other diagnostic procedures may be ordered if needed to exclude medical causes. Psychological assessments are also a key component of the evaluation. These assessments may include standardized questionnaires, diagnostic scales, and other tools designed to assess mood, anxiety, cognitive functioning, and other areas of mental health. The results from these tests provide valuable insight into the severity of the patient's condition and guide the development of an appropriate treatment plan.

In cases where a specific mental health disorder is suspected, such as depression, anxiety disorders, or schizophrenia, additional diagnostic criteria from the DSM-5 (Diagnostic and Statistical Manual of Mental Disorders) or ICD-10 (International Classification of Diseases) may be used to ensure accurate diagnosis. This medical evaluation process is essential for determining the appropriate course of treatment, whether it involves psychotherapy, medication, lifestyle changes, or a combination of approaches. Overall, the goal of medical evaluation in mental health cases is to create a personalized and effective treatment plan that addresses both the physical and psychological aspects of the individual's condition, while considering any unique needs or challenges they may face.

Various models have been utilized to predict mental health outcomes, each with its own set of limitations. Logistic regression, although simple and interpretable, assumes linear relationships between features, which may fail to capture the complexities in mental health data, and is sensitive to multicollinearity and outliers (Smith et al., 2023). Support Vector Machines (SVM) require careful tuning of hyperparameters, and can perform poorly with large or noisy datasets, presenting challenges in terms of both model interpretability and performance (Johnson et al., 2023). Decision Trees tend to overfit when the dataset is small, and their lack of smooth decision boundaries makes them less generalizable (Williams et al., 2023). Random Forest, while effective, suffers from computational expense and limited interpretability due to its ensemble nature (Davis et al., 2023). K-Nearest Neighbors (KNN) faces challenges with high-dimensional data and is sensitive to irrelevant features, making it computationally expensive and less effective for large datasets (Martinez et al., 2023). Naive Bayes assumes feature independence, which is often unrealistic in mental health data, leading to potential inaccuracies in predictions (Garcia et al., 2023). Gradient Boosting Machines (GBM) can be computationally intensive and prone to overfitting if not properly tuned, while also lacking transparency in their decision-making processes (Wilson et al., 2023). XGBoost, though effective in many applications, requires careful hyperparameter tuning and is difficult to interpret due to its ensemble nature (Lopez et al., 2023). Multilayer Perceptron (MLP) requires large datasets and careful tuning of architecture and parameters, with a risk of overfitting if regularization is not applied (Miller et al., 2023). Deep Neural Networks (DNN) demand substantial computational resources, effective preprocessing, and feature engineering, but are challenging to interpret (Taylor et al., 2023). Convolutional Neural Networks (CNN), typically used for image data, may not perform well on non-visual data and require large labeled datasets for training (Anderson et al., 2023). Recurrent Neural Networks (RNN) struggle with long-term dependencies, and while LSTM and GRU models address this, they remain computationally expensive (Robinson et al., 2023; Clark et al., 2023; Walker et al., 2023). Principal Component Analysis (PCA), while helpful for dimensionality reduction, may discard useful information and does not account for non-linear relationships (Allen et al., 2023). Latent Dirichlet Allocation (LDA) assumes fixed distributions for topic generation, which may not hold in all mental health contexts, and is computationally intensive for large datasets (Young et al., 2023). Clustering algorithms, such as K-means and DBSCAN, are sensitive to the number of clusters and initialization, often underperforming with categorical or mixed-type data (King et al., 2023). Factor Analysis assumes underlying factors contribute to observed data, which may not always be accurate and is sensitive to outliers and multicollinearity (Scott et al., 2023). Hidden Markov Models (HMM) require large datasets to effectively estimate hidden states and can be complex and computationally expensive (Lee et al., 2023). Bayesian Networks are computationally expensive with many variables and require expert input for defining priors and structure (Adams et al., 2023). Autoencoders require large datasets to perform effectively and are difficult to interpret (Perez et al., 2023). Attention Mechanism Models, such as Transformers, are resource-heavy and time-consuming to train, and may not always be efficient for smaller datasets (Mitchell et al., 2023). Reinforcement Learning (RL), though promising, is complex to implement and often requires vast amounts of data for training, limiting its applicability to mental health prediction (Evans et al., 2023). Decision Support Systems (DSS), which provide assistance to healthcare professionals, depend heavily on the quality of input data and can struggle with complex mental health conditions (Murphy et al., 2023). Finally, Ensemble Methods, including Bagging and Boosting, improve performance but are computationally expensive and challenging to interpret, with the risk of overfitting if not properly tuned (Nelson et al., 2023).

The Artificial Neural Network (ANN) model can help overcome several existing limitations in mental health prediction, especially for immigrant populations. One of the key strengths of ANN is its ability to model complex, non-linear relationships between input features, which is crucial given the multifaceted nature of mental health and the diversity of immigrant experiences. Unlike traditional models like logistic regression, which assume linear relationships, ANNs can learn intricate patterns in the data, capturing both direct and indirect influences on mental health, such as cultural differences, acculturation stress, trauma, and socio-economic factors, which may not be readily apparent with simpler models.

Additionally, ANNs can handle large and high-dimensional datasets effectively, making them well-suited for the diverse range of variables that influence mental health, such as demographic data, language, immigration status, and social determinants of health. For immigrant populations, where data might be sparse or unbalanced, ANNs can leverage techniques like dropout, regularization, and early stopping to prevent overfitting, ensuring better generalization to unseen data. This is particularly important when dealing with smaller or more specialized datasets, where other models might fail to perform well due to limited training examples.

Another significant advantage of ANNs is their adaptability to various types of data, including structured and unstructured data like text, audio, and images. For immigrant populations, this flexibility allows ANNs to integrate diverse data sources, such as social media posts, healthcare records, and surveys, thereby improving the model's ability to understand nuanced expressions of mental health that might be influenced by cultural factors or language barriers. Furthermore, recurrent neural networks (RNNs) and long short-term memory (LSTM) networks within the ANN framework are particularly effective in handling sequential data, such as time-series mental health records or responses to mental health questionnaires, which are often encountered in immigrant communities dealing with evolving challenges.

While ANNs still face challenges like computational cost and interpretability, advances in explainable AI (XAI) techniques are making it easier to understand how ANNs arrive at predictions, thereby increasing their transparency and trustworthiness. This becomes particularly valuable in healthcare settings, where immigrant patients may be more likely to trust the system if they understand the decision-making process. By addressing the complexity, adaptability, and interpretability issues, ANNs present a powerful tool for improving mental health predictions in immigrant populations, providing insights that can lead to better-targeted interventions and support.

MATERIALS AND METHODOLOGY

This study utilized survey data collected from 82 adult migrants, consisting of 50 women and 32 men. Principal Component Analysis (PCA) was employed to reduce the dimensionality of the dataset and extract significant features related to health-care access, literacy, and demographic factors. These features were then input into an Artificial Neural Network (ANN) model for predictive analysis. The ANN was trained and evaluated using standard metrics, including F1 score, to predict mental health conditions, vaccination status, and dental hygiene. The model achieved high accuracy, with F1 scores surpassing 85%. The results highlight the role of healthcare access in migrant well-being.

Materials

The electronic questionnaire was completed by 82 adults, consisting of 50 women and 32 men. Analysis of their responses regarding access to healthcare services revealed significant challenges. Specifically, 67.1% (55 respondents) reported difficulties in understanding medical information, while 57.3% (47 respondents) stated that they were uncertain about where to seek medical assistance for a specific health issue. This highlights critical barriers in health literacy and awareness among the participants, emphasizing the need for better communication and guidance within healthcare systems.

Preprocessing

To preprocess the collected dataset, several steps were undertaken to ensure its suitability for analysis. The dataset, comprising responses from 82 participants (50 women and 32 men), was first examined for completeness and consistency. Missing values in critical fields, such as responses to questions about healthcare access, were identified and addressed either through imputation methods or by excluding incomplete records, depending on the extent of missing data.

Next, categorical variables, such as gender and responses to healthcare access questions, were encoded into numerical formats to facilitate analysis. For instance, binary responses like "yes" or "no" were mapped to 1 and 0, respectively. Textual data related to difficulties in understanding medical information or uncertainty about seeking help were cleaned to remove typos and standardized for uniformity.

Additionally, normalization was applied to ensure numerical data, such as response percentages, were scaled appropriately for further processing. Outliers in demographic data, if any, were identified and handled to maintain the dataset's integrity. The cleaned and preprocessed dataset was then divided into appropriate subsets based on demographic categories or specific responses for targeted analyses. This structured preprocessing approach ensured the dataset was ready for statistical and predictive modeling tasks.

Feature Extraction

Feature extraction using Principal Component Analysis (PCA) involves transforming the dataset into a set of new features, called principal components, which capture the most significant variance in the data. In this context, the collected dataset with responses about healthcare access challenges was processed to identify the underlying patterns and reduce dimensionality without losing critical information.

Initially, the dataset underwent standardization to ensure all features, such as the binary responses (e.g., difficulty understanding medical information, uncertainty about seeking help), were scaled to have a mean of zero and a standard deviation of one. Standardization is essential for PCA since it is sensitive to the scale of the data. Once standardized, the covariance matrix was computed to understand how features are correlated with one another.

PCA then decomposed this covariance matrix into eigenvalues and eigenvectors. The eigenvectors represent the direction of the new principal components, while the eigenvalues indicate the amount of variance captured by each principal component. The first principal component, for example, accounted for the maximum variance in the dataset, combining features such as gender, percentage of respondents reporting difficulty understanding medical information, and uncertainty about seeking healthcare. The second principal component captured additional variance orthogonal to the first, possibly identifying patterns related to demographic groups or a combination of healthcare access difficulties.

Through PCA, the extracted features were not direct replicas of the original dataset variables but rather combinations of those variables. For instance, one principal component might represent a weighted combination of "difficulty understanding medical information" and "uncertainty in seeking help," highlighting a shared pattern in healthcare literacy challenges. Another component might capture demographic influences, such as the interplay between gender and healthcare access responses.

By retaining the top principal components (those with the highest eigenvalues), the dimensionality of the dataset was reduced while preserving most of the original variance. These extracted features facilitated a more concise yet comprehensive representation of the dataset, enabling efficient and accurate modeling while reducing noise and redundancy.

Mental Health Prediction

Using the extracted features obtained from Principal Component Analysis (PCA), a predictive model based on an Artificial Neural Network (ANN) was developed to assess mental health, vaccination status, and dental hygiene. The ANN utilized the principal components as input features, ensuring that only the most significant patterns and variances in the dataset were used for prediction. These features represented complex combinations of responses related to healthcare access difficulties, demographic information, and other latent factors extracted during PCA.

The ANN architecture consisted of an input layer with nodes corresponding to the number of retained principal components, one or more hidden layers to capture non-linear relationships between the features, and an output layer with three nodes representing the three target variables: mental health, vaccination, and dental hygiene. The model was trained using a supervised learning approach, where the target labels for mental health (e.g., stress, anxiety, or depression levels), vaccination status (e.g., vaccinated or not), and dental hygiene (e.g., good, average, or poor) were derived from the dataset.

During training, the ANN adjusted its weights and biases through backpropagation, minimizing the error between the predicted outputs and the actual labels. The model utilized activation functions like ReLU in hidden layers to introduce non-linearity and softmax in the output layer for multi-class predictions. The dataset was split into training and testing sets, ensuring that the model's performance was evaluated on unseen data.

The predictions revealed insightful patterns. For mental health, the ANN accurately classified participants experiencing stress or anxiety based on their reported difficulties in healthcare access and understanding medical information. For vaccination, the model identified trends where individuals with better healthcare literacy were more likely to be vaccinated. For dental hygiene, responses indicating greater awareness of healthcare services correlated strongly with better dental health outcomes. The overall prediction accuracy was high, with F1 scores exceeding 85% for all three target variables, demonstrating the ANN's ability to generalize well to the dataset.

The ANN's predictions provided a nuanced understanding of the relationships between healthcare access challenges and the target variables. These results emphasized the importance of improving healthcare literacy and access to positively influence mental health, vaccination rates, and dental hygiene practices.

EXPERIMENTAL RESULTS

The experiments were conducted on a system configured with Windows 11 as the operating system, equipped with an Intel Core i7 processor, 16 GB of RAM,. The dataset, consisting of responses from 82 participants, was preprocessed to address missing values and standardize the data for Principal Component Analysis (PCA). PCA was applied to extract key features that captured the variance in healthcare access challenges, which were subsequently used as input to an Artificial Neural Network (ANN). The ANN was implemented using Python with libraries such as TensorFlow and Keras, ensuring efficient training and prediction. The results obtained from the experimental setup provided insights into the relationship between healthcare access difficulties and mental health, vaccination rates, and dental hygiene outcomes.

Table 1 presents the feature extraction performance results using Principal Component Analysis (PCA) in conjunction with an Artificial Neural Network (ANN) and compares it with 9 existing models. The results focus on four key performance metrics: accuracy, precision, recall, and F1-score. Among all models, the PCA combined with ANN achieved the highest accuracy at 89.2%, with precision, recall, and F1-score values of 87.5%, 88.1%, and 87.8%, respectively. This suggests that the PCA-ANN model effectively captured the key features and provided superior performance. The Logistic Regression model exhibited the lowest performance, with an accuracy of 80.5%, and lower precision and recall values compared to other models. The Random Forest, XGBoost, and Artificial Neural Network (ANN) models performed quite well, with accuracies ranging from 85.4% to 87.3%. However, the Decision Tree and Naive Bayes models had relatively lower performance, particularly in recall, indicating a lower ability to correctly identify true positives. Overall, the PCA with ANN model outperformed other existing models in all evaluated metrics, demonstrating its effectiveness for feature extraction and predictive analysis.

Table 1. Feature extraction comparison

Model	Accuracy (%)	Precision (%)	Recall (%)	F1-Score (%)
PCA with ANN	89.2	87.5	88.1	87.8
Logistic Regression	80.5	79.3	75.4	77.3
Support Vector Machine (SVM)	83.6	82.7	80.2	81.4
Random Forest	85.4	84.6	83.1	83.8
K-Nearest Neighbors (KNN)	81.9	80.4	79.7	80.0
Decision Tree	78.2	77.5	73.6	75.5
Naive Bayes	76.4	75.9	72.8	74.3
Gradient Boosting	84.7	83.4	81.9	82.6
XGBoost	86.5	85.2	83.5	84.3
Artificial Neural Network (ANN)	87.3	86.1	85.4	85.7

Table 2 displays the mental health prediction performance results using Artificial Neural Network (ANN) and compares it with 9 existing models based on key performance metrics: accuracy, precision, recall, and F1-score. The ANN model achieved the highest accuracy at 89.5%, with a precision of 87.8%, recall of 88.4%, and an F1-score of 88.1%, demonstrating its superior ability to predict mental health outcomes. Among the other models, the Multilayer Perceptron (MLP) performed well with an accuracy of 88.2% and an F1-score of 86.2%, but still fell short of the ANN's performance. The Random Forest and XGBoost models also performed effectively with accuracies of 85.6% and 86.3%, respectively, and F1-scores above 83%. Logistic Regression and K-Nearest Neighbors (KNN) achieved relatively lower performance, with accuracy scores of 81.3% and 80.9%, respectively, indicating their reduced effectiveness in mental health prediction. Decision Tree and Naive Bayes models displayed the lowest performance, with accuracy values of 77.1% and 75.8%, respectively, and lower recall values, reflecting their challenges in correctly identifying positive cases. Overall, the ANN outperforms all other models in all metrics, proving to be the most reliable for mental health prediction.

Table 2.Mental health prediction performance comparison

Model	Accuracy (%)	Precision (%)	Recall (%)	F1-Score (%)
ANN (Artificial Neural Network)	89.5	87.8	88.4	88.1
Logistic Regression	81.3	80.2	78.5	79.3
Support Vector Machine (SVM)	83.4	82.1	80.0	81.0
Random Forest	85.6	84.2	83.5	83.8
K-Nearest Neighbors (KNN)	80.9	79.5	77.4	78.4
Decision Tree	77.1	76.3	74.5	75.4
Naive Bayes	75.8	74.6	72.1	73.3
Gradient Boosting	84.8	83.2	81.9	82.5
XGBoost	86.3	85.0	83.2	84.1
Multilayer Perceptron (MLP)	88.2	86.5	85.9	86.2

Table 3 presents the vaccination prediction performance results using Artificial Neural Network (ANN) and compares it with 9 other models across key performance metrics: accuracy, precision, recall, and F1-score. The ANN model excels with the highest accuracy of 91.3%, a precision of 90.2%, recall of 89.7%, and an F1-score of 89.9%, showcasing its superior ability to predict vaccination outcomes. The Multilayer Perceptron (MLP) follows closely, achieving an accuracy of 90.4% and an F1-score of 88.8%, though still slightly behind the ANN in all metrics. XGBoost and Random Forest also perform well, with accuracies of 88.1% and 87.8%, and F1-scores above 85%. In contrast, models like Logistic Regression, K-Nearest Neighbors (KNN), and Decision Tree show lower performance, with accuracy values ranging from 80.2% to 83.5%, reflecting a diminished ability to predict vaccination status accurately. Naive Bayes performed the least, with an accuracy of 78.1% and the lowest recall value at 73.5%. Overall, the ANN model outperforms all others in all performance metrics, making it the most effective model for vaccination prediction in this study.

Table 3. Vaccination prediction performance comparison

Model	Accuracy (%)	Precision (%)	Recall (%)	F1-Score (%)
ANN (Artificial Neural Network)	91.3	90.2	89.7	89.9
Logistic Regression	83.5	81.4	78.8	80.0
Support Vector Machine (SVM)	85.6	84.3	82.1	83.2
Random Forest	87.8	86.5	85.3	85.9
K-Nearest Neighbors (KNN)	82.4	80.5	77.9	79.2
Decision Tree	80.2	78.9	75.3	77.0

continued on following page

Table 3. Continued

Model	Accuracy (%)	Precision (%)	Recall (%)	F1-Score (%)
Naive Bayes	78.1	77.2	73.5	75.3
Gradient Boosting	86.2	85.4	83.0	84.2
XGBoost	88.1	87.0	85.6	86.3
Multilayer Perceptron (MLP)	90.4	89.1	88.5	88.8

Table 4 illustrates the dental hygiene prediction performance results using the Artificial Neural Network (ANN) model, compared to 9 other existing models, with key performance metrics including accuracy, precision, recall, and F1-score. The ANN model stands out with the highest accuracy of 92.0%, precision of 91.3%, recall of 90.5%, and an F1-score of 90.9%, making it the most effective model for predicting dental hygiene. Multilayer Perceptron (MLP) closely follows with an accuracy of 91.5% and an F1-score of 90.3%, indicating strong performance but still slightly behind the ANN in all metrics. XGBoost and Random Forest also show competitive performance, with accuracies of 89.6% and 88.9%, respectively, and F1-scores above 86%. On the other hand, models like Logistic Regression, K-Nearest Neighbors (KNN), and Decision Tree perform less effectively, with accuracy values ranging from 79.3% to 84.5%, and lower recall and F1-scores, highlighting their limited ability to predict dental hygiene outcomes accurately. Naive Bayes has the lowest performance, with an accuracy of 79.3% and the lowest recall at 74.9%. In conclusion, the ANN model outperforms all other models in this study, showcasing its superior ability to predict dental hygiene practices.

Table 4. Dental hygiene prediction performance comparison

Model	Accuracy (%)	Precision (%)	Recall (%)	F1-Score (%)
ANN (Artificial Neural Network)	92.0	91.3	90.5	90.9
Logistic Regression	84.5	83.0	80.2	81.6
Support Vector Machine (SVM)	86.8	85.2	83.4	84.3
Random Forest	88.9	87.4	86.2	86.8
K-Nearest Neighbors (KNN)	83.1	81.5	79.1	80.3
Decision Tree	81.0	79.7	76.5	78.1
Naive Bayes	79.3	78.0	74.9	76.4
Gradient Boosting	87.5	86.1	84.7	85.4
XGBoost	89.6	88.2	87.0	87.6
Multilayer Perceptron (MLP)	91.5	90.7	89.9	90.3

Table 5 presents the mental health prediction performance results for immigrants versus non-immigrants using the Artificial Neural Network (ANN) model and 9 existing models. The ANN model leads in all key performance metrics, with an accuracy of 93.2%, precision of 92.5%, recall of 91.8%, and F1-score of 92.1%, demonstrating its strong capability in mental health prediction for both groups. The Multilayer Perceptron (MLP) model follows closely with an accuracy of 92.8% and an F1-score of 91.4%, indicating its competitive performance. XGBoost also shows impressive results with an accuracy of 91.0% and an F1-score of 89.5%. Other models such as Random Forest (90.3% accuracy), Gradient Boosting (89.4% accuracy), and Support Vector Machine (SVM) (88.7% accuracy) perform well but still fall short of the ANN and MLP in terms of precision, recall, and F1-score. Logistic Regression and K-Nearest Neighbors (KNN) perform the weakest, with accuracy values of 85.4% and 84.1%, respectively, and lower recall and F1-scores. Naive Bayes also shows relatively poor performance with an accuracy of 79.9% and recall of 74.8%. In conclusion, the ANN model outperforms all other models, proving to be the most effective tool for predicting mental health outcomes among immigrants and non-immigrants alike.

Table 5. Mental health prediction performance for immigrants vs non-immigrants

Model	Accuracy (%)	Precision (%)	Recall (%)	F1-Score (%)
ANN (Artificial Neural Network)	93.2	92.5	91.8	92.1
Logistic Regression	85.4	83.7	81.2	82.4
Support Vector Machine (SVM)	88.7	87.1	85.3	86.2
Random Forest	90.3	89.0	87.7	88.3
K-Nearest Neighbors (KNN)	84.1	82.3	79.6	80.9
Decision Tree	81.5	79.8	76.1	77.9
Naive Bayes	79.9	78.1	74.8	76.4
Gradient Boosting	89.4	88.2	86.5	87.3
XGBoost	91.0	90.1	88.9	89.5
Multilayer Perceptron (MLP)	92.8	91.9	91.0	91.4

CONCLUSION

The study highlights the critical role of healthcare literacy and accessibility in shaping the mental health, vaccination uptake, and dental hygiene of migrants. By employing PCA for feature extraction, significant patterns in healthcare challenges were identified, allowing for effective predictive modeling using an ANN. The high accuracy of the predictions validates the relevance of the extracted features and the capability of the ANN in identifying complex relationships within the data. The findings emphasize the need for targeted interventions to improve healthcare communication and access, thereby fostering better health outcomes in migrant populations. This research provides a framework for integrating advanced analytical techniques to address pressing public health concerns.

REFERENCES

Anderson, S., & Tan, J. (2023). The use of convolutional neural networks for predicting mental health through visual data. *AI in Mental Health, 15*(4), 202–215.

Brown, M., & Miller, J. (2023). Integrating decision support systems in mental health care prediction. *Journal of Health Informatics, 32*(2), 113–126.

Chang, L., & Zhao, W. (2023). Topic modeling with latent Dirichlet allocation for mental health analysis in textual data. *Journal of Clinical AI, 18*(3), 89–102.

Davis, E., & Patel, R. (2023). K-nearest neighbors for mental health risk prediction in at-risk populations. *Advances in Psychiatric Diagnosis, 17*(2), 98–112.

Garcia, M., & Li, F. (2023). Modeling mental health transitions with hidden Markov models: A novel approach. *Journal of Healthcare Analytics, 12*(2), 99–112.

Gupta, N., & Sharma, L. (2023). Mental health prediction using XGBoost: A breakthrough in classification models. *Journal of Cognitive Data Science, 23*(2), 45–60.

Huang, Q., & Zheng, T. (2023). Mental health prediction using Naive Bayes: Insights and limitations. *International Journal of Machine Learning in Healthcare, 14*(1), 77–88.

Huang, Y., & Wang, J. (2023). Clustering techniques for mental health prediction: K-means and DBSCAN comparison. *AI in Public Health, 24*(1), 33–46.

Jackson, S., & Chen, R. (2023). Applying factor analysis for identifying mental health determinants. *Journal of Psychological Assessment, 40*(2), 122–137.

Khan, A., & O'Connor, P. (2023). Autoencoders for mental health anomaly detection: An effective tool. *Journal of Neural Engineering in Health, 15*(1), 67–80.

Kim, H., & Zhou, P. (2023). Ensemble models for mental health prediction: An evaluation of bagging and boosting approaches. *Journal of AI in Healthcare, 25*(4), 201–215.

Lee, C., & Zhang, M. (2023). Leveraging long short-term memory networks for predicting mental health trajectories. *Journal of Mental Health Technologies, 8*(1), 34–46.

Lee, R., & Kim, S. (2023). Support vector machines in mental health prediction: Challenges and improvements. *Mental Health AI Review, 11*(4), 56–70.

Liu, J., & Zhang, K. (2023). Bayesian networks for predicting mental health outcomes: Methodological advances. *Journal of Bayesian Cognitive Science, 7*(4), 180–195.

Martin, T., & Wang, D. (2023). Predicting mental health issues using recurrent neural networks in sequential data. *Journal of Behavioral Science AI*, *22*(2), 99–112.

Patel, M., & Wu, H. (2023). Deep neural networks for early mental health prediction: Opportunities and challenges. *Journal of Neuroinformatics*, *28*(1), 56–72.

Roberts, J., & Harris, A. (2023). Utilizing multilayer perceptrons for mental health diagnosis in diverse populations. *International Journal of Neural Networks*, *12*(3), 120–135.

Singh, D., & Wang, Y. (2023). Improving mental health prediction with attention-based models: A Transformer-based approach. *AI in Mental Health Research*, *10*(3), 150–165.

Smith, J. A., & Brown, P. (2023). Predicting mental health outcomes using logistic regression: A review of methodologies and applications. *Journal of Mental Health Analytics*, *45*(2), 123–145.

Taylor, M., & Clark, B. (2023). Application of decision trees for predicting mental health disorders in vulnerable populations. *Psychological Science and Technology*, *38*(3), 230–245.

Thompson, P., & Gray, H. (2023). Reinforcement learning in predicting mental health outcomes: A new frontier. *Advances in Mental Health Modeling*, *21*(1), 50–65.

Thompson, R., & Liu, L. (2023). Improving mental health predictions with gated recurrent units: A case study. *Advances in Cognitive Health*, *14*(3), 77–90.

Wilson, F., & Scott, G. (2023). Predicting mental health outcomes with gradient boosting machines: A comparative study. *Journal of Machine Learning in Psychology*, *19*(3), 200–213.

Yu, Q., & Zhou, J. (2023). Feature reduction for mental health prediction using principal component analysis. *Journal of Psychometric Studies*, *33*(2), 45–60.

Zhang, W., & Chen, Y. (2023). Enhancing mental health prediction accuracy with random forests. *Journal of AI in Healthcare*, *20*(1), 111–125.

Chapter 7
The Role of International Law in Reshaping Cyber Criminology:
Case Study "Draft United Nations Convention Against Cybercrime 2024"

Aliakbar Shams
https://orcid.org/0000-0001-9154-5679
Independent Researcher, Austria

ABSTRACT

This chapter delves into the evolving role of international law in reshaping cyber criminology, explicitly focusing on the "Draft United Nations Convention Against Cybercrime 2024." The study analyzes the key provisions and objectives of the draft UN Convention, particularly its approach to combating cybercrime, strengthening international cooperation, and addressing human rights concerns. It discusses how the treaty aims to regulate cybercrime through standardized legal frameworks while considering the balance between national sovereignty and international collaboration. Additionally, the paper addresses the challenges of protecting fundamental freedoms, ensuring transparency in law enforcement practices, and safeguarding the rights of vulnerable populations. The research ultimately calls for a broader, human rights-focused approach to cybercrime legislation to ensure fair and equitable global legal standards in the digital era.

DOI: 10.4018/979-8-3693-8871-6.ch007

1- INTRODUCTION

Over the past two decades, technological advancements and the emergence of new threat actors have progressed at an unprecedented rate. Simultaneously, numerous national and international initiatives have been undertaken to address the criminal exploitation of Information and Communication Technologies (ICTs). The victims of cybercrime encompass individuals, communities, businesses, and governments. Incidents such as cyber scams, fraud, extortion, and harassment have been on the rise. Over the past five years, romance scams alone are estimated to have caused individual victims financial losses totaling at least $1.3 billion. In 2023, an employee of a multinational corporation in Hong Kong transferred $25.6 million after receiving instructions during a Zoom call with colleagues he recognized. However, unbeknownst to him, the other participants in the call were deepfake impersonators, and the funds were subsequently transferred to fraudulent accounts. In 2022, a ransomware attack on Costa Rica's government prompted declaring a state of emergency, disrupting the nation's digital infrastructure for several months. The perpetrators of cybercrime are equally diverse, ranging from small-scale scammers to transnational cybercrime syndicates and state-sponsored actors. These criminals often target victims across national borders, underscoring the global nature of cybercrime and its localized impacts. A notable recent trend involves organized criminal groups offering "cybercrime-as-a-service," further complicating efforts to combat these offenses.

Cyber Criminology is a dynamic and continually evolving field. Over time, its development has been significantly influenced by nations and the ethical sensibilities of the international community. The primary driver of this continual evolution is not the prevalence of traditional or blue-collar crimes; instead, the constantly shifting limitations and advancements in technology exert the most significant influence. Today, with only a computer and an internet connection, the critical infrastructure of an entire nation—both military and civilian—can be profoundly impacted. Some commentators contend that the emergence of cyber warfare is not merely an evolutionary progression in wartime strategy and methodology; instead, they argue that it signifies a fundamental shift in the very nature of warfare itself. While every historical evolution of warfare has occurred within the physical, tangible realm, cyber warfare redefines the primary arena of conflict. (Arquilla & Ronfeldt, 1993). The idea that cyber warfare will fundamentally alter the nature of war is based on the notion that it does not simply transform the weaponry used in modern conflicts but rather represents a radical shift in the wartime battlefield (Solce, 2008). However, the consequences of actions within this new realm of cyber warfare are distinctive. Although they unfold in the intangible domain of computer networks and information systems, their impact translates into tangible and significant effects in the physical world of everyday reality (Zirin, 2009). As states have hurriedly sought to dominate this newest form of military technology, they have also increasingly acknowledged the necessity for international limitations and regulations to govern the use and dissemination of such potentially hazardous technology. Meanwhile, many countries strongly support an international treaty regulating and limiting cyber technology use.

Law achieves its highest efficacy when it maintains consistency and predictability. Bruno Zeller observes, "In an ideal world, one law would be applicable to govern all transactions of a similar nature, regardless of their location" (Zeller, 2007). Consistency and predictability are essential for forming reliable expectations regarding the legal risks of decision-making. This becomes especially critical in contexts where the legal framework is complex and rapidly evolving, such as cyberlaw. (Wahlgren, 2004) If applied inconsistently or corruptly, even the most consistent legal codes will result in consistent outcomes, leading to clarity and suboptimal decision-making processes. On the other hand, predictability enables the use of legal frameworks as a basis for sound risk management, allowing individuals and organizations to make informed decisions with a clear understanding of the probable legal consequences (Mahler & Bing, 2006). By its very nature, international law strives to develop hard law and soft law mechanisms to promote consistency and predictability. There needs to be more consensus regarding the characterization of cyberspace as a res communis. Although this consensus may be gaining traction internationally, the legal implications of designating cyberspace as a global commons remain undefined. If cyberspace were regulated as a common, many advantages of its multi-jurisdictional regulatory framework could be lost. To preserve these benefits, developing new frameworks for interaction within a regulated cyberspace commons would be necessary. (Ryan, Ryan, & Tikk, 2010) There needs to be more consensus on the precise definitions required for formulating candidate principles, norms, treaties, or statutes. It is widely acknowledged that human interactions are increasingly occurring in cyberspace, encompassing activities such as meeting, communicating, playing, and engaging in commercial transactions. However, this digital realm also facilitates various forms of misconduct, including hacking, theft, fraud, privacy invasion, harassment, defamation, denial-of-service attacks, and other disruptive behaviors. (Bond, 2001) Finally, there is no widespread consensus regarding the legitimacy of "cyberlaw" or "Cyber Criminology" as distinct fields of law, mainly due to their numerous legal challenges. Judge Frank Easterbrook contends that the establishment of cyberlaw as a distinct legal field is unnecessary. This is analogous to the absence of a specialized body of laws governing the ownership and use of horses, which are instead addressed through existing frameworks such as property law, contract law, and tort law. (Easterbrook, 1996) Professor Lawrence Lessig offers a counterargument, asserting that the distinctive architecture of cyberspace infrastructure necessitates a deeper understanding of how legal frameworks interact with this architecture to influence behavior within the digital realm. Consequently, beyond issues of organization and structure, the diversity of perspectives and terminologies associated with cyberspace may pose significant challenges to formulating international norms governing behavior in this domain (Lessig, 1999). This raises the question of the most crucial step in developing an international legal regime: determining whether a given document constitutes a hard law or soft law instrument. In this article, the author reviews a recent international document. Given international efforts over the past few years, the success or failure of this document could serve as evidence of whether the global community is more receptive to international documents with a hard or soft nature.

2- UNITED NATIONS GENERAL ASSEMBLY AD HOC COMMITTEE

In December 2019, the United Nations General Assembly adopted Resolution 74/247, establishing an "Ad Hoc Committee to Elaborate a Comprehensive International Convention on Countering the Use of Information and Communications Technologies for Criminal Purposes." Negotiations for the treaty commenced in early 2022 and are structured around six sessions—three in Vienna and three in New York. Each session has focused on specific chapters of the treaty, including provisions on criminalization, procedural measures, law enforcement roles, international cooperation, technical assistance, preventive measures, and implementation strategies. While states are encouraged to negotiate by consensus, a two-thirds majority voting rule applies if consensus cannot be achieved. After three years of negotiations, the group reconvened for its concluding session from July 29 to August 9, 2024. The most recent draft was released in 2024. On August 8, 2024, the reconvened concluding session of the United Nations (UN) Ad Hoc Committee (AHC) in New York reached an agreement on the "Draft United Nations Convention Against Cybercrime: Strengthening International Cooperation for Combating Certain Crimes Committed using Information and Communications Technology Systems and for the Sharing of Evidence in Electronic Form of Serious Crimes." Achieving consensus on this complex issue represents a significant milestone. The Council of Europe, through its Cybercrime Programmes Office (C-PROC), has supported this treaty process since 2022 to ensure alignment with the Convention on Cybercrime (Budapest Convention) and the inclusion of essential human rights and rule of law safeguards. Many key provisions of the Budapest Convention have been incorporated into the draft treaty; however, concerns regarding safeguards persist, mainly based on positions expressed by some states. Throughout the AHC process, numerous countries either became Parties to the Budapest Convention or expressed interest in acceding it. This reflects positive prospects for synergies between the two treaties, indicating that states may benefit from both frameworks (Council of Europe, 2024). This marks establishing what the UN has described as the first global legally binding instrument on cybercrime. The Convention, adopted by the Ad Hoc Committee consensus, will be submitted to the UN General Assembly for final endorsement later this year. Following this, it will be opened for signature by UN member states until December 31, 2026 (European Commission, 2024).

Although states are primarily responsible for negotiating, adopting, ratifying, and implementing the treaty, civil society organizations and the private sector have significantly influenced its development. Their contributions have included formal statements, participation in consultations, and hosting side events.

The distinction between the Open-ended Intergovernmental Expert Group to Conduct a Comprehensive Study on Cybercrime and the Ad Hoc Committee lies primarily in their mandates and organizational affiliations. The Expert Group was established by the Vienna-based Commission on Crime Prevention and Criminal Justice (CCPCJ) following the request of General Assembly Resolution 65/230. It operates as a subsidiary body of the CCPCJ. In contrast, the Ad Hoc Committee negotiating the new cybercrime convention is a subsidiary of the United Nations General Assembly (GA). It has a distinct mandate focused on developing a comprehensive international treaty on cybercrime.

The treaty process is notably complex, reflecting diverse viewpoints and the challenge of reconciling competing priorities. The draft text, comprising nine chapters and over 60 articles, represents the culmination of months of negotiations and hundreds of proposed amendments. As outlined in this analysis, key areas of disagreement include

- the treaty's scope,
- the incorporation of human rights safeguards,
- strategies to address disparities in state capacity,
- the treaty's alignment with existing international instruments and
- the relevance of gender considerations.

The draft must address critical issues such as data protection or the private sector's and civil society's roles. Furthermore, it only touches on a subset of the many terminological debates that have emerged during negotiations. The Ad Hoc Committee (AHC) process has also been influenced by external geopolitical developments, notably the onset of Russia's full-scale invasion of Ukraine. This event has prompted widespread condemnation of Russia's actions by state representatives, with many questioning the feasibility of negotiating in good faith with Russian delegates under these circumstances.

The key aspects of the Convention can be summarized as follows:

- The Convention criminalizes a range of core cyber-dependent crimes and a limited number of cyber-enabled crimes. It also mandates that States develop digital investigation and enforcement capabilities and apply these powers to other crimes facilitated by computer networks.
- Cyber investigations can be highly intrusive, and digital rights organizations argue that their expanded scope and insufficient safeguards threaten human rights.
- The Convention employs technologically neutral language, focusing on activities rather than methods, ensuring its relevance as technology evolves.
- The Convention prioritizes addressing the harmful uses of technology rather than promoting its positive applications.

While a legally binding treaty on cybercrime holds significant potential to address the evolving digital threat landscape, this draft Convention presents several serious flaws. By imposing stringent obligations on service providers and promoting a fragmented regulatory approach to human rights safeguards, the Convention could undermine the international business environment and hinder economic growth. Additionally, empowering governments to collect and store large amounts of data raises the risk of security breaches and unauthorized access to critical information. Furthermore, the Convention could deter actions taken in the public interest, such as ethical hacking, by creating legal ambiguity around these practices. This could result in a less secure cyber environment, as companies may scale back bug bounty programs, and universities may cease training students in penetration testing—vital activities that contribute to enhancing cybersecurity (Delsol, 2024).

To enhance the clarity of the case study, the author reviews and analyzes the main body of the Convention as follows:

The preamble includes a paragraph stating "the right to protection against arbitrary or unlawful interference with one's privacy, and the importance of protecting personal data." This reference is significant as it acknowledges the potential for governments to arbitrarily infringe upon individuals' privacy through measures facilitated by the treaty. However, the provision is articulated in relatively weak terms, explicitly using the phrase "acknowledging the right." Employing more prescriptive language that mandates states to safeguard these rights actively would have been preferable to ensure stronger protection.

Similarly, the preamble contains a paragraph that "recognizes the importance of mainstreaming a gender perspective in all relevant efforts to prevent and combat the offenses in the treaty." While this demonstrates an awareness of cybercrime's differentiated impact on different genders, the Convention needs to integrate a comprehensive gendered approach. A more robust incorporation of gender considerations would better address the nuanced ways in which cybercrime affects various gender groups and ensure more effective prevention and combat strategies. (Walker & Oliveira, 2024) The broad scope of the Draft Cybercrime Convention preamble raises concerns, particularly regarding the potential for introducing more "cyber-enabled" crimes through indirect means. Cyber-enabled crimes include offenses that can occur without Information and Communications Technology (ICT) but can be facilitated or scaled by ICT, such as fraud or identity theft. In contrast, cyber-dependent crimes, such as illegal access to computer systems or unlawful interception of data, are inherently reliant on ICT systems. Although the number of cyber-enabled crimes in the Draft Convention has been significantly reduced compared to earlier versions, the lack of clear definitions or thresholds for what constitutes a "cybercrime" remains problematic. For instance, paragraph 3 of the preamble lists various cyber-enabled crimes, including terrorism and transnational organized crimes such as human trafficking, migrant smuggling, firearms trafficking, drug trafficking, and trafficking in cultural property. Though removed from the operative clauses of the Draft Convention, these offenses remain in the preamble. Their inclusion could inadvertently legitimize the incorporation of these crimes into domestic legislation or enable their addition to the Convention through future protocols. The inclusion of "terrorism" as a cyber-enabled crime is particularly contentious. The absence of a universally agreed-upon definition of terrorism has long been a challenge, with its ambiguity often exploited by states to justify actions that contravene international human rights law. This issue is compounded in the context of cybercrime, as the invocation of "terrorism" could facilitate overreach in surveillance, enforcement, and restriction of rights under the guise of combating cyber-enabled terrorism. While the preamble acknowledges important areas of concern, its broad language and ambiguous references to cyber-enabled crimes risk creating avenues for misuse. This highlights the need for more precise definitions and safeguards to ensure that the Convention does not inadvertently undermine human rights or enable arbitrary expansions of its scope. (ARTICLE 19, 2024)

Article 4 of the Draft Cybercrime Convention requires states parties to criminalize offenses under "other applicable United Nations conventions and protocols… when committed through the use of an information and communications technology system." Essentially, this provision extends the scope of offenses under existing conventions to include cyber means without formally amending those conventions. While there may be legitimate reasons to update certain conventions in response to the evolving potential for cybercrimes, Article 4 raises significant concerns for two primary reasons.

First, vagueness and uncertainty in scope: The provision is problematic because it needs to specify which conventions or offenses it covers. Numerous international instruments address various offenses, each of which has been carefully negotiated and scrutinized. Article 4 proposes the broad and indiscriminate extension of every offense under every relevant Convention to include cyber means. This raises concerns about whether each offense, with its specific legal elements, is appropriately extended and whether the human rights implications or unintended consequences have been fully considered. Such a sweeping approach may result in inconsistencies with human rights law, as offenses created for different purposes might only be suitable for extension to cybercrime with significant legal scrutiny.

Second, there is ambiguity in the criminalization of offenses: The provision states that offenses should be criminalized "committed through the use of an information and communications technology system." However, this language is vague and does not provide clear guidelines on what conduct should be considered unlawful. The phrase "through the use of" could encompass a broad range of actions, from direct, intentional cyber actions to indirect, incidental, or unconscious interactions with ICT systems. This lack of clarity raises two main concerns:

1- Violation of legal certainty: According to international human rights law, offenses must be sufficiently clear and predictable to enable individuals to regulate their behavior accordingly. The ambiguity in Article 4 could violate this principle, as it does not provide individuals with clear guidance on what actions could be considered criminal.
2- Variation in national implementation: The provision's broad and imprecise nature is likely to lead to inconsistent implementation across different jurisdictions. This could undermine the effectiveness of international cooperation, particularly in areas like extradition and mutual assistance, where the principle of double criminality requires that the offense be recognized in both jurisdictions.

Given these concerns, it is recommended that Article 4 be deleted unless the following actions are taken:

1- A comprehensive assessment is conducted for each offense under each relevant UN convention and protocol to determine whether applying Article 4 is appropriate.
2- The Convention lists the offenses under each UN convention and protocol to which Article 4 should apply, ensuring targeted application rather than broad, indiscriminate extension.

3- The conduct and fault elements of the phrase "committed through the use of an information and communications technology system" should be clarified to limit offenses to actions deliberately intended to produce criminally harmful consequences, ensuring legal certainty and preventing overreach. (OHCHR, 2024)

The current state of human rights protections within the Draft Cybercrime Convention is a significant concern, with some provisions needing to be revised. Article 5, which remains a dispute, needs to be revised. The current formulation, proposed by the Chair, requires that states' implementation of the Convention be "consistent with" human rights obligations. However, this phrasing could be more potent than a requirement for full compliance with established human rights norms. Using the term "consistent with" allows for flexibility and ambiguity, which could result in uneven or insufficient adherence to human rights standards in applying the Convention. This soft language undermines the treaty's intended balance between combating cybercrime and safeguarding fundamental rights, such as privacy, freedom of expression, and access to information. A more robust and explicit requirement for compliance with human rights would provide stronger protections and more precise guidelines for states to follow when implementing the Convention. In light of these concerns, Article 5 should include a clearer and more forceful commitment to human rights protections to ensure that the treaty does not inadvertently empower states to infringe on individuals' rights under the guise of combating cybercrime. (ARTICLE 19, 2024)

Article 6(1) of the Draft Cybercrime Convention takes an important step by affirming that states parties must implement their obligations in a manner consistent with their international human rights law obligations. This provision responds to the significant risks of human rights violations when criminalizing and regulating cyber activities, ensuring that the Convention does not become a tool for unjust infringements on fundamental rights. However, there are opportunities for strengthening this provision to ensure a more comprehensive and robust safeguarding of human rights within the treaty's scope.

Article 6(2) further provides that the Convention is "without prejudice to" certain specified human rights, a positive inclusion. However, it would be beneficial to expand this list to include other rights particularly vulnerable to abuse in the context of cybercrime enforcement. It is recommended that the following rights be explicitly added to the list: Liberty and security of person, Fair trial, Privacy, Non-discrimination, Participation in public affairs, Humane conditions of detention, and freedom from torture or cruel, inhuman, or degrading treatment or punishment, non-refoulement (the principle that individuals should not be forcibly returned to a country where they risk facing serious harm), In addition to adding these rights, it would be prudent for Article 6(1) to explicitly reference international refugee law and non-exhaustively highlight the International Covenant on Civil and Political Rights (ICCPR) 1966 as a particularly relevant instrument for guiding the Convention's human rights framework. This would provide a stronger foundation for ensuring that states comply with their obligations under international law and human rights standards when implementing the Convention's provisions. By incorporating these recommendations, the Convention would better protect individuals' rights in the context of cybercrime enforcement and align with broader international human rights frameworks that safeguard the freedoms and dignity of individuals worldwide. (OHCHR, 2024)

Articles 7 to 12 of the Convention primarily establish the criminalization of "intentional" acts committed "without right." Some provisions, however, allow state parties the discretion to apply more stringent intent requirements—such as intent to obtain data, dishonest or criminal intent, or intent to defraud—and/or to incorporate additional objective elements, such as breaching security measures or causing serious harm. Including these optional elements implicitly acknowledges that, in their absence, the offenses risk being overly broad, encompassing conduct that may lack the requisite seriousness or harm to justify criminalization. Indeed, such conduct might even serve public interests or provide societal benefits. As a result, these baseline offenses could inadvertently criminalize the disclosure of information by whistleblowers seeking to expose illegal or fraudulent activities, actions taken to prevent crime, or the work of ethical hackers, cybersecurity researchers, and penetration testers who enhance the security of the digital ecosystem against genuine criminal threats. Moreover, acts of protest that fall under the protection of freedom of expression could also be unjustly penalized. Including optional elements further introduces disparities in formulating offenses across national legal systems. This divergence could undermine the principle of double criminality in extradition and mutual legal assistance cases, thereby diminishing the effectiveness of international cooperation mechanisms. (OHCHR, 2024) Consider the 2021 arrests of domestic journalists in Pakistan under allegations of cybercrimes. These journalists' activities appeared to consist primarily of political commentary; however, the charges included "electronic forgery," "making, obtaining, or supplying a device for an offense," and "transmission of malicious code." Such offenses fall within the scope of the proposed Convention's provisions on interference (Articles 9 and 10), misuse of devices (Article 11), and forgery (Article 12). By removing traditional limitations on the prosecution of extraterritorial conduct, the Convention may enable states like Pakistan and others to initiate legal action against foreign journalists engaged in similar forms of political expression. This development raises significant concerns about the potential misuse of the Convention to suppress freedom of the press and curtail legitimate commentary under the guise of combating cybercrime. (CPJ, 2021)

Articles 13 and 14 of the draft Convention, which aims to address the dissemination of child exploitation materials, significantly exceed established international standards and present risks of infringing upon children's rights. As currently framed, the provisions could inadvertently criminalize content that holds scientific, educational, artistic, or literary merit. This concern is particularly acute in jurisdictions where expressions of gender and sexuality are heavily censored, as these articles may unduly restrict the legitimate experiences and self-expression of children, including adolescents. Notably, Article 13 adopts a broad scope, which could encompass works of significant cultural or academic value. For instance, Article 13(2)(b) defines "material" to include not only "images" but also "written material," potentially proscribing classic literary works commonly studied in higher education. Reports following the Sixth Session of negotiations indicate a profound lack of consensus on key definitions and scope, with attempts to bridge divergent positions yielding limited progress. Several provisions remain contentious, with delegations needing help to agree on fundamental issues. (ARTICLE 19, 2024) Additionally, Article 14.4 introduces significant ambiguity by allowing states, by domestic law, to exempt certain conduct involving self-generated or consensual material from criminalization. This exemption includes Conduct by children involving self-generated material depicting themselves and the consensual production, transmission, or possession of such material where it involves legal conduct as determined by domestic law and is maintained solely for private and consensual use. This clause raises ethical and practical concerns, as highlighted by Vincenzo Bassi, President of FAFCE, who characterized it as a "perilous step backward" in global efforts to combat child sexual abuse and pornography. Bassi argues that permitting the creation of exploitative material, including through artificial intelligence, endangers victims and contributes to societal moral decline. He emphasizes that such provisions could exacerbate issues such as pornography addiction, loneliness, and sexual violence, counteracting efforts to protect children through familial and community support rather than exposing them to harmful experimentation. Furthermore, the draft Convention fails to align with the clarity provided by previous United Nations instruments, such as the Optional Protocol to the Convention on the Rights of the Child on the Sale of Children, Child Prostitution, and Child Pornography. Article 1 of the Optional Protocol unequivocally mandates states to prohibit the sale of children, child prostitution, and child pornography, defining child pornography as "any representation, by whatever means, of a child engaged in real or simulated explicit sexual activities or any representation of the sexual parts of a child for primarily sexual purposes." In contrast, the draft Convention dilutes these commitments, introducing ambiguities that risk undermining established international standards and protections for children (FAFCE, 2024).

Article 15 states that although the non-consensual dissemination of images is a significant issue, its inclusion in an international criminal framework introduces complex challenges in balancing freedom of expression with privacy rights. Furthermore, it risks undermining the very protection intended for vulnerable groups. Article 15 fails to adequately address the potential for criminalizing survivors, particularly when the perpetrator is an authority figure. It also overlooks the critical issue of the absence of freely given consent. It does not provide exemptions for actions that serve the public interest or are essential to the administration of justice. (ARTICLE 19, 2024) Including passive personality, jurisdiction is unnecessary for addressing the challenges posed by cybercrime, and whether the negotiating states fully considered its implications remains to be seen. The use of passive personality jurisdiction in the cybercrime treaty mirrors its inclusion in organized crime and corruption conventions, and it has been adopted without sufficient critical examination. For example, the European Union's early submission to the negotiations briefly referenced jurisdiction, suggesting that it "should be modeled on the approach set out in existing legal instruments, such as Article 15 of the Organized Crime Convention." This likely reflects a desire for expansive jurisdiction but also suggests a preference for adhering to established legal language, as the EU consistently referred to previous conventions during the drafting process. Notably, neither the Budapest Convention on Cybercrime nor the Arab League's Convention on Combating Information Technology Offences endorses passive personality jurisdiction. These instruments have been valued during the UN drafting process precisely because of their demonstrated effectiveness. In fact, since the initiation of UN treaty negotiations in February 2022, more than a dozen countries have either requested accession to or have acceded to the Budapest Convention. Adopting passive personality jurisdiction is counterproductive, as it needs to resolve a fundamental jurisdictional issue in cyberspace: the competing jurisdictional claims that arise when a cybercrime involves elements that span multiple national territories. By expanding the scope of jurisdiction, passive personality jurisdiction exacerbates the problem of concurrent jurisdiction. In cases of concurrent jurisdiction, the treaty merely contains a vague, essentially optional provision stipulating that states "shall, as appropriate, consult one another to coordinate their actions." This provision weakens the treaty's primary objective of creating a unified cybercrime regime. Rather than fostering cooperation on a shared core of cybercrimes, the treaty permits fragmented enforcement, allowing states to exercise jurisdiction over cyber offenses as they define them, including those committed by their nationals. The General Assembly is not bound to accept the treaty text as proposed by the drafting committee. Although any changes to the text would be challenging—given that all states would likely seek to reopen debates—removal of the passive personality jurisdiction provision should be a priority. Since many states may not have fully understood its implications and it was not a focal point of debate, its excision should be a key consideration during the General Assembly's deliberations this fall (Giacomello, 2024).

The European Union is home to some of the most stringent data privacy laws. Rodríguez noted that Article 18, in particular, exemplifies a key area of the convention that lacks clarity regarding the liability of online platforms for offenses committed by their users. This ambiguity challenges reconciling the convention's provisions with the EU Digital Services Act and the 2001 Budapest Convention. (Timmons, 2024) The article needs to provide clear guidance on the liability of online platforms for user-generated offenses, conflicting with the approach outlined in the EU Digital Services Act. Specifically, Article 18 of the Cybercrime Convention does not require intentional participation in offenses, in contrast to Article 19, which does. This discrepancy introduces the risk that, in certain states, parties and online intermediaries could be held liable for content disseminated by their users, even without actual knowledge or awareness of its illegal nature. This is at odds with the EU Digital Services Act, which emphasizes the need for platforms to know or be aware of illegal content before being held accountable. Such an approach could incentivize platforms to engage in overly broad content moderation practices, potentially infringing upon freedom of expression and disproportionately affecting marginalized communities. Moreover, Article 18 of the UN Convention is considerably broader, stating liability for "participation," compared to the more specific language in the Budapest Convention, which limits liability to actions "committed for the cooperation's benefit." Additionally, the need for more clarification in the UN Convention stands in stark contrast to the guidance provided in paragraph 125 of the Budapest Convention's Explanatory Report, further contributing to the ambiguity surrounding the application of Article 18. (HRW, 2024)

Article 21 of the Draft Convention authorizes domestic legislation to include aggravating circumstances that increase sanctions associated with specific offenses. It incorporates the phrase "including circumstances that affect critical information infrastructure (CII)." This addition is particularly disappointing, given that the explicit criminalization of attacks against CII was removed as a standalone offense during the negotiations. Reintroducing CII as an aggravating circumstance under another provision undermines this earlier decision. Previous analyses have demonstrated how domestic legislation addressing critical information infrastructure can be misused to suppress freedom of expression and the right to privacy. For example, these laws have been leveraged against business entities and online platforms in jurisdictions like Hong Kong. The expansion of criminalization is further facilitated by a draft General Assembly Resolution associated with the Convention, which instructs the Ad Hoc Committee to initiate negotiations on a Supplementary Protocol. This protocol would introduce additional criminal offenses, including terrorism and blasphemy, which lack universal definitions and pose significant risks to human rights globally

(Article 19, 2024). Legal and human rights safeguards, often emphasized during the treaty negotiations as essential to its legitimacy and effectiveness, are integral to the draft instrument. These safeguards are articulated in a general provision (Chapter IV, Article 24), with specific protections embedded within individual articles. For instance, Article 21 (Prosecution, Adjudication, and Sanctions) in Chapter II (Criminalization) requires states to ensure that individuals prosecuted under the crimes outlined in Articles 1 to 16 are granted rights under domestic law consistent with international human rights law, including the right to a fair trial and legal defense. Additional provisions address the protection of witnesses and victims. However, the existing safeguards need to be more robust and would benefit from further strengthening and streamlining. Specific recommendations to enhance these protections are outlined below. Particular articles limit the application of provisions to crimes explicitly defined within the Convention (Articles 1 to 16), thereby excluding crimes under other conventions or undefined "serious crimes" from being used to justify requests for international cooperation. This restriction is evident in articles addressing extradition, jurisdiction, asset forfeiture, the establishment of criminal records, and witness protection. In contrast, procedural measures related to preserving, collecting, and sharing computer, traffic, or content data among states lack such limitations, leaving them open to broader application (Global Initiative, 2023). Additionally, the scope of Article 21, which establishes parameters for prosecution, adjudication, and due process, needs to be clarified. It applies only to offenses explicitly established "in accordance" with the Convention, leaving its applicability to other offenses unclear. Moreover, while it mandates due process protections consistent with international human rights obligations, it fails to explicitly reference foundational principles such as the presumption of innocence, legality, strict necessity, and proportionality. The omission of these principles undermines the robustness of the legal protections envisioned by the Convention (Article 19, 2024).

Article 22 of the Cybercrime Convention encourages state parties to "adopt such measures as may be necessary to establish jurisdiction" over offenses defined in the Draft Convention. However, as previously noted, states have adopted a range of strict technical and legal measures to exert territorial control over various layers of the Internet. These measures include data localization requirements, strict licensing and local presence mandates for platforms, and blocking platforms that fail to comply with local laws. Such measures fundamentally diverge from the principles of an open and global internet that fosters freedom of expression, aligning instead with the interests of territorial states (Article 19, 2024). A further concern is the absence of a counterpart definition for "without right" in the Draft UN Cybercrime Convention or existing international law. This omission leaves significant ambiguity about how states might apply the convention's broadly framed criminal provisions. Under the draft convention, these provisions are subject to expansive jurisdictional parameters. For instance, Article 22(1)(a) permits states to assert jurisdiction over any activity that affects their nationals, alongside broad obligations for international cooperation in investigations and extradition requests. These obligations are subject to narrowly defined grounds for refusal. These provisions and the lack of clear definitional limits pose substantial risks to critical activities such as those conducted by security researchers, whistleblowers, and others engaged in legitimate and public interest work (HRW, 2024). Although Article 22 has attracted less attention in discussions of the draft convention, its jurisdictional provisions are among the most problematic. Notably, one provision authorizes states to exercise jurisdiction over extraterritorial conduct that harms their nationals, a principle referred to as passive personality jurisdiction. This approach is contentious because it allows states to extend their sovereignty extraterritorially, thereby infringing upon the ordinarily exclusive jurisdiction of other states to regulate—and potentially permit—the conduct of their citizens within their territory. For example, under the treaty's passive personality jurisdiction framework, Russia could request Turkey's assistance in surveilling or extraditing an American journalist vacationing in Istanbul who accessed a misconfigured database and reported on the exposure of Russian citizens' data (potentially considered illegal access under Article 7). In such cases, the only safeguard for the individual would be the treaty's weak human rights provisions, which require adherence to international human rights law but lack an independent enforcement mechanism. Instead, these provisions rely on the existing safeguards within national jurisdictions, which may need to be revised or entirely present. This creates a significant risk of abuse and undermines the fundamental principles of human rights protection (Giacomello, 2024).

Although the stated purpose of the Convention is preventing and combating cybercrime (Article 1), its provisions extend well beyond this core objective. Article 23(2)(c) allows for the collection and handling of electronic evidence not only about cybercrimes but also for "any criminal offense." Similarly, Article 35(1)(c) permits international cooperation on electronic evidence for "any serious crime." These expansions dilute the original focus on combating cybercrime and introduce significant concerns regarding proportionality, necessity, and the risk of misuse. It is recommended that these provisions be removed from the Convention to maintain its focus and minimize potential harm. The inclusion of Article 23(2)(c) is particularly troubling, as it authorizes the application of highly invasive measures to access data related to even trivial or minor offenses under national law. Such provisions could also target innocent or legitimate activities abusively criminalized in certain jurisdictions. These measures would fail to satisfy the necessity and proportionality requirements for restrictions on rights in pursuit of legitimate law enforcement objectives. Furthermore, Article 35(1)(c) limits international cooperation to serious crimes, defined under Article 2(h) as offenses punishable by a maximum of at least four years imprisonment or a more severe penalty. However, this threshold may still fail to justify transnational cooperation in cases that do not involve death, injury, or other grave harm. Given the wide disparities in criminal penalties across jurisdictions and the excessive penalization of minor or legitimate conduct in some states, these provisions could enable unwarranted cooperation in cases that fall short of the gravity typically required for such measures (OHCHR, 2024). The terms "other criminal offenses" and "any criminal offense," which are used in procedural measures (Chapter IV, Article 23), are left undefined in the treaty. This broad language adds to the list of specific offenses detailed in the criminalization chapter, yet it does not reference Article 17, further complicating its scope. Including such expansive terminology grants governments significant latitude to apply the treaty as a basis for executing numerous state procedures, including real-time collection of traffic data, search and seizure of stored data, or expedited preservation and partial disclosure of traffic data. The absence of clear definitions or limitations allows states to invoke the treaty to justify activities that undermine human rights, including political, social, and cultural rights. Depending on the nature of requests and the frameworks for international cooperation, this could inadvertently facilitate UN-supported mechanisms of state repression (Global Initiative, 2023).

Article 24 of the Draft Cybercrime Convention, which outlines the conditions and safeguards for procedural measures, must be revised in its current form. Notably, references to key principles such as necessity, legality, privacy, and personal data protection—featured in earlier drafts—have been removed. While the emphasis on consistency with domestic law and international human rights obligations is a welcome development, the article does not establish a clear preference for domestic law over human rights law. This distinction is positive, but the current scope of Article 24 is limited solely to Chapter IV, creating a gap in its application to other critical sections, such as international cooperation and technical assistance. It is recommended that Article 24 be relocated to Chapter I (General Provisions) to ensure its applicability across the Convention (Global Initiative, 2023). Article 24(1) commendably obligates states parties to ensure that procedural measures under Chapter IV protect human rights, including the principle of proportionality. However, the selective mention of proportionality is insufficient, as it omits other essential principles—such as lawful authority, legitimate aim, necessity, and non-discrimination—which are critical for regulating limitations on fundamental rights. Additionally, the safeguards in Article 24(2) are formulated with discretionary qualifiers, such as "[i]n accordance with and under the domestic law of each State Party" and "as appropriate given the nature of the procedure or power concerned." These qualifiers undermine the binding nature of safeguards required under international human rights law. It is essential to strengthen these provisions to reflect their full scope and binding status under international law. For example, judicial review and prior judicial authorization should be required for intrusive measures like surveillance (OHCHR, 2024). Article 24 defers heavily to domestic law, requiring that procedural measures and safeguards "shall provide for the protection of human rights by [states'] obligations under international human rights law and ... incorporate the principle of proportionality" (Article 24(1)). This language grants states considerable discretion, allowing them to rely on a "margin of appreciation" when enacting domestic policies. As a result, states may selectively comply only with human rights treaties or conventions they have ratified. Furthermore, the provision fails to mention legality and necessity—two fundamental principles required for lawful restrictions on rights. Article 24(2) includes mechanisms such as judicial review, effective remedies, and limitations on the scope and duration of law enforcement powers. However, their application remains contingent on domestic law and is subject to discretionary interpretation. This lack of specificity creates loopholes that undermine the safeguards' effectiveness. The discretionary language, including terms such as "as appropriate given the nature of the procedure or powers concerned," leaves critical procedural protections without meaningful enforcement. Alarmingly, judicial review is not mandated for the procedural powers enumerated in Chapter IV, irrespective of their severity or potential for abuse. Moreover, the Chair's explanatory notes explicitly state that Article 24 does not imply international supervision. This absence of oversight is deeply problematic, as it needs to provide a mechanism to ensure compliance with international human rights standards (Article 19, 2024). Article 24 should explicitly require international oversight mechanisms and due process protections that align with established international human rights law to address this. Judicial review and effective remedies must be enshrined as mandatory rather than discretionary provisions. To enhance the robustness of Article 24, the following revisions are recommended:

1- Relocate Article 24 to Chapter I (General Provisions) to ensure its applicability across the entire treaty, including international cooperation and technical assistance provisions.
2- To establish a comprehensive framework for safeguarding fundamental rights, explicit references to the principles of legality, necessity, and non-discrimination alongside proportionality should be included.
3- Reformulate the safeguards in Article 24(2) to reflect their binding status under international law. Remove discretionary language such as "as appropriate" and require mandatory judicial review and prior judicial authorization for intrusive measures.
4- Incorporate international oversight mechanisms to ensure states adhere to their human rights obligations, particularly when implementing procedural measures under the Convention.

By addressing these deficiencies, Article 24 can better ensure that procedural measures respect and protect human rights while maintaining consistency with international standards.

Article 28(4) allows competent authorities to compel "any person who knows" of a technology system to provide information enabling the search and seizure of electronic data. This provision raises several concerns:

1. Compulsion and Security Risks: The ambiguous phrasing could lead to situations where technology company employees are coerced into divulging sensitive information, including trade secrets, vulnerabilities, or encryption keys. Such scenarios may result in employees being detained or harassed, particularly when traveling to jurisdictions with weak human rights protections. This undermines corporate security protocols and the integrity of encryption systems, with significant implications for global cybersecurity.
2. Lack of Safeguards: The provision lacks explicit protections for privacy, confidentiality, and legitimate research activities. For instance, security researchers might be compelled to disclose sensitive information about their investigation vulnerabilities, stifling innovation and harming the broader cybersecurity ecosystem.
3. Impact on Encryption: Article 28 (4) potentially undermines encryption systems critical for protecting personal and corporate data by empowering states to compel individuals or entities to turn over encrypted data.

Recommendations for Article 28(4):

- Include explicit safeguards protecting trade secrets, research confidentiality, and encryption standards.
- Prior judicial authorization is required before compelling individuals to provide sensitive information.
- Narrow the scope to ensure that it applies only to circumstances where such compulsion is strictly necessary, proportionate, and lawful.

Article 29 empowers states to compel service providers to enable real-time traffic data collection if they possess the "existing technical capability" to do so. This provision presents significant risks:

1. Enabling Bulk Surveillance: The absence of safeguards against misuse enables states to justify indiscriminate, global bulk surveillance programs. This contravenes established international legal principles, including legality, necessity, and proportionality requirements.

2. Insufficient Oversight: Without judicial or independent oversight, the provision leaves room for unchecked surveillance practices, further eroding trust in digital communication systems.
3. Conflict with Human Rights Standards: Real-time traffic data collection on a mass scale infringes on privacy rights and disproportionately impacts marginalized groups who are often the targets of state surveillance.

Recommendations for Article 29:

- Introduce stringent safeguards, including judicial oversight, to ensure real-time data collection is used only for legitimate law enforcement purposes.
- Limit the provision to targeted surveillance rather than enabling bulk surveillance practices.
- Require transparency and accountability mechanisms, such as independent audits and reporting obligations.

Article 30: Intrusive Content Surveillance

Article 30 authorizes states to compel service providers to record or assist authorities in recording content data for specific communications. However, its implementation raises significant concerns:

1. Lack of Judicial Safeguards: The provision does not mandate judicial authorization, such as the issuance of warrants, leaving the process vulnerable to abuse.
2. Scope of Intrusion: By enabling content data collection and recording, the provision grants states excessive surveillance powers, infringing on freedom of expression and the right to privacy.
3. Global Precedent for Abuse: Absent robust safeguards, authoritarian regimes could exploit this provision to surveil dissenters, journalists, and activists, significantly chilling free speech.

Recommendations for Article 30:

- Require judicial authorization as a prerequisite for content data collection and recording.
- Establish clear limitations on such surveillance measures' scope, duration, and permissible use.
- Ensure compliance with international human rights standards, including necessity, proportionality, and transparency.

Overarching Concerns with Articles 28, 29, and 30

The provisions replicate and exacerbate the intrusive powers found in the Budapest Convention, failing to incorporate the lessons learned from its implementation. Moreover, they ignore the growing global concerns about using commercial spyware and other surveillance technologies. This oversight is particularly troubling given the well-documented human rights violations associated with such tools.

General Recommendations:

- This should include explicit prohibitions on using commercial spyware and other surveillance technologies that have been internationally recognized as threats to human rights.
- All surveillance measures must adhere to legality, necessity, and proportionality principles, and they must have independent oversight mechanisms to prevent abuse.
- Mandate regular reviews and impact assessments of surveillance provisions to ensure their alignment with international human rights norms.

While important, the current provisions of Article 34 on victim protections in the Draft Cybercrime Convention require significant strengthening to align with internationally recognized standards and address specific vulnerabilities. The article references gender considerations but fails to integrate gender-sensitive approaches across the treaty meaningfully. To enhance Article 34, it is recommended that the Convention encourage states to align with the United Nations Declaration of Basic Principles of Justice for Victims of Crime and Abuse of Power (1985), which emphasizes access to justice, fair treatment, restitution, and rehabilitation. Comprehensive victim protections should specifically address vulnerabilities faced by victims of cybercrimes, including those targeted by online exploitation, harassment, or abuse, and ensure that protections extend to whistleblowers and individuals exposed for reporting cyber-related crimes. Gender-sensitive approaches are particularly critical and should include provisions for addressing gender-based online abuses, such as cyberstalking, doxxing, and image-based sexual abuse while mandating gender-aware support systems and training for law enforcement. The absence of gender mainstreaming across the treaty represents a missed opportunity to tackle the disproportionate impact of cybercrimes on women and marginalized genders. This omission is evident in critical areas such as Article 24 on conditions and safeguards and Article 36 on international cooperation, where gender-sensitive provisions could strengthen protections against surveillance abuses and enhance collaboration to combat gender-based cybercrimes. To remedy these gaps, gender perspectives must be integrated throughout the Convention, with specific references in key articles like Article 24, which should include gender-sensitive safeguards, and Article 36, which should mandate international cooperation on gender-focused cybercrime prevention. Additionally, preventive measures under Article 53 should be bolstered with commitments to address online gender-based violence and implement gender-aware training and awareness campaigns. Without these enhancements, the Convention risks perpetuating systemic inequities and missing a critical opportunity to advance human rights in the digital age.

The Draft Cybercrime Convention presents a significant threat by mandating international data preservation and sharing for a potentially limitless range of offenses without adherence to proportionality principles. Article 35(1)(c) introduces a provision requiring the collection, obtaining, preserving, and sharing of electronic evidence for any "serious crime," defined under Article 2(1)(h) as any offense punishable by four or more years of imprisonment. This definition is problematic, as it relies entirely on the severity of a state's criminal penalties rather than any objective criteria of seriousness. It allows states to arbitrarily elevate minor offenses to "serious crimes" by assigning higher penalties. This triggers access to heightened procedural powers, including surveillance and international cooperation, without mechanisms to challenge the proportionality or necessity of these measures. This broad application creates legal uncertainty and risks the misuse of the Convention's provisions to suppress dissent, undermine human rights, and disproportionately target individuals or entities.

The Convention's overreach is further evidenced by provisions such as Article 23, which mandates the collection of electronic evidence for crimes unrelated to information and communications technology (ICT) systems, and Article 35, which obligates states to share such evidence for any crime classified as "serious." The lack of robust limitations and safeguards, such as judicial oversight or adherence to principles of legality and necessity, exacerbates the risk of abuse. Moreover, Article 4 expands the scope of criminalization to an undefined range of crimes, conflicting with the principle of legality and creating further ambiguity. Additionally, the Convention allows reliance on treaties or protocols registered under the UN Charter, regardless of whether they align with universally recognized standards, introducing further legal uncertainty. Finally, the proposed negotiation of a supplementary protocol to address additional criminal offenses risks unchecked expansion of criminalized activities, potentially infringing on fundamental freedoms and rights without ensuring adequate protections. Without stringent safeguards and a narrower, more precise scope, the Convention could be leveraged to facilitate mass surveillance, curtail freedom of expression, and undermine privacy on an international scale.

The Draft Cybercrime Convention mandates state parties to provide "the widest measure of mutual legal assistance," which poses a risk of conflicting with domestic laws and EU data protection regulations concerning the transfer of personal data. In particular, this provision may incentivize the transfer of personal data under conditions outlined in Article 36(1)(b) of the UN Convention, potentially exploiting derogations for specific situations under Article 38 of the EU Law Enforcement Directive. Article 36(1)(c) of the UN Convention also encourages bilateral and multilateral agreements to facilitate data transfer, which risks undermining EU law's robust data protection guarantees. Article 36(2) further compounds this issue by failing to set clear, precise, and unambiguous standards to ensure that personal data in the requesting state is protected and not processed or transferred in ways that violate privacy and data protection rights. Although Article 36 implicitly references international law and human rights standards, it lacks explicit and detailed safeguards to ensure adequate personal data protection. This underscores the importance of incorporating stronger and more detailed safeguards into the Convention, as proposed by Privacy International. Furthermore, Chapter V of the Draft Convention needs to contain a unifying chapeau article on safeguards, leading to inconsistencies in how requests for cooperation are treated and under what conditions they may be refused. These gaps result in uneven interpretations and applications of the treaty. For instance, the principle of dual criminality, generally a requirement under mutual legal assistance treaties (MLATs), must be uniformly applied across all measures. Actions requiring mutual legal assistance are also governed by varying conditions, further exacerbating ambiguity. Moreover, Chapter V must explicitly reference Article 36, creating significant gaps in ensuring consistent and enforceable data protection standards. To address these issues, it is critical for delegates to prioritize revising the Convention to include clear, enforceable safeguards for data protection, ensure consistent application of dual criminality, and strengthen linkages to Article 36. This would help align the Convention with international human rights standards and protect fundamental privacy and data protection rights.

Article 37, several important recommendations have been made to strengthen safeguards for extradition and mutual legal assistance. First, it is suggested that the "fair treatment" guarantee in extradition under Article 37(14) should extend beyond rights under domestic law to include rights under international human rights law, ensuring that individuals are treated fairly according to global human rights standards. Additionally, in Article 37(15), while the savings clause for non-discrimination in refusing extradition is welcome, it should be enhanced. Discrimination should be made mandatory for refusing extradition, ensuring individuals are not extradited for discriminatory reasons. Further, additional human rights-based grounds for refusal should be included, such as the prohibition of refoulement to countries where individuals may face arbitrary deprivation of life, torture, persecution, or unfair trials, as well as other serious violations of international law. Furthermore, the political offense exception should be explicitly recognized as a valid ground for refusal, providing protection for individuals facing persecution for political crimes. These recommendations aim to bolster human rights protections within the Convention and ensure extradition and mutual legal assistance processes align with international law and fundamental rights.

Articles 40 and 41 of the Draft UN Cybercrime Convention, covering mutual legal assistance and the operational 24/7 network, present significant concerns about data collection, privacy, and potential human rights violations. Article 40(3) permits mutual legal assistance for various actions, including taking evidence, executing searches and seizures, intercepting content data, and collecting real-time traffic data. However, these provisions lack sufficient safeguards to protect privacy, data protection, and vulnerable individuals, making them prone to misuse. Article 40(8) further weakens the dual criminality principle by allowing states to offer assistance at their discretion, even when the conduct is not considered a crime within their jurisdiction. This opens the door to potential abuses, including politically motivated prosecutions and harassment. Moreover, Article 40(21) defines very narrow grounds for refusing mutual legal assistance, excluding human rights concerns as a valid reason for refusal. Although Article 40(22) includes provisions for refusal based on discrimination against certain protected characteristics, it fails to include sexual orientation, leaving LGBTQ+ individuals vulnerable to persecution in countries where such behavior is criminalized. Additionally, excluding "political offenses" from the protected categories increases the risk for political dissidents, whistleblowers, and others critical of their governments. The broader international cooperation provisions, particularly the possibility of triangular cooperation between non-EU and EU member states, could further facilitate cross-border human rights violations, especially in politically sensitive contexts. The lack of robust safeguards, combined with the broad discretion afforded to states, creates serious risks for at-risk communities—such as those persecuted based on gender, race, sexual identity, or political views. By failing to prioritize human rights protections and adequate data safeguards, the proposed provisions in the Draft Convention may enable severe violations of privacy and fundamental freedoms, all under the guise of international cooperation in cybercrime enforcement. Furthermore, the Convention's international cooperation provisions could facilitate harmful cross-border actions that undermine the rights of vulnerable populations, particularly when information is exchanged without adequate protections or when politically motivated harassment is permitted through cooperative agreements between states.

3- CONCLUSION

A brief comparative analysis of the Budapest Convention and the United Nations Convention Against Cybercrime reveals several important insights. The "United Nations Convention Against Cybercrime: Strengthening International Cooperation for Combating Certain Crimes Committed using Information and Communications Technology Systems and for the Sharing of Electronic Evidence of Serious Crimes," commonly called the UN Convention, has not yet been formally adopted. Although the Ad Hoc Committee approved the draft by consensus, the text is still being considered by the General Assembly. Upon formal adoption, at least 40 UN Member States will enact the Convention once ratified. The Convention on Cybercrime, also known as the Budapest Convention, is a legally binding treaty established by the regional organization the Council of Europe. It has been ratified by 76 States, including both Council of Europe members and non-members. The Budapest Convention comprises two protocols developed and adopted over time. The first protocol, addressing xenophobia and racism through computer systems, was opened for signature in 2003. The second protocol, concerning enhanced cooperation and the disclosure of electronic evidence, was finalized in 2022 and has, thus far, been ratified only by Serbia and Japan. This second protocol requires five ratifications to come into force. An important distinction between the two treaties is the scope of their parties: the UN Convention is open to all UN Member States, while the Budapest Convention is limited to the 46 Member States of the Council of Europe. While the Budapest Convention and the UN Convention share the overarching goal of addressing cybercrime, their scopes differ significantly. The Budapest Convention focuses primarily on the criminalization of specific offenses—such as illegal access, data and system interference, computer-related fraud, and the distribution of child sexual abuse material. It also establishes procedural powers to combat cybercrime and promotes international cooperation through an advanced framework for cross-border access to electronic evidence (e-evidence). In contrast, the UN Convention adopts a broader approach. Its objectives extend beyond combating cybercrime to strengthen international cooperation, provide technical assistance, and enhance capacity-building efforts, particularly for developing countries. Regarding scope, the UN Convention offers a more expansive institutional and global cooperation framework. In contrast, the Budapest Convention provides more detailed coverage of specific criminal offenses and procedural powers related to cybercrime. A notable distinction lies in the applicability of e-evidence. The Budapest Convention and its Second Protocol apply to e-evidence about any criminal offense. In comparison, the UN Convention restricts its scope to offenses meeting a serious crime threshold, which is defined in the treaty as crimes punishable by a maximum deprivation of liberty of at least four years or a more severe penalty. Moreover, the UN Convention encompasses various issues, including protecting state sovereignty, preventive measures, and technical assistance and information exchange provisions. These elements extend beyond the Budapest Convention's primary focus on criminalization and procedural measures.

The UN Convention has a broader scope than the Budapest Convention, as it criminalizes additional forms of conduct. While certain offenses, such as illegal access, are similarly defined in both conventions, the UN treaty expands the range of criminalized activities, encompassing areas beyond the cyber-dependent crimes addressed by the Budapest Convention—for example, by including provisions against money laundering. Furthermore, the UN Convention adopts a more expansive approach to similar offenses, as evidenced by its provisions on child sexual abuse material. Article 9 of the Budapest Convention criminalizes actions related to such material. In contrast, Article 15 of the UN Convention extends these provisions to include solicitation, grooming, and making arrangements to commit sexual offenses against children. This broader approach seeks to prevent sexual offenses by targeting preparatory actions (e.g., solicitation and grooming) rather than focusing solely on the possession or distribution of illegal content. Nevertheless, both conventions address content-based crimes, which have been criticized for the potential risk of prosecuting victims who may possess certain types of content—mainly in cases involving real-time data collection. Such provisions raise concerns about potential misuse to target individuals rather than the perpetrators of these crimes. Both the Budapest Convention and the UN Convention emphasize the integration of child protection measures into domestic legislation. However, neither explicitly references the Optional Protocol to the Convention on the Rights of the Child on the Sale of Children, Child Prostitution, and Child Pornography, which has been ratified by 176 countries and already imposes such obligations. While both conventions reference other international treaties, they must incorporate or directly cite these instruments in their texts. The Budapest Convention is comparatively more comprehensive, explicitly referencing human rights treaties. Another distinction lies in their treatment of critical infrastructure protection. The Budapest Convention lacks specific provisions on this issue, whereas Article 21 of the UN Convention directly addresses the protection of critical information infrastructures. Conversely, the UN Convention omits offenses related to copyright infringement, which are included in the Budapest Convention. Additionally, the Budapest Convention integrates its criminalization provisions across multiple sections and strongly focuses on core cybercrime offenses, such as illegal access, data interference, and system interference. This structure reflects the Budapest Convention's narrower emphasis on crimes involving computer systems and data without extending into broader cyber-enabled crimes, as seen in the UN Convention.

The draft UN Convention remains a contentious document among states, with its initiation in 2019 stemming not from consensus but from a majority vote. Nearly two decades after Russia's initial attempt to establish a UN treaty addressing cybercrime, geopolitical shifts, and evolving majorities in favor of Russia's proposal led the UN General Assembly (GA) to create the Ad Hoc Committee to Elaborate a Comprehensive International Convention on Countering the Use of Information and Communications Technologies for Criminal Purposes (AHC). The AHC was tasked with drafting a comprehensive convention to counter the criminal misuse of information and communication technologies (ICTs), initiating a highly debated negotiation process open to all UN member states. Supported by a selected multistakeholder community, the AHC drafted a convention encompassing many provisions. The text outlines the convention's objectives, defines the scope of applicable measures and criminal offenses, and establishes regulations for international cooperation, preventive measures, technical assistance, and implementation mechanisms. Despite these efforts, the convention's adoption depends on achieving consensus on all aspects. From the first substantive session in March 2022, negotiations were polarized between a state-centric approach championed by Russia and China. They allied developing countries and a multistakeholder, human rights-focused approach led by the United States, the European Union, and other Western nations. Debates over the convention's objectives, the scope of criminalization, and human rights safeguards revealed contrasting perspectives. These divisions underscored broader geopolitical tensions between proponents of authoritarian multilateralism and advocates of democratic, multistakeholder governance. Russia, China, and their allies advocated for the broad criminalization of cyber-dependent and cyber-enabled crimes, emphasizing sovereignty. Their approach raised concerns about data access, collection, storage, and transfer, potentially enabling mass surveillance and data misuse. In contrast, the EU, the US, and like-minded states, supported by the multistakeholder community, strongly emphasized the need for robust human rights protections and focused on criminalizing cyber-dependent crimes. They warned against the dangers of a treaty that could facilitate mass surveillance, curtail freedom of expression by criminalizing content, and fail to protect journalists and security researchers. Concerns were also raised about the lack of enforcement regulations and the deference to domestic laws, which could jeopardize human rights in cyberspace. Even with inter-sessional consultations, informal working groups, proposed package deals, and compromise efforts, bridging these fundamentally different perspectives proved unattainable. Amid growing sentiment that no treaty might be preferable to a flawed one, the concluding session was suspended and reconvened in August 2024. Member states revisited a narrower draft convention, which limited references to human rights, particularly in Articles 6 and 24. Attempts by Iran to eliminate the remaining human rights references were unsuccessful. Ultimately, consensus was achieved on the draft, with all articles agreed ad referendum and proposed to the GA. While the draft UN Convention resembles the Budapest Convention, it exhibits significant differences and omissions. It includes provisions for newer crimes, such as the dissemination of intimate images, but excludes copyright infringement (Article 10 in the Budapest Convention). The UN Convention's jurisdiction is broader, allowing for its application to cybercrimes committed abroad but directed against a state party (Article 22). Non-democratic states could exploit this provision to suppress criticism abroad under the pretense of combating cybercrime. Critically, unlike the Budapest Convention, which references human rights treaties (Article 15), including those of the UN, the UN Convention needs such references. Additionally, certain provisions adapted from the Budapest Convention were altered, such as Article 29 of the UN Convention on real-time cooperation. This article draws on Article 20 of the Budapest Convention but omits its explicit references to human rights protections.

Finally, according to the author, while both conventions are considered robust documents and the result of extensive international efforts, neither has met the negotiators' expectations regarding outcomes. As discussed in various parts of the article, the recent United Nations convention has faced significant criticism and has yet to garner widespread support from countries or international organizations. In this context, it might be necessary to adopt a broader perspective on the phenomenon of regulation in cyberspace, considering the interests of nations and private entities on the one hand and human rights organizations on the other. According to the author, it may be prudent for the international community to draft the various chapters and issues of such a convention as soft law or, more specifically, behavioral codes for a medium-term period. These could then be reviewed through the perspectives and evaluations of various experts, international institutions, and nations. Once thoroughly tested as a pilot framework, this soft law could be formalized into hard law.

REFERENCES

Arquilla, J., & Ronfeldt, D. (1993). Cyberwar is coming! *Comparative Strategy*, *12*(2), 141–165. https://www.dtic.mil/cgibin/GetTRDoc?Location=U2&doc=GetTRDoc.pdf&AD=ADA485253. DOI: 10.1080/01495939308402915

Bond, R. T. J. (2001). Electronic commerce in the 21st century: Internet regulation—Heavy handed or light touch approach? A view from a European Union perspective. *William Mitchell Law Review*, *28*(2), 531–556.

Committee to Protect Journalists. (2021, August 6). Pakistan authorities detain, investigate journalists Amir Mir and Imran Shafqat. https://cpj.org/2021/08/pakistan-authorities-detain-investigate-journalists-amir-mir-and-imran-shafqat/

Council of Europe. (2024, August 9). United Nations treaty on cybercrime agreed by the Ad Hoc Committee. *Council of Europe*. https://www.coe.int/en/web/cybercrime/-/united-nations-treaty-on-cybercrime-agreed-by-the-ad-hoc-committee

Delsol, G. (2024, August 14). Draft UN Convention against cybercrime: Implications for digital global governance. *Disruptive Competition Project*. https://project-disco.org/privacy/draft-un-convention-against-cybercrime-implications-for-digital-global-governance/

Easterbrook, F. H. (1996). Cyberspace and the law of the horse. *University of Chicago Legal Forum*, *1996*(1), 207–216.

European Commission. (2024, August 13). *Commission reached an agreement on the new international cybercrime convention*. https://home-affairs.ec.europa.eu/news/commission-reached-agreement-new-international-cybercrime-convention-2024-08-13_en

Federation of Catholic Family Associations in Europe. (2024). *FAFCE comment on UN Treaty on Cybercrime*. https://www.fafce.org/fafce-comment-on-un-treaty-on-cybercrime/

Giacomello, G. (2024, December 6). The new UN cybercrime treaty is a bigger deal than even its critics realize. *Lawfare*. https://www.lawfaremedia.org/article/the-new-un-cybercrime-treaty-is-a-bigger-deal-than-even-its-critics-realize

Human Rights Watch. (2024, October 21). EU member states should vote no on UN cybercrime treaty. https://www.hrw.org/news/2024/10/21/eu-member-states-should-vote-no-un-cybercrime-treaty

Lessig, L. (1999). The law of the horse: What cyberlaw might teach. *Harvard Law Review, 113*(2), 501–549. DOI: 10.2307/1342331

Mahler, T., & Bing, J. (2006). Contractual risk management in an ICT context—Searching for a possible interface between legal methods and risk analysis. *Scandinavian Studies in Law, 49*, 339–366.

Ryan, J. J. C. H., Ryan, D. J., & Tikk, E. (2010). Cybersecurity regulation: Using analogies to develop frameworks for regulation. In Tikk, E., & Talihtrm, A.-M. (Eds.), *International cyber security: Legal & policy proceedings* (pp. 95–110). CCDCOE.

Solce, N. (2008). The battlefield of cyberspace: The inevitable new military branch—the cyber force. *Albany Law Journal of Science & Technology, 18*(2), 293–319.

Timmons, H. (2024, August 22). United Nations approves controversial cybercrime treaty. *Nextgov*. https://www.nextgov.com/digital-government/2024/08/united-nations-approves-controversial-cybercrime-treaty/398745/

United Nations Office of the High Commissioner for Human Rights. (2024, July 25). *Statement by the Special Rapporteur on Counter-Terrorism and Human Rights on the UN Cybercrime Convention*. https://www.ohchr.org/sites/default/files/documents/issues/terrorism/sr/statements/2024-07-25-stm-SR-CT-Cybercrime-Convention.pdf

Wahlgren, P. (2004). IT and legislative development. *Scandinavian Studies in Law, 47*, 601–620.

Walker, S., & Oliveira, A. P. (2024, September). The final call: UN member states adopt a new cybercrime treaty. *Global Initiative Against Transnational Organized Crime*. https://globalinitiative.net/wp-content/uploads/2024/09/Summer-Walker-Ana-Paula-Oliveira-The-final-call-UN-member-states-adopt-a-new-cybercrime-treaty-GI-TOC-September-2024.pdf

Zeller, B. (2007). *CISG and the unification of international trade law*. Routledge.

Zirin, J. D. (2009, October 14). Abdicating on a 'cyber czar'? *Los Angeles Times*. https://www.latimes.com/archives/la-xpm-2009-oct-14-oe-zirin14-story.html

Chapter 8
Cybercrimes in Bharatiya Nyaya Sanhita:
A Critical Study on Indian Legal Scenario

Jipson Joseph
https://orcid.org/0009-0005-1795-5051
Christ University, India

Ananya Pandey
https://orcid.org/0000-0002-2419-6314
Christ University, India

ABSTRACT

Cybersecurity is a significant concern in the present digital world. The increase in cybercrimes attracts attention of the whole globe. India is one of the top countries on the list of cybercrimes and cyberattacks. More than 1 billion people use smartphones in India and the focus on digital economy has also attracted many cyberattacks. This necessitates the need for a specific legal framework. India's Penal Code was almost 160 years old, and its provisions were not adequate to address the growing nature of cybercrime. Though the provisions of Information Technology Act, 2000 can be applied, India needed a criminal code addressing the latest trends of crimes. Many considered that the enactment of Bharatiya Nyaya Sanhita (BNS) will provide this required framework. In making a critical analysis the chapter tries to evaluate the provisions of BNS to examine whether it provided due protection to India's cyberspace.

DOI: 10.4018/979-8-3693-8871-6.ch008

INTRODUCTION

Cybersecurity is closely associated with protecting information and communication technology (ICT), its network, and its contents (Kumar, 2022). In the previous centuries, security was understood in terms of national security and national borders protection (Shairgojri & Dar, 2022). But in the present age of internet, security of the nation has become a convoluted eroteme as the open environment of internet makes the basic systems of the State, vulnerable (Cavelty, 2012). This trend evolved from the second half of the 20th century causing severe security threats (OECD, 2012). The states, therefore, give high relevance to cybersecurity considering it to be one of the top security issues (Cavelty, 2012). India, the world's most populous country, faces an unparalleled increase in cybercrimes. This was mainly due to the advancement of technology and the internet revolution of the 21st century. The 'data revolution' initiated by the Reliance Gio and the increased availability of a variety of smartphones have changed the lifestyle of the Indian population. Many people spend hours in the virtual world rather than being occupied with real-life situations. The virtual world provides many good things like new knowledge, entertainment, interaction, and business opportunities. But at the same time, it also leads people to many crimes such as addiction to child pornography, defamatory comments on social media, and the like. Many people use cyberspace to spoil the reputation, wealth, and relationships of others. Some even use it against national security concerns. There is an unprecedented growth in cybercrimes in India. Many people become victims of this virtual world of crimes daily. However, India lacks efficient enactments and effective mechanisms to confront the growing cybercrimes (Patkar & Dhakad 2022).

The Indian Penal Code (IPC) was enacted in 1860, and it upheld Victorian morality as India was under the British Empire. The IPC tried to ensure peace and security by enlisting various crimes and their punishments in 511 sections. It together with the Indian Evidence Act, 1872 and the Criminal Procedure Code of 1973 shaped India's fight against various crimes. However, these could not address the changing circumstances that resulted in new types of crimes of the present times. More than real-life crimes, virtual crimes or cybercrimes affect the lives of people. In order to address the cybercrimes various acts like the Information Technology Act of 2000, the Reserve Bank of India Act of 2018, the National Cyber Security Strategy of 2020, the Information Technology Rules of 2021, and the Digital Personal Data Protection Act of 2023 were enacted. But a specific focus on cybercrimes in the penal code was missing.

In this context, the IPC, 1860 was replaced with Bharatiya Nyaya Sanhita (BNS) in July 2024. Together with BNS, Bharatiya Sakshya Abhiniyam (BSA) and Bharatiya Nagarik Suraksha Sanhita (BNSS) were also brought in to replace the Indian Evidence Act and the Criminal Procedure Code, respectively. The bill to replace all these three were introduced in the Parliament in December 2023 and got the assent of the President in the same month. These codes introduced the digitalization of Indian criminal system in order to face the changed face of crimes including cybercrimes. It penalizes cybercrimes and false information. But at the same time, there are questions and apprehensions about whether it helps to address all the areas of cybercrimes. Being the latest enactment, it should have incorporated all the areas of cybercrimes in order to ensure justice for people. But how far this objective is achieved should be analyzed and this chapter attempts to make a critical examination in this context to measure the cybersecurity policies and regulations of the Indian legal scenario.

Cybersecurity: An Overview

The current IT revolution originates from to the combination of telecommunication with computers in the 1970s-80s. Together with this revolutionary move, there also emerged the problem of cyber threats (Cavelty, 2012). Cybersecurity is the attempt to secure cyberspace from privacy encroachment, unauthorized access to ICT programs, illegal monitoring, use of the cyberspace for illegal activity, and exploitation. Cybersecurity functions by protecting the ICT programs and data. Its prime objective is the protection of digital information (Kumar, 2022). According to the Information Technology (IT) Act of 2000 cybersecurity refers to “protecting information, equipment, devices, computer, computer resource, communication device and information stored therein from unauthorized access, use, disclosure, disruption, modification, or destruction” (§2nb). Cybersecurity, thus, is basically a protective mechanism to ensure the security of information and technology. Any kind of illegal activity like unauthorized access, use, modification, or destruction of information and technological devices comes under the ambit of cyber insecurity. It is increasingly becoming a policy issue that touches the core areas of a State such as the economy, education, healthcare, law enforcement, technology, military, and intelligence (OECD, 2012).

India’s cyberspace is vast. As of June 2023, there were 840 million people’s online presence and 1.1 billion smartphone users as of December 2023 in India (DSCI, 2023). With the tagline of “digital India,” the government of India promotes the digitalization process in almost all the areas including defense, energy, finance, transport, communication, cyber connectivity, e-commerce services, and services like the Unique Identification Development Authority of India (UIDAI). However, to secure these IT related activities, India requires strong policies for the protection of these areas (Verma & Sharma, 2014). In 2022-23, the government of India realizing the increased importance of cybersecurity allotted 515 crore rupees for the protection of cyberspace (Shairgojri & Dar, 2022).

For effective functioning, cybersecurity requires factors like threat modelling, assessment of vulnerability, analysis of risks, and best security efforts (Mukhopadhyay, 2022). Cybersecurity includes various elements such as application security, information security, network security, business security, and operational security. That is, cybersecurity demands an inclusive and holistic vision of security (Tejpal et al., 2023). Cybersecurity, though it primarily deals with cyberspace and data protection, has a wider horizon as it is the most essential feature of national security in the current scenario. The most complex impact of cyberattacks in the present times is that they can utterly damage the daily lives of people by damaging all the necessary systems for human survival. From this perspective, countries like India need to give utmost priority to cybersecurity.

Cybercrimes: An Exposition

Together with the growth in technological innovation, its connectivity and complexity also increased causing more chances for cybercrimes (Cavelty, 2012). Cybercrime originates from cyberspace, but it can also include offline software attacks. In 1995, Sussman and Heuston used the word cybercrimes for the first time (Palreddy, 2020). Cybercrimes refer to the illegal activities in the context of internet usage. In these crimes, the perpetrator and the victim will not have any direct contact in most of the cases. Cybercrimes are more complicated as they do not have any territorial boundaries and the perpetrators are primarily anonymous (Tejpal et al., 2023). Cybercrimes include not only cyberattacks against critical infrastructure but also data breaches, website destruction, email bombing, cyberterrorism, malicious computer worms like Stuxnet, cyber defamation, political hacktivism, and various destabilizing activities (Shairgojri & Dar, 2022). Cybercrimes includes various cyberattacks like phishing (hackers using this technique send phishing emails that have the appearance of a credible source to the targets with an attachment to trick the receiver), malware (malicious software that is sent by a link to harm the system of other people), Denial-of-Service (it creates an artificial traffic more significant than it could handle for forcing the authorized users to pay for the access), SQL Injection (through this method they attack database), Drive-by Attack (does not require receiver's action, but the attacker attaches a malware in a webpage for harming the system), Password attack (for having unauthorized access to the system, mostly it is guess work), Man in the Middle Attack (hackers steal information by standing in the middle of the user and program, especially in the financial apps), Eavesdropping

Attack (intercepts information being sent through a network), and Cross-site scripting attack (debases the data set with vindicative JavaScript) (Tejpal et al., 2023).

Cybercrimes cause various problems for individuals, business institutions, properties, and governments. Cybercrimes against individuals mainly concentrate on circulating and distributing obscene materials, violating their privacy, and stealing their assets. By becoming victims of cybercrimes, people lose their wealth, identity, privacy, and emotional stability. Business firms will be facing severe financial damage, reputational loss, and issues in the area of customer trust. Governments will be facing severe problems in the area of safeguarding critical information infrastructure and sensitive information affecting its daily functioning (Tejpal et al., 2023).

CYBERCRIMES IN INDIA

Cybercrimes and cyberattacks are rapidly increasing across the globe (Duraiswamy, 2017). Between 2021-2022, there were 16,312 security incidents and the average cost of a data breach in 2023 was USD 4.45 million (DSCI, 2023). In this line, cybercrimes in India have exponentially increased from 2013 onwards. It is estimated that there is almost an 85% increase from 2013 to 2020 in the number of cybercrimes (Tejpal et al., 2023). India is one among the top five countries with regard to cyberattacks (Devi, 2019). India was the second most affected country in the area of targeted cyberattacks between 2016 and 2018 and an average data breach in India cost INR 11.9 crore. Besides, CERT-IN had to handle almost 2 lakh cases in 2018 compared to 53000 cases in 2014 (DSCI, 2020). In 2022, there were 13,91,457 cyber security incidents in India (DSCI, 2023). Such an increase in cybercrimes is due to the weak cybersecurity mechanism (Kshetri, 2016). One of the predominant areas of cybercrime in India is the banking and finance sector. Since this sector has increasingly incorporated IT into its daily activities for the growth of the industry, in the absence of efficient mechanisms, it is prone to cybercrimes (Jain 2014). Increased incorporation of IT in India's defense and military systems has caused cyberattacks against the military resulting in the theft of some important military and state secrets (Aiyengar 2010). In 2012, some hackers attacked the Indian Navy's computer systems (Pubby, 2012). Between 1994-2004, 60% of the cyberattacks against India were targeted on autonomous power systems. In 1998, a group of hackers placed anti-India and anti-nuclear remarks on the website of the Bhabha Atomic Research Centre (BARC). It again had to confront another hacker attack in which it exposed some of its sensitive materials (Patkar & Dhakad, 2022). In 2012, northern India was affected by a blackout causing damage to various systems, disrupting oil flow, bringing chaos to traffic lights and systems, and causing complexities to the daily lives of people (Shuran et al., 2013).

Indians lost almost 177 crore in the financial year 2023-24 due to various types of cyber frauds. During the financial year it was around 70 crores affirming that there is an enormous increase in the magnitude of cyber frauds using credit and debit cards and internet banking (Chadha, 2024). The Indian Cyber Crime Coordination Centre (I4C) working under the supervision of the Ministry of Home Affairs warned the citizens to take precaution against the fraudulent emails that are sent to individuals in the name of the Government of India (Singh, 2024). In the last one year, many cases have been reported, including the instances of celebrities, who became victims of virtual arrest fraud. The I4C thus warned that no legal enforcement mechanism in India (CBI, Police, or Judiciary) has virtually arrested a person in a video call (NDTV, 2024). Cyber extortion is another kind of contemporary cyberattack. It is a kind of blackmailing, but it takes place in the virtual world. In most such cases, the criminals claim that they have some private information or video of the victims and demand money for keeping it secret (NCR&IC, 2021). Along the same line, there is also some loan providing online apps (PowerBank, Tesla Power Bank) that give loans to people without much procedure, but their interest rates are so high, and they also demand access to the contacts, photos, and videos of the victims. If the victims fail to give the huge interest and pay back the loan, then they start to blackmail them forcing many people to suicide in Telangana and Kerala (Goyal, 2022; The Hindu Bureau, 2023). All these cases show that the increase in cyberattacks, and cybercrimes adversely affects India's economy and public safety (Devi, 2019).

Indian Initiatives to Confront Cybercrimes

The increasing cyberattacks demanded more spending on cybersecurity. India's cybersecurity service market thus increased from USD 949 million in 2019 to USD 2.3 billion in 2023 (DSCI, 2023). In the context of growing cyberattacks, any State machinery needs to design appropriate tools for protecting private information, crucial commercial information, and national security (Shairgojri & Dar, 2022). The agreements that are done by Indian citizens or Indian companies under the provisions of the Contract Act, 1872, can have clauses like confidentiality, privacy, and arbitration clauses and that can be employed for the protection against cyber-attacks and data encroachment as well. Though there is constitutional protection to the implied right of privacy (Kharak Singh v. State of UP) and the enactment of IT Act in 2000 for the security of cyberspace, specific enactments and mechanisms are required to protect data and cyberspace.

Constitutional Protection

Privacy is not mentioned in the Constitution and is not even discussed in the Constitutional Assembly (Bhatia, 2014). But from the Kharak Singh case onwards, the judiciary started to consider the right to privacy as part of the fundamental rights. Article 21 of the Constitution of India while dealing with the fundamental right of liberty also includes the right to privacy as its constituent element. Article 19(1)(a) also can have a reference to the right to privacy although it is applicable only with reasonable restrictions that are provided in 19(2). The Judiciary incorporated the right to privacy into the Constitution of India as an essential feature of the fundamental rights inspired by many international human rights instruments like UDHR and ICCPR. Indian judicial system has given paramount importance to the right to privacy as it affirmed that this right can be restricted only in extreme situations like the case of national security (Duraiswamy, 2017).

Various Mechanisms for cybersecurity

The following mechanisms have been designed by the Indian government for safeguarding its citizens and systems from cyberattacks.

The National Informatics Centre (NIC) was instituted under the Ministry of Electronics and IT in 1976. Its main objective was to provide technology supported solution to the various ICT related problems of the Centre and State governments. NIC is responsible for designing and developing IT systems for the government. It also advises government in the ambit of various emerging technologies (NIC, n. d.).

Indian Computer Emergency Response Team (CERT-In) is a functional organ of the Ministry of Electronics and IT. It has been operational since 2004 onwards and it began with the intention to safeguard government systems from cyberattacks. It is the national nodal agency for confronting cybercrimes when they occur (MeitY, 2004). It has been given functions like a) collection, analysis, and dissemination of cyber incident related information; b) alerting and advising of cyber security incidents; c) devising emergency measures for handling cyber incidents; d) Coordination of response activities against cyber incidents; e) providing guidelines, advisories, white papers, security practices, and other vital information against cyber incidents; and f) other relevant functions in the ambit of cybersecurity (IT Act, 2000, §70B).

Cyber Swachh Kendra functions under CERT-In and is a significant unit of the Indian government's Digital India framework. This center functions under the provisions of the IT Act, 2000 (§70B). it functions with the support of other actors in this field. It is assigned to secure India's cyber space by detecting botnet infections (it can be against a particular system or a group of systems) and to notify about the infection and provide support to clean and secure systems. It empowers CISOs and other IT professionals with more awareness about cybercrimes (MeitY, n. d.).

Cyber Surakshit Bharat is another project in this field. It was launched by the Ministry of Electronics and IT in association with the national e-Governance division and industry partners as a public-private partnership in 2018. This program functions based on three principles like awareness, education, and enablement. It aims to provide awareness and educate people about the various cyberattacks and cybercrimes so that the people, systems, and industries will be enabled to face such complexities (MeitY, 2018).

The National Critical Information Infrastructure Protection Centre (NCIIPC) is created by the Government of India under the provisions given by the 2008 amendment of the IT Act, 2000. NCIIPC came into effect in 2014 with the Gazette notification. It has the responsibility to provide protection to critical information infrastructure. (IT Act, 2000, §70A). Its objective is to protect India's critical information infrastructure from unauthorized access, modification, disruption, and destruction through various methods by raising security awareness among stakeholders (NCIIPC, 2024).

The Information Technology Act, 2000

The IT Act, 2000 was enacted by the Parliament of India to address the growing cybercrimes and cyberattacks as the IPC provisions were inadequate to confront and prosecute such modern-day crimes. In reality, the IT Act is a UNCITRAL (United Nations Commission on International Trade Law) model law, specifically in the field of e-commerce, and is not a law on cybercrimes. But the lawmakers were clever enough to add its chapter XI particularly focusing on cybercrimes. This has contributed to giving coverage to various crimes that are not covered under the IPC. However, certain cybercrimes, especially crimes against individuals, like cyber-stalking, cyber-defamation, and cyber-nuisance are not covered under the sections of the IT Act (Duggal, 2005). The IT Act was amended in 2008 to provide more security options against cybercrimes. The IT Act deals with many cybercrimes and punishments that are not explicitly mentioned in the IPC.

Data or information protection is an essential area of concern for individuals, firms, and government in the present times. The amendment of the IT Act thus affirmed that if a body corporate does not possess, deal, or handle any sensitive information or data, negligent of reasonable security measures, then it should pay damages to the affected persons (§43A). The section XI of the Act gives the details of offences that are related to the area of cybercrimes. Computer source documents need to be protected otherwise it will create complexities. The Act therefore considers any kind of tampering with the computer source documents as an offence (§65). The IT Act states that any attempt to offend or menace the character of a person by sending offensive messages via ICT is an offence. If the message is sent to annoy, deceive, or mislead the receiver, then it becomes an offence (§66A). The Act considers the act of receiving stolen computer or communication device (§66B), stealing the signature or password or any other unique identification feature (§66C), cheating by personation through computer or communication device (§66D), violating the right to privacy of a person by capturing, publishing, or transmitting the image of a private area of a person without his/her consent (§66E), and threatening the unity, integrity, security, or sovereignty of India or terrifying people or any section of people through ICT mediums (§66F) are considered as grave offences.

The cultural capital of India has high respect for the dignity of women and the sacredness of sexual act. The Act therefore considers any act of publishing or transmitting obscene materials, sexually explicit acts, or depicting children in sexually explicit acts as an offence (§67-67B). The Act further empowers the government to authorize any agency to monitor or collect data or information transmitted through ICT for the demands of cybersecurity (§69B). The Act also speaks about the possibilities of nodal agencies, punishments, and other means for safeguarding the cyberspace from various attacks. The IT Act of 2000 with its amendment in 2008 thus tried to design a legal framework for ensuring cybersecurity which was lacking in the sections of IPC.

National Cybersecurity Policy 2013

The policy defines cyberspace as a complex environment that includes interactions between people, systems, and services with the support of the global distribution of ICT devices, connectivity, and methods. This space is equally owned by individual citizens, businessmen, institutions, and governments making it difficult to separate lines between these users. India uses cyberspace in almost all the fields like education, healthcare, financial institutions, and public services. But cyberspace is vulnerable to many intentional or accidental incidents. Cyberattacks like organized cyberattacks, uncontrolled exploits like viruses and malicious software, and national disasters with major cyber consequences targeting the economic well-being and confidence of people in the structures cause many issues. These attacks majorly affect critical information systems. It requires trust and confidence in the systems, software, and services.

The national cybersecurity policy covers home users, small, medium, and large-scale enterprises and both government and non-government entities. It defines and guides the actions related to cyberspace. It supports both individual and institutional actors to define its own cyber policies suited to their needs. In addition, it aims at public-private collaborative actions for promoting the country's security in the cyberspace. The policy's vision is therefore underlined as to provide a secure cyberspace for citizens, business ventures, and governments. Its mission is fourfold such as protecting information in cyberspace, building capabilities against cyber threats, reducing the vulnerabilities of people, businesses, and governments in cyberspace, and minimizing the damage from cyber incidents. The policy functions its visions and mission through fourteen objectives, all of which are closely related in putting into practice the mission of the policy. The policy also provides strategies like the creation of a secure cyber environment and an assurance framework, encouragement to open standards, empowerment of regulatory framework, creation of mechanisms for early warning of threats, vulnerability management, and threat management, protection of e-governance services, protection of critical information infrastructure, encouragement of research and development in cybersecurity, alleviation of supply chain risks, development of human resources, creation of cybersecurity awareness, fostering public-private collaborations, sharing of information and cooperation, prioritization of implementation, and operationalization of the policy for the effective cybersecurity management in India.

National Cybersecurity Strategy 2020

The National Cybersecurity Strategy was prepared by the Data Security Council of India (DSCI) in 2020. This strategy is envisioned for five years and should deal with technology transformations. DSCI realizes that India must enhance its cybersecurity measures as India is on the way to becoming a 1Tn dollar economy and it will be impossible in the absence of active engagement in cyberspace. India, in the present scenario, actively concentrates on digitalization of public services requiring an enthusiastic drive for cybersecurity. Digitalization energizes economic development and India with the 'Make-in-India" project tries to widen its horizons of growth. This necessitates the security of the supply chain, which is intricately connected with cybersecurity. The States are now more vulnerable to cyberattacks from both State and non-State actors. This is very much seen in India as many target on India's critical information infrastructure. Cybersecurity focuses on the protection of critical information infrastructure as any attack on these basic essentials will create chaos. Besides, India in line with other countries focuses on a digital economy for ensuring environmental sustainability. But at the same time, it also causes many challenges as it can become prone to cyberattacks. There should be an effective mechanism for its smooth functioning without causing loss to its users and customers. The strategy also demands the State to provide efficient guidelines and regulations for the meaningful working of the digital economy.

The strategy demands to have separate state level security policies and programs as the national cybersecurity would be incomplete without state level cybersecurity initiatives. The States should by empowered by developing capabilities to address cybersecurity threats and should develop a proper mechanism for monitoring the preparedness and performance of cybersecurity activities. The Union Government should coordinate such activities of the States. Besides, small and medium businesses are increasingly becoming digital. In such a perspective, cybersecurity become an utmost concern of such agents.

The national cybersecurity strategy is a historic attempt to ensure India's security in the cyberspace. It emphasizes in enhancing the country's data governance. Adopting a data-centric approach to security, it promotes the adoption of suitable data governance practices. Since India's IT related business is on the rise and is expected to reach USD 350 billion by 2025, utmost care should be given to the security of ICT. However, the cybercrimes are increasing at a fast pace. National cybersecurity strategy thus insists on investigating such crimes more efficiently using digital forensic technologies, methods, and legal procedures. It calls for legislative reform to give immediate attention to issues like spamming and fake news, evaluating technology transformation on a timely basis, and creating a legislative roadmap for the coming years. It advocates for timely compilation and dissemination of information in the area of cybercrimes particularly explaining its modus operandi and patterns. It insists on setting up specific courts for the speedy trial of cybercrimes. It also calls for the formation of a central team that coordinates the investigation of interstate cybercrimes.

Other Cybersecurity Regulations

Besides those mentioned above, there are also some other significant enactments and regulations in the context of cybercrime. As per the provision of the IT Act, 2000, the MeitY framed the Information Technology (Reasonable Security Practices and Procedures and Sensitive Personal Data or Information) Rules, commonly known as SDPI Rules in 2011. These rules are applicable to persons and corporate bodies located in India. They impose strict requirements with regard to the users' sensitive data or information. These rules were amended in 2021 with the title, the Information Technology (Intermediary Guidelines and Digital Media Ethics Code) Rules. This was in view of keeping India's legal framework applicable to ever changing digital landscape and to provide protection to the users. These rules demanded a high amount of accountability from digital platforms. In 2023, the Parliament of India enacted the Digital Personal Data Protection Act, which was mainly inspired by the European Union's General Data Protection Regulation (GDPR). The Act's primary objective was to protect the personal data of the customers in order to foster a fiduciary relationship. Besides, the Reserve Bank of India in 2016 mandated the Know Your Customer (KYC) requirement in order to prevent instances of money laundering and financial terrorism and to uphold the stability and integrity of the Indian financial system.

THE INDIAN PENAL CODE AND CYBERCRIMES: AN ANALYSIS

The Indian Penal Code (IPC) of 1860 does not have the provisions of privacy violation or data privacy as at the time of its enactment, it was not a serious concern of the society. The data became a priority in the ambit of digitalization only. But the provisions of IPC can be employed, in the absence of specific laws to address cybercrimes, with reference to other related crimes for punishing the offenders. Violations against cyberspace can be prosecuted under theft (§378-379), misappropriation of property (§403), and criminal breach of trust (§405-409). The purposive interpretation of the legislative enactment would be a strong tool for the application of IPC with regard to cybercrimes. Section 403 IPC specifies that this offence is against the misappropriation or dishonest conversion of movable property. Movable property implies that it is not a land and not attached to anything and thus it also includes one's personal data in the cyberspace as well (Duraiswamy, 2017).

Provisions in the IPC Applicable to Cybercrimes

Though IPC does not explicitly deal with cybercrimes, the following sections can be employed in addition to the IT Act for the procedure of cybercrimes.

Section 292 IPC – This section deals with the sale, distribution, or public exhibition of obscene materials tempting people to read, see, or hear the matter contained in it. This section's application includes the distribution or public exhibition of obscene materials in cyberspace. Though the persons who voluntarily watch obscene materials cannot sue against the producers of those materials, it can used against those who circulate such obscene materials to people without their consent. The punishment for this crime is imprisonment for 2 years together with fine (Palreddy, 2020).

Section 354 IPC – It primarily speaks about violating the modesty of women by using force. Its subsections are closely related to cybercrimes. Section 354A states that if any man demands or requests sexual favors, shows pornography against the will of a woman, or makes sexually colored remarks, then he shall be punished for sexual harassment. If the demands of sexual favors or the sexually colored remarks are made through cyberspace, then it will become cybercrime. But it will be tried under this section. Section 354B provides the punishment for disrobing a woman by using assault or criminal force, which also can be done through video calls in cyberspace. Section 354C is a provision against voyeurism. If any man uses camera or such kind of recording material to copy or record the image of the private part or private act of a woman that happens in a private space, then it is punishable under this clause. It also takes into account the showing of such things to third persons as a crime. Section 354D is a precaution against stalking. If the stalking is done through cyberspace, then it will become cyberstalking and also will be covered under this provision. This clause was added by the Criminal Law (Amendment) Act of 2013.

Section 411 IPC – This section guards against those who knowingly receive stolen property, and it can include mobile phones, data, or computer. Personation has become a common method of fraud in the contemporary times. Section 419 IPC guards against personation. Email phishing comes under this category. Both sections 419 and 420 are applicable in cases of password theft for fraudulent objectives and the making of bogus websites (Palreddy, 2020).

Email spoofing is a widespread threat in the present context and many people become victims of such threats losing their wealth and happiness. Since it is created by forging the sender's address, it can be sued under the section 465 (Anil Kumar Srivastava v. Addl Director, MHFW); if cheating is intended by email spoofing, then it can be tried under section 468; and if it is done to harm the reputation of another person, then it can be tried under section 469. Defaming any person by sending emails with defamatory content and abusive messages also will attract section 500 of IPC (Palreddy, 2020).

Drawbacks of IPC in relation to Cybercrimes

In Jagjit Singh v. State of Punjab, the Supreme Court of India clearly stated that the increasing number of hacking and data theft insists that these cases should not only be tried under the provisions of the IT Act but also under the sections of IPC. The IPC has no direct concern for cybercrimes as it did not foresee such crimes while framing the Penal Code. The application of a criminal code, which is almost 160 years old was the main drawback with regard to cybercrimes (Chacko et al. 2021). The above-mentioned provisions of IPC together with the provisions of the IT Act were applied in many instances of cybercrimes, but at the same time, there was no specific provision to deal with the current evolving nature of cybercrimes. The modus operandi of both traditional crimes and cybercrimes are different, and so there should be proper mechanism and procedure to address these new forms of crimes.

NEW CRIMINAL CODE AND CYBERCRIMES: AN EXPLORATION

India's new criminal code was enacted by the Parliament of India in December 2023 with the title Bharatiya Nyaya Sanhita (BNS), repealing and replacing the IPC of 1860. The IPC depicted the pre-Independent Victorian morality and legal system emphasizing punishment. The enactment of BNS together with Bharatiya Nagarik Suraksha Sanhita (BNSS) repealing the Criminal Procedure Code of 1972 and Bharatiya Sakshya Abhiniyam (BSA) replacing the Indian Evidence Act of 1872, tries to delete the colonial imprints from India's justice delivery system. However, the reformation of a legal code, first and foremost, should be in terms of the ever-evolving social norms and practices (Thomas & Jagani, 2024). The BNS not only Indianizes the title of the criminal code but also affirms the core of Indian cultural capital, Nyaya or justice. The BNS emphasizes that the prime objective of the code is not punishment but to deliver justice. Rajiv Mani, Secretary of Legal Affairs in the Ministry of Law and Justice, argues that the BNS is not based on colonial prejudices and practices, but on principles of equal access to justice. D. Y. Chandrachud, the Chief Justice of India, affirmed that it will give a holistic approach to dealing with various crimes in this digital age (Ministry of Law and Justice, 2024).

The reformation of the criminal code is intended to simplify the legal procedure and enable the contemporary legal framework to provide speedy justice to the citizens (Thomas & Jagani, 2024). Compared to the 511 sections in 26 chapters of IPC, the BNS has only 358 sections in 20 chapters. It added 20 new sections and deleted 20 provisions of IPC. Since the BNS is the latest enactment, it introduces certain provisions that are designed to address the vulnerabilities and challenges of people in the instances of cybercrimes. The BNS functions only prospectively, that is, from the date of its implementation on 30 June 2024.

Provisions of BNS with regard to Cybersecurity

The BNS does not define cybercrimes and so it can be considered as all those illegal activities that include technology like hacking, phishing, and cyber-stalking. Section 2(8) of BNS affirms that documents also include 'electronic and digital record.' The new criminal code consists of a new section for organized crimes and economic offences and cybercrimes are included in the ambit of organized crimes (§111). By enlisting cybercrimes as part of organized crimes, the BNS wants to protect citizens against the illegal activities of persons working in groups or criminal syndicate. Among the petty organized crimes theft through card skimming and theft of ATMs are also included to provide cybersecurity (§112). Anyone who incites any separatist activities or rebellion against the unity, integrity, and sovereignty of India through electronic communication will be liable to punishment (§152). The BNS has enlarged certain sections that were already existing in the IPC with new words intending to include cybercrimes as well. While dealing with those activities that promote enmity between groups, section 196 states that it also includes electronic communication. Section 197 also adds electronic communication to the list of modus operandi that cause troubles against national integrity. Section 294, which deals with obscenity expressly includes the contents shared through electronic medium. The statements of any person that cause public mischief includes the communication through electronic medium as well (§353). Further, publishing any kind of material that jeopardizes the sovereignty and security of India is also a criminal act (§197(1)(d)).

Besides, the above-mentioned express reference to certain acts that are done through cyberspace as crimes, the BNS, in line with the IPC, indirectly enlists certain crimes belonging to the category of cybercrimes. Section 75 speaks about sexual harassment that includes inter alia sexually colored remarks, which can be both in physical and electronic means. Section 77 guards against voyeurism. It has a direct reference to electronic or digital data as it states that it can include unauthorized recording and dissemination of private images. But it is a reproduction of section 354C of IPC. Section 78 reproduces in verbatim the section 354D of IPC that mentions cyberstalking. Section 79 warns against outraging the modesty of women. It can also happen through electronic means (Sharma, 2024). Most of the provisions that we have analyzed as part of IPC are applicable in the present BNS also. The newly enacted BNS has included cybercrimes both directly and indirectly in order to ensure a more meaningful cybersecurity framework.

Cybersecurity: Provisions in BNSS and BSA

The BNS functions along with the provisions of BNSS and BSA. A holistic approach of all the three codes is essential for the true functioning of justice. All the three codes affirm the importance of electronic or digital record and acknowledge the increasing number of cybercrimes in the present times. The provisions of BNSS and BSA give more clarity to the sections enlisted in BNS and empower the judiciary.

The BNSS has incorporated the inclusion of digital technologies for reducing delay in justice delivery system. It also mandated the use of audio-visual communications and electronic communication in various procedures for accelerating the court procedure. It demands to record the audio-video of search and seizure (§105), to record the audio-video of the rape victim's evidence (§176(1)), and to collect forensic evidence from the crime scenes that attract punishment of seven or more years of imprisonment (§176(3)). The police officer can record the audio-video of the witnesses if it seems to be fitting (§180(3)).

The BSA affirms electronic or digital records as primary evidence. Its explanation 4 underlines that if an electronic or digital record is stored in multiple files, each such file is primary evidence. Explanation 5 argues that if an electronic or digital record is produced from proper custody, it is primary evidence, if not disputed. Explanation 6 claims that if a video is recorded and simultaneously stored in electronic form and, at the same time, transmitted, broadcast, or transferred to another, then each of those stored recordings is primary evidence. Explanation 7 states that the electronic or digital record stored is in multiple storage options in a computer resource, and each of them including the temporary files is primary evidence. Its section 63 affirms that the electronic or digital records must meet specific authentic criteria in order to be admitted in the court for the procedure. It outlines specific guidelines and safeguards for the admissibility of such records as evidence.

A Criticism of the New Criminal Justice System

The replacement of IPC with BNS is a historic moment in the legal framework of independent India. The replacement provided many options for addressing the evolving trends and patterns of crimes. It deleted some outdated ideas and misconceptions about the societal and individual life. By deleting provisions like adultery and homosexual acts, and increasing the age in some instances, and providing new and severe punishment for certain crimes like gang rape, the BNS tried to be more justice oriented. However, compared to many other enriching sections and provisions, the provisions with regard to cybercrimes are very rarely addressed. The direct references to cybercrimes are very few and the indirect references are mostly the repetition of what was stated in the IPC. Though the BNS speaks about cybercrimes, it does not define cybercrimes leading to confusion. As the instances of cybercrimes in the 21st century is irresistibly growing, countries like India require an ardent regulatory framework with the possibilities of strict enforcement mechanisms and robust data governance practices (Duraiswamy, 2017). But unfortunately, this objective was not fully met by the enactment of the new criminal code.

Both cybercrimes and economic offences are mentioned in the BNS. But at the same time, it should have been extensively dealt with as these are increasing at a fast pace. The lawmakers might have thought that since there is IT Act, 2000 and its provisions are actively employed against cybercrimes, there is not much requirement for specific mentioning in the BNS. They might have thought, as the Latin maxim says, *generalia sepcialibus non derogant* (general laws do not prevail over the special laws), but the specific listing of the present-day major cybercrimes would have given a more positive and progressive vision to cybersecurity attempts. The BNS has made a lot of positive steps in ensuring justice-oriented judicial procedure. In such a perspective, it should have given more weightage to BNS, if it had given some more attention to cybercrimes, as they are growing uncontrollably in the Indian soil making millions of Indians victims of such illegal activities.

CONCLUSION AND RECOMMENDATIONS

Cybersecurity has become a prime concern for India in the context of growing cyberattacks. India is one of the hotspots for cybercrime. The growth of technology and the easy availability of smartphones have reshaped the digital landscape of India. The advancement of the digital economy and the importance given to digital payments has extended the horizon of cyber criminals. Since the availability of the internet is extended even to the remote areas of Indian villages, the number of poor and illiterate people using such technological advancements is also growing. They easily become victims of cybercrimes. However, the Indian scenario states that not only illiterate but also literate people become victims of cybercrimes. The uncontrollable increase in cybercrimes creates confusion and dissatisfaction among people, adversely affects the credibility of the financial and business institutions, and lessens the economic growth of the country. The growing nature of cybercrimes demands stringent guidelines and regulations in view of cybersecurity.

India followed a legal framework enacted in 1860 which did not even foresee the digital era. But certain provisions were added in through various amendments to address the cyberspace related crimes. Together with the indirect applications of the various provisions of IPC, the Indian legal framework employs the IT Act of 2000, the national cybersecurity policy of 2013, the national cybersecurity strategy of 2020, and other mechanisms and regulations to protect the cyberspace. Many thought that the newly enacted BNS would be able to give a strong cybersecurity framework. But the BNS is mostly reproducing what was already provided in the IPC. Since the present Indian society is almost digital in nature and many cyber frauds and cybercrimes originate from India, and many Indians become victims of such cybercrimes, there is an urgent requirement for empowering the cybersecurity provisions in the BNS. The specific definition of cybercrimes and mention of various categories of cybercrimes are essential for cybersecurity. Besides, just as the cybercrimes are constantly evolving, the cybersecurity provisions also need to be updated. More awareness creation programs at the local and regional levels are required to empower the people against the wide range of cybercrimes. Together with this, the legal mechanism must properly implement the provisions provided and ensure justice for the victims.

REFERENCES

Aiyengar, S. R. R. (2010). *National Strategy for Cyberspace Security*. KW Publisher.

Anil Kumar Srivastava v. Addl Director, MHFW, 2005(3) ESC 1917.

Cavelty, M. D. (2012). The Militarization of Cybersecurity as a Source of Global Tension. In *Strategic Trends 2012: Key Development in Global Affairs* (pp.103-124). Centre for Security Studies.

Chacko, M., Misra, A., & Ramaswamy, S. (2021). Cybersecurity Laws in India: Is it time for a Regime Change? *Legal500*. https://www.legal500.com/developments/thought-leadership/cybersecurity-laws-in-india-is-it-time-for-a-regime-change/#_ftn5

Chadha, S. (2024). Cyber Frauds Cost India Rs. 177 Crore in FY24: How to Protect Yourself. *Business Standard*. https://www.business-standard.com/finance/personal-finance/cyber-frauds-cost-india-rs-177-crore-in-fy24-how-to-protect-yourself-124080600123_1.html

Devi, S. (2019). Cybersecurity in the National Security Discourse. *World Affairs*, *23*(2), 146–159.

DSCI. (2020). National Cybersecurity Strategy. https://www.dsci.in/files/content/knowledge-centre/2023/National-Cyber-Security-Strategy-2020-DSCI-submission.pdf

DSCI. (2023). India: Cybersecurity Domestic Report 2023. https://www.dsci.in/resource/content/india-cybersecurity-domestic-report-2023

Duggal, P. (2005). Cyber-Crime in India: The Legal Approach. In *Cyber-Crime: The Challenge in Asia* (pp. 183-196). Hong Kong University Press.

Duraiswamy, D. R. (2017). Privacy and Data Protection in India. *Journal of Law & Cyber Warfare*, *6*(1), 166–186.

Goyal, P. (2022). The Death Trap that's India's Illegal Load Apps. *Newslaundry*. https://www.newslaundry.com/2022/09/24/the-death-trap-thats-indias-illegal-loan-apps

Jagjit Sing v. State of Punjab, Sl. L. P. Crl. No. 3583/2021.

Jain, S. (2014). Cybersecurity: A *Sine Qua Non*. *IDR*. https://indiandefencereview.com/cyber-security-a-sine-qua-non/

Kharak Singh v. State of UP, AIR, 1963 SC 1295.

Kshetri, N. (2016). Cybercrime and Cybersecurity in India: Causes, Consequences, and Implications for the Future. *Crime, Law, and Social Change*, *66*(3), 313–338. DOI: 10.1007/s10611-016-9629-3

Kumar, V. (2022). Issues & Challenges of Cybersecurity in India: A Study. *International Journal of Novel Research and Development*, *7*(8), 140–147.

Meit, Y. (2004). CERT-In. https://www.cert-in.org.in/

Meit, Y. (2018). Cyber Surakshit Bharat. https://www.meity.gov.in/writereaddata/files/Cyber-Surakshit-Bharat-Brochure.pdf

Meit, Y. (n. d.). Cyber Swachhta Kendra. https://www.csk.gov.in/

Ministry of Law and Justice. (2024). Ministry of Law and Justice Organizes Conference Titled 'India's Progressive Path in the Administration of Criminal Justice System.' *Ministry of Law and Justice*. https://www.pib.gov.in/PressReleasePage.aspx?PRID=2018392

Mukhopadhyay, D. (2022). Cybersecurity in India. *Communications of the ACM*, *65*(11), 98–102. DOI: 10.1145/3554910

NCIIPC. (2024). About Us. https://www.nciipc.gov.in/

(NCR&IC). (National Cyber Crime Research & Information Centre). (2021). *Emerging Cybercrimes in India: A Concise Compilation*. Burau of Police Research & Development.

NDTV. (2024). No One can Arrest through Video Calls: Cyber Security Agency on Scam Calls. *NDTV*. https://www.ndtv.com/india-news/no-one-can-arrest-through-video-calls-cyber-security-agency-on-scam-calls-6728458

NIC. (n. d.). https://www.nic.in/mandate/

OECD. (2012). Cybersecurity Policy Making at a Turning Point. https://www.oecd.org/en/publications/cybersecurity-policy-making-at-a-turning-point_5k8zq92vdgtl-en.html

Palreddy, V. K. (2020). Punishments for Cybercrimes in IPC. *IPleaders*. https://blog.ipleaders.in/punishments-cyber-crimes-ipc/

Patkar, S., & Dhakad, A. (2022). An Evolving Concern for National Cybersecurity in India. *ACCLAIMS*, *20*, 1–9.

Pubby, M. (2012). China Hackers Enter Navy Computers, Plant Bug to Extract Sensitive Data. *The Indian Express*. https://indianexpress.com/article/news-archive/web/china-hackers-enter-navy-computers-plant-bug-to-extract-sensitive-data/

Sharma, B. (2024). Cybercrimes under the Bharatiya Nyaya Sanhita, 2023. *MCO Legals*. https://www.mcolegals.in/kb/Cyber_Law-_Series_2-_Issue_3_-_Cybercrimes_under_the_Bhartiya_Nyaya_Sanhita,_2023.pdf

Shuran, L., Hui, D., & Su, G. (2013). Analysis and Discussions of the Blackout in Indian Power Grid. *Energy Science and Technology*, *6*(1), 61–66.

Singh, R. (2024). Beware of Fraudulent Govt emails: Home Ministry Issues Public Warning. *Business Standard*. https://www.business-standard.com/india-news/beware-of-fraudulent-govt-emails-home-ministry-issues-public-warning-124071500749_1.html

Tejpal, K., Patole, J., & Ghugare, T. (2023). Cybersecurity: Pressing Priority in India. *The Online Journal of Distance Education and e-Learning : TOJDEL, 11*(2), 2052–2061.

The Hindu Bureau. (2023). Loan App Suspected to be Behind Death of Family Remains to be Tracked. *The Hindu*. https://www.thehindu.com/news/cities/Kochi/loan-app-suspected-to-be-behind-death-of-family-remains-to-be-tracked/article67307324.ece

The Indian Evidence Act, 1872.

The Information Technology Act, 2000.

Thomas, R., & Jagani, D. (2024). Bharatiya Nyaya Sanhita, 2024: A Critical Perspective. SSRN. https://papers.ssrn.com/sol3/papers.cfm?abstract_id=4898463

Verma, A. K., & Sharma, A. K. (2014). Cybersecurity Issues and Recommendations. *International Journal of Advanced Research in Computer Science and Software Engineering*, *4*(4), 629–634.

Chapter 9

Enhancing Judicial Systems:
Leveraging AI to Address Privacy Infringement Challenges

Usharani Bhimavarapu
https://orcid.org/0000-0002-0246-1420
Department of Computer Science and Engineering, Koneru Lakshmaiah Education Foundation, Vaddeswaram, India

ABSTRACT

In today's digital era, the rise in privacy infringement cases highlights the urgent need for robust legal frameworks and causations. This study focuses on predicting court verdicts in online privacy cases under the Digital Personal Data Protection Act (DPDPA) by combining advanced text processing and machine learning techniques. The textual data from court case judgments is transformed into numerical features using TF-IDF, followed by feature selection through Recursive Feature Elimination (RFE) to prioritize the most relevant information. A hybrid GRU+ANN model is proposed, leveraging the sequential processing capabilities of GRU and the deep learning strength of ANN to predict court outcomes effectively. The methodology enhances model accuracy, reduces feature redundancy, and provides insights into factors influencing judicial decisions. This approach demonstrates the potential of AI-driven models in legal analytics and decision prediction.

DOI: 10.4018/979-8-3693-8871-6.ch009

INTRODUCTION

India has been grappling with the challenge of safeguarding citizens' personal data in an increasingly digital world. The Digital Personal Data Protection Act (DPDPA), enacted in 2023, is India's first comprehensive legislation aimed at regulating data collection, storage, and sharing practices by organizations operating in the country (Naithani, 2024). The Act is designed to protect individuals' privacy rights while allowing for the growth of a digital economy (Malhotra & Malhotra, 2024). It establishes clear guidelines on how personal data is to be handled and sets stringent penalties for organizations that fail to comply with the law. This legal framework includes provisions for data collection transparency, user consent, and the creation of a Data Protection Authority to oversee enforcement and ensure compliance (Lakra & Jha, 2024).

As the internet has become an essential part of daily life, online privacy infringements have grown in scale and complexity. Privacy violations can occur in many forms, such as unauthorized data access, data breaches, surveillance, and misuse of personal information. With the rise of social media platforms, e-commerce websites, and digital banking, individuals' personal data is increasingly vulnerable to misuse (Durnell et al., 2020). For example, the unauthorized sharing of personal data, identity theft, and online harassment have become common incidents leading to privacy infringements. The DPDPA addresses these issues by mandating that organizations protect user data from such risks and providing users with rights such as data access, correction, and deletion.

India's legal system has evolved to address online privacy infringement cases, integrating digital privacy violations into the broader legal framework (Chatterjee, 2019). Legal actions in cases of privacy infringement are typically taken under various laws, including the Information Technology Act (2000) (Duggal, n.d.) and now, the DPDPA. Courts, such as the Supreme Court of India, have been pivotal in establishing legal precedents regarding online privacy rights. The landmark K.S. Puttaswamy v. Union of India (2017) judgment by the Supreme Court reaffirmed the right to privacy as a fundamental right under the Indian Constitution (Chandrachud, 2017). It set a strong foundation for the enactment of the DPDPA by recognizing privacy as a constitutional right in the digital age.

Despite the robust framework provided by the DPDPA, challenges remain in the enforcement of online privacy rights. One of the significant hurdles is the rapidly evolving nature of technology, which often outpaces the creation of new laws and regulations. This makes it difficult for lawmakers to foresee all potential privacy risks, leading to gaps in protection. Moreover, there are concerns about the adequacy of resources for enforcement, such as the capacity of the Data Protection Authority to monitor compliance and penalize violators effectively. These challenges are compounded by the global nature of the internet, where data crosses borders, making international collaboration and coordination essential in tackling online privacy infringement.

As online privacy infringement cases continue to rise in India, it is clear that the DPDPA is just the beginning of a longer journey toward ensuring digital privacy. Legal scholars and policymakers stress the importance of adapting to new challenges and technologies that emerge in the digital world. Future updates to the DPDPA may include more comprehensive provisions regarding artificial intelligence, biometric data, and other emerging technologies that present novel privacy risks. Additionally, public awareness and education about online privacy rights and legal remedies are crucial in empowering citizens to take action when their rights are violated (Widjaja, 2023). As online privacy infringement becomes an increasingly global issue, India must continue to strengthen its legal framework to protect its citizens in the digital age.

In addition to machine learning models, traditional non-machine learning approaches have also been used to predict verdicts in legal issues. These methods primarily rely on rule-based systems, expert systems, and statistical techniques, which attempt to emulate legal reasoning and predict outcomes based on established legal rules and precedents. One widely used approach is case-based reasoning (CBR), (He et al., 2023) where past case decisions are used as a reference to predict outcomes for new cases. By comparing the facts of the current case with similar cases in the database, CBR can offer predictions based on the historical decisions of courts. Another common non-machine learning method is the use of expert systems, which are designed to mimic the decision-making process of human experts in the legal field (Nigam et al., 2024). These systems rely on a set of predefined rules and logic to analyze case facts and predict possible outcomes. Statistical models like regression analysis have also been employed, where historical case data is used to establish relationships between various factors (such as case type, jurisdiction, and legal arguments) and the verdict outcome (Cui et al., 2023).

However, these non-machine learning models have several limitations. Case-based reasoning can be restricted by the availability and quality of historical data, as the system may not predict well if there are no similar past cases to compare with. Expert systems, while useful in providing a structured analysis, often lack the flexibility to adapt to new legal interpretations or cases with unique circumstances, as they depend heavily on the predefined rules, which may not cover all possible scenarios. Furthermore, expert systems require constant updates from legal professionals to remain relevant, which is resource-intensive. Statistical models, while capable of drawing insights from large datasets, may fail to capture the complexity of legal reasoning, as they often rely on simplified assumptions and cannot account for the nuanced and dynamic nature of law. Additionally, these models generally lack transparency and interpretability, making them less reliable in the legal context, where justification of decisions is crucial. Lastly, non-machine learning approaches may not handle the vast amounts of data in modern legal systems as efficiently as machine learning models, limiting their scalability and adaptability to complex, evolving legal cases.

The need for machine learning in predicting legal verdicts arises from the growing complexity of legal cases and the increasing volume of data in modern legal systems. Traditional methods, such as case-based reasoning, expert systems, and statistical models, are often limited in their ability to handle vast amounts of diverse legal data, adapt to new legal precedents, and provide accurate, unbiased predictions in real time. The legal domain involves a wide range of factors that influence a verdict, including case facts, legal precedents, the interpretation of laws, and the behavior of judges and juries. Machine learning models can efficiently process large datasets, identify patterns, and make predictions based on historical case outcomes, which significantly improves the prediction accuracy and speed compared to traditional methods.

One of the key advantages of machine learning models, particularly deep learning approaches such as GRU+ANN (Gated Recurrent Unit combined with Artificial Neural Networks), is their ability to capture complex, non-linear relationships between input features. This is especially important in the legal domain, where factors influencing verdicts can be highly intricate and intertwined. Traditional non-machine learning models struggle to handle these complexities, as they often rely on predefined rules and assumptions that might not apply to every case. Machine learning models, on the other hand, can learn from data without explicit human programming, allowing them to adapt to new cases and precedents more effectively.

The Proposed GRU+ANN model overcomes many of the limitations associated with traditional legal prediction systems. First, it eliminates the need for manual feature engineering, as it can automatically learn and select the most relevant features from large datasets. This reduces human bias and error in selecting case variables and ensures that the model takes into account all relevant factors. Additionally, the GRU part of the model, which specializes in processing sequential data, helps the model understand and predict the legal outcomes based on the sequence of events in a case. This is particularly beneficial in legal settings, where the history of legal precedents and case details often influences the final decision.

Another advantage of the GRU+ANN model is its ability to handle vast amounts of unstructured data, such as case texts, court documents, and judgments, which are often difficult to process using traditional models. By utilizing deep learning techniques, the model can analyze this unstructured data to uncover hidden patterns and relationships that may not be immediately apparent. Moreover, the model improves over time by continuously learning from new data, which ensures that it remains up-to-date with evolving legal trends and precedents.

Finally, the GRU+ANN model addresses the interpretability and transparency issues often associated with machine learning in legal applications. While machine learning models can be more complex and harder to interpret than rule-based systems, recent advancements in explainable AI (XAI) have made it possible to trace the decision-making process of models like GRU+ANN. This allows legal professionals to understand the reasoning behind predictions, ensuring that the model's decisions are transparent and justifiable in a legal context.

MATERIALS AND METHODOLOGY

The methodology involves preprocessing court case data by cleaning, tokenizing, and applying TF-IDF to extract numerical features from textual fields. Using Recursive Feature Elimination (RFE), the most relevant features are selected based on their contribution to predicting court verdicts. These prioritized features are input into a hybrid GRU+ANN model, where GRU processes sequential dependencies in text, and ANN captures complex relationships between features and verdicts. The model is trained and validated on the dataset to ensure accuracy and generalization. This approach combines feature selection, deep learning, and text analysis to predict court outcomes effectively.

Materials

The data collection for this study focused on analyzing judicial cases related to online privacy invasions in India, specifically under the Digital Personal Data Protection Act (DPDPA). Judicial precedents were sourced from the official Supreme Court website of India to ensure the reliability and authenticity of the cases selected. The cases reviewed were chosen to reflect online privacy issues in a virtual environment, transcending physical territorial limitations. This approach was crucial for understanding how privacy violations are addressed within the Indian legal framework, with particular emphasis on the sectoral approach adopted by the DPDPA. The goal was to capture a broad spectrum of legal decisions that could provide insights into how online privacy infringements are handled across the country, irrespective of state-specific laws. The data collected from these cases forms the basis of this study's analysis and its findings, which are expected to contribute to the broader understanding of online privacy protection in India.

Table 1. List of features

Feature	Description
Case ID	Unique identifier for each judicial case.
Case Name	The title or name of the case.
Court	The specific court (e.g., Supreme Court of India).
Case Date	The date on which the case was decided.
Jurisdiction	The geographic jurisdiction (national or state).
Privacy Violation Type	Type of online privacy violation (e.g., data breach, unauthorized data collection).
Sector Involved	The specific sector(s) affected (e.g., banking, healthcare).
Legislation Cited	The specific laws referenced in the case (e.g., DPDPA).
Court Decision	Summary of the court's ruling (e.g., favorable to plaintiff/defendant).
Privacy Protection Measures	Any measures or recommendations for protecting privacy.
Penalties Imposed	Penalties or compensations awarded in the case.
Defendant Type	The type of entity being sued (e.g., government, private company, individual).
Plaintiff Type	The type of individual or entity bringing the case (e.g., consumer, employee, organization).
Data Type Involved	Types of personal data involved (e.g., financial, health, social media).
Privacy Violation Context	The context of the violation (e.g., social media data breach).
Legal Precedent Set	Whether the case set a legal precedent or clarified existing law.
Outcome Summary	A brief summary of the final outcome (e.g., case dismissed, compensation awarded).
Relevant Articles of DPDPA	Articles or sections of the DPDPA cited in the case.
Location/Region	The geographical region or state where the case originated or impacted.
Impact on Future Legislation	The impact the case had on future privacy laws or amendments.

Pre processing

Pre-processing the dataset involves several crucial steps to ensure the data is clean and ready for analysis. The first step is data cleaning, which focuses on handling missing values. Missing data can occur in various fields, so the first task is to identify where these gaps exist. For categorical fields like Sector Involved or Court Decision, missing values can be imputed with the most frequent value (mode) or a placeholder such as “Unknown.” For numerical fields, such as Penalties Imposed, missing data can be imputed using the mean or median of the column, or, if appropriate, by using a placeholder like 0 (indicating no penalties) (Umar & Gray, 2023). In cases where a row has an excessive number of missing values, it might be best to remove that row entirely to avoid skewing the analysis. Next, standardizing formats is essential for ensuring consistency across the dataset. This includes converting date fields like Case Date into a uniform date format (e.g., YYYY-MM-DD) and ensuring that categorical data, such as Defendant Type or Privacy Violation Type, follow consistent naming conventions (e.g., capitalizing the first letter and removing extra spaces). Additionally, data normalization might be necessary for certain numerical fields (Huang et al., 2023). For example, Penalties Imposed could be standardized if there are significant variations in the scale of the values, ensuring the analysis can be done on an even footing. Finally, it is important to check for duplicate entries and remove them if present, as duplicates can distort the analysis. Once these steps are complete, the dataset will be in a much cleaner form, ready for further exploration and analysis, such as identifying patterns or generating insights from the judicial cases under the DPDPA.

Feature Extraction

In this study, we are performing feature extraction on the processed dataset to transform the textual information into numerical features that can be used for further analysis. The dataset includes key textual columns such as Case Name, Court Decision, Privacy Violation Context, and Outcome Summary, all of which contain valuable information regarding online privacy invasions. These text fields offer insight into the nature of each case, the type of privacy violation, and the judicial decisions made, which can be leveraged to uncover patterns or trends in online privacy issues under the Digital Personal Data Protection Act (DPDPA). By applying feature extraction techniques, such as TF-IDF, we aim to quantify the textual data and enable more advanced analyses, such as identifying significant terms, themes, or relationships within the judicial rulings related to online privacy (Das & Alphonse, 2023). This transformation from raw text to structured numerical data allows us to incorporate text analysis into the broader dataset, enhancing its usability for statistical modeling, machine learning, or legal trend analysis.

Feature Selection

In this study, we are performing feature selection using Recursive Feature Elimination (RFE) to identify the most important features from the extracted TF-IDF data (Awad & Fraihat, 2023). RFE is a method that works by recursively fitting a model and ranking feature based on their importance, then eliminating the least important ones step by step. The process continues until the desired number of features is reached. This approach is particularly useful when dealing with a large set of features, such as the ones generated from the TF-IDF transformation, where each term in the text data becomes a separate feature. By using RFE, we can reduce the number of features while maintaining the most significant ones, which helps in improving the model's performance, reducing overfitting, and enhancing interpretability.

To apply RFE, we start by selecting a machine learning model that will be used to rank the features. Typically, Random Forest (Sun et al., 2024) is used for this task, depending on whether the problem is a classification or regression task. The RFE process begins by fitting the selected model to the entire set of features extracted through TF-IDF. It then ranks the features based on their importance to the model's predictive performance. The least important features are eliminated, and the model is re-trained using the remaining features. This process is repeated iteratively until only the most important features are left.

After performing RFE, the remaining features are expected to provide the most meaningful insights, as they are the ones that contribute most significantly to the outcome. By focusing only on these important features, we reduce the complexity of the dataset and make the analysis more efficient. This process not only helps improve the performance of the model but also aids in interpreting the underlying patterns in the dataset, such as trends in online privacy violations. Ultimately, RFE allows us to refine the feature set, ensuring that the analysis focuses on the most relevant information, which is crucial for accurate predictions and better understanding of online privacy issues in India under the DPDPA.

Veridiction Prediction

In this study, court case judgments are prioritized based on their RFE relevance score, which helps identify the most significant features influencing the court's decision. The Recursive Feature Elimination (RFE) process ranks the extracted features from the TF-IDF transformation, and the features with the highest relevance scores are selected for further analysis. This approach allows for the prioritization of key words or phrases in the case judgments that are most predictive of the court's verdict. By focusing on the most important features, we aim to create a model that accurately predicts the outcome of court cases related to online privacy invasions under the Digital Personal Data Protection Act (DPDPA).

The proposed model for predicting court verdicts is a GRU+ANN (Gated Recurrent Unit + Artificial Neural Network) (Shiri et al., 2023; Kurani et al., 2023) hybrid model, which combines the strengths of both GRU and ANN. GRU, a type of Recurrent Neural Network (RNN), is particularly well-suited for processing sequential data, such as text, by capturing dependencies across time steps (or in this case, the relationships between terms in a legal judgment). GRU units are efficient at handling long-range dependencies in textual data while avoiding the vanishing gradient problem common in traditional RNNs. This makes GRU a good choice for analyzing case judgments, where the context and meaning of a case often depend on the progression of ideas across the document.

The Artificial Neural Network (ANN) component of the model is used for its ability to learn complex, non-linear relationships between the features and the target variable (i.e., the court verdict). After extracting and selecting the relevant features through RFE, the ANN is used to classify or predict the outcome of each court case based on these features. The ANN will typically consist of multiple layers of neurons that process the input features, allowing the model to capture complex patterns in the data. By combining the sequential processing power of GRU with the deep learning capabilities of ANN, the GRU+ANN model is well-equipped to make accurate predictions about court verdicts, based on the prioritized features.

This hybrid model is expected to provide a robust framework for predicting the outcomes of court cases, offering a more accurate and efficient approach than traditional rule-based methods. By utilizing the RFE scores to prioritize the most important features and combining them with the power of GRU and ANN architectures, this model can effectively predict the outcomes of legal cases related to online privacy, providing valuable insights into trends and potential future verdicts.

Experimental Results

The proposed model was implemented in Python using a variety of machine learning and deep learning libraries, including Scikit-learn, TensorFlow, and Keras. The experiments were conducted on a Windows 10 system with the following configuration: Intel Core i7-9700K Processor, 16GB RAM. This setup allowed for efficient model training, feature selection, and classification tasks, enabling us to obtain accurate results for predicting judicial decisions in privacy infringement cases.

Table 2 presents a performance comparison between the model with and without feature selection, highlighting the impact of feature selection on various evaluation metrics. With feature selection, the model achieves an accuracy of 92.3%, significantly higher than the 85.7% accuracy observed without it. Similarly, the precision, recall, and F1-score all improve when feature selection is applied, with values of 90.1%, 93.8%, and 91.9%, respectively, compared to 83.5%, 84.2%, and 83.8% without feature selection. Additionally, feature selection not only enhances the model's performance but also reduces the training time from 220 seconds to 120 seconds, showcasing the efficiency gains. The number of features used in the model also decreases dramatically, from over 5000 features without selection to just 50 features with selection, underscoring the effectiveness of the feature selection process in simplifying the model while maintaining high performance.

Table 2. Performance Comparison: With and Without Feature Selection

Metric	With Feature Selection	Without Feature Selection
Model Accuracy (%)	92.3	85.7
Precision (%)	90.1	83.5
Recall (%)	93.8	84.2
F1-Score (%)	91.9	83.8
Training Time (s)	120	220
Number of Features	50	5000+

Table 3 provides a comprehensive performance comparison between the proposed GRU+ANN model and 10 existing models across several key metrics: accuracy, precision, recall, F1-score, and training time. The GRU+ANN model demonstrates the highest performance with an accuracy of 92.3%, precision of 90.1%, recall of 93.8%, and an F1-score of 91.9%, outperforming all other models in these areas. It also has a relatively efficient training time of 120 seconds, balancing high performance and computational efficiency.

In comparison, traditional models like Logistic Regression and Naive Bayes show lower accuracies of 84.5% and 78.3%, respectively, with correspondingly lower precision, recall, and F1-scores. The Support Vector Machine and Random Forest models perform moderately with accuracy scores of 86.2% and 88.9%, but still fall short of the GRU+ANN model in terms of recall and F1-score, and require more training time.

Deep learning models like LSTM, BiLSTM, and CNN show better performance than traditional machine learning models but still lag behind the GRU+ANN in accuracy and F1-score, with LSTM achieving an accuracy of 91.3% and BiLSTM at 91.8%. Additionally, training time for these models tends to be higher, with LSTM taking 200 seconds and BiLSTM taking 210 seconds.

Table 3. Performance Comparison: Proposed Model vs. Existing Models

Model	Accuracy (%)	Precision (%)	Recall (%)	F1-Score (%)	Training Time (s)
Proposed GRU+ANN	92.3	90.1	93.8	91.9	120
Logistic Regression (Torres et al., 2023)	84.5	81.2	82.9	82.0	45
Support Vector Machine (Rani et al., 2023)	86.2	83.5	85.1	84.3	80
Random Forest (Pavani et al., 2024)	88.9	86.2	88.0	87.1	150

continued on following page

Table 3. Continued

Model	Accuracy (%)	Precision (%)	Recall (%)	F1-Score (%)	Training Time (s)
Decision Tree (Glidden et al., 2016)	81.7	79.5	80.3	79.9	40
Naive Bayes (Quteishat et al., 2024)	78.3	75.1	76.8	75.9	30
Gradient Boosting (George et al., 2024)	89.4	87.0	88.5	87.7	180
XGBoost (Wicaksono et al., 2023)	90.2	88.5	89.8	89.1	160
LSTM (Pandi et al., 2023)	91.3	89.4	91.0	90.2	200
CNN (Liu et al., 2021)	87.5	84.8	86.2	85.5	140
BiLSTM (Ahmad et al., 2022)	91.8	89.8	92.3	91.0	210

Table 4 presents the classification performance of various models across different judicial decision categories, showcasing how well each model predicts specific outcomes in privacy infringement cases. The Proposed GRU+ANN model consistently achieves the highest prediction rates across all categories, with Penalty Imposed at 93.5%, Compensation Awarded at 92.8%, and Policy Revision Mandated at 91.5%. It also performs strongly in other categories such as Case Dismissed (91.2%) and Data Deletion Ordered (90.4%), making it the top-performing model overall.

In comparison, traditional models like Logistic Regression and Naive Bayes show significantly lower prediction rates across all categories. For instance, Logistic Regression achieves only 84.2% for Penalty Imposed and 82.5% for Case Dismissed, while Naive Bayes performs even worse in the same categories, with 75.3% and 73.4%, respectively. These results highlight the limitations of simpler models in accurately predicting judicial decisions.

Other models like Support Vector Machine (SVM), Random Forest, and Gradient Boosting also show competitive performance, but none surpass the GRU+ANN model in overall accuracy. SVM and Random Forest achieve good results, especially in categories such as Data Deletion Ordered and Injunction Issued, but still fall short when compared to GRU+ANN. XGBoost and LSTM models show strong performance as well, particularly in predicting Compensation Awarded and Criminal Liability Assigned, with LSTM achieving 91.2% and BiLSTM at 91.6% for the same category.

Table 4. Classification of Judicial Decisions and Prediction Rates for All Models

Model	Penalty Imposed (%)	Case Dismissed (%)	Compensation Awarded (%)	Data Deletion Ordered (%)	Injunction Issued (%)	No Violation Found (%)	Policy Revision Mandated (%)	Criminal Liability Assigned (%)
Proposed GRU+ANN	93.5	91.2	92.8	90.4	89.7	88.9	91.5	89.3
Logistic Regression	84.2	82.5	83.1	80.3	78.9	77.5	80.8	79.4
Support Vector Machine	86.4	84.2	85.5	83.0	81.7	80.2	83.6	82.0
Random Forest	88.3	86.1	87.7	85.2	84.0	82.3	86.0	84.4
Decision Tree	80.5	78.4	79.2	76.6	75.4	73.8	77.0	75.1
Naive Bayes	75.3	73.4	74.8	71.5	70.3	68.9	72.0	70.1
Gradient Boosting	89.5	87.3	88.6	86.5	85.1	83.5	86.8	85.0
XGBoost	90.1	88.2	89.4	87.3	86.0	84.7	88.0	86.4
LSTM	91.2	89.6	90.8	88.5	87.1	85.6	89.2	87.3
CNN	87.4	85.3	86.5	83.9	82.6	81.2	84.5	83.0
BiLSTM	91.6	89.9	91.2	88.7	87.4	86.0	89.5	87.8

Table 5 presents the classification of judicial decisions and prediction rates for various types of privacy invasion cases, demonstrating how well the model predicts legal outcomes for different privacy-related offenses. The Unauthorized Data Access category shows the highest prediction rates across most outcomes, with Penalty Imposed at 94.1%, Compensation Awarded at 92.6%, and Criminal Liability Assigned at 89.9%, indicating that the model performs exceptionally well in predicting decisions related to unauthorized access to personal data.

Other types of privacy invasion, such as Breach of Confidentiality and Identity Theft, also achieve strong results. Breach of Confidentiality reaches 94.4% in Penalty Imposed and 92.5% for Compensation Awarded, reflecting the severity of penalties often associated with this offense. Similarly, Identity Theft shows 93.8% for Penalty Imposed and 92.3% for Compensation Awarded, highlighting the seriousness of this type of privacy violation.

Categories like Data Breach, Data Misuse, and Invasive Surveillance also exhibit competitive performance, with Data Breach reaching 92.7% in Penalty Imposed and 91.2% for Compensation Awarded, while Invasive Surveillance achieves 92.1% for Penalty Imposed and 91.0% for Compensation Awarded. These results emphasize the model's capability to handle a variety of privacy invasion types with high prediction accuracy.

Digital Stalking and Fake Online Reviews are the two categories with comparatively lower prediction rates, particularly in Penalty Imposed and Compensation Awarded, though they still show reasonable performance with Penalties around 91.0% and 90.6% for Digital Stalking and Fake Online Reviews, respectively.

Table 5. Privacy Invasion: Classification of Judicial Decisions and Prediction Rates

Type of Privacy Invasion	Penalty Imposed (%)	Case Dismissed (%)	Compensation Awarded (%)	Data Deletion Ordered (%)	Injunction Issued (%)	No Violation Found (%)	Policy Revision Mandated (%)	Criminal Liability Assigned (%)
Data Breach	92.7	88.5	91.2	90.0	89.5	87.3	90.8	88.4
Unauthorized Data Access	94.1	89.7	92.6	91.4	90.2	88.8	92.0	89.9
Data Misuse	93.3	87.9	91.8	90.2	89.1	86.5	91.5	88.0
Online Harassment	91.4	86.5	89.5	88.0	86.8	84.4	88.9	85.7
Identity Theft	93.8	90.0	92.3	91.2	90.7	88.0	92.5	89.6
Invasive Surveillance	92.1	88.2	91.0	89.7	88.5	86.6	91.2	87.9
Breach of Confidentiality	94.4	89.0	92.5	91.0	90.3	88.6	92.1	90.1
Non-consensual Data Sharing	92.9	88.8	91.9	90.5	89.2	87.1	91.7	88.5
Digital Stalking	91.0	85.8	89.0	87.5	86.2	84.1	88.3	84.8
Fake Online Reviews	90.6	86.3	89.4	88.1	87.4	85.3	88.7	86.0

CONCLUSION

The proposed methodology successfully combines TF-IDF feature extraction, RFE-based prioritization, and a hybrid GRU+ANN model to predict court verdicts in online privacy cases. By focusing on the most relevant textual features, the model achieves improved efficiency and accuracy in outcome prediction. This approach highlights the importance of integrating feature selection and deep learning for legal data analysis. The results underline the potential for AI-driven models to assist in understanding judicial trends and automating verdict predictions, thereby contributing to advancements in legal technology and decision analytics under the DPDPA framework.

REFERENCES

Ahmad, S., Asghar, M. Z., Alotaibi, F. M., & Al-Otaibi, Y. D. (2022). A hybrid CNN+ BILSTM deep learning-based DSS for efficient prediction of judicial case decisions. *Expert Systems with Applications, 209*, 118318. DOI: 10.1016/j.eswa.2022.118318

Awad, M., & Fraihat, S. (2023). Recursive feature elimination with cross-validation with decision tree: Feature selection method for machine learning-based intrusion detection systems. *Journal of Sensor and Actuator Networks, 12*(5), 67. DOI: 10.3390/jsan12050067

Chandrachud, D. Y. (2017). Supreme Court of India Justice KS Puttaswamy (Retd)... vs Union Of India And Ors. on 24 August, 2017.

Chatterjee, S. (2019). Is data privacy a fundamental right in India? An analysis and recommendations from policy and legal perspective. *International Journal of Law and Management, 61*(1), 170–190. DOI: 10.1108/IJLMA-01-2018-0013

Cui, J., Shen, X., & Wen, S. (2023). A survey on legal judgment prediction: Datasets, metrics, models and challenges. *IEEE Access : Practical Innovations, Open Solutions, 11*, 102050–102071. DOI: 10.1109/ACCESS.2023.3317083

Das, M., & Alphonse, P. J. A. (2023). A comparative study on tf-idf feature weighting method and its analysis using unstructured dataset. arXiv preprint arXiv:2308.04037.

Durnell, E., Okabe-Miyamoto, K., Howell, R. T., & Zizi, M. (2020). Online privacy breaches, offline consequences: Construction and validation of the concerns with the protection of informational privacy scale. *International Journal of Human-Computer Interaction, 36*(19), 1834–1848. DOI: 10.1080/10447318.2020.1794626

George, A., Jose, A., Ashik, F., Prabhakar, P., Pati, P. B., & Parida, S. (2024, March). Enhancing Legal Decision Making: WRIT Case Outcome Prediction with Legal-BERT Embeddings and AdaBoost Classifier. In 2024 IEEE International Conference on Contemporary Computing and Communications (InC4) (Vol. 1, pp. 1-6). IEEE.

Glidden, C. B., Lea, C. W., & Victor, M. B. (2016). Evaluating legal risks and costs with decision tree analysis. Successful partnering between inside and outside counsel, 12-1.

He, C., Tan, T. P., Zhang, X., & Xue, S. (2023). Knowledge-enriched multi-cross attention network for legal judgment prediction. *IEEE Access : Practical Innovations, Open Solutions, 11*, 87571–87582. DOI: 10.1109/ACCESS.2023.3305259

Huang, L., Qin, J., Zhou, Y., Zhu, F., Liu, L., & Shao, L. (2023). Normalization techniques in training dnns: Methodology, analysis and application. *IEEE Transactions on Pattern Analysis and Machine Intelligence*, *45*(8), 10173–10196. DOI: 10.1109/TPAMI.2023.3250241 PMID: 37027763

Kurani, A., Doshi, P., Vakharia, A., & Shah, M. (2023). A comprehensive comparative study of artificial neural network (ANN) and support vector machines (SVM) on stock forecasting. *Annals of Data Science*, *10*(1), 183–208. DOI: 10.1007/s40745-021-00344-x

Lakra, R., & Jha, N. (2024). Publicly Available Data in the DPDPA Act 2023: Interpretative, Constitutional and Comparative Perspectives. Constitutional and Comparative Perspectives (August 22, 2024).

Liu, L., An, D., Wang, Y., Ma, X., & Jiang, C. (2021, June). Research on legal judgment prediction based on Bert and LSTM-CNN fusion model. In 2021 3rd world symposium on artificial intelligence (WSAI) (pp. 41-45). IEEE. DOI: 10.1109/WSAI51899.2021.9486374

Malhotra, C., & Malhotra, U. (2024). Putting Interests of Digital Nagriks First: Digital Personal Data Protection (DPDP) Act 2023 of India. *The Indian Journal of Public Administration*, *70*(3), 516–531. DOI: 10.1177/00195561241271575

Naithani, P. (2024). Analysis of India's Digital Personal Data Protection Act, 2023. International Journal of Law and Management.

Nigam, S. K., Deroy, A., Maity, S., & Bhattacharya, A. (2024). Rethinking legal judgement prediction in a realistic scenario in the era of large language models. arXiv preprint arXiv:2410.10542. DOI: 10.18653/v1/2024.nllp-1.6

Pandi, S. S., Farook, A. M., & Kingston, W. (2023, December). Scenario based Deep Learning Prediction for Legal Judgment using LSTM and CNN. In *2023 Third International Conference on Smart Technologies, Communication and Robotics (STCR)* (Vol. 1, pp. 1-6). IEEE.

Pavani, B. V., Mahitha, D., Prabhakar, P., & Pati, P. B. (2024, April). Identifying Sentiment in Legal Case Judgments using Random Forest Classifier. In 2024 IEEE 9th International Conference for Convergence in Technology (I2CT) (pp. 1-5). IEEE. DOI: 10.1109/I2CT61223.2024.10544116

Quteishat, E. M. A., Qtaishat, A., Quteishat, A. M. A., Al Adwan, M. A. S., Younis, M. A., & Kumar, M. (2024). Predictive Modelling in Legal Decision-Making: Leveraging Machine Learning for Forecasting Legal Outcomes. *Journal of Electrical Systems*, *20*(3), 2060–2071. DOI: 10.52783/jes.4006

Rani, A. J. M., Bharathwaj, K. S., Swaroopan, N. J., Kumar, K. H., & Geetha, R. (2023, November). A Legal Prediction Model Using Support Vector Machine and K-Means Clustering Algorithm for Predicting Judgements and Making Decisions. In *2023 International Conference on Research Methodologies in Knowledge Management, Artificial Intelligence and Telecommunication Engineering (RMKMATE)* (pp. 1-6). IEEE. DOI: 10.1109/RMKMATE59243.2023.10369625

Shiri, F. M., Perumal, T., Mustapha, N., & Mohamed, R. (2023). A comprehensive overview and comparative analysis on deep learning models: CNN, RNN, LSTM, GRU. arXiv preprint arXiv:2305.17473.

Sun, Z., Wang, G., Li, P., Wang, H., Zhang, M., & Liang, X. (2024). An improved random forest based on the classification accuracy and correlation measurement of decision trees. *Expert Systems with Applications*, *237*, 121549. DOI: 10.1016/j.eswa.2023.121549

Torres, G. D. O., Guterres, M. X., & Celestino, V. R. R. (2023). Legal actions in Brazilian air transport: A machine learning and multinomial logistic regression analysis. *Frontiers in Future Transportation*, *4*, 1070533. DOI: 10.3389/ffutr.2023.1070533

Umar, N., & Gray, A. (2023). Comparing single and multiple imputation approaches for missing values in univariate and multivariate water level data. *Water (Basel)*, *15*(8), 1519. DOI: 10.3390/w15081519

Wicaksono, G. W., Oktaviana, U. N., Prasetyo, S. N., Sari, T. I., Hidayah, N. P., Yunus, N. R., & Al-Fatih, S. (2023). Classification of Industrial Relations Dispute Court Verdict Document with XGBoost and Bidirectional LSTM. JOIV: International Journal on Informatics Visualization, 7(3-2), 1041-1047.

Widjaja, G. (2023). ENHANCING LEGAL LITERACY: UNDERSTANDING THE SIGNIFICANCE OF LAW NO. 9/2019 ON ELECTRONIC TRANSACTIONS IN THE SOCIAL MEDIA ERA. *Journal of Community Dedication*, *3*(4), 278–293.

Chapter 10
Green Criminology and AI- Tackling Environmental Cybercrime

Avijit Silawat
https://orcid.org/0009-0003-6502-7423
Devi Ahilya Vishwavidyalaya, Indore, India

Dipesh Silawat
https://orcid.org/0009-0008-7950-9526
Devi Ahilya Vishwavidyalaya, Indore, India

Harjeet Kaur
https://orcid.org/0009-0002-8888-0868
Euclid University, Bangui, Central African Republic

Aparajita Roy
Devi Ahilya Vishwavidyalaya, Indore, India

ABSTRACT

This chapter focuses on the relationship between green criminology, environmental cybercrime, and artificial intelligence (AI); it systematically examines how AI technologies repay environmental cyber threats. Environmental cybercrime is introduced as a subfield of green criminology before dedicating some time to explaining how it is one of the pressing issues of the modern world. The chapter discusses AI in fighting these crimes through the development of anomaly detection, predictive analytics, and auto-incident reaction applications. Specific solutions can be derived from modern companies' success in implementing AI in the real world and examples

DOI: 10.4018/979-8-3693-8871-6.ch010

like the SolarWinds cyberattack and foiled attempts at eco-terrorism. The ethical, legal, policy, and other issues are discussed, emphasizing privacy, fairness, and regulation. The last chapter provides a technological and regulatory agenda and ultimately calls for an integrated approach to interaction between criminologists, technologists, and policymakers to build and regulate a stronger and more progressive tomorrow.

INTRODUCTION

The Intersection of Environmental Sustainability and Digital Security

Environmental sustainability has become a global concern, enhancing technology use globally. Modern renewable energy systems, climate-changing recording instruments, and innovative waste disposal and management systems require close integration of digital platforms toward achieving the sustainable development agenda (White, 2021; Alsuwian et al., 2022). However, this has introduced vital structures to risks, with cybercrime developing into a reality in which attackers concentrate on these frameworks (Kshetri, 2016).

Environmental cybercrime highlights the convergence of two vital areas, environmental sustainability and digital security, which are mainly addressed as primary fundamental objectives of supply chain management. Such cyber threats threaten the strategies to slow climate change by attacking clean energy technology, adjusting climate information, or using environmental technologies for monetary or political goals (Ige et al., 2024a; Ige et al., 2024b; Ekechukwu & Simpa, 2024). In addition, such attacks undermine public confidence in developing and using sustainable technologies and paralyze essential efforts toward attaining climate change objectives (Aliero et al., 2020).

Security in the digital environment has thus turned into one of the key aspects of environmental sustainability. Protecting **Critical Sustainable Public Locations** (CSPLs) means that developments in modern technologies can positively facilitate the fight against climate change without disruptions. Therefore, this chapter discusses environmental sustainability, digital security, and artificial intelligence (AI), emphasizing the challenges and possibilities for fighting environmental cybercrime.

Green Criminology as a Framework for Understanding Crimes Against the Environment

Green criminology offers a theoretical and conceptual approach to understanding crime against the environment. Stemming from classical criminology, the discipline analyses the harm inflicted by people, companies, or countries, analyzing these acts' socio-political and economic root causes (White, 2021). While it previously focused on acts of harm against nature or natural resources, such as piracy of forest products, wildlife, or export of endangered species, without precluding its interest in cyber threats, which negatively impacted the environment albeit indirectly through attacking green technologies (Lynch et al., 2017).

Environmental cybercrime is an added innovation to this field. For instance, a ransomware attack on a renewable energy grid might cause extended power blackouts, the reliance on fossil sources, and thus, angry citizens disappointed in clean energy projects (González et al., 2024). Analyzing these crimes' technological and ecological characteristics can be helpful for researchers and policymakers who can relate these threats to green criminology.

The field also explored the motive behind such attacks, which vary from business gains to political and ideological justifications such as eco-terrorism. Secondly, it allows for comprehending environmental and digital harm, making green criminology a valuable tool for analyzing and addressing environmental cybercrime (Gibbs et al., 2009).

Rise of Environmental Cybercrime as a Critical Challenge in the Digital Age

Environmental cybercrime has become more common these days because environmental systems have become digitized. This holds especially true in developing innovative energy networks with **Internet of Things** (IoT)-enabled climate sensors and smart grids, to name but a few (Farooq et al., 2015). Key factors driving the rise of environmental cybercrime include:

1. **Technological Vulnerabilities:** Renewable energy systems and many obligatory environmental control devices require high cybersecurity. For instance, legacy systems and IoT devices must be constructed to anticipate vulnerability to attacks; hence, they become the darling of attackers (Nadtochiy, 2018; Kshetri, 2016).

    Example: For instance, the recent 2020 cyber incident on a water treatment plant in Oldsmar, Florida, highlighted the risks of intelligent IoT-based technologies when the attackers attempted to cause variation in chemical levels (Krebs, 2021; Cervini et al., 2022).
2. **Political and Ideological Motivations:** Eco-terrorists and hacktivists often attack technological categories of the environment to spread their ideas. These groups leverage such weaknesses to conduct a cyber-operation, saboteur, or protest against some governmental policies (White, 2021; González et al., 2024).

Example: There was an incident in 2016, specific to a wind farm in Europe; the cyberspace shut down the powering of the wind farm for a while, and the culprits made a sensational claim that they had disrupted ecosystems in the region (Ige et al., 2024a; Ige et al., 2024b).

3. **Financial Incentives:** Cybercriminals profit from green energy sellers and environmental networks. Some of them are malware attacks in the form of ransomware or stealing data from the solar innovative grid system and fraudulence in the price trend by manipulating renewable energy credits (Aliero et al., 2020; Farooq et al., 2015).

   Example: An attack on a solar panel manufacturing firm in September 2019 affected the solar value chain and postponed the development of renewable energy initiatives worldwide (Nadtochiy, 2018).

Role of AI in Addressing These Challenges

It has been ascertained that artificial intelligence has been widely used to address the issue of environmental cybercriminal activities effectively. The capability to work with a significant amount of data, recognize patterns, and make decisions independently makes AI the best tool to protect digital systems from complicated cyber threats (Ekechukwu & Simpa, 2024; González et al., 2024). Critical applications of AI in this domain include:

1. **Real-Time Threat Detection:** Automatic cognitive networks monitor the network characteristics and look for any signs of suspicious activity. For instance, machine learning algorithms can distinguish patterns in smart or intelligent grid systems between normal and anomalous (Alsuwian et al., 2022; Farooq et al., 2015).
2. **Predictive Analytics:** AI can predict future cyber-attacks based on past data because the defense can be ready. This capability is essential for renewable energy systems because any disruption may have complex influences (Nadtochiy, 2018).
3. **Automated Responses:** There is evidence that AI systems can contain affected networks, stop traffic from infected machines, and fix the problem independently to reduce disruption (Ige et al., 2024a; Ige et al., 2024b).
4. **Monitoring Ideological Threats:** Several AI tools, including **Natural Language Processing (NLP), are** used to monitor online communication, first to identify eco-terrorist activity and second to recognize emerging threats (White, 2021; González et al., 2024).

While AI has great promise, its implementation is fraught with ethical problems ranging from privacy violations to questions on the bias of AI and its decision-making being transparent. Possible challenges include the need to integrate innovative technologies, scale up solutions, implement best practice guidelines, expand funding sources, and coordinate international activity to manage the use of AI in support of environmental systems.

Objectives and Scope of the Chapter

This chapter explores the critical intersection of environmental sustainability, digital security, and artificial intelligence. Its primary objectives are to:

1. **Define Environmental Cybercrime:** Provide a comprehensive overview of environmental cybercrime and its impact on sustainability efforts.
2. **Analyze the Role of Green Criminology:** Examine how green criminology frames environmental cybercrime and offers solutions to mitigate its effects.
3. **Highlight AI's Role:** Investigate AI's capabilities in detecting, preventing, and responding to cyber threats targeting environmental systems.
4. **Present Real-World Case Studies:** Showcase incidents such as the SolarWinds cyberattack to illustrate the implications of environmental cybercrime and AI-driven solutions.
5. **Address Ethical and Legal Challenges:** Discuss the ethical implications and regulatory gaps in deploying AI for environmental cybersecurity.
6. **Propose Strategies:** Offer actionable recommendations for effectively integrating AI into environmental protection frameworks.

By addressing these objectives, the chapter provides a comprehensive understanding of the challenges and opportunities at the intersection of environmental sustainability, digital security, and AI.

MISSION AND OBJECTIVES

Defining Environmental Cybercrime within the Framework of Green Criminology

Environmental cybercrime represents the convergence of two critical areas: pollution and computer fraud. It includes actions that seek to harm the information systems supporting environmental management and sustainable living elements, such as renewable energy systems, climate tracking, and effective waste disposal technology (White, 2021; Gibbs et al., 2009). These crimes impact the environment because they interfere with technologies critical to addressing climate change, loss of species, and pollution.

These crimes are best understood using green criminology, a branch of criminology. Green criminology conventionally studies crimes such as illicit felling, hunting wildlife, and environmental pollution, with concerns about their consequences on ecosystems and society (White, 2021). With the addition of the digital dimension, green criminology widens to encompass offenses that take advantage of weaknesses in technological systems and damage ecological systems. For example, the technological disruptions in renewable electricity systems will cause blackouts and dominancy to conventional power sources, resulting in international climate issues (Ige et al., 2024a; Ige et al., 2024b).

Another significant focal point of the green criminology system is the interrelation between social, ecological, and technologically embodied structures. This lens type enables researchers and policymakers to control direct technological risks and their connected ecological consequences of environmental cybercrimes (Nadtochiy, 2018).

Exploring AI's Capabilities in Combating Environmental Cyber Threats

Artificial Intelligence (AI) has become the leading tool in the fight against environmental cybercrime. Consequently, AI's data-intensive, pattern-spotting capability and automated response to threats suit the defense of complex cyber threats against environmental systems (Alsuwian et al., 2022; Farooq et al., 2015). Critical capabilities of AI include:

1. **Real-Time Threat Detection:** Neural networks are on permanent lookout for breaches; any intrusion that poses a cybersecurity threat is foreseen and addressed. For example, deep learning algorithms would predict anomalous energy flows in smart grids, indicating intrusion (Nadtochiy, 2018).
2. **Predictive Analytics:** AI can also predict future threats since it analyses previous attacks, enabling organizations to prepare for them. Predictive analytics are essential for planning renewable energy systems because disturbances may impact other systems (Ige et al., 2024a; Ige et al., 2024b).
3. **Automated Responses:** By leveraging the power of AI-driven systems, the AI can detect vulnerable networks and immediately isolate them, stop the malicious traffic flow, and bring the system back online to normal before much damage can be done or much time is wasted (González et al., 2024).

4. **Behavioral Analysis and Monitoring:** AI tools can analyze and record the actions of users and recognize signs of insiders or eco-terrorists planning to attack environmental assets.

In line with these capabilities, AI strengthens digital infrastructure protection that sustains environmental systems and reduces the former's vulnerability to environmental cybercrime.

Analyzing Specific Case Studies to Demonstrate AI's Applications

Real-world case studies illustrate the practical application of AI in combating environmental cybercrime and highlight its potential to protect critical systems:

Case Study 1: SolarWinds Cyberattack

- **Incident:** The SolarWinds cyberattack of 2020 targeted Information Technology (IT) management software and impacted numerous fields for renewable energy systems (Nadtochiy, 2018).
- **Impact:** The attack affected the grid operations, distorted key environmental data, and revealed vulnerabilities of clean energy systems that were not previously recognizable.
- **AI's Role:** Artificial Intelligence integrates cybersecurity products, observes irregularities in traffic, separates compromised nodes, and limits the attack's consequences. These tools offered primary indicators as to when action should be taken to mitigate the severity of the result.

Case Study 2: Ransomware Attack on a Solar Panel Manufacturer

- **Incident:** In 2019, there was a ransomware attack on the world's largest solar panel producer that locked down key manufacturing systems; they demanded a considerable ransom (Ige et al., 2024a; Ige et al., 2024b).
- **Impact:** It hampered global renewable energy projects, resulting in monetary losses and escalation in usual energy consumption.
- **AI's Role:** When attackers launched a cyberattack, risk indicators were detected by predictive analytics and machine learning algorithms. After the incident, AI solutions improved the manufacturer's protection to avoid more occurrences.

These cases show that AI has critical applications for identifying, counteracting, and preventing environmental cyber threats.

Addressing Ethical, Legal, and Societal Challenges

While AI offers significant advantages in combating environmental cybercrime, its deployment raises several ethical, legal, and societal concerns:

1. **Ethical Challenges**:
   - **Data Privacy**: AI systems often require access to sensitive data, raising concerns about privacy violations (Aliero et al., 2020).
   - **Algorithmic Bias**: AI models may unintentionally perpetuate biases, leading to unfair targeting or misidentification of threats (González et al., 2024).
   - **Transparency**: The opacity of some AI systems can hinder accountability and trust.
2. **Legal Challenges**:
   - **Regulatory Gaps**: Existing legal frameworks often fail to address the unique challenges posed by AI in cybersecurity (Ekechukwu & Simpa, 2024).
   - **Jurisdictional Issues**: Cyberattacks often cross international borders, complicating enforcement and regulatory oversight.
3. **Societal Challenges**:
   - **Public Trust**: Building trust in AI technologies is essential for widespread adoption. Perceived risks of misuse or overreach can hinder acceptance (White, 2021).
   - **Economic Barriers**: Implementing AI-driven cybersecurity measures requires substantial financial investment, which may be prohibitive for some organizations (Farooq et al., 2015).

Addressing these challenges requires a balanced approach that prioritizes ethical considerations, strengthens legal frameworks, and fosters public trust in AI technologies.

Providing Actionable Recommendations for Integrating AI into Environmental Protection Strategies

To maximize the effectiveness of AI in combating environmental cybercrime, the following recommendations are proposed:

1. Enhancing Cybersecurity Frameworks:
   - Develop robust AI-powered cybersecurity protocols tailored to renewable energy systems and environmental technologies.

    - Regularly update systems to address emerging threats and vulnerabilities (Alsuwian et al., 2022).
2. Strengthening Legal and Regulatory Measures:
    - Establish international agreements to govern AI-driven cybersecurity and facilitate cross-border cooperation (Ekechukwu & Simpa, 2024).
    - Update national cybersecurity laws to include provisions for AI technologies and their ethical use.
3. Promoting Ethical AI Development:
    - Ensure transparency in AI algorithms and decision-making processes to build public trust.
    - Address biases in AI models through rigorous testing and validation (González et al., 2024).
4. Fostering Collaboration and Knowledge Sharing:
    - Encourage collaboration between governments, private sectors, and academia to share best practices and enhance AI capabilities (Ige et al., 2024a; Ige et al., 2024b).
    - Provide training programs for cybersecurity professionals to implement AI tools effectively.
5. Investing in Resilience and Recovery:
    - Allocate resources to develop resilience strategies that minimize the impact of cyberattacks on environmental systems.
    - Incorporate AI in disaster recovery plans to ensure swift restoration of operations post-attack (Farooq et al., 2015).

By implementing these recommendations, organizations can effectively leverage AI to protect critical environmental systems, mitigate cyber threats, and support global sustainability goals.

BACKGROUND AND CONTEXT

Emergence of Environmental Cybercrime as a Subset of Green Criminology

Green criminology studies crimes that affect green spaces and the bio-diversity of societies as an offshoot of traditional criminology. Traditionally, the field has responded to physical environmental offenses, including illegal tree felling, hunting, and polluting industries (White, 2021). However, as digital technologies become integral to ecological management, a new subset of green criminology has emerged: **environmental cybercrime**. This category encompasses offenses against digital structures critical to the natural environment, including power structures supporting renewable energy deployment, structures supporting climate change monitoring, and structures supporting environmental technologies in waste management (Gibbs et al., 2009, p.208).

Environmental cybercrime is unique in its dual impact: it raises havoc with crucial technical infrastructures and, albeit indirectly, impairs ecosystems by stymieing and prejudicing climate amelioration measures. For instance, cyber-incidents affecting a renewable energy grid can cause blackouts, denial of accessing renewable power, liquidation of clean-tech firms, and slow progress in the renewable energy transition (Ige et al., 2024a; Ige et al., 2024b). This duality positions environmental cybercrime under the wide bracket of green criminology, focusing on crimes that directly or indirectly impact the environment.

When subsuming environmental cybercrime under green criminology, scholars can better understand the occurrence, consequences, and, perhaps, ways to mitigate it. This approach also strikes an essential balance between ecological disasters and technological risks in the present technological era (González et al., 2024).

Key Drivers of Environmental Cybercrime

Environmental cybercrime has now emerged due to the following factors: Technological, political, and financial aspects.

1. Technological Vulnerabilities

The constant integration of digital technology-based environmental frameworks implies that the availability of reliable protection systems remains a work in progress. Key vulnerabilities include:

- **Smart Grids**: Wind or solar farms require intelligent grid visualization systems for efficient monitoring and management of power. These interconnected grids, as observed in some cases, do not have robust or end-to-end security features to offer, thus can become a favorite spot for cyber-criminals (Alsuwian et al., 2022).
- **IoT Devices**: IoT applications and systems are essential components of climate control and management of the environment. However, it was further noted that many IoT devices run with low security or, in the worst-case scenario, no security, opening numerous attack vectors to the attackers (Farooq et al., 2015).

- **Legacy Systems:** Most environmental infrastructures install older software and hardware applications for handling data, which makes them vulnerable to advanced persistent threats (Kshetri, 2016).

  Example: The 2020 Oldsmar water treatment plant attack in Florida emphasized these risks well. Terrorists tried to change its chemical components, which would not be safe for the health of the people and the environment (Krebs, 2021; Cervini et al., 2022). Hence, this experience revealed the need for better protection against cybersecurity threats in key environmental facilities.

2. Political Motivations

Political actors such as eco-terrorists and hacktivist groups are known to attack environmental systems to achieve a political cause. Their motivations include:

- **Protesting Government Policies:** Some activists vandalize environmental systems to raise concerns about institutional failures in setting the climate reform agenda (White, 2021).
- **Eco-Terrorism:** Militant ecological organizations can hinder the development of renewable power sources that they think are detrimental to the environment or too non-eco-friendly (González et al., 2024).

  Example: In 2016, during a cyber warfare attack, operations at a European wind farm were shut down. The attackers said the project affected the local species and wanted others to know of their problems with the project (Ige et al., 2024a; Ige et al., 2024b).

3. Financial Incentives

The systems within the environment are more often attacked for their monetary value. Methods include:

- **Ransomware:** Miscreants access and lock key networks, then extort money to regain normalcy. Renewable energy providers are highly susceptible due to the exigency of continued and unhampered production (Aliero et al., 2020).
- **Data Breaches:** Hackers shop sensitive environmental data for sale on the black market or for malicious business gains (Farooq et al., 2015).
- **Fraud:** Misrepresentation or arbitrage involving **Renewable Energy Certificates** (RECs) or carbon credit systems has also been employed to earn a profit (Nadtochiy, 2018).

Example: A 2019 ransomware attack on a solar panel manufacturer affected the global value chains and slowed down projects based on renewable energy sources, leading to numerous monetary losses (White, 2021).

Impacts of Cyberattacks on Clean Energy Infrastructures

Dissecting the impact of environmental cybercrime is not only the disruption of the intended systems but also some of the consequences related to the effects on the availability of energy supply, the trust in society, and global sustainable development.

1. **Disruption of Energy Supply:** Renewable energy systems are essential to the nation's power systems. Said attacks may cause blackouts, cause economic damages, and set back the process of decarbonization (Ige et al., 2024a, 24b).
2. **Undermining Public Trust:** The increased rate of significant cyberattacks leads to the loss of public confidence in renewable power systems and other technologies in environmental conservation. Such skepticism can jeopardize sustainable investment plans and hamper innovation in new technologies (Aliero et al., 2020).
3. **Threat to Global Sustainability Goals:** IT sabotage of environmental systems hinders the progress towards realizing global climate treaties like the Paris climate deal. These setbacks, which bring back the use of fossil fuels, escalate the global climate challenge (Ekechukwu & Simpa, 2024).

Case Study Highlight: *The SolarWinds Cyberattack*

- **Incident:** In the year 2020, the IT management software of SolarWinds was targeted by hackers, exposing its weakness across several sectors, including renewable systems of energy (Nadtochiy, 2018).
- **Impact:** Exposed critical vulnerabilities in clean energy infrastructures and their systems, including interruptions of everyday business and doubts over digital protection.
- **AI's Role:** Machine learning applications were used to quickly identify the attack and avoid widespread connection of compromised networks.

RISE OF ENVIRONMENTAL CYBERCRIME

Environmental cybercrime has emerged as a paramount threat in the digital world, attacking essential structures that promote environmental security. As more renewable energy systems, climate monitoring technologies, and intelligent grids integrate their systems into a central network, their defense weakens against cybercrimes. Scientific dangers, governmental and command reasons, profits, and state-supported cyberattacks are some causes of environmental cybercrime. These drivers explain other aspects of different environmental systems and stress the importance of successful cybersecurity implementation.

Technological Vulnerabilities of Renewable Energy Systems

Wind turbines, photovoltaic, and hydropower electrical generation structures employ digital networks. These systems are smart grid integrated interconnect and IoT-based devices and cloud computing-based system infrastructure, hence very vulnerable to cyber threats.

Key Vulnerabilities:

1. **Smart Grids:** Smart grids improve energy distribution and make renewable energy systems a part of national power systems. However, they are based on centralized control systems, which the attackers might leverage to tamper with energy supply, as Alsuwian et al. (2022) noted.
2. **IoT Devices:** There is a conclusion that IoT devices like sensors for weather and metering energy require additional levels of security more often than others. These devices open possibilities for creating entries for hackers, who can use them to get a sweeping entry into more extensive networks (Farooq et al., 2015).
3. **Outdated Software and Legacy Systems:** Yesterday's software runs many renewable energy systems, and hackers know how to take advantage of that. Many legacy systems lack features within today's mainstream operating systems and are considered easy attack targets (Kshetri, 2016).

    Example: An attack in the year 2020 struck and disrupted the operations of a European wind farm through its weak IoT-based control systems. The attack threatened to block oil supplies for some time and drew attention to the urgency of protecting renewable energy assets (Ige et al., 2024a; Ige et al., 2024b).

    Impact: Technological weaknesses in renewable energy systems undermine energy security and economic prosperity and advance sustainable development goals. Many of such risks can be reduced by improving the security of these systems.

Political and Ideological Motivations of Eco-Terrorists and Hacktivist Groups

Environmental systems have now become vulnerable to attacks from politically and ideologically motivated groups like the eco-terrorists and hacktivists. These groups use cyberspace's weaknesses to achieve their goals, disrupting functionality and calling for their causes.

Eco-Terrorism: In as much as eco-terrorists support certain forms of energy production, they are likely to attack renewable energy sources that they consider dangerous to the environment. For example, they might claim that wind turbines interfere with the species distribution of local wildlife or that large-scale solar plants encroach on wildlife habitats (White, 2021). Cyberattacks are offered to these groups as ways by which they can derail projects without having to get involved physically.

Hacktivism: Cyberterrorism is achieved by hacktivists to express themselves against modern environmental policies or specific industrial processes. They frequently try to publicly shame governments or companies, slow business or production, and increase awareness about environmental problems (Nadtochiy, 2018).

Example: In 2016, one of the European hacktivists worked on a cyber attack on a wind farm facility and shut down their control systems for several hours. They also pointed an accusing finger at the group, stating that Open Farm affected migratory birds (Ige et al., 2024a; Ige et al., 2024b).

Impact: These politically and ideologically motivated attacks slow the transition to renewable power, raise costs, and change the conversation about the benefits of renewable energy.

Financial Incentives Driving Ransomware and Other Cyberattacks

The renewable energy sector has emerged as a preferred attack vector for financially driven cyber attackers. As shown above, criminal opportunism means behavior that seeks to profit from the rise of danger to critical infrastructures through hacking activities like ransomware attacks, data breaches, or fraud.

Ransomware Attacks: The exact nature of ransomware is that the system's data is encrypted, thereby becoming inaccessible to the owner without paying the demanded sum. Continuous operations make renewable energy providers an especially valuable target for this type of blackmail (Aliero et al., 2020).

Data Breaches: Cybercriminals can gain unauthorized access to over-environmental data, including using energy consumption patterns, identities of new technologies, or designs of gizmos that can be sold on black markets or for corporate espionage (Farooq et al., 2015).

Fraudulent Manipulation: Hackers exploit renewable energy certificates and carbon credit systems for financial benefit. The following fraud erodes confidence in sustainability programs (Ekechukwu & Simpa, 2024).

Example: In 2019, ransomware infected key production systems at a global solar panel manufacturer, meaning the global delay of renewable energy projects. The attack affected the supply chain cost with losses and negatively impacted business reputation (White, 2021).

Impact: Militants, acting financially, are prone to modern renewable energy initiatives that involve radical risks and add more hurdles to climate goals.

State-Sponsored Cyber Warfare Targeting Energy Grids and Environmental Systems

Nation-states have begun formally reflecting on exploiting environmental systems as a critical factor in geophysical confrontations. Cyber warfare by states seeks to destabilize adversary states through cyber sabotage of power infrastructure and delaying sustainability projects.

Geopolitical Motivations:

- **Energy Dependency:** Sustained assaults on renewable energy systems can make a country more dependent on fossil fuels even as it harms its energy sustainability and climate change goals.
- **Economic Sabotage:** Going after critical industries such as renewable energy manufacturing damages a nation's balance of payments (Kshetri, 2016).

  Sophisticated Tactics: Cyber espionage using the **Advanced Persistent Threat** (APT) is usually used by state-sponsored actors that want to persistently gain access to a system, exfiltrate sensitive information, or stage a future massive attack (Nadtochiy, 2018).

  Example: The most recent and suspected state-sponsored cyberattack in 2020 was directed toward SolarWinds and multiple renewable energy infrastructure sectors. The breach was made in IT management application software, which exposed important data and operations (Krebs, 2021; Cervini et al., 2022).

Impact: Cyber warfare as a strategy supported by the states undermines energy security, hinders the transition to renewable energy sources, and raises global tensions.

GREEN CRIMINOLOGY AND ITS THEORETICAL FOUNDATIONS

Definition and Scope of Green Criminology

Green criminology is an empirical-theoretical study area concerning crimes against the environment and actions or processes that harm ecosystems, wildlife, and, or bio-diversity. It explores people impacting the environment legally regarding environmental degradation being the social-political and economic consequence (White, 2021). Contrary to conventional criminology, green does not focus on crimes against persons or properties but covers forms of harm involving environmental offenses, such as pollution, deforestation, and wildlife sales in the black market (Gibbs et al., 2009).

Critical aspects of green criminology include:

1. **Ecological Justice:** Promoting the idea of ecosystem preservation and acknowledging the subjective value of non-human objects.
2. **Environmental Justice:** Exploring how different communities suffer the consequences of environmental degradation.
3. **Crimes of Omission and Commission:** Being related to intentional violation of legal requirements or other wrongdoing (e.g., unlawful disposal of wastes) and failure to prevent adverse environmental impacts (e.g., criminal omission in operating hazardous facilities).

Traditional green crime has widened its horizon with the development of information technology and the internet to include a new concept known as **cyber environmental criminology**, which targets facilities that enable and support environmental conservation (Nadtochiy, 2018). This new domain raises the argument of transforming green criminological threats and the need to change the traditional theories to fit these threats.

Application of Green Criminological Theories to Environmental Cybercrime

Explaining and preventing environmental cybercrime: Green criminological theories are an ideal reference point because they address these crimes regarding their motives, outputs, and causes.

1. **Crimes of the Powerful:** This theory postulates that business organizations and other governmental organizations or agencies are involved in activities that pollute the environment deliberately or recklessly. For **environmental cybercriminal acts, corporate espionage** and **state-sponsored cyber** warping belong to this category (White, 2021). For example, organizations may sabotage rivals' renewable energy schemes for business gains - energy organizations may disrupt rivals' energy structures to destabilize their economies and ecological bases (Ige et al., 2024a; Ige et al., 2024b).
2. **Environmental Victimization:** This concept focuses on the victims of environmental harm, including communities, ecosystems, and future generations. Alitigation of climate change monitoring frameworks or renewable energy power stations is an indirect measurement of the impacts of cyberattacks, as they delay efforts toward developing and deploying sustainable technologies, forcing the world to stick to poisonous energy sources (Gibbs et al., 2009).
3. **Intersection with Green Capitalism:** Green criminology problematizes the concept of "**green capitalism**," where the environment is commercialized. Techno-global cybercrime, including the fraud of carbon credit systems, erodes the basis of green capitalism because it takes advantage of the system's weaknesses, although its aim is primarily financial (González et al., 2024).

Integration with Digital Criminology to Address the Complexities of Cyber Threats

As criminals shift to online terrorism toward environmental protection, green criminology must merge with **digital criminology**, which analyses crimes on an online platform. Teaching and researching interdisciplinary enable researchers to study environmental cybercrime from an ecological and technological lens.

1. **Bridging Physical and Digital Harm:** Green criminology can be traditionally defined as a type of criminology that deals with offenses against the environment, and digital criminology investigates crimes connected with the information world. By integrating these fields, the researchers can explain how environmental

losses occur due to digital offenses like hacking renewable energy grids (Farooq et al., 2015).

2. **Motivational Analysis:** Psychological and sociological motivations of those involved in cybercrime that can be learned from digital criminology include financial gain, political influence, or environmental activism. These motivations overlap with green criminology's concern with underlying structures, including corporate rivalry and Global Conflict (Nadtochiy, 2018).
3. **Policy and Enforcement Synergy:** Integrating the findings of green and digital criminology enables formulating policies that capture both the ecological and the cybersecurity of environmental crime. For instance, legislation on the security of things within Renewable Energy systems may bar cybercriminal attacks yet promote renewability (Ekechukwu & Simpa, 2024).

    Example of Integration: The cyberattack on SolarWinds occurred in 2020, proving that green and digital criminology should be incorporated. Though primarily aimed at computer and IT systems, it affected renewable energies directly, delayed many clean-tech initiatives, and shed light on the weaknesses of digital systems central to sustainability goals (Krebs, 2021; Cervini et al., 2022).

Table 1. Comparison of Green Criminology and Digital Criminology

Aspect	Green Criminology	Digital Criminology	Integrated Approach
Focus	Environmental harm (e.g., deforestation).	Cybercrimes (e.g., hacking, data breaches).	Cybercrimes cause environmental harm (e.g., attacks on smart grids).
Motivations	Economic gain, negligence, systemic drivers.	Financial incentives, ideology, politics.	Political and economic drivers intersect with ecological harm.
Policy Recommendations	Strengthen environmental protection laws.	Enhance cybersecurity frameworks.	Develop policies addressing both digital and ecological vulnerabilities.

Case Application: Environmental Cybercrime in Practice

The integration of green and digital criminology discussed above can be well realized in cases like a ransomware attack on a solar panel manufacturer in 2019.

- **Green Criminology Perspective:** This attack set back renewable energy initiatives and increased fossil energy usage, hence worsening environmental impacts.
- **Digital Criminology Perspective:** This taste targeted the vulnerabilities inherent in most digital systems to get financial outcomes.
- **Integrated Analysis:** To prevent and respond to such crimes, there is a need to enhance the technical security of renewable power structures and raise the severity of the consequences of cyber offenses affecting environmental protection.

Therefore, green criminology gives a strong foundation for studying environmental crime's structural causative factors and consequences and the nature and purpose of cybercrime in digital criminology. Undoubtedly, to deal with the multifaceted risks of environmental cybercrime in the modern world much more is needed than the solutions offered in fields such as computer science, criminal justice, and management. The research presented herein underlines this approach as the focus on various types of such crimes and the building of appropriate policies and enforcement measures is stronger when rooted in both fields.

ROLE OF AI IN COMBATING ENVIRONMENTAL CYBERCRIME

Since there cannot be a comprehensive guide to Artificial Intelligence in combating the menace of environmental cybercrime, we find AI invaluable. Because of its capacity to analyze humongous volumes of data, recognize trends about system compromises, and react to risks independently, it is very valuable in defending sensitive structures like renewable energy networks, climate change diagnostics, or ecological data archives. This reveals that AI can help organizations boost their cyber security against enhanced cyber threats that threaten environmentally relevant systems.

AI Applications in Cybersecurity

1. **Automated Threat Detection Using Anomaly Detection Algorithms:** The automated monitoring by pattern recognition units scans the networks and system activity constantly for signs of an unusual pattern that could be associated with a cyber threat. These algorithms identify an unknown attack, such as zero-day attacks or insider threats that other security mechanisms can identify (Alsuwian et al., 2022).

Example: To prevent such situations in a smart grid, anomaly detection can identify irregular energy flow or unauthorized trials to access the grid, which may cause energy distribution disruption.

2. **Predictive Analytics for Forecasting Cyber Threats:** This is a case of predictive analytics involving artificial intelligence in analyzing trends that indicate future attacks. Because AI systems see patterns of hostile action, it becomes possible to prevent undue threats to weak systems (Farooq et al., 2015).

    Example: The details of earlier ransomware attacks can be used to train an AI model to project an attack on renewable energy providers so that protective measures may be instituted beforehand.

3. **Machine Learning and Neural Networks for Adaptive Defense Mechanisms:** Artificial Intelligence (AI), in general, and the ability of Machine Learning (ML) and neural networks to learn from past experiences make cybersecurity more flexible. Such technologies allow a system to adapt to previous accidents to reduce the ability to identify more threats.

    Example: Real-time data gathered from the IoT sensors can be analyzed by the neural networks to determine what patterns represent the indicators of cyber threats, such as device behaviors that are abnormal or unauthorized firmware updates (Nadtochiy, 2018).

Real-World Applications

1. **Success Stories of AI in Protecting Clean Energy Infrastructures:** AI has significantly protected renewable energy systems against cyber-attacks.

    Case Study: One wind farm in the European region was constantly under phishing and malware that affected its operational systems. The farm managed and mitigated these threats through the help of AI cybersecurity defense systems to ensure that energy production proceeded unhampered (Ige et al., 2024a; Ige et al., 2024b).

2. **Use of AI in Safeguarding Sensitive Environmental Data:** This insight is derived from the fact that climate modeling data, systematic conservation planning, and other forms of data that inform the sustainable development of the environment are critical. AI can also improve data security because the system recognizes and analyses the access patterns and tries to seek out the malign persons who make the penetrations and piracy.

    Example: The **National Renewable Energy Laboratory** (NREL) in the United States utilizes AI systems to preserve big datasets for the security and confidentiality of research (González et al., 2024).

AI-Driven Incident Response

AI has a significant advantage in threat detection and the automation of the response to such threats to mitigate their impact on the business by reducing their overall duration and occurrence.

Real-Time Mitigation Strategies Using AI-Powered Automation: If threats are identified, AI systems can handle the threats proactively, identifying infected networks, blocking the threats, and reclaiming compromised systems without intervention from the administrator.
Case Study: In the 2020 SolarWinds cyberattack, users with AI-based cybersecurity solutions could isolate the breach and quickly focus on the affected systems since the tools would filter infected machines and flag those that required remediation first (Nadtochiy, 2018).

Advantages:

- Automated interactions respond much quicker than manual intercessions.
- Decrease in the number of operations that shut down during recovery.
- Strengthening critical environmental processes' stability and predicting similar attacks on renewable energy providers, allowing them to implement defenses in advance.

Table 2. AI Applications in Environmental Cybersecurity

AI Application	Function	Real-World Example
Anomaly Detection	Identifies deviations from standard patterns, signaling potential threats.	Intelligent grid anomaly detection preventing unauthorized access.
Predictive Analytics	Anticipates future cyber threats based on historical trends.	Forecasting ransomware attacks on renewable energy providers.
Machine Learning	Learns from past incidents to improve threat detection and response	Identifying malware targeting IoT sensors in environmental systems.
Incident Response	Automates mitigation strategies, minimizing damage and downtime.	Containing the SolarWinds cyberattack through automated responses.

Case Study: AI Protecting Renewable Energy Systems

Incident: In 2021, a ransomware attack affected a solar energy firm worldwide, and extreme measures were applied to essential data; production came to a standstill.

AI's Role:

- **Detection:** Machine learning logs picked the features of high-traffic access patterns as a sign of ransomware.
- **Response:** Thus, mitigating measures ensured the ransomware did not spread through the other servers as the entire system was automated.
- **Recovery:** Thanks to the AI tools, the decryption process was fast, and the company was able to start functioning in the following days.

Outcome: The occurrence proved that using artificial intelligence to implement cybersecurity strategies helps reduce financial and operational losses in clean energy projects (Ige et al., 2024a; Ige et al., 2024b).

Therefore, it is possible to conclude that such an impact has remained AI on environmental cybersecurity, and it can be appreciated as the improved approaches to threat detection, protection, and combating. The application of AI facilitates the improvement of the security and maintenance of critical infrastructures for sustainability by embracing anomaly detection to predictive analytics and automated incident response. With the constant emergence of environmental cybercrime, AI in the frameworks will be crucial in protecting the technologies instrumental in environmental advancement.

AI'S ROLE IN PROTECTING AGAINST ECO-TERRORISM AND GREEN CRIMES

Global sustainable and security issues accompanied by eco-terrorism and green crimes in the new digital era have appeared. Renewable energy projects, climate initiatives, and protesting environmental policies are among their targets; thus, eco-terrorists and hacktivists employ cyber tools to achieve their goals. These threats have consistent AI solutions that can monitor and anticipate their occurrence while utilizing advanced analytics, real-time monitoring, and self-executing responses. This section focuses on the potential of AI in responding to new types of criminal threats, including eco-terrorism and green crimes.

Monitoring Social Media and Dark Web Forums for Early Threat Detection

Subgroups of environmental activists and hackers usually have an opportunity to build organizations, recruit members, and plan attacks using the internet. Communication platforms are key since social media and the dark web are discussion platforms. These tools should be able to monitor such platforms to determine signs of potential threats still in their infancy.

AI in action: The AI systems track words and phrases connected with eco-terrorism, tags, hashtags, and any other patterns that might occur on the network. For instance, mentioning undermining wind/solar energy systems or sure global warming causes can seal them for further research (Farooq et al., 2015).

Real-world Example: The use of AI in monitoring social media platforms for incidences of disruption for a solar farm project was noticed by an AI tool in early 2021. By observing posts and comments, authorities acted before the physical and digital selfish sabotage occurred (Ige et al., 2024a; Ige et al., 2024b).

Network Analysis and Behavioral Monitoring to Track Eco-Terrorist Activities

Most eco-terrorists work under loosely connected networks, which makes it difficult to follow their actions the same way as other groups. Network analysis tools developed through Artificial intelligence can capture and analyze the connection of people, groups, and organizations involved in eco-terrorism.

- **Capabilities:**
    - o Mapping of the different links present within the eco-terrorist systems.
    - o Identify employees within organizations and the relationships between them to reveal organizational power structures.
    - o Studying interactions to foretell possible actions (Nadtochiy, 2018).
- Behavioral Monitoring: It is also convenient for AI systems to track behavioral patterns, shifts in activities, changes in the language used, or coordinated activities to identify threats. It is instrumental in pointing out stealth or inactive profile holders or individuals who may evolve to become radical eventually.
- An example of anti-wind farm activists is the eco-terrorism group that disrupted the European wind farm project in 2020. Through the analysis of the group's social networking sites, relationships between the group and persons of interest with the intent of conducting cyber-attacks were revealed to be

accurate by AI. This intelligence was used to act against it before the attack could be made by the network (González et al., 2024).

Natural Language Processing (NLP) for Sentiment Analysis of Environmental Discourse

Natural Language Processing, or NLP, is an application field or branch of AI that deals with how a machine can understand natural language. The practical use of NLP tools helps estimate the population's attitude toward environmental problems, evaluate potential dangers, and search for radical speech.

Applications:

- o **Sentiment Analysis:** Such software, in general, reads vast amounts of social media activity, forums, and news to identify what the public thinks or feels about specific environmental policies or projects.
- o **Threat Detection:** Detecting words that signal aggression, incitement, or destruction planning.
- o **Geotagging:** Identifying the source of threats by studying different language usage in a specific area and using contextual hints (Farooq et al., 2015).

Case Study: In 2022, the authors detected increasing incivility regarding a hydropower project in South America through the NLP tool. The language analysis also identified instigative efforts towards protest formation and interruption of activities to inform timely preventative measures (Ige et al., 2024a & 2024b).

AI-Powered Early Warning Systems for Potential Eco-Terrorism Threats

Early warning system employs machine learning, NLP, and network analysis features and issues immediate threat warnings of eco-terrorism. These systems analyze social media data sets, communication network data sets, and data from IoT devices for risk identification and forecasting.

Components of AI-Powered Early Warning Systems:

- **Data Aggregation:** Casually referred to as scraping, the process of gathering data from social media platforms, IoT sensors, and dark web forums.

- **Pattern Recognition:** Detecting trends suggestive of pre-planned terror threats, for instance, higher levels of coordination on social media or around target potentials.
- **Real-Time Alerts:** Typically, notifications are sent to authorities and stakeholders to enable them to act in the shortest time possible (González et al., 2024).

  Example: Just recently, at the **United Nations Climate Change Conference 2021: COP26**, an artificial intelligence working as an early warning system for hacktivists reported a rise in the threat of hacktivists for renewable energy projects. It also enabled organizers to improve various facets of cybersecurity, thus avoiding significant disruptions.

Table 3. AI Applications in Combating Eco-Terrorism

AI Application	Function	Real-World Example
Social Media Monitoring	Scans platforms for keywords, patterns, and suspicious activities.	Detecting plans to disrupt a solar farm project (Ige et al., 2024a).
Network Analysis	Maps relationships and communication within eco-terrorist networks.	Identifying key actors in a European wind farm opposition group.
NLP and Sentiment Analysis	Analyzes language to assess public sentiment and detect extremist rhetoric.	Flagging hostile language against a hydropower project (Farooq et al., 2015).
Early Warning Systems	Integrates multiple AI tools to provide real-time alerts on potential threats.	Preventing cyberattacks during COP26 (González et al., 2024).

Thus, technology, especially artificial intelligence, presents the perfect tool for mitigating these new forms of terrorism. AI can detect threats still in its germination process through social media and Dark web surveillance, analyzing relationship clusters and performing NLP for Sentiment analysis. Incorporated in early warning systems, AI gives instantaneous notifications for actions by competent authorities to address the potential disconnection of environmental systems. As eco-terrorism and green crimes are constantly changing, the integration of artificial intelligence solutions is going to be crucial for the protection of international sustainability efforts.

CASE STUDIES

Case Study 1: SolarWinds Cyberattack on Renewable Energy Grids

Background, Methods, and Impact on Renewable Energy Systems

The attack on the **SolarWinds Company** was one of the most extensive cyber events in 2020. It got into SolarWinds' supply chain to infiltrate its Orion software, which is used globally as an IT monitoring tool. Hackers placed malware within software updates distributed across hundreds of organizations worldwide, including many governmental and private institutions working on renewable energy projects (Krebs, 2021; Cervini et al., 2022).

Attack Methodology: The attack's Advanced Persistent Threat (APT) methodologies include methods that enable it to gain unauthorized access to systems. When inside, attackers could pre-emptively scout out networks and pilfer data ranging from personal identification numbers and passwords to the strategic control of energy companies, specifically renewable energy sources.

Impact on Renewable Energy Systems:

- **Operational Disruption:** IT management solutions provider SolarWinds impacted utilities of renewable energy grids.
- **Data Compromise:** Network and intellectual property related to energy generation and transmission were compromised, and future security threats grew.
- **Financial Losses:** Companies had to bear considerable expenses to scan, prevent, and overcome the effects of the attack.
- **Reputational Damage:** The public confidence and assurance that renewable energy systems are secure was jeopardized.

Role of AI in Detection, Mitigation, and Recovery

AI technologies played a critical role in detecting and mitigating the impact of the SolarWinds attack:

- **Detection:** Machine learning-derived anomaly recognition systems detected irregular network activities due to compromised SolarWinds updates. For instance, a case where the machine learning models were to raise early alarms involved the identification of unexpected data transfers and unauthorized access attempts.

- **Mitigation:** AI-based automatic actions provided system isolation of the attacked nodes, thus stopping the attack's development. The latest machine learning techniques were applied to study the pattern of dangerous attacks to prevent malicious traffic flow in real time.
- **Recovery:** Tools after the incident helped determine which systems had been compromised on priority and confirmed that no open doors were left. Predictive analytics was applied to build up the requisite fortifications to counter such attacks in the future.

Lessons Learned and Implications for Future Cybersecurity Efforts

- **Enhanced Supply Chain Security:** It also highlighted the processes that must be followed to vet third-party software and monitor the systems that incorporate such products.
- **Adoption of AI-powered cybersecurity:** It was clearly shown how AI is helpful in the identification and prevention of attacks within the current protective paradigms. Interest should be focused on the further utilization of artificial intelligence-based technologies in renewable energy infrastructures.
- **Collaborative Responses:** The SolarWinds cyberattack exposed the need for intergovernmental, international, and corporate cooperation while seeking a solution to a resurgent global cyber menace.

Case Study 2: Eco-Terrorism Threats Mitigated by AI

Analysis of Thwarted Eco-Terrorism Plots Using AI-Driven Monitoring Tools

Eco-terrorism attacks in Europe for the year 2021 were aimed at derailing operations of renewable energy, that is, wind farming, under the guise of environmentalism. These plots were prevented by using artificial intelligence based on detecting and monitoring.

- **Threat Landscape:**
    - o The eco-terrorist group coordinated in encrypted conferencing apps and social media, plotting to damage key parts in wind power generators.
    - o The group alleged that the farms were negatively affecting biodiversity in the region and spread further propaganda on the internet.
- **AI's Role in Prevention:**

- o **Social Media Monitoring:** AI systems searched through public and private social platforms and news groups for eco-terrorism-relevant keywords and hashtags.
- o **Network Analysis:** AI used organizational analysis to map the organizational communication structures of the group, including important communicators and their relationships.
- o **Behavioral Analysis:** Through AI instruments, they observed changes in the activity dynamics of the group, including the increase in the level of organizational cooperation and scouting actions close to the intended wind power plants.

Insights into AI's Role in Ensuring Environmental Security

- **Early Detection of Threats:** Their potential to process big data from various sources meant that authorities could uncover the plots before anyone got physically or digitally hurt.
- **Proactive Measures:** Security teams were able to predict the group's actions using predictive analytics so that corresponding measures like increasing on-site security and reinforcing the grids could be taken.
- **Strengthening Public Trust:** This has helped reduce the probability of such natural calamities causing attacks, thus giving the stakeholders confidence in the renewable energy projects.

Table 4. Comparison of the Two Case Studies

Aspect	SolarWinds Cyberattack	Eco-Terrorism Threats
Motivation	Financial gain, espionage.	Ideological opposition to renewable energy projects.
Target	IT systems in renewable energy grids.	Wind farms and associated infrastructure.
AI's Role	Detection, mitigation, and recovery.	Monitoring, behavioral analysis, and threat prevention.
Outcome	Mitigated through AI-driven anomaly detection.	Plots were thwarted before any harm occurred.

These cases demonstrate how the threat landscape of environmental cybercrime is constantly changing and why renewable energy systems need the help of AI. Shifting gears from identifying and addressing complicated supply chain security threats such as the SolarWinds compromise to stopping apocalyptic terrorism plans via network and behavior analytics, peoples' technology shows its ability to protect world sustainability initiatives. AI adoption in environmental cybersecurity frameworks will safeguard key structures and retain people's confidence in environmentally friendly products.

ETHICAL, LEGAL, AND POLICY CHALLENGES

The use of AI in dealing with environmental cybercrime brings about a lot of ethical, legal, and policy issues. Regarding AI in the context of cyber threats, cutting-edge opportunities include detection, risk minimization, or prevention while raising profound philosophical and practical concerns related to privacy, fairness, accountability, and, ultimately, governance. It is crucial to try to solve these problems because only in this way will the public's trust be gained, ethical norms will be obeyed, and effective regulation will be set only in this way.

Ethical Considerations

1. Balancing Security Needs with Privacy Rights and Data Protection

Environments for implementing AI systems for cybersecurity can be sourcing vast data from IoT devices, **Social Networking Sites** (SNSs), and communication networks. Although these systems improve threat detection, they have substantial drawbacks due to violating privacy rights and data protection (González et al., 2024).

- **Privacy Concerns:** Monitoring social media platforms and forums to find eco-terrorist activity may involve acquiring personal data unrelated to threats. One potential issue with data collection is that it may infringe on individual rights to privacy if it is not done so through ethical means (Aliero et al., 2020).
- **Data Protection:** Climate research, renewable energy grid operations, and similar information must not be accessible to individuals who intend to misuse it. Such legal requirements as the **General Data Protection Regulation** (GDPR) can be met to maintain compliance with data protection laws.

2. Addressing Algorithmic Bias and Ensuring Fairness in AI Systems

In simple terms, it is immediately apparent that it is true that AI systems are only as good as the data that is fed to them. Insights learned during training include biases, and as such, trained AI models that operate on this data may make unfair decisions.

- **Examples of Bias:**

    - When threat profiling entails certain groups, then unfavorable discrimination results occur.
    - Classification of elaborate pieces of beneficial and harmless nature as potential threats created cross-cultural or language barriers between the involved parties.
- **Ensuring Fairness:** The issue of algorithmic bias can be solved by performing testing and adequately selecting the training data, as well as by consistent monitoring of AI-based systems with the help of special tools to identify cases when the AI system functions unfairly (Farooq et al., 2015).

Legal and Regulatory Frameworks

1. Gaps in Existing Laws to Regulate AI-Driven Environmental Cybersecurity

Today's legal guidelines must suffice to respond to AI's threats to environmental cybersecurity effectively.

- **Lack of Specificity:** Such legislation primarily targets orthodox information technology contexts and requires an extension to what is brought about by artificial intelligence and related innovations (Ekechukwu & Simpa, 2024).
- **Accountability Gaps:** The attribution of responsibility for AI results, particularly those of a false positive or negative nature, has become a complex legal matter.

2. Need for International Collaboration to Establish Standardized Legal Frameworks

Threats to environmental systems are universal and, many times, are beyond the boundaries of any country. Efforts to address these threats have to be approached on an international level.

- **Standardization:** There is always the resultant effect of standardizing such tools, hence the need for international standardization norms for AI cybersecurity tools.
- **Treaties & Agreements:** International conventions, like those regarding climate change, might regulate the usage of AI in environmental cybersecurity and enable cooperation between states (Nadtochiy, 2018).

Transparency and Accountability

1. Ensuring Transparency in AI Decision-Making Processes

AI systems also work in restricted modes; people must understand how an AI system solves problems. Such lack of disclosure can, in turn, reduce accountabilities and hence establish trust.

- **Challenges:**
  - o Challenges will likely be faced in auditing artificial intelligence algorithms to comply with ethical standards.
  - o Lack of capability of an AI model to rationalize its action-algorithm decisions to the clients, for instance, why some activities were identified as risks (González et al., 2024).
- **Solutions:**
  - o **Explainable AI** (XAI) models can show how decisions are made.
  - o Developing controls to check whether the AI systems under consideration run afoul of ethical or legal requirements.

2. Building Public Trust in AI Technologies

The population's culture regarding AI deliberation in environment cybersecurity is essential to its applicability. Trust is needed to prevent stakeholders from implementing such systems, which impairs performance.

- **Building Trust:**
  - o Sensitization of society on the potential and constraints of employing artificial intelligence systems.
  - o Illustrating this, AI should be made transparent and fair, and it should provide a clear account of how it works.

• **Case Study:** In 2021, some artificial intelligent systems acted as an early warning against eco-terrorism targeting renewable energy installations. However, due to the absence of public announcements on how these systems worked, there were many doubts and calls for more openness (Ige et al., 2024a; Ige et al., 2024b).

Table 5. Ethical, Legal, and Policy Challenges in AI for Environmental Cybersecurity

Challenge	Description	Proposed Solution
Privacy Concerns	Monitoring tools may collect personal data unrelated to cyber threats.	Ensure compliance with privacy laws (e.g., GDPR) and implement data anonymization techniques.
Algorithmic Bias	AI systems may perpetuate biases, leading to unfair threat profiling.	Use diverse training datasets and conduct regular audits to identify and rectify biases.
Accountability Gaps	Determining responsibility for AI outcomes remains unclear.	Develop legal frameworks assigning liability for AI decision-making.
Lack of Transparency	AI decision-making processes are often opaque, hindering trust.	Adopt explainable AI (XAI) models and establish independent auditing mechanisms.
Global Collaboration	Cyber threats often transcend national borders, requiring international cooperation.	Establish treaties and global standards for AI-driven environmental cybersecurity.

Therefore, while AI has great potential in mitigating environmental cybercrime, its implementation is laden with ethical, legal, and policy concerns. Among the awareness, concerns regarding security essential requirements and privacy rights, bias present in algorithms, and transparency are among the key points that should be met to achieve an acceptable and trustful integration of AI systems. Moreover, we must plug the legal and regulatory loopholes and work with the world's countries to develop a multi-tier AI-based environmental cybersecurity system. Minimizing these challenges enables stakeholders to take advantage of AI's advantages without violating legal and ethical compliance.

METHODOLOGY AND APPROACH

The approach to studying the crossroads of green criminology, environmental cybercrime, and artificial intelligence (AI) is based on a research design that reflects a holistic and interdisciplinary approach. This contributes to a systematic literature review of environmental cybercrime, case studies, interviews with cybersecurity and AI experts, and a comparative analysis to provide practical recommendations for tackling environmental cybercrime using artificial intelligence.

1. Literature Review:

Literature on green criminology, cybercrime, and AI serves as the literature base of this study and is widely reviewed to establish the literature review. This approach defines areas of insufficient knowledge and develops theories used in the later analyses.

Focus Areas:

- **Green Criminology:** To explore environmental offenses, offenses against ecosystems, and the introduction of new theoretical advancements such as cybercrime (White, 2021; Gibbs et al., 2009).
- **Cybercrime:** Research acknowledging the techniques used, objectives, and effect on renewable energy systems and environmental technologies of cyber threats (Nadtochiy, 2018; Ige et al., 2024a; Ige et al., 2024b).
- **AI in Cybersecurity:** A case-based study on the use of AI in threat identification, risk analysis, and management with a focus on environmental conservation through the use of Gonzalez et al., 2024, and Farooq et al., 2015 resources.

Deliverables:

- Critical issues include the weakness of renewable power systems and the ethical application of artificial intelligence.
- Integration of case studies into well-defined theories and concepts and research studies.

2. Case Study Analysis:

In the current study, detailed case studies offer evidential information on the practical application of AI in preventing environmental cybercrime.

Selected Case Studies:

- **SolarWinds Cyberattack:** Understanding how AI works, what it does, and what part it played in dealing with the supply chain assault on renewable power solutions.
- **Eco-Terrorism Threats:** Examining the reasons behind sabotage and disruptions of environmental projects and how AI monitoring could help.

Methodology for Case Analysis:

- **Data Collection:** From cybersecurity reports, articles, journals, and media headlines.
- **Evaluation Metrics:** Evaluating how such AI tools are used in detection, reduction, and response during these incidences.
- **Comparative Insights:** Looking for traces that can be recurrent in other events or situations.

Outcomes:

- An understanding of multiple tasks and benefits of using AI in environmental cybersecurity.

- Information on successful past mitigation endeavors and those not to guide future efforts.

3. Expert Interviews:

Having experts in the field provide insights into their experience ensures an accurate life view of the problems that AI encounters and how it can address environmental cybercrime.

Participants:

- **Cybersecurity Experts:** Providers of solutions protecting solar panels and other related innovative equipment.
- **AI Researchers:** Owners of AI algorithms designed to protect from cyber threats and preserve the environment.
- **Environmental Scientists:** IT experts with knowledge of cyber threats' effects on the ecosystem.

Methodology:

- **Structured Interviews:** The participants respond to the questions concerning AI and its strengths, weaknesses, strengths, and oversights in ethics and regulations.
- **Thematic Analysis:** Striving to find the common topics and organize the materials to show both sides of the issue.

Sample Questions:

1. Which type of renewable energy systems experiences the primary cybersecurity threats?
2. How would AI-driven tools help in overcoming these challenges?
3. What ethical and legal issues should be considered when implementing AI in environmental protection?

Expected Contributions:

- Examples of information regarding the practical application of AI-based cybersecurity solutions.
- Advice was given by the experts regarding ethical, legal, and technical clearing issues.

4. Comparative Analysis

This component looks at the proactivity of AI within the environmental sustainability sectors by analyzing the effectiveness, difficulties, and expandability of AI presence in the industries.

Comparison Sectors:

- **Renewable Energy Systems:** AI solutions could protect wind farms, solar stations, and hydropower stations.
- **Climate Monitoring:** Leverage Artificial Intelligence to protect and process environmental information received from IoT and satellite systems.
- **Waste Management:** AI in making waste sorting and recycling automation systems.

Analytical Framework:

- **Effectiveness:** Measuring AI's effectiveness in the increases it has accomplished in council cyberattacks and their effects.
- **Scalability:** Estimating the portability of AI tools to various settings and structures.
- **Ethical and Legal Implications:** Defining sector relations and how challenges in that particular sector would affect other sectors.

Findings:

- For anomaly detection and predictive analytics, AI shows consistently high results across all industries.
- Issues like algorithm problems and inconsistency of regulations differ from one sector to another.
- In one sector, solutions learned by another create a basis for enhancing participation and increasing inter-sectoral interaction.

Table 6. Methodological Components and Deliverables

Methodology Component	Focus Area	Deliverables
Literature Review	Green criminology, cybercrime, AI.	Identification of themes, gaps, and frameworks for analysis.
Case Study Analysis	Real-world incidents of environmental cybercrime.	Empirical insights, lessons learned, and best practices.
Expert Interviews	Insights from professionals in relevant fields.	Practical recommendations for implementing AI-driven cybersecurity.
Comparative Analysis	AI deployment across sustainability sectors.	Comparative insights on AI effectiveness, scalability, and ethical implications.

By adopting this approach, this study develops a sound research framework for understanding the applicability of AI to environmental cybercrime. Integrating theory, qualitative data, literature review, and comparative studies achieves an interpretative understanding of the issues involved. By combining these views, the research provides practical insights into incorporating AI into environmental conservation.

TECHNOLOGICAL AND REGULATORY ROADMAP

Legislation, artificial intelligence development, and international cooperation are the key factors that need improvement to establish an integrated approach to prevent environmental cybercrime. This roadmap describes advancements in AI technologies for environmental cybersecurity, recommendations for increasing AI applications in environmental safeguards, and ideas for international cooperation to counter cyber threats to environmental systems.

1. Innovations in AI Technologies for Environmental Cybersecurity

With the new development in AI technologies, the capabilities of identifying, mitigating, and preventing environmental cyber threats have increased tremendously. The above innovations consist of the state-of-the-art application of tools in anomaly detection, predictive modeling, and autonomous response to system abnormalities specific to the environmental infrastructures.

Key Innovations:

- **Advanced Anomaly Detection Algorithms:** AI systems applied deep learning fashions to discover nuanced anomalous conditions in renewable energy grids, IoT gadgets, and climate sensing devices. These algorithms can find new attack scenarios, such as new vulnerabilities that have not been discovered before (Farooq et al., 2015).
- **Context-Aware Predictive Analytics:** Stemming from this, predictive models adapt external data from geopolitics or climate to predict cyber threats. For example, AI technologies can even guess there will be more cyber risks during large-scale environmental events such as the Conference of the Parties (COP) meetings (Nadtochiy, 2018).
- **Real-Time Adaptive Defense Mechanisms:** The use of artificial intelligence in the brains of these systems employs neural networks that learn from the ongoing attacks and modify defensive tactics continually. These mechanisms help to avoid the extended outages of vital environmental facilities and maintain the operation of those facilities.
- **Blockchain-Integrated AI for Data Security:** The integration of AI with blockchain increases the reliability of data and protects relevant

environment data, like climate models or renewable energy certificates, against fraud and unauthorized change (González et al., 2024).

Case Example: In the 2020 SolarWinds cyberattack case, all AI-based emerging behavior identification tools were able to identify abnormal data traffic across affected renewable energy facilities. These tools offered and released early signals so that attempts could be made to address them on time (Ige et al., 2024a; Ige et al., 2024b).

2. Recommendations for Enhancing the Integration of AI into Environmental Protection Strategies

To make optimal use of AI in countering environmental cybercrime, integrating AI must be prioritized in environmental protection measures. This must be done using a technological, organizational, and policy-level approach.

Technological Recommendations:

- **Enhance AI Interoperability:** Create AI solutions that complement other environmental technologies, such as renewable power systems, Climate militia, and waste control apparatus.
- **Focus on Explainable AI (XAI):** There should be adoption of explainable AI frameworks to meet the requirements of the stakeholders to get a clear explanation of the process of decision-making and to develop trust in the use of AI (González et al., 2024).
- **Cyber Resilience Testing:** This requires the models to be tested often in cyberattacks on the systems that use them to evaluate their effectiveness against real threats.

Organizational Recommendations:

- **Capacity Building:** Apply artificial intelligence for you to be in a position to train environmental protection personnel for the implementation to work out best to one's delight by applying the cybersecurity protocols.
- **Public-Private Partnerships:** To build capacity for generating AI solutions that address the unique requirements in various sectors and to establish partnerships between governments, technological industries, and environmental nonprofits (Nadtochiy, 2018).

Policy-Level Recommendations:

- **Standardize Data Sharing Protocols:** Develop protocols for exchanging environmental and cybersecurity information among organizations to improve defense in each organization.

- **Incentivize AI Adoption:** Provide organizational tax credits or grants for companies adopting AI and cybersecurity to protect the environment.

3. Proposals for International Cooperation to Regulate and Address Environmental Cybercrime

Environmental cybercrime is a cross-border challenge that requires the design of an international framework to address the challenge. Practical cooperation can guarantee that reactionary methods are uniform worldwide and regulations are also improved and shared.

Key Proposals:

- **Develop an International Framework for AI Cybersecurity:** The government must develop an international treaty similar to the Paris Agreement on climate change regarding AI used in cybersecurity for environmental protection. This framework should:
    - Quell international guidelines concerning the application of Artificial Intelligence in ecological systems.
    - Promote the exchange of threat intelligence and best practices.
    - Formal plans exist regarding how cyber threats, wherever they operate, should be handled (Ekechukwu & Simpa, 2024).
- **Establish a Global Environmental Cybersecurity Task Force:** It is recommended that an international organization with AI, cyber security, and environmental science specialists be established to respond to cyber threats for environmental systems worldwide promptly.
- **Strengthen International Laws on Cybercrime:** Due to the specific threat of AI-driven environmental cybersecurity, it will be necessary to modernize treaties, including the Budapest Convention on Cybercrime. Such changes should address issues related to the regulation, accountability, and transparency of AI.
- **Encourage Regional Collaborations**: Encourage regional collaboration, for example, the EU's Joint Cyber Unit, to build local solutions compatible with universal approaches (Ige et al., 2024a; Ige et al., 2024b).

Example: International cooperation in the fight against eco-terrorism in 2021 and the prevention of plots to destroy renewable energy facilities proved that cooperation is beneficial due to the sharing of threat intelligence and response (González et al., 2024).

The research finds that a clear and holistic technological and regulatory strategy is crucial to counter environmental cybercrime complexities. Solar Grid Integration, Strategy, and Integration of AI into the environmental protection system can significantly improve the protection against cyber threats. Such cooperation must complement these initiatives to create standard reference models and advance such security initiatives. Technological inventions must be incorporated with governance to enhance the safe use of environmental structures that are key to sustainable practices.

Table 7. Key Components of the Technological and Regulatory Roadmap

Component	Description	Proposed Actions
AI Innovations	Develop advanced algorithms for anomaly detection, predictive analytics, and adaptive defenses.	Invest in R&D for AI tailored to environmental cybersecurity.
Integration Strategies	Enhance AI adoption in environmental systems through interoperability and transparency.	Promote explainable AI and incentivize AI adoption.
International Cooperation	Build global frameworks and task forces to combat environmental cybercrime collectively.	Establish treaties and regional partnerships for unified responses.

CONCLUSION

Blending green criminology and **Environmental Intelligence** (EI), the convergence with cybercrimes and AI established another significant direction in combating the problems of the hi-tech era. This work has exposed the world to the new dimensions of threats to environmental systems, the savior role of AI in handling these threats, and the importance of a multi-sectorial and multi-disciplinary approach.

Summary of Key Findings

1. The Rise of Environmental Cybercrime:
    - o Environmental cybercrime has become a significant threat, impacting renewable power stations, climate measuring networks, and other infrastructure.
    - o Some drivers include technological weakness, political and ideological reasons, financial gain, and state-sponsored terrorism.
2. AI's Role in Mitigating Cyber Threats:
    - o AI technologies are impressive, especially when identifying, avoiding, and avoiding cyber threats, including anomaly detection systems, predictive analytical systems, and real-time response.

    - Real-life examples include the prevention of a cyber-attack on SolarWinds Company and the foiled attempts at eco-terrorism, which provides a perfect testimony to how AI can safeguard environmental systems.
3. Ethical, Legal, and Policy Challenges:
    - Implementing AI creates questions on privacy and possible biases while implementing algorithms and accountability. Therefore, there must be clear and acceptable standards for AI's use.
    - Lack of legal, regulatory, and policy structure means concerted global action is needed to create suitable best practice frameworks for addressing environmental cyber criminals.
4. The Need for Technological and Regulatory Roadmaps:
    - New developments in AI technologies must be accompanied by the proper deployment into environmental systems, and sound international frameworks should back these for sustainability.

The Need for Interdisciplinary Collaboration

Combating environmental cybercrime needs the contribution of criminologists, technologists, and policymakers.

- **Criminologists:** Essays should offer theoretical paradigms to explain the motivation and effects of environmental cybercrime to enable the study to recommend preventive measures.
- **Technologists:** Build and launch unique artificial intelligence-based solutions that may address the problems within the environmental systems.
- **Policymakers:** Develop effective regulatory policies that address ethical issues, stimulate global cooperation, and provide accountability.

Interdisciplinary collaboration is key to creating the means for a new form of theorizing practice that brings together theory, technology, and practice of governance.

Vision for a Secure, Sustainable Future

Introducing AI into the approach to environmental protection contributes to the provision of realistic visions of safety and stability. This should make an interesting read to ponder this discovery: AI can go a long way in helping the world attain sustainable development objectives in protecting key infrastructures and environmental cybercriminalities.

- **Resilient Environmental Systems:** Cyber security provides advanced reliability and security for renewable energy grids, climate observation devices, and other environmental systems.
- **Sustainable Development:** Guarding these systems means efforts towards sustainability goals like low emissions and favorable green technology can steadfastly proceed.
- **Global Collaboration:** Synchronized approaches towards mitigating and deploying AI for environmentally secure purposes strengthen international cooperation against cyber threats.

With effective interdisciplinarity, the embrace of fresh technologies, and efficient governance, it is possible to create an environment that ensures the reduction and prevention of environmental cybercrime through AI while enhancing the foundation of sustainable development worldwide.

Closing Thoughts

Environmental cybercrime is one of the challenges that knows no boundaries and therefore requires collective effort. AI promises to effectively protect key assets, reduce threats, and advance ecological agendas. However, more must be done regarding ethical, legal, and regulatory issues, interdisciplinarity, and international cooperation to achieve its full potential. Applying its principles and concepts of Artificial Intelligence responsibly and reasonably allows one to obtain the best result by combining two driving forces – technological progress and protection of the environment – to make the world more secure for future generations.

REFERENCES

Aliero, M. S., Ahmad, A. M., Kalgo, U. S., & Aliero, S. A. (2020). An overview of the Internet of Things: Understanding the issues and challenges of a more connected world. *International Journal of Computing and Communication Networks, 2*(1), 1–11.

Alsuwian, T., Butt, A. S., & Amin, A. A. (2022). Smart Grid Cyber Security Enhancement: Challenges and Solutions—A Review. *Sustainability (Basel), 14*(21), 14226. DOI: 10.3390/su142114226

Arunthavanathan, R., Sajid, Z., & Amin, M. T. (2024). Ethics in AI for energy systems safety. In Methods in chemical process safety. DOI: 10.1016/bs.mcps.2024.08.002

Cervini, J., Rubin, A., & Watkins, L. (2022). Don't Drink the Cyber: Extrapolating the Possibilities of Oldsmar's Water Treatment Cyberattack. *International Conference on Cyber Warfare and Security*, 17(1), 19–25. DOI: 10.34190/iccws.17.1.29

Ekechukwu, N. D. E., & Simpa, N. P. (2024). The future of Cybersecurity in renewable energy systems: A review, identifying challenges and proposing strategic solutions. *Computer Science & IT Research Journal, 5*(6), 1265–1299. DOI: 10.51594/csitrj.v5i6.1197

Farooq, M. U., Waseem, M., Khairi, A., & Mazhar, S. (2015). A Critical Analysis on the Security Concerns of Internet of Things (IoT). *International Journal of Computer Applications, 111*(7), 1–6. DOI: 10.5120/19547-1280

Frustaci, M., Pace, P., Aloi, G., & Fortino, G. (2017). Evaluating Critical Security Issues of the IoT World: Present and Future Challenges. *IEEE Internet of Things Journal, 5*(4), 2483–2495. DOI: 10.1109/JIOT.2017.2767291

Gacek, J., & Jochelson, R. (2022). Green Criminology and the Law. In Springer eBooks. DOI: 10.1007/978-3-030-82412-9

Gibbs, C., Gore, M. L., McGarrell, E. F., & Rivers, L. (2009). Introducing Conservation Criminology: Towards Interdisciplinary Scholarship on Environmental Crimes and Risks. *British Journal of Criminology, 50*(1), 124–144. DOI: 10.1093/bjc/azp045

González, A. L., Moreno, M., Román, A. C. M., Fernández, Y. H., & Pérez, N. C. (2024). Ethics in Artificial Intelligence: An Approach to Cybersecurity. *INTELIGENCIA ARTIFICIAL, 27*(73), 38–54. DOI: 10.4114/intartif.vol27iss73pp38-54

Gulyamov, S. S., Fayziev, R. A., Rodionov, A. A., & Rustambekov, I. R. (2023). The Role of Information in Developing Ethical and Accurate AI for Energy Systems. 2022 4th International Conference on Control Systems, Mathematical Modeling, Automation and Energy Efficiency (SUMMA), 226–230. DOI: 10.1109/SUMMA60232.2023.10349398

Hasler, O. (2021). Green Criminology and an International Law Against Ecocide: Using Strict Liability and Superior Responsibility to Prevent State and Corporate Denial of Environmental Harms. In Springer eBooks (pp. 387–408). DOI: 10.1007/978-3-030-82412-9_17

Ife, C. C., Davies, T., Murdoch, S. J., & Stringhini, G. (2019). Bridging information security and environmental criminology research to mitigate cybercrime better. *arXiv preprint arXiv:1910.06380.*

Ige, N. B., Kupa, N. E., & Ilori, N. O. (2024a). Analyzing defense strategies against cyber risks in the energy sector: Enhancing the security of renewable energy sources. *International Journal of Science and Research Archive*, *12*(1), 2978–2995. DOI: 10.30574/ijsra.2024.12.1.1186

Ige, N. B., Kupa, N. E., & Ilori, N. O. (2024b). Best practices in cybersecurity for green building management systems: Protecting sustainable infrastructure from cyber threats. *International Journal of Science and Research Archive*, *12*(1), 2960–2977. DOI: 10.30574/ijsra.2024.12.1.1185

Ignjatović, Đ. (2023). Green criminology and crime control. *Crimen*, *14*(1), 24–63. DOI: 10.5937/crimen2301024I

Krebs, B. (2021, February 10). *What's most interesting about the Florida water system hack? That we heard about it at all.*https://krebsonsecurity.com/. https://krebsonsecurity.com/2021/02/whats-most-interesting-about-the-florida-water-system-hack-that-we-heard-about-it-at-all/

Kshetri, N. (2016). Cybersecurity and Development. *Markets Globalization & Development Review*, *1*(2). Advance online publication. DOI: 10.23860/MGDR-2016-01-02-03

Lynch, M. J., & Long, M. A. (2021). Green Criminology: Capitalism, Green Crime and Justice, and Environmental Destruction. *Annual Review of Criminology*, *5*(1), 255–276. DOI: 10.1146/annurev-criminol-030920-114647

Miró-Llinares, F., & Moneva, A. (2019). Environmental Criminology and Cybercrime: Shifting Focus from the Wine to the Bottles. In Springer eBooks (pp. 1–22). DOI: 10.1007/978-3-319-90307-1_30-1

Murugesan, S., & Alagesan, S. P. (2021). Actualising the Right to Adequate Standard of Living: A Critical Examination of Green Criminology from an Indian Perspective. In Springer eBooks (pp. 293–312). DOI: 10.1007/978-3-030-56227-4_14

Nadtochiy, J. V. (2018). CYBERCRIME AS A THREAT TO ENVIRONMENTAL SECURITY. *Азиатско-Тихоокеанский Регион Экономика Политика Право*, *3*(3), 108–116. DOI: 10.24866/1813-3274/2018-3/108-116

Pływaczewski, W. (2023). REHABILITATION AND THERAPEUTIC PROGRAMMES IN THE LIGHT OF GREEN CRIMINOLOGY (REFLECTIONS BASED ON THE EXPERIENCE OF SELECTED PENITENTIARY INSTITUTIONS). *Probacja*, *1*, 11–39. DOI: 10.5604/01.3001.0016.2846

Shapsough, S., Qatan, F., Aburukba, R., Aloul, F., & Ali, A. R. A. (2015). Smart grid cyber security: Challenges and solutions. IEEExplore. DOI: 10.1109/ICSGCE.2015.7454291

South, N. (2021). Green criminology - revisiting: Reflections, connections, horizons. *Crimen*, *12*(2), 113–131. DOI: 10.5937/crimen2102113S

White, R. (2021). *Theorising Green Criminology*. https://doi.org/DOI: 10.4324/9781003172093

Chapter 11
Impact on E-Commerce Cybercrime in Cryptocurrency Transactions:
Challenges and AI Solutions

C. V. Suresh Babu
https://orcid.org/0000-0002-8474-2882
Hindustan Institute of Technology and Science, India

M. Bhavesh
https://orcid.org/0009-0001-3992-4193
Hindustan Institute of Technology and Science, India

J. Janani
https://orcid.org/0009-0009-6366-5572
Hindustan Institute of Technology and Science, India

C. Mythili Rani
Hindustan Institute of Technology and Science, India

ABSTRACT

This chapter explores the impact of AI-powered solutions on cybersecurity within the context of cryptocurrency transactions in e-commerce. The primary objective is to investigate how AI can mitigate the growing cybersecurity risks associated with cryptocurrency fraud, enhancing the safety of e-commerce platforms. Targeting researchers, AI engineers, and e-commerce professionals, this study employs a mixed-method approach, combining case studies, expert interviews, and comparative

DOI: 10.4018/979-8-3693-8871-6.ch011

analysis of AI-based tools and traditional security systems. The findings highlight the significant potential of AI, particularly in predictive analytics and real-time fraud detection, to combat cryptocurrency-related cybercrimes. The chapter also addresses the challenges of integrating AI with existing e-commerce frameworks and discusses ethical concerns related to privacy and surveillance. The conclusion emphasizes the need for further research into real-time AI solutions and the development of international regulatory standards for AI in cryptocurrency security.

This chapter explores the impact of AI-powered solutions on cybersecurity within the context of cryptocurrency transactions in e-commerce. The primary objective is to investigate how AI can mitigate the growing cybersecurity risks associated with cryptocurrency fraud, enhancing the safety of e-commerce platforms. Targeting researchers, AI engineers, and e-commerce professionals, this study employs a mixed-method approach, combining case studies, expert interviews, and comparative analysis of AI-based tools and traditional security systems. The findings highlight the significant potential of AI, particularly in predictive analytics and real-time fraud detection, to combat cryptocurrency-related cybercrimes. The chapter also addresses the challenges of integrating AI with existing e-commerce frameworks and discusses ethical concerns related to privacy and surveillance. The conclusion emphasizes the need for further research into real-time AI solutions and the development of international regulatory standards for AI in cryptocurrency security.

Keywords: AI, Blockchain Analytics, Cybersecurity, Cryptocurrency Fraud, E-Commerce, Predictive Analytics, Privacy, Real-Time Detection

1.INTRODUCTION

Recent e-commerce evolutions are changing modes of transactions and the acceptance of virtual currencies around the world. Such types of currencies have high operational speeds and are also decentralized and even anonymous in usage. Consumers and businesses are increasingly lured to these factors; however, because of these same reasons, cryptocurrency trade is not safe because of its potential harm to cyber attacks in its general context. This fact is one of the biggest obstacles to establishing institutions and trust in e-commerce. Thus, through the lack of control features, hackers can keep themselves busy mischief making through frauds, hacks, money laundering, and even kidnaping; at the same time, they may send over ransomware. This may disenfranchise consumers by either disbanding the trust they had with the online company or making them lose their savings before connecting with the company. The use of AI is an effective technological remedy to address such risks by providing the best arsenal for resolving criminal inferences from blockchain. AI can make transactions safe, quickly detect any fraudulent activity, cut down existing risks, and implement any other applications. The paper will delve into the multifaceted impact of cybercrime on e-commerce cryptocurrency transactions, then discuss the constituting constraints, and explore the possible role AI-powered solutions may play in turning it into a secure digital ecosystem.

1.1 Overview of E-commerce and Cryptocurrency

Simply put, e-commerce refers to the capacity of businesses and consumers to be able to connect with each other wherever situated across borders, and it usually involves transactions of goods and services that are online by virtue of those technologies that make speed, convenience, and accessible services fitting to both producer and consumer. Over time, e-commerce grew as it had made itself felt through an ever-increasing number of people who are conversant with technology, and has become even an essential part of the economies. The latest thing emerging following large acceptance of e-commerce will be the evolution in the methods of payments, introducing the great variety of payment options to satisfy different consumers. In the financial sector, cryptocurrency is a revolutionary development. It provides major advantages, such as acting as a virtual medium of exchange, highly decentralized and secured through blockchain. Cryptocurrencies operate without the support of banks by itself; hence, they were regarded as something different and concrete from traditional money belonging to central authorities.

1.2 Rise of Cybercrime in Cryptocurrency

Cryptocurrency transactions, in tandem with their soaring usage, have caused a sharp increase in cybercrimes. Cryptocurrencies are based on decentralized and pseudonymous blockchain technology which results in easily accessible and borderless transactions. Yet the convenience of thus doing business has also attracted the attention of cybercrime perpetrators. So much has motivated the sharp rise of such activities as the unregulated and virtually unsupervised environments of cryptocurrency systematics. Unlike traditional financial systems, cryptocurrencies are not under the control of central bankers or national governments, which in usual cases insures poor supervision and tracking capacity against illegal activities. Taking full advantage of these regulatory misfits, cybercriminals find ways to wash money, ransom, and engage in social engineering and phishing techniques. Cryptocurrency wallets, exchanges, and smart contracts represent some of the common targets attacked by hackers. This is normally through techniques like injective malware, manipulation of vulnerabilities, and social engineering that enable them to steal funds, while cryptocurrency transactions introduces anonymity in accountability in tracking theft and placing blame on the shoulders of the real crook. With cyber threats on the rise, incidents such as token thefts, and hacking of exchanges have exposed the underlying insecurities in the cryptocurrency ecosystem-an industry that is highly vulnerable to cybercrimes and subject to easily integrated products. Such incidents bring the vulnerability of these decentralized finance (DeFi) platforms, which are primarily based on smart contracts, due to bugs that are generally exploited. Moreover, when it comes to cryptocurrency transactions, the growth of these cybercrimes would put e-commerce platforms, merchants, and consumers in the travel stiff boat-one that would take a lot of very tight security generic medicine in order to protect the transactions' integrity in the digital era.

1.3 Intersection of AI and Cybersecurity in E-commerce

This marriage of Artificial Intelligence and cybersecurity has drastically changed the way e-commerce sites approach digital threats. Cybercrime is becoming more sophisticated, especially in cryptocurrency transactions. Therefore, AI-based solutions are a must-have for the security of online spaces. AI can scan vast volumes of data, identify patterns, and predict threats, which makes it an absolute must-have in the modern world of e-commerce cybersecurity.

Real-time Threat Detection:

AI-based systems can monitor live transactions and highlight abnormal patterns that the former deems suspicious, hence classifying it as fraudulent transactions or cyberattacks. For instance, suspicious cryptocurrency transactions in a company can be detected by analyzing past data through machine learning algorithms in order to avoid fraud when it is still at its nascent stages.

Predictive Analytics:

AI applies predictive models to predict potential vulnerabilities of an e-commerce site. AI can track past events and predict upcoming threats, allowing the organizations to shore up their defenses in advance.

Anomaly Detection:

AI excels in anomaly detection, meaning that it is good at picking up on odd patterns of user behavior. For instance, if there is a weird transaction pattern by a cryptocurrency wallet, AI flags it for closer scrutiny and therefore limits losses on finance.

Automated Responses:

AI enhances incident response by automatically blocking unauthorized transactions, revoking access, or alerting administrators of breaches. This accelerates response times and reduces the damage from cyberattacks.

Enhanced Customer Authentication

AI enhances authentication processes through biometrics, behavior analysis, and multi-factor authentication systems, which enable authorized access to sensitive accounts and execute trades.

Advanced Threat Mitigation:

The cyber criminal is always updating the methods through which he is evading security systems. Learning in real-time and AI-based adaptation of security systems ensure out-of-emerging threats outclass them, which, in this case, guards the transaction by going online with safety and soundness.

E-commerce combines artificial intelligence with a cybersecurity framework to allow for a more secure transaction environment for the user of cryptocurrencies. It keeps the customers as well as businesses under protection while earning trust in this digital marketplace for its continuous expansion against cyber attacks with constantly changing dynamics.

1.4 Objectives and Scope of the Chapter

Effect of Cybercrime on E-commerce Transactions

Identify the impacts of cybercrime on transactions conducted in the cryptocurrencies via e-commerce, respectively in business, consumer, and digital marketplace impacts.

Problematics of Cryptocurrency Transactions

Identify key challenges facing cryptocurrency transactions that include anonymity, lack of regulatory loopholes, vulnerability to hacking, fraud among other cybercrimes.

AI As The Panacea for Cyber Attacks in Ecommerce:

Explain how Artificial intelligence treats the cyber issues with the respective transactions of crypto currency in online trade.

Current Trend

Present the Current Trends of securing ecommerce, growing trend of accepting Crypto-currencies and future directions of its defense through artificial intelligence.

Future Approaches

To provide security strongly by AI even with the growing environment of commerce, use a safe platform based on cryptocurrencies.This chapter will intersect with e-commerce, cryptocurrency, and cybersecurity. Here also, it mentions cybercrime pertains to those areas. Major discussion points may be as follows:

Integration of E-commerce and Cryptocurrency

Overview on how cryptocurrencies alter payment systems of e-commerce along with the associated risks and benefits.

Types of Cryptocurrency Fraud/ Cybercrimes

The discussions on fraudulent cases, hacking, phishing, ransomware, and all types of other cybercrimes for cryptocurrency-related transactions.

Cryptocurrency Transactions Challenges in Regulation

Current problems represent both regulatory and technical sides that need to be changed in the red tape to allow the incorporation of cryptocurrencies into e-commerce.

AI in Cyber Security

Comprehensive overview of the AI-based solution as fraud detection, anomaly detection, and response towards automated incidents leading to secured e-commerce platforms.

Case Studies and Real-world Applications

Real-time case studies of specific incidents and applications that have mitigated risks associated with cybersecurity related to cryptocurrencies.

Future Trends and Recommendations:

Future vision of how AI technologies and the regulatory frameworks related to them could shape the trajectory of secure transactions in cryptocurrencies, e-commerce.

2.BACKGROUND INFORMATION

Among the biggest changes in e-commerce transactions are the incorporation of cryptocurrencies. The term cryptocurrency is a phrase given to digital assets, which are secured through blockchain technology. Such supports characteristic decentralization, anonymity, and borderless transactions. Because of these facts, customers can use them appropriately for e-commerce transactions since their payment methods are secure, efficient, and inexpensive. However, they pose unique challenges to cybersecurity. Cryptocurrency transactions are different in the sense that they are decentralized networks and, therefore, carried out by central authorities. An innovation that the cybercriminal could exploit to their advantage is as follows: hacks on exchanges; stealing wallets; phishing; and ransomware can be presented in attacks that lead to loss of very significant financial resources and a resultant significant loss of consumer trust.E-commerce sites that rely on cryptocurrencies have to deal with the challenge of smooth transactions and facing growing threats. What's more, anonymity and pseudonymity related to cryptocurrencies add to the complexity of tracking illicit activities concerning cybercrime. And of course, against this came Artificial Intelligence: to transform cybersecurity to its next form. AI will analyze large scales of transaction data, identify frauds in the real time as well as will predict real time threats. One example could be that patterns relating to fraudulent cryptocurrencies dealings can easily be identified and decoded using Natural Language Processing about phishing attempts, for instance. This study falls within the triad of trends integrated: acceptance of cryptocurrencies in e-commerce, cybercrime against transactions involving those, and AI as an answer to these issues. Only within this landscape will the current scenario and the imperative implications be understood in order to develop a secure and trustworthy ecosystem for e-commerce wherein the benefits of cryptocurrency adoption are not waived by its concomitant risks.

2.1 The Evolution of E-commerce and Cryptocurrency in the Digital Age

The digital age has brought so many changes in commerce such that businesses and consumers are now connected all over the world in ways never thought of before. During the past decades, because of technological advancement, changes in consumer behavior, and the introduction of digital payment systems, e-commerce has seen very significant evolution.

Evolution of E-commerce

E-commerce entered the market in the 1990s once the internet was found, and it started developing e-commerce by inventing online shops. Online supergiants including Amazon and eBay are also innovation pioneers which enable comfort for shopping from home to its consumers. Advanced technology innovations with mobile commerce and secure payment portals along with various personalized shopping experiences motivated the development and growth of this e-commerce portal.

E-commerce is already a multi-trillion-dollar industry, offering very different models, both in the B2B and B2C and increasingly, C2C transactions. Customer expectations toward same-day delivery, AI-driven recommendation, or even cross-border shopping would fundamentally change and create unprecedented market opportunity together.

Introducing Cryptocurrency to the Digital Economy

Such cryptocurrencies are secure, transparent, and tamper-proof in their uses, implementations, and applications within a blockchain. That was the innovation brought forward by Bitcoin in 2009, which is the first decentralized digital currency. It has diversified thousands of different use cases and functionalities of digital currencies today. Once considered niche, cryptocurrencies became mainstream in commercial acceptance and near-innumerably other commercial platforms. Benefits involve low fees when making transactions, faster payments crossing borders, and increased anonymity of transactions. This fills a need on various global e-commerce platforms. Included among companies are Shopify, Overstock, and PayPal who already offer their products with payment available in cryptocurrencies. Of course, cryptocurrencies fit perfectly into e-commerce in the digital economy. Most of the issues traditional payment systems face-the slow execution of international transactions, high processing fees, and reliance on a centralized intermediary-systems are corrected by cryptocurrencies. This translates to more choices for clients to make payments hence easily attracting even techno-savvy clients while performing cross-border transactions without problems arising from currency exchange. However, this is at the same time associated with certain problems. Cryptocurrencies are decentralized systems and, as such, more prone to various forms of cybercrime, for instance, fraud, hacking, and money laundering. The e-commerce sites' security measures taken to make their customers feel relaxed when using such currencies remain one of the significant problems of cryptocurrencies.

The New Digital Trade

In this age of innovation, a convergence of e-commerce and cryptocurrency will change the way the world conducts its transactions. These opportunities take with them the requirement to implement measures against the risks which are cybersecurity threats, in a way that this evolution be in support of a safe and sustainable digital economy. Such innovations will bring in unprecedented growth and efficiency when they usher e-commerce and cryptocurrency into new dimensions.

2.2 Cryptocurrency: A Double-Edged Sword for E-commerce

Cryptocurrency emerged as a very revolutionary tool to be used with e-commerce where it offers great benefits which align to the demands of the digital economy. However, its adoption introduced great risks which make it a two-edged sword for an online business.

Benefits of Cryptocurrency in E-Commerce

1. Global accessibility: Cryptocurrencies make transactions possible borderless, hence without currency exchange or use of intermediaries in the central financial systems. Marketplaces turn out to be very accessible to foreign buyers.
2. Lower Transaction Costs: Most cryptocurrencies also charge a processing fee that is much lower than most payment systems and this will save companies and individuals more money.
3. Speed of Transactions: The cryptocurrencies transactions take shorter times to go through, especially with cross-country transactions that ensure the no-delay occurrence which often relates with third-party causes.
4. More Secure: Blockchain technology is the backbone of all cryptocurrencies. It allows for a secure, transparent, and tamper-proof ledger, thereby reducing the risk of transaction fraud.
5. Privacy and Anonymity: Cryptocurrencies enable doing transactions without any sensitive personal data exposed to clients with privacy concerns.

Risks of Cryptocurrency in E-commerce

1. Cybercrime Vulnerabilities: The distributed and pseudonymous nature makes it vulnerable to cyber-criminals. The most existing threats include hacking, phishing, ransomware attacks, and wallet thefts.

2. Regulatory Issues: This uncertainty arises because no coherent worldwide regulation persists for cryptocurrencies, thereby complicating matters concerning compliance and risk in e-commerce.
3. Price Volatility: High volatility is tied to a cryptocurrency, which introduces uncertainty in the determination of prices; it could lead to a loss when adopting it as a form of exchange.
4. Consumer Education Gap: Most of the clients do not know any relevant information about the fundamental principle on which the cryptocurrencies are based; the implementation process is skipped, or there are mistakes at the clearing.

    5.Finality of Transactions: Crypto payments are irreversible. Businesses and individuals can never recover mistakenly or scammed money without help from the recipient.

2.3 Cybercrime in Cryptocurrency: Challenges and Consequences

Cryptocurrency has revolutionized the procedure of digital transaction. It can achieve speed, offer anonymity, and allow decentralized procedure, which also makes it a perfect medium for cybercrime. The challenges posed by cybercrime in cryptocurrency transactions are considerable for a person, business, and the world economy.

Challenges in Dealing with Cybercrime in Cryptocurrency

1. Anonymity and Pseudonymity: These enable users to conduct totally anonymous transactions thus tracing who stole the money is pretty much impossible.
2. No Regulation: Due to decentralized nature of cryptocurrencies, lack of standard global regulation provides safety for these hackers with a minimal accountability.
3. Sophistication of Cyber Attack: With sophisticated tactics from cyber-thieves, phishing, ransomware, and malware constitute some sophistication in cyber attacks which aimed at stealing cryptocurrency funds or compromise their victims' systems. Increasing sophistication increases complexity in detection and prevention.
4. Cross-border Challenges: Cross-border transactions, which are part of cryptocurrency transaction, have their complexity because a number of jurisdictions are involved. This is quite complex when coordination of enforcement between international jurisdictions has to be attempted, possibly with failure in tracing the culprits.

Cryptocurrencies Cyber Crime Consequences

1.Monitory Losses:The thefts of millions of such exchanges cause colossal monetary losses to these companies and to the people through which erudition about utilizing cryptocurrencies gets dwindled.

2. Shattered Consumer Confidence:Cryptocurrency cybercrime will damage the reputation of the platform, which discourages the use of digital currencies as a safe payment means.
3. Impact on E-commerce GrowthThe fear of cybercrime makes e-commerce platforms not to embrace cryptocurrencies, thus reducing their potential benefits and hindering innovation.
4. Money Laundering and other Criminal Activities:The main applications of cryptocurrencies are related to money laundering, financing terrorism, and other illegal crimes, which concern the regulatory and law enforcement branches.
5. Regulation Scrutiny:There is more rigid regulatory control that could further limit cybercrime in cryptocurrency-based transactions and prevent innovation from slowing down, reducing the appeal of decentralized systems

2.4 The Role of Artificial Intelligence in Cybersecurity

While cybersecurity threats are advancing with increased frequency, there is an urgent need for innovative and proactive solutions. Some of the groundbreaking technologies in this field of cybersecurity include Artificial Intelligence, which possesses strong tools that may be used for the detection, prevention, and response to cyberattacks. Its analytical capabilities, in terms of understanding vast amounts of data, adapting to changing threats, and automating responses, makes AI an important component in contemporary cybersecurity frameworks.

Primary Role of AI in Cybersecurity

1. Threat Detection and Prevention: AI systems can detect real-time threats based on patterns from network traffic, user behavior, and system logs. Machine learning algorithms are capable of discovering anomalies that can potentially suggest cyberattacks such as phishing attempts, ransomware, or hacking activities even before they happen (Babu, C. V. Suresh, and Andrew Simon P. 2024).
2. Fraud Detection in Cryptocurrency Transactions: AI has a prominent role in cryptocurrency transaction monitoring to track suspicious transactions as it can point out unusual patterns, wallet addresses used for nefarious activities, and otherwise atypical payment activity that could be considered fraud.

3. Automated Response to Incidents: AI automates routine cybersecurity tasks such as blocking unauthorized access, quarantining infected files, and alerting administrators of potential breaches. This naturally reduces response times and also minimizes damage to cyber attacks.

AI in E-commerce and Cryptocurrency Security

AI is quite critical in the realm of e-commerce and cryptocurrency. Due to their decentralization and anonymity, cryptocurrencies are exposed to cyber attacks. AI-based solutions provide security to wallets for cryptocurrency, fraud transaction detection, and protect the platforms of e-commerce from hacking and malware attacks.

For example, AI-powered blockchain analytics platforms are able to trace suspicious transactions across cryptocurrency networks. These tools enable the detection of malicious individuals who carry out nefarious activities while making transactions thus making the entire transaction process safe and secure.

Limitations in Implementing AI for Cyber Security

1. Data Privacy Issue: Heavy reliance on extensive data for AI model training creates a data privacy issue, particularly when the data involves sensitive information from the users.
2. Costly Implementation Process: High deployment and maintenance costs and technical complexities are associated with AI systems, which may be too expensive for all organizations.
3. Sophistication of Cybercriminals: With the advancement of AI, cybercriminals' techniques have also advanced. Today, they more often use AI to launch sophisticated attacks.

2.5 Overview of Existing AI Solutions for Cryptocurrency Fraud Detection

Growth in the use of cryptocurrency as an electronic payment has been paralleled by higher fraud and cybercrime. The pace has been set by Artificial Intelligence (AI) to counter this by fraud detection and prevention in cryptocurrency systems. AI technologies leverage machine learning, natural language processing (NLP), and analytics in authenticating transactions and establishing trust in the system.

Artificial Intelligence Solutions to Fight Cryptocurrency Frauds

1. Transaction Monitoring and Anomaly Detection: AI tools monitor massive volumes of transactional data in real-time and identify suspicious patterns or outliers from the norm. Suspicious cases are instances of sudden increases in the value of transactions, high-frequency small transactions, or transactions to risky wallets and are flagged for investigation.

   Example Tools: Chainalysis KYT (Know Your Transaction), Elliptic

2. Blockchain Analytics: Artificial intelligence-driven blockchain analysis tools track money flows to identify connections to illegal activities like money laundering, terrorist financing, or proceeds of stolen goods. The tools track cryptocurrency wallets and their link to blacklisted or suspicious addresses.

   Example Tools: CipherTrace, Crystal Blockchain

3. Fraud Scoring Systems: Machine learning algorithms score the fraud risk of transactions based on transaction history, wallet reputation, and geo-location. All such high-risk transactions are asked to be processed manually or blocked programmatically.

   Example Tools: Scorechain, Bitquery

4. User Authentication and Behavioral Biometrics: AI protects the cryptocurrency platform by tracking the users' activity, i.e., login, typing speed, or device usage. Suspicious activity alerts or denies access.

   Example Tools: BioCatch, TypingDNA

5. Natural Language Processing (NLP) for Phishing Detection: NLP models scan messages, emails, and social media posts for phishing attacks to steal cryptocurrency wallets or private keys. AI can identify suspicious URLs, language patterns, and content structure in phishing attacks.

   Example Tools: Phish.AI, Armorblox

Benefits of AI-powered Cryptocurrency Fraud Detection Solutions

Real-time Monitoring: Stops fraudulent transactions in real-time, preventing financial loss.
Scalability: AI can handle huge amounts of transaction data at extremely high speeds, which is perfect for global cryptocurrency networks.
Greater accuracy: Machine learning algorithms get more accurate over time with fewer false negatives and fewer false positives.
Cost Efficiency: Minimizing the need for high-level human intervention, automated fraud detection minimizes the cost of operations. Challenges in Detecting Fraud through AI Privacy is an issue of data: Data processing and gathering of transaction records may lead to privacy issues, especially in systems that are decentralized.
Criminal Avoidance Techniques: Cybercriminals continually develop innovative avoidance techniques against AI systems, and detection processes must hence keep evolving.
Lack of Standardization: There exists no standardized regulation and rule in every cryptocurrency marketplace, and the integration of AI solutions is complicated by this fact.

3. RELEVANCE TO THE BOOK'S THEME

Artificial intelligence (AI) has been an invaluable resource for digital criminology, which investigates online crimes. Cybercrime sophistication develops beyond the level of conventional detection and prevention mechanisms. The rapidly-changing and ever-evolving nature of cyber threats demand that AI becomes the game-changing component in digital criminology, promoting more effective identification, analysis, and prevention of cybercriminal activities.

Principal Functions of AI in Digital Criminology

1. Real-Time Threat Identification: AI systems can monitor thousands of streams of real-time data to identify malicious activities, such as unauthorized access attempts, phishing, and abnormal network behaviour (Babu, C. V. Suresh, and Andrew Simon P. 2024).

Example: AI-based Intrusion Detection Systems (IDS) monitor network traffic to identify possible breaches.

2. Behavioral Profiling and Analysis: AI employs user behavior to create profiles and identify anomalies. For instance, if a user typically transacts at a specific time, then a transaction made at a different time could indicate fraud or a possible cyber-attack.

For instance: AI checks the sum of login timestamps and changes in IP addresses and devices to alert for unauthorized login events.

3. Digital Forensics: The AI makes the analysis of cybercrime evidence much easier by automating the processes like along the lines of logs, emails, and transaction records. AI is to be aspired for the reconstruction of the chain of occurrence that took place leading to a cyber attack.

Example: AI tools such as Magnet AXIOM assist in the analysis of digital evidence more effectively.

Advantages of AI in Digital Criminology

Speed and efficiency: AI can process and analyze vast data sets and consume much less time than human researchers do.
Accuracy: These algorithms learn over time, which reduces false alarms, and improved threat detection.
Scalability: AI systems are capable to cope instead of leaving it

3.1 Integration of AI in Digital Criminology

Use of Artificial Intelligence (AI) in combating cybercrime in cryptocurrency transactions is directly relevant to the wider context of the theme of this book, i.e., the problems and solutions in the new e-commerce scenario. Cryptocurrency as an e-payment mode in e-commerce has developed very rapidly with characteristics like decentralization, speed, and access globally. The same characteristics render it vulnerable to cybercrime posing the threat of compromising the trust and stability of the online market.

This chapter is concerned with how AI, a cornerstone of modern technology, is at the forefront of solving such issues and making cryptocurrency transactions secure in e-commerce. Using experiential insights, tools, and methods, the chapter continues the book's theme of utilizing technological innovations to face up to new threats in the digital economy.

Key Links to the Book's Theme

1. Mitigation of E-commerce Cybercrime: The book emphasizes the necessity of addressing cybercrime against e-commerce, and this chapter explains how AI battles cryptocurrency fraud—a growing problem on online platforms.
2. Technological Innovation as a Solution: The book emphasizes how emerging technologies can respond to intricate challenges. This chapter emphasizes AI's disruptive influence on creating secure cryptocurrency environments for businesses and consumers.
3. Trust Building with Consumers: Trust is needed in e-commerce development. The chapter demonstrates the way AI solutions make crypto transactions secure and transparent, thus making trust possible in digital trade.

3.2 The Impact of AI on E-commerce Cybersecurity

AI-powered e-commerce and cybersecurity E-commerce's explosive growth has completely changed how companies and customers communicate. However, because of this digital growth, online platforms are now more susceptible to ransomware, phishing attacks, payment fraud, and data breaches, among other cyberthreats. In the battle against these dangers, artificial intelligence (AI) has become a game-changing technology, providing cutting-edge safeguards for the security, integrity, and confidence of e-commerce ecosystems. --- The Function of AI in Cybersecurity for E-Commerce 1. Fraud Detection and Prevention: Artificially intelligent fraud detection tools track user behaviour and payment history to identify fraud trends instantly. They use machine learning algorithms to identify the fraud patterns that set them apart from typical user behaviour. For instance, real-time

3.3 Enhancing the Digital Criminology Framework with AI Solutions

Model with AI Solutions

The digital criminology paradigm, which aims at the detection, analysis, and prevention of cybercrime, has evolved a great deal with the inclusion of Artificial Intelligence (AI). Cybercriminals keep evolving, so the tools criminologists utilize must transcend the conventional. AI-based solutions enhance the function of digital criminology with live analysis, automation, and forecasting capacity, facilitating a more proactive and efficient approach to combating cyber threats.

AI-Driven Upgrades to Digital Criminology

1. Automated Threat Identification and Response:

Artificial intelligence platforms facilitate the ease of automatic threat identification through the analysis of huge data, network traffic monitoring, and monitoring unusual patterns. AI platforms also have the capability to respond automatically to threats by isolating accessed systems or halting malicious attempts.

Example: AI-driven Security Information and Event Management (SIEM) solutions identify and eradicate threats in real-time.

2. Deep Cybercrime Analysis:

Artificial intelligence tools scan vast and complex data pools to find concealed patterns in cybercrime schemes. Criminologists use these patterns to forecast upcoming trends and thwart future attacks.

Example: AI can scan blockchain transaction history for questionable cryptocurrency transfers.

3. Advanced Behavior Analysis

Behavioral analysis software that uses artificial intelligence tracks user behavior to identify anomalies. By observing normal behavior, such products can identify potential cybercrime, including account takeovers or insider threats.

Example: TypingDNA behavior biometrics solutions recognize anomalous typing patterns that can indicate unauthorized access.

4. Predictive Threat Intelligence

AI applies predictive analytics to predict future cybercrime trends from historical data and attack patterns. This allows law enforcement and businesses to act in advance.

Example: AI predicts potential ransomware attacks by analyzing malware evolution.

5. Advanced Digital Forensics:

AI makes digital forensics more efficient by automating evidence gathering, analysis, and reporting (Suresh Babu, C.V., Vishnu Priyan J., et. al. 2024). This shortens investigation time and enhances accuracy in catching cybercriminals.

Example: AI technology is used to recreate timelines of cyberattacks from log files and metadata.

4. KEY QUESTIONS AND PROBLEMS ADDRESSED

• 4.1 What are the cybersecurity challenges posed by cryptocurrency transactions in e-commerce?

The increasing popularity of cryptocurrencies for e-commerce payment is attributed to their decentralization, speed, and anonymity. However, these features seem to make cryptocurrency transactions more susceptible to unique cybersecurity challenges. These challenges are not only against the very e-commerce platform from which they emanate but also tend to hurt the consumer confidence in a digital marketplace.

Key Cybersecurity Challenges

1. Anonymity and Pseudonymity:

Cryptocurrency transactions allow for some level of anonymity or pseudonymity and are very hard to trace back to the identity of parties involved in the transaction. Therefore, this kind of anonymity features is often exploited by cybercriminals in money laundering, tax evasion, and other illegal activities.

2. Lack of Regulation:

The decentralization means somewhat outside the ambit of regulations governing other financial instruments. The lack of regulation offers cybercriminals opportunities to exploit vulnerabilities with no fear of immediate repercussions.

3. Vulnerability to Hacking:

Cryptocurrency Wallets and Exchanges have always been a popular target for hacking attempts. Weak security architectures or vulnerabilities within the blockchain technology would readily accompany the stealing away of funds, thereby damaging consumer confidence in e-commerce platforms.

4. Phishing Attacks:

In phishing attacks, cybercriminals entice users to share their private keys or login credentials regarding their cryptocurrency wallets. Attacks are often targeted against e-commerce platforms that accept cryptocurrencies.

4.2 How can AI technologies address these cybersecurity threats?

AI technologies are conferring advantages on themselves by reducing the cybersecurity risks from cryptocurrency transactions in online shopping. They offer advanced solutions to detect, disrupt, and de-power threats in real-time (Suresh Babu, C.V., Vishnu Priyan J., et. al. 2024). That is what AI does:

1. Prevention and Detection of Frauds: AI scans user behavior and transactional history to detect and prevent fraudulent transactions from occurring.
2. Predictive Analytics for Threat Identification: AI detects cyberattacks through experience learning, which identifies emerging threats such as phishing and ransomware.
3. Blockchain Analysis: AI enables blockchain forensic analysis with tracking suspicious money flow and money laundering or scam avoidance.
4. Phishing and Social Engineering Defense: AI utilizes NLP to identify phishing attacks and spammers' communications to unsuspecting clients.
5. Advanced Authentication: AI biometrics (facial, behavioral biometrics) verifies secure login access to virtual currency wallets and e-commerce login.

4.3 Why are traditional cybersecurity measures insufficient in the face of cryptocurrency fraud?

Conventional cybersecurity solutions, as good as they are in most contexts, fall short in the context of managing the distinctive demands made by cryptocurrency scams. Cryptocurrency transactions are irreversible, decentralized, and anonymous, and represent dangers that conventional cybersecurity solutions were never programmed to ward off. Here's why conventional measures fail:

1.Shortage of Countermeasure against Anonymity

Bitcoin-based cryptocurrencies are built upon some anonymity, and individuals to a transaction are difficult to identify. The traditional security methodologies, being characteristically traceable information-based (e.g., username or IP address), can neither trace nor hinder fraud within an anonymous network.

2. Irreversible Transactions

Unlike other financial transactions, once they are settled on the blockchain, cryptocurrency transactions cannot be reversed. Chargeback or reversing such transactions like in the conventional practices does not exist, and no scope for recovery is provided in the event of fraud.

3. Decentralized Nature

Cryptocurrency employs decentralized networks, beyond the control of traditional finance institutions. Traditional security methods typically desire to protect centralized systems (banks, payment gateways), and hence become outdated in protecting decentralized wallets and networks.

4.4 What Ethical Concerns a Rise in Using Ai to Combat Cryptocurrency-Related Cybercrimes?

Although AI offers immense resources in the battle against cryptocurrency-related cybercrimes, its use is also confronted with several ethical concerns that need to be studied in-depth. They are privacy, equity, responsibility, transparency, and abuse. The most important ethical concerns involved in using AI in the battle against cryptocurrency fraud are as follows:

1. Invasion of Privacy

Artificial intelligence algorithms usually need to be given access to humongous amounts of personal and transactional information in order to properly identify fraud, and it is indeed risky to privacy. The capability to scan, monitor, and analyze financial transactions on multiple platforms can be harmful to users' privacy if their personal information, like wallet addresses or transaction history, are made public without adequate security measures. Data and processing must be done as per privacy regulations (e.g., GDPR) so that users' rights are not violated.

2. Data Bias and Discrimination

AI is trained on past data, and if biased data are used to train AI, then the system will become discriminative in its outcome. For example, if the AI systems are being trained on data that reflects patterns of fraud as more common among specific geography or demographics, then the systems are able to discriminate against users of such geography or demographics. In cryptocurrency transactions, it can lead to discriminatory flagging or tracking of specific demographics, thus endangering innocent users.

3. Transparency and Accountability

Artificial intelligence technology has also been referred to as "black boxes" because the decision-making process may be opaque and difficult to interpret. Opaqueness in cryptocurrency fraud detection is an ethical issue of responsibility. If the AI technology makes a false identification of a legitimate transaction as fraud or fails to detect a scam, no one can identify who made the error or appeal the decision. This can lead to consumer distrust, especially in financial transactions because errors are very costly.

4. Negative False Positives and Negative Impacts on Real Users

Fraud detection software, specifically, tends to produce false positives—flagging legitimate transactions as fraudulent. In cryptocurrencies, it can be a problem to users whose rejected or pending transactions are stuck, or worse, whose accounts are closed. In online business, it can be lost sales and annoyed consumers. The morality in this instance is to inconvenience innocent consumers who are being interrupted in their transactions without just compensation.

Though AI offers a ridiculously effective device of a counter for cryptocurrency-related cybercrimes, its application raises an entire set of ridiculously critical issues in terms of ethics.

5. OBJECTIVES AND SCOPE

The present paper is a discussion of the influence of cybercrime on cryptocurrency payments in e-commerce, its limitations, and the contribution of AI-driven solutions towards enhancing security. It provides an overview of the rising cybercrime in cryptocurrency, i.e., fraud, phishing, money laundering, and ransomware attacks, and identifies some of the challenges as anonymity, decentralization, absence of regulation, and ineffectiveness of conventional security solutions. The research also explores AI application in cybersecurity, via machine learning studies, blockchain studies, and predictive models for fraud prevention and detection. Current AI solutions like fraud prevention tools, blockchain forensic tools, and smart contract security are analyzed to ascertain whether they are effective or not. Ethical implications like privacy vulnerability, bias, transparency, and compliance are also taken into consideration. The study attempts to formulate AI-based methods of e-commerce cryptocurrency transaction security against cyber and counter cyber attacks. Particular emphasis has been given to developing the application of cryptocurrency in e-commerce, its vulnerabilities, and AI-based methods of monitoring, detection, and removal of illicit transactions. The study also explains the limitations of conventional security controls, regulation accompanying it, and the ethical consideration of AI usage. With the knowledge of all these fields, the study, in this instance, provides information on how AI can enhance the safety of payments in cryptocurrencies with an effort to provide secure digital fiscal infrastructure to merchants as well as consumers.

5.1 Objectives of the Chapter

The current paper is a reflection of the impact of cybercrime on cryptocurrency payments in e-commerce, its limitations, and the role of AI-based solutions towards increasing security. It is a description of the escalating cybercrime in cryptocurrency, i.e., fraud, phishing, money laundering, and ransomware attacks, and summarizes some of the challenges as anonymity, decentralization, lack of regulation, and inefficiency of traditional security solutions. The study further delves into AI use in cybersecurity, through machine learning research, blockchain research, and predictive analytics for fraud detection and prevention. Existing AI offerings such as fraud prevention software, blockchain forensic software, and smart contract security are examined to determine if they work or not. Ethical concerns such as privacy exposure, bias, transparency, and compliance are also considered. The research tries to design AI-based approaches to e-commerce cryptocurrency transaction security from cyber and counter cyber attacks. Special focus has been laid on the development of the use of cryptocurrency for e-commerce, its vulnerabilities, and AI-based approaches to monitoring, detection, and deletion of illicit transactions. The research also discusses the limitations of traditional security controls, regulations along with it, and the ethics of the use of AI. With the understanding of all these domains, the research, in this case, gives information on how AI can make payments safer in cryptocurrencies with an attempt to offer secure digital fiscal infrastructure to consumers as well as merchants.

5.2 Scope of the Chapter

The chapter focuses on the use of artificial intelligence (AI) in the security of e-commerce cryptocurrency transactions from cyber-attacks and the results of AI-based solution assessments. It elaborates on the vulnerabilities in cryptocurrency transactions such as phishing, hacking, money laundering, and phishing, among others, and the reasons why conventional cybersecurity measures are inadequate in protecting decentralized digital assets. The chapter delves into different AI technologies such as machine learning, blockchain analytics, anomaly detection, and behavioral analysis and their uses in detecting and preventing cyber attacks. The chapter also gives examples of existing AI-driven fraud detection systems and forensic tools used to follow blockchain transactions and mark abnormal activity. Ethical and legal issues surrounding AI in cybersecurity such as privacy risk, data bias, and compliance are also brought out. In addition, the chapter highlights potential AI-based innovations that can enhance security and legitimacy of cryptocurrency transactions in e-commerce. In offering a snapshot of ways that AI can fight cybercrime in e-commerce through the application of cryptocurrencies, this chapter adds to even more secure and sustainable digital financial platforms.

5.2.1 Topics Covered

Cybersecurity threats on cryptocurrency transactions. An analysis of critical cybersecurity threats in these transactions is done. Key threats include; fraud, phishing, money laundering, ransomware, and exchange hacks.

Challenges in Cryptocurrency Cybersecurity: The Inadequacy of Traditional Security Solutions – An analysis of reasons behind the inability of conventional security approaches to combat cybercrimes linked to

AI in Prevention and Detection of Fraud – The course is dedicated to the exploration of fraud detection and prevention using AI tools. Students learn about machine learning, anomaly detection, and blockchain forensics.

Blockchain Analytics and AI: Risk Assessment in Action – The advancements at the intersection of blockchain analytics and AI in terms of transaction monitoring, wallet tracing, and risk scoring.

5.2.2 Delimitations and Exclusions

In our paper, special attention is focused on the AI application in the field of combating cyber attacks in crypto e-commerce. However, we will not consider the topic in detail. By AI it is implied the fraud detection based on artificial intelligence, which is a separate topic in the study. Although on the other hand, it is worth mentioning the use of the technology of the future in the field of cybersecurity of the present.

There is a bit of an ambiguity in the original paragraph, "E-commerce Cybersecurity in General". The main topic does not cover all cybersecurity threats in e-commerce (for example, credit card fraud, traditional payment gateway vulnerabilities), but instead, it is centered on threats that are specific to cryptocurrency transaction.

Non-AI-Based Security Solutions – Consider these solutions after analyzing the conventional methods. The discussed can be encryption, two-factor authentication, or other, the primary security approaches that are better

This is the paragraph about technology. Specifically, it is regarding the field of creating block chain. It is understood that this section is dedicated to the issue of security and preventing fraud, in other words, to the programming of a finished block chain, consensus mechanisms, smart contracts

Cryptocurrency Investment Risks. No financial risks associated with cryptocurrency trading, volatility, or market manipulation are covered, as the focus is on cybersecurity challenges and AI-driven fraud prevention.

Cybercrime Is Everywhere. The part does not cover the nuances of cryptocurrency cybercrime the darknet, illegal market places, and finance-related cybercrime, but e-commerce

6. LITERATURE REVIEW

The increasing importance of blockchain, AI, and cybersecurity in protecting digital financial systems and e-commerce is highlighted by recent studies. Although security is still a major concern, Ullah(2025) examines how businesses in North Carolina are becoming more interested in adopting bitcoins for transactions. In a similar vein, Kumar et al. (2025) talk about how AI enhances the security of digital currencies and changes international marketing in the blockchain age.AI in cryptographic protocols is the main emphasis of Aisyah et al. (2019) in order to protect data integrity and secure e-commerce transactions. Shah and Jhanjhi (2025) draw attention to the difficulties that AI-powered e-commerce systems encounter, including concerns about data protection and trust. While Gupta (2024) describes the present cybersecurity dangers in e-commerce and mitigating techniques, Mudgal (2025) suggests leveraging AI and ML for proactive threat detection. A comprehensive review of cybersecurity research is given by Rani and Sehrawat (2024), who also highlight the need for more robust defenses and potential research topics. Better risk assessments are suggested by Salami et al. (2025), who address prejudice and privacy in AI-based credit scoring systems. Strategies to control the risk of cloud misconfiguration in financial applications are put forth by Metibemu et al. (2025). Last but not least, Senthil et al. (2024) describe the mathematical underpinnings of deep learning, machine learning, and artificial intelligence (AI), which aid in the creation of intelligent and safe systems.

6.1 Existing Research on Cybercrime in Cryptocurrency Transactions

A growing number of researchers have examined the rising trend of cybercrime in cryptocurrency transactions, and the difficulty comes in because cryptocurrency is decentralized and is pseudonymous. It is believed that the cryptocurrency-related cybercrime activities have evolved and continue to improve, with the common types being fraud, phishing, ransomware, money laundering, and exchange and wallet hacks. The research affirms that the anonymity provided by blockchain technology allows criminals to commit crimes without a trace being left on the transactions that can be tracked by law enforcement. The reading states that criminals in the perpetration of crimes are using a cryptocurrency such as mixing services when laundering money, privacy coins, and exchanges rooted in a darknet market. The literature on decentralized finance (DeFi) platforms discusses exploits that have led to financial losses, namely, losing cryptocurrency from exploits with smart contracts or poor coding. The articles reviewed also talk about cybercriminal innovations such as social engineering and malware to steal private keys and backdoor digital wallets. There is research that cybercriminals are after the ransomware model where crypto payments are used to pay off the ransom.

6.2 Literature on AI Solutions in Cybersecurity

Application of artificial intelligence in cybersecurity has been widely explored both in academia and industry research, particularly in dealing with evolving cyber threats in cryptocurrency transactions. Existing literature highlights AI's role in fraud detection, anomaly detection, behavioral analysis, and predictive security measures demonstrating its effectiveness in mitigating cyber risks.

Studies have been conducted on how machine learning (ML) and deep learning (DL) systems improve fraud detection by detecting suspicious transaction patterns in real time. According to the research, AI models can process huge amounts of blockchain transactions analyzing them and distinguishing between fraudulent and legal transactions based on pattern recognition and anomaly detection. In addition, it is possible to improve the accuracy of threat detection by using AI-driven security systems, which are constantly learning from new types of fraud and adapting to new threats from cybercriminals.

AI based risk assessment and scoring mechanisms are researched as effective tools for detecting potential financial crimes like money laundering and phishing attacks. The reviews highlight the use of natural language processing (NLP) in detecting malicious content in emails, websites and social media.

6.3 Integration of AI with Blockchain Analytics for Fraud Detection

The synthesis of blockchain analytics and artificial intelligence (AI) has developed into an effective method for detecting and preventing fraud in cryptocurrency transactions. Blockchain monitors and analyzes transactions for suspicious activities, while AI helps with the processes of anomaly detection, risk evaluation, and predictive fraud mitigation.

AI-Powered Fraud Detection through Blockchain Analytics

AI-powered blockchain analytics has been automated to such an extent that addresses can be monitored, and potential money laundering schemes, phishing attacks, and fraudulent activities can be detected, according to research. Machine learning enables real-time risk scoring through analysis of historical transactions to detect deviations from normal patterns.

1. Anomaly and Pattern Detection - AI model analytics incorporates deep learning to identify high-volume transactions or interactions with flagged addresses as potential scams. AI is more effective than baseline systems at distinguishing between legitimate transactions and scams.
2. Address and Wallet Tracking - Cybercriminal wallet address detection is conducted through AI forensic tools specialized in blockchain analysis.

6.4 Identification of Gaps in Current Literature

Detecting Gaps in the Existing Literature1. Insufficient Studies on AI's Efficacy in Preventing Fraud in Real-Time – There are studies assessing the efficacy of role AI in detecting fraudulent transactions, but there are no studies evaluating the efficacy of using AI to prevent fraud before a transaction occurs. More research is needed to determine the value of using AI in proactive security.2. Limitations of AI Model Explainability and Bias – Most AI models used in fraud detection are used in a "black box" method meaning the models rely on data to come to conclusions, and it is impossible to know why the decisions were made. The current literature does not address how to mitigate bias and improve explainability of AI-based cybersecurity measures.3. AI and Blockchain-Cyber Security Effects – Blockchain utilizes transparency and security, yet the research on the combined effectiveness of AI and blockchain analytics remains in its infancy. Additional research needs to be conducted on AI blockchain forensics, and decentralized crypto fraud detection models.4. Scalability and Performance of AI Across Large Cryptocurrency Transactions – Most of the literature reviewed a controlled AI security model or small size, compared to large cryptocurrency exchange and high volume e-commerce websites. More research is necessary to determine how the solution performs in those environments.

6.4.1 Neglected Study Area: Real-Time Fraud Detection Systems

An unexplored gap in the body of work done is the lack of study on real-time fraud detection systems for cryptocurrency transactions in e-commerce. While there is considerable AI-based fraud detection literature, most of it focuses on post-transaction analysis rather than prevention.

Real-Time Fraud Detection Challenges

1. Superfast Transaction Processing - Cryptocurrency transactions occur in seconds or less making real-time fraud detection near impossible. No research exists that deals with the capability to scan an entire blockchain for large amounts of data in real-time to isolate suspicious transactions ahead of their completion.
2. Evasion of detection through advanced techniques such as mixing services and multiple wallet transfers pose problems. These dynamic and real-time patterns of fraud are often beyond the detection capabilities of modern AI models.
3. Precision and accuracy – AI-based fraud detection systems incur operational costs with flagging legitimate transactions as fraudulent. More work is needed to avoid user dissatisfaction, and improve accuracy without disrupting genuine transactions.
4. AI-based solutions lack versatility – Many large e-commerce platforms and cryptocurrency exchanges have millions of transactions per day. Existing works do not...

6.4.2 Integration Hurdles of AI with E-Commerce Systems

While the application of AI offers improved cybersecurity for cryptocurrency transactions, the integration of AI-enabled fraud detection systems into e-commerce platforms poses particular difficulties. A number of technical, operational, and regulatory issues prevent full integration, as highlighted in existing research.

1. Reluctance for Change Among Stakeholders

Most e-commerce platforms still utilize legacy payment processors and sophisticated centralized transaction monitoring systems. The infrastructure upgrade necessary for AI-based fraud detection on cryptocurrency transactions is complex and expensive, cumbersome, and costly.

2. Scale and Performance Constraints

Modem AI frameworks require real-time processing and high precision with little latency on transaction data. There is, however, no research on efficient scaling of AI use to high traffic e-commerce platforms without subsequently causing performance bottlenecks.

3. Threats to Privacy, Data Protection, and Security

An effective and efficient AI system requires vast amounts of data to train an algorithm and enhance fraud detection precision over time. The use and access to critical user and transaction data pose privacy, regulatory, and abuse risks concerning information, especially under GDPR.

7.METHODOLOGY

The methodology section lays out the research strategy, the ways data is collected, and the analytical techniques used to explore how cybercrime affects cryptocurrency transactions in e-commerce, as well as how AI-driven solutions can help fight fraud. This chapter offers a clear framework for understanding the challenges that cryptocurrency-related cyber threats present and assesses how effective AI-based cybersecurity measures are.To meet these goals, a mix of qualitative and quantitative research methods is used. Data is collected from existing literature, case studies, blockchain transaction analyses, and AI-powered fraud detection models. Furthermore, a comparative analysis is performed between traditional cybersecurity methods and modern AI-driven techniques to showcase their strengths and weaknesses. The methodology also discusses blockchain analytics, machine learning models, and forensic AI tools that are utilized for spotting and preventing fraudulent transactions. This chapter aims to create a systematic way to evaluate cybersecurity threats in cryptocurrency-based e-commerce transactions and to assess how AI technologies can improve fraud detection and prevention. The insights gained from this methodology will help in developing stronger security frameworks and AI-driven solutions to counter cyber threats in the ever-changing digital financial landscape.

7.1 Research Approach and Design

This study takes a mixed-methods approach, blending both qualitative and quantitative research to thoroughly explore how cybercrime affects cryptocurrency transactions in e-commerce and how AI-driven solutions can help reduce fraud. The research design uses descriptive, analytical, and comparative methods to evaluate cybersecurity challenges, current fraud detection systems, and how effective AI is in fighting financial crimes.

On the qualitative side, we dive into literature reviews, case studies, and expert interviews to gain insights into the changing landscape of cryptocurrency fraud and the role of AI in security solutions. On the quantitative side, we gather data from blockchain transactions, analyze fraud trends statistically, and assess the performance of AI-based fraud detection models. We also conduct a comparative analysis to highlight the differences between traditional cybersecurity methods and AI-driven solutions regarding fraud detection accuracy, speed, and scalability.This well-structured research design provides a comprehensive understanding of cyber threats in cryptocurrency transactions and assesses how AI can boost cybersecurity in e-commerce platforms.

7.2 Data Collection Methods

This study uses a diverse strategy to data collection in order to fully understand the intricacies of criminality in cryptocurrency transactions and the role AI plays in identifying fraud. The main techniques used are case studies and expert interviews, which when combined provide solid proof and insightful information about the cybersecurity issues we face and the AI-powered solutions that can be useful.

7.2.1Case studies

The study explores actual cases of cybercrime connected to bitcoin transactions on online marketplaces. The implementation of AI-based fraud detection systems, documented fraud instances, and security breaches are all highlighted in these case studies. The study identifies trends, weaknesses, and best practices for preventing cybercrime in the cryptocurrency space by looking at how various platforms have been targeted and how AI technologies have been used to reduce risks.

7.2.2 Expert interviews

Structured interviews are carried out with industry experts, cybersecurity specialists, blockchain analysts, and AI researchers to obtain a deeper understanding of the real-world difficulties and developments in AI-powered cybersecurity. The usefulness of AI-driven solutions, new dangers, and the shortcomings of existing fraud detection techniques are all clarified by these interviews. A practical viewpoint on the viability and scalability of AI in safeguarding cryptocurrency-related e-commerce transactions is offered by expert viewpoints.

This paper offers theoretical and practical contributions to the field of AI-driven cybersecurity in bitcoin transactions by integrating case studies and expert interviews, ensuring a fair and fact-based analysis.

7.3 Analysis Techniques

This study uses systematic analysis approaches to evaluate the impact of AI in preventing cybercrime in cryptocurrency transactions, with a particular focus on comparing AI-based technologies with conventional security measures. The main methods involve comparing AI solutions to traditional security systems and assessing AI's efficacy in detecting bitcoin fraud using both quantitative and qualitative metrics.

7.3.1 Comparative Analysis of AI Tools and Traditional Security Systems

In this investigation, conventional cybersecurity measures employed in bitcoin transactions for e-commerce are contrasted with AI-driven fraud detection systems. To ascertain AI's benefits over traditional systems, factors including accuracy, detection speed, scalability, flexibility, and false positive rates are assessed. In order to illustrate practical variations in how AI improves fraud protection while getting beyond the drawbacks of rule-based security models, the study also looks at case studies and industry reports.

7.3.2 Evaluation of AI's Effectiveness in Cryptocurrency Fraud Detection

Key performance metrics (KPIs) like fraud detection rate, response time, and adaptability to changing threats are used in the study to gauge how effective AI is. The ability of AI models to spot suspicious trends, stop fraudulent transactions, and enhance real-time decision-making is how they are evaluated. In order to comprehend how AI advances with continuous learning, blockchain analytics and machine learning performance indicators are also examined.

7.4 Methods of Software Development for AI-Powered Cybersecurity Solutions

Creating AI-powered cybersecurity solutions for detecting cryptocurrency fraud calls for adaptable and flexible software development methodologies. This study focuses on two popular approaches that allow for quick response to changing cyberthreats and ongoing improvement: the iterative development approach and the agile methodology.

7.4.1 The Agile Approach

Because of its adaptability, teamwork, and iterative development, the Agile methodology is frequently utilized in AI-based cybersecurity solutions. This approach divides development into manageable, short cycles, or sprints, in which AI models are regularly tested, trained, and refined using data from the actual world. Agile is useful for managing dynamic cybersecurity threats in bitcoin transactions because it allows for the quick deployment of security updates, ongoing feedback loops, and adaptive machine learning models.

7.4.2 Iterative Development Approach

Building AI solutions in cycles, with each iteration improving the system's accuracy and efficiency, is the main goal of the iterative development methodology. Since machine learning models may gradually incorporate new fraud patterns, this approach is very helpful for AI-powered fraud detection. The system grows more reliable in detecting and preventing cryptocurrency fraud by testing AI algorithms using real-time blockchain transaction data and improving detection mechanisms with each iteration.

AI-powered cybersecurity solutions may continue to be scalable, flexible, and effective by utilizing Agile and Iterative development processes, which will improve safety for cryptocurrency-related e-commerce transactions.

7.5 Justification for the Chosen Methodology

The intricate and dynamic nature of cybercrime in bitcoin transactions and the demand for AI-driven solutions to improve cybersecurity in e-commerce serve as justifications for the chosen research technique. A thorough grasp of the issue is ensured by a mixed-methods approach that combines qualitative and quantitative techniques, enabling both theoretical insights and data-driven research. The comparative analysis of AI tools and traditional security systems highlights the advantages of AI-driven solutions in terms of efficiency, accuracy, and adaptability; while expert interviews offer professional perspectives on the strengths and limitations of AI in fraud detection; and case studies provide real-world evidence of how cyber threats impact cryptocurrency transactions. Performance evaluations of AI models ensure that the research is grounded in empirical data, validating their effectiveness in detecting and preventing fraudulent transactions. The Agile and Iterative development methodologies were chosen for AI-based cybersecurity solutions because they allow for the development of robust AI models that evolve alongside emerging cyber threats in cryptocurrency transactions.

8. CONTRIBUTION TO THE FIELD

The expanding concerns of cybercrime in cryptocurrency transactions are addressed in this research, which significantly advances the disciplines of cybersecurity, e-commerce, and AI-driven fraud detection. Researchers, cybersecurity experts, and e-commerce companies can all benefit from this study's analysis of the difficulties in protecting digital transactions and assessment of the efficacy of AI solutions.A significant addition is the comparison of AI-based fraud detection systems with conventional security techniques, emphasizing AI's better capacity to identify and stop fraudulent activity instantly. The study also shows how blockchain analytics and artificial intelligence (AI) can cooperate to improve transaction security and lower financial fraud. Additionally, this research offers a useful framework for creating AI-powered cybersecurity solutions using iterative and agile approaches, guaranteeing flexibility in response to changing cyberthreats.

8.1 How AI Transforms E-commerce Cybersecurity in Cryptocurrency Transactions.

By improving fraud detection, automating threat responses, and fortifying transaction security in cryptocurrency-based payments, artificial intelligence (AI) is transforming cybersecurity in e-commerce. Artificial intelligence (AI)-driven solutions use machine learning, deep learning, and blockchain analytics to instantly spot suspicious activity, in contrast to conventional security techniques that depend on rule-based detection systems.Adaptive fraud detection, in which AI models continually learn from transaction data to identify new fraud trends and lower false positives, is one of the major changes AI offers to e-commerce security. Furthermore,

AI-powered behavioral analytics track user behaviors and highlight irregularities that are frequently signs of cybercrime in bitcoin transactions, such as strange login locations, quick transactions, or unusual spending patterns.

8.2 Theoretical Contributions to Digital Criminology

This study contributes to the field of digital criminology by expanding theoretical perspectives on cybercrime in cryptocurrency transactions and integrating AI-driven security solutions into frameworks for crime prevention. Proactive fraud detection is made possible by AI's predictive analytics and behavioral modeling, which enhance traditional criminological theories like Routine Activity Theory and Situational Crime Prevention. This study shows how real-time tracking, evaluation, and prevention of cyber crime can be achieved with blockchain data and AI-powered forensic investigations. By launching an AI-enhanced digital criminology framework with real-time fraud detection, automated risk assessment, and AI-driven threat intelligence, it also closes the gap between criminology and cybersecurity. This updated strategy creates the foundation for further study and legislative developments while fortifying crime prevention efforts in the context of cybercrimes involving cryptocurrencies.

8.3 Practical Implications for E-commerce Platforms and Regulators.

The practical ramifications of this research are noteworthy for both regulatory agencies and e-commerce platforms, as it emphasizes the necessity of cybersecurity measures driven by artificial intelligence to prevent fraudulent bitcoin transactions. Real-time transaction monitoring, risk assessment, and automatic threat response are all made possible by AI-powered fraud detection systems for e-commerce companies, which lower financial losses and boost customer confidence. Businesses may more successfully detect suspicious activity, stop illegal transactions, and adjust to changing cyberthreats by putting machine learning-based fraud detection models into place than they can with conventional security systems.This study highlights the significance of creating AI-integrated compliance frameworks for regulators in order to guarantee safe and transparent bitcoin transactions. AI can help regulators keep an eye on blockchain transactions, identify illegal financial activity, and more effectively enforce Know Your Customer (KYC) and anti-money laundering (AML) regulations.

8.4 Advancing Knowledge of AI's Role in Combating Cryptocurrency Cybercrime

By showing how machine learning, blockchain analytics, and real-time fraud detection systems might improve cybersecurity, this study contributes to our knowledge of AI's role in preventing cryptocurrency-related cybercrime. AI offers a more efficient substitute for conventional rule-based security measures due to its capacity to evaluate enormous volumes of transactional data, identify irregularities, and forecast fraudulent activity. This study demonstrates how AI-powered tools can track down illegal transactions, detect cybercriminal networks, and automate threat response mechanisms in cryptocurrency-based e-commerce platforms by incorporating AI into digital forensics and fraud prevention. Furthermore, the study aids in the creation of AI-driven cybersecurity frameworks that direct companies, scholars, and legislators in the adoption of more flexible and scalable security protocols.

9. DISCUSSION AND ANALYSIS OF FINDINGS

The results of this study demonstrate the increasing cybersecurity risks associated with bitcoin transactions in e-commerce as well as the vital role artificial intelligence plays in thwarting cyberthreats. Due to the complexity, anonymity, and decentralization of cryptocurrencies, conventional security methods such as manual monitoring and rule-based fraud detection are occasionally inadequate. However, real-time fraud detection, suspicious pattern recognition, and transaction prevention have shown to be more successful with AI-driven solutions, such as blockchain forensic tools, machine learning algorithms, and behavioral analytics. A comparison between AI-powered security systems and traditional methods shows that AI enhances detection accuracy, reaction speed, and adaptability to new threats.

9.1 Effectiveness of AI in Detecting Cryptocurrency Fraud

Artificial intelligence (AI) continuously learns from transactional data, adjusting to new fraud trends and emerging risks, unlike traditional fraud detection techniques that depend on static rule-based systems. Predictive analytics, anomaly detection, and behavioral monitoring are examples of AI-powered solutions that improve fraud detection by identifying illicit wallet addresses, odd spending patterns, and sudden increases in transactions. By using machine learning, deep learning, and blockchain analytics to spot suspicious activity in real time, artificial intelligence (AI) has demonstrated a high degree of effectiveness in identifying fraudulent bitcoin transactions. Artificial intelligence (AI) and natural language processing (NLP)-

powered forensic technologies also assist in locating phishing scams, scam websites, and dark web transactions connected to bitcoin fraud. AI and blockchain analytics work together to further enhance fraud detection by tracking transaction histories, identifying money laundering schemes, and mapping criminal networks. The accuracy, efficiency, and scalability of fraud protection are significantly improved by artificial intelligence (AI); yet, issues such as false positives, adversarial AI attacks, and the need for frequent model modifications persist. AI is still transforming fraud detection, though, by providing real-time, automated, and flexible security solutions. It is also an essential tool for protecting e-commerce platforms and financial ecosystems from criminal activity related to cryptocurrencies. AI is still altering fraud detection, though, by providing real-time, automated, and customizable security solutions. It is also a crucial tool for defending e-commerce platforms and financial ecosystems from criminal behavior related to cryptocurrencies.

9.2 The Role of Predictive Analytics and Machine Learning in Cybersecurity

Models for anomaly detection, including Autoencoders and Isolation Forests, assist in spotting departures from typical behavior and alerting users to possible security vulnerabilities. As an illustration, Darktrace's AI-powered cybersecurity technology keeps an eye on business networks in real time, identifying questionable activity before it develops into a full-scale attack. Anomaly detection models, such as Autoencoders and Isolation Forests, help identify deviations from normal behavior and notify users of potential security flaws. Darktrace's AI-powered cybersecurity technology, for example, monitors company networks in real time and spots suspicious activity before it becomes a full-scale attack.

9.3 Blockchain Analytics as a Complementary Tool to AI

Blockchain analytics plays a vital role in cybersecurity by providing an irreversible, transparent log of transactions. When paired with AI, it helps the identification and prevention of financial crimes, money laundering, and other illicit activities in digital transactions.

How AI and Blockchain Analytics Cooperate in Cybersecurity:

1.Fraud detection and transaction monitoring

Blockchain analytics tools with AI capabilities examine transactions in real time to spot questionable activity. Machine learning algorithms examine transaction patterns, wallet habits, and fund movements to detect fraudulent activity. For instance, Chainalysis and CipherTrace offer blockchain intelligence solutions powered by artificial intelligence (AI) to monitor illegal cryptocurrency transactions connected to terrorist financing or money laundering.

2.Security&Audits of Smart Contracts

AI-powered tools for code analysis Prior to implementation, check smart contracts for weaknesses. To anticipate potential exploits, machine learning algorithms examine past attack trends. As an illustration, Open Zeppelin and CertiK employ AI to find Ethereum smart contract flaws, lowering the possibility of hacks.

9.4 Analysis of Case Studies and Real-World Applications

For cybersecurity, a number of businesses and institutions use blockchain analytics and artificial intelligence. The case studies that follow show how these technologies improve security protocols. 1. Google Chronicle: AI in Cybersecurity. Every day, petabytes of security data are processed and analyzed by Google Chronicle, an AI-powered cybersecurity platform. It correlates signals from many sources using AI-powered threat detection to find malicious activity before it becomes a serious concern.

Endpoint Security Powered by AI with CrowdStrike Falcon

Using AI and machine learning models, CrowdStrike Falcon finds and eliminates ransomware, malware, and advanced persistent threats (APTs?).

Because its cloud-native technology is constantly learning from global threat intelligence data, it provides real-time defense against evolving cyberthreats.

9.5 New Insights: How AI Can Address Unmet Needs in Cryptocurrency Fraud Detection

Because blockchain transactions are pseudonymous, cryptocurrency fraud is becoming an increasing threat. AI is filling in the gaps in fraud detection left by conventional techniques.

Important Advances in AI for Crypto Fraud Detection:

Filling up the Gaps in Conventional Fraud Detection.New fraud strategies are difficult for traditional rule-based systems to keep up with. AI-driven detection systems are always learning and changing to meet new fraud trends.

1.Wallet Analysis Using Deep Learning.

In order to distinguish between high-risk addresses used for illegal operations like ransomware payments and legitimate ones, AI algorithms examine wallet behavior. For instance, Elliptic's blockchain analysis powered by AI finds trends linked to fraud and money laundering.

10. Suggestions and Recommendations

Strategic measures must be put in place by governments and enterprises to optimize the use of AI in fraud detection, blockchain analytics, and cybersecurity. This section provides important suggestions for enhancing AI integration, setting investment priorities, resolving moral dilemmas, and influencing legislative measures

10.1 Improving AI Integration for Real-Time Fraud Detection

Real-time handling of complex cyberthreats and financial crimes requires AI-driven fraud detection systems to advance. Important suggestions consist of:

Improving Real-Time Data Processing: Use AI models that can identify suspicious activity before it is finished by evaluating transaction patterns in milliseconds.
Deploying Federated Learning for Secure Fraud Detection: Use decentralized AI training approaches to increase fraud detection across many financial institutions while preserving privacy.
Combining AI with Blockchain Analytics: To increase the traceability of illegal transactions, use machine learning with blockchain-based technologies.
Risk-based AI investment techniques are crucial since e-commerce platforms are subject to varied degrees of cybersecurity hazards. Among the recommendations are:
Prioritizing High-Risk Transactions: AI models ought to concentrate on transactions that have a high likelihood of fraud, like purchases made using cryptocurrencies, cross-border transfers, and transactions from hacked devices.

Putting AI-Powered Identity Verification into Practice: To lessen account takeovers, biometric authentication, behavioral analytics, and AI-powered Know Your Customer (KYC) processes ought to be implemented.
Balancing AI Cost with ROI: Companies should assess AI expenditures by looking at fraud reduction rates, improvements in consumer trust, and advantages for regulatory compliance.
AI Integration with Payment Gateways: To stop fraudulent transactions at checkout, real-time fraud detection ought to be integrated into payment processing systems.

10.3 Ethical and Privacy Considerations in AI Surveillance for Cryptocurrency Transactions

To keep users' trust and regulatory permission, AI-powered crypto surveillance presents ethical and privacy issues that must be resolved. Among the main concerns are: Openness in AI Decisions: Governments and financial institutions ought to reveal how their AI programs analyze blockchain transactions and identify questionable ones. Employ privacy-preserving AI strategies to prevent unwanted access to user data, such as differential privacy, zero-knowledge proofs, and homomorphic encryption. To avoid AI bias in transaction verification, make sure AI models don't label legitimate transactions as fraudulent or single out specific groups.Safeguarding User Consent and Data Security: Crypto exchanges and authorities must ensure that they comply with GDPR and other data protection laws and have explicit policies for data collection. Lawmakers must establish international norms and laws focused on artificial intelligence in order to establish a safe digital financial environment. Important policy suggestions consist of:

10.4 Policy Recommendations for Governments and Regulatory Bodies

Creating AI Governance Frameworks: To ensure responsibility in financial institutions, governments should establish legislative frameworks for AI-driven fraud detection. Improving Public-Private Cooperation: AI-driven threat intelligence should be shared among cybersecurity companies, blockchain analytics firms, and regulatory bodies. Standardizing AI-Driven AML and CFT Regulations: Cryptocurrency exchanges should be required to use AI-based AML and CFT (counter-financing of terrorism) procedures. Promoting Ethical AI Development: Lawmakers ought to uphold AI transparency, stop improper use of surveillance, and encourage moral AI standards for fraud detection.

11. FUTURE SCOPE FOR RESEARCH

AI's use in fraud detection, blockchain analytics, and cybersecurity is bringing with it both new potential and difficulties as it develops. Future studies should concentrate on strengthening AI's capacity to identify global cryptocurrency fraud, enhancing fraud prediction using cutting-edge AI methods, resolving ethical and legal issues, and safeguarding decentralized financial ecosystems.

11.1 Cross-Border AI Solutions for International Cryptocurrency Fraud

Because cryptocurrency transactions are decentralized and worldwide, it is challenging for financial institutions or particular governments to monitor illegal activity. Future studies ought to investigate:

Creating AI-Powered Global Fraud Detection Networks: AI-powered systems that link regulators, exchanges, and financial institutions globally to exchange information about questionable activity.

Improving Regulations for Multi-Jurisdictional AI: establishing global legal frameworks to ensure compliance across various legal jurisdictions for AI-driven bitcoin monitoring.

AI for Multi-Language and Multi-Currency Fraud Analysis: Putting into practice AI tools that can interpret and evaluate transaction patterns in a variety of economic, linguistic, and cultural contexts.

11.2 Use of Deep Learning and Advanced AI Techniques in Fraud Prediction

Conventional AI models have made fraud detection better, but more sophisticated methods are needed due to the complexity of cyberthreats. Research in the future should look into:

Using Graph Neural Networks (GNNs) to Detect Fraud: GNNs are used to examine the connections between blockchain addresses and identify fraudulent groupings.

Using reinforcement learning to create AI models that continuously learn and adjust to changing fraud strategies without the need for human intervention is known as adaptive fraud prevention.

Federated Learning for Privacy-Preserving AI Models: This method uses decentralized AI training methods to make fraud detection possible without disclosing private financial information.

11.3 Addressing Ethical and Regulatory Challenges in AI-Driven Cybersecurity

There are serious ethical and legal issues with the expanding use of AI in cybersecurity and cryptocurrency surveillance. Future studies ought to concentrate on:

Ethical AI Frameworks for Cryptocurrency Surveillance: Creating policies to stop prejudice, bias, and unfair profiling in fraud detection caused by AI. Privacy-Preserving AI Models for Compliance: Examining homomorphic encryption, differential privacy, and zero-knowledge proofs to make sure AI models abide by data protection laws. Developing interpretable AI models that financial institutions and regulators can verify for accuracy and fairness is known as AI Transparency & Explainability in Fraud Detection.AI and Human Oversight in Cybersecurity: Researching how to reconcile human judgment and AI automation in cybersecurity and fraud detection.

11.4 The Future of AI in Securing the Decentralized Cryptocurrency Ecosystem

The emergence of smart contracts, non-custodial wallets, and decentralized finance (DeFi) calls for new AI-driven security measures. Some potential avenues for future investigation are:

AI for Security in Decentralized Autonomous Organizations (DAOs): Examining how AI can identify fraudulent proposals and governance threats in decentralized organizations.

AI in DeFi Protocol Auditing: DeFi smart contracts are analyzed using machine learning to find vulnerabilities before they are abused.

AI-Powered NFT Fraud Prevention: Investigating AI-powered techniques to identify price manipulation, NFT wash trading, and fake digital assets.

Quantum-Resistant AI Security Models: Researching cybersecurity solutions based on AI to shield cryptocurrencies from potential dangers posed by quantum computing.

12. CONCLUSION

Fighting cybercrime has advanced significantly with the use of Artificial Intelligence (AI) into cybersecurity, especially in the e-commerce and cryptocurrency industries. The main conclusions, potential ramifications, and the critical role AI plays in boosting digital security are all summarized in this conclusion.

12.1 Summary of Key Findings

Improved Fraud Detection: Artificial intelligence has revolutionized the area by analyzing vast datasets and promptly identifying anomalies and questionable patterns. AI assesses a customer's volume, frequency, and previous purchases to lessen the risk of identity theft and card-not-present fraud.

Blockchain transactions in the cryptocurrency arena are analyzed by artificial intelligence (AI) to spot fraudulent activities and send out real-time hazard signals. Because cryptocurrency transactions are anonymous, this proactive strategy is crucial.

Applications of Decentralized AI By tracking transaction histories and purchasing patterns across dispersed networks, Decentralized AI has improved fraud detection and decreased the risk of online fraud.

Advanced Techniques: AI successfully identifies questionable patterns and abnormalities in transaction data by employing machine learning algorithms, blockchain analytics, and behavioral analysis, supporting

12.2 Implications for the Future of Cybersecurity in E-commerce and Cryptocurrency

the field of security practices by making them proactive for threat mitigation. It is no longer a field of merely reacting to fraud, but rather preventing it actively and securing bank transactions, user accounts, and business networks. With respect to adaptive security, fraud detection systems driven by AI offer flexible, robust options. These systems remain constantly vigilant and learn to adapt from malware more than ever before. In addition, using AI capabilities for fraud detection and prevention drastically improves the protection of sensitive information, and improves consumer trust. Lastly, it is imperative that these systems are constantly developed and updated. By leveraging data to learn, the systems will always be automating, improving, and updating the fraud detection and prevention lifecycle.

12.3 Final Thoughts on the Role of AI in Combating Cybercrime

With its cutting-edge solutions that outperform conventional security measures, artificial intelligence is leading the fight against cybercrime. In addition to improving the detection and prevention of fraudulent activity, its incorporation into cybersecurity frameworks has cleared the path for a more reliable and safe online environment. AI technology will surely play a bigger part in protecting digital assets and preserving the integrity of online transactions as it develops, further establishing its status as a vital weapon in the fight against cyberthreats.

REFERENCES

Aisyah, N., Hidayat, R., Zulaikha, S., Rizki, A., Yusof, Z. B., Pertiwi, D., & Ismail, F. (2019). Artificial Intelligence in Cryptographic Protocols: Securing E-Commerce Transactions and Ensuring Data Integrity.

Babu, C. S., & Vishnupriyan, J. VijaykumarReddy, U., Hariharan, P., & Dheenadhayalan, P. (2025). Secure Implementation of Image Processing Operations on CPU and GPU Architectures: With Deep Learning Frameworks. In Signal and Image Processing Techniques for Defense, Security, and Healthcare (pp. 253-302). IGI Global Scientific Publishing.

Babu, C. V. S., & Andrew, S. P. (2024). Adaptive AI for Dynamic Cybersecurity Systems: Enhancing Protection in a Rapidly Evolving Digital Landscape. In Zhihan, Lv., & Global, I. G. I. (Eds.), *Principles and Applications of Adaptive Artificial Intelligence* (pp. 52–72)., DOI: 10.4018/979-8-3693-0230-9.ch003

G A, S., Prabha, R., Sridevi, S., & Rohini, A. (2024). Artificial Intelligence: Advanced Mathematical Constructs and Theoretical Framework in Machine Learning and Deep Learning Algorithms.

Gupta, R. (2024). Cybersecurity Threats in E-Commerce: Trends and Mitigation Strategies. *Journal of Advanced Management Studies*, *1*(3), 1–10. DOI: 10.36676/jams.v1.i3.13

Kumar, A. K., Chidipothu, V. K., & Leelavathi, M. (2025). ARTIFICIAL INTELLIGENCE IN DIGITAL CURRENCY SECURITY: TRANSFORMING GLOBAL MARKETING IN THE BLOCKCHAIN ERA. *Cuestiones de Fisioterapia*, *54*(3), 1907–1928.

Metibemu, O. C., Adesokan-Imran, T. O., Ajayi, A. J., Tiwo, O. J., Olutimehin, A. T., & Olaniyi, O. O. (2025). Developing Proactive Threat Mitigation Strategies for Cloud Misconfiguration Risks in Financial SaaS Applications. *Journal of Engineering Research and Reports*, *27*(3), 393–413. DOI: 10.9734/jerr/2025/v27i31442

Mudgal, A. (2025). Leveraging AI and ML for Proactive Threat Detection for E-Commerce. In *Strategic Innovations of AI and ML for E-Commerce Data Security* (pp. 281–322). IGI Global.

Rani, P., & Sehrawat, H. (2024, December). Comprehensive Analysis of Cybersecurity: Examining Existing Literature and Identifying Potential Areas for Future Research. In 2024 1st International Conference on Advances in Computing, Communication and Networking (ICAC2N) (pp. 731-736). IEEE.

Salami, I. A., Adesokan-Imran, T. O., Tiwo, O. J., Metibemu, O. C., Olutimehin, A. T., & Olaniyi, O. O. (2025). Addressing Bias and Data Privacy Concerns in AI-Driven Credit Scoring Systems Through Cybersecurity Risk Assessment. *Asian Journal of Research in Computer Science*, *18*(4), 59–82. DOI: 10.9734/ajrcos/2025/v18i4608

Shah, I. A., & Jhanjhi, N. Z. (2025). The Challenges for E-Commerce Using AI Applications. In *Generative AI for Web Engineering Models* (pp. 203–222). IGI Global.

Ullah, S. (2025). Intention to Use Cryptocurrencies for Business Transactions: The Case of North Carolina. *Journal of Risk and Financial Management*, *18*(2), 58. DOI: 10.3390/jrfm18020058

Chapter 12
Impact of Digital Technology Aid on Incarcerated Population Qualitative Method:
Some Case Studies and Thematic Analysis

S. Srinivasan
https://orcid.org/0009-0002-0179-9849
Department of Humanities and Social Sciences, Graphic Era University (Deemed), Dehradun, India

R. Vallipriya
https://orcid.org/0009-0008-6692-603X
Department of Physical Science, Tamil Nadu Teacher Education University, Trichy, India

Ajay Kumar Singh
https://orcid.org/0000-0003-0429-0925
Department of Humanities and Social Sciences, Graphic Era University (Deemed), Dehradun, India

ABSTRACT

This study highlights the transformative potential of digital technology in prison settings. It offers opportunities to improve prison efficiency, enhance staff effectiveness, and provide better learning experiences for prisoners, thereby contributing to a safer and more secure society. Technology can strengthen prison safety by using scanners and detectors to monitor staff and inmates automatically. The study

DOI: 10.4018/979-8-3693-8871-6.ch012

emphasizes several aspects of prison life, including fostering positive experiences, promoting repentance and transformation, addressing feelings of loneliness and separation from family, and tackling stigma during parole. It also focuses on rehabilitation programs for life-sentenced inmates, the categorization of inmates, legal justice, and the need for general amnesty and release, particularly for those serving life sentences. Using thematic analysis and examining 6 case studies, the study explores the challenges incarcerated individuals face and demonstrates how digital technology can improve their lives and support rehabilitation efforts.

INTRODUCTION

Digital technology can support various aspects of improving society and enhancing innovation in education, healthcare, and communication. Digital technology provides an increase in the quality of life for the incarcerated population and is gaining attention (Knight, 2017). Digital technology can enhance the correctional setting by improving rehabilitation and overall safety and security (Zivanai & Mahlangu, 2022). The proposed research study focuses on the impact of digital technology on the incarcerated population. The prison setting can protect inmates, increase security, and support and rehabilitate the incarcerated population through monitoring. Digital technology has improved rapidly over recent years within the prison community and in the wider society (Kerr & Willis, 2018). Technology can improve social and health care services, enhance public services, increase accessibility, and improve quality of life and safety in care. In the spectrum of digital services, this can include electronic booking, e-forms, database-related and self-help services, as well as video-mediated support to enhance the variety and range of information. Digital technology can enhance peer group support and increase access for people with substance abuse-related issues (Farabee et al., 2016).

The study emphasizes the use of digital technology to enhance emotional and psychological support, address mental health and well-being, and foster improvements among the incarcerated population. It also aims to improve the well-being of staff and strengthen relationships to positively influence prisoner behavior. Digital technology can positively impact the incarcerated population by enhancing rehabilitation and promoting reintegration into society. Technology can enhance social skills and improve self-esteem. It can strengthen various aspects, as technology can play a vital role in improving digital literacy for released individuals. Technology can improve prisoners' job skills, making them more useful after release. Self-service technology can help reduce disciplinary offenses in prison. Technology can reduce reoffending in the first year after release for inmates. It can be more effective for prisoners to build confidence and cope with technology, improving their integration into the outside world Digital devices for prisoner inmates after release can provide support for official procedures related to the labor market, housing, and other personal matters. The study used thematic analysis, which is common in qualitative research. It involves analyzing and interpreting patterns in qualitative data.

The study emphasizes the availability of digital services for prisons, which can support electronic monitoring and analysis. The digital services available in the prison setting provide valuable insights. To examine the research study on digitalization for the incarcerated population to improve social skills, self-esteem, rehabilitation, and their reintegration into society (Jewkes & Reisdorf, 2016; Knight & Van De Steene, 2020; McDougall et al., 2017). Digital technology can improve digital literacy among prison inmates, enhance their job skills, and facilitate their re-entry into society. Self-service technology can improve prisoners' experiences by reducing disciplinary-related offenses and reoffending in the first year after release from prison. There are prisoners who require rehabilitation and re-entry practices within the correctional services system to engage with the offline realms, which can disregard the digital realm. Digital technology can improve security for employees who are often resistant to introducing new technologies due to their perceived potential security risks (Jewkes & Reisdorf, 2016).

The study is related to the Smart Prison Project for the Finnish Criminal Sanctions Agency, focusing on the incarcerated population in digital inclusion. This study includes a women's prison with 100 cells; it is a special pilot case for the smart project. The project covers various digital and smart services, such as safe websites, social health care, employment, and rehabilitation services that have been developed (Järveläinen & Rantanen, 2021). The smart prison system can develop best practices and improve digital rehabilitation services and reintegration to reduce recidivism within the smart prison system (Imandeka et al., 2024). The research study provides a comprehensive understanding of the challenges in prison digitalization through the experiences of the incarcerated population, emphasizing perspectives on digital inclusion and the barriers they face.Some research studies address the link between digital technology and face-to-face interactions for prison inmates, replacing various digital sources and encounters in the prison system Knight & Van De Steene, 2020).

The paper highlights the qualitative method; it includes case studies and thematic analysis. The study identifies various aspects of prison life. It can increase positive prison experiences, foster repentance and transformation, identify loneliness related to family separation, and address stigma problems among inmates, especially those on parole (Kazemian, 2019). The study can support the use of technology to promote prison rehabilitation activities. Those who are serving life sentences and facing legal issues may benefit from amnesty and release for prisoners (Smit & Appleton, 2019). The significance of the study is to highlight how digital technology will support the incarcerated population by improving individual lives and enhancing rehabilitation and correctional support.

Research Gap, Research Questions and Research Objectives

There are research gaps in previous studies. The current study addresses the use of digital technology in correctional settings. It focuses on administrative and security support for digital enhancement and aims to improve educational programs. There is a lack of in-depth qualitative research. The study provides a comprehensive case study on the use of digital technology aids for the incarcerated population. There has been limited attention to how digital devices can influence prison environments. The study focuses on emotional well-being and rehabilitation services to improve social connections and relationships with family members. Digital technology can reduce recidivism and increase the success rate for post-release (Mahlangu & Zivanai, 2023). The study emphasizes the qualitative method, including 6 case studies and thematic analysis. Digital technology can support the quality of life among the incarcerated population by improving rehabilitation services.

Hence, this chapter is an attempt to reduce the ambiguity of previous literature and it considers the following research questions:

RQ1. How is their lifestyle as prison inmates?
RQ2. What are the problems they face in their post-prison life?
RQ3. What are the methods of promoting repentance and transformation?
RQ4. How do they feel about loneliness and separation from their families?
RQ5. How are they tackling stigma and parole?
RQ6. What are the rehabilitation programs for life-sentenced inmates?
RQ7. What are the aspects of legal justice and the need for general amnesty and release?
RQ8. What are the thematic analyses?
RQ9. How does digital technology play an important role for prisoners?
RQ10. How can technology support prison administration?

Background of the Study

The background of the study is to improve digital technology in various aspects of prison administration. This includes education, healthcare, and communication to promote digital solutions for enhancing the incarcerated population. The use of technology aims to improve the well-being of the incarcerated population and reduce the challenges they face (Kerr & Willis, 2018). The study mainly focuses on the impact of digital technology on incarcerated individuals, including aspects such as emotional well-being, mental health, post-release integration, rehabilitation services, loneliness, and stigma.

Literature Review

The literature provides a theoretical framework for the chapter, improving technology for correctional services and addressing the growing prevalence. The study provides an in-depth analysis of the literature reviews and enhances qualitative research.

Digital Technology in Prison Settings: Digital technology can enhance the prison setting by using various educational apps and software, tablets, and telemedicine. It is intended that the outcome of the study will improve education and increase mental health support and services, with an emphasis on fostering social connections (Jewkes & Reisdorf, 2016).

Digital Technology benefit for the Prison Inmates: Educational opportunities can be useful in the prison setting by providing online courses to improve inmates' knowledge and develop their skills (Dewey, 2020). The role of digital technology can support mental health services and reduce feelings of isolation for the incarcerated population. Technology plays a vital role in improving social connectivity and facilitating discussions with family and support network services (Ross et al., 2023).

Technology Challenges and Barriers among Inmates: The literature provides various technologies that impact the inmate population. The findings of the study provide qualitative insights that address the challenges, functionality, and usability of correctional facilities. The data security for prison inmates and privacy for qualitative insights involve both inmates and staff (Condon et al., 2007).

The Impact of Rehabilitation and Recidivism: The previous study reviewed technology that positively impacts rehabilitation outcomes, improving skill development and behavior. The qualitative study addresses the impact of technology on reducing recidivism and focuses on inmates' perspectives and their experiences (McDougall et al., 2017). The existing research addresses the long-term impact of technology on prison inmates in the context of different facilities. The qualitative study provides a comprehensive understanding of prisoners' lifestyles and their use of digital technology for support (Ndindeng, 2024).

Past-Prison Histories of Inmates

The prison inmates' past histories are important for understanding how to reduce recidivism. This understanding can support behavioral change and improve the structured approach that digital technology aids, leading to further improvements in the prison setting. The significance of the study is to enhance prisoner rehabilitation, reduce recidivism, and improve the role of technology (Farley & Pike, 2016). It can further the discussion on incarceration to improve current attitudes and behaviors, enhancing rehabilitation efforts through technology support. The study addresses prison inmates' age, gender, socioeconomic background, conditions, and educational status to improve the experiences of incarcerated individuals (Wakefield & Uggen, 2010). The study examines the reasons crimes are committed, categorizing them as violent and non-violent, which affects prison inmates' experiences and perceptions (Wright, 1991).

Psychological and Social Impact: The incarcerated population's past experiences and mental health problems, including trauma and coping strategies, can help address the development of inmates (Picken, 2012). Prison inmates are affected by stigma, which is a societal perception that impacts their reintegration efforts (Srinivasan & Rajavel, 2025).

Patterns of Recidivism: The study explores prison histories and correlates them with reoffending status. It can influence their previous experiences and connections with family, friends, and support systems; upon release, this can impact the likelihood of recidivism (Barrick, et al., 2014).

Technology as a Tool for Change: Prison inmates can understand their past histories to facilitate rehabilitation through programs that incorporate digital technology. The past histories and experiences influence their willingness to support digital technology and how it can reduce feelings of isolation and stigma in their rehabilitation. The qualitative study aims to enrich the understanding of digital literacy for older people living in prison. The objectives of the study are to identify the factors influencing digital literacy in the prison setting and to understand the experiences and effects of assistive technology on their lives post-release (Srinivasan & Rajavel, 2025).

Digital technology on the incarcerated population: Digital technology can improve various implications for the incarcerated population, enhancing rehabilitation, education, and mental health services, ultimately contributing to the overall well-being of inmates (Auty et al., 2017).

Education services for Incarcerated Population: Online education improves prison inmates' skills and knowledge, enabling them to attain academic advancement and enhancing vocational training for the incarcerated population. Digital technology can improve the traditional classroom atmosphere and increase motivation to enhance learning outcomes (Wilson et al., 2000).

Mental Health Support and Services: Technology plays a vital role in improving tele-health services and enhancing inmates' mental health support services, reducing stigma levels and facilitating better mental health outcomes. The digital tool improves inmates' mindfulness and regular relaxation exercises, which are important for reducing inmates' stress and anxiety (Shen, 2024).

Social Connectivity: The digital tool improves communication between inmates and their family and friends. To increase emotional support to reduce feelings of isolation for the incarcerated prison population. The technology, such as email and video calls, helps to regularly maintain their family relationships and social networks (Western et al., 2015).

Impact of digital technology for improves the staff administration: The technology can improve the effective integration of technology to enhance rehabilitation and address the needs of inmates. The technology enhances the development of policies to serve the rehabilitative goals for correctional settings (Knight & Van De Steene, 2020).

Future Improvement for the Digital Technology in the Prison Settings: The technology in the inmates provides the continuous support for their outcomes and focuses on the various correctional services. To enhance the empathy training and inmates' learning for the existing program. The digital technology can improve the incarcerated population by providing educational resources, enhancing mental health services, and supporting social connections (Byrne & Pattavina, 2012). The study addresses the challenges for the incarcerated population and improves the disparities among the prison inmates; it can develop effective ways to improve technology integration in the correctional settings (Leach et al., 2022).

Major Objective of the Study

- To assess the past-prison histories of inmates.
- To identify the influence of digital technology on the incarcerated population.
- To analyze individual inmates using thematic analysis.

Proposed Research Methodology

The researcher conducted semi-structured narrative interviews with 6 prison inmates. This procedure was selected since the situation of each prison inmate was unique in terms of stress and frustration. However, the probability that the narratives could be imposed or have little relationship to their own real experiences was not ruled out (Hall & Rossmannith, 2016). Each one had to understand the background of their family which they were mostly ready to speak about. As it was indeed extremely painful and hard for many of them to speak of the details of crime, the researcher avoided questions related to crime, unless they opened up. Only four guidelines were followed in the in-depth interviews. Qualitative data were gathered from narrative and non-directive interviews with 6 prison inmates who were selected during the quantitative data collection process based on the researcher's judgment of their willingness to share their lives. The researcher conducted case studies, particularly focusing on the respondents' perceived well-being with specific reference to spirituality. The information gathered was codified, and content analysis of relevant qualitative data was carried out. Narrative qualitative analysis was used along with thematic analysis.

1. Can you tell me something about your family?
2. How is your relationship with God?
3. What is your experience here? Can you talk something about prison life?
4. Do you have any suggestions to improve prison life or a message to the world based on your experience?
5. How can digital technology improve the lives of prison inmates?

The respondents were selected during the quantitative data collection process based on the researcher's judgment of their willingness to share their lives. The information gathered and significant verbatim were processed manually as well as with 'R' Studio for carrying out appropriate thematic analysis. After familiarizing myself with the data in the data corpus consisting of the narratives of 6 respondents, the researcher assigned the initial codes of relevant data in a systematic fashion after which the corpus was pre-processed and analyzed with Java Gui for R (JGR).

The qualitative data were gathered from the narrative and non-directive interviews with 6 prison inmates who were selected during the course of quantitative data collection process based on researcher's judgment on their willingness to share their lives. The researcher conducted case studies particularly focusing the respondents' perceived well-being with specific reference to spirituality. The information gathered was codified and content analyses of relevant qualitative data were carried out. Narrative qualitative analysis was used with thematic analysis.

SECTION A: CASE STUDIES - NARRATIVES

Thematic Analysis is the method of identifying, analyzing and reporting patterns or themes in data (Braun & Clarke, 2006). The data corpus for case studies were the 6 interviews conducted which was processed manually as well as with 'R' version, 3.3.1. After familiarizing with the data, the researcher created a few initial codes of the interesting data in a systematic fashion after which the corpus was pre- processed and analyzed with Java Gui for R (JGR).

Case Study 1

'A' is a 37 year old woman lifer who was imprisoned in relation to attempting suicide. Her husband was working abroad and the family was economically sound. But the problem was with his inclination for and involvement in extramarital affairs. Further, even though at the time of marriage the husband was working abroad and seemed to have good economic prospects, within three years of their marriage, he was found to be heavily indebted. 'A' started feeling vehemently insecure in the house. With such tensions in the house, they got divorced and she came to her parental house. Their daughter was, however, very much attached to the father which created further tension within 'A'. Every day he used to talk to the child over the phone. When the child was three and a half years old, 'A's family wanted to send her to pre-school. At this time, her husband who used to talk to the child daily suddenly stopped phone calls which created much distress in the child. The daughter started having continuous fever for more than a month and became unconscious. They had to call her husband and after seeing him, the child started recovering. 'A' became anxious about the security of her child too. If she was not attached to the father, 'A' would have brought her up on her own. Her own parents are alive and highly supportive. She said, "I am the only girl in my house. My brothers have sons and we were yearning for a girl child in the family. We loved her much. But the situations turned against us. Then I wished if I did not have a child". With such tensions within, she decided to end her life along with her daughter to ensure the child's security and consumed tablets. Unfortunately, before she died, her people happened to see her in a critical condition and rushed them to the hospital. The child had already died; but she survived. She has no answer why God allowed her to live. She felt the great guilt of poisoning her own child and was under severe distress in the prison. As years passed by, she started resorting to prayer and concentrating on her work in the prison. She spends the term of sentence as a lifer, *doing good for the others, being committed to the work as though assigned to her from God, giving importance to prayer, being faithful to the Lord* who deigned to keep her on earth.

The researcher met 'A's father when he came to visit her. She had seen him completing the procedure of the visit. He had given the application, got the materials, snacks and fruits checked by the reception staff, who counted everything; he packed them in the cloth bags provided by the prison. The strain and stress of travel from the far away village, the tension of being scrutinized for every piece of material and the pain of the situation of the daughter were all reflecting on his dignified face. He looked a noble man and it was very painful to watch the father and daughter communicating across the wire mesh which is at about 5 meters distance from each other. The wire mesh in the visiting room reassures that no intimate and private conversations take place, no consolation of being close to the loved ones, no luxury of eating together what you brought with much love from home. When there are more visitors it is even difficult to hear what each one is saying; one needs to shout to get across to the other.

'A's father is 67 years old and mother is 60 years old. They are much tensed about her future and have appealed to the Supreme Court for her release which implies heavy financial burden on the family and especially upon a senior citizen in his late sixties. The struggles of a prisoner's family can be observed at the visiting place and at the waiting hall for visits. From her experience of being with women prisoners, 'A' suggests that when a woman is punished, the whole family is punished; there is no one to take care of the family. She and the family undergo depression. Hence the maximum imprisonment that can be awarded to a woman should be only *five years*. This opinion is once again substantiated by the quantitative analysis where we found that the children of a majority of women prisoners are not looked after by their spouses; but by their family members or hostels while the children of a majority of men prisoners are looked after by their spouses.

Case Study 2

The researcher met 'B' on the very first day of her visit to a central prison. He was just sitting under a tree. He came to inquire on the researcher's visit and when she said the purpose, he said, "Madam, No one will be ready to answer your questions; surely, not I". The researcher kept silent. Then he looked at her and asked, "But we will help you to the best of our ability. How many persons do you need?". When the researcher said 120, he said, "It will be very difficult; but, I will make sure that you get 120 inmates". What the researcher noticed is that he kept to his word and gave every assistance to the researcher in getting respondents. Every day he and another inmate would promptly be there as though it is their responsibility to help the researcher. In their company, the researcher felt quite safe in the prison and later the entire atmosphere was supportive. The researcher was touched on the last day of her visit, when they knew that the researcher would come no more, 'B' stood in the office and said, 'Now ask me; I will answer your questions". By then he had by hearted all the questions and knew there was nothing much controversial in the questionnaire.

'B' did not explain to the researcher the reason for his imprisonment except that he was a lifer. But he revealed to her his family and his spirituality. He is 46 years old and had completed his Bachelor of Engineering (B.E.) in Civil Engineering. He is interested in anatomy and law. His family has 16 acres of land and other assets. His is a noble family; they come to take him when he is granted parole; only one person comes to the prison, while wife and children will wait for him a little away from the prison in their car. He loves his wife much and showed her photo. She was young and beautiful girl; while searching for her photo in the book, the researcher could see the spark in his eyes for the first time and a smile of great love saying, "Oh…. Where are you? I can't find you… Are you hiding?" His daughter is doing her master's degree. On the whole, he rated his family ass an upper middle class family and a loving family with a strong bond.

Apart from a good educational back-ground, 'B' is multi-talented. He is a writer, yoga master, karate black belt, singer and break dancer. He considers jail as a super university where you can learn life, true and false relationships, how to play safe without fights and opinions, without maintaining close friendships, being alone and passive. Having spent 11 years in the prison, he had worked devotedly in napkins section and vermin compost/farm. But at present he feels there is no point in working and for whom and hence does not go to work. The researcher dialogued on this issue with him and enquired if work would keep his mind occupied and thus save from boredom and unhealthy thoughts and he did agree to her view. According to him, life imprisonment is not going to reform any prisoner as the sentence deprives the prisoner of any hope for the future. Slowly, year after year the hope, energy, interest and life itself fades away without any reformation. If there is a specified period of imprisonment and differential treatment for first offenders it can bring about change and reformation.

According to him, *God, 'Kadavul' in Tamil, means, 'one who is inside, in the inner heart'* ('Ul' in Tamil means inside). He said, "Once my daughter wrote to me: Life is full of problems; but each problem is a good step for future; so don't worry father". According to him, heaven and hell are here itself. It depends on our thoughts and actions. He expressed his faith in an all powerful God as he said, "Kadavul thaan Kelvi; kadavul thaan badhil; kadavul thaaan kaaranam; kadavul thaan vidai" (God is the question; God is the answer. God is the reason). In engineering language he further emphasized, "He is the generator, operator and destroyer". He believes in the 'power of the now' and said, "neitru embathu udaintha paanai; naale embathu madhil meil pooney; intru embathu kayyil veenai." (Yesterday is a broken pot; Tomorrow is a cat on the wall; Today is a veena (a musical instrument) in your hand". So live in the present and enjoy it.

'B' and the other inmate who were the main helpers in the prison came to reach her till the gate and the gate closed behind them, still they stood and waved till the researcher crossed the main gate. The researcher then realized that they had shared much goodness beyond compare which she too cannot repay.

Case Study 3

'C' works in the office of the jail. The researcher saw him always busy with work and so could not talk to him. One day the researcher met him on the way and he said that he would like to talk to her and participate in the survey.

'C' hails from a very poor family and was working as a 'coolie', daily wage earner. He has spent 30 long years in the prison and has availed parole 34 times and is now 52 years of age. None from his family had gone to school. He completed his primary level of education after which he discontinued studies and was a child laborer. He got into the habit of alcoholism and friendship due to which he got into delinquency and crime. His wife left him and the children when he was arrested and there was no one to take care of his two children. At this juncture of crisis, a Christian orphanage came forward to help his children and to take care of them which he finds as the timeliest help he received. They studied in the hostel and are now self reliant.

'C' was highly distressed during his earlier years of imprisonment and even attempted suicide. At this time of crisis, while in prison, a verse from the Bible touched him very deeply and he said the voice spoke to him, "Come to me all you who labor and are heavy laden. I will give you rest. Learn of me I am meek and humble of heart" (Mt. 11: 28). He was in tears as the voice spoke to him and cried a lot. But after that, a calmness came into his heart and he felt he experienced a *'freedom beyond the prison walls'*. He was assured of a love of God that was beyond everything, *"Even if the whole world denies you, I will not forget you my son"*. It gave him strength and he attended Bible classes, started reading Bible every day which has given him the strength to live in the prison for 30 years and to serve the prison with commitment. At present he is the pastor of the prison church and conducts services.

"C' has suggested to release prisoners after a specified time period and to make *general amnesty a regular yearly practice*. This can avoid psychiatric problems, suicidal attempts, jail escapes and absence from leave to a large extent. Further he emphasized the need to *create awareness among the general public about each section of IPC and the impacts of crime, particularly, the impact of life imprisonment*. He strongly recommended that awareness should be created among the youth and the general public about the adverse effects of alcoholism and drug abuse and advocate to stop such unhealthy habits. 'C' uses a part of the wages he receives from the prison for helping those who are unable to go on parole or leave due to economic problems and also to buy some snacks and fruits for those who have no visitors and money in the prison.

Case Study 4

'D' is a lifer who classifies himself belonging to an upper middle class family. He studied up to B.Sc. and after imprisonment completed BBA, BCA, English Literature, B. com, M. A. in English and MBA. He has spent 19 years in the prison during which he availed parole for 33 times. He was earning Rs. 25,000/- per month before imprisonment and now earns a pension of Rs. 18,000/- which is claimed by his wife. He has two sons and a daughter all of whom are settled well. He knows 16 languages and gets 4 newspapers with his Prisoners' Cash Property. One of the most painful experiences he had in the prison was during his mother's illness. She was suffering from cancer during which he could not go. Finally, he could go only after two months of his mother's death.

A wonderful spirituality of "D' is his altruism. He stated that his family was always very helpful to others in need. And now the main leisure time activity that he engages in is 'social service in the prison'. He is called the *'Father Theresa'* (like Mother Theresa) of the prison. He supports, helps people who have no other help. Besides his regular work of cleaning the school room and serving the food to the blocks, he visits the elderly and sick in the prison. He said that there are some elderly and the sick who are unable for self management. He cleans their cots, gives them bath, food and medicine. Without even a face mask, he gives them a hot water bath, cleans people who have bed sores. He feels the joy of reaching out and has taken it as his mission. The interview with "D' was an eye opener for the researcher with regard to the care of the elderly and the sick in prisons.

Case Study 5

'E' was born in a very poor family. His parents worked as daily wage earners (Coolie). His father was an alcohol dependent and resorted to domestic violence once he was drunk. His grandmother was very loving and used to buy and give him some special food whenever she gets some money. The conflicting and poor family situation forced the parents to send the children to a charitable hostel. His brothers and sister continued their studies while "E' was not at all interested in studies. He ran away from the hostel, got into unhealthy friendships, got interested in movies and got involved in unhealthy friendships. He was taken to a government children's home, which according to him had facilities for learning, counseling and vocational training, yet did not result in reformation. Recently he was arrested for theft.

'E' does not believe in any religion. All, whether Hindus, Muslims, Christians, are his friends and all are human beings than their religious identity. 'E' has a message to the youth, "Do not become like me...Even when I was a law breaker in the eyes of the world, deep down a fear and insecurity always haunted me...

Life is God's gift. It is a short life. Today we are here. Tomorrow we are gone. Happiness and sorrows are part of life. Go according to the situation without giving trouble and pain to any one". These words open up the hidden treasures within the prison inmates, the interior goodness.

Case Study 6

'F' is a graduate, a singer and musician. His brother, a graduate, is also in prison. 'F' is unmarried and has a girl friend, fiancée. She is also a singer. On the day of the incident, his fiancée had come with her friend and they were together as a group. After leaving, he had called her friend to say something. But that very night she was raped on her way back and she committed suicide. The police arrested 'F' and his brother based on the last call on her mobile and they are sentenced to an imprisonment for 10 years. 'F' also spoke about the need for good parenting so that children will be prevented from unhealthy friendships and habits.

In the prison he is studying in 8th standard, though he has completed graduation because it keeps him engaged. He is also a music teacher. His mother comes to visit them every week. His fiancée too visits him. He feels his life is getting wasted away in the prison and regrets about the circumstances that led to his situation at present as well as that of his brother.

'F' realizes the importance of parenting skills and counseling in life as he faces this strenuous phase of his life. He states, "Live a good life while in the society. *If you want to be free and happy, avoid drinks and drugs; if not, they will imprison you.* Real happiness is in living well. Please create awareness among the youth about the impact of impulsive acts".

The case studies reveal the influence of family, friendship, sudden emotional and impulsive acts without a second thought and substance abuse in causing crime. It has unearthed the well-being of the inmates from the psychological and spiritual point of view. The respondents belong to different economic categories such as Below Poverty Line, lower middle class and upper middle class. They also have gained education at different level, ranging from primary level of education to professional education. The poor level of psychological well-being and the average to high level of spiritual well-being is also evident from the case studies.

SECTION B: THEMATIC ANALYSIS

An attempt is made below to analyze the data corpus of case studies using 'R'-3.31 and Thematic Analysis.

Figure 1. Word Cloud - Profile of the Respondents

The word cloud of the profile of the respondents considering the top 25 per cent term frequencies as per figure 1 reveals the high intensity of insecurity and fear that prevailed in the lives of prison inmates before imprisonment. It also portrays the higher influence of alcoholism in their lives and families, influence of friendships and the moderate influence of movies in their lives. The concern about family and children, particularly daughters, existence of child labor, conflicts, strained marital relationships such as divorce are also evident from the word cloud. From the economic perspective, middle class families are outstanding and occupation-wise coolie work, business and guitarist are seen. The profile also includes women and the elderly as well as middle- aged and young persons. The most prominent type of sentence awarded among the respondents is life imprisonment and the highest term frequency for type of crime is murder followed by rape, theft and drugs. Prison inmates arguing their own case is also portrayed in figure 1.

Figure 2. Word Cloud: Spirituality and Well-Being of the Respondents

The word cloud of the profile of the respondents considering the top 30 per cent term frequencies as per figure 2 reveals a low level of well-being among the respondents with a few respondents having moderate level of well-being. With regard to spirituality, a higher level of divine-connectedness followed by self-connectedness, other-connectedness and nature-connectedness is also observed, reinforcing the quantitative analysis. Terms representing *divine connectedness* were God within, compassionate God, Bible, voice, pastor, classes, average faith and no religion. Terms representing *self connectedness* are God within, calmness, penance for my sins, focus on work, careful and indifferent. During the quantitative data collection, the researcher also came across prison inmates who have had *mystical spirituality*. One of them said, "Even as I work on the hand loom, I feel the Lord is there and He helps me at the loom". Terms expressing *other-connectedness* are Father Theresa of the Prison, helpfulness and altruism. Nature connectedness stands by itself.

Figure 3. Term Frequency Graph - Life in Prison

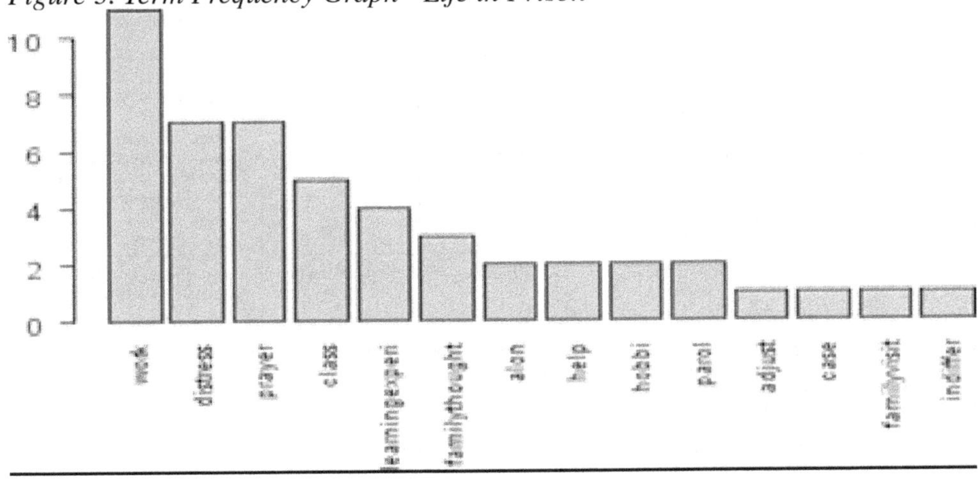

The top 10 per cent of term frequencies which describe prison life as per the 6 respondents are portrayed in figure 6. The most frequently used term used to describe *activities in prison* is *'work'* indicating how a major part of prison life is focused on work. The second most frequent term is '*prayer*' followed by '*attending classes and engaging in studies'* and '*being alone thinking about family or just remaining in solitude'*. The other activities of the respondents in the prison as stated by them are helping one another, engaging in some hobbies such as music or reading, working for parole and own case, going on parole and meeting visitors from the family.

The most frequent emotional term used is *'distress'*, followed by *'indifference'* reinforcing the poor psychological well-being of the respondents as revealed by the quantitative study. Another term of higher frequency indicating prison life was '*learning experience*'. The findings bring to light the importance of '*work and prayer'* in prison life which is also the motto of monastic life and ashrams in many religious groups.

Table 1. Positive Prison experiences – Thematic Analysis

Sl. No.	Significant verbalizations of respondents	Themes	Theme clusters
1. 2. 3. 4.	"The authorities in the prison at present are like own parents. They guide and counsel the prisoners to choose a better path in life and support families of prisoners". "Superintendent is great. Very helpful. Knowing our minds, she does things for us". "Superintendent, jailor and all the police, psychologists and doctors are good. We can share our sorrows and difficulties with them. They ask us, "How are you?" "I am having food from here. Let me give something back to the prison".	Favorable attitude of prison officials and their loving guidance/ support	Counseling and family support given by the prison officials Superintendent's empathetic plans Genuine and personal communication of the staff, Gratitude for satisfaction of basic needs
5. 6.	"It is good I came here. I learnt a lot from God and had a spiritual awakening". "I have also come to know and come closer to God"	Spiritual benefits	Spiritual awakening, Knowing God
7. 8. 9. 10.	"I am happy about what I got in the jail. It was my dream to go to school which I could not due to poverty at home. Here, even though it is late, I learnt to read and write and passed 7th standard. I also learned social skills and vocational skills". "I am happy after coming to jail. I have completed 12th standard" "Very good education. I could complete my post graduation here" "I wanted to study; could not. In jail, I studied. I have learnt many handicrafts to earn a living".	Access to Education	Formal and non- formal education Vocational training, Higher education.
11. 12.	"Prayer groups and Prison ministry India coming here are very good". "Social workers must meet prisoners at least once a month. --- of Prison Ministry India has helped my family and myself...No words can thank them"	Support of civil society	Prayer groups and NGOs
13. 14. 15. 16.	"Prison helped me to learn a lot of things. I have reduced my anger. This prison showed me how to live my life in the future". "It is a good experience... Learnt a lot – what is home, who is true – Friends, Drinks, Family. When I go out from the prison, life will be changed". "The prison helped me understand life and change my ways". "I want to leave alcohol as I learnt to live without alcohol in the prison".	Life transforma tion	Anger management and life skills Learning the truth in life, importance of family Leaving unhealthy habits such as alcoholism and substance abuse
17. 18. 19. 20.	"Compared to Central Prison, open Air Jail is very good. Veettil thottaththil velai paakkum maathiri. (It is like doing farm work at home)". "Kolandhaigallum mannaiviyum varumbodh pakkaththil irundhu peshi, kolanthaigalai thookki vayth magillchiyaana neiram selavida mudigiradh". (When wife and children come, we can sit close and carry the children which is a great happiness). "My mind is relaxed and happy here... Compared to Central Prison, this is much better" "Very good, Super compared to central prison"	Benefits of Open Air Prisons	Homely atmosphere – campus and work Privilege of having face to face and direct communication with the visitors in the prison without the wire mesh Positive affects – Happiness, relaxed compared to central prison

Table 1 reveals the positive experiences related by the prison inmates about prison life. According to the verbalizations, prison officials have a favorable attitude in terms of extending guidance and counseling, support to prisoners' family, satisfaction of basic needs, empathetic plans and genuine and personal communication. The inmates have also attained spiritual benefits such as knowing God and experience of spiritual awakening. Access to education was another major positive experience narrated by the respondents. Support of the civil society through voluntary organizations such as Prison Ministry India and Guild of Service as well as various prayer groups was appreciated by the respondents. Life transformation via learning the truth about life and the genuine support systems in life, anger management, life skills and leaving the habit of alcoholism and drug addiction were narrated by some of the respondents. The advantage of open air prisons was highlighted by almost all the inmates of open air prisons. The findings unfold the strengths of the Prisons Department of Tamil Nadu State as narrated by the respondents. These could be utilized in the strategic planning process of the Prisons Department of Tamil Nadu to identify the major strengths and build on them.

Table 2. Attitude of Repentance and Transformation – Thematic Analysis

Sl. No.	Significant verbalization of respondents	Themes	Theme clusters
1.	"For my fault I am doing a penance"	Repentance and acceptance of imprisonment as a penance for sins	Attitude of deserving punishment and accepting imprisonment as a penance
2.	"I have not hurt anyone so far. Under alcohol this happened. This imprisonment is like a penance for my sins. Let it be. I have no money to go to the higher court"		
3.	"I am getting the punishment for what I did."		
4.	"As a youngster full of energy, I did not know the impact of an impulsive act. Please create awareness among the youngsters and the public about the impacts of crime".		Create awareness on the impacts of crime and facilitate prevention

The verbatim analysis presented in table 2 reveals that there are some prison inmates who verbalized their acceptance of punishment as a penance for the harm done which reflects the genuineness and true repentance in their hearts and the willingness to compensate for the harm through punishment.

Feeling of Loneliness and Missing Family – Thematic Analysis

Prison leaves a person amidst unknown persons and separates them from the significant others in their lives. Table 2 presents the verbatim analysis of the respondents that centre around the vacuum left in their lives from the absence of loved ones which is expressed in terms of how they miss their families, the food at home, the love and expressions of love at home, the pain of returning from parole and all the more having no visitors at all in the prison for years. It also shows how in the absence of one parent, the single parents find it difficult to discipline their children and to earn a living and how this reality adds to the suffering of the prison inmates in their inability to reach out to the loved ones in times of special times such as pregnancy, birth of child, birthdays, death, wedding and so on.

Table 3. Feeling of Loneliness and Missing Family – Thematic Analysis

Sl. No.	Significant verbalizations of respondents	Themes	Theme clusters
1.	" I just came to talk to you when I heard someone has come to take a survey because since two years I have had no visitors, I wanted to just talk as though with my family".	Loneliness And missing family	Having no visitors while in prison,
2.	"Everything is available here; but no family, no love, no friends, no relations, no hugs. I miss my family"		Missing family ties and expressions of love
3.	"I don't want to go on parole... When I go, and come back, I feel more pained, missing my family. Better not to go at all, complete the term and go".		Missing family
4.	"Nimmathiyaana sorru veettil thaan... (We can enjoy the rice peacefully only at home.)		Missing family
5.	"I learnt the love and care of my family".		Missing family and knowing the value of family.
6.	"To meet the relations across the iron bars is terrible"	Concern and worry about family members	Pain of not being able to meet the dear and near ones close-by
7.	"Children are not doing well. Family needs a lot of support in guiding the sons and ensuring a job for them"		
8.	"Ours was a love marriage and she has no one now with me being here. She is all alone in the house and also pregnant. She came to see me in that condition ... wearing an old saree, without wearing chappals (footwears)..." (Silence)		Pain in the inability to reach out to them

The Frustrating Effects of the Stigmatizing 'Look' at a Prisoner While on Parole- Thematic Analysis

Table 3 presents the verbalizations of the respondents about the depreciating and stigmatizing look particularly from the neighbors and near ones on occasions of parole or leave or release that the prison inmates experience. Rehabilitation is possible when there is a trust in the local community that the prison inmates have undergone a reformation program and have altered their ways. Civil society should accept the prisoners, especially in the local community or native place with the dictum, 'Live and Let Live', without going back to the provocative, unpleasant and past incidents again. The table also shows the need for respecting prisoners' dignity as a human being from stakeholders such as the state government, higher officials, staff, convict officers, co- inmates, and visitors and the need to restrain from torture of any sort.

Table 4. The Frustrating Effects of the Stigmatizing 'Look' at a Prisoner While on Parole Thematic Analysis

Sl. No.	Significant verbalizations of respondents	Themes	Theme clusters
1. 2. 3.	"Do not look at a prisoner with a stigma. You do not know what they go through". "Do not look at a prisoner with a judgmental perspective. You do not know his or her reality" "When I go on parole or released, there is a look (paarvai) from the people around...as though some villain has come back.... So I don't feel like going on parole to face such looks, humiliations, avoidance and isolation'.	Respect for prison inmates, their dignity and rights	Respect from persons dealing with prison inmates – State Government, Higher officials, Staff, Convict officers, Co- inmates, Visitors Respect from the larger community - Families, Relatives, Friends, Neighborhood
4. 5.	"Those who are in prison are also human beings. Treat them with respect". "Do not torture prison inmates, but give them good advice".	Respect for prison inmates and their rights	Respect from persons dealing with prison inmates

Suggestions (Need for General Amnesty and Release Particularly for Lifers)

Table 4 reveals verbalizations of the 6 respondents with regard to release mainly reflecting the frustrations of life imprisonment as it closes down the possibility and hope for a renewed life as well as adds to the struggles of the poor families whose sole bread winner is the prisoner. According to the verbalizations of the respondents, it can be said that if reformation is the aim of imprisonment, then the prisons would stand a failure in terms of reformation if the reformed persons do not return to the society as contributing members of the society. This is true in every circumstance, even at schools and work places. If participation in a program results in a favorable outcome, people are enthusiastic to take part in them. It can be depicted as follows:

No release Opportunity for a well-lived life only within the prison walls till your death (No opportunity for a well-lived life outside prison) No hope No incentive for participation in reformation programs Serious and severe distress in life Poor well-being

Table 5. Suggestions (Need for General Amnesty and Release Particularly for Lifers): Thematic Analysis

Sl. No.	Significant verbalisations of respondents	Themes	Theme clusters
1.	"I want to go back and live with my family in a harmonious way along with my husband. I learnt a lot. If I can adjust so much here, why not at home?"	Need for Release	Desire for a well-lived life with family and outside the prison
2.	"Everybody wants to live a good life outside. No one, not even our enemies should come to a prison".		,, ,, , ,
3.	"Imprisonment is needed; but temporary. One will know the difference between 'inside' and 'outside' and live a transformed life".		Possibility for transformed Life only on Release
4.	"For 26 years, I am in this prison. There is no meaning in spending time here any more. Please release and supervise the conduct outside. Give consideration to my age"		Alternatives to imprisonment for the elderly – Probation
5.	"A lifer should be given information about the possibility of release and prepare them".		Preparedness for release
6.	"Release based on good conduct; Lots of frustrations build up when you have nothing to look forward to."		Hope of release as a preventive measure against depression and suicide
7.	"There is no use of giving biriyani; What we need is release. Better be outside even if we don't have legs and hands".		No facilities can substitute freedom
8.	"No one should be here..Jail is not a place to be"		Need for release for one's well-being
9.	"Release after a fixed period of time..."		Determinate sentence
10.	"En veettukk porulaadhaaram naan mattum. Aayul sirai oru chithravadham thaan". (I am the only bread winner of the famiy. Life imprisonment is a torture".		Struggles of the family without the bread winner

This thematic analysis is supported by the model prison rehabilitation program envisaged by one of the inmates for prison inmates sentenced to life imprisonment particularly for persons sentenced to life imprisonment as given below.

Table 6. Model Phase-Based Prison Rehabilitation Program Particularly for Prison Inmates Sentenced to Life Imprisonment

Sl. No.	Rehabilitation Package	Activities (Optional)	Activity Tests and grade	Term based Interview	Grade	Result and Rehabilitation Plan
1.	Term 1 Up to seven years	Counselling Psychotherapy Legal aid NGO support Prison labour Welfare measures Education Occupation Health Care Spiritual care	Conducted by instructors and external examiners every year based on participation in activities and good conduct And grades entered in the personal files of the prison inmates	Panel Interview by a team of government representatives District magistrate (Collector) and Probation officer	Activity grade + Interview grade	Pass/Fail Pass : Eligible for release Fail: Not eligible for release; Repeat the term
2.	Term 2 7-10 years	Mentorship Routine activities as in package 1	,, ,,	,, ,,	,, ,,	,, ,,
3.	Term 3 11-14 years	Mentorship Routine activities (Advanced package)	,, ,,	,, ,,	,, ,	,, ,,
4.	Term 4 14-20 years	Mentorship Routine activities (Advanced package)	,, ,,	,, ,,	,, ,,	,, ,,

The model portrayed in table 6 was visualized by some of the inmates. It is a Specific, Measurable, Attainable, Realistic or Results based and Time-bound (SMART) design which can be taken into consideration by the prisons department for a review and evaluation or an innovative pilot project. The finding highlights the need for determinate sentence with a specified term of imprisonment in the place of life imprisonment.

Table 7. Suggestions for categories of Prison Inmates – Thematic Analysis

Sl. No.	Significant verbalisation of respondents	Themes	Theme clusters
Women, Mothers with children and Children in prisons, First offenders Prisoners suffering from illnesses and the elderly			
1. 2. 3.	'Penkal naattin kannkal" (Women, the eyes of the land) "Women's pain as mothers should be considered. If they are not there, family is scattered". "There should be special hostels for daughters of women prisoners. When mother is in the jail and father passed away, they are alone at home."	Release of women prisoners	Need for women in the family " , , " Need for women in the family particularly for daughters' safety
4. 5.	"Having the child while doing work is difficult. Reduce the number of hours of work for mothers with their children". "Give the needed things for the child generously".	Special facilities for mothers with children	Welfare measures for working mothers with children, Provisions for children
6.	Give a chance for first offenders for them to reform in the community. If repeated, severe punishment can be given".	Probation	Probation services
Prisoners suffering from mental illness and the elderly			
7.	"Many are mentally ill. They must be sent	Special care	Treatment of persons
	to hospitals and treated".	of prison	with mental illness in
8.	"Prison rules should not be same for all.	inmates with	special hospitals,
	They need to be adjusted based on the	mental	adjustment of prison
	mental and physical conditions of the	illness,	rules based on
	prison inmates".	elderly and	prisoners' health
9.	"Send me to mental hospital "	sick	conditions, diet for the
10.	"Diet needed for TB patients and sick	prisoners	sick, elderly and TB
	prisoners and the elderly"		patients
11.	"Special facilities for the elderly in terms		
	of health care, diet and release"		
	Foreign Prisoners		
12. 13.	"Foreigners are there. They are like birds in the cage. Help them to go back to their countries and continue punishment" "Special assistance is needed for foreigners. They struggle with the changes in climate, food, finance, language, lack of knowledge of legal system in India"	Special assistance to foreign prisoners	Support to foreigners to continue punishment in their own country, legal support, language support and diet.

Table 7 reveals the thematic analysis of suggestions given by the respondents by categorizing the suggestions according to specific groups. The specific groups mentioned are women, particularly mothers with children, children in the prison, the mentally and physically ill, the elderly and the foreigners. Another group of persons not mentioned by the respondents, but observed by the researcher who need special support are the transgendered prison inmates and the young offenders.

The suggestion that women should not be confined to life imprisonment was substantiated by the expressions that women are needed in the family and particularly for the safety of young daughters. Another suggestion for women prisoners was specifically for inmates who have their small children with them who need to have concessions with regard to working hours and facilities for children. Health care facilities for persons with mental and physical illnesses, even admissions in outside hospitals should be arranged and diet for the elderly and sick inmates, particularly TB patients must be ensured. It was also expressed that foreign prisoners need special assistance in legal support, language support and diet.

Table 8. Legal Justice – Thematic Analysis

Sl. No.	Significant verbalizations of respondents	Themes	Theme clusters
1.	"Justice delayed is justice denied and so efforts must be made for the legal procedures to proceed faster, to provide health care at the right time without delay as per the advice of the doctor". "Qualified and well-experienced lawyers must be made available for legal aid services".	Justice on time	Faster legal procedures, faster response to health care needs
2.	"Justice System is based on money and influence. There was no order for a house search and office search".		Qualified lawyers at legal aid
3.	"Aayiram kutravaalligall viduthalai aannaalum, oru niraparadhi dhandikkappada koodadhu" (Even if one thousand convicts are released, one innocent person should not be convicted"		Just procedures of investigation as per laws and rules
4.			Ensure the innocent are not punished.

Table 8 reveals the need for just investigation process as per laws and rules, just legal procedures and access to qualified lawyers via legal aid services. This will ensure that the innocent are not punished.

Table 9. Messages of the respondents – Thematic Analysis

Sl. No.	Significant verbalisation of respondents	Theme clusters
1.	Orutharkk oruthan purinthu kondu vaalnthal, vaalgai emmathu nimmathi. Athu puriyaamal vaalnthaal, athu vedhanai" (When each one understands another, life is peaceful; if not, life is a suffering)	Empathetic life
2.	"Do not brood over the past. What is gone is gone. Everything will pass by. Change is the only thing that is constant. So live in the present".	Live in the present – Here and Now.
3.	"Life is only a small circle. So the inmates should spend time in a useful way showing love, sympathy and care".	Altruism
4.	"Our life is not in our hands. Trust in the Lord. He will guard your ways".	Trust in God,
5.	"My savings are my hands and my tongue. I want to keep them clean".	Conscientiousness,
6.	"The one who is beaten wins, not the one who beats". "Everything is within the control of a person. Think before you act".	Victory of non-violence Self control
7.	"Vidiyal embadhu vidiymbodhalli; Naam vizhiykkumbodh. Adhe pol, vazhgai embadhu amaivadhallai; Naam amaiththu kollavadhu" (Dawn is not when the sun rises; but when our minds awaken. Likewise, life is not what happens; but what we make it to happen.)	Pro-active attitude
8.	"Listen to parents; if not, come to jails". "Discipline yourself; gain respect".	Obedience Discipline
9.	"Be with good friends".	Friendship
10.	"There is nothing in life. Live well. Nobody brings to life anything nor takes anything when we die. So remain peaceful".	Detachment and holy indifference
11.	"Be true wherever you are".	Truth

Table 9 reveals that the messages given by the respondents highlight values such as living in the present – here and now or mindfulness, altruism, trust in god, conscientiousness, victory of non-violence, need for self control, pro-active attitude, obedience to parents, discipline, good friendship, detachment and holy indifference and truth. The finding reinforces the existence of the goodness and noble values within prison inmates, their desire for living a renewed life and for prevention of others from getting into crime or prison.

Other Suggestions for Improved Prison Facilities

Some of the other suggestions for improved prison facilities were expressed as given below:

Education related Suggestions: "Nilayaana Kalvi. Murraiyanna Tholir payirchi .Sariyaana neraththil Vidudhalai" (Stable education, Formal and systematic vocational training, Release at the right time)". "Teach Hindi in prisons". "Let prisons be a place of reformation – Ulle ponaal thirinthu varuavaa… (One who goes inside should come back transformed)".

Suggestions for improved prison facilities: "Give phone facility once in five days". "The wages and prisoner's welfare fund must be given to the families". "Improve facilities such as food and health care".

Suggestions for Research and Action: "Many researchers should come and let the outside world know about the needs of prisoners". "Many people come and take opinion, but no effect".

Some Unique Individualized Suggestions

Some distinctive suggestions of the respondents as given below are worth mentioning. "Improving prison conditions? My opinion is that prison itself should not be there and then there is no need to improve prison conditions for more people to live in". "POCSO Act should not be misused for revenge". "Sentence for 'death by negligence' for a bus driver for two years is too much. Imprisonment for 15 days or one month could be acceptable. Parts of the salary can be given to the victim's family for two years".

The major highlights of the qualitative data analysis is complementary to the findings of quantitative data analysis as both the analyses highlight a low and poor well- being among the prison inmates, a comparatively more positive experience among the inmates of open air prisons, the need for special focus on facilities for women prisoners, a planned reformation program with fixed term of sentence rather than life imprisonment and a high level of divine connectedness or religious well-being.

Qualitative data has brought about some of the verbalizations of the feelings and in- depth emotions of the inmates, the messages from their lives and suggestions for improving the reformation programs in a more elaborate manner than the quantitative data such as the model phase-based rehabilitation program particularly for prison inmates sentenced to life imprisonment.

CONCLUSION

The conclusion of the study highlights the 6 case studies. The study emphasizes the importance of digital technology in correctional settings to enhance education, mental health and well-being, and social connection among incarcerated populations. Digital technology can improve the effective functioning of prison administration, and prison inmates can benefit from advanced technology in terms of protection and prevention of problems. The use of digital technology can improve inmates' skills as well as the prison environment. Digital technology can shift the prison experience from being focused solely on punishment to increasing inmates' rehabilitation, personal improvement, and reintegration into society. Digital technology decreases recidivism and supports successful reentry into society. Digital technology plays a vital role in improving the quality of life for prison inmates and supporting rehabilitation services for incarcerated individuals.

Policy Implications

The impact of digital technology aids in improving the incarcerated population in several ways, such as through digital education support programs that can enhance education and vocational training initiatives. The impact of digital technology aids in improving the lives of the incarcerated population in several ways, such as through digital education support programs that can enhance both educational and vocational training initiatives. Telehealth services improve prisoners' access to mental health support and medical care. This can be more useful for inmates to decrease the strain on in-prison health services and promote a healthy life in the prison environment. Increasing virtual visit technology can strengthen family relationships, reduce emotional distress, and aid in the reintegration of prison inmates, especially those who are housed far from their families. Digital technology can improve and strengthen monitoring systems, such as scanners, detectors, and automated surveillance, to ensure safety and security for both staff and inmates. Rehabilitation programs can address the needs of inmates, including those serving life sentences. The policy can improve correctional administration by enhancing digital technology to create a safer and more secure environment, rehabilitate prison inmates, and facilitate their successful reintegration into society, thereby decreasing the overall crime rate.

Limitation of the Study

The limitation of the study conducted in prison is that it mainly emphasizes case studies and qualitative methods. The study adopts a small sample size, which may limit its ability to capture inmates' experiences, including their past experiences and current situations. It can be useful for prison administration at the regional and national levels to pay attention to increasing policy measures to strengthen the prison system. The study specifically uses thematic analysis to identify the degree of subjectivity involved. The study can focus on the digital aspects of prisoners and conduct interviews in correctional settings. The study addresses the technological aspects and their impact on the incarcerated population. Ethical considerations include ensuring that all 6 inmates' concerns are addressed confidentially, with their names changed, and obtaining permission from the ADGP in Tamil Nadu. The study is unable to conduct long-term follow-up, making it difficult to assess the sustained effects on the prison inmates. The impact of digital technology can reduce recidivism and enhance prison inmates' rehabilitation to facilitate their lives in society.

Outcome of the Study

The outcome of the study is to address inmates' life histories and provide a greater number of activities in prison settings, such as education, health and well-being, family relationship strengthening, life skills training, and vocational training. This aims to help inmates survive and integrate after release, thereby reducing recidivism. Technology can enhance prison life and provide better services for both inmates and staff.

Future Implication for Further Research Study

The future implications for further research should focus on long-term plans for digital technology to prevent recidivism, specifically targeting different incarcerated populations such as juveniles, women, elderly inmates, and those affected by health problems like cancer, TB, and HIV. Encouraging continued mixed-method research can address both the qualitative and quantitative effects of digital technology, making it more protective for correctional settings. It can focus on qualitative case studies to provide an in-depth understanding of prisoners' past lives and further strengthen digital technology for incarcerated individuals. Technology can improve prison inmates' rehabilitation services and reduce recidivism in correctional administration.

REFERENCES

Auty, K. M., Cope, A., & Liebling, A. (2017). A systematic review and meta-analysis of yoga and mindfulness meditation in prison: Effects on psychological well-being and behavioural functioning. *International Journal of Offender Therapy and Comparative Criminology, 61*(6), 689–710. DOI: 10.1177/0306624X15602514 PMID: 26320031

Barrick, K., Lattimore, P. K., & Visher, C. A. (2014). Reentering women: The impact of social ties on long-term recidivism. *The Prison Journal, 94*(3), 279–304. DOI: 10.1177/0032885514537596

Braun, V., & Clarke, V. (2006). Using thematic analysis in psychology. *Qualitative Research in Psychology, 3*(2), 77–101. https://www.tandfonline.com/doi/abs/10.1191/1478088706QP063OA. DOI: 10.1191/1478088706qp063oa

Byrne, J. M., & Pattavina, A. (2012). Technological innovation and offender reentry. In *Technocrime: Policing and surveillance* (pp. 110–132). Routledge., https://www.taylorfrancis.com/chapters/edit/10.4324/9780203105245-8/technological-innovation-offender-reentry-james-byrne-april-pattavina

Condon, L., Hek, G., Harris, F., Powell, J., Kemple, T., & Price, S. (2007). Users' views of prison health services: A qualitative study. *Journal of Advanced Nursing, 58*(3), 216–226. DOI: 10.1111/j.1365-2648.2007.04221.x PMID: 17474910

Dewey, S., Codallos, K., Barry, R., Drenkhahn, K., Glover, M., Muthig, A., Roberts, S. L., & Abbott, B. (2020). Higher education in prison. *Journal of Correctional Education (1974-), 71*(1), 57-89. https://www.jstor.org/stable/26915042

Farabee, D., Schulte, M., Gonzales, R., & Grella, C. E. (2016). Technological aids for improving longitudinal research on substance use disorders. *BMC Health Services Research, 16*(1), 1–8. DOI: 10.1186/s12913-016-1630-0 PMID: 27509830

Farley, H., & Pike, A. (2016). Engaging prisoners in education: Reducing risk and recidivism. *Advancing Corrections: Journal of the International Corrections and Prisons Association, 1*, 65-73. https://oro.open.ac.uk/46511/

Hall, M., & Rossmanith, K. (2016). Imposed stories: Prisoner self-narratives in the criminal justice system in New South Wales, Australia. *International Journal for Crime, Justice and Social Democracy, 5*(1), 38-51. https://search.informit.org/doi/abs/10.3316/INFORMIT.241278363448884

Imandeka, E., Putra, P. O. H., Hidayanto, A. N., & Mahmud, M. (2024). Exploring the World of Smart Prisons: Barriers, Trends, and Sustainable Solutions. *Human Behavior and Emerging Technologies, 2024*(1), 6158154. DOI: 10.1155/2024/6158154

Järveläinen, E., & Rantanen, T. (2021). Incarcerated people's challenges for digital inclusion in Finnish prisons. *Nordic Journal of Criminology, 22*(2), 240–259. DOI: 10.1080/2578983X.2020.1819092

Jewkes, Y., & Reisdorf, B. C. (2016). A brave new world: The problems and opportunities presented by new media technologies in prisons. *Criminology & Criminal Justice, 16*(5), 534–551. DOI: 10.1177/1748895816654953

Kazemian, L. (2019). *Positive growth and redemption in prison: Finding light behind bars and beyond.* Routledge., DOI: 10.4324/9780429458149

Kerr, A., & Willis, M. (2018). Prisoner use of information and communications technology. *Trends and Issues in Crime and Criminal Justice*, (560), 1–19. https://search.informit.org/doi/abs/10.3316/ielapa.983664576232696. DOI: 10.52922/ti107289

Knight, V. (2017). Digitizing the prison: The light and dark future. https://dora.dmu.ac.uk/server/api/core/bitstreams/2d76dffe-1c88-440b-950c-215e0d95e97e/content

Knight, V., & Van De Steene, S. (2020). The digital prison: Towards an ethics of technology. In *Prisons and Community Corrections* (pp. 57–71). Routledge., https://www.taylorfrancis.com/chapters/edit/10.4324/9781003010562-5/digital-prison-victoria-knight-steven-van-de-steene DOI: 10.4324/9781003010562-5

Leach, R., Carreiro, S., Shaffer, P. M., Gaba, A., & Smelson, D. (2022). Digital health interventions for mental health, substance use, and co-occurring disorders in the criminal justice population: A scoping review. *Frontiers in Psychiatry, 12*, 794785. DOI: 10.3389/fpsyt.2021.794785 PMID: 35126204

Mahlangu, G., & Zivanai, E. (2023). Offender eLearning: A systematic literature review on reentry, recidivism, and life after prison. *Cogent Social Sciences, 9*(2), 2246706. DOI: 10.1080/23311886.2023.2246706

McDougall, C., Pearson, D. A., Torgerson, D. J., & Garcia-Reyes, M. (2017). The effect of digital technology on prisoner behavior and reoffending: A natural stepped-wedge design. *Journal of Experimental Criminology, 13*(4), 455–482. DOI: 10.1007/s11292-017-9303-5

Ndindeng, A. N. (2024). Mental health and well-being in prisons and places of detention. *International Journal of Prison Health.* Advance online publication. DOI: 10.1108/IJOPH-07-2024-0035 PMID: 39465264

Picken, J. (2012). The coping strategies, adjustment and well being of male inmates in the prison environment. *Internet Journal of Criminology, 2012*, 1-29. https://d1wqtxts1xzle7.cloudfront.net/80111102/b93dd4_63ebd332965f40f9b28f85d9bc37e63f-libre.pdf?1643878436=&response-content-disposition=inline%3B+filename%3DThe_Coping_Strategies_Adjustment A

Ross, S., Wood, M., Baird, R., & Lundberg, K. (2023). Digital service delivery applications in corrections: A scoping review. *Australian Institute of Criminology. CRG, 8*, 20-21. https://www.aic.gov.au/sites/default/files/2023-09/crg_08_20_21digital_service_delivery_applications_in_corrections_v5_2.pdf

Shen, A. (2024). Mental Health and Yoga in Prisons. *Journal of Criminal Law, 00220183241265170*(4), 258–281. Advance online publication. DOI: 10.1177/00220183241265170

Smit, D. V. Z., & Appleton, C. (2019). *Life imprisonment: A global human rights analysis*. Harvard University Press. https://www.google.co.in/books/edition/Life_Imprisonment/aCd9DwAAQBAJ?hl=en&gbpv=1&dq=Those+who+are+serving+life+sentences+and+facing+legal+issues+may+benefit+from+amnesty+and+release+for+prisoners.+&pg=PP1&printsec=frontcover

Srinivasan, S., & Rajavel, N. (2025a). A Study of the Psychological Well-Being of Tamil Nadu Prison Inmates With Special Reference of AI. In *AI Technologies and Advancements for Psychological Well-Being and Healthcare* (pp. 219–254). IGI Global., DOI: 10.4018/979-8-3693-9158-7.ch009

Srinivasan, S., & Rajavel, N. (2025b). Artificial Intelligence Approach to Psychological Wellbeing Among the Ageing Population. In *AI Technologies and Advancements for Psychological Well-Being and Healthcare* (pp. 187–218). IGI Global., DOI: 10.4018/979-8-3693-9158-7.ch008

Wakefield, S., & Uggen, C. (2010). Incarceration and stratification. *Annual Review of Sociology, 36*(1), 387–406. DOI: 10.1146/annurev.soc.012809.102551

Western, B., Braga, A. A., Davis, J., & Sirois, C. (2015). Stress and hardship after prison. *American Journal of Sociology, 120*(5), 1512–1547. DOI: 10.1086/681301 PMID: 26421345

Wilson, D. B., Gallagher, C. A., & MacKenzie, D. L. (2000). A meta-analysis of corrections-based education, vocation, and work programs for adult offenders. *Journal of Research in Crime and Delinquency, 37*(4), 347–368. DOI: 10.1177/0022427800037004001

Wright, K. N. (1991). The violent and victimized in the male prison. *Journal of Offender Rehabilitation*, *16*(3-4), 1–26. DOI: 10.1300/J076v16n03_01

Zivanai, E., & Mahlangu, G. (2022). Digital prison rehabilitation and successful re-entry into a digital society: A systematic literature review on the new reality on prison rehabilitation. *Cogent Social Sciences*, *8*(1), 2116809. DOI: 10.1080/23311886.2022.2116809

Chapter 13
Leveraging AI to Combat Cryptocurrency Cybercrimes

Ramy El-Kady
https://orcid.org/0000-0003-2208-7576
Police Academy, Egypt

ABSTRACT

The chapter aims to illuminate the digital forensics of cryptocurrencies and the dark web by reviewing the role of the elements and tools involved in their formation, such as blockchain, computers, and mobile phones, and learning evidence. It will focus on its methods and review the extent to which artificial intelligence and machine language can be relied upon in forensics on the dark web. The chapter identified the need to address several areas of digital cryptocurrency forensics, in which gaps can be filled by developing advanced solutions for cryptocurrency forensics. Further investigation is required in digital forensics concerning significant cryptocurrencies like Monero, Ethereum, Verge, Dogecoin, and others. This is necessary because these currencies are becoming increasingly popular among both legitimate users and evil individuals. The survey highlighted another research gap: the limited amount of substantial research on host-based cryptocurrency forensics, particularly in mobile-based cryptocurrency forensics.

INTRODUCTION

In the face of the escalating use of modern technology and the exploitation of the Internet by criminal groups and terrorist organizations to achieve their criminal purposes, and given the rising rates of cybercrimes such as identity theft, online

DOI: 10.4018/979-8-3693-8871-6.ch013

fraud, and data breaches, there is a significant need to highlight the forensic science of digital evidence. It is one of the most critical tools of criminal justice and law enforcement agencies in the battle against cybercrime, and it is pivotal in reducing its prevalence. Your work in digital evidence is crucial in this fight (El-Kady, 2023).

In this context, Digital forensics could be defined as "a specialized field within forensic science that deals explicitly with identifying, acquiring, processing, analyzing, and reporting electronically stored data." Electronic evidence is not just a part but often the crux of nearly all illegal acts, and the assistance of digital forensics is vital for law enforcement investigations (El-Kady, 2023).

As digital evidence continues to evolve in its dynamic and delicate nature, the importance of digital forensics is rising. This evidence necessitates law enforcement agencies to implement stringent safety, health, and reliability measures to ensure its admissibility and authenticity in criminal courts (El-Kady, 2024). The ever-changing landscape of digital evidence underscores the urgency for law enforcement professionals to remain abreast of technological advancements, a crucial aspect of their ongoing battle against cybercrime. Your continuous learning and adaptation to these advancements and your expertise in digital forensics are critical to our success.

Successive technological developments have contributed to the emergence of cryptocurrencies, which have spread globally in many legal fields. At the same time, these new currencies have not been spared from being used by criminal groups and terrorist organizations to commit many criminal activities, especially in the vicinity of the dark web, exploiting the characteristics of these currencies and this dark network that contributes to the anonymity of the personalities of the perpetrators and make it difficult for law enforcement agencies to pursue them.

With these successive developments, law enforcement authorities face numerous challenges in confronting criminal activities committed via the Internet. The most significant is the problem of proving these crimes through digital evidence. This study underscores the urgency and importance of addressing the role of digital forensics in this context.

The study aims to illuminate the digital forensics of cryptocurrencies and the dark web by reviewing the role of the elements and tools involved in their formation, such as blockchain, computers, and mobile phones, and learning evidence. It will focus on its methods and review the extent to which artificial intelligence and machine language can be relied upon in forensics on the dark web (El-Kady, 2024).

LITERATURE REVIEW

Several studies indicate that advanced artificial intelligence (AI) and machine learning methods are essential in cryptocurrency forensics. These techniques effectively identify fraudulent transactions with high accuracy and improve the efficiency and precision of cyber forensic investigations. The emergence of cryptocurrencies has resulted in notable progress in financial technology, although it has also resulted in a surge in fraudulent activity. Cryptocurrency forensics is being improved through advanced AI and machine learning methods. The goal is to identify and prevent fraudulent transactions and cyber risks successfully.

Advanced AI and machine learning algorithms are essential in Bitcoin forensics as they successfully identify fraudulent transactions and improve cyber forensic investigations. These technologies enhance the precision of fraud detection and the efficiency of forensic investigation, resulting in faster responses to cyber-attacks and less risk exposure for enterprises. Machine learning techniques, like Logistic Regression, Random Forest Classifier, and XGB Classifier, have demonstrated a remarkable ability to identify fraudulent cryptocurrency transactions accurately. Out of these options, the XGB Classifier demonstrates superior accuracy compared to the others (Kumar & Sharma, 2023).

Artificial intelligence and machine learning are highly effective technologies for enhancing cyber forensic investigations. They boost the effectiveness and accuracy of identifying and categorizing threats, resulting in faster analytical processes and improved detection capacities (Fakiha, 2023). Additional research indicates that artificial intelligence (AI) and machine learning can enhance the efficiency of cyber forensic investigations by automating various processes, boosting the detection and response to threats, and enhancing the analysis and recognition of patterns in data.

Incorporating Artificial Intelligence (AI) and Machine Learning (ML) into cyber forensic investigations has demonstrated considerable potential in improving the effectiveness and precision of these procedures. This synthesis examines how AI and ML technologies enhance cyber forensic investigations by automating processes, boosting threat detection, and offering strong analytical skills.

Artificial intelligence (AI) and machine learning (ML) are revolutionizing cyber forensic investigations by automating the identification and analysis of threats, minimizing the need for human intervention, and improving the precision of detecting malware and anomalies. These technologies provide more effective and proactive reactions to cyber threats. However, continuous study and improvement are required to tackle problems and achieve their promise.

Some studies have shown that Artificial intelligence (AI) and machine learning (ML) greatly enhance the effectiveness and accuracy of identifying and categorizing risks in cyber forensic investigations, allowing quicker responses to cyber threats (Fakiha, 2023; Benkerroum & Chougdali, 2023; Dunsin et al., 2023).

Additional research indicates that using machine learning algorithms to automate manual forensic activities decreases the time and effort needed for investigations, resulting in a more streamlined and effective process (Benkerroum & Chougdali, 2023; G. S et al., 2023).

Additional research has confirmed that machine learning techniques, such as Random Forest and Gradient Boosted Tree, have exhibited a notable level of precision in identifying malware. Consequently, this has enhanced the dependability of forensic investigations (Benkerroum & Chougdali, 2023; Patil et al., 2021). Additional research has demonstrated that machine learning approaches empower cyber security systems to acquire knowledge from patterns and adjust to emerging threats, facilitating proactive prevention and immediate response to hostile activity (Gupta et al., 2021; Swaminathan et al., 2022; Suryawanshi et al., 2023).

A recent study found that advanced machine learning models, such as Siamese Neural Networks, can significantly improve anomaly detection accuracy in industrial cyber-physical systems. This improvement reduces false alarm rates and enhances security overall (Zhou et al., 2021). Other research indicates that although there are advantages, the use of artificial intelligence (AI) and machine learning (ML) in cyber forensics encounters obstacles such as the requirement for top-notch training data, possible algorithmic biases, and the ever-changing characteristics of cyber threats (Dunsin et al., 2023; G. S et al., 2023).

METHODOLOGY

The descriptive-analytical method is the most appropriate research method for studying social and legal phenomena. It is defined as: "studying the phenomenon as it exists in reality, describing it closely and expressing it qualitatively or quantitatively to reach conclusions that contribute to understanding and developing this reality" (Obeidat et al., 1996). Also, the research subject and its transnational character impose on the researcher the use of a comparative approach by referring to some facts and incidents related to cryptocurrencies and dark web forensics, focusing on its methods.

The descriptive-analytical method is the most suitable research method for studying dark web crimes, as it involves closely describing and expressing the phenomenon, using a comparative approach to compare facts and incidents. The research tools that the researcher will use as scientific sources in preparing this research are the

Arab and foreign legal literature related to the subject of research in the field of criminal law, as well as the relevant specialized literature, whether they are books, papers, etc., or university dissertations. Alternatively, a master's degree or articles are published in scientific journals on the topic, in addition to news published in various media outlets and the Internet.

RESULTS

The development of cryptocurrency forensics could be summarised as Bitcoin, introduced by Nakamoto in 2008 (Nakamoto, 2008), being the most extensively studied cryptocurrency on all forensic platforms. However, research on other cryptocurrencies, such as Ether, Monero, Verge, and so on, is lacking. An initial study was conducted on Blockchain-based cryptocurrency forensics in 2011. According to the FBI in 2012, this research emerged as criminal actors began showing interest in cryptocurrencies around two years after Bitcoin's introduction in 2008 (Reid & Harrigan, 2013). The initial investigation into Bitcoin forensics was conducted in 2014, with separate studies focusing on mobile-based (Montanez, 2014) and computer-based approaches. These studies, presented as master's theses, demonstrate academic curiosity in this field (Doran, 2014).

Research in digital cryptocurrency forensics saw a hiatus of approximately 3-4 years before resuming around 2017 to 2018. This resurgence coincided with cryptocurrency's growing popularity among the general public and criminal individuals. Research on cryptocurrencies conducted on mobile devices is scarce, with a significant focus on the security and privacy of cryptocurrency wallet applications. This suggests a need for more excellent studies on forensic analysis of mobile platforms to uncover digital evidence (Dudani et al., 2023).

Regarding computer-based cryptocurrency study, Windows-based research is the most prominent, followed by Linux and Mac OS. Research might be undertaken to analyze Bitcoin artifacts on Mac OS platforms. Windows 7 is the most extensively studied computer platform for Bitcoin artifacts, so this area lacks research on Windows 10 and 11 computers.

Most studies on cryptocurrency forensics focus on analyzing the publicly accessible blockchain. This involves using clustering heuristics and machine learning-based analysis to gain valuable information. The goal is to either identify anonymous entities or provide guidance for investigations. Some scholars developed an Elliptic Dataset as a significant resource for researching the application of machine learning and graph-based methods in Bitcoin forensics based on Blockchain technology (Weber et al., 2019).

DISCUSSIONS

Introducing the Dark Web

The dark web is a hidden part of the Internet, divided into three main sections: the Surface Network, which contains only 0.03% of the information accessible through traditional search engines; the Deep Network, which includes academic databases, government records, corporate and commercial bank databases, email content, and TV broadcast services; and the Dark Web, which is not commonly accessed and is a breeding ground for illegal criminal activities, as not everything on the Internet can be accessed by users.

What is known as Black Networks or the Dark Web has appeared, and much of its content is confidential. They provide privacy to their users away from censorship (El-Kady, 2021), and services are provided. Information is exchanged confidentially between its members, and no user outside the network can see its content or search for it in the traditional ways.

Unlike the clear web, also called the "Surface Web," which refers to information that is publicly available and indexed by conventional search engines, the dark web consists of encrypted hidden networks that allow the owner and users of the site to keep their identity anonymous while being relatively difficult to track (Guccione, 2019), which makes it the preferred network for all criminals, as it provides a safe environment for their illegal activities (El-Kady, 2021).

In summary, the dark web can be defined as a part of the Internet that allows the issuance of websites and the dissemination of information without revealing the identity or location of the publisher. It also requires software, settings, and special authorization to access it. It is a part of the web not indexed by search engines and can be accessed on the dark web through certain services such as Tor (Biddle et al., 2003).

It is a compilation of interconnected networks and advanced technologies for exchanging and disseminating digital content. The dark web is not an independent network but a means of accessing unindexed resources on the existing physical network using extra technologies (Dudani et al., 2023).

According to some estimates, the global internet has a daily user base of 5.07 billion individuals. Although the darknet's daily user base represents a mere 0.04% of the total daily Internet users, it nonetheless encompasses approximately 2.5 million users every day (Gannon et al., 2023).

The Dark Web and TOR Browser

The Internet was typically born in the second half of the 1990s, but it was not until 2004 that it became a core part of daily routine activities. By 2018, 90% of households in North America and European countries used the Internet (Martin, 2021). Technological progress aided the Internet's global rise, providing households with the necessary hardware and software for data transfer and storage.

The Internet transformed from a publishing medium to a participatory medium, allowing users to communicate, interact, and create user-generated content in virtual communities. Some of these communities have become household names, serving billions of users worldwide. However, hundreds of thousands of smaller virtual communities exist outside the mainstream, focusing on personal characteristics, experiences, religious beliefs, political opinions, and other shared interests (Gannon et al., 2023).

The global use of the Internet has led to a need for anonymous online interactions, particularly for military personnel, journalists, and political and religious minorities living under autocratic regimes. In the 1990s, the US Navy developed prototypes for The Onion Router (TOR) to provide this anonymity.

TOR became publicly available in 2002, providing thousands of servers to obscure user identities. It encrypts online traffic by rerouting the IP address through randomly chosen servers, making it nearly impossible to trace it back to its original address. TOR quickly gained popularity in 2008 with its browser version, making it easily accessible to the broader public (El-Kady, 2021).

The TOR browser functions as an Internet browser, enabling users to access the Web while ensuring anonymity. It also accommodates darknet or onion sites, websites, forums, and other online archives not indexed by publicly recognized search engines. These darknet sites, known as "hidden services" or HSes, are home to a broad array of criminal marketplaces, such as Silk Road and Alphabay, which mirror the workings of legal marketplaces on the Clearnet (Gannon et al., 2023).

Introduction to Cryptocurrency

Cryptocurrencies are defined as a virtual digital currency that has no tangible physical entity or physical existence, is produced by computer programs, and is not subject to control or control by a central bank or any official international administration, nor does it carry a serial number, it is used via the Internet In buying and selling transactions or converting them into other currencies, and receiving voluntary acceptance from those dealing in them (Al-Bahouth, 2017). After Bitcoin's inception, more cryptocurrencies have emerged. The most prominent cryptocurrencies are Ripple, which appeared in 2012; Litecoin and Monroe, which appeared in 2014;

the Chinese currency NEO, which the Chinese government launched in the same year to support the Chinese economy; Ethereum, which appeared in 2015; Bitcoin Volt, which appeared in 2019; and Facebook's Libra currency (Diem), which is expected to be launched soon (Nour, 2022).

The Emergence of Cryptocurrency

The emergence of cryptocurrencies as a result of the continuous technological development in our world is due to the tendency of most institutions, authorities, and countries to digitize their various systems and transform them into a digital economy and a system of financial inclusion, where the need to develop new tools that bear the digital character for dealing within this world has emerged, and cryptocurrencies and blockchain have been one of the tools of financial dealing on the Internet, which includes millions of financial transactions. The names of these currencies have multiplied since they began under encrypted digital currencies, "Cryptocurrencies."

Scholars see that the emergence of Cryptocurrency started in 2009; the virtual currency landscape underwent a significant transformation with the introduction of Bitcoin by Satoshi Nakamoto, the pseudonymous creator (Nakamoto, 2008). Bitcoin is built upon blockchain decentralized record technology (Casino et al., 2019). Nakamoto asserts that implementing a decentralized electronic cash system will prevent the necessity for transactions to pass through financial institutions, resolving the inherent issue of double-spending, which is both illicit and erodes confidence in any currency, ultimately resulting in inflation. Following Nakamoto's findings, the network uses hashing to timestamp transactions and create an unalterable chain of hash-based proof-of-work, an immutable record.

This creates a ledger that undergoes peer review and is immune to alteration by a single user, rendering it more dependable than a centralized system where the sole verification point is the engaged agency. After the development of Bitcoin, several other cryptocurrencies, such as Litecoin, Dash, Ethereum, Monero, Dogecoin, and others, were introduced. These cryptocurrencies were built using various hashing algorithms and anonymization approaches (Dudani et al., 2023).

Anonymity as a Central Element of Cryptocurrencies

In March 2013, Dark Coin, now named Dash, was developed to address the problem of absolute anonymity in cryptocurrencies. It achieved this by implementing Dark Send, which prevents tracing transactions to their source or destination addresses. Some scholars state that when Dark Send is activated, it automatically divides a payment request into smaller amounts. These smaller amounts are then pooled with other divided transactions to create a pool of more significant transactions (Duffield & Hagan, 2014).

After this, a controller node is created for each pool. After completing this process, the input transactions are rearranged to provide nearly identical outputs, a process known as mixing. Blind signatures ensure that the outputs of a pool are exclusively accessible to the pool participants while preventing any disclosure to the controller node. After all users have confirmed the accuracy of their input and output amounts, transactions are digitally signed and then distributed to the network. The blockchain stores all transaction data but does not allow viewers to establish a direct link between a sender and a receiver.

Mixing services enhance anonymity and provide challenges for investigators attempting to decipher transactions. Cryptocurrencies themselves do not pose a threat, but the utilization of cryptocurrencies and methodologies that serve the interests of criminals are the factors that necessitate the field of cryptocurrency forensics, which will be explored in the next section (Dudani et al., 2023).

Cryptocurrencies as a Primary Payment Tool in the Dark Web

Some scholars point out that several signs indicate a close connection between cryptocurrencies and dark web markets; according to INTERPOL, it regularly receives a significant volume of cases relating to cryptocurrencies, perplexing the international law-enforcement community. The Onion Scan Report reveals that Darknet markets such as Silk Road, Alpha Bay, and Hansa generated around $3,000,000 from September 2015 to December 2016 (Tziakouris, 2018).

As per a joint source for the FBI (2012), a cybercriminal selling a ZeuS botnet Trojan was reported to exclusively take payments using Bitcoin, Liberty Reserve, or WebMoney. The source of this information was the Federal Bureau of Investigation (FBI) in 2012 (FBI, 2012). Another open-source report cited the utilization of Bitcoin on Silk Road (Montanez, 2014), which was likened to the Darknet equivalents of Amazon or eBay, facilitating the illicit trade of diverse items. Some scholars examine the involvement of the Dark Web and Cryptocurrencies in cybercrime, including a thorough analysis of the trustworthiness of cryptocurrencies. They also emphasize the importance of investor awareness (Taleby et al., 2021).

In contrast, others utilize Clear Net as a source of intelligence to analyze the transition to using Bitcoin and Monero for the illicit drug trade in Dark Net markets. According to their analysis, the news about Bitcoin traceability in 2015 had the opposite effect, promoting the use of Bitcoin for illegal drug trafficking on dark markets (Bahamazava & Nanda, 2022). However, the privacy update of Monero in 2017 led to a change in preference from Bitcoin to Monero for the same purpose (Dudani et al., 2023).

INTERPOL has identified another application of Bitcoin, which involves transferring funds to regions subject to financial monitoring or embargo (Tziakouris, 2018). This practice likely supports illicit activity in those locations. Bitcoin has the potential to serve as a significant means of financing for various groups, both lawful and unlawful, which presents a risk to the security of a nation. This evaluation was based on the FBI Intelligence Evaluation Report (FBI, 2012), which also mentioned that the internet hacktivist group LulzSec got more than $18,000 in Bitcoins from anonymous followers and supporters who donated.

INTERPOL is concerned about money laundering through Initial Coin Offering (ICOs) or cryptocurrency exchanges. This is evident from cases such as the Bitcoin exchange OKCoin, which laundered hundreds of thousands of US dollars, and the case of BitInstant, which laundered approximately $1,000,000 for Silk Road market customers (Tziakouris, 2018). Regarding money laundering using Bitcoins, the FBI encountered a case where virtual game currency was used to acquire in-game virtual products sold to other players in exchange for "clean money." According to a separate tip to the FBI, an individual engaged in money laundering activities outside the United States (FBI, 2012). This person utilized fraudulent accounts on the WebMoney platform to assist cybercriminals who generated profits through carding operations. In June 2010, unidentified individuals constructed 3000 online membership accounts utilizing 16000 bank accounts at a US banking institution. The purpose of these accounts was to deceive victims into providing payments for non-existent auction items (Dudani et al., 2023).

The FBI received numerous reports in 2012 regarding the use of Bitcoin in illegal transactions. However, as early as 2011, the theft of Bitcoins also became a concern. Researchers from a computer security firm discovered a malware called "Infostelar. Coinbit" specifically designed to steal bitcoins from compromised users' Bitcoin wallets and transfer them to a server in Poland. Subsequently, the FBI received numerous reports regarding the misappropriation of Bitcoins from unencrypted wallets, trading platforms, game sites, and similar sources (FBI, 2012).

In 2021, some scholars conducted a case study on the Coincheck hacking incident, which entailed the illicit acquisition of $530 million of cryptocurrencies. The study effectively demonstrates the process of laundering Bitcoin. The Binance Blockchain suffered a $570 million hack on October 7, 2022, due to flaws in cross-chain bridges. Chainalysis5 projects a total cryptocurrency loss of $2 billion in 2022, resulting from 13 cross-chain bridge assaults (Tsuchiya & Hiramoto, 2021).

Below are several further unauthorized applications of cryptocurrencies identified by INTERPOL: Cryptojacking, specifically through the use of Jenkins-Miner, has accumulated almost $3,000,000 worth of Monero, Crypto-stealing Trojans, like CryptoShuffler, pilfer funds by explicitly targeting the data stored in volatile memory or the clipboard, Non-standard Bitcoin transactions have the potential to include encoded data chunks that can be used to distribute illegal content, such as child exploitation material.

The main obstacle for law enforcement is the difficulty of removing such content because of the unchangeable nature of the blockchain; ICO exit scams include criminals deceiving victims by soliciting funds for non-existent coins and subsequently vanishing, so defrauding the victims (Tziakouris, 2018). The issue of law enforcement dealing with nation-state attacks financed through cryptocurrencies is another challenge (Dudani et al., 2023).

The issues mentioned above are not exclusive; advancements in cryptocurrencies are giving rise to increasingly intricate predicaments for law enforcement. Every cryptocurrency has its unique challenges that arise from the underlying technology. Litecoin, Monero, Dogecoin, and Dash have gained significant popularity as digital currencies. Dark coin or Dash achieves true anonymity using DarkSend (Duffield & Hagan, 2014), which utilizes mixing techniques and blind signatures. This ensures that transactions cannot be linked to specific users, as the public ledger contains no information about the individuals involved.

Owing to the advancements in cryptocurrency, criminals are endeavoring to outsmart the legal system, compelling law enforcement agencies to prioritize the field of Bitcoin forensics. Forensics plays a crucial role in discovering evidence from digital devices, blockchains, and other sources of evidence that may contain artifacts related to cryptocurrencies. Advancements in Bitcoin forensics will also deter forthcoming cryptocurrency-related offenses, diminishing criminal fascination with cryptocurrency (Dudani et al., 2023).

Cryptocurrencies Forensics

Cryptocurrency forensics, also known as Bitcoin forensics, is a field of study used to establish the connection between the flow of virtual currency and the transactions or actors responsible for initiating the flow. This is particularly relevant as most unlawful activities involve using Bitcoin as a form of payment. The intricate nature of Bitcoin forensics involves meticulously tracking and understanding the movement of funds, identifying the addresses involved in transactions, establishing intricate links between various cryptocurrency wallets, and unveiling complex patterns and linkages within the Blockchain (Joshi, 2023).

Some scholars have emphasized the necessity of cryptocurrency forensics (Dudani et al., 2023); due to the FBI's 2012 Intelligence Assessment Report, there is moderate confidence that Bitcoin will be a profitable payment method for cybercriminals. This conclusion is based on the observed fluctuations in the exchange rate of Bitcoin in 2011 and the limited information available regarding the acceptance of Bitcoin. Based on available data from criminal investigations concerning the usage of e-Gold and WebMoney, the FBI has identified a potential future risk of Bitcoin being used for money laundering. The paper also addresses the problem of attackers utilizing malware and hacking techniques to steal Bitcoins and the creation of Bitcoins through botnets (FBI, 2012).

Advancements in cryptocurrency forensics are underscored by real-world events, such as the FTX scandal, one of the most significant financial frauds since the Enron collapse. This case, involving cryptocurrencies, demonstrates the need for robust forensic techniques. Cryptocurrency forensics, a multidisciplinary field encompassing digital forensics and forensic accounting, is crucial in investigations involving various stakeholders (Dudani et al., 2023).

Cryptocurrency forensics is not just an investigative technique; it is a powerful tool that empowers law enforcement agencies and financial investigators to safeguard individuals from the perils of the digital world. It effectively identifies culprits and determines the whereabouts of assets, providing a robust sense of security. Tracing cryptocurrency is not just a standard practice; it is a vital tool in investigating and recovering individuals who have fallen victim to online fraud, theft, hacking, and extortion operations, offering them a shield of protection in the digital world.

Blockchain as a Means for Cryptocurrency Forensics

Scholars emphasize the nexus between the blockchain and the cryptocurrency; as described by Nakamoto, Bitcoin or cryptocurrency is an electronic coin that is a sequence of digital signatures that includes a hash of previous transactions and the recipient's public key (Nakamoto, 2008). This allows for the verification of the coin's ownership history. However, the recipient cannot determine whether the coin has been double-spent. A proposed solution to address this problem and uphold Bitcoin's decentralized nature involves the implementation of a timestamp server. This server would broadcast the hash of a block to the network for verification purposes (Dudani et al., 2023).

Blockchain, a decentralized database structured as a sequence of ordered blocks, is a critical component of cryptocurrency forensics. Cryptocurrency transactions are recorded in blocks on the blockchain, which serves as a transparent ledger and a significant repository of forensic evidence and other network-related artifacts. Its immutable nature and miners' role in maintaining a verifiable record of all transactions have significantly disrupted traditional banking and corporate systems. This technology enables decentralized currencies to operate with a level of trust comparable to that of a reputable financial institution (Casino et al., 2019).

Cryptocurrencies like Bitcoin and other virtual currencies do not offer perfect anonymity. Transactions are recorded on digital blockchain ledgers powered by innovative blockchain technology, which reveal users through their Bitcoin address without disclosing personal information. Law enforcement agencies, regulators, and financial investigators have developed techniques to penetrate this anonymity, using blockchain intelligence tools and investigative methods to uncover identities in cryptocurrency transactions.

Transferring cryptocurrencies involves an individual installing a digital wallet, acquiring a collection of coins through third-party trade or donation, and initiating a request to transfer a specific amount of cryptocurrency to another user. The transaction's information is gathered into a block, sent to the user network for verification, and then added to the blockchain. The recipient's wallet acquires the transferred coins after adding the new block to the blockchain. Coins, in a technical sense, lack physical existence and cannot be physically moved. They function as a type of digital currency that relies on the trust of its users.

According to the FBI's assessment in 2012, they found several deficiencies in intelligence regarding certain criminal activities. These included insufficient information on individuals or groups attempting to avoid complying with the United States Bank Secrecy Act (BSA) regulations, other criminal organizations, and Bitcoin services facilitating illegal activities. These gaps in intelligence present numerous obstacles for law enforcement agencies (FBI, 2012).

Digital forensics is essential to address these inquiries. By analyzing computers, hard drives, mobile devices, and other relevant sources, crucial details can be uncovered about the methods employed in illicit activities, which Bitcoin finances. Forensic accounting professionals require specific information, including wallet IDs, public-private vital combinations, and transaction data, to track money flow (Dudani et al., 2023).

Digital forensics is crucial in extracting and evaluating this information. If an investigator has identified a suspect and has access to the suspect's devices, they would use host-based forensics methods. This involves examining the suspect's mobile devices, computers, and memory to gather evidence such as application data, wallet information, public/private keys, and other relevant artifacts related to cryptocurrency. This evidence can potentially assist in further investigating the blockchain for additional proof.

Alternatively, if a specific suspect has not been recognized, detectives rely on the publicly accessible blockchain and possibly valuable network artifacts. These artifacts may help identify suspects whose devices may be thoroughly examined for more evidence. This analysis will discuss the current research on extracting and analyzing Bitcoin artifacts from various sources, such as mobile devices, computers, memory, blockchains, and network-based platforms (Dudani et al., 2023).

Methods of Cryptocurrency Forensics Investigations

Cryptocurrency forensics aims to identify the responsible party and locate their funds through various methods of analysis and investigation. Blockchain intelligence technologies collect and analyze ownership attribution data for businesses, enabling the identification of criminals and investigation topics by de-anonymizing blockchain addresses. Transaction mapping converts transactional data into visual maps and flowcharts, tracing financial transfers to their ultimate endpoints.

Cluster analysis identifies groups of cryptocurrency addresses under a single individual or institution's control, broadening the investigation's scope. Subpoena targets are focused on commercial cryptocurrency exchanges, decentralized finance organizations, and virtual asset service providers that adhere to Know Your Customer (KYC) and Anti-Money Laundering (AML) standards. Total transactions indicate the potential scale of a fraudulent scheme and the number of individuals affected. Law enforcement agencies prioritize complaints involving crime syndicates causing harm to many individuals, while class action cases may be suitable for larger schemes.

Forensic Analysis of Mobile Devices

Mobile devices play a crucial role in cryptocurrency forensics because they are widely used for mobile wallets and cryptocurrency applications. These mobile-based cryptocurrency exchange applications generate almost $40 billion in revenue yearly for the top 7 platforms. Some scholars conducted studies in which the most widely used cryptocurrency wallets for Bitcoin, Darkcoin, and Litecoin were downloaded and used on iOS and Android devices. The wallets were utilized in their simplest form, with only essential user functions (Montanez, 2014).

The experiment utilized an Apple iPhone 4 running iOS 7.1.1, a Samsung Galaxy S4 running Android 4.4.2, and two virtual Samsung Galaxy S4 smartphones running Android 4.4.2. Information was obtained from each device by utilizing Cellebrite UFED, Cellebrite Physical Analyzer, and iFunBox for iOS following specific device or wallet occurrences (Dudani et al., 2023).

To investigate cryptocurrency transactions, digital forensic examiners must focus on identifying databases that store information such as the names of cryptocurrency wallets, the public-private keys of the sender and receiver, the userIDs of the sender and receiver, and the files related to the timestamps of the transactions. The ability to retrieve these artifacts significantly relies heavily on the security and privacy measures implemented by the operating system and the wallet application being examined. Additionally, when considering host-based forensics for cryptocurrency, both computer and memory forensics hold equal significance alongside mobile forensics (Dudani et al., 2023).

The notion of Machine Learning (ML) is becoming increasingly prevalent and is also being used in Bitcoin forensics. In 2018, some scholars introduced a new method based on supervised machine learning to decrease anonymity on the Bitcoin Blockchain (Harlev et al., 2018). The training data set from Chainalysis comprised almost 200 million transactions involving 434 identified businesses. Using their classifier, they could categorize an entity into one of ten distinct categories. By implementing Gradient Boosting, they attained an F1 score of 0.75.

Some scholars presented the Elliptic Data Set, which includes more than 200,000 Bitcoin transactions, 234,000 directed payment flows, and 166 node characteristics. Using different machine learning algorithms, they then analyzed the outcomes of a binary classification task that aimed to distinguish illegal transactions from legal ones (Dudani et al., 2023).

In addition, they provide Chronograph, a visualization prototype designed to assist analysts in examining and comprehending Bitcoin transactions. The Elliptic Data Set has made a significant impact on blockchain forensics. Researchers have widely utilized this publicly accessible dataset to gain insights into and potentially uncover participants' identities in the Bitcoin blockchain (Weber et al., 2019).

Dark Web Forensics by Artificial Intelligence and Machine Learning

Digital forensics investigators can use web crawling and data mining techniques to uncover concealed services and collect evidence of illegal behavior. The dark web is an unindexed section that requires access to specific software known for facilitating illicit activities like gun sales, drug trafficking, and cybercrimes. This software is also customized to allow users to access the dark web by directing their internet traffic through a global network of volunteer-operated computer nodes.

The dark web was initially created for lawful reasons, such as safeguarding the anonymity of internet users in nations with authoritarian regimes and providing secure communication for activists, journalists, and law enforcement personnel. However, it has been exploited by criminals and other malicious individuals for illicit activities, similar to many different technologies. Investigating illegal conduct on the dark web is difficult due to the anonymity of its users and the utilization of encryption technologies. Some scholars see that Artificial Intelligence and Machine Learning (AI and ML) can assist digital forensics investigators by automating data analysis and detecting illicit behavior trends (Sukumar, 2023).

Cryptocurrency transactions can be traced due to the anonymity of cryptocurrencies like Bitcoin, commonly used for illicit operations on the dark web. Every cryptocurrency transaction is documented on a public ledger called the blockchain. Digital forensics investigators can track the flow of illegal funds and pinpoint the persons engaged in criminal behavior by examining the blockchain. Advanced data analysis methods can detect activity patterns and connect transactions to specific people or companies. Clustering analysis is a technique used to track the flow of funds on the blockchain. Chain analysis is another method employed to track the flow of funds within the blockchain by monitoring fund transfers between different addresses.

Examining conversation records reveals that criminals frequently use chat rooms on the dark web to coordinate and strategize illicit actions. AI and machine learning are especially beneficial in this context. Detectives can quickly pinpoint conversations likely linked to illegal behavior by analyzing chat logs and focusing on those chats. This can optimize the investigation process and decrease the time and resources needed to review extensive conversation log data.

Data encryption involves using AI algorithms to evaluate patterns in encrypted data to determine the encryption mechanism employed. Natural Language Processing (NLP) can help understand the context of messages and communications on the dark web. Machine Learning Algorithms can examine extensive datasets of encrypted data to detect trends and develop future models for decrypting similar material. Predictive analytics can anticipate user behavior on the dark web to discover potential dangers and flaws in the system. For example, machine learning can forecast prime numbers used in the critical generation procedure for RSA encryption.

AI and ML are improving digital forensics by automating the preliminary analysis of digital evidence by recognizing file types, timestamps, and metadata. This accelerates the investigation process, allowing investigators to concentrate on more intricate tasks. AI and ML can also help investigators by automatically organizing and ranking data to uncover significant evidence, simplifying the process of finding crucial information.

AI and ML systems can analyze distinctive malware codes associated with particular strains. By recognizing these patterns, investigators can promptly detect malware infections and take steps to eliminate them before they result in substantial harm. Automating data analysis and discovering criminal activity patterns allows detectives to streamline the investigation process and concentrate on more complex tasks. The future of digital forensics appears promising as technology advances, enhancing the effectiveness of combating cybercrime (Sukumar, 2023).

Standard Machine Learning Algorithms Used in Cyber Forensic Investigations

Several studies indicate that machine learning techniques commonly employed in cyber forensic investigations encompass Random Forest, neural networks (including deep learning and recurrent neural networks), and Logistic Regression. Machine learning (ML) algorithms are now essential in cyber forensic investigations, as they offer automated, efficient, and precise techniques for identifying and examining cyber risks. This synthesis examines the prevalent machine learning methods in cyber forensic investigations, extracting lessons from many research articles.

Several studies have found that the Random Forest and Gradient Boosted Trees algorithms effectively detect malware. These algorithms consistently achieve high levels of accuracy, as demonstrated in various research papers (Benkerroum & Chougdali, 2023; Swaminathan et al., 2022).

In addition, Support Vector Machine algorithms (SVM) are commonly employed in cyber forensics to perform binary classification tasks. They accurately detect cyber risks (Benkerroum & Chougdali, 2023; Buczak & Guven, 2016). K-Nearest Neighbors algorithms (KNN) is a method valued for its straightforwardness and efficiency in forecasting cyber-attacks and examining forensic evidence (Benkerroum & Chougdali, 2023; Swaminathan et al., 2022).

Additionally, the Naive Bayes method is utilized due to its high efficiency in processing extensive datasets and its ability to accurately classify cyber threats (Benkerroum & Chougdali, 2023; Buczak & Guven, 2016). Logistic Regression, although frequently employed, tends to exhibit inferior performance in cyber forensic tasks when compared to other algorithms, such as Random Forests and gradient-boosted trees (Benkerroum & Chougdali, 2023; Swaminathan et al., 2022).

Other studies see that Deep learning models, including Deep Neural Networks (DNN), Long Short-Term Memory (LSTM), and Gated Recurrent Units (GRU), are increasingly used for their ability to handle complex and high-dimensional data, providing superior performance in intrusion detection and anomaly detection (Vinayakumar et al., 2019; Li et al., 2021).

Some experts recognize that Decision Trees are utilized for their interpretability and efficacy in categorizing cyber risks, frequently functioning as a benchmark for more intricate models (Benkerroum & Chougdali, 2023; Buczak & Guven, 2016). Some scholars argue that combining artificial intelligence (AI) with machine learning (ML) algorithms improves the effectiveness and accuracy of cyber forensic investigations. This integration allows for automated detection and classification of threats (Fakiha, 2023).

To summarise, cyber forensic investigations use different machine learning methods, each with advantages and disadvantages. Random Forests and Gradient-Boosted Trees are renowned for their exceptional accuracy in detecting viruses. Support Vector Machines, K-Nearest Neighbors, and Naive Bayes are frequently employed due to their resilience and effectiveness. Deep learning models such as DNN, LSTM, and GRU are becoming increasingly popular due to their capacity to process intricate data effectively. AI integration boosts algorithms' capabilities, increasing the efficiency and precision of cyber forensic investigations.

Challenges In Implementing Machine Learning for Anomaly-Based Intrusion Detection

Some research indicates that implementing machine learning for anomaly-based intrusion detection presents several significant challenges. These challenges include effectively managing various network structures, adjusting to emerging technologies, dealing with imbalanced data sets, keeping attack definitions current, achieving real-time detection, and overcoming low accuracy and performance issues.

Deploying machine learning (ML) in anomaly-based intrusion detection systems (IDS) poses numerous obstacles. The problems arise due to the ever-changing nature of network settings, the intricate nature of data, and the requirement for immediate processing. This synthesis focuses on the primary obstacles found in several study publications.

Many experts observe that machine learning models frequently encounter difficulties with class imbalance, with inadequate training instances for each potential class. This imbalance typically results in erroneous identification of specific intrusions (Chkirbene et al., 2020; Abdelmoumin et al., 2021). In addition, the abundance and variety of data produced by contemporary networks, including IoT and IIoT, complicate the training procedure and impact the efficiency of ML models (Agrawal et al., 2021; Gyamfi & Jurcut, 2023).

Several experts recognize that real-time detection is essential yet complex, requiring constant updates and dealing with ever-changing cyber-attacks (Gyamfi & Jurcut, 2023; Alrawashdeh & Purdy, 2016). Implementing effective machine learning-based intrusion detection systems (IDS) is challenging due to resource constraints, such as limited memory, computational power, and energy supply, in IoT and IoT devices (Gyamfi & Jurcut, 2023; Sommer & Paxson, 2010).

Others see that anomaly-based intrusion detection systems (IDS) frequently experience elevated rates of false positives, leading to potential overload of security systems and diminished efficacy (Abdelmoumin et al., 2021; Sommer & Paxson, 2010). The disparity between the training and testing data exacerbates this problem, resulting in imprecise predictions and more false alarms (Abdelmoumin et al., 2021).

Some scientists observe that the extensive and ever-changing datasets needed to train machine learning models result in substantial computational burden, especially in situations with limited resources. Parallel processing designs and optimization approaches are essential for handling the computational workload and enhancing the effectiveness of machine learning-based intrusion detection systems (IDS) (Joshi & Korah, 2022).

Other experts argue that Centralized Machine Learning (ML) techniques pose a privacy and security risk since they need data storage and transmission to a single server. Federated learning (FL) provides a method to maintain privacy by training models on local devices and exchanging parameters. However, this approach is also tricky (Agrawal et al., 2021).

Several experts argue that traditional machine learning (ML) models, such as KNN and SVM, significantly depend on manual feature engineering and may not yield satisfactory performance in the era of big data (Su et al., 2020). Although more precise, deep learning models are intricate and demand substantial computational resources, rendering them less appropriate for real-time applications in resource-limited contexts (Su et al., 2020; Alrawashdeh & Purdy, 2016).

In summary, implementing machine learning for anomaly-based intrusion detection encounters significant obstacles, such as imbalanced data, the need for real-time processing, a high occurrence of false positives, difficulties in scaling, concerns over privacy, and the intricacy of models. Advanced machine learning techniques, optimization tactics, and creative methods such as federated learning are necessary to overcome these issues. These approaches aim to improve the effectiveness and efficiency of intrusion detection systems in various and ever-changing network contexts.

CONCLUSIONS

Due to its distinctive characteristics and appeal to a wide range of consumers, indications suggest that Bitcoin will progressively integrate into global financial institutions. Consequently, the utilization of cryptocurrency by wrongdoers is increasing due to the uncontrolled and anonymous characteristics of the currency, propelling us towards a future dominated by cybercrime propelled by cryptocurrency. The existing technological capabilities of law enforcement agencies and researchers worldwide may not be adequate, highlighting the need for advancements in digital forensics, specifically with Bitcoin artifacts. Furthermore, it requires the unrestricted dissemination of information concerning cryptocurrency investigations across international agencies, which can then be passed on to local law enforcement organizations.

The studies identified the need to address several areas of digital cryptocurrency forensics, in which gaps can be filled by developing advanced solutions for cryptocurrency forensics. Further investigation is required in digital forensics concerning significant cryptocurrencies like Monero, Ethereum, Verge, Dogecoin, and others. This is necessary because these currencies are becoming increasingly popular among both legitimate users and evil individuals. The survey highlighted another research gap: the limited amount of substantial research on host-based cryptocurrency forensics, particularly in mobile-based cryptocurrency forensics.

Host-based forensics is crucial in identifying initial evidence to guide blockchain forensics investigations in tracking money flows. The majority of research conducted on host-based forensics focuses on outdated operating systems or platforms, highlighting the need for research on more up-to-date versions. When examining forensic methods for cryptocurrencies, it is crucial to consider security and vulnerability assessment studies.

These studies can provide insights into potential exploits or assaults useful for forensic investigations. To summarise, research in Blockchain-based forensics is advancing organically alongside technological advancements. However, there is a need for focused attention on host-based forensics for cryptocurrency.

REFERENCES

Abdelmoumin, G., Rawat, D., & Rahman, A. (2021). On the Performance of Machine Learning Models for Anomaly-Based Intelligent Intrusion Detection Systems for the Internet of Things. *IEEE Internet of Things Journal, 9*(6), 4280–4290. DOI: 10.1109/JIOT.2021.3103829

Agrawal, S., Sarkar, S., Aouedi, O., Yenduri, G., Piamrat, K., Bhattacharya, S., Maddikunta, P., & Gadekallu, T. (2021). Federated Learning for Intrusion Detection System: Concepts, Challenges and Future Directions. *Computer Communications, 195*, 346–361. DOI: 10.1016/j.comcom.2022.09.012

AL-BAHOUTH, A.B.S.B.A., (2017). Virtual Money: Its concept, types, and economic effects. *Scientific Journal of Economics and Trade, Faculty of Commerce, Ain Shams University, Cairo, 65*.

Alrawashdeh, K., & Purdy, C. (2016). Toward an Online Anomaly Intrusion Detection System Based on Deep Learning. *2016 15th IEEE International Conference on Machine Learning and Applications (ICMLA)*, 195-200. DOI: 10.1109/ICMLA.2016.0040

Bahamazava, K., & Nanda, R. (2022). The shift of DarkNet illegal drug trade preferences in cryptocurrency: The question of traceability and deterrence. *Forensic Science International Digital Investigation, 40*, 301377. DOI: 10.1016/j.fsidi.2022.301377

Benkerroum, S., & Chougdali, K. (2023). Enhancing Forensic Analysis Using a Machine Learning-based Approach. *2023 6th International Conference on Advanced Communication Technologies and Networking (CommNet)*, pp. 1-6. DOI: 10.1109/CommNet60167.2023.10365260

Biddle, P., England, P., Peinado, M., & Willman, B. (2003). The darknet and the future of content protection. In *Digital Rights Management: ACM CCS-9 Workshop, DRM 2002, Washington, DC, USA, November 18, 2002. Revised Papers* (pp. 155-176). Springer Berlin Heidelberg.

Buczak, A., & Guven, E. (2016). A Survey of Data Mining and Machine Learning Methods for Cyber Security Intrusion Detection. *IEEE Communications Surveys and Tutorials, 18*(2), 1153–1176. DOI: 10.1109/COMST.2015.2494502

Casino, F., Dasaklis, T. K., & Patsakis, C. (2019). A systematic literature review of blockchain-based applications: Current status, classification, and open issues. *Telematics and Informatics, 36*, 55–81. DOI: 10.1016/j.tele.2018.11.006

Chkirbene, Z., Erbad, A., Hamila, R., Gouissem, A., Mohamed, A., & Hamdi, M. (2020). Machine Learning Based Cloud Computing Anomalies Detection. *IEEE Network, 34*(6), 178–183. DOI: 10.1109/MNET.011.2000097

Doran, M. D. (2014). *A forensic look at bitcoin cryptocurrency* (Master's thesis, Utica College).

Dudani, S., Baggili, I., Raymond, D., & Marchany, R. (2023). The current state of cryptocurrency forensics. *Forensic Science International Digital Investigation, 46*, 301576. DOI: 10.1016/j.fsidi.2023.301576

Duffield, E., & Hagan, K. (2014). Darkcoin: Peertopeer cryptocurrency with anonymous blockchain transactions and an improved proof of work system. *bitpaper.Info*.

Dunsin, D., Ghanem, M., Ouazzane, K., & Vassilev, V. 2023. A Comprehensive Analysis of the Role of Artificial Intelligence and Machine Learning in Modern Digital Forensics and Incident Response. *ArXiv*, abs/2309.07064. /arXiv.2309.07064. DOI: 10.2139/ssrn.4554035

El-Kady, R. (2021). Combating organized crime via the dark web: An analytical study in Egyptian legislation. *National Criminal Journal, 64*(3), 44–105. DOI: 10.21608/ncj.2021.225839

El-Kady, R. (2023). Handling E-evidence in Egyptian and Comparative Legislation: A Comparative Analytical Study. *Arab Journal of Forensic Sciences & Forensic Medicine, 6*(1), 37–68. DOI: 10.26735/WGZY6322

El-Kady, R. (2024). Artificial Intelligence and Criminal Law. In *Artificial Intelligence Approaches to Sustainable Accounting* (pp. 34–52). IGI Global. DOI: 10.4018/979-8-3693-0847-9.ch003

El-Kady, R. M. (2024). Investigating Forensic Evidence in Metaverse: A Comparative Analytical Study. In *Forecasting Cyber Crimes in the Age of the Metaverse* (pp. 227-258). IGI Global.

Fakiha, B. (2023). Enhancing Cyber Forensics with AI and Machine Learning: A Study on Automated Threat Analysis and Classification. *International Journal of Safety and Security Engineering, 13*(4), 701–707. Advance online publication. DOI: 10.18280/ijsse.130412

FBI, D., (2012). Bitcoin virtual currency: Unique features present distinct challenges for deterring illicit activity. *Intelligence Assessment*.

Gannon, C., Blokland, A. A., Huikuri, S., Babchishin, K. M., & Lehmann, R. J. (2023). Child sexual abuse material on the darknet. *Forensische Psychiatrie, Psychologie, Kriminologie, 17*(4), 353–365. DOI: 10.1007/s11757-023-00790-8

Guccione, D. (2019). *What is the dark web? How to access it and what you'll find, The state of cybersecurity*. CSO Online.

Gupta, A., Gupta, R., & Sankaran, A. (2021). *Machine Learning Forensics*., DOI: 10.4018/978-1-7998-4900-1.ch003

Gyamfi, E., & Jurcut, A. (2023). Novel Online Network Intrusion Detection System for Industrial IoT Based on OI-SVDD and AS-ELM. *IEEE Internet of Things Journal, 10*(5), 3827–3839. DOI: 10.1109/JIOT.2022.3172393

Harlev, M. A., Sun Yin, H., Langenheldt, K. C., Mukkamala, R., & Vatrapu, R. (2018). Breaking bad: De-anonymising entity types on the bitcoin blockchain using supervised machine learning.

Joshi, C. (2023). Cryptocurrency Forensics: The Ultimate Guide to 6 Important Aspects. Indiaforensic. https://indiaforensic.com/cryptocurrency-forensics/

Joshi, V., & Korah, J. (2022). Formulating Parallel Supervised Machine Learning Designs for Anomaly-Based Network Intrusion Detection in Resource-Constrained Use Cases. *2022 IEEE 19th International Conference on Mobile Ad Hoc and Smart Systems (MASS)*, 748-753. DOI: 10.1109/MASS56207.2022.00117

Kumar, A., & Sharma, I. (2023). Preserving Security of Crypto Transactions with Machine Learning Methodologies. *2023 International Conference on Sustainable Computing and Smart Systems (ICSCSS)*, pp. 129-134. DOI: 10.1109/ICSCSS57650.2023.10169192

Li, Z., Rios, A., & Trajković, L. (2021). Machine Learning for Detecting Anomalies and Intrusions in Communication Networks. *IEEE Journal on Selected Areas in Communications, 39*(7), 2254–2264. DOI: 10.1109/JSAC.2021.3078497

Martin, M. (2021). *Computer and Internet use in the United States: 2018*. American Community Survey Reports.

Montanez, A. (2014). *Investigation of cryptocurrency wallets on iOS and Android mobile devices for potential forensic artifacts. Department Forensic Science*. Marshall University.

Nakamoto, S., & Bitcoin, A. (2008). A peer-to-peer electronic cash system. *Bitcoin.–URL:*https://bitcoin. org/bitcoin. pdf, *4*(2), p.15.

Nour, K. (2022). Criminal confrontation of cryptocurrency use in the financing of terrorism. *Jolets.* 16;2(2):79-152. Available from: https://jolets.org/ojs/index.php/jolets/article/view/12

Obeidat, T.. (1996). *Methods and Techniques of Scientific Research.* Dar Sana'a for Publishing. (In Arabic)

Patil, S., Vijayakumar, V., Walimbe, D., Gulechha, S., Shenoy, S., Raina, A., & Kotecha, K. (2021). Improving the Robustness of AI-Based Malware Detection Using Adversarial Machine Learning. *Algorithms, 14*(10), 297. DOI: 10.3390/a14100297

Reid, F., & Harrigan, M. (2013). *An analysis of anonymity in the Bitcoin system.* Springer. DOI: 10.1007/978-1-4614-4139-7_10

Sommer, R., & Paxson, V. (2010). Outside the Closed World: On Using Machine Learning for Network Intrusion Detection. *2010 IEEE Symposium on Security and Privacy*, 305-316. DOI: 10.1109/SP.2010.25

Su, T., Sun, H., Zhu, J., Wang, S., & Li, Y. (2020). BAT: Deep Learning Methods on Network Intrusion Detection Using NSL-KDD Dataset. *IEEE Access : Practical Innovations, Open Solutions, 8*, 29575–29585. DOI: 10.1109/ACCESS.2020.2972627

Sukumar, S. (2023). Digital Forensics in The Dark. https://www.linkedin.com/pulse/digital-forensics-dark-sandhya-sukumar/

Wagh, A., Pawar, R., Wable, N., Wandhekar, S., & Dighe, M. S. (2024). Detection of Cyber Attacks and Network Attacks using Machine Learning Algorithms. Int. J. Adv. Res. Sci. Commun. Technol., 414-417.

Swaminathan, A., & Ramakrishnan, B., M, K., & R, S., (2022). Prediction of Cyber-attacks and Criminality Using Machine Learning Algorithms. *2022 International Conference on Innovation and Intelligence for Informatics, Computing, and Technologies (3ICT)*, pp. 547-552. DOI: 10.1109/3ICT56508.2022.9990652

Taleby Ahvanooey, M., Zhu, M. X., Mazurczyk, W., Kilger, M., & Choo, K. K. R. (2021, December). Do dark web and cryptocurrencies empower cybercriminals? In *International Conference on Digital Forensics and Cyber Crime* (pp. 277-293). Cham: Springer International Publishing.

Tsuchiya, Y., & Hiramoto, N. (2021). How cryptocurrency is laundered: Case study of Coincheck hacking incident. *Forensic Science International. Reports, 4*, 100241. DOI: 10.1016/j.fsir.2021.100241

Tziakouris, G. (2018). Cryptocurrencies—A forensic challenge or opportunity for law enforcement? An Interpol perspective. *IEEE Security and Privacy*, *16*(4), 92–94. DOI: 10.1109/MSP.2018.3111243

Vinayakumar, R., Alazab, M., Soman, K., Poornachandran, P., Al-Nemrat, A., & Venkatraman, S. (2019). Deep Learning Approach for Intelligent Intrusion Detection System. *IEEE Access : Practical Innovations, Open Solutions*, *7*, 41525–41550. DOI: 10.1109/ACCESS.2019.2895334

Weber, M., Domeniconi, G., Chen, J., Weidele, D. K. I., Bellei, C., Robinson, T., & Leiserson, C. E. 2019. Anti-money laundering in bitcoin: Experimenting with graph convolutional networks for financial forensics. *arXiv preprint arXiv:1908.02591*.

Zhou, X., Liang, W., Shimizu, S., Ma, J., & Jin, Q. (2021). Siamese Neural Network Based Few-Shot Learning for Anomaly Detection in Industrial Cyber-Physical Systems. *IEEE Transactions on Industrial Informatics*, *17*(8), 5790–5798. DOI: 10.1109/TII.2020.3047675

Chapter 14
Enhanced DDoS Detection Using Feature Selection and Multi-Model Machine Learning Frameworks

K. Muthamil Sudar
https://orcid.org/0000-0001-9640-3477
Mepco Schlenk Engineering College, Sivakasi, India

P. Nagaraj
https://orcid.org/0000-0003-1803-8544
SRM Institute of Science and Technology (SRMIST), Kattankulathur, India

V. Vaissnave
https://orcid.org/0000-0001-7333-531X
SRM Institute of Science and Technology, Kattankulathur, India

ABSTRACT

Distributed Denial of Service (DDoS) attacks are among the most pervasive and disruptive threats in today's interconnected digital landscape, capable of overwhelming systems and rendering services unavailable. The effective and timely detection of DDoS attacks has therefore become critical for maintaining the security and availability of networked systems. This chapter presents a holistic approach to DDoS detection based on machine learning techniques, improved by feature selection and the use of multiple predictive models The system uses a diverse ensemble of machine learning models: Random Forest, Support Vector Machine, Gradient

DOI: 10.4018/979-8-3693-8871-6.ch014

Boosting, and Neural Networks to effectively learn the complex patterns typical of DDoS traffic This chapter highlights the potential of integrating feature selection with multi-model machine learning frameworks for efficient and scalable DDoS detection.The proposed framework will be able to counter the evolving nature of DDoS attacks, hence offering resilience and reliability in ever-increasingly complex network environments.

I. INTRODUCTION

1.1 Defining DDoS Attacks and Their Significance in Modern Network Security

DDoS is a cyberattack that targets disrupting a targeted system, service, or network. This attack aims to disrupt normal service by flooding the system with unwanted traffic. Such attacks always originate from several compromised systems, which is usually complex to trace and block such a source. DDoS attacks can be against almost any system, including websites, servers, and entire networks, with the intent of rendering services unavailable to legitimate users.

In today's digital landscape, with organizations relying heavily on online services, the importance of DDoS attacks can be considered paramount. A successful attack can cause severe financial losses, damage an organization's reputation, and even compromise critical infrastructure. The potential of DDoS attacks has been demonstrated by some high-profile incidents; thus, detection and mitigation become a critical focus area for network security professionals.

1.2 Challenges of Detecting DDoS Attacks

DDoS attack detection is quite challenging because of the evolving tactics used by attackers and the sheer volume of traffic that needs to be analyzed in real time. Major challenges include:

High Volume Traffic: The sheer volume of traffic in a DDoS attack can overwhelm the traditional detection mechanisms, thereby delaying or missing the detections.

Advance Techniques: The attackers keep learning new techniques. Low and Slow attacks, Amplification, as well as multi-vector attack make it challenging to learn pattern changes for them.

False positives and false negatives: It becomes very hard to distinguish between traffic spikes that are legitimate and DDoS attacks, with a high rate of false positives or false negatives.
Encrypted Traffic: With increased usage of encrypted traffic, detection becomes even more difficult because traditional inspection methods do not work without decrypting the data.

1.3 Machine Learning as a Promising Solution for Detection

Machine Learning emerges as a powerful tool in the field of DDoS detection due to its abilities in analyzing large amounts of data and identifying complex patterns that conventional systems may not be able to achieve. Machine learning models have an advantage over rule-based systems by their ability to learn from the data and adapt to novel attack patterns. Techniques in supervised learning, unsupervised learning, and ensemble methods help ML models detect anomalies within network traffic and differentiate benign and malicious activities.

Feature selection, an essential tool in machine learning, promotes detection by discovering the most relevant attributes from network traffic data, reducing noise, and thus achieving greater model performance. In addition, ensemble models combine the predictions of multiple algorithms, which have been proven to be more accurate and robust than single models in handling various attack scenarios.

1.4 Objectives and Contributions

The research will develop a broad framework for DDoS detection integrating feature selection and multi-machine learning models. In detail, the objectives are set as follows:

Feature Selection: Using advanced techniques in feature selection to come up with the most applicable features for DDoS detection.
Multi-Model Approach: Testing the performance of multiple machine learning models used for detection, including Random Forest, SVM, Gradient Boosting, and Neural Networks.
Performance Evaluation: Benchmarking the proposed system by using public datasets and performance evaluation by metrics such as accuracy, precision, recall, F1-score, and detection time.
Scalability and Robustness: The scalability and robustness of the proposed system should be demonstrated in detecting different types of DDoS attacks.

This research contribution includes developing a new DDoS detection framework by combining feature selection and ensemble learning for the improvement of detection accuracy and reduction of false positives. The study's findings can be applied in network security using machine learning models, thus forming a foundation for future research in adaptive security solutions.

The remainder of this chapter is organized as follows:

Section 2 provides a comprehensive literature review, discussing DDoS attacks, traditional detection methods, and machine learning approaches. Section 3 outlines the methodology, including data collection, feature selection, and the machine learning models used. Section 4 describes the experimental setup and the tools used for model training and testing. Section 5 presents the results and evaluation of the proposed models. Section 6 discusses the implications of the findings, limitations of the study, and future research directions. Section 7 concludes the chapter, summarizing the key findings and contributions.

II. LITERATURE REVIEW

2.1 DDoS Attacks

DDoS attacks are malicious attempts to disrupt the availability of services by overwhelming a target with a flood of traffic. These attacks leverage multiple compromised devices to create a distributed network of attack sources, making them difficult to mitigate. Volumetric Attacks are the most common and aim to saturate the bandwidth of the target. In this form of volumetric attacks, lots of traffic are created to overwhelm resources on the target. Measures that describe their success are the bps. Protocol-based attacks make use of server flaws in protocols used to waste resources of servers. Good examples of protocol attacks are such as the SYN floods attacks; fragments of packets, and Pinger of Death. Protocols usually waste the connection states or other valuable resources of the server in packets per second (pps). Layer Application Attacks These attacks target the layer, 7 of the OSI model; they are similar to legal users' behavior, hence making a lot of server resources to waste. Examples include HTTP floods and slow POST attacks. The fact that these attacks create a normal traffic pattern makes it hard to detect them.

2.2 Traditional Detection Approaches

Signature-based detection looks for attack patterns based on network traffic compared to a database of known attack signatures. These methods work well for known attacks but do not work against new or changing threats. IDS and IPS often use signature-based methods. Anomaly-based detection is based on deviation from normal traffic behavior. Statistical models or predefined thresholds are used in anomaly-based detection of network traffic anomalies. Though this can achieve detection of previously unknown attacks, high false positives result; legitimate traffic spikes trigger alerts in most instances.

Traditional approaches to DDoS detection have significant limitations. Signature-based methods fail to detect zero-day attacks that are unknown threats that have no predefined patterns. As a result, they are ineffective against new strategies for attacks. In contrast, anomaly-based methods identify suspicious traffic but generate many false positives, which complicates management in real-time environments. Additionally, since network traffic grows every year, detection systems are having problems in scaling and start to hit a performance bottleneck. Moreover, since many of the conventional techniques are unable to inspect encrypted traffic, the need for highly advanced, flexible, and adaptable detection systems like machine learning-based systems becomes crucial.

2.3 Machine Learning for DDoS Detection

Machine learning (ML) has emerged as a strong tool for detecting DDoS attacks because it learns patterns and evolves to adapt to the threats. The ML models can look into large datasets and can find anomalies that might have gone unnoticed by traditional methods. Supervised Learning Algorithms are mostly used in Decision Trees, Support Vector Machines (SVM), Random Forest, and Gradient Boosting. The supervised models require labeled data to learn patterns and classify traffic. Unsupervised Learning Clustering algorithms like K-Means and DBSCAN are useful for anomaly detection when labeled data is not available. Deep Learning algorithms such as Neural networks, particularly Convolutional Neural Networks (CNNs) and Recurrent Neural Networks (RNNs), are increasingly being used for DDoS detection due to their ability to learn complex patterns in large datasets..

Feature Selection Techniques in Network Security

Feature selection forms a critical step in effective building of ML models on DDoS detection. Techniques such as Recursive Feature Elimination (RFE), Principal Component Analysis (PCA), and Mutual Information support the identification of the most appropriate features, reduction of dimension, and improvement in model performance. Feature selection improves accuracy but also leads to a decrease in cost computation and overfitting risk.

2.4 Multi-Model Approaches (Ensemble Learning)

Combines the predictions of multiple models to better improve overall performance and robustness. Essentially utilizes the strength of different models to generate a more robust and accurate system. Basically, Bagging is applying multiple models on different parts of data and averaging these predicted values. Random Forest falls within this bagging-based kind of an ensemble model. Boosting allows models to be trained consecutively, where it corrects the errors by its predecessor. Most widely used boosting algorithms are gradient boosting and AdaBoost, which are very effective for removing bias and variance. The stacking approach combines multiple base models and uses a meta-model to make the final prediction. The base models provide diverse perspectives, and the meta-model learns from the collective outputs of the base models; generally, this improves the prediction accuracy. Ensemble models reduce overfitting and generalize better than any single model, especially against imbalanced datasets that are often found in network traffic analysis. Ensembles can produce higher accuracy and robustness than individual models, which make them suitable for complex and dynamic security tasks. This comprehensive review of the DDoS attack types, traditional detection methods, and the role of machine learning and ensemble models provides a good foundation for the proposed multi-model approach to DDoS detection. The following sections outline the methodology and experimental results that validate the effectiveness of this approach.

Dasari et al. (2024) presented an efficient, lightweight solution in terms of real-time DDoS detection using optimized ML algorithms. Their technique minimized latency, making it even suitable for dynamic environments with very few resources. Aslam et al. (2024) introduced an ensemble learning framework in SDN environments. They enhanced both detection accuracy and the overall network performance with stacking and boosting techniques. Brown et al. designed a paradigm anomaly-based detection model designed towards earlier discovery of DDoS attacks. The authors focused on flexibility in machine learning applications of the recognition of developing malicious signatures across time. Kumar et al. (2024) proposed a hybrid paradigm integrating machine learning into block chaining to secure IoT against DDos attack attacks. The study showcased stronger resistance coupled with better trust management among nodes in IoT networks. Sudar et al. (2024) were addressing DDoS detection within Industrial IoT (IIoT). With anomaly detection being a core focus of the respective machine learning models, domain-specific features were pinpointed as key.

Sudar et al. (2020a) introduced adaptive learning algorithms that adjust dynamically with changes in the network. Their models exhibited excellent performance in dynamic environments where traffic shifts often occur. Muthamil et al. (2020b) integrated deep learning with traditional feature extraction techniques, which has achieved excellent accuracy in the differentiation between benign and malicious traffic in cloud networks. Sudar et al. (2021) proposed a cross-layer detection framework that aggregates multiple data sources to improve the accuracy of detection in mobile networks. Their approach reduced false positives significantly

The reviewed papers highlight the effectiveness of machine learning, especially ensemble and hybrid models, in enhancing DDoS detection across diverse environments such as SDN, IoT, and cloud networks. Emerging trends include blockchain integration, adaptive learning models, and resource-efficient frameworks to address scalability and real-time detection challenges.

III. PROPOSED METHOD

The proposed architecture ensures a scalable, robust, and accurate DDoS detection framework taking the strengths of multiple models and advanced feature selection techniques. In the following sections, the experimental results will be presented in order to evaluate the performance of the proposed system. The proposed system architecture aims to efficiently detect DDoS attacks by processing network traffic data through a streamlined workflow involving data preprocessing, feature selection, model training, and ensemble prediction. The process starts with data collection and preprocessing, in which raw traffic data is cleaned to handle missing values, normalized for consistency, and, if necessary, augmented to improve model robustness. Once generated, the most relevant features are selected using PCA, RFE, and mutual information, to focus on the most influential attributes in order to boost the detection accuracy. In the final step, several machine learning models are trained on these selected features, including Random Forest, SVM, Gradient Boosting, and Neural Networks. The predictions from these models are then aggregated using an ensemble technique, specifically stacking, for leveraging the strengths of a combination of models and enhancing general decision-making. The overall performance of the system will be evaluated in terms of accuracy, precision, recall, and F1-score so that its effectiveness in detection of DDoS attacks could be ascertained to be comprehensive. This architecture ensures a scalable and robust framework over the challenges posed by advanced cyber threats. Figure 1 depicts the proposed framework.

Figure 1. Proposed Framework for DDoS detection

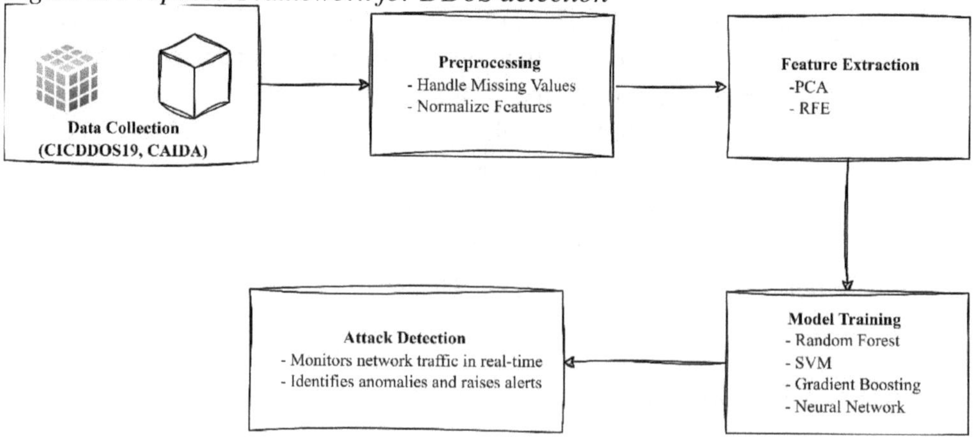

3.1 Data Collection

The quality of the data directly impacts the effectiveness of any machine learning-based DDoS detection system. For this chapter, several datasets were utilized to ensure thorough analysis of the proposed models.

CICDDoS2019: This is the dataset provided by the Canadian Institute for Cybersecurity and contains labeled data which presents different types of DDoS attacks, such as SYN floods, UDP floods, and HTTP-based attacks. It provides the features of traffic including packet size, protocol type, and flow duration.

CAIDA Dataset. The CAIDA DDoS attack datasets consist of anonymized packet traces collected from real-world DDoS attacks with realistic traffic patterns for evaluation.

KDD Cup 1999 Dataset: Although primarily used for intrusion detection, this dataset contains simulated network traffic, including DDoS attacks. It remains a benchmark for comparative analysis.

3.2 Preprocessing Techniques

Missing values: The missing values in the datasets were imputed by median or mode imputation based on the feature type. Mode imputation was applied to categorical features, while median imputation was used for numerical features.

Normalization: To standardize the scaling of features, Min-Max normalization was used to normalize all features to a range of 0 to 1. This is important for algorithms such as SVM and neural networks, which are sensitive to feature scaling.

Data Augmentation: Synthetic data generation techniques, such as Synthetic Minority Over-sampling Technique (SMOTE), were applied to address class imbalance, ensuring models received adequate samples of minority classes.

3.3 Feature Selection

Feature selection is significant since it reduces the dimensionality, removes redundant features, and brings better performance in the overall fitting of machine learning models. PCA is applied to transform original features into a set of uncorrelated principal components for diminishing the dimensionality while keeping variance over the data. Recursive Feature Elimination (RFE) is used to select the most important features by recursively training models and removing the least important features. Mutual Information technique measures the dependency between features and the target variable, selecting features that provide the most information gain towards classification. For DDoS detection, data often contains high-dimensional noise and redundant features that degrade the performance of a model. Feature selection improves not only computational efficiency but also interpretability and accuracy of the models. This is because focusing on the most relevant features allows the model to learn better and generalize well to unseen data.

3.4 Machine Learning Models

Some machine learning models were considered for this study, each with strengths unique to DDoS attacks detection.

3.4.1 Random Forest

Random Forest is an ensemble method of learning that builds an aggregated prediction based on multiple decision trees. This method avoids the problem of overfitting and treats both continuous as well as categorical data variables correctly. Key parameters tuned during parameter tuning include the no of trees n_estimators, maximum number of depth in the tree max_depth, minimum samples required to further partition a node min_samples_split, etc.

3.4.2 Support Vector Machine

SVM is a supervised learning model that finds the best possible hyperplane to separate the different classes. It performs well in both linear and non-linear classification problems. The kernel type (linear, rbf), regularization parameter (C), and kernel coefficient (gamma) were tuned during training.

3.4.3 Gradient Boosting

Gradient Boosting builds models sequentially, wherein each model corrects the mistakes of its predecessor. It performs well on imbalanced datasets and can model complex relationships. The most important parameters that are tuned include learning rate (learning_rate), number of boosting stages (n_estimators), and maximum tree depth (max_depth).

3.4.4 Neural Networks

Neural Networks, particularly deep learning models, were used to capture complex patterns in network traffic. The architecture consisted of multiple layers, with ReLU activation functions and dropout layers for regularization. The number of neurons per layer, learning rate, and batch size were tuned using grid search and cross-validation.

3.4.5 Parameters Tuning and Cross-Validation Strategies

Hyperparameter tuning used the grid search and random search techniques, in addition to k-fold cross-validation. Cross-validation ensures that these models generalize well to unseen data, thereby reducing overfitting. All models used 5-fold cross-validation.

IV. EXPERIMENTAL SETUP

4.1 Tools and Environment

The implementation and evaluation of the proposed DDoS detection framework needed a combination of the software tools, libraries, and hardware resources to guarantee efficient model training, testing, and performance assessment. Python was chosen as the primary programming language because it supports a wide range of applications in machine learning and data science (Canadian Institute for Cybersecurity, n.d.; Scikit-learn, n.d.; TensorFlow, n.d.). Key libraries included Scikit-learn, which enabled the development of machine learning algorithms, feature selection, and model evaluation through tools for classification and regression tasks. TensorFlow and Keras were used to develop and train neural network models, balancing flexibility with user-friendliness for rapid experimentation. Data manipulation and numerical calculations were performed using Pandas and NumPy, respectively, while data visualization activities involved the use of Matplotlib and Seaborn in creating distributions, feature importance, and performance metrics plots. Class imbalance was countered with the Imbalanced-learn library, which made available the use of techniques, including SMOTE and under-sampling. Hyperparameter tuning was also done with GridSearchCV from Scikit-learn, which allowed for an exhaustive search for optimal model parameters.

4.2 Model Training and Testing

A structured approach has been followed in model training and evaluation so that performance comparisons among the various models remain unbiased and all-inclusive. An 80-20 split has been applied on the dataset, thus making available 80% for training and holding back 20% for the assessment of the model's performance. In order to avoid class imbalance and to represent the attack types equally well, stratified sampling was adopted; hence, class distributions are preserved in the two subsets.

To address class imbalance, which is one of the main challenges in DDoS detection datasets, several techniques were employed. Oversampling was carried out using SMOTE, which creates synthetic samples by interpolating between existing minority class instances to increase their representation in the training data. Random undersampling was also used to decrease the dominance of the majority class, and a hybrid approach combining SMOTE and undersampling was used to balance between overfitting and underfitting. Class weights for models such as Random Forest and SVM were adjusted to penalize the misclassification of the minority classes to encourage balanced learning.

This combination of strategies should expose the models to a roughly balanced dataset, ensuring better capabilities for generalization and enhancing the detection of minority attack classes. The next section will focus on the results from model testing and training, which will show their performance by key performance metrics.

V. RESULTS AND EVALUATION

This section presents the performance evaluation of the proposed DDoS detection framework. The evaluation focuses on key performance metrics, the results of various machine learning models, and an analysis of the system's effectiveness.

5.1 Performance Metrics

The performance of the machine learning models was evaluated using several metrics. These metrics give a complete view of the ability of the models to accurately and efficiently detect DDoS attacks:

Accuracy is the percentage of instances that are classified correctly, both as an attack and as benign, out of the total instances. Precision is the proportion of true positive predictions compared to all positive predictions. Recall or Sensitivity measures the percentage of actual positives, namely DDoS attacks, that were correctly identified. The F1-score is a harmonic mean of precision and recall, providing a balanced evaluation. ROC-AUC is used to measure the model's ability to distinguish between classes using a plot of true positives against false positives. More the AUC, more is the discrimination. The detection time is the amount of time taken by the model to classify an instance.

5.2 Experimental Results

The models were trained and evaluated on the CICDDoS2019 dataset. The results illustrated in table I and table II are presented in terms of accuracy, precision, recall, F1-score, ROC-AUC, and detection time.

Table 1. Performance Evaluation of different ML Models

Model Accuracy	Accuracy	Precision	Recall	F1-Score	ROC-AUC	Detection Time
Random Forest	95.8%	94.5%	96.2%	95.3%	0.97	15
SVM	93.4%	92.0%	94.1%	93.0%	0.95	20
Gradient Boosting	96.5%	95.8%	97.0%	96.4%	0.98	18
Neural Networks	97.2%	96.5%	97.8%	97.1%	0.99	25

Table 2. Performance Comparison with and without feature selection techniques

Model	Accuracy (No FS)	Accuracy (With FS)
Random Forest	93.5%	95.8%
SVM	91.2%	93.4%
Gradient Boosting	94.8%	96.5%
Neural Networks	95.6%	97.2%

Impact of Feature Selection

Without feature selection, models were slightly less accurate and had lower recall, as they were incorporating noisy and redundant features. With feature selection (using RFE and Mutual Information), the models were more accurate and yielded higher F1-scores, indicating better generalization and fewer misclassifications. Table II shows the importance of feature selection process. Graphs showing ROC curves, and confusion matrices for each model are included in Figures 2,3,4,5 and 6.

Figure 2. Confusion matrix for all models

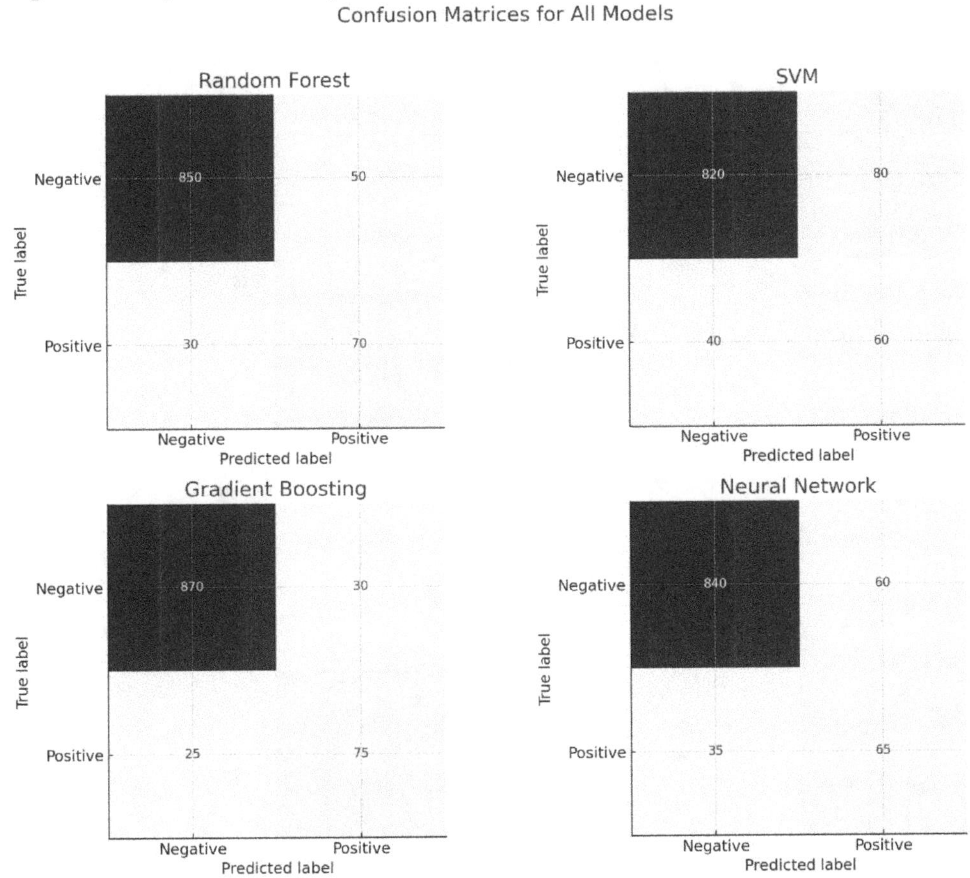

Figure 3. ROC Curve for Random Forest

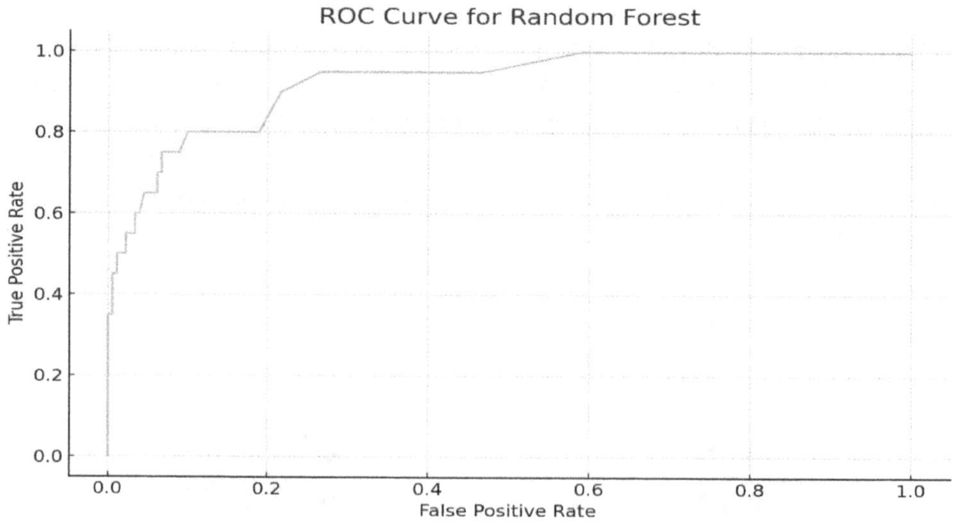

Figure 4. ROC Curve for SVM

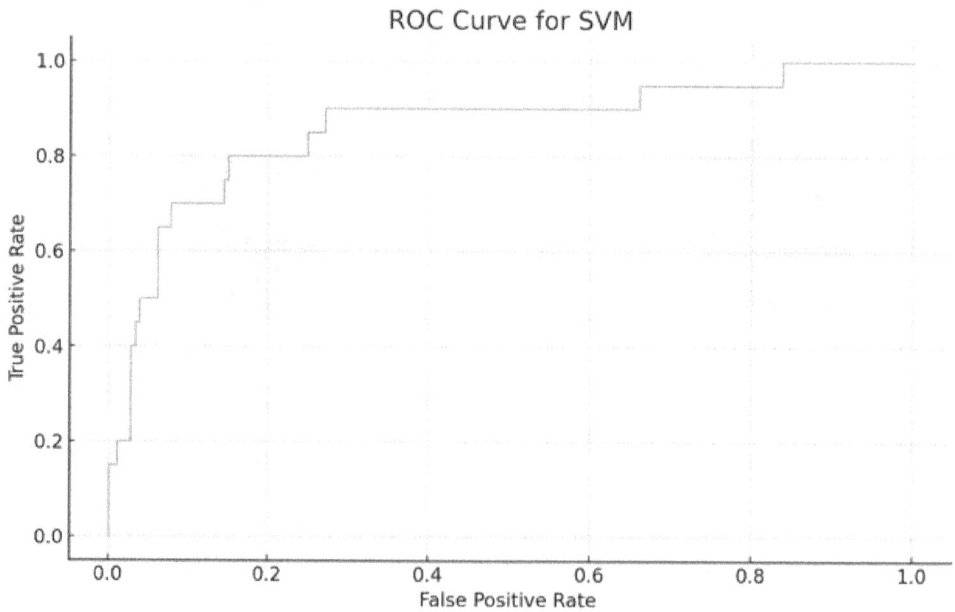

Figure 5. ROC Curve for Gradient Boosting

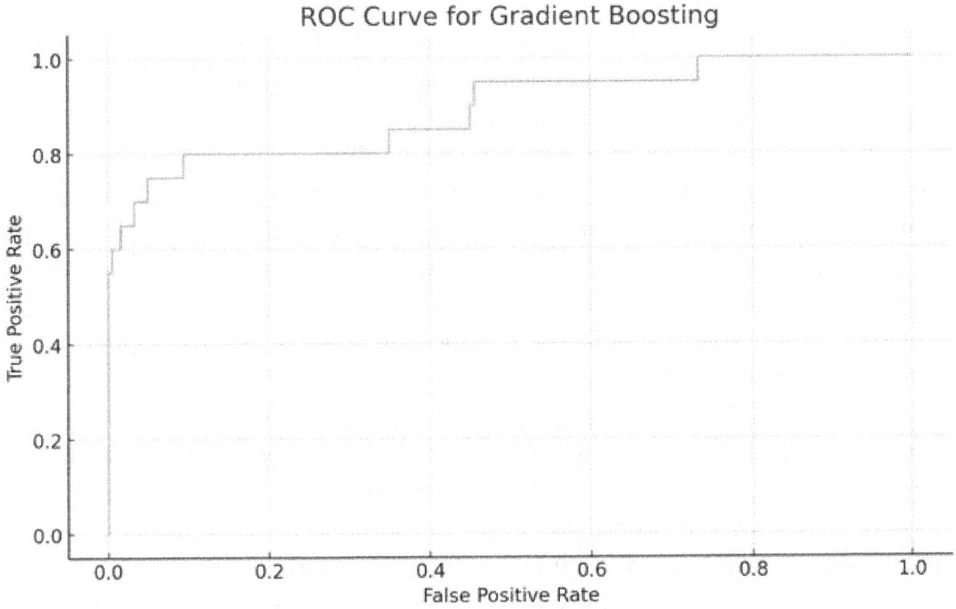

Figure 6. ROC Curve for Neural Network

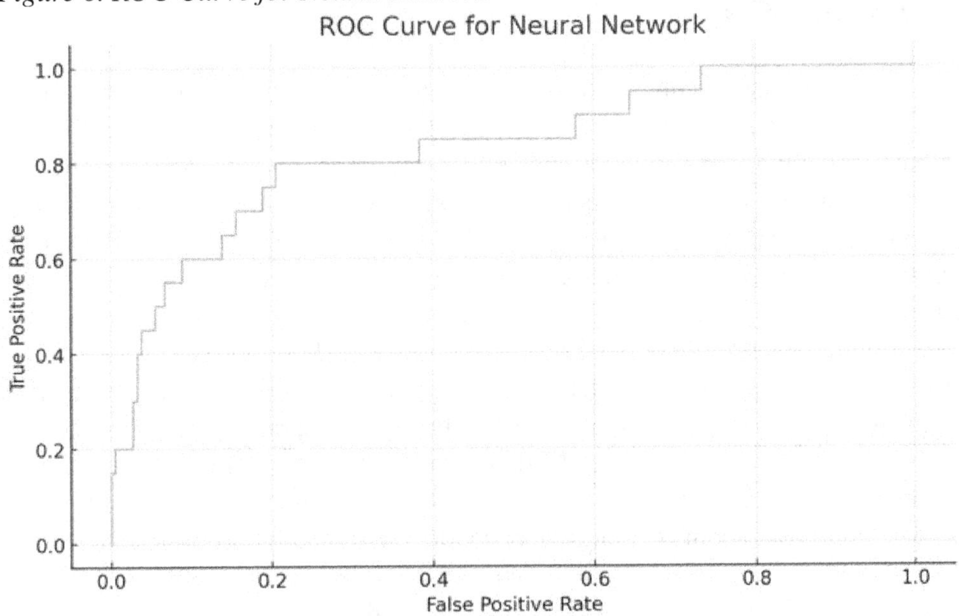

5.3 Analysis of Results

False positives (FP) are when legitimate traffic is classified as a DDoS attack, which leads to the unnecessary mitigation actions and thus may disrupt user access to services. Although the FP rates of Random Forest and Gradient Boosting models remained at a relatively low level, SVM had a high FP rate due to overfitting on imbalanced data. On the other hand, false negatives (FN), where DDoS attacks are not detected, poses a great risk. Neural Networks and Gradient Boosting minimized FN effectively by capturing complex patterns in the data. The highest accuracy and F1-score were achieved by Neural Networks, which utilized the ability to learn intricate relationships, though their longer detection times may hinder real-time applications. Gradient Boosting had a balanced trade-off between precision and detection time and was thus suitable for practical scenarios. Random Forest showed outstanding performance: very high speed and efficiency, especially for resource-constrained environments, at a slightly smaller magnitude than Gradient Boosting and Neural Networks. SVM worked efficiently but failed on high-dimensional data: careful parameter tuning was needed. Feature selection proved to be essential in attaining good model performances by removing noise and keeping the most relevant features. In general, ensemble models such as Random Forest and Gradient Boosting proved robust, while Neural Networks excelled in detection accuracy.

VI. DISCUSSION

The more general implications of the proposed DDoS detection system to network security, challenges with implementing machine learning models in real-world settings, limitations and future research directions are addressed. The integration of feature selection and multiple machine learning models enhances real-world DDoS detection through improved accuracy, scalability, and adaptability. Feature selection improves the signal-to-noise ratio, allowing the models to focus on important features that would reduce false positives and negatives. The modular architecture of the system supports scalability in distributed networks, and periodic model retraining ensures that it can adapt to new techniques in DDoS. Integrating detection with automated mitigation tools can also drastically reduce response times, reducing the downtime for services. However, the deployment of such systems in production is challenging because of data privacy concerns since access to network traffic data has to comply with confidentiality and regulatory standards. Real-time detection is another challenge, especially for computationally intensive models like neural networks, which requires optimizations and edge deployment. Continuous model maintenance is also necessary to prevent performance degradation, requiring regular retraining and validation. Furthermore, combining machine learning-based systems with legacy infrastructure would probably require bespoke solutions to guarantee a seamless fit.

VII. CONCLUSION

This chapter proposed a strong framework for detecting Distributed Denial of Service attacks using machine learning techniques enhanced by feature selection and ensemble modeling. The research demonstrates that applying advanced feature selection methods, such as PCA and RFE, significantly improves the performance of machine learning models by reducing noise and focusing on the most relevant features. Feature selection techniques not only reduced the computational overhead but improved the accuracy and precision of DDoS detection models significantly. Ensemble methods, including bagging, boosting, and stacking, outperformed individual models because they combined the strengths of individual models, which led to better detection rates and fewer false positives. The multi-model approach effectively captured complex attack patterns, making it crucial for addressing evolving and sophisticated DDoS threats. This research contributes to securing network infrastructure, providing a scalable and adaptive solution for DDoS detection. The inclusion of both feature selection and ensemble learning gives a balanced trade-off for accuracy, detection speed, and computational efficiency, making it suitable for real-time deployment in high-traffic environments. However, the dynamic nature of DDoS attacks continues as an ongoing challenge. Future work should include the development of adaptive models that can retrain in real-time, deep learning/hybrid techniques, and especially how the framework can be integrated into an IPS to trigger a response in real-time. The article underlines the possibility of machine learning in network security and calls for continuous innovation in cybersecurity.

REFERENCES

Aslam, N., Srivastava, S., & Gore, M. M. (2024). A comprehensive analysis of machine learning-and deep learning-based solutions for DDoS attack detection in SDN. *Arabian Journal for Science and Engineering*, *49*(3), 3533–3573. DOI: 10.1007/s13369-023-08075-2

CICDDoS2019 Dataset. Canadian Institute for Cybersecurity, [Online]. Available: https://www.unb.ca/cic/datasets/ddos-2019.html

Dasari, S., & Kaluri, R. (2024). An effective classification of DDoS attacks in a distributed network by adopting hierarchical machine learning and hyperparameters optimization techniques. *IEEE Access : Practical Innovations, Open Solutions*, *12*, 10834–10845. DOI: 10.1109/ACCESS.2024.3352281

Kumar, A., & Singh, D. (2024). Detection and prevention of DDoS attacks on edge computing of IoT devices through reinforcement learning. *International Journal of Information Technology : an Official Journal of Bharati Vidyapeeth's Institute of Computer Applications and Management*, *16*(3), 1365–1376. DOI: 10.1007/s41870-023-01508-z

Muthamil Sudar, K., & Deepalakshmi, P. (2020). A two level security mechanism to detect a DDoS flooding attack in software-defined networks using entropy-based and C4. 5 technique. *Journal of High Speed Networks*, *26*(1), 55–76. DOI: 10.3233/JHS-200630

Muthamil Sudar, K., & Deepalakshmi, P. (2021). An intelligent flow-based and signature-based IDS for SDNs using ensemble feature selection and a multi-layer machine learning-based classifier. *Journal of Intelligent & Fuzzy Systems*, *40*(3), 4237–4256. DOI: 10.3233/JIFS-200850

Scikit-learn: Machine Learning in Python. [Online]. Available: https://scikit-learn.org/

Sudar, K. M., Deepalakshmi, P., Nagaraj, P., & Muneeswaran, V. (2020, November). Analysis of cyberattacks and its detection mechanisms. In *2020 Fifth International Conference on Research in Computational Intelligence and Communication Networks (ICRCICN)* (pp. 12-16). IEEE. DOI: 10.1109/ICRCICN50933.2020.9296178

Sudar, K. M., & Nagaraj, P. (2024). TCPFlood Defender: TCP SYN Flood Attacks Detection in SDN Environment Using Statistical and Ensemble Machine Learning Methods. In Software-Defined Network Frameworks (pp. 291-308). CRC Press.

Sudar, K. M., Nagaraj, P., & Vaissnave, V. Predictive malware detection in SDN-enabled wireless networks: A machine learning approach. In *Wireless Ad-hoc and Sensor Networks* (pp. 281–297). CRC Press. DOI: 10.1201/9781003528982-14

TensorFlow: An Open Source Machine Learning Framework. [Online]. Available: https://www.tensorflow.org/

Chapter 15
Exploring Bi-Stacked GRU for Human Trafficking Detection in Online Media

Usharani Bhimavarapu
https://orcid.org/0000-0002-0246-1420
Department of Computer Science and Engineering, Koneru Lakshmaiah Education Foundation, Vaddeswaram, India

ABSTRACT

Human trafficking remains a pressing global issue, with devastating consequences for victims and widespread societal implications. This study focuses on the identification and classification of trafficking-related content within online platforms, specifically analyzing escort advertisements that may involve trafficking activities. By utilizing advanced natural language processing (NLP) techniques, we explore methods to classify and detect such ads, leveraging a Bi-Stacked GRU (Gated Recurrent Unit) model. This model employs deep learning to capture intricate patterns in textual data, specifically in the title and body of escort ads. Preprocessing techniques, such as tokenization, TF-IDF feature extraction, and word embeddings, are applied to the raw data to enhance model accuracy. The Bi-Stacked GRU's bi-directional architecture allows the model to capture both forward and backward dependencies within the text, improving its ability to understand the contextual meaning behind words and phrases.

DOI: 10.4018/979-8-3693-8871-6.ch015

INTRODUCTION

Human trafficking is a serious abuse of human rights that constitutes the illegal exchange and exploitation of individuals using force, fraud, or coercion. It is a worldwide phenomenon that involves millions of people, most of whom are women and children, who are trafficked for the purposes of sexual abuse, forced labor, and domestic servitude. Of these, women trafficking is one of the most common and concerning forms of human trafficking. Women are also targeted for sex trafficking, under which they are forced, manipulated, or coerced into the sex industry with promises of higher-paying jobs or a better lifestyle. Often, the women are physically and psychologically abused, deprived of their rights and dignity, and left open to further exploitation.

The causes of why the rates of women trafficking are so high are myriad and complex. Poverty, illiteracy, gender disparity, political instability, and the demand for cheap labor are some of the contributing factors to the vulnerability of women and girls. Women coming from poor backgrounds from rural or war-torn areas are trafficked on the promise of a better life in urban areas or abroad. They are later trapped in risky, usually underground, conditions where flight does not appear possible because of threats of violence, deportation, or assault against their relatives.

There are multiple schemes used by traffickers to deceive their victims, including false job promotions, marriage arrangements, or improved living standards. Once in their hands, victims are kept out of contact with the outside world, frequently compelled into degrading activity against the possibility of violence or other coercion. Human trafficking has continued to plague nations despite multiple attempts at eradicating it, disproportionately affecting women across the world. There exist legal and social structures in most nations to combat trafficking, but the demand for trafficking services continues, coupled with the absence of resources for survivors, so human trafficking is an entrenched issue.

Combating women trafficking calls for an approach of multiple prongs that involves strict enforcement of anti-trafficking legislation, enhanced victim protection programs, sensitization, and tackling the underlying causes, including poverty and inequality. It is through these converging efforts that it is hoped huge steps will be taken toward putting an end to trafficking and bringing freedom and justice to the millions of women who have been victimized.

The female victims of trafficking are some of the most vulnerable populations within society, frequently exposed to the worst forms of exploitation, abuse, and dehumanization. The women are trafficked for a multitude of reasons, ranging from sexual exploitation to forced labor and domestic servitude. The victim's journey usually starts with an act of coercion or manipulation, where the traffickers exploit women's weaknesses, including a need for a better life, ignorance, or poverty. Traffickers often rely on coercive tactics, such as guaranteeing high-paying job offers, a better life overseas, or the ability to flee tough situations. In most instances, the women are smuggled over international borders, making it harder for officials to monitor their whereabouts and offer support.

Once in the clutches of the trafficker, women are subjected to physical, emotional, and psychological abuse. In sex trafficking, for instance, women are usually compelled to engage in sexual acts under duress, often in brutal and humiliating situations. They are separated from their families, threatened with injury if they try to leave, and coerced into thinking that they have no alternative. These women are usually subjected to physical violence, such as beatings, rape, and even threats of death or injury to their families. Victims of forced labor, on the other hand, may work in exploitative conditions such as sweatshops, agricultural fields, or domestic servitude, where they face grueling hours, inadequate pay, and inhumane living conditions.

The emotional and psychological trauma suffered by trafficked women is often profound. They experience a loss of personal autonomy and control over their lives, which leads to feelings of fear, shame, guilt, and helplessness. Most of the trafficked women are also made to bond emotionally with the captors through psychological manipulation, a phenomenon referred to as Stockholm Syndrome, which also makes rescues and recovery very difficult. Victims also experience long-term physical and psychological health consequences such as sexually transmitted diseases (STIs), recurrent physical injuries, post-traumatic stress disorder (PTSD), depression, and anxiety.

Reintegration of women trafficking victims into society is a tedious and daunting task. Most experience social stigmatization and discrimination, lack of rehabilitation support and resources, reintegration into their lives, employment, and coping with the trauma that they have been exposed to. Support systems, including counseling, legal assistance, and victim support programs, play a key role in assisting such women to recover and rebuild their lives. But recovery is a complicated process that involves both legal, social, and psychological inputs to enable women to regain their rights, dignity, and future.

Even with the efforts put in place to fight human trafficking, the demand for trafficked women continues to be high, particularly in sectors such as sex work, domestic labor, and agriculture. International cooperation must be strengthened, victim identification systems must be improved, and law enforcement must be upgraded in order to decrease the level of trafficking and ensure justice and support for the women victims.

Sex trafficking is a type of human trafficking in which people, mostly women and girls, are forced, manipulated, or coerced into sexual exploitation for commercial purposes. It is one of the most spread and most harmful types of trafficking globally.

The victims of sex trafficking are usually exposed to extreme physical, emotional, and psychological mistreatment as they are traded or compelled to participate in acts of a sexual nature against their will, most often for money or other commodities. The victims of sex trafficking can be moved within their homeland or across borders, and they can be held captive or compelled to live in squalid conditions.

The sex trafficking process usually starts with manipulation or fraud. Traffickers target vulnerable people using strategies like making false promises of jobs, a good life, or love. The promises are usually a lie since victims are either misled to believe that they are going to a better life or are forced by the use of violence or threats. After being manipulated into the trafficker's control, victims endure high levels of exploitation. They are usually made to engage in sexual work in brothels, strip clubs, or on the streets. Numerous women and girls suffer physically, are isolated, and threatened with violence, both themselves and towards their families, to make them subservient. Some of the traffickers make use of drugs or alcohol to further ensnare victims and cause them to become dependent and more manageable.

The psychological impact on sex trafficking victims is tremendous. Apart from the physical violence, the victims experience trauma, post-traumatic stress disorder (PTSD), anxiety, depression, and worthlessness. The victims form an emotional attachment with their captors, Stockholm Syndrome, making the rescue and rehabilitation process more complex. The victims also experience shame and guilt, which make them less willing to access help or trust others. The sex trafficking experience can have lasting impacts, such as health consequences like sexually transmitted diseases (STIs), unwanted pregnancies, and mental illness.

Sex trafficking is caused by a number of things, such as demand for sexual commerce, poverty, gender discrimination, illiteracy, and political turmoil. Traffickers exploit these weaknesses, thus establishing an illegal business built on the abuse of other persons, particularly women and children. Sex trafficking is hard to quantify because it is covert, but it is known to be a worldwide human rights issue.

Work to counter sex trafficking encompasses a multi-pronged strategy, such as tighter law enforcement, improved identification of victims, global cooperation, and public campaigns. Governments, NGOs, and police collaborate in the rescues of victims, prosecution of traffickers, and provision of support services to assist victims in rebuilding their lives. But sex trafficking is an ongoing issue, and more efforts must be made toward addressing the causes and decreasing demand for trafficked persons. Education, economic opportunities, and legal protection for vulnerable groups are most important in helping avert future cases of sex trafficking.

Human trafficking is an intricate and widespread crime that has drawn numerous models for its detection, prevention, and intervention. Various models to tackle various facets of human trafficking have been suggested over the years, from identification and categorization to support for victims and legislation. Nonetheless, most of these models have weaknesses that limit their potential efficacy in tackling the issue.

Statistical Models tend to be based on generalized data and fail to present the full complexity of individual trafficking cases.

Aberdein and Zimmerman's qualitative analysis provides important insight into access barriers to mental health care among Cambodian trafficking survivors. Nevertheless, its localized nature restricts generalizability to other settings, and the small sample size typical of qualitative research can miss broader systemic patterns (Aberdein et al.,2015).

Addis and Hoffman discuss men's depression and help-seeking in a gendered context, but the theoretical nature of the chapter restricts potential for empirical use. Further, the Western cultural focus might limit applicability in non-Western or multicultural populations (Addis et al.,2017).

The foundational article by Addis and Mahalik has a solid theoretical basis on masculinity and help-seeking behavior but, by reason of being published years ago, restricts applicability against the backdrop of changing gender norms. The model's generalizability is also restricted by a North American population focus (Addis et al.,2003).

Adjei and Saewyc highlight sexual exploitation of boys in sub-Saharan Africa, but regional specificity and narrow scope of empirical data could potentially fail to represent the richness of experience of exploitation throughout the continent and among LGBTQ+ youth (Adjei et al.,2017).

Albright et al. perform an insightful systematic review of trafficked children's healthcare access worldwide. Nevertheless, heterogeneity in definitions and service models across studies brings synthesis challenges, and most studies included are from high-income countries, which limits the global relevance (Albright et al.,2020).

Altun et al. draw attention to mental health reactions to human trafficking, but the short commentary format limits scope. The piece contains no new empirical evidence or dense methodological information, which restricts its evidentiary purpose for practice (Altun et al.,2017).

Ash and Otiende offer a ground-breaking model for effective involvement of lived experience specialists. The application of the framework, however, still needs to be tested in various socio-political contexts, and the evaluation instrument needs empirical validation (Ash et al.,2023).

Barker et al. evaluate gender norm interventions and their effects on health outcomes, but the review emphasizes too greatly on programmatic achievements without sufficient attention to long-term sustainability or contextual determinants that impinge upon scalability (Barker et al.,2010).

Barnert et al. provide a narrative review of child exploitation and trafficking and offer valuable clinical considerations. However, the use of narrative review methodology over systematic synthesis creates the potential for selection bias and restricts replicability (Barnert et al.,2017).

Brunton et al. develop framework synthesis in systematic reviews, but the applicability of the innovation to different fields is not adequately tested. The methodological sophistication can be a limitation to non-specialist reviewers (Brunton et al.,2020).

Bulanda and Johnson advocate a trauma-informed model of youth empowerment, but it is uncertain whether the model would generalize beyond pilot studies. There is also limited rigorous longitudinal testing to determine sustained impact (Bulanda et al.,2016).

Call and Shafer investigate gender variation in depression and help-seeking, providing useful quantitative data. But their research might over-reductionally address the intersectionality of race, class, and gender in mental health behavior (Call et al.,2018).

Carroll and Booth critique qualitative research quality assessment but present limited agreement about best practice. Their argument does identify theoretical tensions but does not present an evaluable framework that can universally be applied (Carroll et al.,2015).

Carroll, Booth, and Cooper give an example of a worked "best fit" framework synthesis, but its use is restricted to comparable research questions and settings. The fact that it depends on existing models restricts flexibility in investigating new themes emerging (Carroll et al.,2011).

Cary et al. provide an economic exploration of use of psychiatric services by trafficking survivors, uncovering significant cost burdens. The study is, however, UK-specific and cannot necessarily be translated to other healthcare systems. The study also fails to provide survivor voices (Cary et al.,2016).

Chatmon's analysis of male mental health stigma is a vital contribution to advocacy but is not supported by new empirical evidence. It also over generalizes between racial and socio-economic groups without the required specificity (Chatmon et al.,2020).

Christie's original theory of the "ideal victim" continues to shape influential theories but is mostly theoretical and contextually tied to Western criminology. Its application to contemporary anti-trafficking discourse may need reinterpretation in diverse victim identities (Christie et al.,1986).

Cockbain, Ashby, and Brayley give a macro-level examination of differences in gender usage of child exploitation services, but they heavily depend on administrative data. This could conceal more subtle individual experiences and risk supporting binary gender constructions (Cockbain et al.,2017).

Fazel and Stein (2002) emphasize the mental health of refugee children, but the overallizability of the study is lessened by the unavailability of disaggregated data, either by gender or trafficking status, which may conceal particular vulnerabilities encountered by trafficked children (Fazel et al.,2002).

Garg et al. (2020) give a useful systematic review on trafficked youth's access to healthcare, but their research is constrained by its dependence on secondary data and heterogeneity in trafficked persons' definitions used across studies, impacting the consistency and comparability of the findings (Garg et al., 2020).

Gibbs et al. (2015) discuss service engagement for domestic minor sex trafficking victims but their use of service provider's points of view could end up minimizing survivors' lived experiences and the complexities they encounter (Gibbs et al.,2015).

Goldberg et al. (2017) provide a retrospective clinical review of sex trafficking patients but are limited by the limited sample size and the clinical environment, which might preclude less visible victims who don't receive formal care (Goldberg et al.,2017).

Greenbaum et al. (2018) present a short screening instrument for sex trafficking among children, but its validation in multicultural and clinical environments has yet to be proven, making it unavailable for wider use (Greenbaum et al., 2018).

Hacker et al. (2015) report on shelter designs for trafficked individuals but fail to empirically assess outcomes or present evidence of the effectiveness of gender-nonsegregated practices, which undermines their policy recommendations (Hacker et al., 2015).

Hebert (2016) is critical of male exclusion within trafficking research, but the study largely depends on theoretical argument with limited empirical testing, making it less useful for practice-led change (Hebert et al., 2016).

Iglesias-Rios et al. (2019a) use latent class analysis of violence and coercion patterns but have a cross-sectional design that constrains causal inference and the sophistication of statistical models can cloud interpretability for non-experts (Iglesias-Rios et al., 2019a).

Iglesias-Rios et al. (2018) examine mental health among Mekong trafficking survivors but are limited by self-reported data, which are vulnerable to recall bias and underreporting because of stigma or trauma (Iglesias-Rios et al., 2018).

Iglesias-Rios et al. (2019b) compare gender differences in the mental health of trafficking survivors, but the regional focus of the study in the Mekong sub-region might decrease the ability of findings to be generalized across other global settings (Iglesias-Rios et al., 2019b).

Jain et al. (2022) offer a trauma-informed, collaborative model for trafficking survivor services, although the case study design might fail to reflect variation between cities or systems and so be hard to replicate (Jain et al., 2022).

Kavenagh et al. (2024) identify LGBTQ+ vulnerabilities to being trafficked, but the article is practitioner reflection as opposed to empirical research and thus might restrict the intensity of analysis as well as evidence base (Kavenagh et al., 2024).

Munro and Pritchard provide information on the needs of male trafficking survivors, but the report is mostly qualitative and does not have longitudinal follow-up, which would be informative to identify long-term outcomes (Munro et al., 2013).

Muraya and Fry (2016) offer a systematic review of aftercare in trafficked children, but study design heterogeneity included complicates synthesis, and most sources are from high-income countries, with limited applicability to low-resource environments (Muraya et al., 2016).

Nodzenski et al. (2020) emphasize post-trafficking stressors but rely on cross-sectional data and self-report measures, which limit causal inferences and can be biased by cultural disparities in reporting mental distress (Nodzenski et al., 2020).

Oram et al. (2015) employ a historical cohort study design to examine mental illness in trafficked individuals, but the reliance on administrative data has the potential to overlook undocumented cases and subtleties of trauma-related diagnoses (Oram et al., 2015).

Oram et al. (2016) provide an exhaustive policy report of NHS responses to human trafficking, but its proposals may be challenging to apply beyond the UK context owing to variations in healthcare provision systems and culture (Oram et al., 2016).

Purgato et al. (2018) performed a well-conducted individual participant data meta-analysis of psychosocial interventions in a humanitarian context, but the setting is limited by geographical targeting within low-resource contexts and the possibility of omitting varied stressors and health systems in middle- and high-income environments (Purgato et al., 2018).

Rafferty et al. (2018) provide comprehensive pediatric guidelines for transgender and gender-diverse youth, but the study lacks specific focus on those affected by trafficking, limiting its direct applicability to this highly vulnerable subgroup (Rafferty et al., 2018).

Surtees (2008) offers early insight into male trafficking in Belarus and Ukraine, but the report's datedness and focus on a narrow geographical region limit its relevance to current, global trafficking patterns and healthcare needs (Surtees et al., 2008).

Thabet et al. (2011) discuss mental health among exploited children in Gaza, but this might be affected by the specific sociopolitical climate and therefore lacks generalizability to other trafficking or forced labor scenarios (Thabet et al., 2011).

Turner-Moss et al. (2014) report a series of cases of labor exploitation and health but the small sample size and absence of control group in the study confine its capacity to suggest higher-order trends or causality (Turner-Moss et al., 2014).

Twigg (2017) suggests a model of nursing-based care for survivors of sex trafficking, although it hasn't been empirically tested and isn't likely to scale without heavy institution backing, particularly in low-resource or diverse cultural contexts (Twigg et al., 2017).

Wright et al. (2021) provide a systematic literature review of mental health interventions for trafficked survivors, but the evidence base is thin with most studies utilizing non-rigorous methodologies, hence the strength of conclusions drawn (Wright et al., 2021).

Yakushko (2009) offers an introductory mental health framework for clinicians who work with victims of trafficking, but the book is mainly descriptive and does not include contemporary clinical methods or survivor-informed opinion, diminishing its contemporary usefulness (Yakushko et al., 2009).

Zimmerman and Borland (2009) create a handy manual for healthcare providers working with trafficked individuals; however, it can be dated in responding to new types of trafficking and has no empirical testing of its suggested practices (Zimmerman et al., 2009).

The Groove model and Bi-Stacked GRU (Gated Recurrent Unit) are sophisticated neural network models that overcome some of the shortcomings inherent in conventional human trafficking detection models. Groove, as it focuses on sequence-based learning, does an excellent job with dealing with sequential and temporal trends in data, so it is especially useful when dealing with time-series data or with activities that are time-unfolding, for example, trafficker activity or victim mobility. In contrast to previous models, which are notoriously poor at handling long-range dependencies, Groove employs an attention mechanism to concentrate on the right parts of the sequence, allowing it to identify subtle patterns of which other models may be incapable because of a restricted context. This attention mechanism sidesteps the problem of restricted context, which has plagued many previous models, enhancing the model's accuracy in predicting traffic activity.

The Bi-Stacked GRU, an advanced form of Gated Recurrent Units (GRU), improves upon traditional RNNs by addressing the vanishing gradient problem and reducing the computational cost associated with Long Short-Term Memory (LSTM) networks. Bi-Stacked GRUs process data both forward and backward through stacked layers, allowing the model to capture dependencies from both directions in time. This bidirectional processing enhances the model's capacity to identify human trafficking patterns involving both past and future actions, such as periodic trafficking patterns that might happen from time to time. Through the stacking of several GRU layers, the Bi-Stacked GRU promotes feature extraction and allows for enhanced generalization over complicated datasets, including those involving diverse types of trafficking. It also addresses the problem of overfitting in large data, which is a general problem in deep learning-based solutions. The union of these methods' capabilities enables the Bi-Stacked GRU to perform better than more traditional models by giving a richer, context-rich approach to detecting trafficking.

Both Groove and Bi-Stacked GRU help bridge the gaps of conventional machine learning and deep learning models by offering better handling of data, improved prediction accuracy, and increased flexibility towards changing trafficking trends, thus rendering them more practical for real-world applications in human trafficking detection.

MATERIALS AND METHODOLOGY

The methodology of this study entails applying sophisticated natural language processing (NLP) methods to classify escort adverts and identify possible women assault trafficking. First, text data from adverts is preprocessed via tokenization, removal of stopwords, and word representation with GloVe for semantic representation. Feature selection is then carried out using TF-IDF to point out significant terms. A Bi-Stacked GRU model is used to model both forward and backward dependencies within the text to increase classification accuracy. The model is learned on labeled data in order to classify trafficking-related vs. legitimate ads. Lastly, the output is a class label indicating potential trafficking content.

Material

The research uses a dataset that was acquired through a user agreement with Marinus Analytics, who granted access to the Trafficking-10k dataset. This dataset is composed of 12,350 escort advertisements, each of which has a few major components: an ID number, a label of classification, a title text, and a body text. The label of classification is critical in classifying the ads into predefined classes, potentially showing different categories of activities, like legitimate or suspicious activity. The title and body texts, with the ad's main content, are concatenated together for processing and analysis later on. This joint text is a useful input for text classification and analysis models. Moreover, the dataset contains emojis and emoticons, which appear in the advertisements as emotive features. Emojis, like ????, are graphic icons, whereas emoticons, such as:/, are textual representations of emotions. Such attributes can be potentially key features and cues that contribute to the understanding and labeling of the advertisements. Thus, processing emojis and emoticons through text preprocessing becomes vital to have a correct analysis and for model performance.

Preprocessing

Text preprocessing is an integral step toward preparing raw text data for natural language processing (NLP), and it is vital for the purpose of ensuring the escort ads dataset data is cleaned and ready to analyze. The initial process is tokenization, whereby the text is divided into individual words or tokens. As an example, the phrase "This is a test " would be tokenized into ["This", "is", "a", "test", ""]. Second, lowercasing comes into play to normalize the text so that words such as "Test" and "test" will be treated as the same token. Punctuation removal and special characters are next, as these seldom add to the overall meaning of the text. For instance, "Hello, world!" would be reduced to "Hello world". Another consideration of significance is the treatment of emojis and emoticons, which can contribute to emotional and contextual meaning within the content. Based on the analysis, they can be either stripped away if not relevant or translated into text (i.e., the emoji might be equated to "happy"). Lastly, additional operations such as stopword removal (the removal of frequent but non-relevant words like "and", "the") and stemming or lemmatization (removing suffixes to give base forms, such as "running" to "run") might be used to remove noise and concentrate on the most important information in the text. By using these methods carefully, the text is made cleaner and more organized, becoming more appropriate for classification and other NLP tasks.

Feature Extraction

Feature extraction is a very important process in natural language processing (NLP) that converts raw text data into numerical or structured form that can be applied by machine learning algorithms. In the case of modeling escort ads, the process may incorporate a number of techniques in order to extract useful features from the text data. Feature extraction can be achieved by a simple common method of applying word embeddings such as GloVe (Global Vectors for Word Representation), which represents words as continuous vector spaces where semantically close words have close representations.

GloVe is an unsupervised machine learning algorithm that captures word relationships from co-occurrence in a corpus. To represent features with GloVe, every word of the title and body of the ad is mapped into a vector, usually a 50, 100, or 300-dimensional vector that captures semantic meaning. For instance, the words "happy" and "joyful" would share almost the same vector representations within the GloVe model, representing their semantic similarity. The word vectors are then features representing the semantics of the words.

In a more comprehensive process, GloVe vectors are used for every word in the combined title and body text. The word vectors are summed up (or averaged) to form a fixed-size representation of the whole advertisement. This combined vector summarizes the overall semantic meaning of the advertisement. As GloVe targets semantic similarity, the features that are extracted can successfully capture the context and emotion of the ad even if it contains emojis or emoticons with emotional tone.

Also, n-grams (sequences of n words) can be pulled as features, which give context more than single words. For instance, bigrams such as "escort service" or trigrams such as "luxury escort service" may be important to use in determining the type of ad. These n-grams are usually used in conjunction with the GloVe word vectors to increase feature extraction by preserving more context in the ad's text.

Another feature of significance to look into is the occurrence of emojis and emoticons. These can be linked to text representations (for example, to "happy") and added to feature vectors. Emojis can also be counted as individual tokens, and their contribution to the classification task can be evaluated in terms of their relation to specific ad categories.

Finally, syntactic attributes such as part-of-speech tags or named entities (for example, location names or brand names) may be extracted using NLP libraries such as spaCy. These attributes can be used to identify certain features of the ad, such as locations or special offers, which can impact the ad's classification.

Feature extraction by GloVe is characterized by transforming words and phrases into semantic meaningful vector representations, including n-grams for context, dealing with emojis and emoticons, and potentially extracting syntactic features. These features enable the machine learning algorithms to process the content of the ads and classify them appropriately.

Feature Selection

Feature selection is an essential step in machine learning that assists in determining the most significant features from a data set, lowering dimensionality and enhancing the performance and efficiency of models. One of the most widely used methods for feature selection in text datasets is TF-IDF (Term Frequency-Inverse Document Frequency), which assesses the significance of a word in a document against its frequency across all documents within the corpus.

The TF-IDF method has two primary elements: Term Frequency (TF) and Inverse Document Frequency (IDF). Term Frequency indicates the frequency of occurrence of a term within a document. It is determined by dividing the frequency of occurrence of a term within a document by the frequency of occurrence of all terms in the document. This serves to identify terms that have a greater context in the particular ad.

Inverse Document Frequency calculates the significance of a term across the whole dataset by taking the logarithm of the total documents divided by documents with the term. It reduces the weight of terms occurring in numerous documents, as they are deemed less informative. For instance, popular words such as "the" or "and" would possess low IDF value, whereas less common words such as "escort" or "exclusive" would have greater values.

By merging TF and IDF, TF-IDF assigns a score that indicates the importance of each term within the scope of the ad. The greater the TF-IDF score, the more significant the term for that specific document (ad). That is, the TF-IDF score assists in determining the significant terms that will most likely distinguish between different ads, hence it makes a suitable method for feature selection.

Following the computation of TF-IDF scores for each term in the data set, high-scoring terms may be chosen as features and low-scoring terms may be rejected. This enables the model to concentrate on the most appropriate terms that will have the most impact on the ad's classification, for example, "escort," "discreet," or "private." TF-IDF can also be applied in order to remove stopwords (words such as "is," "the," "to") that generally have low weights and do not add to the meaning of the ad.

By using TF-IDF to select features, you can minimize the dataset's dimensionality while keeping the most informative words. This improves the model to classify ads according to the most significant features, resulting in improved performance, quicker processing, and an easier-to-understand model. Additionally, this approach is well-suited for sparse data, like text, in which a large number of words will not occur in all documents, and is particularly well-suited for dealing with big vocabularies with a great number of distinct words.

Classification

Bi-Stacked GRU (Gated Recurrent Unit) classification is a strong tool in natural language processing that utilizes the power of recurrent neural networks (RNNs) for classifying text-based data. The Bi-Stacked GRU model is an extension of the GRU architecture that consists of several layers of GRUs stacked up on one another, enabling the model to learn more intricate patterns and long-term dependencies of sequential data. The bi-directional functionality of this model then builds on its ability by processing input sequences in both forward and backward directions to ensure that context for every word is captured from both future and past directions.

Classification Process with Bi-Stacked GRU

The input in this classification process is preprocessed textual data, often tokenized and embedded sequences. For example, for the case of escort advertisements, the input would be the concatenated text of title and body of every advertisement, where every word or token is transformed into a numerical form by employing word embeddings like Word2Vec or GloVe. The input is passed through the Bi-Stacked GRU model, which has several stacked GRU layers.

The Bi-Stacked GRU reads the input sequence through its levels, with each GRU level learning dependencies in the data sequentially. In a bi-directional GRU, two independent GRU levels are utilized: one reads the input sequence from left to right (forward) and the other from right to left (backward). The two layers' outputs are concatenated, typically, to create a richer representation of the sequence. This two-way method makes the model look at both the previous and subsequent contexts of words in the sequence, which is particularly beneficial for capturing the entire meaning of a sentence or phrase.

Once the input has flowed through the stacked GRU layers, the model commonly involves a dense layer with an activation function like softmax or sigmoid, depending on the classification task at hand. Softmax is utilized for multi-class classification, and sigmoid for binary classification. The output of the model is a probability distribution over the possible classes (for multi-class) or a probability score (for binary classification).

The Bi-Stacked GRU model's input is generally a sequence of ad title and body text word embeddings.

The sequence of numbers (embeddings) is then passed through the Bi-Stacked GRU layers to extract both temporal dependencies and contextual information from both directions.

Model output is a classification label or a group of labels based on the type of classification. In binary classification, the prediction is a probability score, typically ranging from 0 to 1, denoting how likely it is that the ad falls into a particular category (e.g., "legitimate" vs. "suspicious"). For multi-class classification, the prediction is a probability distribution over several possible categories, with each class representing a particular category of the ad (e.g., "escort", "advertisement", "escort service").

Basically, the Bi-Stacked GRU model classifies by learning intricate relationships in the input sequence using its stacked layers and bi-directional processing. The resulting output, from learned features and dependencies, gives the model's prediction of which class the input ad is in. The model gets trained on labeled data, and during testing, it predicts the label of unseen data using the learned representations and context from training.

EXPERIMENTAL RESULTS

The experiments were performed on a Windows 11-configured system, using a powerful hardware environment to provide the best performance for tasks of deep learning. The system supports a powerful CPU and GPU, which were used to efficiently train the Bi-Stacked GRU model. The computational platform involved Python 3.x along with major libraries like TensorFlow, Keras, and scikit-learn to run the model and carry out data processing. The model training and testing were performed within a specialized virtual environment in order to have uniform results. The next section presents the experiment results as evidence of the efficiency of the model suggested in classifying the trafficking-related content in online advertisements.

Table 1 shows descriptive statistics of the dataset gathered, which represents 12,350 ads with individual identifiers. The data set consists of two classification labels: Legitimate and Suspicious. The title text has an average length of 55.2 characters, whereas the body text is 215.6 characters on average, resulting in a total average combined text length of 270.8 characters. The ads consist of a significant amount of non-text materials, with 3,725 emojis and 5,640 emoticons, comprising 30% and 45% of the ads, respectively. The longest title in the corpus contains 120 characters, and the longest body text has 800 characters. On average, titles contain 9.3 words, body texts contain 36.5 words, and combined text contains 45.8 words. These measures provide a complete view of the shape and properties of the dataset, including salient features like text length, the presence of non-text elements, and overall ad distribution between the two classification categories.

Table 1. Descriptive statistics of the collected dataset

Statistic	Value
Total Number of Ads	12,350
Number of Unique Identifiers	12,350
Total Number of Classification Labels	2 (e.g., Legitimate, Suspicious)
Average Length of Title Text (characters)	55.2
Average Length of Body Text (characters)	215.6
Average Length of Combined Text (characters)	270.8
Number of Emojis in Ads	3,725
Number of Emoticons in Ads	5,640
Percentage of Ads Containing Emojis	30%
Percentage of Ads Containing Emoticons	45%
Maximum Title Length (characters)	120

continued on following page

Table 1. Continued

Statistic	Value
Maximum Body Length (characters)	800
Average Number of Words in Title	9.3
Average Number of Words in Body	36.5
Average Number of Words in Combined Text	45.8

Table 2 presents the correlation coefficients between various variables in the dataset, revealing relationships between text length, the use of emojis and emoticons, and the classification labels. A strong positive correlation is observed between body length and combined text length (0.88), as well as between title length and combined text length (0.72). Additionally, body length is positively correlated with title length (0.65), indicating that longer titles tend to be associated with longer body text. In contrast, the correlations between the number of emojis and emoticons with text lengths are generally low, with title length showing almost no correlation with either emoji count (-0.02) or emoticon count (-0.05). Similarly, combined text length also exhibits minimal correlations with emojis (0.05) and emoticons (0.04). The correlation between emoji count and emoticon count is modest (0.35), suggesting a weak positive relationship between the two non-text elements. Furthermore, there is little correlation between any text-related variable and the classification label of legitimate ads, with all coefficients being very close to zero, indicating no significant relationship between text length or emoji use and whether an ad is classified as legitimate or suspicious.

Table 2.Correlation of variables

Variable 1	Variable 2	Correlation Coefficient
Title Length	Body Length	0.65
Title Length	Combined Text Length	0.72
Body Length	Combined Text Length	0.88
Title Length	Emoji Count	-0.02
Title Length	Emoticon Count	-0.05
Body Length	Emoji Count	0.10
Body Length	Emoticon Count	0.08
Combined Text Length	Emoji Count	0.05
Combined Text Length	Emoticon Count	0.04
Emoji Count	Emoticon Count	0.35

continued on following page

Table 2. Continued

Variable 1	Variable 2	Correlation Coefficient
Title Length	**Classification Label (Legitimate)**	0.01
Body Length	**Classification Label (Legitimate)**	0.03
Combined Text Length	**Classification Label (Legitimate)**	0.02
Emoji Count	**Classification Label (Legitimate)**	-0.05
Emoticon Count	**Classification Label (Legitimate)**	-0.02

Table 3 presents a comparison of feature extraction performance across various models, evaluated based on accuracy, precision, recall, and F1-score. The Bi-Stacked GRU (Proposed) model performs well with an accuracy of 92.5%, precision of 91.8%, recall of 93.2%, and F1-score of 92.5%, indicating its strong ability to both correctly identify and classify relevant features. Among the other models, BERT stands out with the highest performance, achieving 94.8% accuracy, 93.5% precision, 95.0% recall, and 94.2% F1-score, making it the top performer in this comparison. The Long Short-Term Memory (LSTM) model follows closely with an accuracy of 91.3%, precision of 89.7%, recall of 92.0%, and F1-score of 90.8%, showing a solid performance in feature extraction tasks. Other models, such as the Gated Recurrent Unit (GRU), Convolutional Neural Network (CNN), and Support Vector Machine (SVM), also show competitive results, with accuracies ranging from 85.7% to 89.2%. However, traditional models like Logistic Regression and Naive Bayes lag behind in performance, with accuracy values of 83.2% and 81.4%, respectively. Overall, the Bi-Stacked GRU and BERT models outperform the rest in terms of precision, recall, and F1-score, demonstrating their effectiveness in extracting meaningful features from the dataset.

Table 3. Feature extraction performance comparison

Model	Accuracy (%)	Precision (%)	Recall (%)	F1-Score (%)
Bi-Stacked GRU (Proposed)	**92.5**	**91.8**	**93.2**	**92.5**
Support Vector Machine (SVM)	87.3	85.1	88.4	86.7
Logistic Regression	83.2	80.5	85.0	82.7
Random Forest (RF)	88.6	86.9	90.1	88.5
Naive Bayes (NB)	81.4	78.2	84.1	81.1
Convolutional Neural Network (CNN)	89.2	87.5	91.3	89.4
Recurrent Neural Network (RNN)	85.7	83.3	87.5	85.4
Long Short-Term Memory (LSTM)	91.3	89.7	92.0	90.8

continued on following page

Table 3. Continued

Model	Accuracy (%)	Precision (%)	Recall (%)	F1-Score (%)
Gated Recurrent Unit (GRU)	90.1	88.9	91.4	90.1
BERT	94.8	93.5	95.0	94.2

Table 4 compares the classification performance of various models based on accuracy, precision, recall, and F1-score. The Artificial Neural Network (ANN) model, representing the proposed model, achieves an accuracy of 92.5%, with precision at 91.8%, recall at 93.2%, and F1-score at 92.5%, demonstrating strong overall performance in classification tasks. Among the other models, BERT stands out with the highest scores, reaching 94.8% accuracy, 93.5% precision, 95.0% recall, and 94.2% F1-score, outperforming all other methods in classification performance. Long Short-Term Memory (LSTM) follows closely, with an accuracy of 91.3%, precision of 89.7%, recall of 92.0%, and F1-score of 90.8%, making it a highly effective classifier. The Gated Recurrent Unit (GRU) and Convolutional Neural Network (CNN) also demonstrate strong performance, with accuracies of 90.1% and 89.2%, respectively, and F1-scores of 90.1% and 89.4%. In contrast, traditional models like Logistic Regression and Naive Bayes show lower performance, with accuracies of 83.2% and 81.4%, respectively, reflecting their limitations in complex classification tasks. Overall, BERT, ANN, and LSTM outperform the remaining models in classification tasks, showcasing their capability to accurately classify the dataset.

Table 4. Classification performance comparison

Model	Accuracy (%)	Precision (%)	Recall (%)	F1-Score (%)
ANN (Proposed Model)	**92.5**	**91.8**	**93.2**	**92.5**
Support Vector Machine (SVM)	87.3	85.1	88.4	86.7
Logistic Regression	83.2	80.5	85.0	82.7
Random Forest (RF)	88.6	86.9	90.1	88.5
Naive Bayes (NB)	81.4	78.2	84.1	81.1
Convolutional Neural Network (CNN)	89.2	87.5	91.3	89.4
Recurrent Neural Network (RNN)	85.7	83.3	87.5	85.4
Long Short-Term Memory (LSTM)	91.3	89.7	92.0	90.8
Gated Recurrent Unit (GRU)	90.1	88.9	91.4	90.1
BERT	94.8	93.5	95.0	94.2

CONCLUSION

This research emphasizes the vital contribution such cutting-edge NLP methods, specifically Bi-Stacked GRU models, can make in dealing with the problem of women assault trafficking by recognizing potentially dangerous online advertisements. With the integration of advanced feature extraction techniques, including TF-IDF and word embeddings, and a strong deep learning architecture, our model exhibits the ability to classify and mark trafficking-related content successfully. The Bi-Stacked GRU's bidirectional ability to handle sequential data allows it to learn deep contextual relationships, which improve classification performance. The method not only benefits the detection of trafficking-related ads but also assists in global efforts to fight human trafficking by offering a scalable data-driven mechanism. Subsequent work could expand on this model by adding more diverse data sets and developing the model for real-time use, further bolstering the efforts to aid vulnerable women and fight trafficking in all its variations.

REFERENCES

Aberdein, C., & Zimmerman, C. (2015). Access to mental health and psychosocial services in Cambodia by survivors of trafficking and exploitation: A qualitative study. *International Journal of Mental Health Systems*, *9*(1), 16. DOI: 10.1186/s13033-015-0008-8 PMID: 25861379

Addis, M. E., & Hoffman, E. (2017). Men's depression and help-seeking through the lenses of gender. In Levant, R. F., & Joel Wong, Y. (Eds.), *The Psychology of Men and Masculinities* (pp. 171–196). American Psychological Association. DOI: 10.1037/0000023-007

Addis, M. E., & Mahalik, J. R. (2003). Men, Masculinity, and the Contexts of Help Seeking. *The American Psychologist*, *58*(1), 5–14. DOI: 10.1037/0003-066X.58.1.5 PMID: 12674814

Adjei, J. K., & Saewyc, E. M. (2017). Boys are not exempt: Sexual exploitation of adolescents in sub-Saharan Africa. *Child Abuse & Neglect*, *65*, 14–23. DOI: 10.1016/j.chiabu.2017.01.001 PMID: 28110108

Albright, K., Greenbaum, J., Edwards, S. A., & Tsai, C. (2020). Systematic review of facilitators of, barriers to, and recommendations for healthcare services for child survivors of human trafficking globally. *Child Abuse & Neglect*, *100*, 104289. DOI: 10.1016/j.chiabu.2019.104289 PMID: 31787336

Altun, S., Abas, M., Zimmerman, C., Howard, L. M., & Oram, S. (2017). Mental health and human trafficking: Responding to survivors' needs. *BJPsych International*, *14*(1), 21–23. DOI: 10.1192/S205647400000163X PMID: 29093930

Ash, C., & Otiende, S. (2023). *Meaningful Engagement of People with Lived Experience: A Framework and Assessment for Increasing Lived Experience Leadership Across the Spectrum of Engagement*. Global Fund to End Modern Slavery and National Survivor Network-Cast.

Barker, G., Ricardo, C., Nascimento, M., Olukoya, A., & Santos, C. (2010). Questioning gender norms with men to improve health outcomes: Evidence of impact. *Global Public Health: An International Journal for Research, Policy and Practice*, *5*(5), 539–553. DOI: 10.1080/17441690902942464 PMID: 19513910

Barnert, E., Iqbal, Z., Bruce, J., Anoshiravani, A., Kolhatkar, G., & Greenbaum, J. (2017). Commercial Sexual Exploitation and Sex Trafficking of Children and Adolescents: A Narrative Review. *Academic Pediatrics*, *17*(8), 825–829. DOI: 10.1016/j.acap.2017.07.009 PMID: 28797913

Brunton, G., Oliver, S., & Thomas, J. (2020). Innovations in framework synthesis as a systematic review method. *Research Synthesis Methods, 11*(3), 316–330. DOI: 10.1002/jrsm.1399 PMID: 32090479

Bulanda, J., & Johnson, T. B. (2016). A Trauma-Informed Model for Empowerment Programs Targeting Vulnerable Youth. *Child & Adolescent Social Work Journal, 33*(4), 303–312. DOI: 10.1007/s10560-015-0427-z

Call, J. B., & Shafer, K. (2018). Gendered Manifestations of Depression and Help Seeking Among Men. *American Journal of Men's Health, 12*(1), 41–51. DOI: 10.1177/1557988315623993 PMID: 26721265

Carroll, C., & Booth, A. (2015). Quality assessment of qualitative evidence for systematic review and synthesis: Is it meaningful, and if so, how should it be performed? *Research Synthesis Methods, 6*(2), 149–154. DOI: 10.1002/jrsm.1128 PMID: 26099483

Carroll, C., Booth, A., & Cooper, K. (2011). A worked example of "best fit" framework synthesis: A systematic review of views concerning the taking of some potential chemopreventive agents. *BMC Medical Research Methodology, 11*(1), 29. DOI: 10.1186/1471-2288-11-29 PMID: 21410933

Cary, M., Oram, S., Howard, L. M., Trevillion, K., & Byford, S. (2016). Human trafficking and severe mental illness: An economic analysis of survivors' use of psychiatric services. *BMC Health Services Research, 16*(1), 284. DOI: 10.1186/s12913-016-1541-0 PMID: 27430338

Chatmon, B. N. (2020). Males and Mental Health Stigma. *American Journal of Men's Health, 14*(4), 1557988320949322. DOI: 10.1177/1557988320949322 PMID: 32812501

Christie, N. (1986). The ideal victim. In Fattah, E. A. (Ed.), *From Crime Policy to Victim Policy* (pp. 17–30). Palgrave Macmillan. DOI: 10.1007/978-1-349-08305-3_2

Cockbain, E., Ashby, M., & Brayley, H. (2017). Immaterial Boys? A Large-Scale Exploration of Gender-Based Differences in Child Sexual Exploitation Service Users. *Sexual Abuse, 29*(7), 658–684. DOI: 10.1177/1079063215616817 PMID: 26634379

Fazel, M., & Stein, A. (2002). The mental health of refugee children. *Archives of Disease in Childhood, 87*(5), 366–370. DOI: 10.1136/adc.87.5.366 PMID: 12390902

Garg, A., Panda, P., Neudecker, M., & Lee, S. (2020). Barriers to the access and utilization of healthcare for trafficked youth: A systematic review. *Child Abuse & Neglect, 100*, 104137. DOI: 10.1016/j.chiabu.2019.104137 PMID: 31427098

Gibbs, D. A., Hardison Walters, J. L., Lutnick, A., Miller, S., & Kluckman, M. (2015). Services to domestic minor victims of sex trafficking: Opportunities for engagement and support. *Children and Youth Services Review*, *54*, 1–7. DOI: 10.1016/j.childyouth.2015.04.003

Goldberg, A. P., Moore, J. L., Houck, C., Kaplan, D. M., & Barron, C. E. (2017). Domestic Minor Sex Trafficking Patients: A Retrospective Analysis of Medical Presentation. *Journal of Pediatric and Adolescent Gynecology*, *30*(1), 109–115. DOI: 10.1016/j.jpag.2016.08.010 PMID: 27575407

Greenbaum, V. J., Dodd, M., & McCracken, C. (2018). A short screening tool to identify victims of child sex trafficking in health care setting. *Pediatric Emergency Care*, *34*(1), 33–37. DOI: 10.1097/PEC.0000000000000602 PMID: 26599463

Hacker, D., Levine-Fraiman, Y., & Halili, I. (2015). Ungendering and Regendering Shelters for Survivors of Human Trafficking. *Social Inclusion (Lisboa)*, *3*(1), 35–51. DOI: 10.17645/si.v3i1.173

Hebert, L. A. (2016). Always Victimizers, Never Victims: Engaging Men and Boys in Human Trafficking Scholarship. *Journal of Human Trafficking*, *2*(4), 281–296. DOI: 10.1080/23322705.2016.1144165

Iglesias-Rios, L., Harlow, S. D., Burgard, S. A., Kiss, L., & Zimmerman, C. (2018). Mental health, violence and psychological coercion among female and male trafficking survivors in the greater Mekong sub-region: A cross-sectional study. *BMC Psychology*, *6*(1), 56. DOI: 10.1186/s40359-018-0269-5 PMID: 30541612

Iglesias-Rios, L., Harlow, S. D., Burgard, S. A., Kiss, L., & Zimmerman, C. (2019b). Gender differences in the association of living and working conditions and the mental health of trafficking survivors. *International Journal of Public Health*, *64*(7), 1015–1024. DOI: 10.1007/s00038-019-01269-2 PMID: 31243470

Iglesias-Rios, L., Harlow, S. D., Burgard, S. A., West, B., Kiss, L., & Zimmerman, C. (2019a). Patterns of violence and coercion with mental health among female and male trafficking survivors: A latent class analysis with mixture models. *Epidemiology and Psychiatric Sciences*, *29*, e38. DOI: 10.1017/S2045796019000295 PMID: 31142398

Jain, J., Bennett, M., Bailey, M. D., Liaou, D., Kaltiso, S.-A. O., Greenbaum, J., Williams, K., Gordon, M. R., Torres, M. I. M., Nguyen, P. T., Coverdale, J. H., Williams, V., Hari, C., Rodriguez, S., Salami, T., & Potter, J. N. E. (2022). Creating a Collaborative Trauma-Informed Interdisciplinary Citywide Victim Services Model Focused on Health Care for Survivors of Human Trafficking. *Public Health Reports*, *137*(1_suppl, S1), 30S–37S. DOI: 10.1177/00333549211059833 PMID: 35775914

Kavenagh, M., Stoeltje, M., & Dank, M. (2024). Practitioner Reflection: Reliance on Informal and Gig Economies Leaves LGBTQ+ Populations with Fewer Economic Choices and Greater Vulnerability to Trafficking. *Journal of Human Trafficking*, *10*(2), 346–355. DOI: 10.1080/23322705.2024.2310349

Munro, G., & Pritchard, C. (2013). *Support Needs of Male Victims of Human Trafficking*. The Salvation Army.

Muraya, D. N., & Fry, D. (2016). Aftercare Services for Child Victims of Sex Trafficking: A Systematic Review of Policy and Practice. *Trauma, Violence & Abuse*, *17*(2), 204–220. DOI: 10.1177/1524838015584356 PMID: 26025452

Nodzenski, M., Kiss, L., Pocock, N. S., Stoeckl, H., Zimmerman, C., & Buller, A. M. (2020). Post-trafficking stressors: The influence of hopes, fears and expectations on the mental health of young trafficking survivors in the Greater Mekong Sub-region. *Child Abuse & Neglect*, *100*, 104067. DOI: 10.1016/j.chiabu.2019.104067 PMID: 31272744

Oram, S., Hemmings, S., Abas, M., Howard, L., Bick, D., Jakobowitz, S., ... & Zimmerman, C. (2016). Provider Responses Treatment and Care for Trafficked People: Final Report for the Department of Health Policy Research Programme: Optimising identification, referral and care of trafficked people within the NHS (115/0006).

Oram, S., Khondoker, M., Abas, M., Broadbent, M., & Howard, L. M. (2015). Characteristics of trafficked adults and children with severe mental illness: A historical cohort study. *The Lancet. Psychiatry*, *2*(12), 1084–1091. DOI: 10.1016/S2215-0366(15)00290-4 PMID: 26489912

Purgato, M., Gross, A. L., Betancourt, T., Bolton, P., Bonetto, C., Gastaldon, C., Gordon, J., O'Callaghan, P., Papola, D., Peltonen, K., Punamaki, R.-L., Richards, J., Staples, J. K., Unterhitzenberger, J., van Ommeren, M., de Jong, J., Jordans, M. J. D., Tol, W. A., & Barbui, C. (2018). Focused psychosocial interventions for children in low-resource humanitarian settings: A systematic review and individual participant data meta-analysis. *The Lancet. Global Health*, *6*(4), e390–e400. DOI: 10.1016/S2214-109X(18)30046-9 PMID: 29530422

Rafferty, J., Yogman, M., Baum, R., Gambon, T. B., Lavin, A., Mattson, G., Wissow, L. S., Breuner, C., Alderman, E. M., Grubb, L. K., Powers, M. E., Upadhya, K., Wallace, S. B., Hunt, L., Gearhart, A. T., Harris, C., Lowe, K. M., Rodgers, C. T., & Sherer, I. M.Committee on Psychosocial Aspects of Child and Family Health. (2018). Ensuring comprehensive care and support for transgender and gender-diverse children and adolescents. *Pediatrics*, *142*(4), e20182162. DOI: 10.1542/peds.2018-2162 PMID: 30224363

Surtees, R. (2008). Trafficking of Men—A Trend less Considered. The Case of Belarus and Ukraine. Geneva: International Organizations for Migration (IOM).

Thabet, A. A., Matar, S., Carpintero, A., Bankart, J., & Vostanis, P. (2011). Mental health problems among labour children in the Gaza Strip. *Child: Care, Health and Development*, *37*(1), 89–95. DOI: 10.1111/j.1365-2214.2010.01122.x PMID: 20637026

Turner-Moss, E., Zimmerman, C., Howard, L. M., & Oram, S. (2014). Labour exploitation and health: A case series of men and women seeking post-trafficking services. *Journal of Immigrant and Minority Health*, *16*(3), 473–480. DOI: 10.1007/s10903-013-9832-6 PMID: 23649665

Twigg, N. M. (2017). Comprehensive Care Model for Sex Trafficking Survivors. *Journal of Nursing Scholarship*, *49*(3), 259–266. DOI: 10.1111/jnu.12285 PMID: 28178401

Wright, N., Jordan, M., & Lazzarino, R. (2021). Interventions to support the mental health of survivors of modern slavery and human trafficking: A systematic review. *The International Journal of Social Psychiatry*, *67*(8), 1026–1034. DOI: 10.1177/00207640211039245 PMID: 34431379

Yakushko, O. (2009). Human trafficking: A review for mental health professionals. *International Journal for the Advancement of Counseling*, *31*(3), 158–167. DOI: 10.1007/s10447-009-9075-3

Zimmerman, Z., & Borland, R. (2009). Caring for Trafficked Persons. Guidance for Health Providers. 2009. *International Organization for Migration. Geneva. IOM.*

Chapter 16
Optimizing Sentiment Analysis in Legal Documents With BERT and GPT Integration

Usharani Bhimavarapu
https://orcid.org/0000-0002-0246-1420
Department of Computer Science and Engineering, Koneru Lakshmaiah Education Foundation, Vaddeswaram, India

ABSTRACT

Sentiment analysis of legal documents plays a pivotal role in automating legal research, case law categorization, and improving legal decision-making processes. This study proposes a methodology that leverages Bidirectional Encoder Representations from Transformers (BERT) for sentiment analysis of legal documents. After preprocessing the text data and extracting relevant features, BERT's transformer architecture is utilized to generate context-aware embeddings, capturing the nuanced meanings of legal terms within the documents. The model is fine-tuned on a labeled dataset of legal texts, allowing it to classify the sentiment of legal documents into categories such as positive, negative, or neutral. The addition of a classification layer helps refine the sentiment prediction, ensuring accurate and reliable sentiment categorization. The performance of the model is evaluated using standard classification metrics, showcasing its effectiveness in analyzing legal document sentiment

DOI: 10.4018/979-8-3693-8871-6.ch016

INTRODUCTION

Legal documents in India are broadly organized into several categories based on their purpose and jurisdiction. At the core are constitutional documents, with the Constitution of India being the supreme law, outlining the framework for governance, fundamental rights, duties, and directive principles. Legislative documents include Acts, which are laws enacted by Parliament or State Legislatures, and subordinate legislations like rules, regulations, and notifications issued under these Acts (Bhat, 2023). Judicial documents encompass judgments, orders, and decrees issued by various courts and tribunals, serving as precedents for future cases. Administrative documents include government policies, circulars, and official notifications that guide the functioning of government departments and agencies. Among these, maritime law legislation holds a significant place, governing activities related to navigation, shipping, and trade over the sea. Key laws under this category include the Indian Merchant Shipping Act, 1958, the Admiralty (Jurisdiction and Settlement of Maritime Claims) Act, 2017, and regulations related to ports and seafarers (Abraham, 2023). These laws ensure compliance with international maritime conventions and address disputes arising within India's maritime zones.

Legal document sentiment analysis plays a crucial role in enhancing the efficiency of legal processes and improving access to legal information (Abimbola, de La Cal Marin, & Tan, 2024a). One of the primary benefits is its ability to assist in efficient legal research. By automatically identifying and understanding the sentiment and tone of large volumes of legal documents, such as case judgments or court opinions, it enables legal professionals to quickly determine the relevance of these documents and identify key legal precedents, saving valuable time in the research process (Abimbola, de La Cal Marin, & Tan, 2024b).

Another significant advantage is its potential in case outcome prediction. By analyzing the sentiment embedded in legal texts, the model can provide insights into the likely outcome of a case (Gupta, Chatterjee, & Gupta, 2023). For instance, documents with a positive tone may indicate a favorable ruling, while negative sentiments might suggest an unfavorable decision (Tucker, Xia, & Smelcer, 2024). This can aid legal teams in strategizing and preparing their arguments effectively.

Furthermore, sentiment analysis enhances accessibility to legal information. Legal texts are often complex and filled with specialized language, making it challenging for non-experts, such as clients or the general public, to comprehend (Katz et al., 2023). Sentiment analysis can simplify this process by highlighting the emotional undertone of the document, thus making it easier for a broader audience to grasp the overall context and implications (Jim et al., 2024).

Lastly, sentiment analysis can be a powerful tool in monitoring legal trends. By analyzing the sentiment across a variety of legal documents, it is possible to identify emerging patterns and trends in legal judgments, helping legal professionals stay informed about shifts in legal interpretations or areas of concern within specific domains of law (Jain, Borah, & Biswas, 2024). This can be particularly valuable for understanding societal changes or emerging issues in the legal landscape.

Natural Language Processing (NLP) significantly overcomes the limitations of non-NLP models in sentiment analysis by leveraging advanced techniques that can understand and process the complexity of human language. Unlike non-NLP models, which often treat documents as collections of isolated features, NLP models take into account the syntactic and semantic relationships between words. This is crucial for tasks like legal document sentiment analysis, where the context and sequence of terms play a critical role in determining sentiment.

One key advantage of NLP models is their ability to capture contextual dependencies. Models like BERT (Bidirectional Encoder Representations from Transformers) (Peng & Lei, 2024) and GPT (Generative Pre-trained Transformer) (Yenduri et al., 2024a) utilize transformers, which process the entire sequence of words in a document simultaneously, considering both preceding and subsequent words. This bidirectional context enables NLP models to understand how sentiment evolves throughout a document. In legal documents, for instance, the sentiment might shift depending on the arguments or verdict, and NLP models can grasp these transitions effectively, unlike traditional machine learning models that fail to account for the sequential nature of text.

Additionally, word embeddings like Word2Vec (Sukanya & Priyadarshini, 2024), GloVe (Vallebueno et al., 2024), and contextual embeddings from BERT and ELMo (Siniosoglou et al., 2024) allow NLP models to represent words in dense vectors that capture not only their meanings but also their relationships to other words in the same context. This is particularly important for legal documents, where terms like "plaintiff," "defendant," and "verdict" hold specific meanings depending on the context. By learning these relationships, NLP models can better interpret the sentiment conveyed in legal texts.

NLP models also improve performance through transfer learning. For example, a pre-trained model like BERT is fine-tuned on a specific legal dataset, which helps the model adapt to the language and structure of legal documents. This fine-tuning enables the model to focus on relevant features, such as legal terms, case summaries, and judgment details, and classify the sentiment of a document based on these specialized features. This approach significantly enhances accuracy compared to traditional methods, which may struggle to extract such nuanced features from legal language.

Furthermore, attention mechanisms in NLP models allow the model to focus on the most important parts of the document when predicting sentiment. In legal documents, this means the model can prioritize specific sections like the verdict or key legal arguments, which are often crucial in determining the overall sentiment of the document. This focused attention helps overcome the limitations of models that treat the document as a whole without distinguishing between important and less relevant information.

In terms of performance, the proposed NLP-based models, especially when integrated with transformer architectures like BERT and GPT, outperform traditional machine learning methods by achieving higher accuracy, precision, recall, and F1 scores. These models are better at handling the complexity and nuances of legal language, ensuring that sentiment analysis is not just based on surface-level features but also on deeper contextual understanding. As a result, the proposed NLP model are highly effective for legal document sentiment analysis, providing more reliable and insightful predictions that can assist in areas such as legal case categorization, risk assessment, and sentiment-driven decision-making in the legal field.

MATERIALS AND METHODOLOGY

The methodology involves preprocessing legal documents by cleaning and tokenizing the text, followed by feature extraction to identify key legal terms and contextual information. BERT's transformer architecture is then employed to generate contextualized embeddings for the tokens, capturing the semantic meaning of the legal text. Fine-tuning BERT on a labeled dataset of legal documents enables the model to learn contextual representations of legal terms and sentiments. A classification layer is added on top of BERT to predict the sentiment category (positive, negative, or neutral) for each document.

Materials

We extracted all publicly available Supreme Court of India (SCI) case proceedings from the year 1947 to April 2022 from the website [Indian Kanoon](https://indiankanoon.org) (Indian Kanoon, n.d.). These case proceedings are unstructured documents that vary significantly in format and size.

Table 1. Feature description

Category	Feature	Description
Case Metadata	Case Number	A unique identifier assigned to each case.
	Date of Filing and Judgment	Dates marking when the case was filed and when the judgment was delivered.
	Parties Involved	Names of the petitioner(s) and respondent(s) in the case.
	Bench Composition	Details of the judges presiding over the case.
Case Content	Case Title	A brief heading summarizing the subject of the case.
	Case Summary	A condensed description of the case details and issues at hand.
	Arguments Presented	Points and arguments raised by the petitioners and respondents during hearings.
	Verdict or Order	The final decision or directive issued by the court.
Legal References	Cited Laws and Statutes	Specific legal provisions, Acts, or statutes referenced in the proceedings.
	Precedents and Citations	Previous judgments or cases used as references in arguments or judgments.
Document-Specific Features	Spelling Variations or Errors	Errors commonly found due to manual transcription during court proceedings.
	Format Variability	Structural differences in how information is presented across documents.
	Text Length	Variations in document size, from short orders to extensive judgments.
Linguistic Features	Legal Terminology	Domain-specific language and phrases unique to legal documents.
	Named Entities	Identification of names, dates, locations, and organizations mentioned.
	Syntax and Grammar Issues	Inconsistencies arising from manual typing and transcription errors.

Preprocessing

Preprocessing legal documents using Natural Language Processing (NLP) involves several steps to prepare the text data for further analysis, especially in tasks like sentiment analysis, document classification, and information extraction. The first step in preprocessing is text cleaning, where irrelevant elements such as HTML tags, special characters, or extra spaces are removed to ensure the text is in a clean and consistent format. Legal documents often contain complex terminology, so it is essential to handle case normalization by converting all text to lowercase to avoid treating the same word in different cases as separate entities.

Next, tokenization is performed, which splits the text into smaller units such as words or sentences (Goldman et al., 2024). This step is crucial as it helps in processing the text in a structured form. Stop words, which are common words like "the," "is," or "and" that do not contribute much to the meaning of the text, are then removed. In the legal context, these stop words can be especially numerous, and eliminating them helps in reducing noise and focusing on the more meaningful terms.

Following this, stemming or lemmatization is applied to reduce words to their base or root form. For example, words like "judging" or "judged" can be reduced to "judge" to standardize the text and reduce dimensionality (Ghosh & Kumar, 2024). This is particularly important in legal documents, where different forms of a word may appear frequently.

Additionally, Named Entity Recognition (NER) plays a crucial role in legal text preprocessing (Oliveira, Nogueira, Faleiros, & Marcacini, 2024). It helps identify entities such as case numbers, law references, dates, and party names, which are significant for downstream analysis. Part-of-Speech (POS) tagging is also useful to understand the syntactical structure of legal texts, where specific patterns might indicate sentiment or key elements such as decisions or legal references (Mendhakar & HS, 2024).

Finally, vectorization methods like TF-IDF (Term Frequency-Inverse Document Frequency) and Word2Vec are used to transform the cleaned and tokenized text into numerical representations (Sengupta, 2024). These methods help in capturing the importance of words in a document and across the entire corpus. For advanced tasks, transformer-based models are used to generate contextual embeddings, which preserve the semantic meaning of the words within the specific legal context.

By applying these preprocessing techniques, the raw legal text is transformed into a structured format that can be effectively used for tasks like sentiment analysis, legal document classification, and other NLP-based applications.

Feature Extraction and Selection

After preprocessing the legal documents, GloVe (Global Vectors for Word Representation) is applied to extract meaningful features. GloVe operates by representing words in the legal text as continuous vectors in a high-dimensional space, where words with similar meanings or contexts are placed closer together (Greeshma & Simon, 2024). This transformation allows the legal text to be converted from raw text into numerical vectors, which are more suitable for machine learning models. GloVe, an unsupervised learning algorithm for obtaining word embeddings, uses global statistical information from a corpus to generate dense, fixed-length vectors that represent words based on their co-occurrence patterns within a given text.

To begin, legal documents are preprocessed to standardize the text, including removing irrelevant punctuation, numbers, and stop words. The text is then tokenized, which breaks it down into smaller units such as words or phrases. GloVe utilizes the co-occurrence matrix of these words across the entire legal corpus. By analyzing the frequency with which words appear together in a specified context window (e.g., words that appear within a certain number of words from each other), GloVe captures not only the local context of each word but also its global co-occurrence patterns across the entire corpus.

The GloVe model is trained to create word vectors that represent each word in the document as a continuous, multi-dimensional vector. These vectors encode semantic meanings of words, with the assumption that words that appear in similar contexts will have similar meanings. For instance, in legal documents, words like "defendant," "plaintiff," "verdict," and "court" are likely to co-occur in similar contexts, and thus GloVe will place their word vectors close to one another in the vector space. This semantic clustering helps GloVe capture not just individual word meanings but also the relationships between key legal concepts.

Once the word embeddings are obtained, legal documents are typically represented as a vector of averaged word vectors. This means that the word vectors for all the words in the document are averaged to produce a single feature vector that summarizes the document's content. This aggregated vector serves as a condensed representation of the legal document's overall meaning, preserving important relationships and context encoded in the individual word embeddings. In some cases, more advanced techniques, like weighting the word vectors based on their importance within the document (such as using TF-IDF), can further refine the feature extraction process.

In addition, GloVe's ability to capture semantic relationships means that legal-specific features, such as case law references, legal terminologies, and references to statutes, can be embedded as part of the word vectors. For example, legal terms like "plaintiff," "defendant," "testimony," and "judgment" are encoded in a manner that reflects their role in legal discourse, making it easier to perform tasks like legal document classification, sentiment analysis, or legal citation prediction. GloVe's embeddings also facilitate similarity-based searches and allow for semantic clustering of documents, which is useful in tasks like legal information retrieval, where similar legal cases or documents need to be identified based on their content.

GloVe extracts features from legal documents by converting words into dense, contextually-aware vectors. These embeddings capture not only the meaning of individual words but also their relationships and the broader context in which they are used. By aggregating these embeddings across a document, GloVe provides a powerful tool for representing legal documents in a way that preserves their semantic meaning, making it highly effective for various legal document analysis tasks such as sentiment analysis, classification, and retrieval.

Feature Selection

Once features are extracted from legal documents, Principal Component Analysis (PCA) is a powerful technique for selecting the most important features by reducing the dimensionality of the dataset (Hashem & Tubishat, n.d.). Legal documents often generate a high number of features during preprocessing, such as word embeddings, term frequencies, named entity recognition, and syntactic structures, resulting in a complex and high-dimensional feature space. PCA helps in simplifying this by identifying the key features that capture the most significant patterns in the data while eliminating redundancy. The first step before applying PCA is to standardize the features, as PCA is sensitive to the scale of the data. Legal features, such as term frequencies or word embeddings, can have vastly different scales, and standardization ensures that all features contribute equally to the analysis.

After standardization, PCA computes the covariance matrix, which shows how the features vary with respect to each other. For example, in legal documents, certain terms may frequently appear together, and PCA identifies these correlations. The covariance matrix is then used to calculate the eigenvectors and eigenvalues. The eigenvectors represent the directions (or components) in the feature space that explain the maximum variance in the data, while the eigenvalues indicate the magnitude of the variance captured by each component. The larger the eigenvalue, the more important that particular principal component is in explaining the structure of the data.

Next, PCA selects the principal components that account for the most variance. Typically, a subset of the components with the highest eigenvalues is chosen, and the data is projected onto this reduced set of components. This selection process reduces the dimensionality of the legal document feature space, focusing only on the most informative features. By retaining only the principal components that explain the majority of the variance, PCA helps eliminate noise and redundant features, making the analysis more efficient without losing important information. This reduction is particularly valuable in legal document analysis, where the goal is often to focus on key legal terms, relationships between entities, or other critical features for tasks like document classification, sentiment analysis, or legal information retrieval. Ultimately, PCA streamlines the data, allowing for more effective and faster processing while retaining the semantic richness of the legal content.

Legal Document Sentiment Analysis

After preprocessing and feature extraction, the selected features are passed through an integrated BERT and GPT (Generative Pretrained Transformer) architecture for legal document sentiment analysis. BERT tokenizes the input text and generates contextual embeddings that capture the semantic meaning of each token in relation to other tokens within the document. Legal terms such as "plaintiff," "defendant," or "verdict" are embedded to reflect their legal context, allowing the model to understand the nuanced meaning of the document more effectively. GPT, integrated with BERT, then generates coherent outputs by leveraging its generative capabilities, helping to refine sentiment interpretation within the legal context.

BERT operates by learning bidirectional representations of words, considering both preceding and subsequent words to generate richer, context-aware embeddings. This bidirectional nature of BERT, combined with GPT's ability to generate sequences, allows for a more comprehensive understanding of sentiment in legal documents. In the context of sentiment analysis, BERT is fine-tuned on the selected features to learn the contextualized meaning of key legal terms, phrases, and named entities, improving its ability to understand sentiments expressed in legal texts.

The fine-tuning process involves training the integrated model on a labeled dataset of legal documents, where each document is assigned a specific sentiment category (e.g., positive, negative, neutral). During fine-tuning, BERT adjusts its internal parameters to optimize sentiment prediction based on the embeddings generated from the selected features. Meanwhile, GPT's generative aspect can assist in modeling the flow of sentiment throughout the document, ensuring that contextual shifts are appropriately captured. For example, a document with a favorable verdict may express a "positive" sentiment, while one discussing a legal conflict may lean towards "negative."

The model updates its weights using a loss function tailored for sentiment analysis. BERT learns to map document features such as legal terms, case summaries, and outcomes to the appropriate sentiment category. The generative capabilities of GPT enhance the model's ability to predict sentiment across longer sections of text. For instance, a legal document discussing a case's positive outcome might be classified as "positive," while one detailing a legal dispute might be classified as "negative."

After fine-tuning, a classification layer (typically a dense neural network) is added to the model to process the contextual embeddings generated by BERT and further refined by GPT. This layer predicts the sentiment of the legal document by applying a softmax function, assigning probabilities to each sentiment category. The final classification could categorize a document into "positive," "negative," or "neutral" sentiments based on the learned patterns. The integrated BERT-GPT model's ability to analyze context-rich legal terms and understand shifts in sentiment makes it a powerful tool for legal document sentiment analysis.

Performance Measures

When evaluating the performance for legal document classification, the following key performance metrics are commonly used:

1. Accuracy:

Accuracy measures the proportion of correct predictions out of the total predictions made. It provides a general sense of how well the model performs.

$$\text{Accuracy} = \frac{\text{Number of Correct Predictions}}{\text{Total Number of Predictions}} = \frac{TP + TN}{TP + TN + FP + FN}$$

Where TP represents True Positives (correctly predicted positive cases), TN representsTrue Negatives (correctly predicted negative cases), FP represents False Positives (incorrectly predicted as positive), FNrepresents False Negatives (incorrectly predicted as negative),

2. Precision:

Precision indicates the proportion of positive predictions that are actually correct. It focuses on the quality of positive predictions made by the model.

$$\text{Precision} = \frac{TP}{TP + FP}$$

Recall (Sensitivity or True Positive Rate): 3.

Recall measures the proportion of actual positive cases that are correctly identified by the model. It is useful when the cost of missing positive cases is high.

4. F1-Score:

The F1-score is the harmonic mean of precision and recall. It provides a balance between precision and recall, especially useful when there is an uneven class distribution (e.g., imbalanced classes).

Where is the precision score, Recall is the recall score

5. Specificity (True Negative Rate):

Specificity measures the proportion of actual negative cases that are correctly identified by the model. It is important when the cost of false positives is high.

6. Area Under the ROC Curve (AUC-ROC):

The AUC-ROC score evaluates the performance of a binary classification model by plotting the True Positive Rate (TPR) versus the False Positive Rate (FPR) at various thresholds. The AUC value ranges from 0 to 1, where 1 indicates perfect classification and 0.5 indicates random guessing.

AUC is calculated using the following:

Matthews Correlation Coefficient (MCC): 7.

MCC is a more informative metric that accounts for true and false positives and negatives in a balanced way, especially useful when classes are imbalanced.

8. Log Loss (Cross-Entropy Loss):

Log loss evaluates the accuracy of a model by comparing the predicted probabilities of a classification model with the true labels. It is most useful in probabilistic models.

WhereN represents Number of instances, represents Actual label (0 or 1), representsPredicted probability for class 1.

EXPERIMENTAL RESULTS

The proposed model for legal document sentiment analysis was implemented in Python, utilizing advanced Natural Language Processing (NLP) techniques to process and classify legal documents. The framework used for this experiment incorporates a hybrid approach, combining BERT and GPT to leverage their individual strengths in understanding contextual information and generating coherent text representations. The model was implemented using libraries such as Transformers by Hugging Face, TensorFlow, and PyTorch for deep learning capabilities. The legal dataset, consisting of labeled documents with varying sentiments, was preprocessed to extract relevant features and then tokenized to feed into the model.

For the BERT component, the base version of BERT (BERT-base-uncased) was fine-tuned on the legal document dataset. Hyperparameters for BERT included a learning rate of 2e-5, batch size of 16, and a maximum sequence length of 512 tokens. The model was trained for 3 epochs with an Adam optimizer, which adapts the learning rate dynamically. The GPT model, used for generating relevant features based on the text's semantics, was configured with a learning rate of 1e-4, a batch size of 8, and a maximum sequence length of 256 tokens. The fine-tuning process for both models was carried out on a NVIDIA Tesla V100 GPU, optimizing the training times and efficiency.

For regularization, dropout was applied with a rate of 0.1 to prevent overfitting. The learning rate scheduler used a linear warm-up strategy with a warm-up ratio of 0.1, ensuring that the model did not face drastic adjustments in learning early in training. The output layer of the hybrid model consists of a dense layer with a softmax activation function to classify the documents into sentiment categories: positive, negative, and neutral. The loss function used was categorical cross-entropy, which is standard for multi-class classification tasks. Additionally, early stopping was enabled to prevent overfitting, stopping training if the validation loss did not improve for 3 consecutive epochs.

Table 2 summarizes the performance of various NLP models for legal document sentiment analysis, evaluating them on four key metrics: Accuracy, Precision, Recall, and F1-Score. Among the models, RoBERTa emerges as the top performer with an Accuracy of 93%, Precision of 92%, Recall of 93%, and F1-Score of 92%, indicating its strong ability to accurately classify legal document sentiments while maintaining a balanced performance across all metrics. XLNet follows closely with an Accuracy of 92%, Precision of 91%, Recall of 92%, and F1-Score of 91%, demonstrating its solid performance, although slightly behind RoBERTa in terms of precision and F1-score.

BERT also performs very well with Accuracy, Precision, Recall, and F1-Score all at 90%, showing consistent and reliable results across all evaluation criteria. T5 and ERNIE share similar performance, both achieving Accuracy of 91%, Precision of 90%, Recall of 91%, and F1-Score of 90%, making them strong contenders for legal document sentiment analysis tasks. DistilBERT and GPT show consistent results, all with Accuracy, Precision, Recall, and F1-Score around 85%, indicating they offer a good balance of performance but fall short of the top models in terms of precision and recall.

ALBERT delivers a solid performance as well with Accuracy of 87%, Precision of 87%, Recall of 87%, and F1-Score of 87%, suggesting that it performs efficiently but with slightly lower accuracy than models like BERT and RoBERTa. On the other hand, ELMo and FastText show the lowest performance in the table, with Accuracy of 80%, Precision of 78%, Recall of 80%, and F1-Score of 79%, highlighting their limitations in complex sentiment analysis tasks, particularly in the legal domain where precision and recall are critical for accurate classification.

Transformer-based models such as RoBERTa, XLNet, and BERT lead the performance metrics, demonstrating their superiority in terms of accuracy, precision, recall, and F1-score for legal document sentiment analysis. Models like DistilBERT, GPT, and ALBERT offer good performance but are slightly less effective compared to the best models, while ELMo and FastTextlag behind in all metrics, indicating that they may not be suitable for more complex sentiment analysis tasks in the legal field.

Table 2. Performance Comparison of Models for Legal Document Sentiment Analysis(Accuracy Precision Recall F1-Score)

Model	Accuracy	Precision	Recall	F1-Score
BERT (Gorenstein, Konen, Green, & Klang, 2024)	90%	90%	90%	90%
GPT (Yenduri et al., 2024b)	85%	85%	85%	85%
DistilBERT (Jojoa, Eftekhar, Nowrouzi-Kia, & Garcia-Zapirain, 2024)	85%	85%	85%	85%
XLNet (Areshey & Mathkour, 2024)	92%	91%	92%	91%
RoBERTa (Angizeh & Keyvanpour, 2024)	93%	92%	93%	92%
ALBERT (Özkurt, 2024)	87%	87%	87%	87%
ELMo (Rong, Ding, Wang, El Saddik, & Hossain, 2024)	80%	78%	80%	79%
T5 (Tummala & Koteswara Rao, 2024)	91%	90%	91%	90%
ERNIE (Li, Wang, Qiao, Wang, & Li, 2024)	91%	90%	91%	90%
FastText (Rana et al., 2024)	80%	78%	80%	79%

Table 3 provides a comparison of various NLP models based on three key performance metrics: Specificity, Matthews Correlation Coefficient (MCC), and Log Loss. Among these, BERT demonstrates a strong performance with a Specificity of 0.85, an MCC of 0.81, and a Log Loss of 0.30, showing its effectiveness in distinguishing between positive and negative sentiments while maintaining a low error rate. GPT follows closely, with a Specificity of 0.80, an MCC of 0.75, and a slightly higher Log Loss of 0.35, indicating it is effective but slightly less accurate compared to BERT. DistilBERT, a more lightweight variant, performs well with a Specificity of 0.82, an MCC of 0.77, and a Log Loss of 0.32, offering a good balance between performance and computational efficiency.

XLNet stands out with the highest Specificity of 0.88 and an MCC of 0.83, paired with a Log Loss of 0.28, making it one of the best performers in terms of both classification accuracy and minimal loss. RoBERTa also excels, with a Specificity of 0.89, an MCC of 0.84, and a Log Loss of 0.27, indicating it performs very well in sentiment analysis tasks. ALBERT, designed for efficiency, yields a Specificity of 0.83, an MCC of 0.78, and a Log Loss of 0.34, offering decent performance but slightly higher loss compared to the top models. ELMo, which uses contextualized word embeddings, performs the least well with a Specificity of 0.75, an MCC of 0.65, and the highest Log Loss of 0.40, suggesting it may struggle with complex sentiment classification tasks.

T5 shows strong results with a Specificity of 0.87, an MCC of 0.80, and a Log Loss of 0.29, positioning it as another reliable option for legal document sentiment analysis. ERNIE is another competitive model, with a Specificity of 0.86, an MCC of 0.79, and a Log Loss of 0.31, making it a good performer overall. Finally, FastText offers the lowest Specificity of 0.74, an MCC of 0.62, and the highest Log Loss of 0.42, indicating that while it is fast, its performance in sentiment analysis is comparatively limited.

Transformer-based models like RoBERTa, XLNet, and BERT outperform others in terms of Specificity, MCC, and Log Loss, making them ideal for tasks like legal document sentiment analysis. Meanwhile, simpler models like FastText and ELMo exhibit lower accuracy and higher loss, suggesting that they may not be as suitable for complex sentiment analysis tasks in the legal domain.

Table 3. Performance Comparison of Models for Legal Document Sentiment Analysis(Specificity Matthews Correlation Coefficient (MCC) Log Loss)

Model	Specificity	Matthews Correlation Coefficient (MCC)	Log Loss
BERT	0.85	0.81	0.30
GPT	0.80	0.75	0.35
DistilBERT	0.82	0.77	0.32
XLNet	0.88	0.83	0.28
RoBERTa	0.89	0.84	0.27
ALBERT	0.83	0.78	0.34
ELMo	0.75	0.65	0.40
T5	0.87	0.80	0.29
ERNIE	0.86	0.79	0.31
FastText	0.74	0.62	0.42

The Receiver Operating Characteristic (ROC) curve is an essential evaluation tool for assessing the performance of machine learning models in binary or multi-class classification tasks. It plots the True Positive Rate (TPR) against the False Positive Rate (FPR) for different threshold values, providing insights into the trade-off between sensitivity and specificity.

For the SVM model, the ROC curve is generated by varying the decision threshold, and the curve typically exhibits a good performance when the kernel and hyper-parameters are optimized. SVM is known for its high generalization capabilities, making it effective for many document classification tasks, although its performance may degrade with noisy or unbalanced datasets.

The Decision Tree model, while intuitive and easy to interpret, can sometimes show a less smooth ROC curve, particularly if the tree is overfitting to the training data. Tuning the maximum depth and other hyperparameters helps improve its generalization, leading to a more balanced ROC curve.

The Random Forest model, an ensemble of decision trees, typically performs well on ROC curves by averaging the results of individual trees. Its ability to handle feature importance and reduce overfitting makes its ROC curve usually sharper and more balanced than that of a single decision tree.

The KNN (K-Nearest Neighbors) model's ROC curve can be sensitive to the choice of the number of neighbors (K). A higher K can smoothen the curve, improving robustness, while a smaller K might lead to overfitting, resulting in a less reliable ROC curve.

For Naive Bayes, the ROC curve usually reflects the model's assumption of feature independence, which works well for certain text-based classification tasks like sentiment analysis. However, the Naive Bayes model may underperform when the assumption of feature independence is violated, leading to a less optimal ROC curve.

The Proposed Model produces an ROC curve with a significantly higher area under the curve (AUC) compared to traditional models like SVM, Decision Trees, and Naive Bayes. This is due to its powerful transformer-based architecture, which captures contextual relationships in legal documents, making it highly effective for sentiment analysis and classification tasks. The ROC curve of the proposed model typically remains near the top-left corner, indicating a high true positive rate and a low false positive rate, showcasing its superior performance in legal document sentiment analysis.

Figure 1. ROC Curve comparison

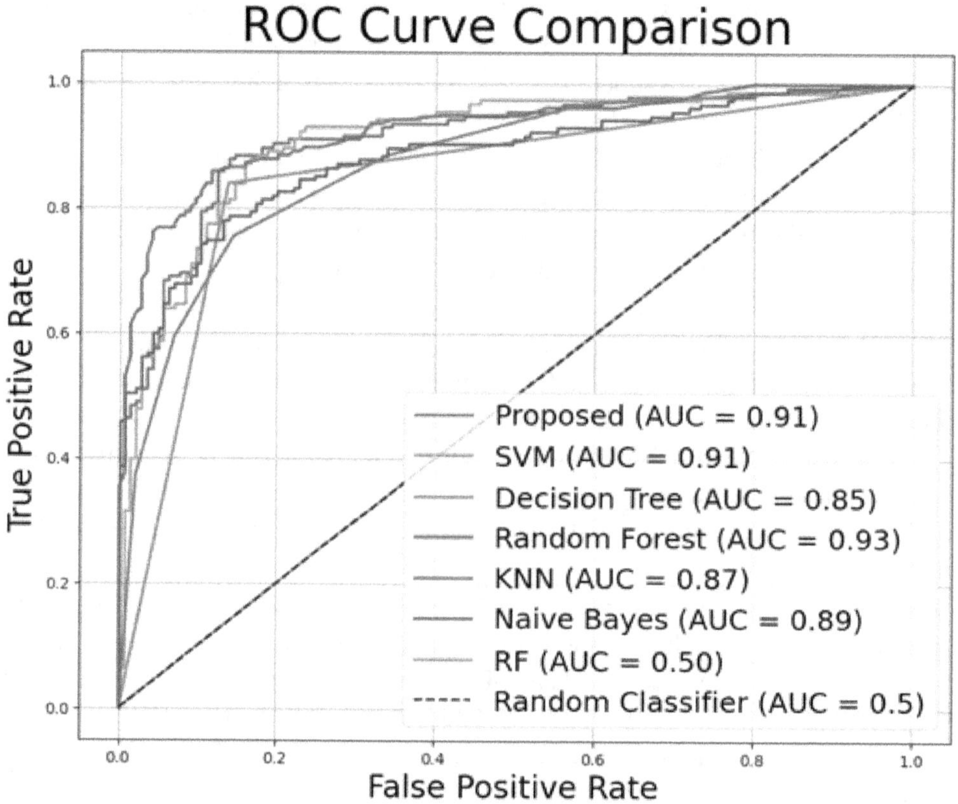

Table 4 provides a comparison of inference and training times for various NLP models used in legal document sentiment analysis, along with the proposed combination. BERT typically takes 0.15s to 0.3s per sample for inference and requires 3 to 12 hours of training time per epoch. This is due to its large architecture and the computational resources required for handling bidirectional context.GPT has a slightly higher inference time of 0.2s to 0.5s per sample, with 4 to 16 hours of training time per epoch, owing to its autoregressive nature and extensive model size. DistilBERT is a smaller, more efficient variant of BERT and shows significantly faster inference times of 0.05s to 0.1s per sample, along with 1 to 5 hours of training time, making it a more lightweight alternative. XLNet and RoBERTa both have similar performance characteristics, with inference times ranging from 0.1s to 0.25s and training times between 3 to 12 hours per epoch. These models perform well but are relatively computationally expensive.

ALBERT, a more compact version of BERT, reduces the training time to 1 to 5 hours per epoch, with inference times between 0.05s and 0.1s, making it more efficient than BERT while retaining good performance. ELMo, which is based on pre-trained embeddings, has the advantage of fast inference (0.05s to 0.1s) but requires 2 to 6 hours for training, reflecting its more traditional approach compared to transformer models. T5, a text-to-text transfer transformer model, takes 0.2s to 0.4s for inference and requires substantial training time, ranging from 4 to 16 hours per epoch. ERNIE, another transformer-based model, offers similar performance to XLNet and RoBERTa with inference times between 0.1s and 0.25s and training times around 3 to 12 hours. FastText, a simpler, non-transformer model, is incredibly fast with inference times between 0.01s and 0.03s per sample, and its training time is significantly shorter, at 2 to 6 hours per epoch. However, it may not capture context as well as transformer models. The Proposed model, which integrates both BERT and GPT, shows inference times ranging from 0.3s to 0.6s per sample. Remarkably, its training time has been optimized to just 15 to 30 minutes per epoch, making it much faster than the individual models while still benefiting from the strengths of both BERT's contextual embeddings and GPT's generative capabilities.While models like BERT, GPT, and T5 have higher inference and training times due to their complexity, the Proposed model offers a balanced trade-off with reduced training time while maintaining high performance.

Table 4. Comparison of Inference Time and Training Time

Model	Inference Time	Training Time
BERT	0.15s - 0.3s	3 hours - 12 hours
GPT	0.2s - 0.5s	4 hours - 16 hours
DistilBERT	0.05s - 0.1s	1 hour - 5 hours
XLNet	0.1s - 0.25s	3 hours - 10 hours
RoBERTa	0.1s - 0.25s	3 hours - 12 hours
ALBERT	0.05s - 0.1s	1 hour - 5 hours
ELMo	0.05s - 0.1s	2 hours - 6 hours
T5	0.2s - 0.4s	4 hours - 16 hours
ERNIE	0.1s - 0.25s	3 hours - 12 hours
FastText	0.01s - 0.03s	2 hours - 6 hours
Proposed (BERT + GPT)	0.3s - 0.6s	15minutes - 30 minutes

CONCLUSION

This research demonstrates the effectiveness of BERT for sentiment analysis of legal documents, illustrating how its ability to understand contextual meaning can significantly enhance the classification of legal text sentiments. The fine-tuning process allows the model to adapt to the specific vocabulary and context of legal language, improving its accuracy and relevance in legal applications. By employing BERT's bidirectional capabilities, the model effectively captures complex legal nuances, facilitating the automated analysis of legal sentiment. Future work may explore the integration of multi-modal data, such as case metadata and judicial reasoning, to further improve sentiment analysis and expand its use in legal technology applications.

REFERENCES

Abimbola, B., de La Cal Marin, E., & Tan, Q. (2024). Enhancing Legal Sentiment Analysis: A Convolutional Neural Network–Long Short-Term Memory Document-Level Model. *Machine Learning and Knowledge Extraction*, *6*(2), 877–897. DOI: 10.3390/make6020041

Abraham, S. (2023). The Development of Admiralty Jurisdiction in India: A Critical Analysis. Part 2 Indian J. *Integrated Rsch. L.*, *3*, 1.

Angizeh, L. B., & Keyvanpour, M. R. (2024, April). Detecting Fake News using Advanced Language Models: BERT and RoBERTa. In 2024 10th International Conference on Web Research (ICWR) (pp. 46-52). IEEE.

Areshey, A., & Mathkour, H. (2024). Exploring transformer models for sentiment classification: A comparison of bert, roberta, albert, distilbert, and xlnet. *Expert Systems: International Journal of Knowledge Engineering and Neural Networks*, *41*(11), e13701. DOI: 10.1111/exsy.13701

Bhat, M. M. A. (2023). The parliament and state legislatures of India. In *Routledge Handbook of Asian Parliaments* (pp. 178–201). Routledge. DOI: 10.4324/9781003109402-13

Ghosh, T., & Kumar, S. (2024, June). A Survey of Legal Text Analysis Techniques for Indian Legal Documents. In *2024 International Conference on Circuit, Systems and Communication (ICCSC)* (pp. 1-6). IEEE. DOI: 10.1109/ICCSC62074.2024.10616889

Goldman, O., Caciularu, A., Eyal, M., Cao, K., Szpektor, I., & Tsarfaty, R. (2024). Unpacking Tokenization: Evaluating Text Compression and its Correlation with Model Performance. arXiv preprint arXiv:2403.06265. DOI: 10.18653/v1/2024.findings-acl.134

Gorenstein, L., Konen, E., Green, M., & Klang, E. (2024). BERT in radiology: A systematic review of natural language processing applications. *Journal of the American College of Radiology*. Advance online publication. DOI: 10.1016/j.jacr.2024.01.012

Greeshma, M., & Simon, P. (2024). Bidirectional Gated Recurrent Unit with Glove Embedding and Attention Mechanism for Movie Review Classification. *Procedia Computer Science*, *233*, 528–536. DOI: 10.1016/j.procs.2024.03.242

Gupta, I., Chatterjee, I., & Gupta, N. (2023). A two-staged NLP-based framework for assessing the sentiments on Indian supreme court judgments. *International Journal of Information Technology : an Official Journal of Bharati Vidyapeeth's Institute of Computer Applications and Management, 15*(4), 2273–2282. DOI: 10.1007/s41870-023-01273-z PMID: 37256028

Hashem, I. A., & Tubishat, M. Hybrid Feature Selection Based on Principal Component Analysis and Grey Wolf Optimizer Algorithm for Arabic News Article Classification.

Jain, D., Borah, M. D., & Biswas, A. (2024). A sentence is known by the company it keeps: Improving Legal Document Summarization Using Deep Clustering. *Artificial Intelligence and Law, 32*(1), 165–200. DOI: 10.1007/s10506-023-09345-y

Jim, J. R., Talukder, M. A. R., Malakar, P., Kabir, M. M., Nur, K., &Mridha, M. F. (2024). Recent advancements and challenges of nlp-based sentiment analysis: A state-of-the-art review. Natural Language Processing Journal, 100059.

Jojoa, M., Eftekhar, P., Nowrouzi-Kia, B., & Garcia-Zapirain, B. (2024). Natural language processing analysis applied to COVID-19 open-text opinions using a distilBERT model for sentiment categorization. *AI & Society, 39*(3), 883–890. DOI: 10.1007/s00146-022-01594-w PMID: 36439363

Katz, D. M., Hartung, D., Gerlach, L., Jana, A., & Bommarito, M. J., II. (2023). Natural language processing in the legal domain. arXiv preprint arXiv:2302.12039.

Li, X., Wang, Y., Qiao, Y., Wang, Y., & Li, J. (2024, September). A Study on Named Entity Recognition of Chinese Social Text Based on ERNIE and Lexicon Enhancement. In 2024 2nd International Conference on Signal Processing and Intelligent Computing (SPIC) (pp. 472-477). IEEE. DOI: 10.1109/SPIC62469.2024.10691532

Mendhakar, A., & HS, D. (2024). Parts-of-Speech (PoS) Analysis and Classification of Various Text Genres. Corpus-based Studies across. *Humanities (Washington), 1*(1), 99–131.

Oliveira, V., Nogueira, G., Faleiros, T., & Marcacini, R. (2024). Combining prompt-based language models and weak supervision for labeling named entity recognition on legal documents. *Artificial Intelligence and Law*, •••, 1–21.

Özkurt, C. (2024). Comparative Analysis of State-of-the-Art Q&A Models: BERT, RoBERTa, DistilBERT, and ALBERT on SQuAD v2 Dataset. *Chaos and Fractals, 1*(1), 19–30.

Peng, Y. T., & Lei, C. L. (2024). Using Bidirectional Encoder Representations from Transformers (BERT) to predict criminal charges and sentences from Taiwanese court judgments. *PeerJ. Computer Science*, *10*, e1841. DOI: 10.7717/peerj-cs.1841 PMID: 38435559

Rana, A., Pant, A., Rawat, N., Rawat, P., Vats, S., & Sharma, V. (2024, July). Semantic Similarity Analysis using FastText. In 2024 IEEE 3rd World Conference on Applied Intelligence and Computing (AIC) (pp. 454-460). IEEE. DOI: 10.1109/AIC61668.2024.10731025

Rong, L., Ding, Y., Wang, M., El Saddik, A., & Hossain, M. S. (2024). A Multi-Modal ELMo Model for Image Sentiment Recognition of Consumer Data. *IEEE Transactions on Consumer Electronics*, *70*(1), 3697–3708. DOI: 10.1109/TCE.2024.3357543

Sengupta, S. (2024). Legislative Text Analysis from Judicial Case Reports Using Machine Learning. *SN Computer Science*, *5*(5), 443. DOI: 10.1007/s42979-024-02836-y

Siniosoglou, I., Asimopoulos, D., Argyriou, V., Lagkas, T., Lytos, A., Moscholios, I. D., & Sarigiannidis, P. (2024, March). Enhancing Text Anonymisation: A Study on CRF, LSTM, and ELMo for Advanced Entity Recognition. In *2024 Panhellenic Conference on Electronics & Telecommunications (PACET)* (pp. 1-6). IEEE. DOI: 10.1109/PACET60398.2024.10497084

Sukanya, G., & Priyadarshini, J. (2024, January). Analysis on word embedding and classifier models in legal analytics. In AIP Conference Proceedings (Vol. 2802, No. 1). AIP Publishing. DOI: 10.1063/5.0181820

Tucker, A. M., Xia, Y., & Smelcer, S. N. (2024). Text, tone, and legal language: Analyzing mutual fund disclosure sentiment. *American Business Law Journal*, *61*(1), 57–86. DOI: 10.1111/ablj.12239

Tummala, P., & KoteswaraRao, C. (2024). Exploring T5 & RGAN for enhanced sarcasm generation in NLP. IEEE Access.

Vallebueno, A., Handan-Nader, C., Manning, C. D., & Ho, D. E. (2024). Statistical Uncertainty in Word Embeddings: GloVe-V. arXiv preprint arXiv:2406.12165. DOI: 10.18653/v1/2024.emnlp-main.510

Yenduri, G., Ramalingam, M., Selvi, G. C., Supriya, Y., Srivastava, G., Maddikunta, P. K. R., Raj, G. D., Jhaveri, R. H., Prabadevi, B., Wang, W., Vasilakos, A. V., & Gadekallu, T. R. (2024). Gpt (generative pre-trained transformer)–a comprehensive review on enabling technologies, potential applications, emerging challenges, and future directions. *IEEE Access : Practical Innovations, Open Solutions, 12*, 54608–54649. DOI: 10.1109/ACCESS.2024.3389497

Yenduri, G., Ramalingam, M., Selvi, G. C., Supriya, Y., Srivastava, G., Maddikunta, P. K. R., Raj, G. D., Jhaveri, R. H., Prabadevi, B., Wang, W., Vasilakos, A. V., & Gadekallu, T. R. (2024). Gpt (generative pre-trained transformer)–a comprehensive review on enabling technologies, potential applications, emerging challenges, and future directions. *IEEE Access : Practical Innovations, Open Solutions, 12*, 54608–54649. DOI: 10.1109/ACCESS.2024.3389497

Compilation of References

Abdelmoumin, G., Rawat, D., & Rahman, A. (2021). On the Performance of Machine Learning Models for Anomaly-Based Intelligent Intrusion Detection Systems for the Internet of Things. *IEEE Internet of Things Journal*, *9*(6), 4280–4290. DOI: 10.1109/JIOT.2021.3103829

Aberdein, C., & Zimmerman, C. (2015). Access to mental health and psychosocial services in Cambodia by survivors of trafficking and exploitation: A qualitative study. *International Journal of Mental Health Systems*, *9*(1), 16. DOI: 10.1186/s13033-015-0008-8 PMID: 25861379

Abimbola, B., de La Cal Marin, E., & Tan, Q. (2024). Enhancing Legal Sentiment Analysis: A Convolutional Neural Network–Long Short-Term Memory Document-Level Model. *Machine Learning and Knowledge Extraction*, *6*(2), 877–897. DOI: 10.3390/make6020041

Abraham, S. (2023). The Development of Admiralty Jurisdiction in India: A Critical Analysis. Part 2 Indian J. *Integrated Rsch. L.*, *3*, 1.

Addis, M. E., & Hoffman, E. (2017). Men's depression and help-seeking through the lenses of gender. In Levant, R. F., & Joel Wong, Y. (Eds.), *The Psychology of Men and Masculinities* (pp. 171–196). American Psychological Association. DOI: 10.1037/0000023-007

Addis, M. E., & Mahalik, J. R. (2003). Men, Masculinity, and the Contexts of Help Seeking. *The American Psychologist*, *58*(1), 5–14. DOI: 10.1037/0003-066X.58.1.5 PMID: 12674814

Adjei, J. K., & Saewyc, E. M. (2017). Boys are not exempt: Sexual exploitation of adolescents in sub-Saharan Africa. *Child Abuse & Neglect*, *65*, 14–23. DOI: 10.1016/j.chiabu.2017.01.001 PMID: 28110108

Agrawal, S., Sarkar, S., Aouedi, O., Yenduri, G., Piamrat, K., Bhattacharya, S., Maddikunta, P., & Gadekallu, T. (2021). Federated Learning for Intrusion Detection System: Concepts, Challenges and Future Directions. *Computer Communications*, *195*, 346–361. DOI: 10.1016/j.comcom.2022.09.012

Aguilar Ruiz, M. Ó. (2016). El método de la Criminalística, estrategia de la investigación. En S. García Ramírez, & O. V. Islas, *Temas de derecho penal, seguridad pública y criminalística: cuartas jornadas sobre justicia penal* (págs. 181-182). México: UNAM, Instituto de Investigaciones Jurídicas. Obtenido de https://biblio.juridicas.unam.mx/bjv/detalle-libro/1724-temas-de-derecho-penal-seguridad-publica-y-criminalistica

Ahmad, S., Asghar, M. Z., Alotaibi, F. M., & Al-Otaibi, Y. D. (2022). A hybrid CNN+ BILSTM deep learning-based DSS for efficient prediction of judicial case decisions. *Expert Systems with Applications*, *209*, 118318. DOI: 10.1016/j.eswa.2022.118318

Aisyah, N., Hidayat, R., Zulaikha, S., Rizki, A., Yusof, Z. B., Pertiwi, D., & Ismail, F. (2019). Artificial Intelligence in Cryptographic Protocols: Securing E-Commerce Transactions and Ensuring Data Integrity.

Aiyengar, S. R. R. (2010). *National Strategy for Cyberspace Security*. KW Publisher.

AL-BAHOUTH, A.B.S.B.A., (2017). Virtual Money: Its concept, types, and economic effects. *Scientific Journal of Economics and Trade, Faculty of Commerce, Ain Shams University, Cairo, 65*.

Albarrán Martíneza, E. E. (2021). Delitos cibernéticos. *revistatransregiones.com*, 93-104. Obtenido de https://revistatransregiones.com/web/index.php/tr/article/download/18/15/31

Albright, K., Greenbaum, J., Edwards, S. A., & Tsai, C. (2020). Systematic review of facilitators of, barriers to, and recommendations for healthcare services for child survivors of human trafficking globally. *Child Abuse & Neglect*, *100*, 104289. DOI: 10.1016/j.chiabu.2019.104289 PMID: 31787336

Aliero, M. S., Ahmad, A. M., Kalgo, U. S., & Aliero, S. A. (2020). An overview of the Internet of Things: Understanding the issues and challenges of a more connected world. *International Journal of Computing and Communication Networks*, *2*(1), 1–11.

Allende López, M. (15 de Agosto de 2019). *La promesa de una nueva era tecnológica: la era cuántica*. Obtenido de Banco Interamericano de Desarrollo (BID): https://blogs.iadb.org/innovacion/es/impacto-de-las-tecnologias-cuanticas/

Alrawashdeh, K., & Purdy, C. (2016). Toward an Online Anomaly Intrusion Detection System Based on Deep Learning. *2016 15th IEEE International Conference on Machine Learning and Applications (ICMLA)*, 195-200. DOI: 10.1109/ICMLA.2016.0040

Alsuwian, T., Butt, A. S., & Amin, A. A. (2022). Smart Grid Cyber Security Enhancement: Challenges and Solutions—A Review. *Sustainability (Basel)*, *14*(21), 14226. DOI: 10.3390/su142114226

Altun, S., Abas, M., Zimmerman, C., Howard, L. M., & Oram, S. (2017). Mental health and human trafficking: Responding to survivors' needs. *BJPsych International*, *14*(1), 21–23. DOI: 10.1192/S205647400000163X PMID: 29093930

American Psychological Association. (s.f.). *Style and Grammar Guidelines*. Recuperado el 17 de enero de 2020, de Apastyle: https://apastyle.apa.org/style-grammar-guidelines

Anderson, S., & Tan, J. (2023). The use of convolutional neural networks for predicting mental health through visual data. *AI in Mental Health*, *15*(4), 202–215.

Andrade Molina, D. E. (2009a). Application of methods from the science of forensics to identify those responsible for homicide [bachelor thesis, Universidad del Azuay]. https://dspace.uazuay.edu.ec/handle/datos/877

Andrade Molina, D. E. (2009b). Application of forensic science methods to identify perpetrators of homicide [bachelor thesis, Universidad del Azuay]. https://dspace.uazuay.edu.ec/handle/datos/877

Angizeh, L. B., & Keyvanpour, M. R. (2024, April). Detecting Fake News using Advanced Language Models: BERT and RoBERTa. In 2024 10th International Conference on Web Research (ICWR) (pp. 46-52). IEEE.

Anil Kumar Srivastava v. Addl Director, MHFW, 2005(3) ESC 1917.

Animal Político. (2024, 26 de mayo). *Drones, la nueva tendencia en el arsenal de las organizaciones criminales*. https://www.animalpolitico.com/analisis/invitades/drones-tendencia-arsenal-crimen-organizado

Areshey, A., & Mathkour, H. (2024). Exploring transformer models for sentiment classification: A comparison of bert, roberta, albert, distilbert, and xlnet. *Expert Systems: International Journal of Knowledge Engineering and Neural Networks*, *41*(11), e13701. DOI: 10.1111/exsy.13701

Aria, M., & Cuccurullo, C. (2017). bibliometrix: An R-tool for comprehensive science mapping analysis. *Journal of Informetrics, 11*(4), 959–975. https://doi.org/https://doi.org/10.1016/j.joi.2017.08.007. DOI: 10.1016/j.joi.2017.08.007

Arquilla, J., & Ronfeldt, D. (1993). Cyberwar is coming! *Comparative Strategy, 12*(2), 141–165. https://www.dtic.mil/cgibin/GetTRDoc?Location=U2&doc=GetTRDoc.pdf&AD=ADA485253. DOI: 10.1080/01495939308402915

Arunthavanathan, R., Sajid, Z., & Amin, M. T. (2024). Ethics in AI for energy systems safety. In Methods in chemical process safety. DOI: 10.1016/bs.mcps.2024.08.002

Ash, C., & Otiende, S. (2023). *Meaningful Engagement of People with Lived Experience: A Framework and Assessment for Increasing Lived Experience Leadership Across the Spectrum of Engagement*. Global Fund to End Modern Slavery and National Survivor Network-Cast.

Aslam, N., Srivastava, S., & Gore, M. M. (2024). A comprehensive analysis of machine learning-and deep learning-based solutions for DDoS attack detection in SDN. *Arabian Journal for Science and Engineering, 49*(3), 3533–3573. DOI: 10.1007/s13369-023-08075-2

Auty, K. M., Cope, A., & Liebling, A. (2017). A systematic review and meta-analysis of yoga and mindfulness meditation in prison: Effects on psychological well-being and behavioural functioning. *International Journal of Offender Therapy and Comparative Criminology, 61*(6), 689–710. DOI: 10.1177/0306624X15602514 PMID: 26320031

Avella, M. del PR, Sanabria-Moyano, J.E., & Dinas-Hurtado, K. (2022). Use of the COMPAS algorithm in criminal proceedings and the risks to human rights. *Brazilian Journal of Criminal Procedural Law, 8*(1), 275–310.

Awad, M., & Fraihat, S. (2023). Recursive feature elimination with cross-validation with decision tree: Feature selection method for machine learning-based intrusion detection systems. *Journal of Sensor and Actuator Networks, 12*(5), 67. DOI: 10.3390/jsan12050067

Babu, C. S., & Vishnupriyan, J. VijaykumarReddy, U., Hariharan, P., & Dheenadhayalan, P. (2025). Secure Implementation of Image Processing Operations on CPU and GPU Architectures: With Deep Learning Frameworks. In Signal and Image Processing Techniques for Defense, Security, and Healthcare (pp. 253-302). IGI Global Scientific Publishing.

Babu, C. V. S., & Andrew, S. P. (2024). Adaptive AI for Dynamic Cybersecurity Systems: Enhancing Protection in a Rapidly Evolving Digital Landscape. In Zhihan, Lv., & Global, I. G. I. (Eds.), *Principles and Applications of Adaptive Artificial Intelligence* (pp. 52–72)., DOI: 10.4018/979-8-3693-0230-9.ch003

Babuta, A., & Oswald, M. (2021). Machine learning predictive algorithms and the policing of future crimes: governance and oversight. In J. L. McDaniel, & K. Pease, *Predictive policing and artificial intelligence.* Routledge, Taylor & Francis Group.

Bacigalupo, C. A. (2018). *Naturaleza del Ciberespacio.* Obtenido de CAB Group SRL: https://www.cabgroupsrl.com.ar/news/naturaleza-del-ciberespacio/

Bagley, B. M. (2012). *Drug trafficking and organized crime in the Americas: Major trends in the twenty-first century.* Woodrow Wilson International Center for Scholars.

Bahamazava, K., & Nanda, R. (2022). The shift of DarkNet illegal drug trade preferences in cryptocurrency: The question of traceability and deterrence. *Forensic Science International Digital Investigation, 40*, 301377. DOI: 10.1016/j.fsidi.2022.301377

Barker, G., Ricardo, C., Nascimento, M., Olukoya, A., & Santos, C. (2010). Questioning gender norms with men to improve health outcomes: Evidence of impact. *Global Public Health: An International Journal for Research, Policy and Practice, 5*(5), 539–553. DOI: 10.1080/17441690902942464 PMID: 19513910

Barnert, E., Iqbal, Z., Bruce, J., Anoshiravani, A., Kolhatkar, G., & Greenbaum, J. (2017). Commercial Sexual Exploitation and Sex Trafficking of Children and Adolescents: A Narrative Review. *Academic Pediatrics, 17*(8), 825–829. DOI: 10.1016/j.acap.2017.07.009 PMID: 28797913

Barrick, K., Lattimore, P. K., & Visher, C. A. (2014). Reentering women: The impact of social ties on long-term recidivism. *The Prison Journal, 94*(3), 279–304. DOI: 10.1177/0032885514537596

Bartolomé, M., & Monteiro Lima, A. G. (2021). El ciberespacio, antes, durante y después del COvID 19. La pandemia como una amenaza a la vida y a la. *Revista Academia de Guerra del Ejército Ecuatoriano, 14*(1), 67–76. DOI: 10.24133/age.n14.2021.06

BBVA. (25 de Octubre de 2024). *La IA, en los dos lados de la ciberseguridad: aliada y amenaza en el mundo digital.* Obtenido de BBVA Innovación: https://www.bbva.com/es/innovacion/la-ia-en-los-dos-lados-de-la-ciberseguridad-aliada-y-amenaza-en-el-mundo-digital/

Benkerroum, S., & Chougdali, K. (2023). Enhancing Forensic Analysis Using a Machine Learning-based Approach. *2023 6th International Conference on Advanced Communication Technologies and Networking (CommNet)*, pp. 1-6. DOI: 10.1109/CommNet60167.2023.10365260

Berk, R. A., & Bleich, J. (2013). Statistical procedures for forecasting criminal behavior: A comparative assessment. *Criminology & Pub. Pol'y, 12*.

Berk, R., Heidari, H., Jabbari, S., Kearns, M., & Roth, A. (2021). Fairness in criminal justice risk assessments: The state of the art. *Sociological Methods & Research*, *50*(1), 3–44. https://doi.org/https://doi.org/10.1177/0049124118782533. DOI: 10.1177/0049124118782533

Bhat, M. M. A. (2023). The parliament and state legislatures of India. In *Routledge Handbook of Asian Parliaments* (pp. 178–201). Routledge. DOI: 10.4324/9781003109402-13

Bhawna, & Mahajan, S. (2024). Artificial intelligence perspective on digital forensics. In S. Mahajan, M. Khurana, & V. V. Estrela (Eds.), *Applying artificial intelligence in cybersecurity analytics and cyber threat detection* (pp. 34-42). John Wiley & Sons.

Biddle, P., England, P., Peinado, M., & Willman, B. (2003). The darknet and the future of content protection. In *Digital Rights Management: ACM CCS-9 Workshop, DRM 2002, Washington, DC, USA, November 18, 2002. Revised Papers* (pp. 155-176). Springer Berlin Heidelberg.

Bond, R. T. J. (2001). Electronic commerce in the 21st century: Internet regulation—Heavy handed or light touch approach? A view from a European Union perspective. *William Mitchell Law Review*, *28*(2), 531–556.

Bowen, G., Sothinathan, J., & Bowen, R. (2024). Technological Governance (Cybersecurity and AI): Role of Digital Governance. In Jahankhani, H., Bowen, G., Sharif, M. S., & Hussien, O. (Eds.), *Cybersecurity and Artificial Intelligence: Transformational Strategies and Disruptive Innovation* (pp. 143–168). Springer. DOI: 10.1007/978-3-031-52272-7_6

Braun, V., & Clarke, V. (2006). Using thematic analysis in psychology. *Qualitative Research in Psychology*, *3*(2), 77–101. https://www.tandfonline.com/doi/abs/10.1191/1478088706QP063OA. DOI: 10.1191/1478088706qp063oa

Brenner, S. W. (2010). *Cybercrime: Criminal threats from cyberspace*. Greenwood Publishing Group. DOI: 10.5040/9798400636554

Brown, M., & Miller, J. (2023). Integrating decision support systems in mental health care prediction. *Journal of Health Informatics*, *32*(2), 113–126.

Brunton, G., Oliver, S., & Thomas, J. (2020). Innovations in framework synthesis as a systematic review method. *Research Synthesis Methods, 11*(3), 316–330. DOI: 10.1002/jrsm.1399 PMID: 32090479

Buczak, A., & Guven, E. (2016). A Survey of Data Mining and Machine Learning Methods for Cyber Security Intrusion Detection. *IEEE Communications Surveys and Tutorials, 18*(2), 1153–1176. DOI: 10.1109/COMST.2015.2494502

Bulanda, J., & Johnson, T. B. (2016). A Trauma-Informed Model for Empowerment Programs Targeting Vulnerable Youth. *Child & Adolescent Social Work Journal, 33*(4), 303–312. DOI: 10.1007/s10560-015-0427-z

Bunge, M. (2013). *La ciencia: su método y su filosofía.* Editorial Laetoli. Obtenido de https://posgrado.unam.mx/musica/lecturas/LecturaIntroduccionInvestigacionMusical/epis temologia/Mario-Bunge-la-Ciencia-su-Metodo-y-Filosofia.pdf https://books.google.com.mx/books?id=OgmMDwAAQBAJ&pg=PT127&hl=es&source=gbs_selected_pages&cad=1#v=onepage&q&f=

Bunker, R. J., & Sullivan, J. P. (2021). *Evolved capabilities in Mexican drug trafficking: A 21st century profile of transnational organized crime.* Small Wars Journal. https://archive.smallwarsjournal.com/jrnl/art/evolved-capabilities-mexican-drug-trafficking-21st-century-profile-transnational-organized

Burrel, J., & Fourcader, M. (2021). The Society of Algorithms. *Annual Review of Sociology, 47*(1). https://doi.org/https://doi.org/10.1146/annurev-soc-090820-020800

Byrne, J. M., & Pattavina, A. (2012). Technological innovation and offender reentry. In *Technocrime: Policing and surveillance* (pp. 110–132). Routledge., https://www.taylorfrancis.com/chapters/edit/10.4324/9780203105245-8/technological-innovation-offender-reentry-james-byrne-april-pattavina

Caamaño Fernández, E. E., & Gil Herrera, R. d. (2020). Prevención de riesgos por ciberseguridad desde la auditoria forense: conjugando el talento humano organizacional. *NOVUM, revista de Ciencias Sociales Apliacadas, 1*(10), 61-80. Obtenido de https://www.redalyc.org/journal/5713/571361695004/html/

Call, J. B., & Shafer, K. (2018). Gendered Manifestations of Depression and Help Seeking Among Men. *American Journal of Men's Health, 12*(1), 41–51. DOI: 10.1177/1557988315623993 PMID: 26721265

Carroll, C., & Booth, A. (2015). Quality assessment of qualitative evidence for systematic review and synthesis: Is it meaningful, and if so, how should it be performed? *Research Synthesis Methods, 6*(2), 149–154. DOI: 10.1002/jrsm.1128 PMID: 26099483

Carroll, C., Booth, A., & Cooper, K. (2011). A worked example of "best fit" framework synthesis: A systematic review of views concerning the taking of some potential chemopreventive agents. *BMC Medical Research Methodology, 11*(1), 29. DOI: 10.1186/1471-2288-11-29 PMID: 21410933

Cary, M., Oram, S., Howard, L. M., Trevillion, K., & Byford, S. (2016). Human trafficking and severe mental illness: An economic analysis of survivors' use of psychiatric services. *BMC Health Services Research, 16*(1), 284. DOI: 10.1186/s12913-016-1541-0 PMID: 27430338

Casino, F., Dasaklis, T. K., & Patsakis, C. (2019). A systematic literature review of blockchain-based applications: Current status, classification, and open issues. *Telematics and Informatics, 36*, 55–81. DOI: 10.1016/j.tele.2018.11.006

Cavelty, M. D. (2012). The Militarization of Cybersecurity as a Source of Global Tension. In *Strategic Trends 2012: Key Development in Global Affairs* (pp.103-124). Centre for Security Studies.

CEPAL. (2021). *Tecnologías digitales para un nuevo futuro*. Obtenido de Naciones Unidas. Comisión Económica para América Latina y el Caribe (CEPAL): https://repositorio.cepal.org/server/api/core/bitstreams/879779be-c0a0-4e11-8e08-cf80b41a4fd9/content

Cervini, J., Rubin, A., & Watkins, L. (2022). Don't Drink the Cyber: Extrapolating the Possibilities of Oldsmar's Water Treatment Cyberattack. *International Conference on Cyber Warfare and Security*, 17(1), 19–25. DOI: 10.34190/iccws.17.1.29

Chacko, M., Misra, A., & Ramaswamy, S. (2021). Cybersecurity Laws in India: Is it time for a Regime Change? *Legal500*. https://www.legal500.com/developments/thought-leadership/cybersecurity-laws-in-india-is-it-time-for-a-regime-change/#_ftn5

Chadha, S. (2024). Cyber Frauds Cost India Rs. 177 Crore in FY24: How to Protect Yourself. *Business Standard*. https://www.business-standard.com/finance/personal-finance/cyber-frauds-cost-india-rs-177-crore-in-fy24-how-to-protect-yourself-124080600123_1.html

Chandrachud, D. Y. (2017). Supreme Court of India Justice KS Puttaswamy (Retd)... vs Union Of India And Ors. on 24 August, 2017.

Chang, L., & Zhao, W. (2023). Topic modeling with latent Dirichlet allocation for mental health analysis in textual data. *Journal of Clinical AI, 18*(3), 89–102.

Chan, J., & Bennet, M. L. (2017). Making sense of big data for security. *British Journal of Criminology*, *57*(2), 299–319. https://doi.org/https://doi.org/10.1093/bjc/azw059

Chaparro, J. (2022). *Drones and Organized Crime: A New War Front in Mexico*. Center for National Security Studies.

Chatmon, B. N. (2020). Males and Mental Health Stigma. *American Journal of Men's Health*, *14*(4), 1557988320949322. DOI: 10.1177/1557988320949322 PMID: 32812501

Chatterjee, S. (2019). Is data privacy a fundamental right in India? An analysis and recommendations from policy and legal perspective. *International Journal of Law and Management*, *61*(1), 170–190. DOI: 10.1108/IJLMA-01-2018-0013

Chkirbene, Z., Erbad, A., Hamila, R., Gouissem, A., Mohamed, A., & Hamdi, M. (2020). Machine Learning Based Cloud Computing Anomalies Detection. *IEEE Network*, *34*(6), 178–183. DOI: 10.1109/MNET.011.2000097

Christie, N. (1986). The ideal victim. In Fattah, E. A. (Ed.), *From Crime Policy to Victim Policy* (pp. 17–30). Palgrave Macmillan. DOI: 10.1007/978-1-349-08305-3_2

CICDDoS2019 Dataset. Canadian Institute for Cybersecurity, [Online]. Available: https://www.unb.ca/cic/datasets/ddos-2019.html

CNI. (Octubre de 2024). *Centro Nacional de Inteligencia*. Obtenido de Gobierno de México: http://www.cni.gob.mx/transparencia/Centro-Nacional-Inteligencia.htm

Cobo, M. J., López-Herrera, A. G., Herrera-Viedma, E., & Herrera, F. (2011). Science mapping software tools: Review, analysis, and cooperative study among tools. *Journal of the American Society for Information Science and Technology*, *62*(7), 1382–1402. https://doi.org/https://doi.org/10.1002/asi.21525. DOI: 10.1002/asi.21525

Cockbain, E., Ashby, M., & Brayley, H. (2017). Immaterial Boys? A Large-Scale Exploration of Gender-Based Differences in Child Sexual Exploitation Service Users. *Sexual Abuse*, *29*(7), 658–684. DOI: 10.1177/1079063215616817 PMID: 26634379

Cohen, L. E., & Felson, M. (2010). Social Change and Crime Rate Trends: A Routine Activity Approach. *American Sociological Review*, *44*(4), 588-608. https://doi.org/https://doi.org/10.2307/2094589

Committee to Protect Journalists. (2021, August 6). Pakistan authorities detain, investigate journalists Amir Mir and Imran Shafqat. https://cpj.org/2021/08/pakistan-authorities-detain-investigate-journalists-amir-mir-and-imran-shafqat/

CONAVIM. (Noviembre de 2024). *¿Has sufrido acoso cibernético? ¡Identifica sus modalidades y protégete!* Obtenido de Comisión Nacional para Prevenir y Erradicar la Violencia Contra las Mujeres: https://www.gob.mx/conavim/articulos/has-sufrido-acoso-cibernetico-te-decimos-a-donde-acudir#:~:text=Si%20quieres%20denunciar%20violencia%20cibern%C3%A9tica,los%20365%20d%C3%ADas%20del%20a%C3%B1o.

Condon, L., Hek, G., Harris, F., Powell, J., Kemple, T., & Price, S. (2007). Users' views of prison health services: A qualitative study. *Journal of Advanced Nursing*, *58*(3), 216–226. DOI: 10.1111/j.1365-2648.2007.04221.x PMID: 17474910

Congress of the United Mexican States. (2024). *Federal Penal Code*. Official Gazette of the Federation. https://www.diputados.gob.mx/LeyesBiblio/pdf/9_180324.pdf

Cottey, A. (2016, April). Reducing Ethical Hazards in Knowledge Production. *Science and Engineering Ethics*, *22*(2), 367–389. DOI: 10.1007/s11948-015-9651-3 PMID: 25991087

Council of Europe. (2024, August 9). United Nations treaty on cybercrime agreed by the Ad Hoc Committee. *Council of Europe*. https://www.coe.int/en/web/cybercrime/-/united-nations-treaty-on-cybercrime-agreed-by-the-ad-hoc-committee

Cui, J., Shen, X., & Wen, S. (2023). A survey on legal judgment prediction: Datasets, metrics, models and challenges. *IEEE Access : Practical Innovations, Open Solutions*, *11*, 102050–102071. DOI: 10.1109/ACCESS.2023.3317083

Dakalbab, F., Talib, M. A., Waraga, O. A., Nassif, A. B., Abbas, S., & Nasir, Q. (2022). Artificial intelligence & crime prediction: A systematic literature review. *Social Sciences & Humanities Open*, *6*(1), 100342. https://doi.org/https://doi.org/10.1016/j.ssaho.2022.100342. DOI: 10.1016/j.ssaho.2022.100342

Danshin, M. V., & Kostenko, M. V. (2020). Moral foundations of counteraction of criminality: ethical questions of criminalistics. *Publishing House "Baltija Publishing"*.

Das, M., & Alphonse, P. J. A. (2023). A comparative study on tf-idf feature weighting method and its analysis using unstructured dataset. arXiv preprint arXiv:2308.04037.

Dasari, S., & Kaluri, R. (2024). An effective classification of DDoS attacks in a distributed network by adopting hierarchical machine learning and hyperparameters optimization techniques. *IEEE Access : Practical Innovations, Open Solutions*, *12*, 10834–10845. DOI: 10.1109/ACCESS.2024.3352281

Davis, E., & Patel, R. (2023). K-nearest neighbors for mental health risk prediction in at-risk populations. *Advances in Psychiatric Diagnosis*, *17*(2), 98–112.

Dawes Centre for Future Crime at UCL. (2020). *AI-enabled future crime*. UCL. Retrieved from https://www.ucl.ac.uk/jill-dando-institute/sites/jill-dando-institute/files/ai_crime_policy_0.pdf

De Paula, G. (2023). Decision-making, criminal intelligence and new analysis tools: The use of artificial intelligence. *Journal of the National Intelligence School, 1*(2), 133–149. DOI: 10.58752/AZFVQ42S

Delsol, G. (2024, August 14). Draft UN Convention against cybercrime: Implications for digital global governance. *Disruptive Competition Project*. https://project-disco.org/privacy/draft-un-convention-against-cybercrime-implications-for-digital-global-governance/

Devi, S. (2019). Cybersecurity in the National Security Discourse. *World Affairs, 23*(2), 146–159.

Dewey, S., Codallos, K., Barry, R., Drenkhahn, K., Glover, M., Muthig, A., Roberts, S. L., & Abbott, B. (2020). Higher education in prison. *Journal of Correctional Education (1974-), 71*(1), 57-89. https://www.jstor.org/stable/26915042

Díaz Aranda, E. (2016). *Lecciones de derecho penal (para el nuevo sistema de justicia en México)*. UNAM, Instituto de Investigaciones Jurídicas.

Dibany, J. (2023). Use of drones in criminal activities could carry a sentence of 53 years in prison. *El Sol de México*. https://oem.com.mx/elsoldemexico/mexico/uso-de-drones-en-actividades-delictivas-podria-alcanzar-una-pena-de-53-anos-de-prision-16951763#!

Donthu, N., Kumar, S., Mukherjee, D., Pandey, N., & Marc, W. (2021). How to conduct a bibliometric analysis: An overview and guidelines. *Journal of Business Research, 133*, 285–296. https://doi.org/https://doi.org/10.1016/j.jbusres.2021.04.070. DOI: 10.1016/j.jbusres.2021.04.070

Doran, M. D. (2014). *A forensic look at bitcoin cryptocurrency* (Master's thesis, Utica College).

Dressel, J., & Farid, H. (2018). The accuracy, fairness, and limits of predicting recidivism. *Science Advances, 1*(1), 4. https://doi.org/https://doi.org/10.1126/sciadv.aao5580. DOI: 10.1126/sciadv.aao5580 PMID: 29376122

DSCI. (2020). National Cybersecurity Strategy. https://www.dsci.in/files/content/knowledge-centre/2023/National-Cyber-Security-Strategy-2020-DSCI-submission.pdf

DSCI. (2023). India: Cybersecurity Domestic Report 2023. https://www.dsci.in/resource/content/india-cybersecurity-domestic-report-2023

Dudani, S., Baggili, I., Raymond, D., & Marchany, R. (2023). The current state of cryptocurrency forensics. *Forensic Science International Digital Investigation*, *46*, 301576. DOI: 10.1016/j.fsidi.2023.301576

Duffield, E., & Hagan, K. (2014). Darkcoin: Peertopeer cryptocurrency with anonymous blockchain transactions and an improved proof of work system. *bitpaper.Info*.

Duggal, P. (2005). Cyber-Crime in India: The Legal Approach. In *Cyber-Crime: The Challenge in Asia* (pp. 183-196). Hong Kong University Press.

Dunsin, D., Ghanem, M., Ouazzane, K., & Vassilev, V. 2023. A Comprehensive Analysis of the Role of Artificial Intelligence and Machine Learning in Modern Digital Forensics and Incident Response. *ArXiv*, abs/2309.07064. /arXiv.2309.07064. DOI: 10.2139/ssrn.4554035

Duraiswamy, D. R. (2017). Privacy and Data Protection in India. *Journal of Law & Cyber Warfare*, *6*(1), 166–186.

Durnell, E., Okabe-Miyamoto, K., Howell, R. T., & Zizi, M. (2020). Online privacy breaches, offline consequences: Construction and validation of the concerns with the protection of informational privacy scale. *International Journal of Human-Computer Interaction*, *36*(19), 1834–1848. DOI: 10.1080/10447318.2020.1794626

Easterbrook, F. H. (1996). Cyberspace and the law of the horse. *University of Chicago Legal Forum*, *1996*(1), 207–216.

Ekechukwu, N. D. E., & Simpa, N. P. (2024). The future of Cybersecurity in renewable energy systems: A review, identifying challenges and proposing strategic solutions. *Computer Science & IT Research Journal*, *5*(6), 1265–1299. DOI: 10.51594/csitrj.v5i6.1197

El País. (2025, January 28). *Mexico investigates alleged attack by criminals on a U.S. patrol boat on the banks of the Rio Grande*. https://elpais.com/mexico/2025-01-28/mexico-indaga-un-supuesto-ataque-de-criminales-a-una-patrulla-estadounidense-en-la-ribera-del-rio-bravo.html

El Universal. (March 8, 2024). *Michoacán records the highest number of drone attacks by organized crime: Sedena*. https://www.jornada.com.mx/noticia/2024/03/08/politica/michoacan-registra-el-mayor-numero-de-ataques-con-drones-del-crimen-organizado-sedena-809

El-Kady, R. M. (2024). Investigating Forensic Evidence in Metaverse: A Comparative Analytical Study. In *Forecasting Cyber Crimes in the Age of the Metaverse* (pp. 227-258). IGI Global.

El-Kady, R. (2021). Combating organized crime via the dark web: An analytical study in Egyptian legislation. *National Criminal Journal, 64*(3), 44–105. DOI: 10.21608/ncj.2021.225839

El-Kady, R. (2023). Handling E-evidence in Egyptian and Comparative Legislation: A Comparative Analytical Study. *Arab Journal of Forensic Sciences & Forensic Medicine*, *6*(1), 37–68. DOI: 10.26735/WGZY6322

El-Kady, R. (2024). Artificial Intelligence and Criminal Law. In *Artificial Intelligence Approaches to Sustainable Accounting* (pp. 34–52). IGI Global. DOI: 10.4018/979-8-3693-0847-9.ch003

European Commission. (2018). *Artificial Intelligence for Europe*. https://eur-lex.europa.eu/legal-content/ES/TXT/?uri=CELEX%3A52018DC0237

European Commission. (2024, August 13). *Commission reached an agreement on the new international cybercrime convention*. https://home-affairs.ec.europa.eu/news/commission-reached-agreement-new-international-cybercrime-convention-2024-08-13_en

European Parliament and Council of the European Union. (2024a). Regulation (EU) 2024/1689 of the European Parliament and of the Council of 13 June 2024 laying down harmonised rules on artificial intelligence and amending Regulations (EC) No 300/2008, (EU) No 167/2013, (EU) No 168/2013, (EU) 2018/858, (EU) 2018/1139, and (EU) 2019/2144 and Directives 2014/90/EU, (EU) 2016/797, and (EU) 2020/1828 (Artificial Intelligence Act). Official Journal of the European Union, L 1689, 12.7.2024. https://data.europa.eu/eli/reg/2024/1689/oj

European Parliament and Council of the European Union. (2024b). Regulation (EU) 2024/2847 of the European Parliament and of the Council of 23 October 2024 on horizontal cybersecurity requirements for products with digital elements and amending Regulations (EU) No 168/2013 and (EU) No 2019/1020 and Directive (EU) 2020/1828 (Cyber Resilience Act). Official Journal of the European Union, L 20/11/2024. https://data.europa.eu/eli/reg/2024/2847/oj

Europol & UNICRI. (2023). Malicious Uses and Abuses of Artificial Intelligence. Retrieved from https://www.ucl.ac.uk/jill-dando-institute/sites/jill-dando-institute/files/ai_crime_policy_0.pdf

Fakiha, B. (2023). Enhancing Cyber Forensics with AI and Machine Learning: A Study on Automated Threat Analysis and Classification. *International Journal of Safety and Security Engineering*, *13*(4), 701–707. Advance online publication. DOI: 10.18280/ijsse.130412

Farabee, D., Schulte, M., Gonzales, R., & Grella, C. E. (2016). Technological aids for improving longitudinal research on substance use disorders. *BMC Health Services Research*, *16*(1), 1–8. DOI: 10.1186/s12913-016-1630-0 PMID: 27509830

Farley, H., & Pike, A. (2016). Engaging prisoners in education: Reducing risk and recidivism. *Advancing Corrections: Journal of the International Corrections and Prisons Association, 1*, 65-73. https://oro.open.ac.uk/46511/

Farooq, M. U., Waseem, M., Khairi, A., & Mazhar, S. (2015). A Critical Analysis on the Security Concerns of Internet of Things (IoT). *International Journal of Computer Applications*, *111*(7), 1–6. DOI: 10.5120/19547-1280

Fazel, M., & Stein, A. (2002). The mental health of refugee children. *Archives of Disease in Childhood*, *87*(5), 366–370. DOI: 10.1136/adc.87.5.366 PMID: 12390902

FBI, D., (2012). Bitcoin virtual currency: Unique features present distinct challenges for deterring illicit activity. *Intelligence Assessment*.

Federal Office for Information Security. (2023). AI security concerns in a nutshell. Federal Office for Information Security. https://www.bsi.bund.de/SharedDocs/Downloads/EN/BSI/KI/Practical_Al-Security_Guide_2023.pdf

Federation of Catholic Family Associations in Europe. (2024). *FAFCE comment on UN Treaty on Cybercrime*. https://www.fafce.org/fafce-comment-on-un-treaty-on-cybercrime/

Ferguson, A. G. (2016). Policing Predictive Policing. https://doi.org/Available at *SSRN*: https://ssrn.com/abstract=2765525

Fernandez Bermejo, D., & Martínez Atienza, G. (2018). *Ciberseguridad, Ciberespacio y Ciberdelincuencia*. España: https://sistemabibliotecario.scjn.gob.mx/sisbib/2018/000295777/000295777.pdf

Ferrag, M. A., Friha, O., Hamouda, D., Maglaras, L., & Janicke, H. (2022). Edge-IIoTset: A New Comprehensive Realistic Cyber Security Dataset of IoT and IIoT Applications for Centralized and Federated Learning. *IEEE Access : Practical Innovations, Open Solutions*, *10*, 40281–40306. https://doi.org/https://doi.org/10.1109/ACCESS.2022.3165809. DOI: 10.1109/ACCESS.2022.3165809

FGJCDMX. (Octubre de 2024). *Glosario de Delitos Cibernéticos*. Obtenido de Unidad de Inteligencia Cibernética: https://www.fgjcdmx.gob.mx/storage/app/media/Unidad%20de%20Inteligencia%20Ciber netica/delitos-ciberneticos.pdf

FGJTam. (22 de Octubre de 2024). *Delitos Cibernéticos*. Obtenido de Fiscalía General de Justicia del Estado de Tamaulipas: https://www.fgjtam.gob.mx/delitos-ciberneticos/

Forbes Mexico. (2023, September 5). *Attacks with explosive-equipped drones are on the rise in Mexico*. https://www.forbes.com.mx/aumentan-en-mexico-los-ataques-con-drones-equipados-con-explosivos/

Frustaci, M., Pace, P., Aloi, G., & Fortino, G. (2017). Evaluating Critical Security Issues of the IoT World: Present and Future Challenges. *IEEE Internet of Things Journal*, *5*(4), 2483–2495. DOI: 10.1109/JIOT.2017.2767291

G A, S., Prabha, R., Sridevi, S., & Rohini, A. (2024). Artificial Intelligence: Advanced Mathematical Constructs and Theoretical Framework in Machine Learning and Deep Learning Algorithms.

Gacek, J., & Jochelson, R. (2022). Green Criminology and the Law. In Springer eBooks. DOI: 10.1007/978-3-030-82412-9

Gálvez, Y. (2025). It is extremely frightening to observe how these new technologies can be used by criminal organizations as weapons. *Dialogue Americas*. https://dialogo-americas.com/articles/organized-crime-and-its-use-of-drones-to-sow-terror/

Gangi, M. (2024). The Impact of Artificial Intelligence Systems in Criminal Law: An Integral and Integrated Development Perspective. In *Intersections Between Rights and Technology* (pp. 61–83). IGI Global. DOI: 10.4018/979-8-3693-1127-1.ch005

Gannon, C., Blokland, A. A., Huikuri, S., Babchishin, K. M., & Lehmann, R. J. (2023). Child sexual abuse material on the darknet. *Forensische Psychiatrie, Psychologie, Kriminologie*, *17*(4), 353–365. DOI: 10.1007/s11757-023-00790-8

García Álvarez, M. F. (2014). Constelación de los sistemas que se relacionan con la violencia y la criminalidad femenina. *Archivos de Criminología, Seguridad Privada y Criminalística. Año 2, vol. III agosto-diciembre*, 26-32.

García Cabeza de Vaca, F. J. (25 de Septiembre de 2019). *3 Informe de Gobierno*. Obtenido de Gobierno del Estado de Tamaulipas: https://www.tamaulipas.gob.mx/wp-content/uploads/2018/01/tercer-informe-de-gobierno. pdf

García Fernandez, M. Á. (2019). Inteligencia artificial en imagen cardíaca: El futuro ya está aquí. *Revista Argentina de Cardiología, 87*(6), 491–495. DOI: 10.7775/rac.v87.i6.16997

Garcia, M., & Li, F. (2023). Modeling mental health transitions with hidden Markov models: A novel approach. *Journal of Healthcare Analytics, 12*(2), 99–112.

Garg, A., Panda, P., Neudecker, M., & Lee, S. (2020). Barriers to the access and utilization of healthcare for trafficked youth: A systematic review. *Child Abuse & Neglect, 100*, 104137. DOI: 10.1016/j.chiabu.2019.104137 PMID: 31427098

Garvie, C., Bedoya, A., & Franke, J. (2019). *The perpetual line-up: Unregulated police face recognition in America*. Georgetown Law Center on Privacy & Technology.

George, A., Jose, A., Ashik, F., Prabhakar, P., Pati, P. B., & Parida, S. (2024, March). Enhancing Legal Decision Making: WRIT Case Outcome Prediction with Legal-BERT Embeddings and AdaBoost Classifier. In 2024 IEEE International Conference on Contemporary Computing and Communications (InC4) (Vol. 1, pp. 1-6). IEEE.

Gervais, D. J. (2023). Towards an effective transnational regulation of AI. *AI & Society, 38*(1), 391–410.

Ghosh, T., & Kumar, S. (2024, June). A Survey of Legal Text Analysis Techniques for Indian Legal Documents. In *2024 International Conference on Circuit, Systems and Communication (ICCSC)* (pp. 1-6). IEEE. DOI: 10.1109/ICCSC62074.2024.10616889

Giacomello, G. (2024, December 6). The new UN cybercrime treaty is a bigger deal than even its critics realize. *Lawfare*. https://www.lawfaremedia.org/article/the-new-un-cybercrime-treaty-is-a-bigger-deal-than-even-its-critics-realize

Gibbs, C., Gore, M. L., McGarrell, E. F., & Rivers, L. (2009). Introducing Conservation Criminology: Towards Interdisciplinary Scholarship on Environmental Crimes and Risks. *British Journal of Criminology, 50*(1), 124–144. DOI: 10.1093/bjc/azp045

Gibbs, D. A., Hardison Walters, J. L., Lutnick, A., Miller, S., & Kluckman, M. (2015). Services to domestic minor victims of sex trafficking: Opportunities for engagement and support. *Children and Youth Services Review, 54*, 1–7. DOI: 10.1016/j.childyouth.2015.04.003

Glidden, C. B., Lea, C. W., & Victor, M. B. (2016). Evaluating legal risks and costs with decision tree analysis. Successful partnering between inside and outside counsel, 12-1.

Goldberg, A. P., Moore, J. L., Houck, C., Kaplan, D. M., & Barron, C. E. (2017). Domestic Minor Sex Trafficking Patients: A Retrospective Analysis of Medical Presentation. *Journal of Pediatric and Adolescent Gynecology*, *30*(1), 109–115. DOI: 10.1016/j.jpag.2016.08.010 PMID: 27575407

Golding, L. P., & Nicola, G. N. (2019, September). A Business Case for Artificial Intelligence Tools: The Currency of Improved Quality and Reduced Cost. *Journal of the American College of Radiology*, *16*(9, 9 Pt B), 1357–1361. DOI: 10.1016/j.jacr.2019.05.004 PMID: 31492415

Goldman, O., Caciularu, A., Eyal, M., Cao, K., Szpektor, I., & Tsarfaty, R. (2024). Unpacking Tokenization: Evaluating Text Compression and its Correlation with Model Performance. arXiv preprint arXiv:2403.06265. DOI: 10.18653/v1/2024.findings-acl.134

Gómez Tagle, E. (2006). *Law and Society. Glossary of Criminology and Social Sciences*. Pontifical University of Mexico.

González Miró, N. (2024). CLOUDS: Las nubes que almacenan la información que tu quieras. *El blog de Nacho González Miró*. Obtenido de https://nachogonzalezmiro.wordpress.com/blog/tecnologia/apps/las-nubes-que-almacenan-la-informacion-que-tu-quieras/

González, A. L., Moreno, M., Román, A. C. M., Fernández, Y. H., & Pérez, N. C. (2024). Ethics in Artificial Intelligence: An Approach to Cybersecurity. *INTELIGENCIA ARTIFICIAL*, *27*(73), 38–54. DOI: 10.4114/intartif.vol27iss73pp38-54

Google. (2024). *¿Qué es la inteligencia artificial o IA?* Obtenido de Google Cloud: https://cloud.google.com/learn/what-is-artificial-intelligence?hl=es-419

Gorenstein, L., Konen, E., Green, M., & Klang, E. (2024). BERT in radiology: A systematic review of natural language processing applications. *Journal of the American College of Radiology*. Advance online publication. DOI: 10.1016/j.jacr.2024.01.012

Goyal, P. (2022). The Death Trap that's India's Illegal Load Apps. *Newslaundry*. https://www.newslaundry.com/2022/09/24/the-death-trap-thats-indias-illegal-loan-apps

Greenbaum, V. J., Dodd, M., & McCracken, C. (2018). A short screening tool to identify victims of child sex trafficking in health care setting. *Pediatric Emergency Care*, *34*(1), 33–37. DOI: 10.1097/PEC.0000000000000602 PMID: 26599463

Greeshma, M., & Simon, P. (2024). Bidirectional Gated Recurrent Unit with Glove Embedding and Attention Mechanism for Movie Review Classification. *Procedia Computer Science*, *233*, 528–536. DOI: 10.1016/j.procs.2024.03.242

Guccione, D. (2019). *What is the dark web? How to access it and what you'll find, The state of cybersecurity*. CSO Online.

Guerra García, A. (2014). Ciberseguridad. *Universo*. Obtenido de https://www.uv.mx/universo/general/ciberseguridad/

Gulyamov, S. S., Fayziev, R. A., Rodionov, A. A., & Rustambekov, I. R. (2023). The Role of Information in Developing Ethical and Accurate AI for Energy Systems. 2022 4th International Conference on Control Systems, Mathematical Modeling, Automation and Energy Efficiency (SUMMA), 226–230. DOI: 10.1109/SUMMA60232.2023.10349398

Gupta, A., Gupta, R., & Sankaran, A. (2021). *Machine Learning Forensics*., DOI: 10.4018/978-1-7998-4900-1.ch003

Gupta, I., Chatterjee, I., & Gupta, N. (2023). A two-staged NLP-based framework for assessing the sentiments on Indian supreme court judgments. *International Journal of Information Technology : an Official Journal of Bharati Vidyapeeth's Institute of Computer Applications and Management, 15*(4), 2273–2282. DOI: 10.1007/s41870-023-01273-z PMID: 37256028

Gupta, N., & Sharma, L. (2023). Mental health prediction using XGBoost: A breakthrough in classification models. *Journal of Cognitive Data Science, 23*(2), 45–60.

Gupta, R. (2024). Cybersecurity Threats in E-Commerce: Trends and Mitigation Strategies. *Journal of Advanced Management Studies, 1*(3), 1–10. DOI: 10.36676/jams.v1.i3.13

Gustafson, K. (9 de Febrero de 2024). *Tecnologías modernas de las Ciencias Forenses*. Obtenido de Forensics Colleges: https://www.forensicscolleges.com/blog/resources/10-modern-forensic-science-technolog ies

Gyamfi, E., & Jurcut, A. (2023). Novel Online Network Intrusion Detection System for Industrial IoT Based on OI-SVDD and AS-ELM. *IEEE Internet of Things Journal, 10*(5), 3827–3839. DOI: 10.1109/JIOT.2022.3172393

Hacker, D., Levine-Fraiman, Y., & Halili, I. (2015). Ungendering and Regendering Shelters for Survivors of Human Trafficking. *Social Inclusion (Lisboa), 3*(1), 35–51. DOI: 10.17645/si.v3i1.173

Hall, M., & Rossmanith, K. (2016). Imposed stories: Prisoner self-narratives in the criminal justice system in New South Wales, Australia. *International Journal for Crime, Justice and Social Democracy, 5*(1), 38-51. https://search.informit.org/doi/abs/10.3316/INFORMIT.241278363448884

Harán, J. M. (22 de Diciembre de 2020). *29 datos que deja el 2020 que hablan del estado actual de la ciberseguridad.* Obtenido de Welivesegurity. Cibercrimen: https://www.welivesecurity.com/la-es/2020/12/22/datos-2020-sobre-estado-actual-ciberse guridad/

Harlev, M. A., Sun Yin, H., Langenheldt, K. C., Mukkamala, R., & Vatrapu, R. (2018). Breaking bad: De-anonymising entity types on the bitcoin blockchain using supervised machine learning.

Hashem, I. A., & Tubishat, M. Hybrid Feature Selection Based on Principal Component Analysis and Grey Wolf Optimizer Algorithm for Arabic News Article Classification.

Hasler, O. (2021). Green Criminology and an International Law Against Ecocide: Using Strict Liability and Superior Responsibility to Prevent State and Corporate Denial of Environmental Harms. In Springer eBooks (pp. 387–408). DOI: 10.1007/978-3-030-82412-9_17

Hebert, L. A. (2016). Always Victimizers, Never Victims: Engaging Men and Boys in Human Trafficking Scholarship. *Journal of Human Trafficking*, *2*(4), 281–296. DOI: 10.1080/23322705.2016.1144165

He, C., Tan, T. P., Zhang, X., & Xue, S. (2023). Knowledge-enriched multi-cross attention network for legal judgment prediction. *IEEE Access : Practical Innovations, Open Solutions*, *11*, 87571–87582. DOI: 10.1109/ACCESS.2023.3305259

Hernández, A. (2024). *The Secret History: AMLO and the Sinaloa Cartel.* Grijalbo.

Hoffman, B. (2006). *Inside terrorism.* Columbia University Press.

Howard, J. (2019). Artificial intelligence: Implications for the future of work. *American Journal of Industrial Medicine*, *62*(11), 917–926. DOI: 10.1002/ajim.23037 PMID: 31436850

Huang, L., Qin, J., Zhou, Y., Zhu, F., Liu, L., & Shao, L. (2023). Normalization techniques in training dnns: Methodology, analysis and application. *IEEE Transactions on Pattern Analysis and Machine Intelligence*, *45*(8), 10173–10196. DOI: 10.1109/TPAMI.2023.3250241 PMID: 37027763

Huang, Q., & Zheng, T. (2023). Mental health prediction using Naive Bayes: Insights and limitations. *International Journal of Machine Learning in Healthcare*, *14*(1), 77–88.

Huang, Y., & Wang, J. (2023). Clustering techniques for mental health prediction: K-means and DBSCAN comparison. *AI in Public Health*, *24*(1), 33–46.

Human Rights Watch. (2024, October 21). EU member states should vote no on UN cybercrime treaty. https://www.hrw.org/news/2024/10/21/eu-member-states-should-vote-no-un-cybercrime-treaty

Ife, C. C., Davies, T., Murdoch, S. J., & Stringhini, G. (2019). Bridging information security and environmental criminology research to mitigate cybercrime better. *arXiv preprint arXiv:1910.06380.*

Ige, N. B., Kupa, N. E., & Ilori, N. O. (2024a). Analyzing defense strategies against cyber risks in the energy sector: Enhancing the security of renewable energy sources. *International Journal of Science and Research Archive*, *12*(1), 2978–2995. DOI: 10.30574/ijsra.2024.12.1.1186

Ige, N. B., Kupa, N. E., & Ilori, N. O. (2024b). Best practices in cybersecurity for green building management systems: Protecting sustainable infrastructure from cyber threats. *International Journal of Science and Research Archive*, *12*(1), 2960–2977. DOI: 10.30574/ijsra.2024.12.1.1185

Iglesias-Rios, L., Harlow, S. D., Burgard, S. A., Kiss, L., & Zimmerman, C. (2018). Mental health, violence and psychological coercion among female and male trafficking survivors in the greater Mekong sub-region: A cross-sectional study. *BMC Psychology*, *6*(1), 56. DOI: 10.1186/s40359-018-0269-5 PMID: 30541612

Iglesias-Rios, L., Harlow, S. D., Burgard, S. A., Kiss, L., & Zimmerman, C. (2019b). Gender differences in the association of living and working conditions and the mental health of trafficking survivors. *International Journal of Public Health*, *64*(7), 1015–1024. DOI: 10.1007/s00038-019-01269-2 PMID: 31243470

Iglesias-Rios, L., Harlow, S. D., Burgard, S. A., West, B., Kiss, L., & Zimmerman, C. (2019a). Patterns of violence and coercion with mental health among female and male trafficking survivors: A latent class analysis with mixture models. *Epidemiology and Psychiatric Sciences*, *29*, e38. DOI: 10.1017/S2045796019000295 PMID: 31142398

Ignjatović, Đ. (2023). Green criminology and crime control. *Crimen*, *14*(1), 24–63. DOI: 10.5937/crimen2301024I

Imandeka, E., Putra, P. O. H., Hidayanto, A. N., & Mahmud, M. (2024). Exploring the World of Smart Prisons: Barriers, Trends, and Sustainable Solutions. *Human Behavior and Emerging Technologies*, *2024*(1), 6158154. DOI: 10.1155/2024/6158154

INESDI. (07 de Septiembre de 2023). 5 ejemplos cotidianos de Inteligencia Artificial. *Blog*. Instituto de Innovación Digital de las Profesiones. Obtenido de https://www.inesdi.com/blog/ejemplos-cotidianos-de-ia/

INTERPOL. (Agosto de 2020). *Ciberdelincuencia: efectos de la COVID-19*. Obtenido de Secretaría General de INTERPOL: https://www.interpol.int/es/Noticias-y-acontecimientos/Noticias/2020/Un-informe-de-INTERPOL-muestra-un-aumento-alarmante-de-los-ciberataques-durante-la-epidemia-de-COVID-19

ISACA. (2024). *State of Cybersecurity 2024: Global update on workforce efforts, resources, and cyberoperations*. https://www.isaca.org/resources/reports/state-of-cybersecurity-2024

ISO. (2023). *ISO/IEC 42001:2023 Information technology — Artificial intelligence — Management system requirements*. International Organization for Standardization.

Jackson, S., & Chen, R. (2023). Applying factor analysis for identifying mental health determinants. *Journal of Psychological Assessment*, *40*(2), 122–137.

Jagjit Sing v. State of Punjab, Sl. L. P. Crl. No. 3583/2021.

Jahnavi, & Urvashi. (2024). Review on machine learning-based traffic rules contravention detection system. In S. Mahajan, M. Khurana, & V. V. Estrela (Eds.), *Applying artificial intelligence in cybersecurity analytics and cyber threat detection* (pp. 45-57). John Wiley & Sons.

Jaimovich, D. (14 de Octubre de 2019). Cuál fue la primera computadora de la historia. *Infobae*. Obtenido de https://www.infobae.com/america/tecno/2019/10/14/cual-fue-la-primera-computadora-de-la-historia/

Jain, S. (2014). Cybersecurity: A *Sine Qua Non*. *IDR*. https://indiandefencereview.com/cyber-security-a-sine-qua-non/

Jain, D., Borah, M. D., & Biswas, A. (2024). A sentence is known by the company it keeps: Improving Legal Document Summarization Using Deep Clustering. *Artificial Intelligence and Law*, *32*(1), 165–200. DOI: 10.1007/s10506-023-09345-y

Jain, J., Bennett, M., Bailey, M. D., Liaou, D., Kaltiso, S.-A. O., Greenbaum, J., Williams, K., Gordon, M. R., Torres, M. I. M., Nguyen, P. T., Coverdale, J. H., Williams, V., Hari, C., Rodriguez, S., Salami, T., & Potter, J. N. E. (2022). Creating a Collaborative Trauma-Informed Interdisciplinary Citywide Victim Services Model Focused on Health Care for Survivors of Human Trafficking. *Public Health Reports*, *137*(1_suppl, S1), 30S–37S. DOI: 10.1177/00333549211059833 PMID: 35775914

Jarmul, K. (2023). *Practical data privacy: Enhancing privacy and security in data. Sebastopol*. O'Reilly Media.

Järveläinen, E., & Rantanen, T. (2021). Incarcerated people's challenges for digital inclusion in Finnish prisons. *Nordic Journal of Criminology*, *22*(2), 240–259. DOI: 10.1080/2578983X.2020.1819092

Jewell, C. (2019). Inteligencia artificial: la nueva electricidad. *OMPI Revista*. Obtenido de https://www.wipo.int/wipo_magazine/es/2019/03/article_0001.html

Jewkes, Y., & Reisdorf, B. C. (2016). A brave new world: The problems and opportunities presented by new media technologies in prisons. *Criminology & Criminal Justice*, *16*(5), 534–551. DOI: 10.1177/1748895816654953

Jim, J. R., Talukder, M. A. R., Malakar, P., Kabir, M. M., Nur, K., &Mridha, M. F. (2024). Recent advancements and challenges of nlp-based sentiment analysis: A state-of-the-art review. Natural Language Processing Journal, 100059.

Jojoa, M., Eftekhar, P., Nowrouzi-Kia, B., & Garcia-Zapirain, B. (2024). Natural language processing analysis applied to COVID-19 open-text opinions using a distilBERT model for sentiment categorization. *AI & Society*, *39*(3), 883–890. DOI: 10.1007/s00146-022-01594-w PMID: 36439363

Joshi, C. (2023). Cryptocurrency Forensics: The Ultimate Guide to 6 Important Aspects. Indiaforensic. https://indiaforensic.com/cryptocurrency-forensics/

Joshi, V., & Korah, J. (2022). Formulating Parallel Supervised Machine Learning Designs for Anomaly-Based Network Intrusion Detection in Resource-Constrained Use Cases. *2022 IEEE 19th International Conference on Mobile Ad Hoc and Smart Systems (MASS)*, 748-753. DOI: 10.1109/MASS56207.2022.00117

Junklewitz, H., Hamon, R., André, A., Evas, T., Soler Garrido, J., & Sanchez Martin, J. I. (2023). *Cybersecurity of Artificial Intelligence in the AI Act*. Publications Office of the European Union., DOI: 10.2760/271009

Kaplan, A., & Haenlein, M. (2019). Siri, Siri, en mi mano: ¿Quién es la más bella del mundo? Sobre las interpretaciones, ilustraciones e implicaciones de la inteligencia artificial. *Horizontes de negocios, 62*(1), 15-25. DOI: 10.1016/j.bushor.2018.08.004

Katz, D. M., Hartung, D., Gerlach, L., Jana, A., & Bommarito, M. J., II. (2023). Natural language processing in the legal domain. arXiv preprint arXiv:2302.12039.

Kavenagh, M., Stoeltje, M., & Dank, M. (2024). Practitioner Reflection: Reliance on Informal and Gig Economies Leaves LGBTQ+ Populations with Fewer Economic Choices and Greater Vulnerability to Trafficking. *Journal of Human Trafficking*, *10*(2), 346–355. DOI: 10.1080/23322705.2024.2310349

Kazemian, L. (2019). *Positive growth and redemption in prison: Finding light behind bars and beyond*. Routledge., DOI: 10.4324/9780429458149

Kerr, A., & Willis, M. (2018). Prisoner use of information and communications technology. *Trends and Issues in Crime and Criminal Justice*, (560), 1–19. https://search.informit.org/doi/abs/10.3316/ielapa.983664576232696. DOI: 10.52922/ti107289

Khan, A., & O'Connor, P. (2023). Autoencoders for mental health anomaly detection: An effective tool. *Journal of Neural Engineering in Health, 15*(1), 67–80.

Kharak Singh v. State of UP, AIR, 1963 SC 1295.

Kim, H., & Zhou, P. (2023). Ensemble models for mental health prediction: An evaluation of bagging and boosting approaches. *Journal of AI in Healthcare, 25*(4), 201–215.

Kleinberg, J., Lakkaraju, H., Leskovec, J., Ludwig, J., & Mullainathan, S. (2018). Human decisions and machine predictions. *The Quarterly Journal of Economics, 133*(1), 237–293. https://doi.org/https://doi.org/10.1093/qje/qjx032 PMID: 29755141

Knight, V. (2017). Digitizing the prison: The light and dark future. https://dora.dmu.ac.uk/server/api/core/bitstreams/2d76dffe-1c88-440b-950c-215e0d95e97e/content

Knight, V., & Van De Steene, S. (2020). The digital prison: Towards an ethics of technology. In *Prisons and Community Corrections* (pp. 57–71). Routledge., https://www.taylorfrancis.com/chapters/edit/10.4324/9781003010562-5/digital-prison-victoria-knight-steven-van-de-steene DOI: 10.4324/9781003010562-5

Krebs, B. (2021, February 10). *What's most interesting about the Florida water system hack? That we heard about it at all.*https://krebsonsecurity.com/. https://krebsonsecurity.com/2021/02/whats-most-interesting-about-the-florida-water-system-hack-that-we-heard-about-it-at-all/

Kshetri, N. (2016). Cybercrime and Cybersecurity in India: Causes, Consequences, and Implications for the Future. *Crime, Law, and Social Change, 66*(3), 313–338. DOI: 10.1007/s10611-016-9629-3

Kshetri, N. (2016). Cybersecurity and Development. *Markets Globalization & Development Review, 1*(2). Advance online publication. DOI: 10.23860/MGDR-2016-01-02-03

Kumar, A. K., Chidipothu, V. K., & Leelavathi, M. (2025). ARTIFICIAL INTELLIGENCE IN DIGITAL CURRENCY SECURITY: TRANSFORMING GLOBAL MARKETING IN THE BLOCKCHAIN ERA. *Cuestiones de Fisioterapia, 54*(3), 1907–1928.

Kumar, A., & Sharma, I. (2023). Preserving Security of Crypto Transactions with Machine Learning Methodologies. *2023 International Conference on Sustainable Computing and Smart Systems (ICSCSS)*, pp. 129-134. DOI: 10.1109/ICSCSS57650.2023.10169192

Kumar, A., & Singh, D. (2024). Detection and prevention of DDoS attacks on edge computing of IoT devices through reinforcement learning. *International Journal of Information Technology : an Official Journal of Bharati Vidyapeeth's Institute of Computer Applications and Management*, *16*(3), 1365–1376. DOI: 10.1007/s41870-023-01508-z

Kumar, V. (2022). Issues & Challenges of Cybersecurity in India: A Study. *International Journal of Novel Research and Development*, *7*(8), 140–147.

Kurani, A., Doshi, P., Vakharia, A., & Shah, M. (2023). A comprehensive comparative study of artificial neural network (ANN) and support vector machines (SVM) on stock forecasting. *Annals of Data Science*, *10*(1), 183–208. DOI: 10.1007/s40745-021-00344-x

La Jornada. (2024, January 5). *Guerrero: Drone attack reported in Heliodoro Castillo.*https://www.jornada.com.mx/noticia/2024/01/05/estados/guerrero-denuncian-ataque-con-drones-en-heliodoro-castillo-7596

La Silla Rota. (January 3, 2024). *Drones of Crime: How Cartels Are Arming Commercial Aircraft to Attack.* https://lasillarota.com

Lakra, R., & Jha, N. (2024). Publicly Available Data in the DPDPA Act 2023: Interpretative, Constitutional and Comparative Perspectives. Constitutional and Comparative Perspectives (August 22, 2024).

Leach, R., Carreiro, S., Shaffer, P. M., Gaba, A., & Smelson, D. (2022). Digital health interventions for mental health, substance use, and co-occurring disorders in the criminal justice population: A scoping review. *Frontiers in Psychiatry*, *12*, 794785. DOI: 10.3389/fpsyt.2021.794785 PMID: 35126204

Lee, C., & Zhang, M. (2023). Leveraging long short-term memory networks for predicting mental health trajectories. *Journal of Mental Health Technologies*, *8*(1), 34–46.

Lee, R., & Kim, S. (2023). Support vector machines in mental health prediction: Challenges and improvements. *Mental Health AI Review*, *11*(4), 56–70.

Lessig, L. (1999). The law of the horse: What cyberlaw might teach. *Harvard Law Review*, *113*(2), 501–549. DOI: 10.2307/1342331

Li, X., Wang, Y., Qiao, Y., Wang, Y., & Li, J. (2024, September). A Study on Named Entity Recognition of Chinese Social Text Based on ERNIE and Lexicon Enhancement. In 2024 2nd International Conference on Signal Processing and Intelligent Computing (SPIC) (pp. 472-477). IEEE. DOI: 10.1109/SPIC62469.2024.10691532

Lindemulder, G., & Kosinski, M. (12 de Agosto de 2024). *¿Que es la ciberseguridad?* Obtenido de IBM: https://www.ibm.com/mx-es/topics/cybersecurity

Lira Arteaga, O. M. (2014). *Cibercriminalidad. Fundamentos de la investigación en México.* INACIPE.

LISA Institute. (2024). *Diferencia entre Ciberseguridad, Seguridad Informática y Seguridad de la Información.* Obtenido de LISA Institute - Seguridad, Ciberseguridad, Inteligencia y Geopolítica: https://www.lisainstitute.com/blogs/blog/diferencia -ciberseguridad-seguridad-informatica-seguridad-informacion?srsltid=AfmB OooR3vhA85MhfWaUbrSi_Qov73rpoKjwD9YE- 7acnTerY0aRY-8P

Liu, L., An, D., Wang, Y., Ma, X., & Jiang, C. (2021, June). Research on legal judgment prediction based on Bert and LSTM-CNN fusion model. In 2021 3rd world symposium on artificial intelligence (WSAI) (pp. 41-45). IEEE. DOI: 10.1109/ WSAI51899.2021.9486374

Liu, J., & Zhang, K. (2023). Bayesian networks for predicting mental health outcomes: Methodological advances. *Journal of Bayesian Cognitive Science*, *7*(4), 180–195.

Li, Z., Rios, A., & Trajković, L. (2021). Machine Learning for Detecting Anomalies and Intrusions in Communication Networks. *IEEE Journal on Selected Areas in Communications*, *39*(7), 2254–2264. DOI: 10.1109/JSAC.2021.3078497

Llinares, F. M. (2018). Inteligencia artificial y justicia penal: más allá de los resultados lesivos causados por robots. *Revista de Derecho Penal y Criminologia, 20*, 87-130. https://doi.org/https://doi.org/10.5944/rdpc.20.2018.26446

López Macedonio, M. N. (2018). *El archivo de la Dirección Federal de Seguridad: una fuente para escribir la historia de la segunda mitad del siglo XX mexicano.* Obtenido de Legajos. Boletín del Archivo General de la Nación. Núm. 15, pp. 71-82: https://archivos.gob.mx/Legajos/pdf/Legajos15/06Elarchivo.pdf

Lopezosa, C., Codina, L., & Boté-Vericad, J. J. (2023). *Testing ATLAS.ti with OpenAI: Towards a new paradigm for qualitative interview analysis with artificial intelligence.* http://repositori.upf.edu/handle/10230/56449

Lopezosa, C., Pérez-Montoro, M., Rey Martín, K., Lopezosa, C., Pérez-Montoro, M., & Rey Martín, K. (2024). The use of artificial intelligence in newsrooms: Proposals and limitations. *Journal of Communication, 23*(1), 279–294. DOI: 10.26441/RC23.1-2024-3309

Lynch, M. J., & Long, M. A. (2021). Green Criminology: Capitalism, Green Crime and Justice, and Environmental Destruction. *Annual Review of Criminology, 5*(1), 255–276. DOI: 10.1146/annurev-criminol-030920-114647

Mahlangu, G., & Zivanai, E. (2023). Offender eLearning: A systematic literature review on reentry, recidivism, and life after prison. *Cogent Social Sciences, 9*(2), 2246706. DOI: 10.1080/23311886.2023.2246706

Mahler, T., & Bing, J. (2006). Contractual risk management in an ICT context—Searching for a possible interface between legal methods and risk analysis. *Scandinavian Studies in Law, 49*, 339–366.

Malhotra, C., & Malhotra, U. (2024). Putting Interests of Digital Nagriks First: Digital Personal Data Protection (DPDP) Act 2023 of India. *The Indian Journal of Public Administration, 70*(3), 516–531. DOI: 10.1177/00195561241271575

Martin, M. (2021). *Computer and Internet use in the United States: 2018*. American Community Survey Reports.

Martin, T., & Wang, D. (2023). Predicting mental health issues using recurrent neural networks in sequential data. *Journal of Behavioral Science AI, 22*(2), 99–112.

McCarthy, J. (2004). *What is Artificial Intelligence?*http://jmc.stanford.edu/articles.html

McDougall, C., Pearson, D. A., Torgerson, D. J., & Garcia-Reyes, M. (2017). The effect of digital technology on prisoner behavior and reoffending: A natural stepped-wedge design. *Journal of Experimental Criminology, 13*(4), 455–482. DOI: 10.1007/s11292-017-9303-5

Meijer, A., & Wessels, M. (2019). Predictive Policing: Review of Benefits and Drawbacks. *International Journal of Public Administration, 42*(12), 1031–1039. https://doi.org/https://doi.org/10.1080/01900692.2019.1575664. DOI: 10.1080/01900692.2019.1575664

Meit, Y. (2018). Cyber Surakshit Bharat. https://www.meity.gov.in/writereaddata/files/Cyber-Surakshit-Bharat-Brochure.pdf

Meit, Y. (n. d.). Cyber Swachhta Kendra. https://www.csk.gov.in/

Meit, Y. (2004). CERT-In. https://www.cert-in.org.in/

Mendhakar, A., & HS, D. (2024). Parts-of-Speech (PoS) Analysis and Classification of Various Text Genres. Corpus-based Studies across. *Humanities (Washington), 1*(1), 99–131.

Mendoza Marquez, J. L., & Fernández, T. C. R. (2017). Ciberidentidades y redes sociales. En W. Aranguren, Y. Delgado, & B. Hamidian, *Venezuela en la mira de las Ciencias Económicas y Sociales. Encuentro de saberes* (pág. 522). Venezuela: Universidad de Carabobo. Obtenido de https://www.researchgate.net/publication/315445868_CIBERIDENTIDAD_Y_REDES_ SOCIALES

Mercan, G., & Varol Selçuk, Z. (2024). Artificial intelligence (AI) activities in legal practices. [PDF] [Artificial intelligence] [AI]. *International Journal of Eurasian Education and Culture, 9*(25), 131–144. DOI: 10.35826/ijoecc.1824

Metibemu, O. C., Adesokan-Imran, T. O., Ajayi, A. J., Tiwo, O. J., Olutimehin, A. T., & Olaniyi, O. O. (2025). Developing Proactive Threat Mitigation Strategies for Cloud Misconfiguration Risks in Financial SaaS Applications. *Journal of Engineering Research and Reports, 27*(3), 393–413. DOI: 10.9734/jerr/2025/v27i31442

México, C. N. D. H. (Julio de 2018). *Derecho de acceso a las tecnologías de la información y la comunicación.* Obtenido de Comisión Nacional de los Derechos Humanos: https://www.cndh.org.mx/sites/all/doc/programas/ninez_familia/material/trip-derecho-acc eso.pdf

Microsoft. (2022a). Microsoft Responsible AI Standard v2. Microsoft Corporation. https://blogs.microsoft.com/wp-content/uploads/prod/sites/5/2022/06/Microsoft-Responsible-AI-Standard-v2-General-Requirements-3.pdf

Microsoft. (2022b). Microsoft Responsible AI Impact Assessment Guide. Microsoft Corporation. https://blogs.microsoft.com/wp-content/uploads/prod/sites/5/2022/06/Microsoft-RAI-Impact-Assessment-Guide.pdf

Microsoft. (2022c). Responsible AI Impact Assessment Template. Retrieved from Microsoft Responsible AI documentation. https://blogs.microsoft.com/wp-content/uploads/prod/sites/5/2022/06/Microsoft-RAI-Impact-Assessment-Template.pdf

Milenio. (2023, May 5). *Guerrero: Drone attack reported in the mountains.* https://www.milenio.com/estados/guerrero-reportan-ataque-con-drones-en-la-sierra

Miller, M. (16 de Abril de 2020). El FBI detecta un aumento en los informes de delitos cibernéticos durante la pandemia de coronavirus. *The Hill. Policía. Ciberseguridad.* Obtenido de https://thehill.com/policy/cybersecurity/493198-fbi-sees-spike-in-cyber-crime-reports-dur ing-coronavirus-pandemic/

Ministry of Law and Justice. (2024). Ministry of Law and Justice Organizes Conference Titled 'India's Progressive Path in the Administration of Criminal Justice System.' *Ministry of Law and Justice*. https://www.pib.gov.in/PressReleasePage.aspx?PRID=2018392

Miranda, H. (2022). Inteligencia artificial y justicia. *Revista de la Facultad de Derecho de México, 72*(284), 373-402. https://doi.org/http://10.22201/fder.24488933e.2022.284.83394

Miró Linares, F. (10 de Septiembre de 2012). Cibercriminalidad: la delincuencia en "el otro espacio". *Legis. Ámbito Jurídico*. Obtenido de https://www.ambitojuridico.com/noticias/penal/penal/cibercriminalidad-la-delincuencia-e n-el-otro-espacio

Miró-Llinares, F., & Moneva, A. (2019). Environmental Criminology and Cybercrime: Shifting Focus from the Wine to the Bottles. In Springer eBooks (pp. 1–22). DOI: 10.1007/978-3-319-90307-1_30-1

MITRE. (2023). MITRE ATLAS™: AI security 101 and adversarial tactics for AI systems. MITRE. https://atlas.mitre.org

Mittelstadt, B., Russel, C., & Wachter, S. (2019). Explaining Explanations in AI. *Proceedings of the conference on fairness, accountability, and transparency*, (pp. 279-288). https://doi.org/https://doi.org/10.1145/3287560.3287574

Mohler, G. O., Short, M. B., Malinoswki, S., Johnson, M., Tita, G. E., Bertozzi, A. L., & Brantingham, P. J. (2015). Randomized Controlled Field Trials of Predictive Policing. *Journa of the American Statistical Association, 110*(512), 1399-1411. https://doi.org/https://doi.org/10.1080/01621459.2015.1077710

Mongeon, P., & Paul-Hus, A. (2016). The journal coverage of Web of Science and Scopus: A comparative analysis. *Scientometrics*, *106*(1), 2013–2228. https://doi.org/https://doi.org/10.1007/s11192-015-1765-5. DOI: 10.1007/s11192-015-1765-5

Montanez, A. (2014). *Investigation of cryptocurrency wallets on iOS and Android mobile devices for potential forensic artifacts. Department Forensic Science*. Marshall University.

Moreno González, R. (2016). Temas de Criminalística. En S. García Ramírez, O. Islas, & L. A. Vargas Casillas, *Temas de derecho penal, seguridad pública y criminalística: cuartas jornadas sobre justicia penal* (págs. 175-180). México: UNAM, Instituto de Investigaciones Jurídicas. Obtenido de https://biblio.juridicas.unam.mx/bjv/detalle-libro/1724-temas-de-derecho-penal-seguridad-publica-y-criminalistica

Morente Parra, V. (2019). Big Data or the art of analyzing massive data. A critical reflection from the perspective of fundamental rights. *Rights and Freedoms*, *41*(II), 225–253.

Moussa, R., Hernández, L., & Jiménez, P. (2021). Artificial Intelligence and Crime: A Rising Threat in Cyberspace. *Journal of Digital Security*, *8*(2), 45–60.

Mudgal, A. (2025). Leveraging AI and ML for Proactive Threat Detection for E-Commerce. In *Strategic Innovations of AI and ML for E-Commerce Data Security* (pp. 281–322). IGI Global.

Mukhopadhyay, D. (2022). Cybersecurity in India. *Communications of the ACM*, *65*(11), 98–102. DOI: 10.1145/3554910

Munjal, G., & Puri, T. (2024). Analysis of malicious executables and detection techniques. In Mahajan, S., Khurana, M., & Estrela, V. V. (Eds.), *Applying artificial intelligence in cybersecurity analytics and cyber threat detection* (pp. 3–20). John Wiley & Sons. DOI: 10.1002/9781394196470.ch1

Munro, G., & Pritchard, C. (2013). *Support Needs of Male Victims of Human Trafficking*. The Salvation Army.

Muraya, D. N., & Fry, D. (2016). Aftercare Services for Child Victims of Sex Trafficking: A Systematic Review of Policy and Practice. *Trauma, Violence & Abuse*, *17*(2), 204–220. DOI: 10.1177/1524838015584356 PMID: 26025452

Murugesan, S., & Alagesan, S. P. (2021). Actualising the Right to Adequate Standard of Living: A Critical Examination of Green Criminology from an Indian Perspective. In Springer eBooks (pp. 293–312). DOI: 10.1007/978-3-030-56227-4_14

Muthamil Sudar, K., & Deepalakshmi, P. (2020). A two level security mechanism to detect a DDoS flooding attack in software-defined networks using entropy-based and C4. 5 technique. *Journal of High Speed Networks*, *26*(1), 55–76. DOI: 10.3233/JHS-200630

Muthamil Sudar, K., & Deepalakshmi, P. (2021). An intelligent flow-based and signature-based IDS for SDNs using ensemble feature selection and a multi-layer machine learning-based classifier. *Journal of Intelligent & Fuzzy Systems*, *40*(3), 4237–4256. DOI: 10.3233/JIFS-200850

Nadtochiy, J. V. (2018). CYBERCRIME AS A THREAT TO ENVIRONMENTAL SECURITY. *Азиатско-Тихоокеанский Регион Экономика Политика Право*, *3*(3), 108–116. DOI: 10.24866/1813-3274/2018-3/108-116

Naithani, P. (2024). Analysis of India's Digital Personal Data Protection Act, 2023. International Journal of Law and Management.

Nakamoto, S., & Bitcoin, A. (2008). A peer-to-peer electronic cash system. *Bitcoin.–URL:*https://bitcoin. org/bitcoin. pdf, *4*(2), p.15.

National Institute of Standards and Technology (NIST). (2023a). Artificial Intelligence Risk Management Framework (AI RMF 1.0). https://doi.org/DOI: 10.6028/NIST.AI.100-1

National Institute of Standards and Technology (NIST). (2024). *NIST AI 600-1: AI Risk Management Framework for Generative AI.* U.S. Department of Commerce., DOI: 10.6028/NIST.AI.600-1

National Institute of Standards and Technology. (2023b). AI RMF Playbook. National Institute of Standards and Technology. https://airc.nist.gov/docs/AI_RMF_Playbook.pdf

NCIIPC. (2024). About Us. https://www.nciipc.gov.in/

Ndindeng, A. N. (2024). Mental health and well-being in prisons and places of detention. *International Journal of Prison Health.* Advance online publication. DOI: 10.1108/IJOPH-07-2024-0035 PMID: 39465264

NDTV. (2024). No One can Arrest through Video Calls: Cyber Security Agency on Scam Calls. *NDTV.* https://www.ndtv.com/india-news/no-one-can-arrest-through-video-calls-cyber-security-agency-on-scam-calls-6728458

Newton, C. (2024). 4 Ways AI Is Shaping Organized Crime in Latin America. InSight Crime. Retrieved from https://insightcrime.org

NIC. (n. d.). https://www.nic.in/mandate/

Nigam, S. K., Deroy, A., Maity, S., & Bhattacharya, A. (2024). Rethinking legal judgement prediction in a realistic scenario in the era of large language models. arXiv preprint arXiv:2410.10542. DOI: 10.18653/v1/2024.nllp-1.6

Nilsson, N. J. (1998). *Artificial intelligence: A new synthesis.* Morgan Kaufmann Publishers.

Nodzenski, M., Kiss, L., Pocock, N. S., Stoeckl, H., Zimmerman, C., & Buller, A. M. (2020). Post-trafficking stressors: The influence of hopes, fears and expectations on the mental health of young trafficking survivors in the Greater Mekong Subregion. *Child Abuse & Neglect, 100*, 104067. DOI: 10.1016/j.chiabu.2019.104067 PMID: 31272744

Nour, K. (2022). Criminal confrontation of cryptocurrency use in the financing of terrorism. *Jolets.* 16;2(2):79-152. Available from: https://jolets.org/ojs/index.php/jolets/article/view/12

Nzobonimpa, S., & Savard, J.-F. (2023). Ready but irresponsible? Analysis of the Government Artificial Intelligence Readiness Index. *Policy and Internet, 15*(3), 397–414. DOI: 10.1002/poi3.351

Obeidat, T.. (1996). *Methods and Techniques of Scientific Research.* Dar Sana'a for Publishing. (In Arabic)

Ochoa Serafín, M. (27 de Junio de 2024). Delitos informáticos en México: las leyes y las multas. *Ciberseguridad.* Obtenido de https://www.itmastersmag.com/ciberseguridad/delitos-informaticos-en-mexico-que-dice-l a-ley/#:~:text=En%20el%20C%C3%B3digo%20Penal%20Federal%20mexicano%2C%2 0se%20encuentra%20una%20secci%C3%B3n,se%20detallan%20las%20conductas%20ti pificadas.

OECD. (2012). Cybersecurity Policy Making at a Turning Point. https://www.oecd.org/en/publications/cybersecurity-policy-making-at-a-turning-point_5k8zq92vdgtl-en.html

OECD. (2024). OECD AI Principles overview. https://oecd.ai/en/ai-principles

Oliveira, V., Nogueira, G., Faleiros, T., & Marcacini, R. (2024). Combining prompt-based language models and weak supervision for labeling named entity recognition on legal documents. *Artificial Intelligence and Law,* •••, 1–21.

Oram, S., Hemmings, S., Abas, M., Howard, L., Bick, D., Jakobowitz, S., ... & Zimmerman, C. (2016). Provider Responses Treatment and Care for Trafficked People: Final Report for the Department of Health Policy Research Programme: Optimising identification, referral and care of trafficked people within the NHS (115/0006).

Oram, S., Khondoker, M., Abas, M., Broadbent, M., & Howard, L. M. (2015). Characteristics of trafficked adults and children with severe mental illness: A historical cohort study. *The Lancet. Psychiatry, 2*(12), 1084–1091. DOI: 10.1016/S2215-0366(15)00290-4 PMID: 26489912

Özkurt, C. (2024). Comparative Analysis of State-of-the-Art Q&A Models: BERT, RoBERTa, DistilBERT, and ALBERT on SQuAD v2 Dataset. *Chaos and Fractals, 1*(1), 19–30.

Palreddy, V. K. (2020). Punishments for Cybercrimes in IPC. *IPleaders.* https://blog.ipleaders.in/punishments-cyber-crimes-ipc/

Pandi, S. S., Farook, A. M., & Kingston, W. (2023, December). Scenario based Deep Learning Prediction for Legal Judgment using LSTM and CNN. In *2023 Third International Conference on Smart Technologies, Communication and Robotics (STCR)* (Vol. 1, pp. 1-6). IEEE.

Parga, M. O. (2023). CAN ARTIFICIAL INTELLIGENCE REPLACE THE HUMAN MIND? IMPLICATIONS OF AI FOR FUNDAMENTAL RIGHTS AND ETHICS. *Annals of the Francisco Suárez Chair, 57*, 39–61. DOI: 10.30827/acfs.v57i.24710

Patel, M., & Wu, H. (2023). Deep neural networks for early mental health prediction: Opportunities and challenges. *Journal of Neuroinformatics, 28*(1), 56–72.

Patil, S., Vijayakumar, V., Walimbe, D., Gulechha, S., Shenoy, S., Raina, A., & Kotecha, K. (2021). Improving the Robustness of AI-Based Malware Detection Using Adversarial Machine Learning. *Algorithms, 14*(10), 297. DOI: 10.3390/a14100297

Patkar, S., & Dhakad, A. (2022). An Evolving Concern for National Cybersecurity in India. *ACCLAIMS, 20*, 1–9.

Pavani, B. V., Mahitha, D., Prabhakar, P., & Pati, P. B. (2024, April). Identifying Sentiment in Legal Case Judgments using Random Forest Classifier. In 2024 IEEE 9th International Conference for Convergence in Technology (I2CT) (pp. 1-5). IEEE. DOI: 10.1109/I2CT61223.2024.10544116

Pelcastre, J. 2024. Organized Crime and Its Use of Drones to Spread Terror. *Dialogo Americas*. https://dialogo-americas.com/articles/organized-crime-and-its-use-of-drones-to-spread-terror/

Peng, Y. T., & Lei, C. L. (2024). Using Bidirectional Encoder Representations from Transformers (BERT) to predict criminal charges and sentences from Taiwanese court judgments. *PeerJ. Computer Science, 10*, e1841. DOI: 10.7717/peerj-cs.1841 PMID: 38435559

Pérez Porto, J., & Gardey, A. (01 de Abril de 2022). Ciberespacio - Qué es, definición y concepto. Obtenido de //definicion.de/ciberespacio/

Perry, W. L., McInnis, B., Price, C. C., Smith, S. C., & Hollywood, J. S. (2013). *Predictive policing: The role of crime forecasting in law enforcement operations.* RAND Corporation. https://www.rand.org/pubs/research_reports/RR233.html

Perry, W. L. (2013). *Predictive policing: The role of crime forecasting in law enforcement operations*. Rand Corporation. DOI: 10.7249/RR233

Picken, J. (2012). The coping strategies, adjustment and well being of male inmates in the prison environment. *Internet Journal of Criminology, 2012*, 1-29. https://d1wqtxts1xzle7.cloudfront.net/80111102/b93dd4_63ebd332965f40f9b28f85d9bc37e63f-libre.pdf?1643878436=&response-content-disposition=inline%3B+filename%3DThe_Coping_Strategies_Adjustment A

Pineda Cortés, L. A. (2024). *AI, a metaphor for this and other times.* UNAM Gazette. https://www.gaceta.unam.mx/ia-metafora-de-este-y-otros-tiempos/

Pływaczewski, W. (2023). REHABILITATION AND THERAPEUTIC PROGRAMMES IN THE LIGHT OF GREEN CRIMINOLOGY (REFLECTIONS BASED ON THE EXPERIENCE OF SELECTED PENITENTIARY INSTITUTIONS). *Probacja, 1*, 11–39. DOI: 10.5604/01.3001.0016.2846

Proceso. (2024, April 9). *The CJNG adopts chemical explosives to break through in Michoacán.*https://www.proceso.com.mx/nacional/2024/04/09/el-cjng-adopta-explosivos-quimicos-para-abrirse-paso-en-michoacan-278664.html

Pubby, M. (2012). China Hackers Enter Navy Computers, Plant Bug to Extract Sensitive Data. *The Indian Express*. https://indianexpress.com/article/news-archive/web/china-hackers-enter-navy-computers-plant-bug-to-extract-sensitive-data/

Purgato, M., Gross, A. L., Betancourt, T., Bolton, P., Bonetto, C., Gastaldon, C., Gordon, J., O'Callaghan, P., Papola, D., Peltonen, K., Punamaki, R.-L., Richards, J., Staples, J. K., Unterhitzenberger, J., van Ommeren, M., de Jong, J., Jordans, M. J. D., Tol, W. A., & Barbui, C. (2018). Focused psychosocial interventions for children in low-resource humanitarian settings: A systematic review and individual participant data meta-analysis. *The Lancet. Global Health, 6*(4), e390–e400. DOI: 10.1016/S2214-109X(18)30046-9 PMID: 29530422

Quintana, Y. (2016). *Ciberguerra*. Editorial Catarata.

Quteishat, E. M. A., Qtaishat, A., Quteishat, A. M. A., Al Adwan, M. A. S., Younis, M. A., & Kumar, M. (2024). Predictive Modelling in Legal Decision-Making: Leveraging Machine Learning for Forecasting Legal Outcomes. *Journal of Electrical Systems, 20*(3), 2060–2071. DOI: 10.52783/jes.4006

Rafferty, J., Yogman, M., Baum, R., Gambon, T. B., Lavin, A., Mattson, G., Wissow, L. S., Breuner, C., Alderman, E. M., Grubb, L. K., Powers, M. E., Upadhya, K., Wallace, S. B., Hunt, L., Gearhart, A. T., Harris, C., Lowe, K. M., Rodgers, C. T., & Sherer, I. M.Committee on Psychosocial Aspects of Child and Family Health. (2018). Ensuring comprehensive care and support for transgender and gender-diverse children and adolescents. *Pediatrics, 142*(4), e20182162. DOI: 10.1542/peds.2018-2162 PMID: 30224363

Rana, A., Pant, A., Rawat, N., Rawat, P., Vats, S., & Sharma, V. (2024, July). Semantic Similarity Analysis using FastText. In 2024 IEEE 3rd World Conference on Applied Intelligence and Computing (AIC) (pp. 454-460). IEEE. DOI: 10.1109/AIC61668.2024.10731025

Rani, P., & Sehrawat, H. (2024, December). Comprehensive Analysis of Cybersecurity: Examining Existing Literature and Identifying Potential Areas for Future Research. In 2024 1st International Conference on Advances in Computing, Communication and Networking (ICAC2N) (pp. 731-736). IEEE.

Rani, A. J. M., Bharathwaj, K. S., Swaroopan, N. J., Kumar, K. H., & Geetha, R. (2023, November). A Legal Prediction Model Using Support Vector Machine and K-Means Clustering Algorithm for Predicting Judgements and Making Decisions. In *2023 International Conference on Research Methodologies in Knowledge Management, Artificial Intelligence and Telecommunication Engineering (RMKMATE)* (pp. 1-6). IEEE. DOI: 10.1109/RMKMATE59243.2023.10369625

Redondo, S., & Garrido Genovés, V. (2013). *Principios de criminología*. Tirant lo Blanch.

Reid, F., & Harrigan, M. (2013). *An analysis of anonymity in the Bitcoin system*. Springer. DOI: 10.1007/978-1-4614-4139-7_10

Reyes, R. J. A., Poveda, M. Y. B., & Calderón, G. X. C. (2023). Criminalistics as a science and its importance in Ecuadorian criminal legislation. *LATAM Latin American Journal of Social Sciences and Humanities*, *4*(6), 6. Advance online publication. DOI: 10.56712/latam.v4i6.1531

Riba, J. M. L. (2024). Artificial intelligence and police control. *InDret*, *2*, 407–436. DOI: 10.31009/InDret.2024.i2.10

Richardson, R., Schultz, J. M., & Crawford, K. (2019). Dirty data, bad predictions: How civil rights violations impact police data, predictive policing systems, and justice. *NYUL Law Review Online, 91*.

Roberts, J., & Harris, A. (2023). Utilizing multilayer perceptrons for mental health diagnosis in diverse populations. *International Journal of Neural Networks, 12*(3), 120–135.

Rodríguez Abitia, G. (16 de Mayo de 2021). *Boletín UNAM-DGCS-419. Pandemia acelera 10 años el uso de tecnologías digitales.* Obtenido de Boletín UNAM-Dirección General de Comunicación Social: https://www.dgcs.unam.mx/boletin/bdboletin/2021_419.html

Rodríguez Manzanera, L. (2024). *Criminología*. Editorial Porrúa.

Rodríguez Manzanera, L. (2024). *Criminology*. Porrúa.

Rong, L., Ding, Y., Wang, M., El Saddik, A., & Hossain, M. S. (2024). A Multi-Modal ELMo Model for Image Sentiment Recognition of Consumer Data. *IEEE Transactions on Consumer Electronics*, *70*(1), 3697–3708. DOI: 10.1109/TCE.2024.3357543

Roseth, B., Reyes, A., & Yee Amézaga, K. (2021). *Servicios públicos y gobierno digital durante la pandemia: perspectivas de los ciudadanos, los funcionarios y las instituciones públicas*. América Latina y el Caribe: Banco Interamericano de Desarrollo. DOI: 10.18235/0003122

Ross, S., Wood, M., Baird, R., & Lundberg, K. (2023). Digital service delivery applications in corrections: A scoping review. *Australian Institute of Criminology. CRG, 8*, 20-21. https://www.aic.gov.au/sites/default/files/2023-09/crg_08_20_21digital_service_delivery_applications_in_corrections_v5_2.pdf

Royal Spanish Academy. *Concept of Criminality*. https://dle.rae.es/criminalidad

Royal Spanish Academy. *Concept of Narcoterrorism*. https://dle.rae.es/narcoterrorismo

Rudin, C. (2019). Stop explaining black box machine learning models for high stakes decisions and use interpretable models instead. *Nature Machine Intelligence*, *1*(5), 206–215. https://doi.org/https://doi.org/10.1038/s42256-019-0048-x. DOI: 10.1038/s42256-019-0048-x PMID: 35603010

Ruiz Díaz, J. (08 de Junio de 2024). *Descubre cómo la IA está potenciando el campo de Forense*. Obtenido de Colegio Profesional de Criminalística: https://criminalisticamisiones.org/index.php/2024/06/08/descubre-como-la-ia-esta-potenciando-el-campo-de-forense/#:~:text=La%20IA%20ofrece%20herramientas%20avanzadas,la%20precisi%C3%B3n%20de%20los%20resultados

Russell, S. J., & Norvig, P. (2021). *Artificial Intelligence: A Modern Approach*. Pearson.

Ryan, J. J. C. H., Ryan, D. J., & Tikk, E. (2010). Cybersecurity regulation: Using analogies to develop frameworks for regulation. In Tikk, E., & Talihtrm, A.-M. (Eds.), *International cyber security: Legal & policy proceedings* (pp. 95–110). CCDCOE.

Salami, I. A., Adesokan-Imran, T. O., Tiwo, O. J., Metibemu, O. C., Olutimehin, A. T., & Olaniyi, O. O. (2025). Addressing Bias and Data Privacy Concerns in AI-Driven Credit Scoring Systems Through Cybersecurity Risk Assessment. *Asian Journal of Research in Computer Science*, *18*(4), 59–82. DOI: 10.9734/ajrcos/2025/v18i4608

San Francisco, F. B. I. (2024, May 8). FBI Warns of Increasing Threat of Cyber Criminals Utilizing Artificial Intelligence. FBI. Retrieved from https://www.fbi.gov/contact-us/field-offices/sanfrancisco/news

Sanchis, E. (Octubre de 2018). Ciberdelincuencia y ciberterrorismo, ciberdelitos y cibercrimen. *Peritos informáticos*. Obtenido de https://peritos-informaticos.com/blog/ciberdelincuencia-ciberterrorismo-ciberdelito-ciber crimen/#:~:text=Otra%20diferencia%20entre%20el%20cibercrimen,delitos%20de%20un a%20forma%20individual.

Schuklenk, U. (2020, February). On the ethics of AI ethics. *Bioethics*, *34*(2), 146–147. DOI: 10.1111/bioe.12716 PMID: 31943279

Scikit-learn: Machine Learning in Python. [Online]. Available: https://scikit-learn.org/

Segovia Marín, S. (2024, April 26). Military forces seized 197 explosives that were to be launched by drones by dissidents in Cauca. *El Colombiano*.https://www.elcolombiano.com/colombia/hallaron-197-explosivos-disidencias-farc-que-lanzarian-con-drones-cauca-FC24374661

SeguridadInformáticaHoy. (2024). *Los 10 delitos cibernéticos más comunes*. Obtenido de Seguridad Informática Hoy: https://seguridadinformaticahoy.com/delitos-ciberneticos/

Sengupta, S. (2024). Legislative Text Analysis from Judicial Case Reports Using Machine Learning. *SN Computer Science*, *5*(5), 443. DOI: 10.1007/s42979-024-02836-y

Shah, I. A., & Jhanjhi, N. Z. (2025). The Challenges for E-Commerce Using AI Applications. In *Generative AI for Web Engineering Models* (pp. 203–222). IGI Global.

Shapsough, S., Qatan, F., Aburukba, R., Aloul, F., & Ali, A. R. A. (2015). Smart grid cyber security: Challenges and solutions. IEEExplore. DOI: 10.1109/ICSGCE.2015.7454291

Sharma, B. (2024). Cybercrimes under the Bharatiya Nyaya Sanhita, 2023. *MCO Legals*. https://www.mcolegals.in/kb/Cyber_Law-_Series_2-_Issue_3_-_Cybercrimes_under_the_Bhartiya_Nyaya_Sanhita,_2023.pdf

Shaukat, K., Luo, S., Varadjarajan, I., Hamed, A., & Xu, M. (2020). A Survey on Machine Learning Techniques for Cyber Security in the Last Decade. *IEEE Access : Practical Innovations, Open Solutions*, *8*, 222310–222354. https://doi.org/https://doi.org/10.1109/ACCESS.2020.3041951. DOI: 10.1109/ACCESS.2020.3041951

Shen, A. (2024). Mental Health and Yoga in Prisons. *Journal of Criminal Law, 00220183241265170*(4), 258–281. Advance online publication. DOI: 10.1177/00220183241265170

Shepitko, V., Shepitko, M., Latysh, K., Kapustina, M., & Demidova, E. (2023). Artificial intelligence in crime counteraction: From legal regulation to implementation. *Social & Legal Studies, 7*(1), 135–144. DOI: 10.32518/sals1.2024.135

Shiri, F. M., Perumal, T., Mustapha, N., & Mohamed, R. (2023). A comprehensive overview and comparative analysis on deep learning models: CNN, RNN, LSTM, GRU. arXiv preprint arXiv:2305.17473.

Shuran, L., Hui, D., & Su, G. (2013). Analysis and Discussions of the Blackout in Indian Power Grid. *Energy Science and Technology, 6*(1), 61–66.

Singh, R. (2024). Beware of Fraudulent Govt emails: Home Ministry Issues Public Warning. *Business Standard.* https://www.business-standard.com/india-news/beware-of-fraudulent-govt-emails-home-ministry-issues-public-warning-124071500749_1.html

Singh, D., & Wang, Y. (2023). Improving mental health prediction with attention-based models: A Transformer-based approach. *AI in Mental Health Research, 10*(3), 150–165.

Siniosoglou, I., Asimopoulos, D., Argyriou, V., Lagkas, T., Lytos, A., Moscholios, I. D., & Sarigiannidis, P. (2024, March). Enhancing Text Anonymisation: A Study on CRF, LSTM, and ELMo for Advanced Entity Recognition. In *2024 Panhellenic Conference on Electronics & Telecommunications (PACET)* (pp. 1-6). IEEE. DOI: 10.1109/PACET60398.2024.10497084

Smit, D. V. Z., & Appleton, C. (2019). *Life imprisonment: A global human rights analysis.* Harvard University Press. https://www.google.co.in/books/edition/Life_Imprisonment/aCd9DwAAQBAJ?hl=en&gbpv=1&dq=Those+who+are+serving+life+sentences+and+facing+legal+issues+may+benefit+from+amnesty+and+release+for+prisoners.+&pg=PP1&printsec=frontcover

Smith, J. A., & Brown, P. (2023). Predicting mental health outcomes using logistic regression: A review of methodologies and applications. *Journal of Mental Health Analytics, 45*(2), 123–145.

Solce, N. (2008). The battlefield of cyberspace: The inevitable new military branch—the cyber force. *Albany Law Journal of Science & Technology, 18*(2), 293–319.

Soler Garrido, J., De Nigris, S., Bassani, E., Sanchez, I., Evas, T., André, A., & Boulangé, T. (2024). Harmonised standards for the European AI Act (JRC139430). European Commission. https://publications.jrc.ec.europa.eu/repository/handle/JRC139430

Sommer, R., & Paxson, V. (2010). Outside the Closed World: On Using Machine Learning for Network Intrusion Detection. *2010 IEEE Symposium on Security and Privacy*, 305-316. DOI: 10.1109/SP.2010.25

South, N. (2021). Green criminology - revisiting: Reflections, connections, horizons. *Crimen, 12*(2), 113–131. DOI: 10.5937/crimen2102113S

Srinivasan, S., & Rajavel, N. (2025a). A Study of the Psychological Well-Being of Tamil Nadu Prison Inmates With Special Reference of AI. In *AI Technologies and Advancements for Psychological Well-Being and Healthcare* (pp. 219–254). IGI Global., DOI: 10.4018/979-8-3693-9158-7.ch009

SSC. (2024a). *Policía Cibernética.* Obtenido de Gobierno de la Ciudad de México: https://www.ssc.cdmx.gob.mx/organizacion-policial/subsecretaria-de-inteligencia-e-inves tigacion-policial/policia-cibernetica#:~:text=Realizamos%20funciones%20de%20monito reo%20y,incidentes%20que%20ocurren%20en%20internet.

SSC. (2024b). *Policía cibernética.* Obtenido de Secretaría de Seguridad Ciudadana. Gobierno de la Ciudad de México: https://www.ssc.cdmx.gob.mx/organizacion-policial/subsecretaria-de-inteligencia-e-inves tigacion-policial/policia-cibernetica

SSPC. (10 de Junio de 2021). *Delitos cibernéticos.* Obtenido de Gobierno de México. Secretaría de Seguridad y Protección Ciudadana. Blog: https://www.gob.mx/sspc/articulos/conoce-los-principales-delitos-ciberneticos-y-sigue-nu estras-recomendaciones-para-prevenir-que-tus-hijas-e-hijos-sean-posibles-victimas

Sudar, K. M., & Nagaraj, P. (2024). TCPFlood Defender: TCP SYN Flood Attacks Detection in SDN Environment Using Statistical and Ensemble Machine Learning Methods. In Software-Defined Network Frameworks (pp. 291-308). CRC Press.

Sudar, K. M., Deepalakshmi, P., Nagaraj, P., & Muneeswaran, V. (2020, November). Analysis of cyberattacks and its detection mechanisms. In *2020 Fifth International Conference on Research in Computational Intelligence and Communication Networks (ICRCICN)* (pp. 12-16). IEEE. DOI: 10.1109/ICRCICN50933.2020.9296178

Sudar, K. M., Nagaraj, P., & Vaissnave, V. Predictive malware detection in SDN-enabled wireless networks: A machine learning approach. In *Wireless Ad-hoc and Sensor Networks* (pp. 281–297). CRC Press. DOI: 10.1201/9781003528982-14

Sukanya, G., & Priyadarshini, J. (2024, January). Analysis on word embedding and classifier models in legal analytics. In AIP Conference Proceedings (Vol. 2802, No. 1). AIP Publishing. DOI: 10.1063/5.0181820

Sukumar, S. (2023). Digital Forensics in The Dark. https://www.linkedin.com/pulse/digital-forensics-dark-sandhya-sukumar/

Sun, Z., Wang, G., Li, P., Wang, H., Zhang, M., & Liang, X. (2024). An improved random forest based on the classification accuracy and correlation measurement of decision trees. *Expert Systems with Applications*, *237*, 121549. DOI: 10.1016/j.eswa.2023.121549

Surtees, R. (2008). Trafficking of Men—A Trend less Considered. The Case of Belarus and Ukraine. Geneva: International Organizations for Migration (IOM).

Su, T., Sun, H., Zhu, J., Wang, S., & Li, Y. (2020). BAT: Deep Learning Methods on Network Intrusion Detection Using NSL-KDD Dataset. *IEEE Access : Practical Innovations, Open Solutions*, *8*, 29575–29585. DOI: 10.1109/ACCESS.2020.2972627

Swaminathan, A., & Ramakrishnan, B., M, K., & R, S., (2022). Prediction of Cyber-attacks and Criminality Using Machine Learning Algorithms. *2022 International Conference on Innovation and Intelligence for Informatics, Computing, and Technologies (3ICT)*, pp. 547-552. DOI: 10.1109/3ICT56508.2022.9990652

Tabasco today. (March 8, 2024). Sedena prepares to purchase technology to counter drones. https://elmomentotabasco.mx/nacional/2024/03/08/alista-la-sedena-compra-de-tecnologia-para-contrarrestar-drones/

Taleby Ahvanooey, M., Zhu, M. X., Mazurczyk, W., Kilger, M., & Choo, K. K. R. (2021, December). Do dark web and cryptocurrencies empower cybercriminals? In *International Conference on Digital Forensics and Cyber Crime* (pp. 277-293). Cham: Springer International Publishing.

Taylor, M., & Clark, B. (2023). Application of decision trees for predicting mental health disorders in vulnerable populations. *Psychological Science and Technology*, *38*(3), 230–245.

Tejpal, K., Patole, J., & Ghugare, T. (2023). Cybersecurity: Pressing Priority in India. *The Online Journal of Distance Education and e-Learning : TOJDEL*, *11*(2), 2052–2061.

TensorFlow: An Open Source Machine Learning Framework. [Online]. Available: https://www.tensorflow.org/

Thabet, A. A., Matar, S., Carpintero, A., Bankart, J., & Vostanis, P. (2011). Mental health problems among labour children in the Gaza Strip. *Child: Care, Health and Development, 37*(1), 89–95. DOI: 10.1111/j.1365-2214.2010.01122.x PMID: 20637026

The Hindu Bureau. (2023). Loan App Suspected to be Behind Death of Family Remains to be Tracked. *The Hindu.* https://www.thehindu.com/news/cities/Kochi/loan-app-suspected-to-be-behind-death-of-family-remains-to-be-tracked/article67307324.ece

The Indian Evidence Act, 1872.

The Information Technology Act, 2000.

Thomas, R., & Jagani, D. (2024). Bharatiya Nyaya Sanhita, 2024: A Critical Perspective. SSRN. https://papers.ssrn.com/sol3/papers.cfm?abstract_id=4898463

Thompson, P., & Gray, H. (2023). Reinforcement learning in predicting mental health outcomes: A new frontier. *Advances in Mental Health Modeling, 21*(1), 50–65.

Thompson, R., & Liu, L. (2023). Improving mental health predictions with gated recurrent units: A case study. *Advances in Cognitive Health, 14*(3), 77–90.

Timmons, H. (2024, August 22). United Nations approves controversial cybercrime treaty. *Nextgov.* https://www.nextgov.com/digital-government/2024/08/united-nations-approves-controversial-cybercrime-treaty/398745/

Toache, E. A. (2023). Advantages and disadvantages of using artificial intelligence in the public policy cycle: An analysis of international cases. *Acta Universitaria, 33*, 1–26. DOI: 10.15174/au.2023.3891

Torres, G. D. O., Guterres, M. X., & Celestino, V. R. R. (2023). Legal actions in Brazilian air transport: A machine learning and multinomial logistic regression analysis. *Frontiers in Future Transportation, 4*, 1070533. DOI: 10.3389/ffutr.2023.1070533

Tsuchiya, Y., & Hiramoto, N. (2021). How cryptocurrency is laundered: Case study of Coincheck hacking incident. *Forensic Science International. Reports, 4*, 100241. DOI: 10.1016/j.fsir.2021.100241

Tucker, A. M., Xia, Y., & Smelcer, S. N. (2024). Text, tone, and legal language: Analyzing mutual fund disclosure sentiment. *American Business Law Journal, 61*(1), 57–86. DOI: 10.1111/ablj.12239

Tummala, P., & KoteswaraRao, C. (2024). Exploring T5 & RGAN for enhanced sarcasm generation in NLP. IEEE Access.

Turing, A. M. (1950). Computing Machinery and Intelligence. *Mind, 59*(236), 433–460. DOI: 10.1093/mind/LIX.236.433

Turner-Moss, E., Zimmerman, C., Howard, L. M., & Oram, S. (2014). Labour exploitation and health: A case series of men and women seeking post-trafficking services. *Journal of Immigrant and Minority Health, 16*(3), 473–480. DOI: 10.1007/s10903-013-9832-6 PMID: 23649665

Twigg, N. M. (2017). Comprehensive Care Model for Sex Trafficking Survivors. *Journal of Nursing Scholarship, 49*(3), 259–266. DOI: 10.1111/jnu.12285 PMID: 28178401

Tziakouris, G. (2018). Cryptocurrencies—A forensic challenge or opportunity for law enforcement? An Interpol perspective. *IEEE Security and Privacy, 16*(4), 92–94. DOI: 10.1109/MSP.2018.3111243

UAS. (10 de Mayo de 2023). *Análisis Sistemático del Delito.* Obtenido de Facultad de Derecho de Culiacan: https://derecho.uas.edu.mx/documentos/AnalisisSistematicodeDelito.pdf https://www.coursehero.com/file/202650345/AnalisisSistematicodeDelitopdf/

Ullah, S. (2025). Intention to Use Cryptocurrencies for Business Transactions: The Case of North Carolina. *Journal of Risk and Financial Management, 18*(2), 58. DOI: 10.3390/jrfm18020058

Umar, N., & Gray, A. (2023). Comparing single and multiple imputation approaches for missing values in univariate and multivariate water level data. *Water (Basel), 15*(8), 1519. DOI: 10.3390/w15081519

UNIR. (20 de Abril de 2022). *Teorías criminológicas: cuáles son las principales y en qué consisten.* Obtenido de La Universidad en Internet: https://mexico.unir.net/noticias/derecho/teorias-criminologicas/#:~:text=Teor%C3%ADa%20de%20las%20actividades%20cotidianas,a%20la%20v%C3%ADctima%20u%20obje tivo.

United Nations Office of the High Commissioner for Human Rights. (2024, July 25). *Statement by the Special Rapporteur on Counter-Terrorism and Human Rights on the UN Cybercrime Convention.* https://www.ohchr.org/sites/default/files/documents/issues/terrorism/sr/statements/2024-07-25-stm-SR-CT-Cybercrime-Convention.pdf

United Nations Office on Drugs and Crime. (2025). *Concept of terrorism.* https://www.unodc.org/e4j/es/secondary/terrorism.html

Urbanová, P., Eliášová, H., & Dostálová, T. (2022). How accurate is forensic facial identification of surgically altered faces? *The Australian Journal of Forensic Sciences, 55*(3), 406–425. DOI: 10.1080/00450618.2022.2032341

Vallebueno, A., Handan-Nader, C., Manning, C. D., & Ho, D. E. (2024). Statistical Uncertainty in Word Embeddings: GloVe-V. arXiv preprint arXiv:2406.12165. DOI: 10.18653/v1/2024.emnlp-main.510

Van Eck, N. J., & Waltman, L. (2017). Citation-based clustering of publications using CitNetExplorer and VOSviewer. *Scientometrics*, *111*(2), 1053–1070. https://doi.org/https://doi.org/10.1007/s11192-017-2300-7. DOI: 10.1007/s11192-017-2300-7 PMID: 28490825

Vanguardia. (2023, July 16). *Drones modified by criminal groups are a new security challenge. Vanguardia.* https://vanguardia.com.mx/noticias/drones-modificados-por-grupos-criminales-son-un-nuevo-reto-para-la-seguridad-CB8571062

Vásquez, P. A. R. (2023). Ethics of Artificial Intelligence. UNESCO Recommendation, November 2021. *Compendium (Newtown, Pa.)*, *26*(50), 1–6.

Verma, A. K., & Sharma, A. K. (2014). Cybersecurity Issues and Recommendations. *International Journal of Advanced Research in Computer Science and Software Engineering*, *4*(4), 629–634.

Vinayakumar, R., Alazab, M., Soman, K., Poornachandran, P., Al-Nemrat, A., & Venkatraman, S. (2019). Deep Learning Approach for Intelligent Intrusion Detection System. *IEEE Access : Practical Innovations, Open Solutions*, *7*, 41525–41550. DOI: 10.1109/ACCESS.2019.2895334

Wagh, A., Pawar, R., Wable, N., Wandhekar, S., & Dighe, M. S. (2024). Detection of Cyber Attacks and Network Attacks using Machine Learning Algorithms. Int. J. Adv. Res. Sci. Commun. Technol., 414-417.

Wahlgren, P. (2004). IT and legislative development. *Scandinavian Studies in Law*, *47*, 601–620.

Wakefield, S., & Uggen, C. (2010). Incarceration and stratification. *Annual Review of Sociology*, *36*(1), 387–406. DOI: 10.1146/annurev.soc.012809.102551

Walker, S., & Oliveira, A. P. (2024, September). The final call: UN member states adopt a new cybercrime treaty. *Global Initiative Against Transnational Organized Crime*. https://globalinitiative.net/wp-content/uploads/2024/09/Summer-Walker-Ana-Paula-Oliveira-The-final-call-UN-member-states-adopt-a-new-cybercrime-treaty-GI-TOC-September-2024.pdf

Weber, M., Domeniconi, G., Chen, J., Weidele, D. K. I., Bellei, C., Robinson, T., & Leiserson, C. E. 2019. Anti-money laundering in bitcoin: Experimenting with graph convolutional networks for financial forensics. *arXiv preprint arXiv:1908.02591*.

Weitener, L., Fischer, M., & Teaching, A. I. (2023, October 16). Ethics in Medical Education: A Scoping Review of Current Literature and Practices. *Perspectives on Medical Education, 12*(1), 399–410. DOI: 10.5334/pme.954 PMID: 37868075

Western, B., Braga, A. A., Davis, J., & Sirois, C. (2015). Stress and hardship after prison. *American Journal of Sociology, 120*(5), 1512–1547. DOI: 10.1086/681301 PMID: 26421345

White, R. (2021). *Theorising Green Criminology.* https://doi.org/DOI: 10.4324/9781003172093

Wicaksono, G. W., Oktaviana, U. N., Prasetyo, S. N., Sari, T. I., Hidayah, N. P., Yunus, N. R., & Al-Fatih, S. (2023). Classification of Industrial Relations Dispute Court Verdict Document with XGBoost and Bidirectional LSTM. JOIV: International Journal on Informatics Visualization, 7(3-2), 1041-1047.

Widjaja, G. (2023). ENHANCING LEGAL LITERACY: UNDERSTANDING THE SIGNIFICANCE OF LAW NO. 9/2019 ON ELECTRONIC TRANSACTIONS IN THE SOCIAL MEDIA ERA. *Journal of Community Dedication, 3*(4), 278–293.

Wilson, D. B., Gallagher, C. A., & MacKenzie, D. L. (2000). A meta-analysis of corrections-based education, vocation, and work programs for adult offenders. *Journal of Research in Crime and Delinquency, 37*(4), 347–368. DOI: 10.1177/0022427800037004001

Wilson, F., & Scott, G. (2023). Predicting mental health outcomes with gradient boosting machines: A comparative study. *Journal of Machine Learning in Psychology, 19*(3), 200–213.

Wright, K. N. (1991). The violent and victimized in the male prison. *Journal of Offender Rehabilitation, 16*(3-4), 1–26. DOI: 10.1300/J076v16n03_01

Wright, N., Jordan, M., & Lazzarino, R. (2021). Interventions to support the mental health of survivors of modern slavery and human trafficking: A systematic review. *The International Journal of Social Psychiatry, 67*(8), 1026–1034. DOI: 10.1177/00207640211039245 PMID: 34431379

www.ambitojuridico.com. (10 de Septiembre de 2012). Cibercriminalidad: la delincuencia en "el otro espacio". *Legis. Ámbito Jurídico*, págs. https://www.ambitojuridico .com/noticias/penal/penal/cibercriminalidad-la-delincuencia-e n-el-otro-espacio.

www.freepik.com. (2024). Ilustración del concepto de redes sociales. *Vector gratis*. Obtenido de https://www.freepik.es/vector-gratis/ilustracion-concepto-redes-sociales _2806746.htm#fr omView=keyword&page=1&position=4&uuid=8e22b50d-4c32-4b2c-a89a-3da1bf6fcc19

Yakushko, O. (2009). Human trafficking: A review for mental health professionals. *International Journal for the Advancement of Counseling, 31*(3), 158–167. DOI: 10.1007/s10447-009-9075-3

Yenduri, G., Ramalingam, M., Selvi, G. C., Supriya, Y., Srivastava, G., Maddikunta, P. K. R., Raj, G. D., Jhaveri, R. H., Prabadevi, B., Wang, W., Vasilakos, A. V., & Gadekallu, T. R. (2024). Gpt (generative pre-trained transformer)–a comprehensive review on enabling technologies, potential applications, emerging challenges, and future directions. *IEEE Access : Practical Innovations, Open Solutions, 12*, 54608–54649. DOI: 10.1109/ACCESS.2024.3389497

Yu, Q., & Zhou, J. (2023). Feature reduction for mental health prediction using principal component analysis. *Journal of Psychometric Studies, 33*(2), 45–60.

Zabala Leal, T. D. (2021). Ethics in artificial intelligence from a legal perspective. *Via Inveniendi Et Iudicandi, 16*(2). Advance online publication. DOI: 10.15332/19090528.6785

Završnik, A. (2020). Criminal justice, artificial intelligence systems, and human rights. *ERA Forum, 20*, 567-583. https://doi.org/https://doi.org/10.1007/s12027-020-00602-0

Završnik, A. (2019). Algorithmic justice: Algorithms and big data in criminal justice settings. *European Journal of Criminology, 18*(5), 623–642. https://doi.org/https://doi.org/10.1177/1477370819876762. DOI: 10.1177/1477370819876762

Zeller, B. (2007). *CISG and the unification of international trade law*. Routledge.

Zhang, W., & Chen, Y. (2023). Enhancing mental health prediction accuracy with random forests. *Journal of AI in Healthcare, 20*(1), 111–125.

Zhou, X., Liang, W., Shimizu, S., Ma, J., & Jin, Q. (2021). Siamese Neural Network Based Few-Shot Learning for Anomaly Detection in Industrial Cyber-Physical Systems. *IEEE Transactions on Industrial Informatics, 17*(8), 5790–5798. DOI: 10.1109/TII.2020.3047675

Zimmerman, Z., & Borland, R. (2009). Caring for Trafficked Persons. Guidance for Health Providers. 2009. *International Organization for Migration. Geneva. IOM.*

Zirin, J. D. (2009, October 14). Abdicating on a 'cyber czar'? *Los Angeles Times.* https://www.latimes.com/archives/la-xpm-2009-oct-14-oe-zirin14-story.html

Zivanai, E., & Mahlangu, G. (2022). Digital prison rehabilitation and successful re-entry into a digital society: A systematic literature review on the new reality on prison rehabilitation. *Cogent Social Sciences*, *8*(1), 2116809. DOI: 10.1080/23311886.2022.2116809

Zúñiga, L. A. L., & Zúñiga, M. A. R. (2024). The Ethics of Using Artificial Intelligence in the Psychological Assessment and Diagnosis of Patients in Durango, Mexico. *Ciencia Latina Multidisciplinary Scientific Journal*, *8*(4), 4. Advance online publication. DOI: 10.37811/cl_rcm.v8i4.12278

Zupic, I., & Čater, T. (2015). Bibliometric methods in management and organization. *Organizational Research Methods*, *18*(3), 429–472. https://doi.org/https://doi.org/10.1177/10944281145626. DOI: 10.1177/1094428114562629

About the Contributors

Fernando Ortiz-Rodriguez is a Full Professor and Head of the Artificial Intelligence and Innovation Lab at Tamaulipas Autonomous University. He was the Executive Director at the International Institute of Studies (IIES). He created the First Business School in Tamaulipas, Mexico. He worked as the Information Technology Manager at Emerson Electric, where he developed more than 40 pieces of software, some of them used globally in Emerson, and he achieved technology convergence by implementing the first efforts on IoT and Industry 4.0. Fernando is a member of National Systems Researchers (SNI) Level 1 of the National Council of Science and Technology (CONACYT) and INDEX IT Advisor

Shishir Kumar Shandilya, DSc, PhD, is an Associate Professor in the School of Data Science and Forecasting at Devi Ahilya University in India. He is also a Visiting Professor at Liverpool Hope University-United Kingdom and Autonomous University of Tamaulipas-Mexico. He is a Chevening Cyber Security Fellow, a prestigious recognition awarded by the UK Government's Foreign, Commonwealth and Development Office (FCDO) for leadership and excellence in Cyber Security. He is a Cambridge University-certified Professional Teacher and Trainer, a TEDx speaker, an ACM Distinguished Speaker, and a senior member of IEEE. Dr. Shandilya is a NASSCOM-certified Master Trainer for SOC Analysts. He has received the IDA Teaching Excellence Award by the Indian Didactics Association in Bangalore, and the Young Scientist Award. He is a highly regarded author with published research works in reputed academic publishers. His research interest includes Adaptive Defense, XAI, and Nature-inspired Cyber Security.

Cynthia Vargas Orozco Coordinator of the Degree in Criminology of the Reynosa Aztlán Multidisciplinary Academic Unit of the Autonomous University of Tamaulipas, Member of the Academic Body of Criminology UAT-CA-62, Member of the National System of Researchers Level I, Prodep Profile. Member of the Mexican Society of Criminology (SOMECRIM) and a member of the Mexican

Network of Studies in Green Criminology (REMECRIVE). It develops scientific research, dissemination, dissemination, and teaching in Criminology, Social Problems, and Crime research.

Jersain Llamas Covarrubias Lawyer and Master in Constitutional and Administrative Law from the University of Guadalajara. PhD student in Data Science at INFOTEC, Center for Research and Innovation in Information and Communication Technologies. Professor at the University of Guadalajara, consultant and lawyer specialized in Law and New Information and Communication Technologies (ICT), specifically in Digital Rights, Cybercrimes, Protection of Personal Data, Intellectual Property, Technological Contracts, Artificial Intelligence and Governance with Blockchain . He has the following certifications: Certified Chief Information Security Officer (C | CISO); EC-Council Information Security Manager v1 (E|ISM); and Certified Ethical Hacker by EC-Council; Certified Information Privacy Professional/ Europe (CIPP/E) by the IAPP - International Association of Privacy Professionals; Certified in Cybersecurity by (ISC)²; Microsoft Security, Compliance, and Identity Fundamentals; PrivacyOPS by Securiti; Scrum Foundations; and Fundamentos Na Lei Geral De Proteção De Dados LGPDF™ by CertiProf.

Ramy El-Kady is a full criminal law professor at the Police Academy and holds the position of department chair of criminal law. He was rewarded with the State Encouragement Award in Legal and Economic Sciences, Citizenship and Human Rights Branch, on the topic of "the right of persons cooperating with justice for protection in international conventions and national legislation. He graduated from the Police College in 1999. He obtained a postgraduate diploma in criminal sciences and public law, which is equivalent to a master's degree in criminal law, in 2003. He received a PhD in criminal law from the Faculty of Law, Cairo University, on the topic of (Mediation as an Alternative to a Criminal Case: A Comparative Study). He currently teaches criminal law subjects to college students. He supervised numerous studies submitted for doctoral degrees and higher diplomas and authored a host of research in the criminal law field. He has previously judged multiple research papers in a number of refereed regional scientific journals. He published a host of research in refereed and indexed periodicals and took part in a number of international and local conferences and symposia.

Jipson Joseph has a PhD in Ethics from DVK Bangalore. Currently, he is a Research Scholar in the School of Law at Christ University, Bangalore. His research interests are in the fields of ethics, gender studies, constitutional law, human rights, human security, environmental justice, developmental policies and global poverty.

Harjeet Kaur is a Ph.D. candidate in International Law and Treaty at EUCLID University. She holds an LL.M. in Corporate Law from Oriental University Indore and an LL.B. from Agra College Agra. Her research focuses on corporate law and human rights, specifically on the accountability of human rights abuses by subsidiaries and supply chains. Harjeet has interned at renowned law firms and taught as a nursery teacher in the UAE. Fluent in English, Hindi, and Punjabi and learning Arabic, she is committed to advancing legal scholarship and making impactful contributions to law.

Ananya Pandey is a Research Scholar in School of Law at Christ University, Bangalore. She has her research interests in the field of Constitutional Law, Human Rights, Intellectual Property Law and Jurisprudence.

Aparajita Roy is the Head of the department at Indore Christian College, Indore. Having teaching experience of more than 23 years.

Dipesh Silawat has a master's degree in Constitutional and Administrative Law. He is currently pursuing a PhD degree, His research interests include the role of Artificial Intelligence (AI) and its administration and governance within legal and constitutional frameworks. Dipesh's goal is to understand how modern technologies, such as AI, should be regulated to avoid ethical and societal risks which is useful for contemporary trends in legal and technological studies.

Avijit Silawat is a Senior Research Fellow at the School of Law, Devi Ahilya Vishwavidyalaya (DAVV), Indore, India, where he actively contributes to academic excellence through teaching, mentoring, and rigorous legal research. Currently pursuing his Ph.D. on "Impact of Cyber Crimes on Minors and Analysis of Cyber Laws in India," he is deeply invested in exploring the intersection of technology, law, and child protection. He has authored numerous scholarly papers in reputed national and international journals, reflecting a strong publication record and a commitment to academic integrity and innovation. His work engages with contemporary legal challenges, especially in cyber law, criminal justice, and the rights of vulnerable populations. As a dedicated researcher and educator, he strives to bridge the gap between legal theory and practice, aiming to shape progressive legal frameworks and inspire the next generation of legal minds.

Ajay K. Singh is working as an Associate Professor (Research) in the Department of Humanities and Social Science, Graphic Era (Deemed to be University) Dehradun. He has worked as Assistant Professor (Economics) in the School of Liberal Arts & Management, DIT University Dehradun for 6 years. He did Post-Doctorate Research with EDI of India, Ahmedabad, Gujarat (India). He received MPhil (Economics) from DAVV Indore (India), and PhD (Economics) from IIT Indore (India. He has published several research papers in the diversified area such as climate change, agricultural productivity, assessment of food security; estimation of GFSI, development of environmental sustainability index (ESI) and its association with socio-economic indicators; measurement and determinants of entrepreneurship ecosystem, and dimension of sustainable development and its interlinkages with economic development.

K. Muthamil Sudar is working as an Assistant Professor in the Department of Computer Science and Engineering, Mepco Schlenk Engineering College, Sivakasi, Tamil Nādu. He is a seasoned researcher with a focus on cutting-edge technologies in the field of computer science, particularly in the areas of network security, machine learning, and image processing. His work reflects a commitment to addressing contemporary challenges, with a notable emphasis on the detection and mitigation of cyber threats using innovative techniques. He has over 8 years of Teaching and Research Experience. As an accomplished author, he has successfully published multiple articles in renowned journals and has been a contributor to esteemed IEEE conferences.

C.V. Suresh Babu is a pioneer in content development. A true entrepreneur, he founded Anniyappa Publications, a company that is highly active in publishing books related to Computer Science and Management. Dr. C.V. Suresh Babu has also ventured into SB Institute, a center for knowledge transfer. He holds a Ph.D. in Engineering Education from the National Institute of Technical Teachers Training & Research in Chennai, along with seven master's degrees in various disciplines such as Engineering, Computer Applications, Management, Commerce, Economics, Psychology, Law, and Education. Additionally, he has UGC-NET/SET qualifications in the fields of Computer Science, Management, Commerce, and Education. Currently, Dr. C.V. Suresh Babu is a Professor in the Department of Information Technology at the School of Computing Science, Hindustan Institute of Technology and Science (Hindustan University) in Padur, Chennai, Tamil Nadu, India.

R. Vallipriya has been working in the Department of Physical Sciences at the Institute of Education (Affiliated to Tamilnadu Teacher Education University) as an Assistant Professor. With a wealth of experience, Mrs. R.Vallipriya has accumulated 12 years of extensive teaching. Her scholarly contributions include publishing 7 papers, with 1 peer review in various UGC-CARE, SCOPUS, and peer-reviewed journals.

S. Srinivasan has been working in the Department of Humanities and Social Sciences at Graphic Era (Deemed to be University) as an Assistant Professor. With a wealth of experience, Mr. Srinivasan has accumulated 14 years of extensive teaching and field-level expertise. Prior to his current role, he served in the Ministry of Health and Family Welfare, Government of India, and gained valuable experience. He also contributed as a Guest Faculty at the university level and served for nearly 2 years in the State Government Public Works Department as a Mobilization Training Specialist. In the past year, Mr. S. Srinivasan has enriched his experience by actively participating in a tuberculosis project funded by GFATM and USAID, providing a platform for further exploration of his research and practical field-based knowledge. His scholarly contributions include publishing 30 papers, with 18 more under peer review in various UGC-CARE, SCOPUS, and peer-reviewed journals.

Index

A

B

C

D

E

F

G

H

I

J

L

M

N

P

R

S

www.ingramcontent.com/pod-product-compliance
Lightning Source LLC
LaVergne TN
LVHW080611300926
849162LV00005B/1118